Strategic Management Process

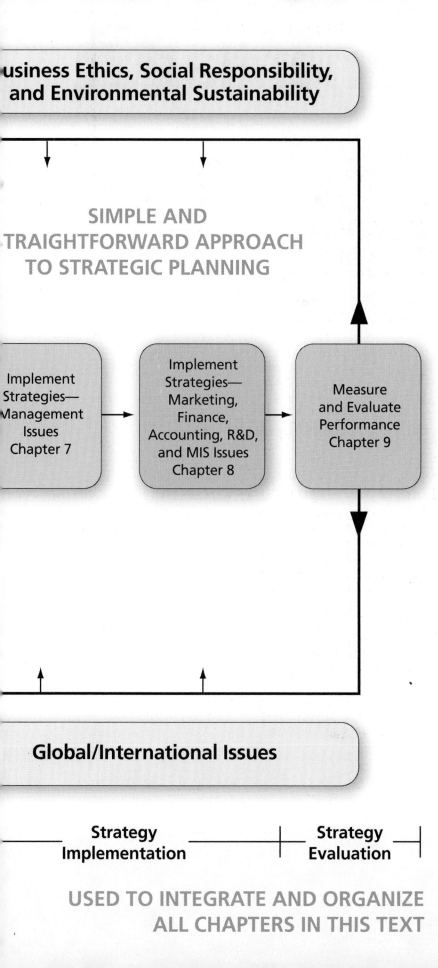

Business Ethics, Social Responsibility, and Environmental Sustainability

SIMPLE AND STRAIGHTFORWARD APPROACH TO STRATEGIC PLANNING

Implement Strategies—Management Issues Chapter 7

Implement Strategies—Marketing, Finance, Accounting, R&D, and MIS Issues Chapter 8

Measure and Evaluate Performance Chapter 9

Global/International Issues

Strategy Implementation

Strategy Evaluation

USED TO INTEGRATE AND ORGANIZE ALL CHAPTERS IN THIS TEXT

THIRTEENTH EDITION

Strategic Management
CONCEPTS

Fred R. David

Francis Marion University
Florence, South Carolina

Prentice Hall

Boston Columbus Indianapolis New York San Francisco Upper Saddle River
Amsterdam Cape Town Dubai London Madrid Milan Munich Paris Montreal Toronto
Delhi Mexico City Sao Paulo Sydney Hong Kong Seoul Singapore Taipei Tokyo

To Joy, Forest, Byron, and Meredith—
my wife and children—
for their encouragement and love.

Editorial Director: Sally Yagan
Editor in Chief: Eric Svendsen
Acquisitions Editor: Kim Norbuta
Product Development Manager: Ashley Santora
Editorial Project Manager: Claudia Fernandes
Editorial Assistant: Meg O'Rourke
Director of Marketing: Patrice Lumumba Jones
Marketing Manager: Nikki Ayana Jones
Marketing Assistant: Ian Gold
Senior Managing Editor: Judy Leale
Associate Production Project Manager:
  Ana Jankowski
Operations Specialist: Ilene Kahn
Art Director: Steve Frim
Text and Cover Designer: Judy Allan

Manager, Visual Research: Beth Brenzel
Manager, Rights and Permissions: Zina Arabia
Image Permission Coordinator: Cynthia Vincenti
Manager, Cover Visual Research & Permissions:
  Karen Sanatar
Cover Art: Vetta TM Collection Dollar Bin:
  istockphoto
Editorial Media Project Manager: Ashley Lulling
Production Media Project Manager: Lisa Rinaldi
Full-Service Project Management: Thistle Hill
  Publishing Services, LLC
Composition: Integra Software Services, Ltd.
Printer/Binder: Courier/Kendallville
Cover Printer: Lehigh-Phoenix Color/Hagerstown
Text Font: 10/12 Times

Credits and acknowledgments borrowed from other sources and reproduced, with permission, in this textbook appear on appropriate page within text.

Many of the designations by manufacturers and seller to distinguish their products are claimed as trademarks. Where those designations appear in this book, and the publisher was aware of a trademark claim, the designations have been printed in initial caps or all caps.

Library of Congress Cataloging-in-Publication Data
David, Fred R.
  Strategic management: concepts / Fred R. David.—13th ed.
    p. cm.
  Includes bibliographical references and index.
  ISBN-13: 978-0-13-612099-5 (pbk.)
  ISBN-10: 0-13-612099-7 (pbk.)
  1. Strategic planning.   I. Title.
HD30.28.D3785 2011
658.4'012—dc22

                                                        2009052034

10 9 8 7 6 5 4 3 2 1

Prentice Hall
is an imprint of

www.pearsonhighered.com

ISBN 10:   0-13-612099-7
ISBN 13: 978-0-13-612099-5

Brief Contents

Contents

Chapter 4
The Internal Assessment 90

Chapter 5
Strategies in Action 130

Chapter 6
Strategy Analysis and Choice 172

Preface

Why the Need for This New Edition?

The global economic recession has created a business world today that is quite different and more complex than it was just two years ago when the previous edition of this text was published. Thousands of businesses have vanished, and consumers have become extremely price sensitive and oftentimes reluctant purchasers of products and services. Very tight credit markets, high unemployment, and millions of new entrepreneurs have also changed the business landscape. Business firms that have survived the last three years of global economic turmoil are today leaner and meaner than ever before. Gaining and sustaining competitive advantage is harder than ever. Social networking and e-commerce have altered marketing to its core since the prior edition. This new edition reveals how to conduct effective strategic planning in this new world order.

Since the prior edition, thousands of liquidations, bankruptcies, divestitures, mergers, alliances, and partnerships captured the news. Corporate scandals highlighted the need for improved business ethics and corporate disclosure of financial transactions. Downsizing, rightsizing, and reengineering contributed to a permanently altered corporate landscape. Thousands of firms began doing business globally, and thousands more closed their global operations. Thousands prospered, and yet thousands failed in the last two years as the global recession spared few. Long-held competitive advantages have eroded as new ones formed. This new edition captures the complexity of this world business environment.

Both the challenges and opportunities facing organizations of all sizes today are greater than ever. There is less room than ever for error in the formulation and implementation of a strategic plan. This new edition provides a systematic effective approach for developing a clear strategic plan, even in the worst of times. Changes made in this edition are aimed squarely at illustrating the effect of new business concepts and techniques on strategic-management theory and practice.

Due to the magnitude of recent changes affecting companies, cultures, and countries, every page of this edition has been updated. The first edition of this text was published in 1986. Since then, this textbook has grown to be one of the most widely read strategic-management books, perhaps the most widely read, in the world. This text is now published in nine languages.

What Is New in This Edition?

This edition includes exciting new features, changes, and content designed to position this text as the clear leader and best choice for teaching strategic management. Here is a summary of what is new in this edition:

- A new Chapter 10, "Business Ethics/Social Responsibility/Environmental Sustainability"; there is extensive new coverage of ethics and sustainability because this text emphasizes that "good ethics is good business." Unique to strategic-management texts, the natural environment discussion is strengthened in this edition to promote and encourage firms to conduct operations in an environmentally sound manner. Respect for the natural environment has become an important concern for consumers, companies, society, and AACSB-International.
- A new Chapter 11, "Global/International Issues"; there is extensive new coverage of cultural and conceptual strategic-management differences across countries. Doing business globally has become a necessity, rather than a luxury in most industries because nearly all strategic decisions today are affected by global issues and concerns. Every case company in this edition does business globally, providing students ample opportunity to evaluate and consider international aspects of doing business.
- A new boxed insert at the beginning of each chapter showcases a company that has done exceptionally well in the 2008–2010 global economic recession and reveals their strategy.

- Hundreds of new examples abound in every chapter.
- A new cohesion case on McDonald's Corporation (2010); this is one of the most successful, well-known, and best managed global companies in the world; students apply strategy concepts to McDonald's at the end of each chapter through new Assurance of Learning Exercises.
- Thirty-two new tables in the chapters to better capture key strategic-management concepts.
- A revised comprehensive strategic management model to reflect the new chapters.
- Extensive new narrative on strategic management theory and concepts in every chapter to illustrate the new business world order.
- On average, 15 new review questions at the end of each chapter.
- Forty-eight new Assurance of Learning Exercises at the end of chapters that apply chapter concepts; the exercises prepare students for strategic-management case analysis.
- Twenty-four new color photographs bring the edition to life and illustrate companies/concepts.
- All new current readings at the end of each chapter; new research and theories of seminal thinkers in strategy development, such as Ansoff, Chandler, Porter, Hamel, Prahalad, Mintzberg, and Barney are provided in the chapters; practical aspects of strategic management, however, are still center stage and the trademark of this text.

This edition continues to offer many special time-tested features and content that have made this text so successful for over 20 years. Historical trademarks of this text that are strengthened in this edition are described below.

Chapters: Time-Tested Features

- This text meets AACSB-International guidelines that support a practitioner orientation rather than a theory/research approach. It offers a skills-oriented approach to developing a vision and mission statement; performing an external audit; conducting an internal assessment; and formulating, implementing, and evaluating strategies.
- The author's writing style is concise, conversational, interesting, logical, lively, and supported by numerous current examples throughout.
- A simple, integrative strategic-management model appears in all chapters and on the inside front cover of the text. This model is widely used for strategic planning among consultants and companies worldwide. One reviewer said, "One thing I have admired about David's text is that he follows the fundamental sequence of strategy formulation, implementation, and evaluation. There is a basic flow from mission/purposes to internal/external environmental scanning to strategy development, selection, implementation, and evaluation. This has been, and continues to be, a hallmark of the David text. Many other strategy texts are more disjointed in their presentation, and thus confusing to the student, especially at the undergraduate level."
- A Cohesion Case follows Chapter 1 and is revisited at the end of each chapter. This Cohesion Case allows students to apply strategic-management concepts and techniques to a real organization as chapter material is covered, which readies students for case analysis in the course.
- End-of-chapter Assurance of Learning Exercises effectively apply concepts and techniques in a challenging, meaningful, and enjoyable manner. Eighteen exercises apply text material to the Cohesion Case; 10 apply textual material to a college or university; another 10 exercises send students into the business world to explore important strategy topics. The exercises are relevant, interesting, and contemporary.
- There is excellent pedagogy in this text, including notable quotes and objectives to open each chapter, and key terms, current readings, discussion questions, and experiential exercises to close each chapter.
- There is excellent coverage of strategy formulation issues, such as business ethics, global versus domestic operations, vision/mission, matrix analysis, partnering, joint

venturing, competitive analysis, governance, and guidelines for conducting an internal/external strategy assessment.

- There is excellent coverage of strategy implementation issues such as corporate culture, organizational structure, outsourcing, marketing concepts, financial analysis, and business ethics.
- A systematic, analytical approach is presented in Chapter 6, including matrices such as the SWOT, BCG, IE, GRAND, SPACE, and QSPM.
- The chapter material is again published in a four-color format.
- A chapters-only paperback version of the text is available.

*The comprehensive strategic-management model is displayed on the inside front cover of the text. At the start of each chapter, the section of the comprehensive strategy model covered in that chapter is highlighted and enlarged so students can see the focus of each chapter in the basic unifying comprehensive model.

Special Note to Students

Welcome to strategic management. This is a challenging and exciting capstone course that will allow you to function as the owner or chief executive officer of different organizations. Your major task in this course will be to make strategic decisions and to justify those decisions through oral and written communication. Strategic decisions determine the future direction and competitive position of an enterprise for a long time. Decisions to expand geographically or to diversify are examples of strategic decisions.

Strategic decision-making occurs in all types and sizes of organizations, from Exxon and IBM to a small hardware store or small college. Many people's lives and jobs are affected by strategic decisions, so the stakes are very high. An organization's very survival is often at stake. The overall importance of strategic decisions makes this course especially exciting and challenging. You will be called upon in this course to demonstrate how your strategic decisions could be successfully implemented.

In this course, you can look forward to making strategic decisions both as an individual and as a member of a team. No matter how hard employees work, an organization is in real trouble if strategic decisions are not made effectively. Doing the right things (effectiveness) is more important than doing things right (efficiency). For example, many American newspapers are faltering as consumers increasingly switch to interactive media for news.

You will have the opportunity in this course to make actual strategic decisions, perhaps for the first time in your academic career. Do not hesitate to take a stand and defend specific strategies that you determine to be the best, based on tools and concepts in this textbook. The rationale for your strategic decisions will be more important than the actual decision, because no one knows for sure what the best strategy is for a particular organization at a given point in time. This fact accents the subjective, contingency nature of the strategic-management process.

Use the concepts and tools presented in this text, coupled with your own intuition, to recommend strategies that you can defend as being most appropriate for the organizations that you study. You will also need to integrate knowledge acquired in previous business courses. For this reason, strategic management is often called a capstone course; you may want to keep this book for your personal library.

A trademark of this text is its practitioner and applications orientation. This book presents techniques and content that will enable you to actually formulate, implement, and evaluate strategies in all kinds of profit and nonprofit organizations. The end-of-chapter Assurance of Learning Exercises allow you to apply what you've read in each chapter to the new McDonald's Cohesion Case and to your own university.

Definitely visit the Strategic Management Club Online at www.strategyclub.com. The templates and links there will save you time in performing analyses and will make your work look professional. Work hard in this course and have fun. Good luck!

Acknowledgments

Many persons have contributed time, energy, ideas, and suggestions for improving this text over 12 editions. The strength of this text is largely attributed to the collective wisdom, work, and experiences of strategic-management professors, researchers, students, and practitioners. Names of particular individuals whose published research is referenced in this edition of this text are listed alphabetically in the Name Index. To all individuals involved in making this text so popular and successful, I am indebted and thankful.

Many special persons and reviewers contributed valuable material and suggestions for this edition. I would like to thank my colleagues and friends at Auburn University, Mississippi State University, East Carolina University, and Francis Marion University. I have served on the management faculty at all these universities. Scores of students and professors at these schools helped shape the development of this text. Many thanks go to the following 15 reviewers of the prior edition whose comments shaped this thirteenth edition:

Moses Acquaah, The University of North Carolina at Greensboro

Charles M. Byles, Virginia Commonwealth University

Charles J. Capps III, Sam Houston State University

Neil Dworkin, Western Connecticut State University

John Frankenstein, Brooklyn College/City University of New York

Bill W. Godair, Landmark College, Community College of Vermont

Carol Jacobson, Purdue University

Susan M. Jensen, University of Nebraska at Kearney

Thomas E. Kulik, Washington University at St. Louis

Jerrold K. Leong, Oklahoma State University

Trina Lynch-Jackson, Indiana University NW, Purdue Calumet, Calumet College of St. Joseph, Indiana Wesleyan University

Raza Mir, William Paterson University

Thomas W. Sharkey, University of Toledo

Jill Lynn Vihtelic, Saint Mary's College

Michael W. Wakefield, Colorado State University–Pueblo

Individuals who develop cases for the North American Case Research Association Meeting, the Midwest Society for Case Research Meeting, the Eastern Case Writers Association Meeting, the European Case Research Association Meeting, and Harvard Case Services are vitally important for continued progress in the field of strategic management. From a research perspective, writing strategic management cases represents a valuable scholarly activity among faculty. Extensive research is required to structure business policy cases in a way that exposes strategic issues, decisions, and behavior. Pedagogically, strategic management cases are essential for students in learning how to apply concepts, evaluate situations, formulate a "game plan," and resolve implementation problems. Without a continuous stream of updated business policy cases, the strategic-management course and discipline would lose much of its energy and excitement.

Professors who teach this course supplement lecture with simulations, guest speakers, experiential exercises, class projects, and/or outside readings. Case analysis, however, is typically the backbone of the learning process in most strategic-management courses across the country. Case analysis is almost always an integral part of this course.

Analyzing strategic-management cases gives students the opportunity to work in teams to evaluate the internal operations and external issues facing various organizations and to craft strategies that can lead these firms to success. Working in teams gives students practical experience solving problems as part of a group. In the business world, important decisions are generally made within groups; strategic-management students learn to deal with overly aggressive group members and also timid, noncontributing group members. This experience is valuable as strategic-management students near graduation and soon enter the working world a full time.

Students can improve their oral and written communication skills as well as their analytical and interpersonal skills by proposing and defending particular courses of action for the case companies. Analyzing cases allows students to view a company, its competitors, and its industry concurrently, thus simulating the complex business world. Through case analysis, students learn how to apply concepts, evaluate situations, formulate strategies, and resolve implementation problems. Instructors typically ask students to prepare a three-year strategic plan for the firm. Analyzing a strategic-management case entails students applying concepts learned across their entire business curriculum. Students gain experience dealing with a wide range of organizational problems that impact all the business functions.

Scores of Prentice Hall employees and salespersons have worked diligently behind the scenes to make this text a leader in strategic management. I appreciate the continued hard work of all those professionals, such as Sally Yagan, Kim Norbuta, Claudia Fernandes, Ann Pulido, and Ana Jankowski.

I also want to thank you, the reader, for investing the time and effort to read and study this text. It will help you formulate, implement, and evaluate strategies for any organization with which you become associated. I hope you come to share my enthusiasm for the rich subject area of strategic management and for the systematic learning approach taken in this text.

Finally, I want to welcome and invite your suggestions, ideas, thoughts, comments, and questions regarding any part of this text or the ancillary materials. Please call me at 910-612-5343, fax me at 910-579-5132, e-mail me at freddavid9@gmail.com, or write me at the School of Business, Francis Marion University, Florence, SC 29501. I sincerely appreciate and need your input to continually improve this text in future editions. Your willingness to draw my attention to specific errors or deficiencies in coverage or exposition will especially be appreciated.

Thank you for using this text.

Fred R. David

About the Author

Dr. Fred R. David is the sole author of two mainstream strategic-management textbooks: (1) *Strategic Management: Concepts and Cases,* and (2) *Strategic-Management Concepts*. These texts have been on a two-year revision cycle since 1986 when the first edition was published. They are among the best if not the best-selling strategic-management textbooks in the world and have been used at more than 500 colleges and universities, including Harvard University, Duke University, Carnegie-Mellon University, Johns Hopkins University, the University of Maryland, University of North Carolina, University of Georgia, San Francisco State University, University of South Carolina, and Wake Forest University.

This textbook has been translated and published in Chinese, Japanese, Farsi, Spanish, Indonesian, Indian, Thai, and Arabic and is widely used across Asia and South America. It is the best-selling strategic-management textbook in Mexico, China, Peru, Chile, Japan, and number two in the United States. Approximately 90,000 students read Dr. David's textbook annually as well as thousands of businesspersons. The book has led the field of strategic management for more than a decade in providing an applications/practitioner approach to the discipline.

A native of Whiteville, North Carolina, Fred David received a BS degree in mathematics and an MBA from Wake Forest University before being employed as a bank manager with United Carolina Bank. He received a PhD in Business Administration from the University of South Carolina, where he majored in management. Currently the TranSouth Professor of Strategic Management at Francis Marion University (FMU) in Florence, South Carolina, Dr. David has also taught at Auburn University, Mississippi State University, East Carolina University, the University of South Carolina, and the University of North Carolina at Pembroke. He is the author of 152 referred publications, including 40 journal articles and 55 proceedings publications. David has articles published in such journals as *Academy of Management Review*, *Academy of Management Executive*, *Journal of Applied Psychology*, *Long Range Planning*, and *Advanced Management Journal*.

Dr. David received a Lifetime Honorary Professorship Award from the Universidad Ricardo Palma in Lima, Peru. He delivered the keynote speech at the twenty-first Annual Latin American Congress on Strategy hosted by the Centrum School of Business in Peru. Dr. David recently delivered an eight-hour Strategic Planning Workshop to the faculty at Pontificia Universidad Catolica Del in Lima, Peru, and an eight-hour Case Writing/Analyzing Workshop to the faculty at Utah Valley State College in Orem, Utah. He has received numerous awards, including FMU's Board of Trustees Research Scholar Award, the university's Award for Excellence in Research given annually to the best faculty researcher on campus, and the Phil Carroll Advancement of Management Award, given annually by the Society for the Advancement of Management (SAM) to a management scholar for outstanding contributions in management research. He recently gave the graduation commencement speech at Troy University.

Strategic Management
CONCEPTS AND CASES

CHAPTER 1
The Nature of Strategic Management

CHAPTER OBJECTIVES

After studying this chapter, you should be able to do the following:

1. Describe the strategic-management process.

2. Explain the need for integrating analysis and intuition in strategic management.

3. Define and give examples of key terms in strategic management.

4. Discuss the nature of strategy formulation, implementation, and evaluation activities.

5. Describe the benefits of good strategic management.

6. Discuss the relevance of Sun Tzu's *The Art of War* to strategic management.

7. Discuss how a firm may achieve sustained competitive advantage.

Assurance of Learning Exercises

Assurance of Learning Exercise 1A
Gathering Strategy Information

Assurance of Learning Exercise 1B
Strategic Planning for My University

Assurance of Learning Exercise 1C
Strategic Planning at a Local Company

Assurance of Learning Exercise 1D
Getting Familiar with SMCO

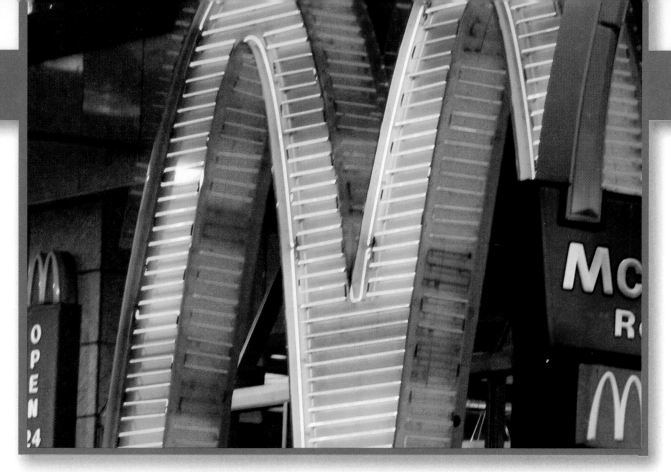

Source: Shutterstock/Photographer Jim Lopes

"Notable Quotes"

"If we know where we are and something about how we got there, we might see where we are trending—and if the outcomes which lie naturally in our course are unacceptable, to make timely change."

—Abraham Lincoln

"Without a strategy, an organization is like a ship without a rudder, going around in circles. It's like a tramp; it has no place to go."

—Joel Ross and Michael Kami

"Plans are less important than planning."

—Dale McConkey

"The formulation of strategy can develop competitive advantage only to the extent that the process can give meaning to workers in the trenches."

—David Hurst

"Most of us fear change. Even when our minds say change is normal, our stomachs quiver at the prospect. But for strategists and managers today, there is no choice but to change."

—Robert Waterman Jr.

"If a man takes no thought about what is distant, he will find sorrow near at hand. He who will not worry about what is far off will soon find something worse than worry."

—Confucius

When CEOs from the big three American automakers, Ford, General Motors (GM), and Chrysler, showed up without a clear strategic plan to ask congressional leaders for bailout monies, they were sent home with instructions to develop a clear strategic plan for the future. Austan Goolsbee, one of President Obama's top economic advisers, said, "Asking for a bailout without a convincing business plan was crazy." Goolsbee also said, "If the three auto CEOs need a bridge, it's got to be a bridge to somewhere, not a bridge to nowhere."[1] This textbook gives the instructions on how to develop a clear strategic plan—a bridge to somewhere rather than nowhere.

This chapter provides an overview of strategic management. It introduces a practical, integrative model of the strategic-management process; it defines basic activities and terms in strategic management.

This chapter also introduces the notion of boxed inserts. A boxed insert is provided in each chapter to examine how some firms are doing really well competing in a global economic recession. Some firms are strategically capitalizing on the harsh business climate and prospering as their rivals weaken. These firms are showcased in this edition to reveal how those companies achieved prosperity. Each boxed insert examines the strategies of firms doing great amid the worst recession in almost 30 years, the biggest stock market decline since 1937, high unemployment, record high and then record low oil prices, low consumer confidence, low interest rates, bankruptcies, liquidations, unavailability of credit, falling consumer demand for almost everything, and intense price competition as

Doing Great in a Weak Economy

McDonald's Corporation

When most firms were struggling in 2008, McDonald's increased its revenues from $22.7 billion in 2007 to $23.5 billion in 2008. Headquartered in Oak Brook, Illinois McDonald's net income nearly doubled during that time from $2.4 billion to $4.3 billion—quite impressive. *Fortune* magazine in 2009 rated McDonald's as their 16th "Most Admired Company in the World" in terms of their management and performance.

McDonald's added 650 new outlets in 2009 when many restaurants struggled to keep their doors open. McDonald's low prices and expanded menu items have attracted millions of new customers away from sit-down chains and independent eateries. Jim Skinner, CEO of McDonald's, says, "We do so well because our strategies have been so well planned out." McDonald's served about 60 million customers

every day in 2009, 2 million more than in 2008. Nearly 80 percent of McDonald's are run by franchisees (or affiliates).

McDonald's in 2009 spent $2.1 billion to remodel many of its 32,000 restaurants and build new ones at a more rapid pace than in recent years. This is in stark contrast to most restaurant chains that are struggling to survive, laying off employees, closing restaurants, and reducing expansion plans. McDonald's restaurants are in 120 countries. Going out to eat is one of the first activities that customers cut in tough times. A rising U.S. dollar is another external factor that hurts McDonald's. An internal weakness of McDonald's is that the firm now offers upscale coffee drinks like lattes and cappuccinos in over 7,000 locations just as budget-conscious consumers are cutting back on such extravagances. About half of McDonald's 31,000 locations are outside the United States.

But McDonald's top management team says everything the firm does is for the long term. McDonald's for several years referred to their strategic plan as "Plan to Win." This strategy has been to increase sales at existing locations by improving the menu, remodeling dining rooms, extending hours, and adding snacks. The company has avoided deep price cuts on its menu items. McDonald's was only one of three large U.S. firms that saw its stock price rise in 2008.

The other two firms were Wal-Mart and Family Dollar Stores.

Other strategies being pursued currently by McDonald's include replacing gasoline-powered cars with energy-efficient cars, lowering advertising rates, halting building new outlets on street corners where nearby development shows signs of weakness, boosting the firm's coffee business, and improving the drive-through windows to increase sales and efficiency.

McDonald's receives nearly two thirds of its revenues from outside the United States. The company has 14,000 U.S. outlets and 18,000 outlets outside the United States. McDonald's feeds 58 million customers every day. The company operates Hamburger University in suburban Chicago. McDonald's reported that first quarter 2009 profits rose 4 percent and same-store sales rose 4.3 percent across the globe. Same-store sales in the second quarter of 2009 were up another 4.8 percent.

Source: Based on Janet Adamy, "McDonald's Seeks Way to Keep Sizzling," *Wall Street Journal* (March 10, 2009): A1, A11. Also, Geoff Colvin, "The World's Most Admired Companies," *Fortune* (March 16, 2009): 76–86.

consumers today purchase only what they need rather than what they want. Societies worldwide confront the most threatening economic conditions in nearly a century. The boxed insert in each chapter showcases excellent strategic management under harsh economic times.

The first company featured for excellent performance in the global recession is McDonald's Corporation, also showcased as the Cohesion Case in this 13th edition. McDonald's is featured as the Cohesion Case also because it is a well-known global firm undergoing strategic change and well managed. By working through McDonald's-related Assurance of Learning Exercises at the end of each chapter, you will be well prepared to develop an effective strategic plan for any company assigned to you this semester. The end-of-chapter exercises apply chapter tools and concepts.

What Is Strategic Management?

Once there were two company presidents who competed in the same industry. These two presidents decided to go on a camping trip to discuss a possible merger. They hiked deep into the woods. Suddenly, they came upon a grizzly bear that rose up on its hind legs and snarled. Instantly, the first president took off his knapsack and got out a pair of jogging shoes. The second president said, "Hey, you can't outrun that bear." The first president responded, "Maybe I can't outrun that bear, but I surely can outrun you!" This story captures the notion of strategic management, which is to achieve and maintain competitive advantage.

Defining Strategic Management

Strategic management can be defined as the art and science of formulating, implementing, and evaluating cross-functional decisions that enable an organization to achieve its objectives. As this definition implies, strategic management focuses on integrating management, marketing, finance/accounting, production/operations, research and development, and information systems to achieve organizational success. The term *strategic management* in this text is used synonymously with the term *strategic planning*. The latter term is more often used in the business world, whereas the former is often used in academia. Sometimes the term *strategic management* is used to refer to strategy formulation, implementation, and evaluation, with *strategic planning* referring only to strategy formulation. The purpose of strategic management is to exploit and create new and different opportunities for tomorrow; *long-range planning,* in contrast, tries to optimize for tomorrow the trends of today.

The term *strategic planning* originated in the 1950s and was very popular between the mid-1960s and the mid-1970s. During these years, strategic planning was widely believed to be the answer for all problems. At the time, much of corporate America was "obsessed" with strategic planning. Following that "boom," however, strategic planning was cast aside during the 1980s as various planning models did not yield higher returns. The 1990s, however, brought the revival of strategic planning, and the process is widely practiced today in the business world.

A strategic plan is, in essence, a company's game plan. Just as a football team needs a good game plan to have a chance for success, a company must have a good strategic plan to compete successfully. Profit margins among firms in most industries have been so reduced by the global economic recession that there is little room for error in the overall strategic plan. A strategic plan results from tough managerial choices among numerous good alternatives, and it signals commitment to specific markets, policies, procedures, and operations in lieu of other, "less desirable" courses of action.

The term *strategic management* is used at many colleges and universities as the subtitle for the capstone course in business administration. This course integrates material from all business courses. The Strategic Management Club Online at www.strategyclub.com offers many benefits for business policy and strategic management students. Professor Hansen at Stetson University provides a strategic management slide show for this entire text (www.stetson.edu/~rhansen/strategy).

Stages of Strategic Management

The *strategic-management process* consists of three stages: strategy formulation, strategy implementation, and strategy evaluation. *Strategy formulation* includes developing a vision and mission, identifying an organization's external opportunities and threats, determining internal strengths and weaknesses, establishing long-term objectives, generating alternative strategies, and choosing particular strategies to pursue. Strategy-formulation issues include deciding what new businesses to enter, what businesses to abandon, how to allocate resources, whether to expand operations or diversify, whether to enter international markets, whether to merge or form a joint venture, and how to avoid a hostile takeover.

Because no organization has unlimited resources, strategists must decide which alternative strategies will benefit the firm most. Strategy-formulation decisions commit an organization to specific products, markets, resources, and technologies over an extended period of time. Strategies determine long-term competitive advantages. For better or worse, strategic decisions have major multifunctional consequences and enduring effects on an organization. Top managers have the best perspective to understand fully the ramifications of strategy-formulation decisions; they have the authority to commit the resources necessary for implementation.

Strategy implementation requires a firm to establish annual objectives, devise policies, motivate employees, and allocate resources so that formulated strategies can be executed. Strategy implementation includes developing a strategy-supportive culture, creating an effective organizational structure, redirecting marketing efforts, preparing budgets, developing and utilizing information systems, and linking employee compensation to organizational performance.

Strategy implementation often is called the "action stage" of strategic management. Implementing strategy means mobilizing employees and managers to put formulated strategies into action. Often considered to be the most difficult stage in strategic management, strategy implementation requires personal discipline, commitment, and sacrifice. Successful strategy implementation hinges upon managers' ability to motivate employees, which is more an art than a science. Strategies formulated but not implemented serve no useful purpose.

Interpersonal skills are especially critical for successful strategy implementation. Strategy-implementation activities affect all employees and managers in an organization. Every division and department must decide on answers to questions, such as "What must we do to implement our part of the organization's strategy?" and "How best can we get the job done?" The challenge of implementation is to stimulate managers and employees throughout an organization to work with pride and enthusiasm toward achieving stated objectives.

Strategy evaluation is the final stage in strategic management. Managers desperately need to know when particular strategies are not working well; strategy evaluation is the primary means for obtaining this information. All strategies are subject to future modification because external and internal factors are constantly changing. Three fundamental strategy-evaluation activities are (1) reviewing external and internal factors that are the bases for current strategies, (2) measuring performance, and (3) taking corrective actions. Strategy evaluation is needed because success today is no guarantee of success tomorrow! Success always creates new and different problems; complacent organizations experience demise.

Strategy formulation, implementation, and evaluation activities occur at three hierarchical levels in a large organization: corporate, divisional or strategic business unit, and functional. By fostering communication and interaction among managers and employees across hierarchical levels, strategic management helps a firm function as a competitive team. Most small businesses and some large businesses do not have divisions or strategic business units; they have only the corporate and functional levels. Nevertheless, managers and employees at these two levels should be actively involved in strategic-management activities.

Peter Drucker says the prime task of strategic management is thinking through the overall mission of a business:

> . . . that is, of asking the question, "What is our business?" This leads to the setting of objectives, the development of strategies, and the making of today's decisions for tomorrow's results. This clearly must be done by a part of the organization that can see the entire business; that can balance objectives and the needs of today against the needs of tomorrow; and that can allocate resources of men and money to key results.[2]

Integrating Intuition and Analysis

Edward Deming once said, "In God we trust. All others bring data." The strategic-management process can be described as an objective, logical, systematic approach for making major decisions in an organization. It attempts to organize qualitative and quantitative information in a way that allows effective decisions to be made under conditions of uncertainty. Yet strategic management is not a pure science that lends itself to a nice, neat, one-two-three approach.

Based on past experiences, judgment, and feelings, most people recognize that *intuition* is essential to making good strategic decisions. Intuition is particularly useful for making decisions in situations of great uncertainty or little precedent. It is also helpful when highly interrelated variables exist or when it is necessary to choose from several plausible alternatives. Some managers and owners of businesses profess to have extraordinary abilities for using intuition alone in devising brilliant strategies. For example, Will Durant, who organized GM, was described by Alfred Sloan as "a man who would proceed on a course of action guided solely, as far as I could tell, by some intuitive flash of brilliance. He never felt obliged to make an engineering hunt for the facts. Yet at times, he was astoundingly correct in his judgment."[3] Albert Einstein acknowledged the importance of intuition when he said, "I believe in intuition and inspiration. At times I feel certain that I am right while not knowing the reason. Imagination is more important than knowledge, because knowledge is limited, whereas imagination embraces the entire world."[4]

Although some organizations today may survive and prosper because they have intuitive geniuses managing them, most are not so fortunate. Most organizations can benefit from strategic management, which is based upon integrating intuition and analysis in decision making. Choosing an intuitive or analytic approach to decision making is not an either–or proposition. Managers at all levels in an organization inject their intuition and judgment into strategic-management analyses. Analytical thinking and intuitive thinking complement each other.

Operating from the I've-already-made-up-my-mind-don't-bother-me-with-the-facts mode is not management by intuition; it is management by ignorance.[5] Drucker says, "I believe in intuition only if you discipline it. 'Hunch' artists, who make a diagnosis but don't check it out with the facts, are the ones in medicine who kill people, and in management kill businesses."[6] As Henderson notes:

> The accelerating rate of change today is producing a business world in which customary managerial habits in organizations are increasingly inadequate. Experience alone was an adequate guide when changes could be made in small increments. But intuitive and experience-based management philosophies are grossly inadequate when decisions are strategic and have major, irreversible consequences.[7]

In a sense, the strategic-management process is an attempt both to duplicate what goes on in the mind of a brilliant, intuitive person who knows the business and to couple it with analysis.

Adapting to Change

The strategic-management process is based on the belief that organizations should continually monitor internal and external events and trends so that timely changes can be made as needed. The rate and magnitude of changes that affect organizations are increasing dramatically as evidenced how the global economic recession has caught so many firms by surprise. Firms, like organisms, must be "adept at adapting" or they will not survive.

Corporate bankruptcies and defaults more than doubled in 2009 from an already bad 2008 year. All industries were hit hard, especially retail, chemicals, autos, and financial. As lenders tightened restrictions on borrowers, thousands of firms could not avoid bankruptcy. Even the economies of China, Japan, and South Korea stalled as demand for their goods from the United States and Europe dried up. China's annual growth slowed from 13 percent in 2007 to 9 percent in 2008 and then 5 percent for 2009. Consumer confidence indexes were falling all over the world as were housing prices.

Nine of 10 stocks in the S&P 1500 lost value in 2008. The Nasdaq composite index fell 40.5 percent in 2008, its worst year ever. S&P 500 stocks lost 38.5 percent of their value in 2008, the worst year since 1937. The Dow Jones Industrial Average lost 33.8 percent of its value in 2008, the worst loss since 1931 as shareholders lost $6.8 trillion in wealth. Only three S&P 500 stocks rose in 2008: Family Dollar up 38 percent, making it the best performer in the S&P 500; Wal-Mart Stores up 18 percent; and McDonald's up nearly 6 percent. The biggest decliner on the Dow in 2008 was GM, whose stock fell 87 percent. Citigroup lost 77 percent of its stock value in 2008. Even General Electric lost 56 percent of its value. Fannie Mae and Freddie Mac each slid 98 percent as did Fleetwood Enterprises, which makes recreational vehicles. And losses were also extensive worldwide. For example, Vanguard's Europe/Pacific Index, composed of stocks firms based on those continents, fell 43 percent in 2008.

To survive, all organizations must astutely identify and adapt to change. The strategic-management process is aimed at allowing organizations to adapt effectively to change over the long run. As Waterman has noted:

> In today's business environment, more than in any preceding era, the only constant is change. Successful organizations effectively manage change, continuously adapting their bureaucracies, strategies, systems, products, and cultures to survive the shocks and prosper from the forces that decimate the competition.[8]

E-commerce and globalization are external changes that are transforming business and society today. On a political map, the boundaries between countries may be clear, but on a competitive map showing the real flow of financial and industrial activity, the boundaries have largely disappeared. The speedy flow of information has eaten away at national boundaries so that people worldwide readily see for themselves how other people live and work. We have become a borderless world with global citizens, global competitors, global customers, global suppliers, and global distributors! U.S. firms are challenged by large rival companies in many industries. To say U.S. firms are being challenged in the automobile industry is an understatement. But this situation is true in many industries.

The need to adapt to change leads organizations to key strategic-management questions, such as "What kind of business should we become?" "Are we in the right field(s)?" "Should we reshape our business?" "What new competitors are entering our industry?" "What strategies should we pursue?" "How are our customers changing?" "Are new technologies being developed that could put us out of business?"

Key Terms in Strategic Management

Before we further discuss strategic management, we should define nine key terms: competitive advantage, strategists, vision and mission statements, external opportunities and threats, internal strengths and weaknesses, long-term objectives, strategies, annual objectives, and policies.

Competitive Advantage

Strategic management is all about gaining and maintaining *competitive advantage*. This term can be defined as "anything that a firm does especially well compared to rival firms." When a firm can do something that rival firms cannot do, or owns something that rival firms desire, that can represent a competitive advantage. For example, in a global economic recession, simply having ample cash on the firm's balance sheet can provide a major competitive advantage. Some cash-rich firms are buying distressed rivals. For example, BHP Billiton, the world's largest miner, is seeking to buy rival firms in Australia and South America. Freeport-McMoRan Copper & Gold Inc. also desires to expand its portfolio by acquiring distressed rival companies. French drug company SanofiAventis SA also is acquiring distressed rival firms to boost its drug development and diversification. Cash-rich Johnson & Johnson in the United States also is acquiring distressed rival firms. This can be an excellent strategy in a global economic recession.

Having less fixed assets than rival firms also can provide major competitive advantages in a global recession. For example, Apple has no manufacturing facilities of its own, and rival Sony has 57 electronics factories. Apple relies exclusively on contract manufacturers for production of all of its products, whereas Sony owns its own plants. Less fixed assets has enabled Apple to remain financially lean with virtually no long-term debt. Sony, in contrast, has built up massive debt on its balance sheet.

CEO Paco Underhill of Envirosell says, "Where it used to be a polite war, it's now a 21st-century bar fight, where everybody is competing with everyone else for the customers' money." Shoppers are "trading down," so Nordstrom is taking customers from Neiman Marcus and Saks Fifth Avenue, T.J. Maxx and Marshalls are taking customers from most other stores in the mall, and even Family Dollar is taking revenues from Wal-Mart.[9] Getting and keeping competitive advantage is essential for long-term success in an organization. The Industrial/Organizational (I/O) and the Resource-Based View (RBV) theories of organization (as discussed in Chapters 3 and 4, respectively) present different perspectives on how best to capture and keep competitive advantage—that is, how best to manage strategically. Pursuit of competitive advantage leads to organizational success or failure. Strategic management researchers and practitioners alike desire to better understand the nature and role of competitive advantage in various industries.

Normally, a firm can sustain a competitive advantage for only a certain period due to rival firms imitating and undermining that advantage. Thus it is not adequate to simply obtain competitive advantage. A firm must strive to achieve *sustained competitive advantage* by

(1) continually adapting to changes in external trends and events and internal capabilities, competencies, and resources; and by (2) effectively formulating, implementing, and evaluating strategies that capitalize upon those factors. For example, newspaper circulation in the United States is steadily declining. Most national newspapers are rapidly losing market share to the Internet, and other media that consumers use to stay informed. Daily newspaper circulation in the United States totals about 55 million copies annually, which is about the same as it was in 1954. Strategists ponder whether the newspaper circulation slide can be halted in the digital age. The six broadcast networks—ABC, CBS, Fox, NBC, UPN, and WB—are being assaulted by cable channels, video games, broadband, wireless technologies, satellite radio, high-definition TV, and digital video recorders. The three original broadcast networks captured about 90 percent of the prime-time audience in 1978, but today their combined market share is less than 50 percent.[10]

An increasing number of companies are gaining a competitive advantage by using the Internet for direct selling and for communication with suppliers, customers, creditors, partners, shareholders, clients, and competitors who may be dispersed globally. E-commerce allows firms to sell products, advertise, purchase supplies, bypass intermediaries, track inventory, eliminate paperwork, and share information. In total, e-commerce is minimizing the expense and cumbersomeness of time, distance, and space in doing business, thus yielding better customer service, greater efficiency, improved products, and higher profitability.

The Internet has changed the way we organize our lives; inhabit our homes; and relate to and interact with family, friends, neighbors, and even ourselves. The Internet promotes endless comparison shopping, which thus enables consumers worldwide to band together to demand discounts. The Internet has transferred power from businesses to individuals. Buyers used to face big obstacles when attempting to get the best price and service, such as limited time and data to compare, but now consumers can quickly scan hundreds of vendor offerings. Both the number of people shopping online and the average amount they spend is increasing dramatically. Digital communication has become the name of the game in marketing. Consumers today are flocking to blogs, short-post forums such as Twitter, video sites such as YouTube, and social networking sites such as Facebook, MySpace, and LinkedIn instead of television, radio, newspapers, and magazines. Facebook and MySpace recently unveiled features that further marry these social sites to the wider Internet. Users on these social sites now can log on to many business shopping sites with their IDs from their social site so their friends can see what items they have purchased on various shopping sites. Both of these social sites want their members to use their IDs to manage all their online identities. Most traditional retailers have learned that their online sales can boost in-store sales as they utilize their Web sites to promote in-store promotions.

Strategists

Strategists are the individuals who are most responsible for the success or failure of an organization. Strategists have various job titles, such as chief executive officer, president, owner, chair of the board, executive director, chancellor, dean, or entrepreneur. Jay Conger, professor of organizational behavior at the London Business School and author of *Building Leaders,* says, "All strategists have to be chief learning officers. We are in an extended period of change. If our leaders aren't highly adaptive and great models during this period, then our companies won't adapt either, because ultimately leadership is about being a role model."

Strategists help an organization gather, analyze, and organize information. They track industry and competitive trends, develop forecasting models and scenario analyses, evaluate corporate and divisional performance, spot emerging market opportunities, identify business threats, and develop creative action plans. Strategic planners usually serve in a support or staff role. Usually found in higher levels of management, they typically have considerable authority for decision making in the firm. The CEO is the most visible and critical strategic manager. Any manager who has responsibility for a unit or division, responsibility for profit and loss outcomes, or direct authority over a major piece of the business is a strategic manager (strategist). In the last five years, the position of chief strategy officer (CSO) has emerged as a new addition to the top management ranks of many organizations, including Sun Microsystems, Network Associates, Clarus, Lante, Marimba, Sapient, Commerce One,

BBDO, Cadbury Schweppes, General Motors, Ellie Mae, Cendant, Charles Schwab, Tyco, Campbell Soup, Morgan Stanley, and Reed-Elsevier. This new corporate officer title represents recognition of the growing importance of strategic planning in the business world.[11]

Strategists differ as much as organizations themselves, and these differences must be considered in the formulation, implementation, and evaluation of strategies. Some strategists will not consider some types of strategies because of their personal philosophies. Strategists differ in their attitudes, values, ethics, willingness to take risks, concern for social responsibility, concern for profitability, concern for short-run versus long-run aims, and management style. The founder of Hershey Foods, Milton Hershey, built the company to manage an orphanage. From corporate profits, Hershey Foods today cares for over a thousand boys and girls in its School for Orphans.

Vision and Mission Statements

Many organizations today develop a *vision statement* that answers the question "What do we want to become?" Developing a vision statement is often considered the first step in strategic planning, preceding even development of a mission statement. Many vision statements are a single sentence. For example, the vision statement of Stokes Eye Clinic in Florence, South Carolina, is "Our vision is to take care of your vision."

Mission statements are "enduring statements of purpose that distinguish one business from other similar firms. A mission statement identifies the scope of a firm's operations in product and market terms."[12] It addresses the basic question that faces all strategists: "What is our business?" A clear mission statement describes the values and priorities of an organization. Developing a mission statement compels strategists to think about the nature and scope of present operations and to assess the potential attractiveness of future markets and activities. A mission statement broadly charts the future direction of an organization. A mission statement is a constant reminder to its employees of why the organization exists and what the founders envisioned when they put their fame and fortune at risk to breathe life into their dreams. Here is an example of a mission statement for Barnes & Noble:

> Our mission is to operate the best specialty retail business in America, regardless of the product we sell. Because the product we sell is books, our aspirations must be consistent with the promise and the ideals of the volumes which line our shelves. To say that our mission exists independent of the product we sell is to demean the importance and the distinction of being booksellers. As booksellers we are determined to be the very best in our business, regardless of the size, pedigree, or inclinations of our competitors. We will continue to bring our industry nuances of style and approaches to bookselling which are consistent with our evolving aspirations. Above all, we expect to be a credit to the communities we serve, a valuable resource to our customers, and a place where our dedicated booksellers can grow and prosper. Toward this end we will not only listen to our customers and booksellers but embrace the idea that the Company is at their service. (www.missionstatements.com)

External Opportunities and Threats

External opportunities and *external threats* refer to economic, social, cultural, demographic, environmental, political, legal, governmental, technological, and competitive trends and events that could significantly benefit or harm an organization in the future. Opportunities and threats are largely beyond the control of a single organization—thus the word *external*. In a global economic recession, a few opportunities and threats that face many firms are listed here:

- Availability of capital can no longer be taken for granted.
- Consumers expect green operations and products.
- Marketing has moving rapidly to the Internet.
- Consumers must see value in all that they consume.
- Global markets offer the highest growth in revenues.

- As the price of oil has collapsed, oil rich countries are focused on supporting their own economies, rather than seeking out investments in other countries.
- Too much debt can crush even the best firms.
- Layoffs are rampant among many firms as revenues and profits fall and credit sources dry up.
- The housing market is depressed.
- Demand for health services does not change much in a recession. For example, Almost Family Inc., a Louisville, Kentucky, provider of home nursing care, more than doubled its stock price in 2008 to $45.
- Dramatic slowdowns in consumer spending are apparent in virtually all sectors, except some discount retailers and restaurants.
- Emerging countries' economies could manage to grow 5 percent in 2009, but that is three full percentage points lower than in 2007.
- U.S. unemployment rates continue to rise to 10 percent on average.
- Borrowers are faced with much bigger collateral requirements than in years past.
- Equity lines of credit often now are not being extended.
- Firms that have cash or access to credit have a competitive advantage over debt-laden firms.
- Discretionary spending has fallen dramatically; consumers buy only essential items; this has crippled many luxury and recreational businesses such as boating and cycling.
- The stock market crash of 2008 left senior citizens with retirement worries, so millions of people cut back on spending to the bare essentials.
- The double whammy of falling demand and intense price competition is plaguing most firms, especially those with high fixed costs.
- The business world has moved from a credit-based economy to a cash-based economy.
- There is reduced capital spending in response to reduced consumer spending.

The types of changes mentioned above are creating a different type of consumer and consequently a need for different types of products, services, and strategies. Many companies in many industries face the severe external threat of online sales capturing increasing market share in their industry.

Other opportunities and threats may include the passage of a law, the introduction of a new product by a competitor, a national catastrophe, or the declining value of the dollar. A competitor's strength could be a threat. Unrest in the Middle East, rising energy costs, or the war against terrorism could represent an opportunity or a threat.

A basic tenet of strategic management is that firms need to formulate strategies to take advantage of external opportunities and to avoid or reduce the impact of external threats. For this reason, identifying, monitoring, and evaluating external opportunities and threats are essential for success. This process of conducting research and gathering and assimilating external information is sometimes called *environmental scanning* or industry analysis. Lobbying is one activity that some organizations utilize to influence external opportunities and threats.

Internal Strengths and Weaknesses

Internal strengths and *internal weaknesses* are an organization's controllable activities that are performed especially well or poorly. They arise in the management, marketing, finance/accounting, production/operations, research and development, and management information systems activities of a business. Identifying and evaluating organizational strengths and weaknesses in the functional areas of a business is an essential strategic-management activity. Organizations strive to pursue strategies that capitalize on internal strengths and eliminate internal weaknesses.

Strengths and weaknesses are determined relative to competitors. *Relative* deficiency or superiority is important information. Also, strengths and weaknesses can be determined by elements of being rather than performance. For example, a strength may involve ownership of natural resources or a historic reputation for quality. Strengths and weaknesses may be determined relative to a firm's own objectives. For example, high levels of inventory turnover may not be a strength to a firm that seeks never to stock-out.

Internal factors can be determined in a number of ways, including computing ratios, measuring performance, and comparing to past periods and industry averages. Various types of surveys also can be developed and administered to examine internal factors such as employee morale, production efficiency, advertising effectiveness, and customer loyalty.

Long-Term Objectives

Objectives can be defined as specific results that an organization seeks to achieve in pursuing its basic mission. *Long-term* means more than one year. Objectives are essential for organizational success because they state direction; aid in evaluation; create synergy; reveal priorities; focus coordination; and provide a basis for effective planning, organizing, motivating, and controlling activities. Objectives should be challenging, measurable, consistent, reasonable, and clear. In a multidimensional firm, objectives should be established for the overall company and for each division.

Strategies

Strategies are the means by which long-term objectives will be achieved. Business strategies may include geographic expansion, diversification, acquisition, product development, market penetration, retrenchment, divestiture, liquidation, and joint ventures. Strategies currently being pursued by some companies are described in Table 1-1.

Strategies are potential actions that require top management decisions and large amounts of the firm's resources. In addition, strategies affect an organization's long-term prosperity, typically for at least five years, and thus are future-oriented. Strategies have multifunctional or multidivisional consequences and require consideration of both the external and internal factors facing the firm.

Annual Objectives

Annual objectives are short-term milestones that organizations must achieve to reach long-term objectives. Like long-term objectives, annual objectives should be measurable, quantitative, challenging, realistic, consistent, and prioritized. They should be established at the

TABLE 1-1 Sample Strategies in Action in 2009

Best Buy

As soon as Best Buy Company became victorious over longtime archrival Circuit City Stores, Best Buy ran head on into a much larger, formidable competitor: Wal-Mart Stores. Based in Richfield, Minnesota, and having 3,900 stores worldwide, Best Buy reported a 20 percent decline in March 2009 earnings as its new rival Wal-Mart gained thousands of the old Circuit City customers. But Best Buy now meets Wal-Mart's prices on electronics items and provides great one-on-one customer service with its blue-shirted employees. Best Buy remains well ahead of Wal-Mart in U.S. electronics sales, but Wal-Mart is gaining strength.

Levi Strauss

San Francisco-based Levi Strauss added 30 new stores and acquired 72 others during the second quarter of 2009. Known worldwide for its jeans, Levi Strauss is expanding and entrenching worldwide while other retailers are faltering in the ailing economy. For that quarter, Levi's revenues in the Americas were up 8 percent to $518 million, although its Europe and Asia/Pacific revenues declined 17 percent and 13 percent respectively. Levi's CEO John Anderson says slim fit and skinny jeans are selling best; and the two most popular colors today are very dark and the distressed look.

New York Times Company

New York Times Company's CEO, Janet Robinson, says her company is selling off assets and investing heavily in Internet technology in order to convince advertisers that the newspaper is getting ahead of technological changes rapidly eroding the newspaper business. Ms. Robinson is considering plans to begin charging customers for access to the newspaper's online content, because online advertising revenues are not sufficient to support the business. The 160-year-old New York Times Company's advertising revenues fell 30 percent in the second quarter of 2009.

TABLE 1-2   Percentage of People Who Smoke in Selected Countries

Country	Percentage	
Greece	50	
Russia		High
Austria		
Spain		
U.K.		
France		
Germany		
Italy		
Belgium		
Switzerland		Low
USA	19	

Source: Based on Christina Passariello, "Smoking Culture Persists in Europe, Despite Bans," *Wall Street Journal* (January 2, 2009): A5.

corporate, divisional, and functional levels in a large organization. Annual objectives should be stated in terms of management, marketing, finance/accounting, production/operations, research and development, and management information systems (MIS) accomplishments. A set of annual objectives is needed for each long-term objective. Annual objectives are especially important in strategy implementation, whereas long-term objectives are particularly important in strategy formulation. Annual objectives represent the basis for allocating resources.

Policies

Policies are the means by which annual objectives will be achieved. Policies include guidelines, rules, and procedures established to support efforts to achieve stated objectives. Policies are guides to decision making and address repetitive or recurring situations.

Policies are most often stated in terms of management, marketing, finance/accounting, production/operations, research and development, and computer information systems activities. Policies can be established at the corporate level and apply to an entire organization at the divisional level and apply to a single division, or at the functional level and apply to particular operational activities or departments. Policies, like annual objectives, are especially important in strategy implementation because they outline an organization's expectations of its employees and managers. Policies allow consistency and coordination within and between organizational departments.

Substantial research suggests that a healthier workforce can more effectively and efficiently implement strategies. Smoking has become a heavy burden for Europe's state-run social welfare systems, with smoking-related diseases costing well over $100 billion a year. Smoking also is a huge burden on companies worldwide, so firms are continually implementing policies to curtail smoking. Table 1-2 gives a ranking of some countries by percentage of people who smoke.

The Strategic-Management Model

The strategic-management process can best be studied and applied using a model. Every model represents some kind of process. The framework illustrated in Figure 1-1 is a widely accepted, comprehensive model of the strategic-management process.[13] This model does not guarantee success, but it does represent a clear and practical approach for formulating, implementing, and evaluating strategies. Relationships among major components of the strategic-management process are shown in the model, which appears in all subsequent

FIGURE 1-1

A Comprehensive Strategic-Management Model

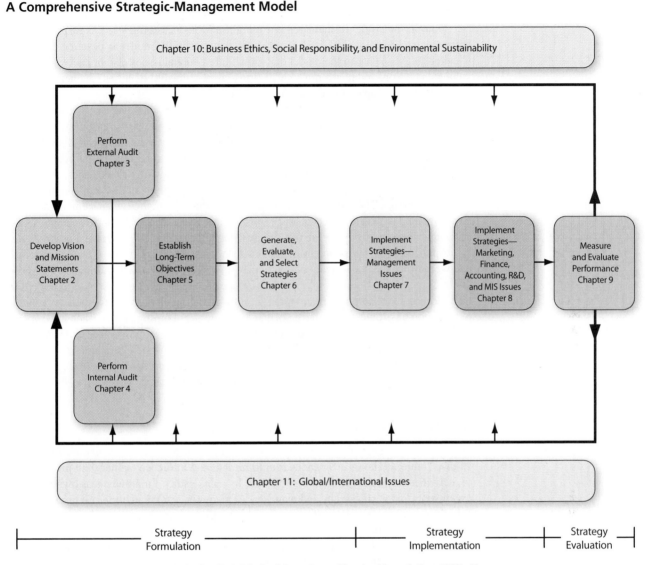

Source: Fred R. David, "How Companies Define Their Mission," *Long Range Planning* 22, no. 3 (June 1988): 40.

chapters with appropriate areas shaped to show the particular focus of each chapter. These are three important questions to answer in developing a strategic plan:

Where are we now?

Where do we want to go?

How are we going to get there?

Identifying an organization's existing vision, mission, objectives, and strategies is the logical starting point for strategic management because a firm's present situation and condition may preclude certain strategies and may even dictate a particular course of action. Every organization has a vision, mission, objectives, and strategy, even if these elements are not consciously designed, written, or communicated. The answer to where an organization is going can be determined largely by where the organization has been!

The strategic-management process is dynamic and continuous. A change in any one of the major components in the model can necessitate a change in any or all of the other components. For instance, a shift in the economy could represent a major opportunity and require a change in long-term objectives and strategies; a failure to accomplish annual objectives could require a change in policy; or a major competitor's change in strategy could require a change in the firm's mission. Therefore, strategy formulation, implementation, and evaluation activities should be performed on a continual basis, not just at the end of the year or semiannually. The strategic-management process never really ends.

Note in the strategic-management model that business ethics/social responsibility/environmental sustainability issues impact all activities in the model as described in full in Chapter 10. Also, note in the model that global/international issues also impact virtually all strategic decisions today, even for small firms, as described in detail in Chapter 11. (Both Chapter 10 and Chapter 11 are new to this edition.)

The strategic-management process is not as cleanly divided and neatly performed in practice as the strategic-management model suggests. Strategists do not go through the process in lockstep fashion. Generally, there is give-and-take among hierarchical levels of an organization. Many organizations semiannually conduct formal meetings to discuss and update the firm's vision/mission, opportunities/threats, strengths/weaknesses, strategies, objectives, policies, and performance. These meetings are commonly held off-premises and are called *retreats*. The rationale for periodically conducting strategic-management meetings away from the work site is to encourage more creativity and candor from participants. Good communication and feedback are needed throughout the strategic-management process.

Application of the strategic-management process is typically more formal in larger and well-established organizations. Formality refers to the extent that participants, responsibilities, authority, duties, and approach are specified. Smaller businesses tend to be less formal. Firms that compete in complex, rapidly changing environments, such as technology companies, tend to be more formal in strategic planning. Firms that have many divisions, products, markets, and technologies also tend to be more formal in applying strategic-management concepts. Greater formality in applying the strategic-management process is usually positively associated with the cost, comprehensiveness, accuracy, and success of planning across all types and sizes of organizations.[14]

Benefits of Strategic Management

Strategic management allows an organization to be more proactive than reactive in shaping its own future; it allows an organization to initiate and influence (rather than just respond to) activities—and thus to exert control over its own destiny. Small business owners, chief executive officers, presidents, and managers of many for-profit and nonprofit organizations have recognized and realized the benefits of strategic management.

Historically, the principal benefit of strategic management has been to help organizations formulate better strategies through the use of a more systematic, logical, and rational approach to strategic choice. This certainly continues to be a major benefit of strategic management, but research studies now indicate that the process, rather than the decision or document, is the more important contribution of strategic management.[15] *Communication is a key to successful strategic management.* Through involvement in the process, in other words, through dialogue and participation, managers and employees become committed to supporting the organization. Figure 1-2 illustrates this intrinsic

FIGURE 1-2

Benefits to a Firm That Does Strategic Planning

benefit of a firm engaging in strategic planning. Note that all firms need all employees on a mission to help the firm succeed.

The manner in which strategic management is carried out is thus exceptionally important. A major aim of the process is to achieve the understanding of and commitment from all managers and employees. Understanding may be the most important benefit of strategic management, followed by commitment. When managers and employees understand what the organization is doing and why, they often feel they are a part of the firm and become committed to assisting it. This is especially true when employees also understand linkages between their own compensation and organizational performance. Managers and employees become surprisingly creative and innovative when they understand and support the firm's mission, objectives, and strategies. A great benefit of strategic management, then, is the opportunity that the process provides to empower individuals. *Empowerment* is the act of strengthening employees' sense of effectiveness by encouraging them to participate in decision making and to exercise initiative and imagination, and rewarding them for doing so.

More and more organizations are decentralizing the strategic-management process, recognizing that planning must involve lower-level managers and employees. The notion of centralized staff planning is being replaced in organizations by decentralized line-manager planning. For example, Walt Disney Co. dismantled its strategic-planning department and gave those responsibilities back to the Disney business divisions. Former CEO Michael Eisner had favored the centralized strategic-planning approach, but CEO Robert Iger dissolved Disney's strategic-planning department within weeks of his taking over the top office at Disney.

The process is a learning, helping, educating, and supporting activity, not merely a paper-shuffling activity among top executives. Strategic-management dialogue is more important than a nicely bound strategic-management document.[16] The worst thing strategists can do is develop strategic plans themselves and then present them to operating managers to execute. Through involvement in the process, line managers become "owners" of the strategy. Ownership of strategies by the people who have to execute them is a key to success!

Although making good strategic decisions is the major responsibility of an organization's owner or chief executive officer, both managers and employees must also be involved in strategy formulation, implementation, and evaluation activities. Participation is a key to gaining commitment for needed changes.

An increasing number of corporations and institutions are using strategic management to make effective decisions. But strategic management is not a guarantee for success; it can be dysfunctional if conducted haphazardly.

Financial Benefits

Research indicates that organizations using strategic-management concepts are more profitable and successful than those that do not.[17] Businesses using strategic-management concepts show significant improvement in sales, profitability, and productivity compared to firms without systematic planning activities. High-performing firms tend to do systematic planning to prepare for future fluctuations in their external and internal environments. Firms with planning systems more closely resembling strategic-management theory generally exhibit superior long-term financial performance relative to their industry.

High-performing firms seem to make more informed decisions with good anticipation of both short- and long-term consequences. In contrast, firms that perform poorly often engage in activities that are shortsighted and do not reflect good forecasting of future conditions. Strategists of low-performing organizations are often preoccupied with solving internal problems and meeting paperwork deadlines. They typically underestimate their competitors' strengths and overestimate their own firm's strengths. They often attribute weak performance to uncontrollable factors such as a poor economy, technological change, or foreign competition.

More than 100,000 businesses in the United States fail annually. Business failures include bankruptcies, foreclosures, liquidations, and court-mandated receiverships. Although many factors besides a lack of effective strategic management can lead to business failure, the planning concepts and tools described in this text can yield substantial financial benefits for any organization. An excellent Web site for businesses engaged in strategic planning is www.checkmateplan.com.

Nonfinancial Benefits

Besides helping firms avoid financial demise, strategic management offers other tangible benefits, such as an enhanced awareness of external threats, an improved understanding of competitors' strategies, increased employee productivity, reduced resistance to change, and a clearer understanding of performance–reward relationships. Strategic management enhances the problem-prevention capabilities of organizations because it promotes interaction among managers at all divisional and functional levels. Firms that have nurtured their managers and employees, shared organizational objectives with them, empowered them to help improve the product or service, and recognized their contributions can turn to them for help in a pinch because of this interaction.

In addition to empowering managers and employees, strategic management often brings order and discipline to an otherwise floundering firm. It can be the beginning of an efficient and effective managerial system. Strategic management may renew confidence in the current business strategy or point to the need for corrective actions. The strategic-management process provides a basis for identifying and rationalizing the need for change to all managers and employees of a firm; it helps them view change as an opportunity rather than as a threat.

Greenley stated that strategic management offers the following benefits:

1. It allows for identification, prioritization, and exploitation of opportunities.
2. It provides an objective view of management problems.
3. It represents a framework for improved coordination and control of activities.
4. It minimizes the effects of adverse conditions and changes.
5. It allows major decisions to better support established objectives.
6. It allows more effective allocation of time and resources to identified opportunities.
7. It allows fewer resources and less time to be devoted to correcting erroneous or ad hoc decisions.
8. It creates a framework for internal communication among personnel.
9. It helps integrate the behavior of individuals into a total effort.
10. It provides a basis for clarifying individual responsibilities.
11. It encourages forward thinking.
12. It provides a cooperative, integrated, and enthusiastic approach to tackling problems and opportunities.
13. It encourages a favorable attitude toward change.
14. It gives a degree of discipline and formality to the management of a business.[18]

Why Some Firms Do No Strategic Planning

Some firms do not engage in strategic planning, and some firms do strategic planning but receive no support from managers and employees. Some reasons for poor or no strategic planning are as follows:

- *Lack of knowledge or experience in strategic planning*—No training in strategic planning.
- *Poor reward structures*—When an organization assumes success, it often fails to reward success. When failure occurs, then the firm may punish.
- *Firefighting*—An organization can be so deeply embroiled in resolving crises and firefighting that it reserves no time for planning.
- *Waste of time*—Some firms see planning as a waste of time because no marketable product is produced. Time spent on planning is an investment.
- *Too expensive*—Some organizations see planning as too expensive in time and money.
- *Laziness*—People may not want to put forth the effort needed to formulate a plan.

- *Content with success*—Particularly if a firm is successful, individuals may feel there is no need to plan because things are fine as they stand. But success today does not guarantee success tomorrow.
- *Fear of failure*—By not taking action, there is little risk of failure unless a problem is urgent and pressing. Whenever something worthwhile is attempted, there is some risk of failure.
- *Overconfidence*—As managers amass experience, they may rely less on formalized planning. Rarely, however, is this appropriate. Being overconfident or overestimating experience can bring demise. Forethought is rarely wasted and is often the mark of professionalism.
- *Prior bad experience*—People may have had a previous bad experience with planning, that is, cases in which plans have been long, cumbersome, impractical, or inflexible. Planning, like anything else, can be done badly.
- *Self-interest*—When someone has achieved status, privilege, or self-esteem through effectively using an old system, he or she often sees a new plan as a threat.
- *Fear of the unknown*—People may be uncertain of their abilities to learn new skills, of their aptitude with new systems, or of their ability to take on new roles.
- *Honest difference of opinion*—People may sincerely believe the plan is wrong. They may view the situation from a different viewpoint, or they may have aspirations for themselves or the organization that are different from the plan. Different people in different jobs have different perceptions of a situation.
- *Suspicion*—Employees may not trust management.[19]

Pitfalls in Strategic Planning

Strategic planning is an involved, intricate, and complex process that takes an organization into uncharted territory. It does not provide a ready-to-use prescription for success; instead, it takes the organization through a journey and offers a framework for addressing questions and solving problems. Being aware of potential pitfalls and being prepared to address them is essential to success.

Some pitfalls to watch for and avoid in strategic planning are these:

- Using strategic planning to gain control over decisions and resources
- Doing strategic planning only to satisfy accreditation or regulatory requirements
- Too hastily moving from mission development to strategy formulation
- Failing to communicate the plan to employees, who continue working in the dark
- Top managers making many intuitive decisions that conflict with the formal plan
- Top managers not actively supporting the strategic-planning process
- Failing to use plans as a standard for measuring performance
- Delegating planning to a "planner" rather than involving all managers
- Failing to involve key employees in all phases of planning
- Failing to create a collaborative climate supportive of change
- Viewing planning as unnecessary or unimportant
- Becoming so engrossed in current problems that insufficient or no planning is done
- Being so formal in planning that flexibility and creativity are stifled[20]

Guidelines for Effective Strategic Management

Failing to follow certain guidelines in conducting strategic management can foster criticisms of the process and create problems for the organization. Issues such as "Is strategic management in our firm a people process or a paper process?" should be addressed.

Even the most technically perfect strategic plan will serve little purpose if it is not implemented. Many organizations tend to spend an inordinate amount of time, money, and effort on developing the strategic plan, treating the means and circumstances under which it will be implemented as afterthoughts! Change comes through implementation and evaluation, not through the plan. A technically imperfect plan that is implemented well will achieve more than the perfect plan that never gets off the paper on which it is typed.[21]

Strategic management must not become a self-perpetuating bureaucratic mechanism. Rather, it must be a self-reflective learning process that familiarizes managers and employees in the organization with key strategic issues and feasible alternatives for resolving those issues. Strategic management must not become ritualistic, stilted, orchestrated, or too formal, predictable, and rigid. Words supported by numbers, rather than numbers supported by words, should represent the medium for explaining strategic issues and organizational responses. A key role of strategists is to facilitate continuous organizational learning and change.

R. T. Lenz offered some important guidelines for effective strategic management:

Keep the strategic-management process as simple and nonroutine as possible. Eliminate jargon and arcane planning language. Remember, strategic management is a process for fostering learning and action, not merely a formal system for control. To avoid routinized behavior, vary assignments, team membership, meeting formats, and the planning calendar. The process should not be totally predictable, and settings must be changed to stimulate creativity. Emphasize word-oriented plans with numbers as back-up material. If managers cannot express their strategy in a paragraph or so, they either do not have one or do not understand it. Stimulate thinking and action that challenge the assumptions underlying current corporate strategy. Welcome bad news. If strategy is not working, managers desperately need to know it. Further, no pertinent information should be classified as inadmissible merely because it cannot be quantified. Build a corporate culture in which the role of strategic management and its essential purposes are understood. Do not permit "technicians" to co-opt the process. It is ultimately a process for learning and action. Speak of it in these terms. Attend to psychological, social, and political dimensions, as well as the information infrastructure and administrative procedures supporting it.[22]

An important guideline for effective strategic management is open-mindedness. A willingness and eagerness to consider new information, new viewpoints, new ideas, and new possibilities is essential; all organizational members must share a spirit of inquiry and learning. Strategists such as chief executive officers, presidents, owners of small businesses, and heads of government agencies must commit themselves to listen to and understand managers' positions well enough to be able to restate those positions to the managers' satisfaction. In addition, managers and employees throughout the firm should be able to describe the strategists' positions to the satisfaction of the strategists. This degree of discipline will promote understanding and learning.

No organization has unlimited resources. No firm can take on an unlimited amount of debt or issue an unlimited amount of stock to raise capital. Therefore, no organization can pursue all the strategies that potentially could benefit the firm. Strategic decisions thus always have to be made to eliminate some courses of action and to allocate organizational resources among others. Most organizations can afford to pursue only a few corporate-level strategies at any given time. It is a critical mistake for managers to pursue too many strategies at the same time, thereby spreading the firm's resources so thin that all strategies are jeopardized. Joseph Charyk, CEO of the Communication Satellite Corporation (Comsat), said, "We have to face the cold fact that Comsat may not be able to do all it wants. We must make hard choices on which ventures to keep and which to fold."

Strategic decisions require trade-offs such as long-range versus short-range considerations or maximizing profits versus increasing shareholders' wealth. There are ethics issues too. Strategy trade-offs require subjective judgments and preferences. In many cases, a lack of objectivity in formulating strategy results in a loss of competitive posture and profitability. Most organizations today recognize that strategic-management concepts and techniques can enhance the effectiveness of decisions. Subjective factors such as attitudes toward risk, concern for social responsibility, and organizational culture will

TABLE 1-3   Seventeen Guidelines for the Strategic-Planning Process to Be Effective

1. It should be a people process more than a paper process.
2. It should be a learning process for all managers and employees.
3. It should be words supported by numbers rather than numbers supported by words.
4. It should be simple and nonroutine.
5. It should vary assignments, team memberships, meeting formats, and even the planning calendar.
6. It should challenge the assumptions underlying the current corporate strategy.
7. It should welcome bad news.
8. It should welcome open-mindness and a spirit of inquiry and learning.
9. It should not be a bureaucratic mechanism.
10. It should not become ritualistic, stilted, or orchestrated.
11. It should not be too formal, predictable, or rigid.
12. It should not contain jargon or arcane planning language.
13. It should not be a formal system for control.
14. It should not disregard qualitative information.
15. It should not be controlled by "technicians."
16. Do not pursue too many strategies at once.
17. Continually strengthen the "good ethics is good business" policy.

always affect strategy-formulation decisions, but organizations need to be as objective as possible in considering qualitative factors. Table 1-3 summarizes important guidelines for the strategic-planning process to be effective.

Comparing Business and Military Strategy

A strong military heritage underlies the study of strategic management. Terms such as *objectives, mission, strengths*, and *weaknesses* first were formulated to address problems on the battlefield. According to *Webster's New World Dictionary*, strategy is "the science of planning and directing large-scale military operations, of maneuvering forces into the most advantageous position prior to actual engagement with the enemy." The word *strategy* comes from the Greek *strategos*, which refers to a military general and combines *stratos* (the army) and *ago* (to lead). The history of strategic planning began in the military. A key aim of both business and military strategy is "to gain competitive advantage." In many respects, business strategy is like military strategy, and military strategists have learned much over the centuries that can benefit business strategists today. Both business and military organizations try to use their own strengths to exploit competitors' weaknesses. If an organization's overall strategy is wrong (ineffective), then all the efficiency in the world may not be enough to allow success. Business or military success is generally not the happy result of accidental strategies. Rather, success is the product of both continuous attention to changing external and internal conditions and the formulation and implementation of insightful adaptations to those conditions. The element of surprise provides great competitive advantages in both military and business strategy; information systems that provide data on opponents' or competitors' strategies and resources are also vitally important.

Of course, a fundamental difference between military and business strategy is that business strategy is formulated, implemented, and evaluated with an assumption of *competition*, whereas military strategy is based on an assumption of *conflict*. Nonetheless, military conflict and business competition are so similar that many strategic-management techniques apply equally to both. Business strategists have access to valuable insights that military thinkers have refined over time. Superior strategy formulation and implementation can overcome an opponent's superiority in numbers and resources.

Both business and military organizations must adapt to change and constantly improve to be successful. Too often, firms do not change their strategies when their environment and competitive conditions dictate the need to change. Gluck offered a classic military example of this:

> When Napoleon won, it was because his opponents were committed to the strategy, tactics, and organization of earlier wars. When he lost—against Wellington, the Russians, and the Spaniards—it was because he, in turn, used tried-and-true strategies against enemies who thought afresh, who were developing the strategies not of the last war but of the next.[23]

Similarities can be construed from Sun Tzu's writings to the practice of formulating and implementing strategies among businesses today. Table 1-4 provides narrative

TABLE 1-4   Excerpts from Sun Tzu's *The Art of War* Writings

- War is a matter of vital importance to the state: a matter of life or death, the road either to survival or ruin. Hence, it is imperative that it be studied thoroughly.
- Warfare is based on deception. When near the enemy, make it seem that you are far away; when far away, make it seem that you are near. Hold out baits to lure the enemy. Strike the enemy when he is in disorder. Avoid the enemy when he is stronger. If your opponent is of choleric temper, try to irritate him. If he is arrogant, try to encourage his egotism. If enemy troops are well prepared after reorganization, try to wear them down. If they are united, try to sow dissension among them. Attack the enemy where he is unprepared, and appear where you are not expected. These are the keys to victory for a strategist. It is not possible to formulate them in detail beforehand.
- A speedy victory is the main object in war. If this is long in coming, weapons are blunted and morale depressed. When the army engages in protracted campaigns, the resources of the state will fall short. Thus, while we have heard of stupid haste in war, we have not yet seen a clever operation that was prolonged.
- Generally, in war the best policy is to take a state intact; to ruin it is inferior to this. To capture the enemy's entire army is better than to destroy it; to take intact a regiment, a company, or a squad is better than to destroy it. For to win one hundred victories in one hundred battles is not the acme of skill. To subdue the enemy without fighting is the supreme excellence. Those skilled in war subdue the enemy's army without battle.
- The art of using troops is this: When ten to the enemy's one, surround him. When five times his strength, attack him. If double his strength, divide him. If equally matched, you may engage him with some good plan. If weaker, be capable of withdrawing. And if in all respects unequal, be capable of eluding him.
- Know your enemy and know yourself, and in a hundred battles you will never be defeated. When you are ignorant of the enemy but know yourself, your chances of winning or losing are equal. If ignorant both of your enemy and of yourself, you are sure to be defeated in every battle.
- He who occupies the field of battle first and awaits his enemy is at ease, and he who comes later to the scene and rushes into the fight is weary. And therefore, those skilled in war bring the enemy to the field of battle and are not brought there by him. Thus, when the enemy is at ease, be able to tire him; when well fed, be able to starve him; when at rest, be able to make him move.
- Analyze the enemy's plans so that you will know his shortcomings as well as his strong points. Agitate him to ascertain the pattern of his movement. Lure him out to reveal his dispositions and to ascertain his position. Launch a probing attack to learn where his strength is abundant and where deficient. It is according to the situation that plans are laid for victory, but the multitude does not comprehend this.
- An army may be likened to water, for just as flowing water avoids the heights and hastens to the lowlands, so an army should avoid strength and strike weakness. And as water shapes its flow in accordance with the ground, so an army manages its victory in accordance with the situation of the enemy. And as water has no constant form, there are in warfare no constant conditions. Thus, one able to win the victory by modifying his tactics in accordance with the enemy situation may be said to be divine.
- If you decide to go into battle, do not anounce your intentions or plans. Project "business as usual."
- Unskilled leaders work out their conflicts in courtrooms and battlefields. Brilliant strategists rarely go to battle or to court; they generally achieve their objectives through tactical positioning well in advance of any confrontation.
- When you do decide to challenge another company (or army), much calculating, estimating, analyzing, and positioning bring triumph. Little computation brings defeat.
- Skillful leaders do not let a strategy inhibit creative counter-movement. Nor should commands from those at a distance interfere with spontaneous maneuvering in the immediate situation.
- When a decisive advantage is gained over a rival, skillful leaders do not press on. They hold their position and give their rivals the opportunity to surrender or merge. They do not allow their forces to be damaged by those who have nothing to lose.
- Brilliant strategists forge ahead with illusion, obscuring the area(s) of major confrontation, so that opponents divide their forces in an attempt to defend many areas. Create the appearance of confusion, fear, or vulnerability so the opponent is helplessly drawn toward this illusion of advantage.

(Note: Substitute the words *strategy* or *strategic planning* for *war* or *warfare*)

Source: Based on *The Art of War* and from www.ccs.neu.edu/home/thigpen/html/art_of_war.html

excerpts from *The Art of War*. As you read through the table, consider which of the principles of war apply to business strategy as companies today compete aggressively to survive and grow.

Conclusion

All firms have a strategy, even if it is informal, unstructured, and sporadic. All organizations are heading somewhere, but unfortunately some organizations do not know where they are going. The old saying "If you do not know where you are going, then any road will lead you there!" accents the need for organizations to use strategic-management concepts and techniques. The strategic-management process is becoming more widely used by small firms, large companies, nonprofit institutions, governmental organizations, and multinational conglomerates alike. The process of empowering managers and employees has almost limitless benefits.

Organizations should take a proactive rather than a reactive approach in their industry, and they should strive to influence, anticipate, and initiate rather than just respond to events. The strategic-management process embodies this approach to decision making. It represents a logical, systematic, and objective approach for determining an enterprise's future direction. The stakes are generally too high for strategists to use intuition alone in choosing among alternative courses of action. Successful strategists take the time to think about their businesses, where they are with their businesses, and what they want to be as organizations—and then they implement programs and policies to get from where they are to where they want to be in a reasonable period of time.

It is a known and accepted fact that people and organizations that plan ahead are much more likely to become what they want to become than those that do not plan at all. A good strategist plans and controls his or her plans, whereas a bad strategist never plans and then tries to control people! This textbook is devoted to providing you with the tools necessary to be a good strategist.

We invite you to visit the David page on the Prentice Hall Companion Web site at http://www.pearsonhighered.com/david/ for this chapter's review quiz.

Key Terms and Concepts

Annual Objectives (p. 13)
Competitive Advantage (p. 9)
Empowerment (p. 17)
Environmental Scanning (p. 12)
External Opportunities (p. 11)
External Threats (p. 11)
Internal Strengths (p. 12)
Internal Weaknesses (p. 12)
Intuition (p. 7)
Long-Range Planning (p. 6)
Long-Term Objectives (p. 13)
Mission Statements (p. 11)
Policies (p. 14)

Retreats (p. 16)
Strategic Management (p. 6)
Strategic-Management Model (p. 14)
Strategic-Management Process (p. 6)
Strategic Planning (p. 6)
Strategies (p. 13)
Strategists (p. 10)
Strategy Evaluation (p. 7)
Strategy Formulation (p. 6)
Strategy Implementation (p. 6)
Sustained Competitive Advantage (p. 9)
Vision Statement (p. 11)

Issues for Review and Discussion

1. Distinguish between long-range planning and strategic planning.
2. Compare a company's strategic plan with a football team's game plan.
3. Describe the three activities that comprise strategy evaluation.

4. How important do you feel "being adept at adapting" is for business firms? Explain.
5. Compare the opossum and turtle to the woolly mammoth and saber-toothed tiger in terms of being adept at adapting. What can we learn from the opossum and turtle?
6. As cited in the chapter, Edward Deming, a famous businessman, once said, "In God we trust. All others bring data." What did Deming mean in terms of developing a strategic plan?
7. What strategies do you believe can save newspaper companies from extinction?
8. Distinguish between the concepts of vision and mission.
9. Your university has fierce competitors. List three external opportunities and three external threats that face your university.
10. List three internal strengths and three internal weaknesses that characterize your university.
11. List reasons why objectives are essential for organizational success.
12. List four strategies and a hypothetical example of each.
13. List six characteristics of annual objectives.
14. Why are policies especially important in strategy implementation?
15. What is a "retreat," and why do firms take the time and spend the money to have these?
16. Discuss the notion of strategic planning being more formal versus informal in an organization. On a 1 to 10 scale from formal to informal, what number best represents your view of the most effective approach? Why?
17. List 10 guidelines for making the strategic-planning process effective. Arrange your guidelines in prioritized order of importance in your opinion.
18. List what you feel are the five most important lessons for business that can be garnered from *The Art of War* book.
19. What is the fundamental difference between business strategy and military strategy in terms of basic assumptions?
20. Explain why the strategic management class is often called a "capstone course."
21. What aspect of strategy formulation do you think requires the most time? Why?
22. Why is strategy implementation often considered the most difficult stage in the strategic-management process?
23. Why is it so important to integrate intuition and analysis in strategic management?
24. Explain the importance of a vision and a mission statement.
25. Discuss relationships among objectives, strategies, and policies.
26. Why do you think some chief executive officers fail to use a strategic-management approach to decision making?
27. Discuss the importance of feedback in the strategic-management model.
28. How can strategists best ensure that strategies will be effectively implemented?
29. Give an example of a recent political development that changed the overall strategy of an organization.
30. Who are the major competitors of your college or university? What are their strengths and weaknesses? What are their strategies? How sucessful are these institutions compared to your college?
31. Would strategic-management concepts and techniques benefit foreign businesses as much as domestic firms? Justify your answer.
32. What do you believe are some potential pitfalls or risks in using a strategic-management approach to decision making?
33. In your opinion, what is the single major benefit of using a strategic-management approach to decision making? Justify your answer.
34. Compare business strategy and military strategy.
35. Why is it important for all business majors to study strategic management since most students will never become a chief executive officer nor even a top manager in a large company?
36. Describe the content available on the SMCO Web site at www.strategyclub.com
37. List four financial and four nonfinancial benefits of a firm engaging in strategic planning.
38. Why is it that a firm can normally sustain a competitive advantage for only a limited period of time?
39. Why it is not adequate to simply obtain competitive advantage?
40. How can a firm best achieve sustained competitive advantage?

Notes

1. Kathy Kiely, "Officials Say Auto CEOs Must Be Specific on Plans," *USA Today* (November 24, 2008): 3B.

2. Peter Drucker, *Management: Tasks, Responsibilities, and Practices* (New York: Harper & Row, 1974): 611.

3. Alfred Sloan, Jr., *Adventures of the White Collar Man* (New York: Doubleday, 1941): 104.

4. Quoted in Eugene Raudsepp, "Can You Trust Your Hunches?" *Management Review* 49, no. 4 (April 1960): 7.

5. Stephen Harper, "Intuition: What Separates Executives from Managers," *Business Horizons* 31, no. 5 (September–October 1988): 16.

6. Ron Nelson, "How to Be a Manager," *Success* (July–August 1985): 69.

7. Bruce Henderson, *Henderson on Corporate Strategy* (Boston: Abt Books, 1979): 6.

8. Robert Waterman, Jr., *The Renewal Factor: How the Best Get and Keep the Competitive Edge* (New York: Bantam, 1987). See also *BusinessWeek* (September 14, 1987): 100. Also, see *Academy of Management Executive* 3, no. 2 (May 1989): 115.

9. Jayne O'Donnell, "Shoppers Flock to Discount Stores," *USA Today* (February 25, 2009): B1.

10. Ethan Smith, "How Old Media Can Survive in a New World," *Wall Street Journal* (May 23, 2005): R4.

11. Daniel Delmar, "The Rise of the CSO," *Organization Design* (March–April 2003): 8–10.

12. John Pearce II and Fred David, "The Bottom Line on Corporate Mission Statements," *Academy of Management Executive* 1, no. 2 (May 1987): 109.

13. Fred R. David, "How Companies Define Their Mission," *Long Range Planning* 22, no. 1 (February 1989): 91.

14. Jack Pearce and Richard Robinson, *Strategic Management,* 7th ed. (New York: McGraw-Hill, 2000): 8.

15. Ann Langley, "The Roles of Formal Strategic Planning," *Long Range Planning* 21, no. 3 (June 1988): 40.

16. Bernard Reimann, "Getting Value from Strategic Planning," *Planning Review* 16, no. 3 (May–June 1988): 42.

17. G. L. Schwenk and K. Schrader, "Effects of Formal Strategic Planning in Financial Performance in Small Firms: A Meta-Analysis," *Entrepreneurship and Practice* 3, no. 17 (1993): 53–64. Also, C. C. Miller and L. B. Cardinal, "Strategic Planning and Firm Performance: A Synthesis of More Than Two Decades of Research," *Academy of Management Journal* 6, no. 27 (1994): 1649–1665; Michael Peel and John Bridge, "How Planning and Capital Budgeting Improve SME Performance," *Long Range Planning* 31, no. 6 (October 1998): 848–856; Julia Smith, "Strategies for Start-Ups," *Long Range Planning* 31, no. 6 (October 1998): 857–872.

18. Gordon Greenley, "Does Strategic Planning Improve Company Performance?" *Long Range Planning* 19, no. 2 (April 1986): 106.

19. Adapted from www.mindtools.com/plreschn.html.

20. Adapted from www.des.calstate.edu/limitations.html and www.entarga.com/stratplan/purposes.html

21. Dale McConkey, "Planning in a Changing Environment," *Business Horizons* (September–October 1988): 66.

22. R. T. Lenz, "Managing the Evolution of the Strategic Planning Process," *Business Horizons* 30, no. 1 (January–February 1987): 39.

23. Frederick Gluck, "Taking the Mystique out of Planning," *Across the Board* (July–August 1985): 59.

Current Readings

Adegbesan, J Adetunji. "On the Origins of Competitive Advantage: Strategic Factor Markets and Heterogeneous Resources Complementarity." *Academy of Management Review* (July 2009): 463–475.

Amabile, Teresa M., and Mukti Khaire. "Creativity and the Role of the Leader." *Harvard Business Review* (October 2008): 100.

Cailluet, Ludovic, and Richard Whittington. "The Crafts of Strategy: Special Issue Introduction by the Guest Editors." *Long Range Planning* 41, no. 3 (June 2008): 241.

Camilus, John C. "Strategy as a Wicked Problem." *Harvard Business Review* (May 2008): 98.

Carroll, Paul B., and Chunka Mui. "Seven Ways to Fail Big." *Harvard Business Review* (September 2008): 82.

Chen, Ming-Jer, and Donald C. Hambrick. "New Academic Fields as Admittance-Seeking Social Movements: The Case of Strategic Management." *The Academy of Management Review* 33, no. 1 (January 2008): 32.

Cummings, Stephen, and Urs Daellenback. "A Guide to the Future of Strategy? The History of Long Range Planning." *Long Range Planning* (April 2009): 234–263.

Davis, Alan, and Eric M. Olson. "Critical Competitive Strategy Issues Every Entrepreneur Should Consider Before Going into Business." *Business Horizons* 51, no. 3 (May–June 2008): 211.

Dominguez, Damian, Hagen Worch, Jachen Markard, Bernhard, Truffer, and Gujer Willi. "Closing the Capability Gap: Strategic Planning for the Infrastructure Sector." *California Management Review* (Winter 2009): 30–50.

Hansen, Morten T. "When Internal Collaboration Is Bad for Your Company." *Harvard Business Review* (April 2009): 82–89.

Joseph, John, and William Ocasio. "Rise and Fall or Transformation? The Evolution of Strategic Planning at the General Electric Company, 1940–2006." *Long Range Planning* 41, no. 3 (June 2008): 248.

Malhotra, Deepak, Gillian, Ku, and Keith J. Murnighan. "When Winning Is Everything." *Harvard Business Review* (May 2008): 78.

McCullough, David. "Timeless Leadership: A Conversation with David McCullough." *Harvard Business Review* (March 2008): 45.

Moldoveanu, Mihnea. "Thinking Strategically About Thinking Strategically: The Computational Structure and Dynamics of Managerial Problem Selection and Formulation." *Strategic Management Journal* (July 2009): 737–763.

Natarajan, Vivek, Sridhar P. Nerur, and Abdul A. Rasheed. "The Intellectual Structure of the Strategic Management Field: An Author Co-citation Analysis." *Strategic Management Journal* 29, no. 3 (March 2008): 319.

Newbert, Scott L. "Value, Rareness, Competitive Advantage, and Performance: A Conceptual-level Empirical Investigation of the Resource-Based View of the Firm." *Strategic Management Journal* 29, no. 7 (July 2008): 745.

Singer, John G. "What Strategy Is Not: Technology- or Platform-Driven Strategy Is a Fast Track to Commoditization." *MIT Sloan Management Review* 49, no. 2 (Winter 2008): 96.

THE COHESION CASE

McDonald's Corporation—2009

Vijaya Narapareddy

University of Denver

www.mcdonalds.com

On May 5, 2009, McDonald's Corporation (MCD, hereafter) and Starbucks went full force campaigning for the attention of coffee connoisseurs. Following its success with McCafés in Europe, MCD surprised Starbucks with its announcement to offer lattes and mochas in its McCafés in the United States. In an attempt to woo rival Starbucks' customers, MCD promised to offer premium taste at bargain prices. This announcement came at a time when Starbucks, hard hit by losses, was closing hundreds of stores in the United States. The MCD–Starbucks fight is everywhere on the tube, in print, and the airwaves. MCD even taunts Starbucks with ads on buses and billboards that read "4 bucks is dumb." Starbucks is retaliating by placing newspaper ads that read "Beware of a cheaper cup of coffee. It comes with a price."

In April 2009, MCD reported strong sales growth in the first quarter of 2009 in spite of recessionary conditions worldwide. MCD sales in the United States increased by 4.7 percent, in Europe by 3.2 percent, and in Asia/Pacific, Middle East, and Africa by 5.5 percent. But as the U.S. dollar gained strength against most currencies, especially the euro, British pound, Australian dollar, Canadian dollar, and the Russian ruble, MCD experienced $642 million in foreign currency translation losses in the first quarter of 2009, as indicated in Exhibit 1. Undeterred, however, MCD is forging ahead with a renewed commitment to allure coffee enthusiasts away from rivals, big and small.

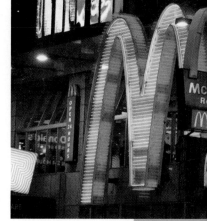

History

MCD was launched in 1940 when brothers Dick and Mac McDonald opened a restaurant in San Bernadino, California. However, the credit of growing the corporation into a franchised, global operation is attributed to Ray Kroc, who acquired equity from the McDonald brothers and took the firm public in 1965. MCD has a really cool history timeline called "Travel in Time with Us" located at the http://www.aboutmcdonalds.com/mcd/our_company/mcd_history.html Web page. It reveals information such as the following:

1979	MCD introduced Happy Meals
1981	MCD opened stores in Spain, Denmark, and the Philippines
1983	MCD entered its 32nd country
1984	Ray Kroc passed away
1987	MCD introduced Fresh Salads
1990	MCD opened a store in Moscow, Russia
1992	MCD opened a store in Warsaw, Poland
1995	MCD's new ad was "Have You Had Your Break Today?"
1996	www.mcdonalds.com Web site introduced
1997	MCD's new ad was "Did Somebody Say McDonald's?"
2001	The Big N'Tasty sandwich introduced
2003	MCD introduced Premium Salads and its "Plan to Win" strategy
2006	MCD introduced Snack Wraps

EXHIBIT 1 **Impact of Foreign Currency Translation ($ in millions, except per share data)**

Quarter ended March 31	2009	2008	Currency Translation Profit/(Loss) in 2009
Revenues	$5,077.4	$5,614.8	(642.4)
Company-operated margins	564.2	659.2	(72.5)
Franchised margins	1,296.0	1,316.2	(109.0)
Selling, general, and administrative expenses	497.3	552.4	43.0
Operating income	1,400.4	1,462.8	(137.9)
Net income	979.5	946.1	(86.2)
Earnings per share—diluted	0.87	0.81	(0.08)

Source: SEC *10-Q*, May 5, 2009.

Today, MCD is the largest global food service retailer, with over 31,000 restaurants in 118 countries serving more than 58 million customers each day. Exhibit 2 shows MCD's global locations. The number of restaurants held and operated by MCD in 2008 and 2009 in each group indicates steady growth in every country of operation except for the United Kingdom, where the growth is flat.

EXHIBIT 2 **MCD's Number of Restaurants Worldwide**

As of March 31	2009	2008	Increase
U.S.	**13,898**	**13,871**	**27**
Europe			
Germany	1,337	1,301	36
United Kingdom	1,192	1,192	—
France	1,135	1,108	27
Spain	393	379	14
Italy	381	363	18
Other	2,212	2,142	70
Total Europe	**6,650**	**6,485**	**165**
APMEA (Asia/Pacific/Middle East/Asia)			
Japan	3,746	3,737	9
China	1,074	911	163
Australia	782	762	20
Taiwan	347	346	1
Other	2,378	2,216	162
Total APMEA	**8,327**	**7,972**	**355**
Other Countries and Corporate			
Canada	1,419	1,408	11
Brazil	563	553	10
Mexico	382	365	17
Other	821	785	36
Total Other Countries and Corporate	**3,185**	**3,111**	**74**
Systemwide restaurants	**32,060**	**31,439**	**621**
Total Countries	**118**	**118**	**—**

Source: SEC *10-K*, dated February 25, 2009.

Internal Issues

Organizational Structure

MCD's top leadership has seen some turnover recently. The position of controller stands vacant, and the McDonald's USA group currently includes new executives to head its East and West Divisions. Exhibit 3 provides a list of MCD's top leadership as well as the firm's organizational chart.

Note that MCD's operations are organized into a geographical structure with four key segments. These four segments are (1) McDonald's—USA, (2) McDonald's—Europe, (3) McDonald's—APMEA (Asia/Pacific, Middle East, and Africa), and (4) McDonald's—Other Countries and Corporate.

Finances

In addition to the steady growth in the number of restaurants, MCD exhibited strong financial performance by geographic segment between 2008 and 2009, even as the worldwide economic crisis negatively impacted MCD's key competitors. As shown in Exhibit 4, revenues and operating margins in the three key segments (United States, Europe, and APMEA) rose steadily in 2006 through 2008, offsetting declines in the "Other and Corporate" segment.

MCD delivers consistently good performance, making it a darling for investors. In April 2009, major industry analysts rated MCD as a "buy," suggesting low levels of risk for investors. MCD's

EXHIBIT 3   McDonald's Corporation: Executive Officers and Organizational Chart

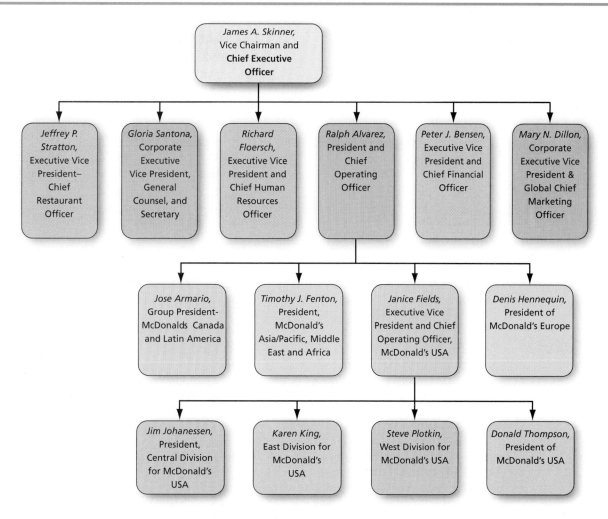

Source: http://www.aboutmcdonalds.com/mcd/our_company/bios.html

EXHIBIT 4   Select Financial Data by Geographic Segment

In millions	2008	2007	2006
U.S.	$ 8,078.3	$ 7,905.5	$ 7,464.1
Europe	9,922.9	8,926.2	7,637.7
APMEA (Asia/Pacific/Middle East/Africa)	4,230.8	3,598.9	3,053.5
Other Countries & Corporate	1,290.4	2,356.0	2,739.9
Total revenues	$23,522.4	$22,786.6	$20,895.2
U.S.	$ 3,059.7	$ 2,841.9	$ 2,657.0
Europe	2,608.0	2,125.4	1,610.2
APMEA	818.8	616.3	364.4
Other Countries & Corporate	(43.6)	(1,704.6)	(198.6)
Total operating income	$ 6,442.9	$ 3,879.0	$ 4,433.0
U.S.	$10,356.7	$10,031.8	$ 9,477.4
Europe	10,532.7	11,380.4	10,413.9
APMEA	4,074.6	4,145.3	3,727.6
Other Countries & Corporate	3,497.5	3,834.2	3,529.4
Businesses held for sale			1,631.5
Discontinued operations			194.7
Total assets	$28,461.5	$29,391.7	$28,974.5
U.S.	$ 837.4	$ 805.1	$ 774.3
Europe	864.1	687.4	504.9
APMEA	360.6	302.8	208.1
Other Countries & Corporate	73.6	97.3	85.4
		43.7	87.0
		10.3	82.2
Total capital expenditures	$ 2,135.7	$ 1,946.6	$ 1,741.9
U.S.	$ 400.9	$ 402.7	$ 390.5
Europe	506.3	473.3	436.4
APMEA	193.4	178.1	171.8
Other Countries & Corporate	107.2	112.6	110.4
		26.1	81.8
		21.3	59.0
	$ 1,207.8	$ 1,214.1	$ 1,249.9

Source: SEC *10-K*, February 25, 2009.

financial statements presented in Exhibit 5 demonstrate the enthusiasm of the analyst community. The MCD income statement provided in the exhibit demonstrates continuous and steady revenue growth. Total revenues grew from $20.9 billion in 2006 to $22.8 billion in 2007 and $23.5 billion in 2008. That translates into an annual growth of about 9.1 percent from 2006 to 2007 and 3.1 percent from 2007 to 2008. Net income shows a slightly different trend. Net income declined by 32.4 percent between 2006 and 2007 but regains momentum by growing 80 percent from 2007 to 2008.

MCD's consolidated balance sheet presented in Exhibit 6 depicts a decline in total assets held by the company from about $29.02 billion in 2006 to about $28.5 billion in 2008. At the same time, both long term debt and retained earnings increased significantly. Because the interest rate on short-term

EXHIBIT 5 McDonald's Consolidated Statement of Income

In millions, except per share data Years ended December 31	2008	2007	2006
REVENUES			
Sales by Company-operated restaurants	**$16,560.9**	$16,611.0	$15,402.4
Revenues from franchised restaurants	**6,961.5**	6,175.6	5,492.8
Total revenues	**23,522.4**	22,786.6	20,895.2
OPERATING COSTS AND EXPENSES			
Company-operated restaurant expenses			
Food & paper	**5,586.1**	5,487.4	5,111.8
Payroll & employee benefits	**4,300.1**	4,331.6	3,991.1
Occupancy & other operating expenses	**3,766.7**	3,922.7	3,802.2
Franchised restaurants–occupancy expenses	**1,230.3**	1,139.7	1,058.1
Selling, general & administrative expenses	**2,355.5**	2,367.0	2,295.7
Impairment and other charges, net	**6.0**	1,670.3	134.2
Other operating (income) expense, net	**(165.2)**	(11.1)	69.1
Total operating costs and expenses	**17,079.5**	18,907.6	16,462.2
Operating income	**6,442.9**	3,879.0	4,433.0
Interest expense–net of capitalized interest of $12.3, $6.9 and $5.4	**522.6**	410.1	401.9
Nonoperating (income) expense, net	**(77.6)**	(103.2)	(123.3)
Gain on sale of investment	**(160.1)**		
Income from continuing operations before provision for income taxes	**6,158.0**	3,572.1	4,154.4
Provision for income taxes	**1,844.8**	1,237.1	1,288.3
Income from continuing operations	**4,313.2**	2,335.0	2,866.1
Income from discontinued operations (net of taxes of $34.5 and $101.9)		60.1	678.1
Net income	**$4,313.2**	$2,395.1	$3,544.2
Per common share–basic:			
Continuing operations	**$ 3.83**	$ 1.96	$ 2.32
Discontinued operations		0.05	0.55
Net income	$ 3.83	$ 2.02	$ 2.87
Per common share–diluted:			
Continuing operations	**$ 3.76**	$ 1.93	$ 2.29
Discontinued operations		0.05	0.54
Net income	$ 3.76	$ 1.98	$ 2.83
Dividends declared per common share	**$ 1.625**	$ 1.50	$ 1.00
Weighted-average shares outstanding–basic	**1,126.6**	1,188.3	1,234.0
Weighted-average shares outstanding–diluted	**1,146.0**	1,211.8	1,251.7

Source: SEC *10-K,* February 25, 2009.

debt for MCD is less than 6 percent for both short- and long-term debt, an increase in MCD's borrowing should not be cause for concern.

Social Responsibility

MCD views its Plan to Win strategy, composed of the 5 P's (people, products, place, price, and promotion) as fundamental to its business success and to becoming better rather than just bigger. This plan aims at delivering exceptional customer experiences by undertaking several initiatives focused on each of the five P's grounded in a set of the corporate values shown in Exhibit 7.

EXHIBIT 6   MCD's Balance Sheet

PERIOD ENDING	31-Dec-08	31-Dec-07	31-Dec-06
Assets			
Current Assets			
Cash and Cash Equivalents	$2,063,400	$1,981,300	$2,136,400
Short Term Investments	—	—	—
Net Receivables	931,200	1,053,800	904,200
Inventory	111,500	125,300	149,000
Other Current Assets	411,500	421,500	435,700
Total Current Assets	**3,517,600**	**3,581,900**	**3,625,300**
Long Term Investments	1,222,300	1,156,400	1,036,200
Property Plant and Equipment	20,254,500	20,984,700	20,845,700
Goodwill	2,237,400	2,301,300	2,209,200
Intangible Assets	—	—	—
Accumulated Amortization	—	—	—
Other Assets	1,229,700	1,367,400	1,307,400
Deferred Long Term Asset Charges	—	—	—
Total Assets	**28,461,500**	**29,391,700**	**29,023,800**
Liabilities			
Current Liabilities			
Accounts Payable	2,506,100	3,634,000	2,739,000
Short/Current Long Term Debt	31,800	864,500	17,700
Other Current Liabilities	—	—	251,400
Total Current Liabilities	**2,537,900**	**4,498,500**	**3,008,100**
Long Term Debt	10,186,000	7,310,000	8,416,500
Other Liabilities	1,410,100	1,342,500	1,074,900
Deferred Long Term Liability Charges	944,900	960,900	1,066,000
Minority Interest	—	—	—
Negative Goodwill	—	—	—
Total Liabilities	**15,078,900**	**14,111,900**	**13,565,500**
Stockholders' Equity			
Misc. Stocks Options Warrants	—	—	—
Redeemable Preferred Stock	—	—	—
Preferred Stock	—	—	—
Common Stock	16,600	16,600	16,600
Retained Earnings	28,953,900	26,461,500	25,845,600
Treasury Stock	(20,289,400)	(16,762,400)	(13,552,200)
Capital Surplus	4,600,200	4,226,700	3,445,000
Other Stockholders' Equity	101,300	1,337,400	(296,700)
Total Stockholders' Equity	**13,382,600**	**15,279,800**	**15,458,300**
Total Liabilities and SE	**$28,461,500**	**$29,391,700**	**$29,023,800**

Source: http://finance.yahoo.com.

EXHIBIT 7 McDonald's Corporation's Values

We place the customer experience at the core of all we do

Our customers are the reason for our existence. We demonstrate our appreciation by providing them with high quality food and superior service, in a clean, welcoming environment, at a great value.

We are committed to our people

We provide opportunity, nurture talent, develop leaders and reward achievement. We believe that a team of well-trained individuals with diverse backgrounds and experiences, working together in an environment that fosters respect and drives high levels of engagement, is essential to our continued success.

We believe in the McDonald's system

McDonald's business model, depicted by the "three-legged stool" of owner/operators, suppliers, and company employees, is our foundation, and the balance of interests among the three groups is key.

We operate our business ethically

Sound ethics is good business. At McDonald's, we hold ourselves and conduct our business to high standards of fairness, honesty, and integrity. We are individually accountable and collectively responsible.

We give back to our communities

We take seriously the responsibilities that come with being a leader. We help our customers build better communities, support Ronald McDonald House Charities, and leverage our size, scope and resources to help make the world a better place.

We grow our business profitably

McDonald's is a publicly traded company. As such, we work to provide sustained profitable growth for our shareholders. This requires a continuing focus on our customers and the health of our system.

We strive continually to improve

We are a learning organization that aims to anticipate and respond to changing customer, employee and system needs through constant evolution and innovation.

Source: http://www.crmcdonalds.com.

MCD has made significant changes to become a socially and environmentally friendly company. It has been recognized for its efforts in inclusive excellence with respect to employing and creating opportunities for minorities. MCD has been listed among the "top 40 companies" by *Black Enterprise Magazine* for 2005 through 2007. It established its first Global Environmental Commitment in 1989. Since then it has been actively seeking to reduce its carbon footprint by using recycled packaging. Additionally, Ronald McDonald's Foundations raise millions of dollars each year for children-centered causes in the community.

According to Skinner, MCD's CEO, "Corporate responsibility means many things to many people. At McDonald's, being a responsible company means living our values to enable us to serve food responsibly, and work toward a sustainable future." (MCD either does not have a written mission statement nor vision statement or these documents are not publicly available because I could not locate either of these at the time this case was written.)

Competitors

The food service industry, also known as the restaurant industry, is large and lucrative with a market capitalization of $104 billion and a price-to-earnings (P/E) ratio of 80.2. Yet it is highly fragmented with over 550,000 restaurants ranging from small local eateries to global giants like MCD and Yum! Brands, Inc. MCD towers over its direct competitors in the industry with a market cap of $59.8 billion in May 2009. Yum! Brands, which has a market cap of only $16.3 billion, and Burger King Holdings, Inc., whose market cap is $2.46 billion, are second and third, respectively. Even though

Wendy's directly competes with MCD in this industry, Wendy's is currently owned by a private holding company, the Wendy's/Arby's Group. A brief summary of competitor financial highlights is provided in Exhibit 8.

Burger King (BKC)

Founded in Miami, Florida, in 1954 under the name "Insta Burger King" by James McLamore and David Edgerton, Burger King Corporation (BKC), a subsidiary of Burger King Holdings, Inc., owns or franchises about 11,500 restaurants in the United States and 70 foreign countries, including Canada, Europe, the Middle East, Africa, the Asia Pacific, and Latin America. Even though it is considered the second largest burger chain in the world, it ranks third in size in the food service industry. With a market capitalization of $2.46 billion, revenues of $2.55 billion, and 41,000 full-time employees, BKC trails behind McDonald's in several categories in the fast-food industry, including operating margins, earnings per share (EPS), and P/E ratio.

In addition to its famous "Whopper sandwich," BKC offers a variety of burgers, chicken sandwiches, breakfast items, and salads that compete directly with MCD. BKC, since the 1980s, has a long-standing contract with the Army and Air Force Exchange Service. As such, every major army and air force location worldwide has a Burger King restaurant on its premises.

Yum! Brands (YUM)

Yum! Brands, Inc., formerly known as TRICON Global Restaurants, Inc., was founded in 1997 and changed its name to Yum! Brands, Inc. in 2002. Yum! operates over 36,000 restaurants in 110 countries. Yum! owns prominent restaurant chains, such as Kentucky Fried Chicken (KFC), Pizza Hut, Taco Bell, Long John Silver's, and A&W. Headquartered in Louisville, Kentucky, it has a market cap of $15.56 billion, has 50,400 employees as of May 7, 2009, and is the closest competitor in size to McDonald's. Headquartered in Louisville, Kentucky, Yum! is considered the second largest in the global fast-food service industry. Offering more than one brand at a single location has helped Yum! increase traffic at a single real estate location. Each of its flagship brands also dominates the segment. For example, Taco Bell holds 60% of the Mexican fast-food segment, KFC holds a respectable 45% of the fast-food chicken business, and Pizza Hut leads the pizza business with a 15% market share in the pizza business segment. In addition to seeking growth through acquisition of prominent brands, since its restructuring in 2006, Yum! has been pursuing aggressive expansion overseas by expanding at the rate of 700 new locations for the seventh consecutive year since 1999. In China alone, it has more than 2,600 restaurants, accounting for 15% of its revenues.

EXHIBIT 8   **McDonald's versus Rivals, Year-end 2008 (B = $billion; M = $million)**

	MCD	YUM	BKC	(Fast) Food Service Industry	SBUX	Specialty Eateries Industry
Market Cap	61.17 B	15.57 B	2.45 B	161.69 M	10.1 B	1.64 B
Employees	400,000	50,400	41,000	5,700	176,000	2,140
Revenue	22.99 B	11.08 B	2.55 B	403.14 M	10.04 B	1.31 B
Gross Margin	37.09%	24.53%	33.13%	21.51%	54.24%	32.2%
Net Income	4.35 B	928 M	192 M	N/A	88 M	N/A
EPS	3.827	1.914	1.402	0.09	0.119	0.12
P/E	14.35	17.65	13.01	17.91	114.79	22.33

MCD = McDonald's Corporation

BKC = Burger King Holdings, Inc.

YUM = Yum! Brands, Inc.

SBUX = Starbucks

Source: Based on http://finance.yahoo.com.

Wendy's (WEN)

Founded in 1969, based in Dublin, Ohio, and operating over 6,600 restaurants, Wendy's International, Inc., owns 1,400 of the 6,600 restaurants. With 44,000 employees in 2007, Wendy's ranks fourth in the industry, behind McDonald's, Yum!, and Burger King. The company is well known for its unique square single, double, or triple made-to-order burgers and fries, and alternative menu items, such as baked potato, chili, and salads. Its new low-priced menus directly compete for market share with MCD. It holds a unique position in the industry as an old-fashioned eating place in the fast-food business and was recognized in 1986 as the most favorite quality brand by *QSR Magazine* for the second year in a row and earned first place for customer satisfaction in the "limited service restaurants" category in that year's American Customer Satisfaction Index survey. With revenues of $2,450 million in 2007, Wendy's currently operates as a subsidiary of the Wendy's/Arby's Group, a private company.

Starbucks Corporation (SBX)

Even though Starbucks is no direct competition for MCD's core business, MCD is now in the fighting ring with Starbucks for the specialty coffee niche. Therefore it is important to view Starbucks as a new direct competitor. Starbucks was founded in 1985 by Howard Schultz, who recently came out of retirement to serve as chairman, CEO, and president. The company is usually grouped with the high-priced, high-margins specialty eateries industry. Starbucks' annual revenues are $10.04 billion, less than half of MCD's. Starbuck's gross margins at 54.24 percent are 17 percent points higher than McDonald's. With 176,000 employees and strong brand recognition, Starbucks is seen as a leader in the specialty eateries industry.

External Threats

Because of its global reach and brand recognition, MCD continues to face significant threats to its aggressive growth strategy at home, one of which is the growing awareness among the medical and scientific community as well as the public of the direct relationship between diet and health. A joint research study recently conducted at the University of California, Berkeley, and Columbia University and published in March 2009 concluded that the presence of a fast-food restaurant within 500 feet of a school is associated with at least a 5.2 percent increase in the obesity rate in that school, suggesting significant health benefits of banning fast-food restaurants close to schools if communities are interested in fighting the growing epidemic of obesity among young adolescents in America.

MCD continues to encounter lawsuits brought about around the world by activists and irate parents of children less than 18 years of age. In 1990, in the McLibel Trial, also known as *McDonald's Restaurants v. Morris & Steel*, activists from a small group known as London Greenpeace with no affiliation with the Greenpeace organization printed and distributed information under the title, *"What's wrong with McDonald's?"* In that printed information that was widely circulated in London, they criticized MCD's environmental, health, and labor record. The corporation wrote to the group demanding them to retract and apologize, but when the two key activists refused to back down, MCD sued them for libel. It turned out to be not only one of the longest cases in British civil law, but it also turned out to be a public relations nightmare for MCD. A documentary film capturing this saga continues to been shown in several countries, including the United States.

MCD's premises continue to draw antiglobalization activists from around the world. In 1999, French activist José Bové vandalized a half-built McDonald's to protest against the introduction of fast food in the region. As recently as 2009, activists vandalized MCD's restaurants during the G-20 summit in protest of the poverty and income inequalities brought about by globalization.

The documentary film, *Super Size Me*, which argued that MCD's menu was contributing to the obesity epidemic and that the company provided no nutritional information about its products, caught MCD executive's attention quickly. Within six weeks after the film's debut, MCD eliminated the supersize option from its meal options.

In April 2006, the global activist organization Greenpeace alleged that MCD, as a client of the agricultural behemoth Cargill, was contributing to the destruction of the Amazon rain forest in Brazil and the invasion of the indigenous people's lands when it bought chickens fed with Brazilian soya. Furthermore, global activists argue that MCD's operations overburden scarce drinking water supply away from the poor local communities by diverting it to the frivolous production of supplies to support MCD.

Unfavorable changes on the sociopolitical, legal, and environmental fronts at home and overseas as well as currency rates may adversely affect MCD without prior notice. Cost of supplies may increase cutting into MCD's gross margins as is evident from its income statement (Exhibit 8). Total operating costs and expenses increased rose from about $16.5 billion in 2006 to $18.9 billion in 2007. Foreign currency translation losses displayed in Exhibit 1 show the extent of damage that global companies like MCD encounter due to the uncertainties in the global environment that no one has control over. In February 2009, MCD cut prices of its popular menu items in China by as much as 40 percent to reverse declining sales.

Conclusion

Success today is no guarantee for success tomorrow. However, McDonald's added 40 restaurants in India in 2008 and another 25 in 2009. Although people in India are predominantly Hindu and revere the cow, thus eating no beef, they love McDonald's, especially Chicken McNuggets, which were first introduced in India in May 2009. MCD's vegetable patties also are a big hit now in India.

For the second quarter, which ended June 30, 2009, MCD had positive global comparable sales in every area of the world, as well as higher revenues, operating income, and earnings per share compared with the prior year. "We're driving results by staying focused on our global business strategy, the Plan to Win," said Chief Executive Officer Jim Skinner. "As consumers find themselves more cash-strapped and time-challenged, they continue to count on McDonald's for value, convenience, and variety across our menu." MCD's second quarter 2009 results included global comparable sales up 4.8% with the United States up 3.5%, Europe up 6.9%, and Asia/Pacific, Middle East and Africa up 4.4% McDonald's Europe delivered strong second quarter comparable sales led by performance in the U.K., France, and Russia. In Asia/Pacific, Middle East, and Africa (APMEA), Australia led the segment's second quarter operating income increase of 34% in constant currencies.

Exhibit 9 provides mid-year 2009 MCD financials:

EXHIBIT 9   **MCD Financial Highlights, Second Quarter 2009 (dollars in millions, except per share data)**

	Quarter ended June 30		Six months ended June 30	
	2009	2008	2009	2008
Revenues	$5,647.2	$6,075.3	$10,724.6	$11,690.1
Operating income	1,681.5	1,654.2	3,081.9	3,117.0
Net income	1,093.7	1,190.5	2,073.2	2,136.6
Earnings per share	0.98	1.04	1.85	1.85

ASSURANCE OF LEARNING EXERCISES

Assurance of Learning Exercise 1A

Gathering Strategy Information

Purpose

The purpose of this exercise is to get you familiar with strategy terms introduced and defined in Chapter 1. Let's apply these terms to McDonald's Corporation (stock symbol = MCD).

Instructions

Step 1   Go to www.mcdonalds.com, which is McDonald's Web site. Click on the word Search. Then type in the words *Annual Report*. Then print the 2009 McDonald's *Annual Report*. This document may be 100 pages, so you may want to print it in your college library or order the report directly from McDonald's as indicated on the Web site. The *Annual Report* contains excellent information for developing a list of internal strengths and weaknesses for MCD.

Step 2   Go to your college library and make a copy of Standard & Poor's Industry Surveys for the restaurant industry. This document will contain excellent information for developing a list of external opportunities and threats facing MCD.

Step 3   Go to the www.finance.yahoo.com Web site. Enter MCD. Note the wealth of information on McDonald's that may be obtained by clicking any item along the left column. Click on Competitors down the left column. Then print out the resultant tables and information. Note that McDonald's two major competitors are Yum! Brands, Inc. and Burger King Holdings.

Step 4   Using the Cohesion Case, the www.finance.yahoo information, the *2009 Annual Report*, and the Industry Survey document, on a separate sheet of paper list what you consider to be MCD's three major strengths, three major weaknesses, three major opportunities, and three major threats. Each factor listed for this exercise must include a %, #, $, or ratio to reveal some quantified fact or trend. These factors provide the underlying basis for a strategic plan because a firm strives to take advantage of strengths, improve weaknesses, avoid threats, and capitalize on opportunities.

Step 5   Through class discussion, compare your lists of external and internal factors to those developed by other students and add to your lists of factors. Keep this information for use in later exercises at the end of other chapters.

Step 6   Be mindful that whatever case company is assigned to your team of students this semester, you can start to update the information on your company by following the steps just listed for any publicly-held firm.

Assurance of Learning Exercise 1B

Strategic Planning for My University

Purpose

External and internal factors are the underlying bases of strategies formulated and implemented by organizations. Your college or university faces numerous external opportunities/threats and has many internal strengths/weaknesses. The purpose of this exercise is to illustrate the process of identifying critical external and internal factors.

External influences include trends in the following areas: economic, social, cultural, demographic, environmental, technological, political, legal, governmental, and competitive. External factors could include declining numbers of high school graduates; population shifts; community relations; increased competitiveness among colleges and universities; rising numbers of adults returning to college; decreased support from local, state, and federal agencies; increasing numbers of foreign students attending U.S. colleges; and a rising number of Internet courses.

Internal factors of a college or university include faculty, students, staff, alumni, athletic programs, physical plant, grounds and maintenance, student housing, administration, fundraising, academic programs, food services, parking, placement, clubs, fraternities, sororities, and public relations.

Instructions

Step 1	On a separate sheet of paper, write four headings: External Opportunities, External Threats, Internal Strengths, and Internal Weaknesses.
Step 2	As related to your college or university, list five factors under each of the four headings.
Step 3	Discuss the factors as a class. Write the factors on the board.
Step 4	What new things did you learn about your university from the class discussion? How could this type of discussion benefit an organization?

Assurance of Learning Exercise 1C

Strategic Planning at a Local Company

Purpose

This activity is aimed at giving you practical knowledge about how organizations in your city or town are doing strategic planning. This exercise also will give you experience interacting on a professional basis with local business leaders.

Instructions

Step 1	Use the telephone to contact business owners or top managers. Find an organization that does strategic planning. Make an appointment to visit with the strategist (president, chief executive officer, or owner) of that business.
Step 2	Seek answers to the following questions during the interview:

- How does your firm formally conduct strategic planning? Who is involved in the process? Does the firm hold planning retreats? If yes, how often and where?
- Does your firm have a written mission statement? How was the statement developed? When was the statement last changed?
- What are the benefits of engaging in strategic planning?
- What are the major costs or problems in doing strategic planning in your business?
- Do you anticipate making any changes in the strategic-planning process at your company? If yes, please explain.

Step 3	Report your findings to the class.

Assurance of Learning Exercise 1D

Getting Familiar with SMCO

Purpose

This exercise is designed to get you familiar with the Strategic Management Club Online (SMCO), which offers many benefits for the strategy student. The SMCO site also offers templates for doing case analyses in this course.

Instructions

Step 1   Go to the www.strategyclub.com Web site. Review the various sections of this site.

Step 2   Select a section of the SMCO site that you feel will be most useful to you in this class. Write a one-page summary of that section and describe why you feel it will benefit you most.

CHAPTER 2
The Business Vision and Mission

CHAPTER OBJECTIVES

After studying this chapter, you should be able to do the following:

1. Describe the nature and role of vision and mission statements in strategic management.

2. Discuss why the process of developing a mission statement is as important as the resulting document.

3. Identify the components of mission statements.

4. Discuss how clear vision and mission statements can benefit other strategic-management activities.

5. Evaluate mission statements of different organizations.

6. Write good vision and mission statements.

Assurance of Learning Exercises

Assurance of Learning Exercise 2A

Evaluating Mission Statements

Assurance of Learning Exercise 2B

Writing a Vision and Mission Statement for McDonald's

Assurance of Learning Exercise 2C

Writing a Vision and Mission Statement for My University

Assurance of Learning Exercise 2D

Conducting Mission Statement Research

Source: Shutterstock/Photographer Dmitriy Shironosov

"Notable Quotes"

"A business is not defined by its name, statutes, or articles of incorporation. It is defined by the business mission. Only a clear definition of the mission and purpose of the organization makes possible clear and realistic business objectives."

—Peter Drucker

"A corporate vision can focus, direct, motivate, unify, and even excite a business into superior performance. The job of a strategist is to identify and project a clear vision."

—John Keane

"Where there is no vision, the people perish."

—Proverbs 29:18

"The last thing IBM needs right now is a vision. (July 1993) What IBM needs most right now is a vision. (March 1996)"

—Louis V. Gerstner Jr., CEO, IBM Corporation

"The best laid schemes of mice and men often go awry."

—Robert Burns (paraphrased)

"A strategist's job is to see the company not as it is ... but as it can become."

—John W. Teets, Chairman of Greyhound, Inc.

"That business mission is so rarely given adequate thought is perhaps the most important single cause of business frustration."

—Peter Drucker

"The very essence of leadership is that you have to have vision. You can't blow an uncertain trumpet."

—Theodore Hesburgh

This chapter focuses on the concepts and tools needed to evaluate and write business vision and mission statements. A practical framework for developing mission statements is provided. Actual mission statements from large and small organizations and for-profit and nonprofit enterprises are presented and critically examined. The process of creating a vision and mission statement is discussed. The global economic recession has resulted in many firms changing direction and thereby altering their entire vision and mission in order to survive. For example, in the Philippines, the largest food and beverage company, San Miguel Corp., recently diversified by purchasing Petron Corp., the country's largest oil refiner. San Miguel also purchased Meralco, formally named Manila Electric, thus broadening its mission to include energy-related businesses.

The boxed insert company examined in this chapter is Wal-Mart, which has a clear vision/mission and strategic plan. Wal-Mart is doing great in the global economic recession.

Doing Great in a Weak Economy

Wal-Mart

When most firms were struggling in 2008, Wal-Mart increased its revenues from $348 billion in 2007 to $378 billion in 2008. Wal-Mart's net income increased too, from $11.2 billion to $12.7 billion—quite impressive. *Fortune* magazine in 2009 rated Wal-Mart as their 11th "Most Admired Company in the World" in terms of their management and performance.

Wal-Mart Stores continues to expand internationally, particularly in emerging countries such as Brazil and India. From 2009 to 2013, Wal-Mart plans to devote 53 percent of its international spending to emerging markets, up from 33 percent in the prior five years. The company plans include remodeling U.S. stores rather than adding new stores and going to smaller stores. Wal-Mart's capital expenditures in the year ending January 2010 were $5.3 billion, up from $4.8 billion the prior year.

As electronics retailer Circuit City was declaring bankruptcy and liquidating in 2008, Wal-Mart was beefing up its electronics product line, directly attacking Best Buy. The two firms today are in a dogfight to obtain the millions of electronics products customers. Best Buy was *Fortune*'s 44th "Most Admired Company in the World" in 2009.

Wal-Mart recently revamped the electronics departments in its 3,500 U.S. stores to make them much more interactive and roomier. The company wants all the business that Circuit City's failure left and also wants all of Best Buy's and Amazon's business. Wal-Mart now carries sophisticated electronics products such as Research in Motion Ltd.'s Blackberry smart phones, Palm Inc.'s Pre smart phone, and Blu-ray disc players. Wal-Mart in June 2009 began selling Dell Inc.'s new Studio One 19 touch-screen computers.

Wal-Mart Stores is bigger than Europe's Carrefour, Tesco, and Metro AG combined. It is the world's number one retailer, with more than 7,870 stores, including about 890 discount stores, 2,970 combination discount and grocery stores (Wal-Mart Supercenters in the United States and ASDA in the United Kingdom), and 600 warehouse stores (Sam's Club). About 55 percent of its Wal-Mart stores are in the United States, but the company continues expanding internationally; it is the number-one retailer in Canada and Mexico and it has operations in Asia (where it owns a 95 percent stake in Japanese retailer SEIYU), Europe, and South America. Founder Sam Walton's heirs own about 40 percent of Wal-Mart.

Wal-Mart is a corporate leader in sustainability. The company in 2009 alone installed rooftop solar arrays on 20 stores and warehouses in California and Hawaii.

A Wal-Mart partner, BP Solar, installs, maintains, and owns these systems.

Perhaps more importantly, Wal-Mart in July 2009 unveiled a new environmental labeling program that requires all its vendors to calculate and disclose the full environmental costs of making their products. All vendors must soon distill that information into Wal-Mart's new labeling system, thus providing product environmental impact information to all Wal-Mart shoppers. This new Wal-Mart program may redefine the whole consumer products labeling process globally by the year 2012.

Source: Based on Geoff Colvin, "The World's Most Admired Companies," *Fortune* (March 16, 2009): 76–86; and Miguel Bustillo, "Wal-Mart Puts Green Movement Into Stores," *Wall Street Journal* (July 16, 2009): Al.

We can perhaps best understand vision and mission by focusing on a business when it is first started. In the beginning, a new business is simply a collection of ideas. Starting a new business rests on a set of beliefs that the new organization can offer some product or service to some customers, in some geographic area, using some type of technology, at a profitable price. A new business owner typically believes that the management philosophy of the new enterprise will result in a favorable public image and that this concept of the business can be communicated to, and will be adopted by, important constituencies. When the set of beliefs about a business at its inception is put into writing, the resulting document mirrors the same basic ideas that underlie the vision and mission statements. As a business grows, owners or managers find it necessary to revise the founding set of beliefs, but those original ideas usually are reflected in the revised statements of vision and mission.

Vision and mission statements often can be found in the front of annual reports. They often are displayed throughout a firm's premises and are distributed with company information sent to constituencies. The statements are part of numerous internal reports, such as loan requests, supplier agreements, labor relations contracts, business plans, and customer service agreements. In a recent study, researchers concluded that 90 percent of all companies have used a mission statement sometime in the previous five years.[1]

What Do We Want to Become?

It is especially important for managers and executives in any organization to agree on the basic vision that the firm strives to achieve in the long term. A vision statement should answer the basic question, "What do we want to become?" A clear vision provides the foundation for developing a comprehensive mission statement. Many organizations have both a vision and mission statement, but the vision statement should be established first and foremost. The vision statement should be short, preferably one sentence, and as many managers as possible should have input into developing the statement.

Several example vision statements are provided in Table 2-1.

What Is Our Business?

Current thought on mission statements is based largely on guidelines set forth in the mid-1970s by Peter Drucker, who is often called "the father of modern management" for his pioneering studies at General Motors Corporation and for his 22 books and hundreds of articles. *Harvard Business Review* has called Drucker "the preeminent management thinker of our time."

TABLE 2-1 Vision Statement Examples

Tyson Foods' vision is to be the world's first choice for protein solutions while maximizing shareholder value. (*Author comment: Good statement, unless Tyson provides nonprotein products*)

General Motors' vision is to be the world leader in transportation products and related services. (*Author comment: Good statement*)

PepsiCo's responsibility is to continually improve all aspects of the world in which we operate—environment, social, economic—creating a better tomorrow than today. (*Author comment: Statement is too vague; it should reveal beverage and food business*)

Dell's vision is to create a company culture where environmental excellence is second nature. (*Author comment: Statement is too vague; it should reveal computer business in some manner; the word* environmental *is generally used to refer to natural environment so is unclear in its use here*)

The vision of First Reliance Bank is to be recognized as the largest and most profitable bank in South Carolina. (*Author comment: This is a very small new bank headquartered in Florence, South Carolina, so this goal is not achievable in five years; the statement is too futuristic*)

Samsonite's vision is to provide innovative solutions for the traveling world. (*Author comment: Statement needs to be more specific, perhaps mention luggage; statement as is could refer to air carriers or cruise lines, which is not good*)

Royal Caribbean's vision is to empower and enable our employees to deliver the best vacation experience for our guests, thereby generating superior returns for our shareholders and enhancing the well-being of our communities. (*Author comment: Statement is good but could end after the word "guests"*)

Procter & Gamble's vision is to be, and be recognized as, the best consumer products company in the world. (*Author comment: Statement is too vague and readability is not that good*)

Drucker says that asking the question "What is our business?" is synonymous with asking the question "What is our mission?" An enduring statement of purpose that distinguishes one organization from other similar enterprises, the *mission statement* is a declaration of an organization's "reason for being." It answers the pivotal question "What is our business?" A clear mission statement is essential for effectively establishing objectives and formulating strategies.

Sometimes called a *creed statement*, a statement of purpose, a statement of philosophy, a statement of beliefs, a statement of business principles, or a statement "defining our business," a mission statement reveals what an organization wants to be and whom it wants to serve. All organizations have a reason for being, even if strategists have not consciously transformed this reason into writing. As illustrated in Figure 2-1, carefully prepared statements of vision and mission are widely recognized by both practitioners and academicians as the first step in strategic management.

Some example mission statements are provided in Table 2-2. Drucker has the following to say about mission statements:

A business mission is the foundation for priorities, strategies, plans, and work assignments. It is the starting point for the design of managerial jobs and, above all, for the design of managerial structures. Nothing may seem simpler or more obvious than to know what a company's business is. A steel mill makes steel, a railroad runs trains to carry freight and passengers, an insurance company underwrites fire risks, and a bank lends money. Actually, "What is our business?" is almost always a difficult question and the right answer is usually anything but obvious. The answer to this question is the first responsibility of strategists. Only strategists can make sure that this question receives the attention it deserves and that the answer makes sense and enables the business to plot its course and set its objectives.[2]

Some strategists spend almost every moment of every day on administrative and tactical concerns, and strategists who rush quickly to establish objectives and implement strategies often overlook the development of a vision and mission statement. This problem is widespread even among large organizations. Many corporations in America have not yet developed a formal vision or mission statement.[3] An increasing number of organizations are developing these statements.

Some companies develop mission statements simply because they feel it is fashionable, rather than out of any real commitment. However, as described in this chapter, firms that develop and systematically revisit their vision and mission statements, treat them as

FIGURE 2-1

A Comprehensive Strategic-Management Model

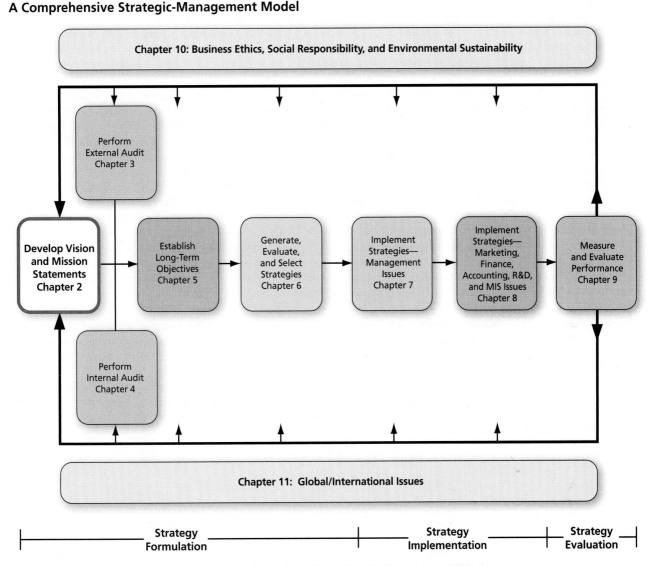

Source: Fred R. David, "How Companies Define Their Mission," *Long Range Planning* 22, no. 3 (June 1988): 40.

living documents, and consider them to be an integral part of the firm's culture realize great benefits. Johnson & Johnson (J&J) is an example firm. J&J managers meet regularly with employees to review, reword, and reaffirm the firm's vision and mission. The entire J&J workforce recognizes the value that top management places on this exercise, and these employees respond accordingly.

Vision versus Mission

Many organizations develop both a mission statement and a vision statement. Whereas the mission statement answers the question "What is our business?" the *vision statement* answers the question "What do we want to become?" Many organizations have both a mission and vision statement.

It can be argued that profit, not mission or vision, is the primary corporate motivator. But profit alone is not enough to motivate people.[4] Profit is perceived negatively by some employees in companies. Employees may see profit as something that they earn and management then uses and even gives away to shareholders. Although this perception is

TABLE 2-2   Example Mission Statements

Fleetwood Enterprises will lead the recreational vehicle and manufactured housing industries (2, 7) in providing quality products, with a passion for customer-driven innovation (1). We will emphasize training, embrace diversity and provide growth opportunities for our associates and our dealers (9). We will lead our industries in the application of appropriate technologies (4). We will operate at the highest levels of ethics and compliance with a focus on exemplary corporate governance (6). We will deliver value to our shareholders, positive operating results and industry-leading earnings (5). *(Author comment: Statement lacks two components: Markets and Concern for Public Image)*

We aspire to make PepsiCo the world's (3) premier consumer products company, focused on convenient foods and beverages (2). We seek to produce healthy financial rewards for investors (5) as we provide opportunities for growth and enrichment to our employees (9), our business partners and the communities (8) in which we operate. And in everything we do, we strive to act with honesty, openness, fairness and integrity (6). *(Author comment: Statement lacks three components: Customers, Technology, and Self-Concept)*

We are loyal to Royal Caribbean and Celebrity and strive for continuous improvement in everything we do. We always provide service with a friendly greeting and a smile (7). We anticipate the needs of our customers and make all efforts to exceed our customers' expectations (1). We take ownership of any problem that is brought to our attention. We engage in conduct that enhances our corporate reputation and employee morale (9). We are committed to act in the highest ethical manner and respect the rights and dignity of others (6). *(Author comment: Statement lacks five components: Products/Services, Markets, Technology, Concern for Survival/Growth/Profits, Concern for Public Image)*

Dell's mission is to be the most successful computer company (2) in the world (3) at delivering the best customer experience in markets we serve (1). In doing so, Dell will meet customer expectations of highest quality; leading technology (4); competitive pricing; individual and company accountability (6); best-in-class service and support (7); flexible customization capability (7); superior corporate citizenship (8); financial stability (5). *(Author comment: Statement lacks only one component: Concern for Employees)*

Procter & Gamble will provide branded products and services of superior quality and value (7) that improve the lives of the world's (3) consumers. As a result, consumers (1) will reward us with industry leadership in sales, profit (5), and value creation, allowing our people (9), our shareholders, and the communities (8) in which we live and work to prosper. *(Author comment: Statement lacks three components: Products/Services, Technology, and Philosophy)*

At L'Oreal, we believe that lasting business success is built upon ethical (6) standards which guide growth and on a genuine sense of responsibility to our employees (9), our consumers, our environment and to the communities in which we operate (8). *(Author comment: Statement lacks six components: Customers, Products/Services, Markets, Technology, Concern for Survival/Growth/Profits, Concern for Public Image)*

Note: The numbers in parentheses correspond to the nine components listed on page 51; author comment also refers to those components.

undesired and disturbing to management, it clearly indicates that both profit and vision are needed to motivate a workforce effectively.

When employees and managers together shape or fashion the vision and mission statements for a firm, the resultant documents can reflect the personal visions that managers and employees have in their hearts and minds about their own futures. Shared vision creates a commonality of interests that can lift workers out of the monotony of daily work and put them into a new world of opportunity and challenge.

The Process of Developing Vision and Mission Statements

As indicated in the strategic-management model, clear vision and mission statements are needed before alternative strategies can be formulated and implemented. As many managers as possible should be involved in the process of developing these statements because through involvement, people become committed to an organization.

A widely used approach to developing a vision and mission statement is first to select several articles about these statements and ask all managers to read these as background information. Then ask managers themselves to prepare a vision and mission statement for the organization. A facilitator, or committee of top managers, should then merge these statements into a single document and distribute the draft statements to all managers. A request for modifications, additions, and deletions is needed next, along with a meeting to revise the document. To the extent that all managers have input into and support the final documents, organizations can more easily obtain managers' support for other strategy formulation, implementation, and evaluation activities. Thus, the process of developing a vision and mission statement represents a great opportunity for strategists to obtain needed support from all managers in the firm.

During the process of developing vision and mission statements, some organizations use discussion groups of managers to develop and modify existing statements. Some organizations hire an outside consultant or facilitator to manage the process and help draft the language. Sometimes an outside person with expertise in developing such statements, who has unbiased views, can manage the process more effectively than an internal group or committee of managers. Decisions on how best to communicate the vision and mission to all managers, employees, and external constituencies of an organization are needed when the documents are in final form. Some organizations even develop a videotape to explain the statements, and how they were developed.

An article by Campbell and Yeung emphasizes that the process of developing a mission statement should create an "emotional bond" and "sense of mission" between the organization and its employees.[5] Commitment to a company's strategy and intellectual agreement on the strategies to be pursued do not necessarily translate into an emotional bond; hence, strategies that have been formulated may not be implemented. These researchers stress that an emotional bond comes when an individual personally identifies with the underlying values and behavior of a firm, thus turning intellectual agreement and commitment to strategy into a sense of mission. Campbell and Yeung also differentiate between the terms *vision* and *mission*, saying that vision is "a possible and desirable future state of an organization" that includes specific goals, whereas mission is more associated with behavior and the present.

Importance (Benefits) of Vision and Mission Statements

The importance (benefits) of vision and mission statements to effective strategic management is well documented in the literature, although research results are mixed. Rarick and Vitton found that firms with a formalized mission statement have twice the average return on shareholders' equity than those firms without a formalized mission statement have; Bart and Baetz found a positive relationship between mission statements and organizational performance; *BusinessWeek* reports that firms using mission statements have a 30 percent higher return on certain financial measures than those without such statements; however, some studies have found that having a mission statement does not directly contribute positively to financial performance.[6] The extent of manager and employee involvement in developing vision and mission statements can make a difference in business success. This chapter provides guidelines for developing these important documents. In actual practice, wide variations exist in the nature, composition, and use of both vision and mission statements. King and Cleland recommend that organizations carefully develop a written mission statement in order to reap the following benefits:

1. To ensure unanimity of purpose within the organization
2. To provide a basis, or standard, for allocating organizational resources
3. To establish a general tone or organizational climate
4. To serve as a focal point for individuals to identify with the organization's purpose and direction, and to deter those who cannot from participating further in the organization's activities
5. To facilitate the translation of objectives into a work structure involving the assignment of tasks to responsible elements within the organization
6. To specify organizational purposes and then to translate these purposes into objectives in such a way that cost, time, and performance parameters can be assessed and controlled.[7]

Reuben Mark, former CEO of Colgate, maintains that a clear mission increasingly must make sense internationally. Mark's thoughts on vision are as follows:

> When it comes to rallying everyone to the corporate banner, it's essential to push one vision globally rather than trying to drive home different messages in different cultures. The trick is to keep the vision simple but elevated: "We make the world's fastest computers" or "Telephone service for everyone." You're never going to get anyone to charge the machine guns only for financial objectives. It's got to be something that makes people feel better, feel a part of something.[8]

A Resolution of Divergent Views

Another benefit of developing a comprehensive mission statement is that divergent views among managers can be revealed and resolved through the process. The question "What is our business?" can create controversy. Raising the question often reveals differences among strategists in the organization. Individuals who have worked together for a long time and who think they know each other suddenly may realize that they are in fundamental disagreement. For example, in a college or university, divergent views regarding the relative importance of teaching, research, and service often are expressed during the mission statement development process. Negotiation, compromise, and eventual agreement on important issues are needed before people can focus on more specific strategy formulation activities.

> "What is our mission?" is a genuine decision; and a genuine decision must be based on divergent views to have a chance to be a right and effective decision. Developing a business mission is always a choice between alternatives, each of which rests on different assumptions regarding the reality of the business and its environment. It is always a high-risk decision. A change in mission always leads to changes in objectives, strategies, organization, and behavior. The mission decision is far too important to be made by acclamation. Developing a business mission is a big step toward management effectiveness. Hidden or half-understood disagreements on the definition of a business mission underlie many of the personality problems, communication problems, and irritations that tend to divide a top-management group. Establishing a mission should never be made on plausibility alone, should never be made fast, and should never be made painlessly.[9]

Considerable disagreement among an organization's strategists over vision and mission statements can cause trouble if not resolved. For example, unresolved disagreement over the business mission was one of the reasons for W. T. Grant's bankruptcy and eventual liquidation. As one executive reported:

> There was a lot of dissension within the company whether we should go the Kmart route or go after the Montgomery Ward and JCPenney position. Ed Staley and Lou Lustenberger (two top executives) were at loggerheads over the issue, with the upshot being we took a position between the two and that consequently stood for nothing.[10]

Too often, strategists develop vision and business mission statements only when the organization is in trouble. Of course, it is needed then. Developing and communicating a clear mission during troubled times indeed may have spectacular results and even may reverse decline. However, to wait until an organization is in trouble to develop a vision and mission statement is a gamble that characterizes irresponsible management. According to Drucker, the most important time to ask seriously, "What do we want to become?" and "What is our business?" is when a company has been successful:

> Success always obsoletes the very behavior that achieved it, always creates new realities, and always creates new and different problems. Only the fairy tale story ends, "They lived happily ever after." It is never popular to argue with success or to rock

the boat. The ancient Greeks knew that the penalty of success can be severe. The management that does not ask "What is our mission?" when the company is successful is, in effect, smug, lazy, and arrogant. It will not be long before success will turn into failure. Sooner or later, even the most successful answer to the question "What is our business?" becomes obsolete.[11]

In multidivisional organizations, strategists should ensure that divisional units perform strategic-management tasks, including the development of a statement of vision and mission. Each division should involve its own managers and employees in developing a vision and mission statement that is consistent with and supportive of the corporate mission.

An organization that fails to develop a vision statement as well as a comprehensive and inspiring mission statement loses the opportunity to present itself favorably to existing and potential stakeholders. All organizations need customers, employees, and managers, and most firms need creditors, suppliers, and distributors. The vision and mission statements are effective vehicles for communicating with important internal and external stakeholders. The principal benefit of these statements as tools of strategic management is derived from their specification of the ultimate aims of a firm:

They provide managers with a unity of direction that transcends individual, parochial, and transitory needs. They promote a sense of shared expectations among all levels and generations of employees. They consolidate values over time and across individuals and interest groups. They project a sense of worth and intent that can be identified and assimilated by company outsiders. Finally, they affirm the company's commitment to responsible action, which is symbiotic with its need to preserve and protect the essential claims of insiders for sustained survival, growth, and profitability of the firm.[12]

Characteristics of a Mission Statement

A Declaration of Attitude

A mission statement is more than a statement of specific details; it is a declaration of attitude and outlook. It usually is broad in scope for at least two major reasons. First, a good mission statement allows for the generation and consideration of a range of feasible alternative objectives and strategies without unduly stifling management creativity. Excess specificity would limit the potential of creative growth for the organization. However, an overly general statement that does not exclude any strategy alternatives could be dysfunctional. Apple Computer's mission statement, for example, should not open the possibility for diversification into pesticides—or Ford Motor Company's into food processing.

Second, a mission statement needs to be broad to reconcile differences effectively among, and appeal to, an organization's diverse *stakeholders*, the individuals and groups of individuals who have a special stake or claim on the company. Thus a mission statement should be *reconcilatory*. Stakeholders include employees, managers, stockholders, boards of directors, customers, suppliers, distributors, creditors, governments (local, state, federal, and foreign), unions, competitors, environmental groups, and the general public. Stakeholders affect and are affected by an organization's strategies, yet the claims and concerns of diverse constituencies vary and often conflict. For example, the general public is especially interested in social responsibility, whereas stockholders are more interested in profitability. Claims on any business literally may number in the thousands, and they often include clean air, jobs, taxes, investment opportunities, career opportunities, equal employment opportunities, employee benefits, salaries, wages, clean water, and community services. All stakeholders' claims on an organization cannot be pursued with equal emphasis. A good mission statement indicates the relative attention that an organization will devote to meeting the claims of various stakeholders.

The fine balance between specificity and generality is difficult to achieve, but it is well worth the effort. George Steiner offers the following insight on the need for a mission statement to be broad in scope:

> Most business statements of mission are expressed at high levels of abstraction. Vagueness nevertheless has its virtues. Mission statements are not designed to express concrete ends, but rather to provide motivation, general direction, an image, a tone, and a philosophy to guide the enterprise. An excess of detail could prove counterproductive since concrete specification could be the base for rallying opposition. Precision might stifle creativity in the formulation of an acceptable mission or purpose. Once an aim is cast in concrete, it creates a rigidity in an organization and resists change. Vagueness leaves room for other managers to fill in the details, perhaps even to modify general patterns. Vagueness permits more flexibility in adapting to changing environments and internal operations. It facilitates flexibility in implementation.[13]

As indicated in Table 2-3, in addition to being broad in scope, an effective mission statement should not be too lengthy; recommended length is less than 250 words. An effective mission statement should arouse positive feelings and emotions about an organization; it should be inspiring in the sense that it motivates readers to action. A mission statement should be enduring. All of these are desired characteristics of a statement. An effective mission statement generates the impression that a firm is successful, has direction, and is worthy of time, support, and investment—from all socioeconomic groups of people.

It reflects judgments about future growth directions and strategies that are based on forward-looking external and internal analyses. A business mission should provide useful criteria for selecting among alternative strategies. A clear mission statement provides a basis for generating and screening strategic options. The statement of mission should be dynamic in orientation, allowing judgments about the most promising growth directions and those considered less promising.

A Customer Orientation

A good mission statement describes an organization's purpose, customers, products or services, markets, philosophy, and basic technology. According to Vern McGinnis, a mission statement should (1) define what the organization is and what the organization aspires to be, (2) be limited enough to exclude some ventures and broad enough to allow for creative growth, (3) distinguish a given organization from all others, (4) serve as a framework for evaluating both current and prospective activities, and (5) be stated in terms sufficiently clear to be widely understood throughout the organization.[14]

A good mission statement reflects the anticipations of customers. Rather than developing a product and then trying to find a market, the operating philosophy of organizations should be to identify customers' needs and then provide a product or service to fulfill those needs.

TABLE 2-3   Ten Benefits of Having a Clear Mission and Vision

1. Achieve clarity of purpose among all managers and employees.
2. Provide a basis for all other strategic planning activities, including the internal and external assessment, establishing objectives, developing strategies, choosing among alternative strategies, devising policies, establishing organizational structure, allocating resources, and evaluating performance.
3. Provide direction.
4. Provide a focal point for all stakeholders of the firm.
5. Resolve divergent views among managers.
6. Promote a sense of shared expectations among all managers and employees.
7. Project a sense of worth and intent to all stakeholders.
8. Project an organized, motivated organization worthy of support.
9. Achieve higher organizational performance.
10. Achieve synergy among all managers and employees.

Good mission statements identify the utility of a firm's products to its customers. This is why AT&T's mission statement focuses on communication rather than on telephones; it is why ExxonMobil's mission statement focuses on energy rather than on oil and gas; it is why Union Pacific's mission statement focuses on transportation rather than on railroads; it is why Universal Studios' mission statement focuses on entertainment rather than on movies. The following utility statements are relevant in developing a mission statement:

Do not offer me things.

Do not offer me clothes. Offer me attractive looks.

Do not offer me shoes. Offer me comfort for my feet and the pleasure of walking.

Do not offer me a house. Offer me security, comfort, and a place that is clean and happy.

Do not offer me books. Offer me hours of pleasure and the benefit of knowledge.

Do not offer me CDs. Offer me leisure and the sound of music.

Do not offer me tools. Offer me the benefits and the pleasure that come from making beautiful things.

Do not offer me furniture. Offer me comfort and the quietness of a cozy place.

Do not offer me things. Offer me ideas, emotions, ambience, feelings, and benefits.

Please, do not offer me *things*.

A major reason for developing a business mission statement is to attract customers who give meaning to an organization. Hotel customers today want to use the Internet, so more and more hotels are providing Internet service. A classic description of the purpose of a business reveals the relative importance of customers in a statement of mission:

It is the customer who determines what a business is. It is the customer alone whose willingness to pay for a good or service converts economic resources into wealth and things into goods. What a business thinks it produces is not of first importance, especially not to the future of the business and to its success. What the customer thinks he/she is buying, what he/she considers value, is decisive—it determines what a business is, what it produces, and whether it will prosper. And what the customer buys and considers value is never a product. It is always utility, meaning what a product or service does for him or her. The customer is the foundation of a business and keeps it in existence.[15]

Mission Statement Components

Mission statements can and do vary in length, content, format, and specificity. Most practitioners and academicians of strategic management feel that an effective statement should include nine components. Because a mission statement is often the most visible and public part of the strategic-management process, it is important that it includes the nine characteristics as summarized in Table 2-4, as well as the following nine components:

1. *Customers*—Who are the firm's customers?
2. *Products or services*—What are the firm's major products or services?
3. *Markets*—Geographically, where does the firm compete?
4. *Technology*—Is the firm technologically current?
5. *Concern for survival, growth, and profitability*—Is the firm committed to growth and financial soundness?
6. *Philosophy*—What are the basic beliefs, values, aspirations, and ethical priorities of the firm?
7. *Self-concept*—What is the firm's distinctive competence or major competitive advantage?
8. *Concern for public image*—Is the firm responsive to social, community, and environmental concerns?
9. *Concern for employees*—Are employees a valuable asset of the firm?

Excerpts from the mission statements of different organizations are provided in Table 2-5 to exemplify the nine essential mission statement components.

TABLE 2-4 Characteristics of a Mission Statement

- Broad in scope; do not include monetary amounts, numbers, percentages, ratios, or objectives
- Less than 250 words in length
- Inspiring
- Identify the utility of a firm's products
- Reveal that the firm is socially responsible
- Reveal that the firm is environmentally responsible
- Include nine components
    customers, products or services, markets, technology, concern for survival/growth/
    profits, philosophy, self-concept, concern for public image, concern for employees
- Reconciliatory
- Enduring

TABLE 2-5 Examples of the Nine Essential Components of a Mission Statement

1. Customers

We believe our first responsibility is to the doctors, nurses, patients, mothers, and all others who use our products and services. (Johnson & Johnson)

To earn our customers' loyalty, we listen to them, anticipate their needs, and act to create value in their eyes. (Lexmark International)

2. Products or Services

AMAX's principal products are molybdenum, coal, iron ore, copper, lead, zinc, petroleum and natural gas, potash, phosphates, nickel, tungsten, silver, gold, and magnesium. (AMAX Engineering Company)

Standard Oil Company (Indiana) is in business to find and produce crude oil, natural gas, and natural gas liquids; to manufacture high-quality products useful to society from these raw materials; and to distribute and market those products and to provide dependable related services to the consuming public at reasonable prices. (Standard Oil Company)

3. Markets

We are dedicated to the total success of Corning Glass Works as a worldwide competitor. (Corning Glass Works)

Our emphasis is on North American markets, although global opportunities will be explored. (Blockway)

4. Technology

Control Data is in the business of applying micro-electronics and computer technology in two general areas: computer-related hardware; and computing-enhancing services, which include computation, information, education, and finance. (Control Data)

We will continually strive to meet the preferences of adult smokers by developing technologies that have the potential to reduce the health risks associated with smoking. (RJ Reynolds)

5. Concern for Survival, Growth, and Profitability

In this respect, the company will conduct its operations prudently and will provide the profits and growth which will assure Hoover's ultimate success. (Hoover Universal)

To serve the worldwide need for knowledge at a fair profit by adhering, evaluating, producing, and distributing valuable information in a way that benefits our customers, employees, other investors, and our society. (McGraw-Hill)

6. Philosophy

Our world-class leadership is dedicated to a management philosophy that holds people above profits. (Kellogg)

It's all part of the Mary Kay philosophy—a philosophy based on the golden rule. A spirit of sharing and caring where people give cheerfully of their time, knowledge, and experience. (Mary Kay Cosmetics)

7. Self-Concept

Crown Zellerbach is committed to leapfrogging ongoing competition within 1,000 days by unleashing the constructive and creative abilities and energies of each of its employees. (Crown Zellerbach)

8. Concern for Public Image

To share the world's obligation for the protection of the environment. (Dow Chemical)

To contribute to the economic strength of society and function as a good corporate citizen on a local, state, and national basis in all countries in which we do business. (Pfizer)

9. Concern for Employees

To recruit, develop, motivate, reward, and retain personnel of exceptional ability, character, and dedication by providing good working conditions, superior leadership, compensation on the basis of performance, an attractive benefit program, opportunity for growth, and a high degree of employment security. (The Wachovia Corporation)

To compensate its employees with remuneration and fringe benefits competitive with other employment opportunities in its geographical area and commensurate with their contributions toward efficient corporate operations. (Public Service Electric & Gas Company)

Writing and Evaluating Mission Statements

Perhaps the best way to develop a skill for writing and evaluating mission statements is to study actual company missions. Therefore, the mission statements presented on pages 44–46 are evaluated based on the nine desired components. Note earlier in Table 2-2 that numbers provided in each statement reveal what components are included in the respective documents. Among the statements in Table 2-2, note that the Dell mission statement is the best because it lacks only one component, whereas the L'Oreal statement is the worst, lacking six of the nine recommended components.

There is no one best mission statement for a particular organization, so good judgment is required in evaluating mission statements. Realize that some individuals are more demanding than others in assessing mission statements in this manner. For example, if a statement merely includes the word "customers" without specifying who the customers are, is that satisfactory? Ideally a statement would provide more than simply inclusion of a single word such as "products" or "employees" regarding a respective component. Why? Because the statement should be informative, inspiring, enduring, and serve to motivate stakeholders to action. Evaluation of a mission statement regarding inclusion of the nine components is just the beginning of the process to assess a statement's overall effectiveness.

Conclusion

Every organization has a unique purpose and reason for being. This uniqueness should be reflected in vision and mission statements. The nature of a business vision and mission can represent either a competitive advantage or disadvantage for the firm. An organization achieves a heightened sense of purpose when strategists, managers, and employees develop and communicate a clear business vision and mission. Drucker says that developing a clear business vision and mission is the "first responsibility of strategists."

A good mission statement reveals an organization's customers; products or services; markets; technology; concern for survival, growth, and profitability; philosophy; self-concept; concern for public image; and concern for employees. These nine basic components serve as a practical framework for evaluating and writing mission statements. As the first step in strategic management, the vision and mission statements provide direction for all planning activities.

Well-designed vision and mission statements are essential for formulating, implementing, and evaluating strategy. Developing and communicating a clear business vision and mission are the most commonly overlooked tasks in strategic management. Without clear statements of vision and mission, a firm's short-term actions can be counterproductive to long-term interests. Vision and mission statements always should be subject to revision, but, if carefully prepared, they will require infrequent major changes. Organizations usually reexamine their vision and mission statements annually. Effective mission statements stand the test of time.

Vision and mission statements are essential tools for strategists, a fact illustrated in a short story told by Porsche former CEO Peter Schultz:

> Three people were at work on a construction site. All were doing the same job, but when each was asked what his job was, the answers varied: "Breaking rocks," the first replied; "Earning a living," responded the second; "Helping to build a cathedral," said the third. Few of us can build cathedrals. But to the extent we can see the cathedral in whatever cause we are following, the job seems more worthwhile. Good strategists and a clear mission help us find those cathedrals in what otherwise could be dismal issues and empty causes.[16]

We invite you to visit the David page on the Prentice Hall Companion Web site at http://www.pearsonhighered.com/david/ for this chapter's review quiz.

Key Terms and Concepts

Concern for Employees (p. 51)
Concern for Public Image (p. 51)
Concern for Survival, Growth, and Profitability (p. 51)
Creed Statement (p. 44)
Customers (p. 51)
Markets (p. 51)
Mission Statement (p. 44)
Mission Statement Components (p. 51)

Philosophy (p. 51)
Products or Services (p. 51)
Reconciliatory (p. 52)
Self-Concept (p. 51)
Stakeholders (p. 49)
Technology (p. 51)
Vision Statement (p. 46)

Issues for Review and Discussion

1. What are some different names for "mission statement," and where will you likely find a firm's mission statement?
2. If your company does not have a vision or mission statement, describe a good process for developing these documents.
3. Explain how developing a mission statement can help resolve divergent views among managers in a firm.
4. Drucker says the most important time to seriously reexamine the firm's vision/mission is when the firm is very successful. Why is this?
5. Explain why a mission statement should not include monetary amounts, numbers, percentages, ratios, goals, or objectives.
6. Discuss the meaning of the following statement: "Good mission statements identify the utility of a firm's products to its customers."
7. Distinguish between the "self-concept" and the "philosophy" components in a mission statement. Give an example of each for your university.
8. When someone or some company is "on a mission" to achieve something, many times they cannot be stopped. List three things in prioritized order that you are "on a mission" to achieve in life.
9. Compare and contrast vision statements with mission statements in terms of composition and importance.
10. Do local service stations need to have written vision and mission statements? Why or why not?
11. Why do you think organizations that have a comprehensive mission tend to be high performers? Does having a comprehensive mission cause high performance?
12. Explain why a mission statement should not include strategies and objectives.
13. What is your college or university's self-concept? How would you state that in a mission statement?
14. Explain the principal value of a vision and a mission statement.
15. Why is it important for a mission statement to be reconciliatory?
16. In your opinion, what are the three most important components that should be included when writing a mission statement? Why?
17. How would the mission statements of a for-profit and a nonprofit organization differ?
18. Write a vision and mission statement for an organization of your choice.
19. Conduct a search on the Internet with the keywords *vision statement* and *mission statement*. Find various company vision and mission statements, and evaluate the documents. Write a one-page single-spaced report on your findings.
20. Who are the major stakeholders of the bank that you do business with locally? What are the major claims of those stakeholders?
21. List seven characteristics of a mission statement.
22. List eight benefits of having a clear mission statement.
23. How often do you think a firm's vision and mission statements should be changed?

Notes

1. Barbara Bartkus, Myron Glassman, and Bruce McAfee, "Mission Statements: Are They Smoke and Mirrors?" *Business Horizons* (November–December 2000): 23.

2. Peter Drucker, *Management: Tasks, Responsibilities, and Practices* (New York: Harper & Row, 1974): 61.

3. Fred David, "How Companies Define Their Mission," *Long Range Planning* 22, no. 1 (February 1989): 90–92; John Pearce II and Fred David, "Corporate Mission Statements: The Bottom Line," *Academy of Management Executive* 1, no. 2 (May 1987): 110.

4. Joseph Quigley, "Vision: How Leaders Develop It, Share It and Sustain It," *Business Horizons* (September–October 1994): 39.

5. Andrew Campbell and Sally Yeung, "Creating a Sense of Mission," *Long Range Planning* 24, no. 4 (August 1991): 17.

6. Charles Rarick and John Vitton, "Mission Statements Make Cents," *Journal of Business Strategy* 16 (1995): 11. Also, Christopher Bart and Mark Baetz, "The Relationship Between Mission Statements and Firm Performance: An Exploratory Study," *Journal of Management Studies* 35 (1998): 823; "Mission Possible," *Business Week* (August 1999): F12.

7. W. R. King and D. I. Cleland, *Strategic Planning and Policy* (New York: Van Nostrand Reinhold, 1979): 124.

8. Brian Dumaine, "What the Leaders of Tomorrow See," *Fortune* (July 3, 1989): 50.

9. Drucker, 78, 79.

10. "How W. T. Grant Lost $175 Million Last Year," *Business Week* (February 25, 1975): 75.

11. Drucker, 88.

12. John Pearce II, "The Company Mission as a Strategic Tool," *Sloan Management Review* 23, no. 3 (Spring 1982): 74.

13. George Steiner, *Strategic Planning: What Every Manager Must Know* (New York: The Free Press, 1979): 160.

14. Vern McGinnis, "The Mission Statement: A Key Step in Strategic Planning," *Business* 31, no. 6 (November–December 1981): 41.

15. Drucker, 61.

16. Robert Waterman Jr., *The Renewal Factor: How the Best Get and Keep the Competitive Edge* (New York: Bantam, 1987); *Business Week* (September 14, 1987): 120.

Current Readings

Baetz, Mark C., and Christopher K. Bart. "Developing Mission Statements Which Work." *Long Range Planning* 29, no. 4 (August 1996): 526–533.

Bartkus, Barbara, Myron Glassman, and R. Bruce McAfee. "Mission Statements: Are They Smoke and Mirrors?" *Business Horizons* 43, no. 6 (November–December 2000): 23.

Brabet, Julienne, and Mary Klemm. "Sharing the Vision: Company Mission Statements in Britain and France." *Long Range Planning* (February 1994): 84–94.

Collins, David J., and Michael G. Rukstad. "Can You Say What Your Strategy Is?" *Harvard Business Review* (April 2008): 82.

Collins, James C., and Jerry I. Porras. "Building a Visionary Company." *California Management Review* 37, no. 2 (Winter 1995): 80–100.

Collins, James C., and Jerry I. Porras. "Building Your Company's Vision." *Harvard Business Review* (September–October 1996): 65–78.

Conger, Jay A., and Douglas A. Ready. "Enabling Bold Visions." *MIT Sloan Management Review* 49, no. 2 (Winter 2008): 70.

Cummings, Stephen, and John Davies. "Brief Case—Mission, Vision, Fusion." *Long Range Planning* 27, no. 6 (December 1994): 147–150.

Davies, Stuart W., and Keith W. Glaister. "Business School Mission Statements—The Bland Leading the Bland?" *Long Range Planning* 30, no. 4 (August 1997): 594–604.

Day, George S., and Paul Schoemaker, "Peripheral Vision: Sensing and Acting on Weak Signals." *Long Range Planning* 37, no. 2 (April 2004): 117.

Gratton, Lynda. "Implementing a Strategic Vision—Key Factors for Success." *Long Range Planning* 29, no. 3 (June 1996): 290–303.

Ibarra, Herminia, and Otilia Obodaru. "Women and the Vision Thing." *Harvard Business Review* (January 2009): 62–71.

Larwood, Laurie, Cecilia M. Falbe, Mark P. Kriger, and Paul Miesing. "Structure and Meaning of Organizational Vision." *Academy of Management Journal* 38, no. 3 (June 1995): 740–769.

Lissak, Michael, and Johan Roos. "Be Coherent, Not Visionary." *Long Range Planning* 34, no. 1 (February 2001): 53.

McTavish, Ron. "One More Time: What Business Are You In?" *Long Range Planning* 28, no. 2 (April 1995): 49–60.

Newsom, Mi Kyong, David A. Collier, and Eric O. Olsen. "Using "Biztainment" to Gain Competitive Advantage." *Business Horizons* (March–April 2009): 167–166.

ASSURANCE OF LEARNING EXERCISES

Assurance of Learning Exercise 2A

Evaluating Mission Statements

Purpose

A business mission statement is an integral part of strategic management. It provides direction for formulating, implementing, and evaluating strategic activities. This exercise will give you practice evaluating mission statements, a skill that is a prerequisite to writing a good mission statement.

Instructions

Step 1	On a clean sheet of paper, prepare a 9 × 3 matrix. Place the nine mission statement components down the left column and the following three companies across the top of your paper.
Step 2	Write *Yes* or *No* in each cell of your matrix to indicate whether you feel the particular mission statement includes the respective component.
Step 3	Turn your paper in to your instructor for a classwork grade.

Mission Statements

General Motors

Our mission is to be the world leader in transportation products and related services. We aim to maintain this position through enlightened customer enthusiasm and continuous improvement driven by integrity, teamwork, innovation and individual respect and responsibility of our employees.

North Carolina Zoo

Our mission is to encourage understanding of and commitment to the conservation of the world's wildlife and wild places through recognition of the interdependence of people and nature. We will do this by creating a sense of enjoyment, wonder and discovery throughout the Park and in our outreach programs.

Samsonite

Our mission is to be the leader in the travel industry. Samsonite's ambition is to provide unparalleled durability, security and dependability in all of its products, through leading edge functionality, features, innovation, technology, contemporary aesthetics and design. In order to fill every niche in the travel market, Samsonite will seek to create strategic alliances, combining our strengths with other partners in our brands.

Assurance of Learning Exercise 2B

Writing a Vision and Mission Statement for McDonald's Corporation

Purpose

There is always room for improvement in regard to an existing vision and mission statement. Currently McDonald's does not have a vision statement or mission statement, so this exercise will ask you to develop one.

Instructions

Step 1   Refer back to page 33, the Cohesion Case, for McDonald's values statement.
Step 2   On a clean sheet of paper, write a one-sentence vision statement for McDonald's.
Step 3   On that same sheet of paper, write a mission statement for McDonald's.

Assurance of Learning Exercise 2C

Writing a Vision and Mission Statement for My University

Purpose

Most universities have a vision and mission statement. The purpose of this exercise is to give you practice writing a vision and mission statement for a nonprofit organization such as your own university.

Instructions

Step 1   Write a vision statement and a mission statement for your university. Your mission statement should include the nine characteristics summarized in Table 2-4.
Step 2   Read your vision and mission statement to the class.
Step 3   Determine whether your institution has a vision and/or mission statement. Look in the front of the college handbook. If your institution has a written statement, contact an appropriate administrator of the institution to inquire as to how and when the statement was prepared. Share this information with the class. Analyze your college's vision and mission statement in light of the concepts presented in this chapter.

Assurance of Learning Exercise 2D

Conducting Mission Statement Research

Purpose

This exercise gives you the opportunity to study the nature and role of vision and mission statements in strategic management.

Instructions

Step 1   Call various organizations in your city or county to identify firms that have developed a formal vision and/or mission statement. Contact nonprofit organizations and government agencies in addition to small and large businesses. Ask to speak with the director, owner, or chief executive officer of each organization. Explain that you are studying vision and mission statements in class and are conducting research as part of a class activity.
Step 2   Ask several executives the following four questions, and record their answers.
    1. When did your organization first develop its vision and/or mission statement? Who was primarily responsible for its development?
    2. How long have your current statements existed? When were they last modified? Why were they modified at that time?
    3. By what process are your firm's vision and mission statements altered?
    4. How are your vision and mission statements used in the firm?
Step 3   Provide an overview of your findings to the class.

CHAPTER 3
The External Assessment

CHAPTER OBJECTIVES

After studying this chapter, you should be able to do the following:

1. Describe how to conduct an external strategic-management audit.

2. Discuss 10 major external forces that affect organizations: economic, social, cultural, demographic, environmental, political, governmental, legal, technological, and competitive.

3. Describe key sources of external information, including the Internet.

4. Discuss important forecasting tools used in strategic management.

5. Discuss the importance of monitoring external trends and events.

6. Explain how to develop an EFE Matrix.

7. Explain how to develop a Competitive Profile Matrix.

8. Discuss the importance of gathering competitive intelligence.

9. Describe the trend toward cooperation among competitors.

10. Discuss market commonality and resource similarity in relation to competitive analysis.

Assurance of Learning Exercises

Assurance of Learning Exercise 3A

Developing an EFE Matrix for McDonald's Corporation

Assurance of Learning Exercise 3B

The External Assessment

Assurance of Learning Exercise 3C

Developing an EFE Matrix for My University

Assurance of Learning Exercise 3D

Developing a Competitive Profile Matrix for McDonald's Corporation

Source: Shutterstock/Photographer Emin Kuliyev

"Notable Quotes"

"If you're not faster than your competitor, you're in a tenuous position, and if you're only half as fast, you're terminal."

—George Salk

"The opportunities and threats existing in any situation always exceed the resources needed to exploit the opportunities or avoid the threats. Thus, strategy is essentially a problem of allocating resources. If strategy is to be successful, it must allocate superior resources against a decisive opportunity."

—William Cohen

"Organizations pursue strategies that will disrupt the normal course of industry events and forge new industry conditions to the disadvantage of competitors."

—Ian C. Macmillan

"If everyone is thinking alike, then somebody isn't thinking."

—George Patton

"It is not the strongest of the species that survive, nor the most intelligent, but the one most responsive to change."

—Charles Darwin

"Nothing focuses the mind better than the constant sight of a competitor who wants to wipe you off the map."

—Wayne Calloway

**Assurance of Learning
Exercise 3E**

Developing a Competitive
Profile Matrix for My
University

This chapter examines the tools and concepts needed to conduct an external strategic management audit (sometimes called *environmental scanning* or *industry analysis*). An *external audit* focuses on identifying and evaluating trends and events beyond the control of a single firm, such as increased foreign competition, population shifts to the Sunbelt, an aging society, consumer fear of traveling, and stock market volatility. An external audit reveals key opportunities and threats confronting an organization so that managers can formulate strategies to take advantage of the opportunities and avoid or reduce the impact of threats. This chapter presents a practical framework for gathering, assimilating, and analyzing external information. The Industrial Organization (I/O) view of strategic management is introduced.

The Chapter 3 boxed insert company pursuing excellent strategies in the midst of a global recession is Dunkin Brands, Inc.

Doing Great in a Weak Economy

Dunkin' Brands, Inc.

Dunkin' Donuts and Baskin-Robbins are under one umbrella company named Dunkin' Brands, Inc. Doughnuts and ice cream go hand-in-hand at this company, which has more than 13,000 locations in more than 40 countries. With more than 7,900 shops in 30 countries (5,800 of which are in North America), Dunkin' Donuts is the world's leading chain of donut shops. Baskin-Robbins is a leading seller of ice cream and frozen snacks with its nearly 6,000 outlets (about half are located in the United States). About 1,100 locations offer a combination of the company's brands. Dunkin' Brands is owned by a group of private investment firms including Bain Capital, The Carlyle Group, and Thomas H. Lee Partners.

Dunkin' Donuts in 2009 launched a $100 million advertising campaign around the theme "You Kin' Do It" that highlights everyday challenges, such as work and traffic. Dunkin' Donuts president Will Kussell says, "We're going to help you get through whatever you have to deal with every day." Dunkin' is also expanding its Dunkin' Deals, which bundles a bagel or sandwich for 99 cents with purchase of a coffee. Franchisee Jim Allen, who owns 18 stores, says, "Dunkin' Deals has been huge in this economy."

In June 2009, Dunkin' Donuts introduced its first 99 cent breakfast wrap. Called the Wake-Up Wrap and supported by the advertising phrase "America Saves at Dunkin'" Dunkin' launched fierce, frontal attacks on both McDonald's and Starbucks as those two firms battled each other over fancy coffee drinks. Dunkin' Donuts' brand marketing officer Frances Allen said: "Starbucks can't do food and McDonald's can't do coffee. We view breakfast as a 'value' meal as noted in our ad 'Breakfast, NOT Brokefast.'" Dunkin' is presently test marketing a six-item breakfast value menu, all priced at 99 cents with any beverage purchase.

Source: Based on Theresa Howard, "Dunkin' Donuts Expects a Solid 2009," *USA Today* (January 2, 2009): 5B.

The Nature of an External Audit

The purpose of an *external audit* is to develop a finite list of opportunities that could benefit a firm and threats that should be avoided. As the term *finite* suggests, the external audit is not aimed at developing an exhaustive list of every possible factor that could influence the business; rather, it is aimed at identifying key variables that offer actionable responses. Firms should be able to respond either offensively or defensively to the factors by formulating strategies that take advantage of external opportunities or that minimize the impact of potential threats. Figure 3-1 illustrates how the external audit fits into the strategic-management process.

Key External Forces

External forces can be divided into five broad categories: (1) economic forces; (2) social, cultural, demographic, and natural environment forces; (3) political, governmental, and legal forces; (4) technological forces; and (5) competitive forces. Relationships among these forces and an organization are depicted in Figure 3-2. External trends and events, such as the

FIGURE 3-1

A Comprehensive Strategic-Management Model

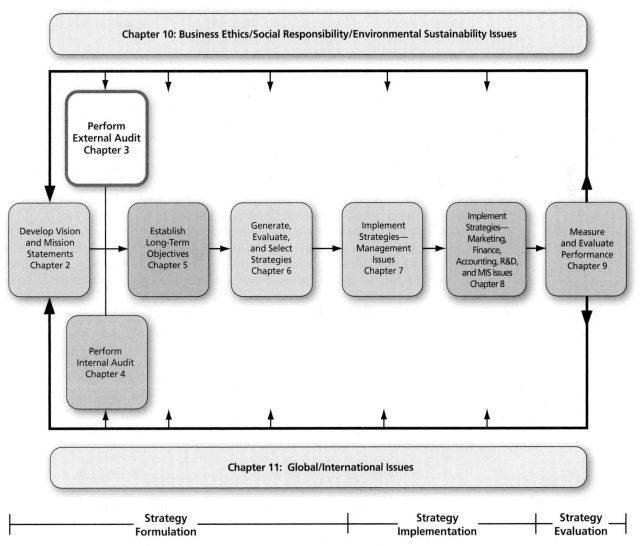

Source: Fred R. David, "How Companies Define Their Mission," *Long Range Planning* 22, no. 3 (June 1988): 40.

FIGURE 3-2

Relationships Between Key External Forces and an Organization

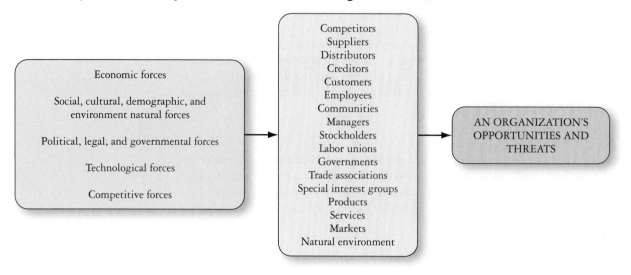

global economic recession, significantly affect products, services, markets, and organizations worldwide. The U.S. unemployment rate climbed to over 9 percent in July 2009 as more than 2.5 million jobs were lost in the United States in 2008—the most since 1945 when the country downsized from the war effort. The rate is expected to rise to 10.1 percent. All sectors witness rising unemployment rates, except for education, health-care services, and government employment. Many Americans are resorting to minimum wage jobs to make ends meet.

Changes in external forces translate into changes in consumer demand for both industrial and consumer products and services. External forces affect the types of products developed, the nature of positioning and market segmentation strategies, the type of services offered, and the choice of businesses to acquire or sell. External forces directly affect both suppliers and distributors. Identifying and evaluating external opportunities and threats enables organizations to develop a clear mission, to design strategies to achieve long-term objectives, and to develop policies to achieve annual objectives.

The increasing complexity of business today is evidenced by more countries developing the capacity and will to compete aggressively in world markets. Foreign businesses and countries are willing to learn, adapt, innovate, and invent to compete successfully in the marketplace. There are more competitive new technologies in Europe and Asia today than ever before.

The Process of Performing an External Audit

The process of performing an external audit must involve as many managers and employees as possible. As emphasized in earlier chapters, involvement in the strategic-management process can lead to understanding and commitment from organizational members. Individuals appreciate having the opportunity to contribute ideas and to gain a better understanding of their firms' industry, competitors, and markets.

To perform an external audit, a company first must gather competitive intelligence and information about economic, social, cultural, demographic, environmental, political, governmental, legal, and technological trends. Individuals can be asked to monitor various sources of information, such as key magazines, trade journals, and newspapers. These persons can submit periodic scanning reports to a committee of managers charged with performing the external audit. This approach provides a continuous stream of timely strategic information and involves many individuals in the external-audit process. The Internet provides another source for gathering strategic information, as do corporate, university, and public libraries. Suppliers, distributors, salespersons, customers, and competitors represent other sources of vital information.

Once information is gathered, it should be assimilated and evaluated. A meeting or series of meetings of managers is needed to collectively identify the most important opportunities and threats facing the firm. These key external factors should be listed on flip charts or a chalkboard. A prioritized list of these factors could be obtained by requesting that all managers rank the factors identified, from 1 for the most important opportunity/threat to 20 for the least important opportunity/threat. These key external factors can vary over time and by industry. Relationships with suppliers or distributors are often a critical success factor. Other variables commonly used include market share, breadth of competing products, world economies, foreign affiliates, proprietary and key account advantages, price competitiveness, technological advancements, population shifts, interest rates, and pollution abatement.

Freund emphasized that these key external factors should be (1) important to achieving long-term and annual objectives, (2) measurable, (3) applicable to all competing firms, and (4) hierarchical in the sense that some will pertain to the overall company and others will be more narrowly focused on functional or divisional areas.[1] A final list of the most important key external factors should be communicated and distributed widely in the organization. Both opportunities and threats can be key external factors.

The Industrial Organization (I/O) View

The *Industrial Organization (I/O)* approach to competitive advantage advocates that external (industry) factors are more important than internal factors in a firm achieving competitive advantage. Proponents of the I/O view, such as Michael Porter, contend that organizational performance will be primarily determined by industry forces. Porter's Five-Forces Model, presented later in this chapter, is an example of the I/O perspective, which focuses on analyzing external forces and industry variables as a basis for getting and keeping competitive advantage. Competitive advantage is determined largely by competitive positioning within an industry, according to I/O advocates. Managing strategically from the I/O perspective entails firms striving to compete in attractive industries, avoiding weak or faltering industries, and gaining a full understanding of key external factor relationships within that attractive industry. I/O research provides important contributions to our understanding of how to gain competitive advantage.

I/O theorists contend that external factors in general and the industry in which a firm chooses to compete has a stronger influence on the firm's performance than do the internal functional decisions managers make in marketing, finance, and the like. Firm performance, they contend, is primarily based more on industry properties, such as economies of scale, barriers to market entry, product differentiation, the economy, and level of competitiveness than on internal resources, capabilities, structure, and operations. The global economic recession's impact on both strong and weak firms has added credence of late to the notion that external forces are more important than internal. Many thousands of internally strong firms in 2006–2007 disappeared in 2008–2009.

The I/O view has enhanced our understanding of strategic management. However, it is not a question of whether external or internal factors are more important in gaining and maintaining competitive advantage. Effective integration and understanding of *both* external and internal factors is the key to securing and keeping a competitive advantage. In fact, as discussed in Chapter 6, matching key external opportunities/threats with key internal strengths/weaknesses provides the basis for successful strategy formulation.

Economic Forces

Increasing numbers of two-income households is an economic trend in the United States. Individuals place a premium on time. Improved customer service, immediate availability, trouble-free operation of products, and dependable maintenance and repair services are becoming more important. People today are more willing than ever to pay for good service if it limits inconvenience.

Economic factors have a direct impact on the potential attractiveness of various strategies. For example, when interest rates rise, funds needed for capital expansion become

TABLE 3-1 Key Economic Variables to Be Monitored

Shift to a service economy in the United States	Import/export factors
Availability of credit	Demand shifts for different categories of goods and services
Level of disposable income	Income differences by region and consumer groups
Propensity of people to spend	Price fluctuations
Interest rates	Export of labor and capital from the United States
Inflation rates	
Money market rates	Monetary policies
Federal government budget deficits	Fiscal policies
Gross domestic product trend	Tax rates
Consumption patterns	European Economic Community (EEC) policies
Unemployment trends	
Worker productivity levels	Organization of Petroleum Exporting Countries (OPEC) policies
Value of the dollar in world markets	
Stock market trends	Coalitions of Lesser Developed Countries (LDC) policies
Foreign countries' economic conditions	

more costly or unavailable. Also, when interest rates rise, discretionary income declines, and the demand for discretionary goods falls. When stock prices increase, the desirability of equity as a source of capital for market development increases. Also, when the market rises, consumer and business wealth expands. A summary of economic variables that often represent opportunities and threats for organizations is provided in Table 3-1.

An economic variable of significant importance in strategic planning is gross domestic product (GDP), especially across countries. Table 3-2 lists the GDP of various countries in Asia for all of 2009. Unlike most countries in Europe and the Americas, most Asian countries expect positive GDP growth in 2009.

Trends in the dollar's value have significant and unequal effects on companies in different industries and in different locations. For example, the pharmaceutical, tourism, entertainment, motor vehicle, aerospace, and forest products industries benefit greatly when the dollar falls against the yen and euro. Agricultural and petroleum industries are hurt by the dollar's rise against the currencies of Mexico, Brazil, Venezuela, and Australia. Generally, a strong or high dollar makes U.S. goods more expensive in overseas markets. This worsens the U.S. trade deficit. When the value of the dollar falls, tourism-oriented firms benefit because Americans do not travel abroad

TABLE 3-2 Expected GDP Growth in 2009 Among Countries in Asia

Country	Percent GDP Growth
China	High (7–8 percent)
India	High (7–8 percent)
Indonesia	Medium (3–4 percent)
Thailand	Medium (3–4 percent)
Philippines	Medium (3–4 percent)
Taiwan	Medium (3–4 percent)
Malaysia	Medium (3–4 percent)
South Korea	Low (1–2 percent)
Hong Kong	Low (1–2 percent)
Singapore	Low (1–2 percent)

Source: Based on Patrick Barta, "Sharp Downturn in Asia Nears," *Wall Street Journal* (October 27, 2008): A9.

as much when the value of the dollar is low; rather, foreigners visit and vacation more in the United States.

A low value of the dollar means lower imports and higher exports; it helps U.S. companies' competitiveness in world markets. The dollar has fallen to five-year lows against the euro and yen, which makes U.S. goods cheaper to foreign consumers and combats deflation by pushing up prices of imports. However, European firms such as Volkswagen AG, Nokia Corp., and Michelin complain that the strong euro hurts their financial performance. The low value of the dollar benefits the U.S. economy in many ways. First, it helps stave off the risks of deflation in the United States and also reduces the U.S. trade deficit. In addition, the low value of the dollar raises the foreign sales and profits of domestic firms, thanks to dollar-induced gains, and encourages foreign countries to lower interest rates and loosen fiscal policy, which stimulates worldwide economic expansion. Some sectors, such as consumer staples, energy, materials, technology, and health care, especially benefit from a low value of the dollar. Manufacturers in many domestic industries in fact benefit because of a weak dollar, which forces foreign rivals to raise prices and extinguish discounts. Domestic firms with big overseas sales, such as McDonald's, greatly benefit from a weak dollar.

Between March and June 2009, the U.S. dollar weakened 11.0 percent against the euro, due to the growing United States debt, which may soon exceed $12 trillion. Table 3-3 lists some advantages and disadvantages of a weak U.S. dollar for American firms.

Rising unemployment rates across the United States have touched off a race among states to attract businesses with tax breaks and financial incentives. New Jersey has promised to send a $3,000 check to every small business that hires a new employee. Minnesota is offering tax-free zones for companies that create "green jobs." Colorado has created a $5 million fund for banks that open credit lines for small businesses. To minimize risk in incentive deals, may states write in claw-back provisions that require companies to return funds if they fail to create the promised number of jobs.

The slumping economy worldwide and depressed prices of assets has dramatically slowed the migration of people from country to country and from the city to the suburbs. Because people are not moving nearly as much as in years past, there is lower and lower demand for new or used houses. Thus the housing market is expected to remain very sluggish well into 2010 and 2011.

TABLE 3-3   Advantages and Disadvantages of a Weak Dollar for Domestic Firms

Advantages	Disadvantages
1. Leads to more exports	1. Can lead to inflation
2. Leads to lower imports	2. Can cause rise in oil prices
3. Makes U.S. goods cheaper to foreign consumers	3. Can weaken U.S. government
4. Combats deflation by pushing up prices of imports	4. Makes it unattractive for Americans to travel globally
5. Can contribute to rise in stock prices in short run	5. Can contribute to fall in stock prices in long run
6. Stimulates worldwide economic recession	
7. Encourages foreign countries to lower interest rates	
8. Raises the revenues and profits of firms that do business outside the United States	
9. Stimulates worldwide economic expansion	
10. Forces foreign firms to raise prices	
11. Reduces the U.S. trade deficit	
12. Encourages firms to globalize	
13. Encourages foreigners to visit the United States	

Social, Cultural, Demographic, and Natural Environment Forces

Social, cultural, demographic, and environmental changes have a major impact on virtually all products, services, markets, and customers. Small, large, for-profit, and nonprofit organizations in all industries are being staggered and challenged by the opportunities and threats arising from changes in social, cultural, demographic, and environmental variables. In every way, the United States is much different today than it was yesterday, and tomorrow promises even greater changes.

The United States is getting older and less white. The oldest members of America's 76 million baby boomers plan to retire in 2011, and this has lawmakers and younger taxpayers deeply concerned about who will pay their Social Security, Medicare, and Medicaid. Individuals age 65 and older in the United States as a percentage of the population will rise to 18.5 percent by 2025. The five "oldest" states and five "youngest" states in 2007 are given in Table 3-4.

By 2075, the United States will have no racial or ethnic majority. This forecast is aggravating tensions over issues such as immigration and affirmative action. Hawaii, California, and New Mexico already have no majority race or ethnic group.

The population of the world surpassed 7.0 billion in 2010; the United States has just over 310 million people. That leaves billions of people outside the United States who may be interested in the products and services produced through domestic firms. Remaining solely domestic is an increasingly risky strategy, especially as the world population continues to grow to an estimated 8 billion in 2028 and 9 billion in 2054.

Social, cultural, demographic, and environmental trends are shaping the way Americans live, work, produce, and consume. New trends are creating a different type of consumer and, consequently, a need for different products, different services, and different strategies. There are now more American households with people living alone or with unrelated people than there are households consisting of married couples with children. American households are making more and more purchases online. Beer consumption in the United States is growing at only 0.5 percent per year, whereas wine consumption is growing 3.5 percent and distilled spirits consumption is growing at 2.0 percent.[2] Beer is still the most popular alcoholic beverage in the United States, but its market share has dropped from 59.5 percent in its peak year of 1995 to 56.7 percent today. For a wine company such as Gallo, this trend is an opportunity, whereas for a firm such as Adolph Coors Brewing, this trend is an external threat.

The trend toward an older America is good news for restaurants, hotels, airlines, cruise lines, tours, resorts, theme parks, luxury products and services, recreational vehicles, home builders, furniture producers, computer manufacturers, travel services, pharmaceutical firms, automakers, and funeral homes. Older Americans are especially interested in health care, financial services, travel, crime prevention, and leisure. The world's longest-living people are the Japanese, with Japanese women living to 86.3 years and men living to 80.1 years on average. By 2050, the Census Bureau projects that the number of Americans age 100 and older will increase to over 834,000 from just under 100,000 centenarians in the

TABLE 3-4 **The Oldest and Youngest States by Average Age of Residents**

Five Oldest States	Five Youngest States
Maine	Utah
Vermont	Texas
West Virginia	Alaska
Florida	Idaho
Pennsylvania	California

Source: Based on U.S. Census Bureau. Also, Ken Jackson, "State Population Changes by Race, Ethnicity," *USA Today* (May 17, 2007): 2A.

United States in 2000. Americans age 65 and over will increase from 12.6 percent of the U.S. population in 2000 to 20.0 percent by the year 2050.

The aging American population affects the strategic orientation of nearly all organizations. Apartment complexes for the elderly, with one meal a day, transportation, and utilities included in the rent, have increased nationwide. Called *lifecare facilities*, these complexes now exceed 2 million. Some well-known companies building these facilities include Avon, Marriott, and Hyatt. Individuals age 65 and older in the United States comprise 13 percent of the total population; Japan's elderly population ratio is 17 percent, and Germany's is 19 percent.

Americans were on the move in a population shift to the South and West (Sunbelt) and away from the Northeast and Midwest (Frostbelt), but the recession and housing bust nationwide has slowed migration throughout the United States. More Americans are staying in place rather than moving. New jobs are the primary reason people move across state lines, so with 3 million less jobs in the United States in 2008–2009 alone, there is less need to move. Falling home prices also have prompted people to avoid moving. The historical trend of people moving from the Northeast and Midwest to the Sunbelt and West has dramatically slowed. The worldwide recession is also reducing international immigration, down roughly 10 percent in both 2008 and 2009. Hard number data related to this information can represent key opportunities for many firms and thus can be essential for successful strategy formulation, including where to locate new plants and distribution centers and where to focus marketing efforts.

A summary of important social, cultural, demographic, and environmental variables that represent opportunities or threats for virtually all organizations is given in Table 3-5.

TABLE 3-5   Key Social, Cultural, Demographic, and Natural Environment Variables

Childbearing rates	Attitudes toward retirement
Number of special-interest groups	Attitudes toward leisure time
Number of marriages	Attitudes toward product quality
Number of divorces	Attitudes toward customer service
Number of births	Pollution control
Number of deaths	Attitudes toward foreign peoples
Immigration and emigration rates	Energy conservation
Social Security programs	Social programs
Life expectancy rates	Number of churches
Per capita income	Number of church members
Location of retailing, manufacturing, and service businesses	Social responsibility
Attitudes toward business	Attitudes toward careers
Lifestyles	Population changes by race, age, sex, and level of affluence
Traffic congestion	Attitudes toward authority
Inner-city environments	Population changes by city, county, state, region, and country
Average disposable income	
Trust in government	Value placed on leisure time
Attitudes toward government	Regional changes in tastes and preferences
Attitudes toward work	Number of women and minority workers
Buying habits	Number of high school and college graduates by geographic area
Ethical concerns	
Attitudes toward saving	Recycling
Sex roles	Waste management
Attitudes toward investing	Air pollution
Racial equality	Water pollution
Use of birth control	Ozone depletion
Average level of education	Endangered species
Government regulation	

Political, Governmental, and Legal Forces

Federal, state, local, and foreign governments are major regulators, deregulators, subsidizers, employers, and customers of organizations. Political, governmental, and legal factors, therefore, can represent key opportunities or threats for both small and large organizations.

For industries and firms that depend heavily on government contracts or subsidies, political forecasts can be the most important part of an external audit. Changes in patent laws, antitrust legislation, tax rates, and lobbying activities can affect firms significantly. The increasing global interdependence among economies, markets, governments, and organizations makes it imperative that firms consider the possible impact of political variables on the formulation and implementation of competitive strategies.

In the face of a deepening global recession, countries worldwide are resorting to protectionism to safeguard their own industries. European Union (EU) nations, for example, have tightened their own trade rules and resumed subsidies for various of their own industries while barring imports from certain other countries. The EU recently restricted imports of U.S. chicken and beef. India is increasing tariffs on foreign steel. Russia perhaps has instituted the most protectionist measures in recent months by raising tariffs on most imports and subsidizing its own exports. Russia even imposed a new toll on trucks from the EU, Switzerland, and Turkmenistan. Despite these measures taken by other countries, the United States has largely refrained from "Buy American" policies and protectionist measures, although there are increased tariffs on French cheese and Italian water. Many economists say the current rash of trade constraints will make it harder for global economic growth to recover from the global recession. Global trade is expected to decrease 2.1 percent in 2009 compared to an increase of 6.2 percent in 2008.[3] Russia has said that "protective tariffs are necessary to allow Russian companies to survive the recession." This view unfortunately is also the view at an increasing number of countries.

Governments are taking control of more and more companies as the global economic recession cripples firms considered vital to the nation's financial stability. For example, France in 2009 took a 2.35 percent equity stake in troubled car-parts maker Valeo SA. President Nicolas Sarkozy of France has created a $20 billion strategic fund to lend cash to banks and carmakers as many governments become more protectionist. The United States of course also is taking equity stakes in financial institutions and carmakers and is "bailing out" companies too.

The UK government in 2009 took a 95 percent stake in the banking giant Royal Bank of Scotland Group PLC in a dramatic move toward nationalization. The government gave the bank $37 billion and insured another $300 billion of the bank's assets. The UK government also recently increased its stake in Lloyds Banking Group PLC to 75 percent. Similarly, the U.S. government has taken over Fannie Mae and Freddie Mac and has raised its stake even in Citigroup to 40 percent.

As more and more companies around the world accept government bailouts, those companies are being forced to march to priorities set by political leaders. Even in the United States, the federal government is battling the recession with its deepest intervention in the economy since the Great Depression. The U.S. government now is a strategic manager in industries from banking to insurance to autos. Governments worldwide are under pressure to protect jobs at home and maintain the nation's industrial base. For example, in France, Renault SA's factory in Sandouville is one of the most unproductive auto factories in the world. However, Renault has taken $3.9 billion in low-interest loans from the French government, so the company cannot close any French factories for the duration of the loan or resort to mass layoffs in France for a year.

Political relations between Japan and China have thawed considerably in recent years, which is good for the world economy because China's low-cost manufactured goods have become essential for the functioning of most industrialized nations. Chinese premier Wen Jiabao addressed the Japanese parliament in 2007, something no Chinese leader has done for more than 20 years, and Japanese prime minister Shinzo Abe has visited Beijing. Japan's largest trading partner is China, and China's third-largest trading partner is Japan—after the European Union, number one, and the United States, number two.

TABLE 3-6 Some Political, Governmental, and Legal Variables

Government regulations or deregulations	Sino-American relationships
Changes in tax laws	Russian-American relationships
Special tariffs	European-American relationships
Political action committees	African-American relationships
Voter participation rates	Import–export regulations
Number, severity, and location of government protests	Government fiscal and monetary policy changes
Number of patents	Political conditions in foreign countries
Changes in patent laws	Special local, state, and federal laws
Environmental protection laws	Lobbying activities
Level of defense expenditures	Size of government budgets
Legislation on equal employment	World oil, currency, and labor markets
Level of government subsidies	Location and severity of terrorist activities
Antitrust legislation	Local, state, and national elections

Local, state, and federal laws; regulatory agencies; and special-interest groups can have a major impact on the strategies of small, large, for-profit, and nonprofit organizations. Many companies have altered or abandoned strategies in the past because of political or governmental actions. In the academic world, as state budgets have dropped in recent years, so too has state support for colleges and universities. Due to the decline in monies received from the state, many institutions of higher learning are doing more fundraising on their own—naming buildings and classrooms, for example, for donors. A summary of political, governmental, and legal variables that can represent key opportunities or threats to organizations is provided in Table 3-6.

Technological Forces

Revolutionary technological changes and discoveries are having a dramatic impact on organizations. CEO Chris DeWolfe of MySpace is using technology to expand the firm's 1,600-person workforce in 2009 even as the economic recession deepens. MySpace expects a 17 percent increase in revenue in 2009. Nearly half of the site's 130 million members worldwide are 35 and older, and 76 million of the members are from the United States. This compares to rival Facebook that has 150 million members worldwide but only 55 million in the United States. MySpace is continually redesigning the site and revamping the way its members can manage their profiles and categorize their friends, and enabling consumers to listen to free streaming audio and songs. Doug Morris, CEO of Universal Music Group, says, "There is a lot of conflict between technology and content, and Chris has successfully brought both together."[4]

The *Internet* has changed the very nature of opportunities and threats by altering the life cycles of products, increasing the speed of distribution, creating new products and services, erasing limitations of traditional geographic markets, and changing the historical trade-off between production standardization and flexibility. The Internet is altering economies of scale, changing entry barriers, and redefining the relationship between industries and various suppliers, creditors, customers, and competitors.

To effectively capitalize on e-commerce, a number of organizations are establishing two new positions in their firms: *chief information officer (CIO)* and *chief technology officer (CTO)*. This trend reflects the growing importance of *information technology (IT)* in strategic management. A CIO and CTO work together to ensure that information needed to formulate, implement, and evaluate strategies is available where and when it is needed. These individuals are responsible for developing, maintaining, and updating a company's information database. The CIO is more a manager, managing the firm's relationship with stakeholders; the CTO is more a technician, focusing on technical issues such as data acquisition, data processing, decision-support systems, and software and hardware acquisition.

Technological forces represent major opportunities and threats that must be considered in formulating strategies. Technological advancements can dramatically affect organizations' products, services, markets, suppliers, distributors, competitors, customers, manufacturing processes, marketing practices, and competitive position. Technological advancements can create new markets, result in a proliferation of new and improved products, change the relative competitive cost positions in an industry, and render existing products and services obsolete. Technological changes can reduce or eliminate cost barriers between businesses, create shorter production runs, create shortages in technical skills, and result in changing values and expectations of employees, managers, and customers. Technological advancements can create new competitive advantages that are more powerful than existing advantages. No company or industry today is insulated against emerging technological developments. In high-tech industries, identification and evaluation of key technological opportunities and threats can be the most important part of the external strategic-management audit.

Organizations that traditionally have limited technology expenditures to what they can fund after meeting marketing and financial requirements urgently need a reversal in thinking. The pace of technological change is increasing and literally wiping out businesses every day. An emerging consensus holds that technology management is one of the key responsibilities of strategists. Firms should pursue strategies that take advantage of technological opportunities to achieve sustainable, competitive advantages in the marketplace.

In practice, critical decisions about technology too often are delegated to lower organizational levels or are made without an understanding of their strategic implications. Many strategists spend countless hours determining market share, positioning products in terms of features and price, forecasting sales and market size, and monitoring distributors; yet too often, technology does not receive the same respect.

Not all sectors of the economy are affected equally by technological developments. The communications, electronics, aeronautics, and pharmaceutical industries are much more volatile than the textile, forestry, and metals industries. A recent article in the *Wall Street Journal* detailed how wireless technology will change 10 particular industries.[5] Table 3-7 provides a glimpse of this article.

TABLE 3-7 Examples of the Impact of Wireless Technology

Airlines—Many airlines now offer wireless technology in flight.

Automotive—Vehicles are becoming wireless.

Banking—Visa sends text message alerts after unusual transactions.

Education—Many secondary (and even college) students may use smart phones for math because research shows this to be greatly helpful.

Energy—Smart meters now provide power on demand in your home or business.

Health Care—Patients use mobile devices to monitor their own health, such as calories consumed.

Hotels—Days Inn sends daily specials and coupons to hotel guests via text messages.

Market Research—Cell phone respondents provide more honest answers, perhaps because they are away from eavesdropping ears.

Politics—President Obama won the election partly by mobilizing Facebook and MySpace users, revolutionizing political campaigns. Obama announced his vice presidential selection of Joe Biden by a text message.

Publishing—eBooks are increasingly available.

Source: Based on Joe Mullich, "10 Industries That Wireless Will Change," *Wall Street Journal* (April 1, 2009): A12.

Competitive Forces

The top U.S. competitors in four different industries are identified in Table 3-8. An important part of an external audit is identifying rival firms and determining their strengths, weaknesses, capabilities, opportunities, threats, objectives, and strategies.

Collecting and evaluating information on competitors is essential for successful strategy formulation. Identifying major competitors is not always easy because many firms have divisions that compete in different industries. Many multidivisional firms do not provide sales and profit information on a divisional basis for competitive reasons. Also, privately held firms do not publish any financial or marketing information. Addressing questions about competitors such as those presented in Table 3-9 is important in performing an external audit.

Competition in virtually all industries can be described as intense—and sometimes as cutthroat. For example, Walgreens and CVS pharmacies are located generally across the street from each other and battle each other every day on price and customer service. Most automobile dealerships also are located close to each other. Dollar General, based in Goodlettsville, Tennessee, and Family Dollar, based in Matthews, North Carolina, compete intensely on price to attract customers. Best Buy dropped prices wherever possible to finally put Circuit City totally out of business.

Seven characteristics describe the most competitive companies:

1. Market share matters; the 90th share point isn't as important as the 91st, and nothing is more dangerous than falling to 89.
2. Understand and remember precisely what business you are in.

TABLE 3-8 **The Top U.S. Competitors in Four Different Industries**

	2008 Sales (in millions)	% Change from 2007	2008 Profits (in millions)	% Change from 2007
Beverages				
Coca-Cola	$31,944	+11	$5,807	−3
Pepsi Bottling	13,796	+2	162	−70
Coca-Cola Enterprises	21,807	+4	(4,394)	−718
Molson Coors Brewing	4774	−23	388	−22
Pharmaceuticals				
Johnson & Johnson	63,747	+4	12,949	22
Pfizer	48,296	0	8,104	0
Merck	23,850	−1	7,808	138
Abbott Laboratories	29,528	+14	4,881	35
Wyeth	22,834	+2	4,418	−4
Construction and Farm Equipment				
Caterpillar	51,324	+14	3,557	0
Deere	28,438	+18	2,053	+13
Terek	9,890	+8	72	−88
Agco	8,425	+23	400	+62
Cummins	14,342	+10	755	+2
Computers				
Hewlett-Packard	118,364	+13	8,329	+15
Sun Microsystems	13,880	0	403	−15
Dell	61,101	0	2,478	−16
Xerox	17,608	+2	230	−80
Apple	32,479	+35	4,834	+38

Source: Based on *Fortune*, April 30, 2008, F50–F73.

TABLE 3-9   Key Questions About Competitors

1. What are the major competitors' strengths?
2. What are the major competitors' weaknesses?
3. What are the major competitors' objectives and strategies?
4. How will the major competitors most likely respond to current economic, social, cultural, demographic, environmental, political, governmental, legal, technological, and competitive trends affecting our industry?
5. How vulnerable are the major competitors to our alternative company strategies?
6. How vulnerable are our alternative strategies to successful counterattack by our major competitors?
7. How are our products or services positioned relative to major competitors?
8. To what extent are new firms entering and old firms leaving this industry?
9. What key factors have resulted in our present competitive position in this industry?
10. How have the sales and profit rankings of major competitors in the industry changed over recent years? Why have these rankings changed that way?
11. What is the nature of supplier and distributor relationships in this industry?
12. To what extent could substitute products or services be a threat to competitors in this industry?

3. Whether it's broke or not, fix it—make it better; not just products, but the whole company, if necessary.
4. Innovate or evaporate; particularly in technology-driven businesses, nothing quite recedes like success.
5. Acquisition is essential to growth; the most successful purchases are in niches that add a technology or a related market.
6. People make a difference; tired of hearing it? Too bad.
7. There is no substitute for quality and no greater threat than failing to be cost-competitive on a global basis.[6]

Competitive Intelligence Programs

What is competitive intelligence? *Competitive intelligence (CI)*, as formally defined by the Society of Competitive Intelligence Professionals (SCIP), is a systematic and ethical process for gathering and analyzing information about the competition's activities and general business trends to further a business's own goals (SCIP Web site).

Good competitive intelligence in business, as in the military, is one of the keys to success. The more information and knowledge a firm can obtain about its competitors, the more likely it is that it can formulate and implement effective strategies. Major competitors' weaknesses can represent external opportunities; major competitors' strengths may represent key threats.

In April 2009, Starwood Hotels & Resorts Worldwide sued Hilton Hotels Corp. for allegedly stealing more than 100,000 confidential electronic and paper documents containing "Starwood's most competitively sensitive information." The complaint alleges that two Starwood executives, Ross Klein and Amar Lalvani, resigned from Starwood to join Hilton and took this information with them. The legal complaint says, "This is the clearest imaginable case of corporate espionage, theft of trade secrets, unfair competition and computer fraud." In addition to monetary awards, Starwood is seeking to force Hilton to cancel the rollout of the Denizen hotel chain. Hilton is owned by Blackstone Group.

Hiring top executives from rival firms is also a way companies obtain competitive intelligence. Just two days after Facebook's COO, Owen Van Natta, left the company in 2009, he accepted the CEO job at MySpace, replacing then CEO and cofounder Chris DeWolfe. Van Natta had previously also been Facebook's COO, chief revenue officer, and vice president of operations. The MySpace appointment now pits CEO Van Natta against his old boss at Facebook, CEO Mark Zuckerberg. Facebook passed MySpace in visitors worldwide in 2008 and is closing in on leadership in the United States. Both firms are fierce rivals in the Internet social-networking business.[7]

A recent article in the *Wall Street Journal* detailed how computer spies recently broke into the Pentagon's $300 billion Joint Strike fighter project, one of the costliest weapons programs ever.[8] This intrusion and similar episodes of late have confirmed that any information a firm has available to anyone within the firm online may be at risk of being copied and/or siphoned away by adversaries or rival firms. A recent Pentagon report says the Chinese military in particular has made "steady progress" in developing online-warfare techniques, but rival firms in many industries have expert computer engineers who may be capable of similar unethical/unlawful tactics.

Many U.S. executives grew up in times when U.S. firms dominated foreign competitors so much that gathering competitive intelligence did not seem worth the effort. Too many of these executives still cling to these attitudes—to the detriment of their organizations today. Even most MBA programs do not offer a course in competitive and business intelligence, thus reinforcing this attitude. As a consequence, three strong misperceptions about business intelligence prevail among U.S. executives today:

1. Running an intelligence program requires lots of people, computers, and other resources.
2. Collecting intelligence about competitors violates antitrust laws; business intelligence equals espionage.
3. Intelligence gathering is an unethical business practice.[9]

Any discussions with a competitor about price, market, or geography intentions could violate antitrust statutes. However, this fact must not lure a firm into underestimating the need for and benefits of systematically collecting information about competitors for Strategic Planning purposes. The Internet has become an excellent medium for gathering competitive intelligence. Information gathering from employees, managers, suppliers, distributors, customers, creditors, and consultants also can make the difference between having superior or just average intelligence and overall competitiveness.

Firms need an effective competitive intelligence (CI) program. The three basic objectives of a CI program are (1) to provide a general understanding of an industry and its competitors, (2) to identify areas in which competitors are vulnerable and to assess the impact strategic actions would have on competitors, and (3) to identify potential moves that a competitor might make that would endanger a firm's position in the market.[10] Competitive information is equally applicable for strategy formulation, implementation, and evaluation decisions. An effective CI program allows all areas of a firm to access consistent and verifiable information in making decisions. All members of an organization—from the chief executive officer to custodians—are valuable intelligence agents and should feel themselves to be a part of the CI process. Special characteristics of a successful CI program include flexibility, usefulness, timeliness, and cross-functional cooperation.

The increasing emphasis on *competitive analysis* in the United States is evidenced by corporations putting this function on their organizational charts under job titles such as Director of Competitive Analysis, Competitive Strategy Manager, Director of Information Services, or Associate Director of Competitive Assessment. The responsibilities of a *director of competitive analysis* include planning, collecting data, analyzing data, facilitating the process of gathering and analyzing data, disseminating intelligence on a timely basis, researching special issues, and recognizing what information is important and who needs to know. Competitive intelligence is not corporate espionage because 95 percent of the information a company needs to make strategic decisions is available and accessible to the public. Sources of competitive information include trade journals, want ads, newspaper articles, and government filings, as well as customers, suppliers, distributors, competitors themselves, and the Internet.

Unethical tactics such as bribery, wiretapping, and computer break-ins should never be used to obtain information. Marriott and Motorola—two U.S. companies that do a particularly good job of gathering competitive intelligence—agree that all the information you could wish for can be collected without resorting to unethical tactics. They keep their intelligence staffs small, usually under five people, and spend less than $200,000 per year on gathering competitive intelligence.

Unilever recently sued Procter & Gamble (P&G) over that company's corporate-espionage activities to obtain the secrets of its Unilever hair-care business. After spending $3 million to establish a team to find out about competitors in the domestic hair-care industry, P&G allegedly took roughly 80 documents from garbage bins outside Unilever's Chicago offices. P&G produces Pantene and Head & Shoulders shampoos; Unilever has hair-care brands such as ThermaSilk, Suave, Salon Selectives, and Finesse. Similarly, Oracle Corp. recently admitted that detectives it hired paid janitors to go through Microsoft Corp.'s garbage, looking for evidence to use in court.

Market Commonality and Resource Similarity

By definition, competitors are firms that offer similar products and services in the same market. Markets can be geographic or product areas or segments. For example, in the insurance industry the markets are broken down into commercial/consumer, health/life, or Europe/Asia. Researchers use the terms *market commonality* and *resource similarity* to study rivalry among competitors. *Market commonality* can be defined as the number and significance of markets that a firm competes in with rivals.[11] *Resource similarity* is the extent to which the type and amount of a firm's internal resources are comparable to a rival.[12] One way to analyze competitiveness between two or among several firms is to investigate market commonality and resource similarity issues while looking for areas of potential competitive advantage along each firm's value chain.

Competitive Analysis: Porter's Five-Forces Model

As illustrated in Figure 3-3, *Porter's Five-Forces Model* of competitive analysis is a widely used approach for developing strategies in many industries. The intensity of competition among firms varies widely across industries. Table 3-10 reveals the average profit margin and return on investment for firms in different industries. Note the substantial variation among industries. For example, the range in profit margin goes from 0 to 18 for food production to computer software, respectively. Intensity of competition is highest in lower-return industries. The collective impact of competitive forces is so brutal in some industries that the market is clearly "unattractive" from a profit-making standpoint. Rivalry among existing firms is severe, new rivals can enter the industry with relative ease, and both suppliers and customers can exercise considerable bargaining leverage. According to Porter, the nature of competitiveness in a given industry can be viewed as a composite of five forces:

1. Rivalry among competing firms
2. Potential entry of new competitors

FIGURE 3-3

The Five-Forces Model of Competition

TABLE 3-10 Intensity of Competition Among Firms in Different
Industries (A through H industries only)

Industry	Year-End Profit Margin		Year-End Return on Investment	
	2006	2008	2006	2008
Aerospace and Defense	6	8	6	8
Airlines	2	−13	2	−14
Apparel	5	9	8	34
Automotive Retailing	1	−8	3	−10
Beverages	7	3	4	2
Chemicals	5	5	5	6
Commercial Banks	16	5	1.3	0.3
Computer Peripherals	8	10	7	12
Computer Software	18	32	8	20
Computers, Office Equipment	6	4	7	5
Diversified Financials	12	−1	1	0
Diversified Outsourcing Services	4	7	5	3
Electronics, Electrical Equipment	7	7	8	9
Energy	3	1	3	2
Engineering, Construction	2	3	4	5
Entertainment	10	−10	4	−3
Financial Data Services	10	12	6	2
Food and Drug Stores	2	2	5	4
Food Consumer Products	5	7	6	7
Food Production	0	1	1	1
Food Services	4	7	7	11
Forest and Paper Products	3	−10	4	−8
General Merchandisers	3	3	5	5
Health Care: Insurance	5	2	8	4
Health Care: Medical Facilities	4	2	4	3
Health Care: Pharmacy	3	3	9	7
Home Equipment/Furnishings	4	1	6	1
Homebuilders	6	−47	6	−43
Hotels, Casinos, Resorts	7	−5	3	0

Source: Based on John Moore, "Ranked Within Industries," *Fortune* (May 4, 2009): F-46–F-60.

3. Potential development of substitute products
4. Bargaining power of suppliers
5. Bargaining power of consumers

The following three steps for using Porter's Five-Forces Model can indicate whether competition in a given industry is such that the firm can make an acceptable profit:

1. Identify key aspects or elements of each competitive force that impact the firm.
2. Evaluate how strong and important each element is for the firm.
3. Decide whether the collective strength of the elements is worth the firm entering or staying in the industry.

Rivalry Among Competing Firms

Rivalry among competing firms is usually the most powerful of the five competitive forces. The strategies pursued by one firm can be successful only to the extent that they provide competitive advantage over the strategies pursued by rival firms. Changes in strategy by one firm may be met with retaliatory countermoves, such as lowering prices, enhancing quality, adding features, providing services, extending warranties, and increasing advertising.

Free-flowing information on the Internet is driving down prices and inflation worldwide. The Internet, coupled with the common currency in Europe, enables consumers to make price comparisons easily across countries. Just for a moment, consider the implications for car dealers who used to know everything about a new car's pricing, while you, the consumer, knew very little. You could bargain, but being in the dark, you rarely could win. Now you can shop online in a few hours at every dealership within 500 miles to find the best price and terms. So you, the consumer, can win. This is true in many, if not most, business-to-consumer and business-to-business sales transactions today.

The intensity of rivalry among competing firms tends to increase as the number of competitors increases, as competitors become more equal in size and capability, as demand for the industry's products declines, and as price cutting becomes common. Rivalry also increases when consumers can switch brands easily; when barriers to leaving the market are high; when fixed costs are high; when the product is perishable; when consumer demand is growing slowly or declines such that rivals have excess capacity and/or inventory; when the products being sold are commodities (not easily differentiated such as gasoline); when rival firms are diverse in strategies, origins, and culture; and when mergers and acquisitions are common in the industry. As rivalry among competing firms intensifies, industry profits decline, in some cases to the point where an industry becomes inherently unattractive. When rival firms sense weakness, typically they will intensify both marketing and production efforts to capitalize on the "opportunity." Table 3-11 summarizes conditions that cause high rivalry among competing firms.

Potential Entry of New Competitors

Whenever new firms can easily enter a particular industry, the intensity of competitiveness among firms increases. Barriers to entry, however, can include the need to gain economies of scale quickly, the need to gain technology and specialized know-how, the lack of experience, strong customer loyalty, strong brand preferences, large capital requirements, lack of adequate distribution channels, government regulatory policies, tariffs, lack of access to

TABLE 3-11   Conditions That Cause High Rivalry Among Competing Firms

1. High number of competing firms
2. Similar size of firms competing
3. Similar capability of firms competing
4. Falling demand for the industry's products
5. Falling product/service prices in the industry
6. When consumers can switch brands easily
7. When barriers to leaving the market are high
8. When barriers to entering the market are low
9. When fixed costs are high among firms competing
10. When the product is perishable
11. When rivals have excess capacity
12. When consumer demand is falling
13. When rivals have excess inventory
14. When rivals sell similar products/services
15. When mergers are common in the industry

raw materials, possession of patents, undesirable locations, counterattack by entrenched firms, and potential saturation of the market.

Despite numerous barriers to entry, new firms sometimes enter industries with higher-quality products, lower prices, and substantial marketing resources. The strategist's job, therefore, is to identify potential new firms entering the market, to monitor the new rival firms' strategies, to counterattack as needed, and to capitalize on existing strengths and opportunities. When the threat of new firms entering the market is strong, incumbent firms generally fortify their positions and take actions to deter new entrants, such as lowering prices, extending warranties, adding features, or offering financing specials.

Potential Development of Substitute Products

In many industries, firms are in close competition with producers of substitute products in other industries. Examples are plastic container producers competing with glass, paperboard, and aluminum can producers, and acetaminophen manufacturers competing with other manufacturers of pain and headache remedies. The presence of substitute products puts a ceiling on the price that can be charged before consumers will switch to the substitute product. Price ceilings equate to profit ceilings and more intense competition among rivals. Producers of eyeglasses and contact lenses, for example, face increasing competitive pressures from laser eye surgery. Producers of sugar face similar pressures from artificial sweeteners. Newspapers and magazines face substitute-product competitive pressures from the Internet and 24-hour cable television. The magnitude of competitive pressure derived from development of substitute products is generally evidenced by rivals' plans for expanding production capacity, as well as by their sales and profit growth numbers.

Competitive pressures arising from substitute products increase as the relative price of substitute products declines and as consumers' switching costs decrease. The competitive strength of substitute products is best measured by the inroads into the market share those products obtain, as well as those firms' plans for increased capacity and market penetration.

Bargaining Power of Suppliers

The bargaining power of suppliers affects the intensity of competition in an industry, especially when there is a large number of suppliers, when there are only a few good substitute raw materials, or when the cost of switching raw materials is especially costly. It is often in the best interest of both suppliers and producers to assist each other with reasonable prices, improved quality, development of new services, just-in-time deliveries, and reduced inventory costs, thus enhancing long-term profitability for all concerned.

Firms may pursue a backward integration strategy to gain control or ownership of suppliers. This strategy is especially effective when suppliers are unreliable, too costly, or not capable of meeting a firm's needs on a consistent basis. Firms generally can negotiate more favorable terms with suppliers when backward integration is a commonly used strategy among rival firms in an industry.

However, in many industries it is more economical to use outside suppliers of component parts than to self-manufacture the items. This is true, for example, in the outdoor power equipment industry where producers of lawn mowers, rotary tillers, leaf blowers, and edgers such as Murray generally obtain their small engines from outside manufacturers such as Briggs & Stratton who specialize in such engines and have huge economies of scale.

In more and more industries, sellers are forging strategic partnerships with select suppliers in efforts to (1) reduce inventory and logistics costs (e.g., through just-in-time deliveries); (2) speed the availability of next-generation components; (3) enhance the quality of the parts and components being supplied and reduce defect rates; and (4) squeeze out important cost savings for both themselves and their suppliers.[13]

Bargaining Power of Consumers

When customers are concentrated or large or buy in volume, their bargaining power represents a major force affecting the intensity of competition in an industry. Rival firms may offer extended warranties or special services to gain customer loyalty whenever the bargaining power of consumers is substantial. Bargaining power of consumers also is higher when the products being purchased are standard or undifferentiated. When this is the case, consumers often can negotiate selling price, warranty coverage, and accessory packages to a greater extent.

The bargaining power of consumers can be the most important force affecting competitive advantage. Consumers gain increasing bargaining power under the following circumstances:

1.   If they can inexpensively switch to competing brands or substitutes
2.   If they are particularly important to the seller
3.   If sellers are struggling in the face of falling consumer demand
4.   If they are informed about sellers' products, prices, and costs
5.   If they have discretion in whether and when they purchase the product[14]

Sources of External Information

A wealth of strategic information is available to organizations from both published and unpublished sources. Unpublished sources include customer surveys, market research, speeches at professional and shareholders' meetings, television programs, interviews, and conversations with stakeholders. Published sources of strategic information include periodicals, journals, reports, government documents, abstracts, books, directories, newspapers, and manuals. The Internet has made it easier for firms to gather, assimilate, and evaluate information.

There are many excellent Web sites for gathering strategic information, but six that the author uses routinely are listed here:

1.   http://marketwatch.multexinvestor.com
2.   http://moneycentral.msn.com
3.   http://finance.yahoo.com
4.   www.clearstation.com
5.   https://us.etrade.com/e/t/invest/markets
6.   www.hoovers.com

Most college libraries subscribe to Standard & Poor's (S&P's) *Industry Surveys*. These documents are exceptionally up-to-date and give valuable information about many different industries. Each report is authored by a Standard & Poor's industry research analyst and includes the following sections:

1.   Current Environment
2.   Industry Trends
3.   How the Industry Operates
4.   Key Industry Ratios and Statistics
5.   How to Analyze a Company
6.   Glossary of Industry Terms
7.   Additional Industry Information
8.   References
9.   Comparative Company Financial Analysis

Forecasting Tools and Techniques

Forecasts are educated assumptions about future trends and events. Forecasting is a complex activity because of factors such as technological innovation, cultural changes, new products, improved services, stronger competitors, shifts in government priorities, changing social values, unstable economic conditions, and unforeseen events. Managers often must rely on published forecasts to effectively identify key external opportunities and threats.

A sense of the future permeates all action and underlies every decision a person makes. People eat expecting to be satisfied and nourished in the future. People sleep assuming that in the future they will feel rested. They invest energy, money, and time because they believe their efforts will be rewarded in the future. They build highways assuming that automobiles and trucks will need them in the future. Parents educate children on the basis of forecasts that they will need certain skills, attitudes, and knowledge when they grow up. The truth is we all make implicit forecasts throughout our daily lives. The question, therefore, is not whether we should forecast but rather how we can best forecast to enable us to move beyond our ordinarily unarticulated assumptions about the future. Can we obtain information and then make educated assumptions (forecasts) to better guide our current decisions to achieve a more desirable future state of affairs? We should go into the future with our eyes and our minds open, rather than stumble into the future with our eyes closed.[15]

Many publications and sources on the Internet forecast external variables. Several published examples include *Industry Week's* "Trends and Forecasts," *BusinessWeek's* "Investment Outlook," and Standard & Poor's *Industry Survey.* The reputation and continued success of these publications depend partly on accurate forecasts, so published sources of information can offer excellent projections. An especially good Web site for industry forecasts is finance.yahoo.com. Just insert a firm's stock symbol and go from there.

Sometimes organizations must develop their own projections. Most organizations forecast (project) their own revenues and profits annually. Organizations sometimes forecast market share or customer loyalty in local areas. Because forecasting is so important in strategic management and because the ability to forecast (in contrast to the ability to use a forecast) is essential, selected forecasting tools are examined further here.

Forecasting tools can be broadly categorized into two groups: quantitative techniques and qualitative techniques. Quantitative forecasts are most appropriate when historical data are available and when the relationships among key variables are expected to remain the same in the future. *Linear regression*, for example, is based on the assumption that the future will be just like the past—which, of course, it never is. As historical relationships become less stable, quantitative forecasts become less accurate.

No forecast is perfect, and some forecasts are even wildly inaccurate. This fact accents the need for strategists to devote sufficient time and effort to study the underlying bases for published forecasts and to develop internal forecasts of their own. Key external opportunities and threats can be effectively identified only through good forecasts. Accurate forecasts can provide major competitive advantages for organizations. Forecasts are vital to the strategic-management process and to the success of organizations.

Making Assumptions

Planning would be impossible without assumptions. McConkey defines assumptions as the "best present estimates of the impact of major external factors, over which the manager has little if any control, but which may exert a significant impact on performance or the ability to achieve desired results."[16] Strategists are faced with countless variables and imponderables that can be neither controlled nor predicted with 100 percent accuracy. Wild guesses should never be made in formulating strategies, but reasonable assumptions based on available information must always be made.

By identifying future occurrences that could have a major effect on the firm and by making reasonable assumptions about those factors, strategists can carry the strategic-management process forward. Assumptions are needed only for future trends and events that are most likely to have a significant effect on the company's business. Based on the best information at the time, assumptions serve as checkpoints on the validity of strategies. If future occurrences deviate significantly from assumptions, strategists know that corrective actions may be needed. Without reasonable assumptions, the strategy-formulation process could not proceed effectively. Firms that have the best information generally make the most accurate assumptions, which can lead to major competitive advantages.

Industry Analysis: The External Factor Evaluation (EFE) Matrix

An *External Factor Evaluation (EFE)* Matrix allows strategists to summarize and evaluate economic, social, cultural, demographic, environmental, political, governmental, legal, technological, and competitive information. Illustrated in Table 3-12, the EFE Matrix can be developed in five steps:

1. List key external factors as identified in the external-audit process. Include a total of 15 to 20 factors, including both opportunities and threats, that affect the firm and its industry. List the opportunities first and then the threats. Be as specific as possible, using percentages, ratios, and comparative numbers whenever possible. Recall that Edward Deming said, "In God we trust. Everyone else bring data."

2. Assign to each factor a weight that ranges from 0.0 (not important) to 1.0 (very important). The weight indicates the relative importance of that factor to being successful in the firm's industry. Opportunities often receive higher weights than threats, but threats can receive high weights if they are especially severe or threatening. Appropriate weights can be determined by comparing successful with unsuccessful competitors or by discussing the factor and reaching a group consensus. The sum of all weights assigned to the factors must equal 1.0.

3. Assign a rating between 1 and 4 to each key external factor to indicate how effectively the firm's current strategies respond to the factor, where 4 = *the response is superior*, 3 = *the response is above average*, 2 = *the response is average*, and 1 = *the response is poor*. Ratings are based on effectiveness of the firm's strategies. Ratings are thus company-based, whereas the weights in Step 2 are industry-based. It is important to note that both threats and opportunities can receive a 1, 2, 3, or 4.

4. Multiply each factor's weight by its rating to determine a weighted score.

5. Sum the weighted scores for each variable to determine the total weighted score for the organization.

Regardless of the number of key opportunities and threats included in an EFE Matrix, the highest possible total weighted score for an organization is 4.0 and the lowest possible

TABLE 3-12 EFE Matrix for a Local Ten-Theatre Cinema Complex

Key External Factors	Weight	Rating	Weighted Score
Opportunities			
1. Rowan County is growing 8% annually in population	0.05	3	0.15
2. TDB University is expanding 6% annually	0.08	4	0.32
3. Major competitor across town recently ceased operations	0.08	3	0.24
4. Demand for going to cinema growing 10% annually	0.07	2	0.14
5. Two new neighborhoods being developed within 3 miles	0.09	1	0.09
6. Disposable income among citizens grew 5% in prior year	0.06	3	0.18
7. Unemployment rate in county declined to 3.1%	0.03	2	0.06
Threats			
8. Trend toward healthy eating eroding concession sales	0.12	4	0.48
9. Demand for online movies and DVDs growing 10% annually	0.06	2	0.12
10. Commercial property adjacent to cinemas for sale	0.06	3	0.18
11. TDB University installing an on-campus movie theatre	0.04	3	0.12
12. County and city property taxes increasing 25% this year	0.08	2	0.16
13. Local religious groups object to R-rated movies being shown	0.04	3	0.12
14. Movies rented from local Blockbuster store up 12%	0.08	2	0.16
15. Movies rented last quarter from Time Warner up 15%	0.06	1	0.06
Total	**1.00**		**2.58**

total weighted score is 1.0. The average total weighted score is 2.5. A total weighted score of 4.0 indicates that an organization is responding in an outstanding way to existing opportunities and threats in its industry. In other words, the firm's strategies effectively take advantage of existing opportunities and minimize the potential adverse effects of external threats. A total score of 1.0 indicates that the firm's strategies are not capitalizing on opportunities or avoiding external threats.

An example of an EFE Matrix is provided in Table 3-12 for a local ten-theatre cinema complex. Note that the most important factor to being successful in this business is "Trend toward healthy eating eroding concession sales" as indicated by the 0.12 weight. Also note that the local cinema is doing excellent in regard to handling two factors, "TDB University is expanding 6 percent annually" and "Trend toward healthy eating eroding concession sales." Perhaps the cinema is placing flyers on campus and also adding yogurt and healthy drinks to its concession menu. Note that you may have a 1, 2, 3, or 4 anywhere down the Rating column. Note also that the factors are stated in quantitative terms to the extent possible, rather than being stated in vague terms. Quantify the factors as much as possible in constructing an EFE Matrix. Finally, note that the total weighted score of 2.58 is above the average (midpoint) of 2.5, so this cinema business is doing pretty well, taking advantage of the external opportunities and avoiding the threats facing the firm. There is definitely room for improvement, though, because the highest total weighted score would be 4.0. As indicated by ratings of 1, this business needs to capitalize more on the "two new neighborhoods nearby" opportunity and the "movies rented from Time Warner" threat. Note also that there are many percentage-based factors among the group. Be quantitative to the extent possible! Note also that the ratings range from 1 to 4 on both the opportunities and threats.

The Competitive Profile Matrix (CPM)

The *Competitive Profile Matrix (CPM)* identifies a firm's major competitors and its particular strengths and weaknesses in relation to a sample firm's strategic position. The weights and total weighted scores in both a CPM and an EFE have the same meaning. However, *critical success* factors in a CPM include both internal and external issues; therefore, the ratings refer to strengths and weaknesses, where 4 = major strength, 3 = minor strength, 2 = minor weakness, and 1 = major weakness. The critical success factors in a CPM are not grouped into opportunities and threats as they are in an EFE. In a CPM, the ratings and total weighted scores for rival firms can be compared to the sample firm. This comparative analysis provides important internal strategic information.

A sample Competitive Profile Matrix is provided in Table 3-13. In this example, the two most important factors to being successful in the industry are "advertising" and

TABLE 3-13 **An Example Competitive Profile Matrix**

Critical Success Factors	Weight	Company 1 Rating	Company 1 Score	Company 2 Rating	Company 2 Score	Company 3 Rating	Company 3 Score
Advertising	0.20	1	0.20	4	0.80	3	0.60
Product Quality	0.10	4	0.40	3	0.30	2	0.20
Price Competitiveness	0.10	3	0.30	2	0.20	4	0.40
Management	0.10	4	0.40	3	0.20	3	0.30
Financial Position	0.15	4	0.60	2	0.30	3	0.45
Customer Loyalty	0.10	4	0.40	3	0.30	2	0.20
Global Expansion	0.20	4	0.80	1	0.20	2	0.40
Market Share	0.05	1	0.05	4	0.20	3	0.15
Total	**1.00**		**3.15**		**2.50**		**2.70**

Note: (1) The ratings values are as follows: 1 = major weakness, 2 = minor weakness, 3 = minor strength, 4 = major strength. (2) As indicated by the total weighted score of 2.50, Competitor 2 is weakest. (3) Only eight critical success factors are included for simplicity; this is too few in actuality.

TABLE 3-14 Another Example Competitive Profile Matrix

Critical Success Factors	Weight	Company 1 Rating	Company 1 Weighted Score	Company 2 Rating	Company 2 Weighted Score	Company 3 Rating	Company 3 Weighted Score
Market share	0.15	3	0.45	2	0.30	4	0.60
Inventory system	0.08	2	0.16	2	0.16	4	0.32
Financial position	0.10	2	0.20	3	0.30	4	0.40
Product quality	0.08	3	0.24	4	0.32	3	0.24
Consumer loyalty	0.02	3	0.06	3	0.06	4	0.08
Sales distribution	0.10	3	0.30	2	0.20	3	0.30
Global expansion	0.15	3	0.45	2	0.30	4	0.60
Organization structure	0.05	3	0.15	4	0.20	2	0.10
Production capacity	0.04	3	0.12	2	0.08	4	0.16
E-commerce	0.10	3	0.30	1	0.10	4	0.40
Customer service	0.10	3	0.30	2	0.20	4	0.40
Price competitive	0.02	4	0.08	1	0.02	3	0.06
Management experience	0.01	2	0.02	4	0.04	2	0.02
Total	**1.00**		**2.83**		**2.28**		**3.68**

"global expansion," as indicated by weights of 0.20. If there were no weight column in this analysis, note that each factor then would be equally important. Thus, having a weight column makes for a more robust analysis, because it enables the analyst to assign higher and lower numbers to capture perceived or actual levels of importance. Note in Table 3-13 that Company 1 is strongest on "product quality," as indicated by a rating of 4, whereas Company 2 is strongest on "advertising." Overall, Company 1 is strongest, as indicated by the total weighted score of 3.15.

Other than the critical success factors listed in the example CPM, factors often included in this analysis include breadth of product line, effectiveness of sales distribution, proprietary or patent advantages, location of facilities, production capacity and efficiency, experience, union relations, technological advantages, and e-commerce expertise.

A word on interpretation: Just because one firm receives a 3.2 rating and another receives a 2.80 rating in a Competitive Profile Matrix, it does not follow that the first firm is 20 percent better than the second. Numbers reveal the relative strengths of firms, but their implied precision is an illusion. Numbers are not magic. The aim is not to arrive at a single number, but rather to assimilate and evaluate information in a meaningful way that aids in decision making.

Another Competitive Profile Matrix is provided in Table 3-14. Note that Company 2 has the best product quality and management experience; Company 3 has the best market share and inventory system; and Company 1 has the best price as indicated by the ratings. Avoid assigning duplicate ratings on any row in a CPM.

Conclusion

Increasing turbulence in markets and industries around the world means the external audit has become an explicit and vital part of the strategic-management process. This chapter provides a framework for collecting and evaluating economic, social, cultural, demographic, environmental, political, governmental, legal, technological, and competitive information. Firms that do not mobilize and empower their managers and employees to identify, monitor, forecast, and evaluate key external forces may fail to anticipate emerging opportunities and threats and, consequently, may pursue ineffective strategies, miss opportunities, and invite organizational demise. Firms not taking advantage of the Internet are technologically falling behind.

A major responsibility of strategists is to ensure development of an effective external-audit system. This includes using information technology to devise a competitive intelligence system that works. The external-audit approach described in this chapter can be used effectively by any size or type of organization. Typically, the external-audit process is more informal in small firms, but the need to understand key trends and events is no less important for these firms. The EFE Matrix and Porter's Five-Forces Model can help strategists evaluate the market and industry, but these tools must be accompanied by good intuitive judgment. Multinational firms especially need a systematic and effective external-audit system because external forces among foreign countries vary so greatly.

We invite you to visit the David page on the Prentice Hall Companion Web site at http://www.pearsonhighered.com/david/ for this chapter's review quiz.

Key Terms and Concepts

Chief Information Officer (CIO) (p. 69)
Chief Technology Officer (CTO) (p. 69)
Competitive Analysis (p. 73)
Competitive Intelligence (CI) (p. 72)
Competitive Profile Matrix (CPM) (p. 81)
Director of Competitive Analysis (p. 73)
Environmental Scanning (p. 60)
External Audit (p. 61)
External Factor Evaluation (EFE) Matrix (p. 80)
External Forces (p. 61)

Industrial/Organization (I/O) (p. 63)
Industry Analysis (p. 60)
Information Technology (IT) (p. 69)
Internet (p. 69)
Lifecare Facilities (p. 67)
Linear Regression (p. 79)
Market Commonality (p. 74)
Porter's Five-Forces Model (p. 74)
Resource Similarity (p. 74)

Issues for Review and Discussion

1. Describe the "process of performing an external audit" in an organization doing strategic planning for the first time.
2. The global recession forced thousands of firms into bankruptcy. Does this fact alone confirm that "external factors are more important than internal factors" in strategic planning? Discuss.
3. Use a series of two-dimensional (two-variable) graphs to illustrate the historical relationship among the following variables: value of the dollar, oil prices, interest rates, and stock prices. Give one implication of each graph for strategic planning.
4. Do you feel the advantages of a low value of the dollar offset the disadvantages for (1) a firm that derives 60 percent of its revenues from foreign countries and (2) a firm that derives 10 percent of its revenues from foreign countries? Justify your opinion.
5. The lingering global recession has greatly slowed the migration of people from (1) region to region across the United States, from (2) city to suburb worldwide, and from (3) country to country across the globe. What are the strategic implications of these trends for companies?
6. Governments worldwide are turning to "nationalization of companies" to cope with economic recession. Examples in the United States include AIG, GM, and Citigroup. What are the strategic implications of this trend for firms that compete with these nationalized firms?
7. Governments worldwide are turning to "protectionism" to cope with economic recession, imposing tariffs and subsidies on foreign goods and restrictions/incentives on their own firms to keep jobs at home. What are the strategic implications of this trend for international commerce?
8. Compare and contrast the duties and responsibilities of a CIO with a CTO in a large firm.
9. What are the three basic objectives of a competitive intelligence program?
10. Distinguish between market commonality and resource similarity. Apply these concepts to two rival firms that you are familiar with.
11. Let's say you work for McDonald's and you applied Porter's Five-Forces Model to study the fast-food industry. Would information in your analysis provide factors more readily to an EFE Matrix, a CPM, or to neither matrix? Justify your answer.
12. Explain why it is appropriate for Ratings in an EFE Matrix to be 1, 2, 3, or 4 for any opportunity or threat.

13. Why is inclusion of about 20 factors recommended in the EFE Matrix rather than about 10 factors or about 40 factors?

14. In developing an EFE Matrix, would it be advantageous to arrange your opportunities according to the highest weight, and do likewise for your threats? Explain.

15. In developing an EFE Matrix, would it be best to have 10 opportunities and 10 threats, or would 17 opportunities (or threats) be fine with 3 of the other to achieve a total of 20 factors as desired?

16. Could/should critical success factors in a CPM include external factors? Explain.

17. Explain how to conduct an external strategic-management audit.

18. Identify a recent economic, social, political, or technological trend that significantly affects the local Pizza Hut.

19. Discuss the following statement: Major opportunities and threats usually result from an interaction among key environmental trends rather than from a single external event or factor.

20. Identify two industries experiencing rapid technological changes and three industries that are experiencing little technological change. How does the need for technological forecasting differ in these industries? Why?

21. Use Porter's Five-Forces Model to evaluate competitiveness within the U.S. banking industry.

22. What major forecasting techniques would you use to identify (1) economic opportunities and threats and (2) demographic opportunities and threats? Why are these techniques most appropriate?

23. How does the external audit affect other components of the strategic-management process?

24. As the owner of a small business, explain how you would organize a strategic-information scanning system. How would you organize such a system in a large organization?

25. Construct an EFE Matrix for an organization of your choice.

26. Make an appointment with a librarian at your university to learn how to use online databases. Report your findings in class.

27. Give some advantages and disadvantages of cooperative versus competitive strategies.

28. As strategist for a local bank, explain when you would use qualitative versus quantitative forecasts.

29. What is your forecast for interest rates and the stock market in the next several months? As the stock market moves up, do interest rates always move down? Why? What are the strategic implications of these trends?

30. Explain how information technology affects strategies of the organization where you worked most recently.

31. Let's say your boss develops an EFE Matrix that includes 62 factors. How would you suggest reducing the number of factors to 20?

32. Discuss the ethics of gathering competitive intelligence.

33. Discuss the ethics of cooperating with rival firms.

34. Visit the SEC Web site at www.sec.gov, and discuss the benefits of using information provided there.

35. Do you agree with I/O theorists that external factors are more important than internal factors to a firm's achieving competitive advantage? Explain both your and their position.

36. Define, compare, and contrast the weights versus ratings in an EFE Matrix.

37. Develop a Competitive Profile Matrix for your university. Include six factors.

38. List the 10 external areas that give rise to opportunities and threats.

Notes

1. York Freund, "Critical Success Factors," *Planning Review* 16, no. 4 (July–August 1988): 20.

2. S&P Industry Surveys, Beverage Industry, 2005.

3. John Miller, "Nations Rush to Establish New Barriers to Trade," *Wall Street Journal* (February 6, 2009): A1.

4. Jon Swartz, "MySpace Forges Ahead Despite Really Tough Times," *USA Today* (February 4, 2009): 3B.

5. Joe Mullich, "10 Industries That Wireless Will Change," *Wall Street Journal* (April 1, 2009): A12.

6. Bill Saporito, "Companies That Compete Best," *Fortune* (May 22, 1989): 36.

7. Jon Swartz, "Ex-Facebook COO Gets Top Job at MySpace," *USA Today* (April 27, 2009): 7B.

8. Evan Perez, "Computer Spies Breach Fighter-Jet Project," *Wall Street Journal* (April 21, 2009): A1.

9. Kenneth Sawka, "Demystifying Business Intelligence," *Management Review* (October 1996): 49.

10. John Prescott and Daniel Smith, "The Largest Survey of 'Leading-Edge' Competitor Intelligence Managers," *Planning Review* 17, no. 3 (May–June 1989): 6–13.

11. M. J. Chen, "Competitor Analysis and Interfirm Rivalry: Toward a Theoretical Integration," *Academy of Management Review* 21 (1996): 106.

12. S. Jayachandran, J. Gimeno, and P. R. Varadarajan, "Theory of Multimarket Competition: A Synthesis and Implications for Marketing Strategy," *Journal of Marketing* 63, 3 (1999): 59; and M. J. Chen. "Competitor Analysis and Interfirm Rivalry: Toward a Theoretical Integration," *Academy of Management Review* 21 (1996): 107–108.

13. Arthur Thompson, Jr., A. J. Strickland III, and John Gamble, *Crafting and Executing Strategy: Text and Readings* (New York: McGraw-Hill/Irwin, 2005): 63.

14. Michael E. Porter, *Competitive Strategy: Techniques for Analyzing Industries and Competitors* (New York: Free Press, 1980): 24–27.

15. horizon.unc.edu/projects/seminars/futuresresearch/rationale.asp.

16. Dale McConkey, "Planning in a Changing Environment," *Business Horizons* 31, no. 5 (September–October 1988): 67.

Current Readings

Capron, Laurence, and Olivier Chatain. "Competitors' Resource-Oriented Strategies: Acting on Competitors' Resources Through Interventions in Factor Markets and Political Markets." *The Academy of Management Review* 33, no. 1 (January 2008): 97.

Coyne, Kevin, and John Horn. "Predicting Your Competitor's Reaction." *Harvard Business Review* (April 2009): 90–110.

Delmas, Magali A., and Michael W. Toffel. "Organizational Responses to Environmental Demands: Opening the Black Box." *Strategic Management Journal* 29, no. 10 (October 2008): 1,027.

Hillman, Amy J., and Gerald D. Keim. "Political Environments and Business Strategy: Implications for Managers." *Business Horizons* 51, no. 1 (January–February 2008): 47.

Kachra, Ariff, and Roderick E. White. "Know-how Transfer: The Role of Social, Economic/Competitive, and Firm Boundary Factors." *Strategic Management Journal* 29, no. 4 (April 2008): 425.

Porter, Michael E. "The Five Competitive Forces That Shape Strategy." *Harvard Business Review* (January 2008): 78.

ASSURANCE OF LEARNING EXERCISES

Assurance of Learning Exercises 3A

Developing an EFE Matrix for McDonald's Corporation

Purpose

This exercise will give you practice developing an EFE Matrix. An EFE Matrix summarizes the results of an external audit. This is an important tool widely used by strategists.

Instructions

Step 1	Join with two other students in class, and jointly prepare an EFE Matrix for McDonald's Corporation. Refer back to the Cohesion Case and to Exercise 1A, if necessary, to identify external opportunities and threats. Use the information in the S&P Industry Surveys that you copied as part of Assurance of Learning Exercise 1A. Be sure not to include strategies as opportunities, but do include as many monetary amounts, percentages, numbers, and ratios as possible.
Step 2	All three-person teams participating in this exercise should record their EFE total weighted scores on the board. Put your initials after your score to identify it as your team's.
Step 3	Compare the total weighted scores. Which team's score came closest to the instructor's answer? Discuss reasons for variation in the scores reported on the board.

Assurance of Learning Exercise 3B

The External Assessment

Purpose

This exercise will help you become familiar with important sources of external information available in your college library. A key part of preparing an external audit is searching the Internet and examining published sources of information for relevant economic, social, cultural, demographic, environmental, political, governmental, legal, technological, and competitive trends and events. External opportunities and threats must be identified and evaluated before strategies can be formulated effectively.

Instructions

Step 1	Select a company or business where you currently or previously have worked. Conduct an external audit for this company. Find opportunities and threats in recent issues of newspapers and magazines. Search for information using the Internet. Use the following six Web sites: http://marketwatch.multexinvestor.com www.hoovers.com http://moneycentral.msn.com http://finance.yahoo.com www.clearstation.com https://us.etrade.com/e/t/invest/markets.
Step 2	On a separate sheet of paper, list 10 opportunities and 10 threats that face this company. Be specific in stating each factor.
Step 3	Include a bibliography to reveal where you found the information.
Step 4	Write a three-page summary of your findings, and submit it to your instructor.

Assurance of Learning Exercise 3C

Developing an EFE Matrix for My University

Purpose

More colleges and universities are embarking on the strategic-management process. Institutions are consciously and systematically identifying and evaluating external opportunities and threats facing higher education in your state, the nation, and the world.

Instructions

Step 1   Join with two other individuals in class and jointly prepare an EFE Matrix for your institution.

Step 2   Go to the board and record your total weighted score in a column that includes the scores of all three-person teams participating. Put your initials after your score to identify it as your team's.

Step 3   Which team viewed your college's strategies most positively? Which team viewed your college's strategies most negatively? Discuss the nature of the differences.

Assurance of Learning Exercise 3D

Developing a Competitive Profile Matrix for McDonald's Corporation

Purpose

Monitoring competitors' performance and strategies is a key aspect of an external audit. This exercise is designed to give you practice evaluating the competitive position of organizations in a given industry and assimilating that information in the form of a Competitive Profile Matrix.

Instructions

Step 1   Gather your information from Assurance of Learning Exercise 1A. Also, turn back to the Cohesion Case and review the section on competitors (pages 33–35).

Step 2   On a separate sheet of paper, prepare a Competitive Profile Matrix that includes McDonald's, Burger King Holdings, and Yum! Brands, Inc.

Step 3   Turn in your Competitive Profile Matrix for a classwork grade.

Assurance of Learning Exercise 3E

Developing a Competitive Profile Matrix for My University

Purpose

Your college or university competes with all other educational institutions in the world, especially those in your own state. State funds, students, faculty, staff, endowments, gifts, and federal funds are areas of competitiveness. Other areas include athletic programs, dorm life, academic reputation, location, and career services. The purpose of this exercise is to give you practice thinking competitively about the business of education in your state.

Instructions

Step 1   Identify two colleges or universities in your state that compete directly with your institution for students. Interview several persons, perhaps classmates, who are aware of particular strengths and weaknesses of those universities. Record information about the two competing universities.

Step 2   Prepare a Competitive Profile Matrix that includes your institution and the two competing insti-
                    tutions. Include at least the following ten factors in your analysis:
                       1. Tuition costs
                       2. Quality of faculty
                       3. Academic reputation
                       4. Average class size
                       5. Campus landscaping
                       6. Athletic programs
                       7. Quality of students
                       8. Graduate programs
                       9. Location of campus
                      10. Campus culture

Step 3   Submit your Competitive Profile Matrix to your instructor for evaluation.

CHAPTER 4
The Internal Assessment

CHAPTER OBJECTIVES

After studying this chapter, you should be able to do the following:

1. Describe how to perform an internal strategic-management audit.

2. Discuss the Resource-Based View (RBV) in strategic management.

3. Discuss key interrelationships among the functional areas of business.

4. Identify the basic functions or activities that make up management, marketing, finance/accounting, production/operations, research and development, and management information systems.

5. Explain how to determine and prioritize a firm's internal strengths and weaknesses.

6. Explain the importance of financial ratio analysis.

7. Discuss the nature and role of management information systems in strategic management.

8. Develop an Internal Factor Evaluation (IFE) Matrix.

9. Explain benchmarking as a strategic management tool.

Assurance of Learning Exercises

Assurance of Learning Exercise 4A
Performing a Financial Ratio Analysis for McDonald's Corporation

Assurance of Learning Exercise 4B
Constructing an IFE Matrix for McDonald's Corporation

Assurance of Learning Exercise 4C
Constructing an IFE Matrix for My University

Source: Shutterstock/Photographer Edyta Pawlowska

"Notable Quotes"

"Like a product or service, the planning process itself must be managed and shaped, if it is to serve executives as a vehicle for strategic decision-making."

—Robert Lenz

"The difference between now and five years ago is that information systems had limited function. You weren't betting your company on it. Now you are."

—William Gruber

"Weak leadership can wreck the soundest strategy."

—Sun Tzu

"A firm that continues to employ a previously successful strategy eventually and inevitably falls victim to a competitor."

—William Cohen

"Great spirits have always encountered violent opposition from mediocre minds."

—Albert Einstein

"The idea is to concentrate our strength against our competitor's relative weakness."

—Bruce Henderson

This chapter focuses on identifying and evaluating a firm's strengths and weaknesses in the functional areas of business, including management, marketing, finance/accounting, production/operations, research and development, and management information systems. Relationships among these areas of business are examined. Strategic implications of important functional area concepts are examined. The process of performing an internal audit is described. The Resource-Based View (RBV) of strategic management is introduced as is the Value Chain Analysis (VCA) concept.

Doing Great in a Weak Economy. How?

Amazon.com, Inc.

Based in Seattle, Washington, Amazon's sales grew 14 percent to $4.65 billion in the second quarter of 2009; the firm's worldwide electronics sales grew 35 percent. CEO Jeff Bezo's strategic plan for Amazon is to make the firm the "Wal-Mart of the Internet" through heavily discounted prices and expansion into more and more product offerings as well as free shipping. Amazon prides itself on offering the lowest prices anywhere on anything, and the firm is charging ahead as brick and mortar retailers falter, declare bankruptcy, and even liquidate. Amazon has no retail stores, just inventory warehouses. Therefore the firm has low fixed costs. Its primary online rival, E-bay, is incurring declining revenues and profits.

Amazon is the largest online bookseller in the United States and is making its Kindle e-books available for reading on Apple's iPhone and iPod Touch devices. E-books is a rapidly growing segment of the publishing business. Barnes & Noble recently acquired e-book firm Fictionwise for $15.7 million, and Google is getting heavily in the e-book business. Sony Electronics recently formed a partnership with Google to compete against Amazon in the growing digital books market. Amazon's Kindle electronic book reader is under attack from the partnership that enables readers to use the Sony Reader device to access more than half a million public domain books from Google's digital book library.

Amazon sold about 500,000 Kindles in 2008 and expects the Kindle could bring $3.7 billion in annual revenue by 2012. In July 2009, Amazon lowered the price of its Kindle product from $359 to $299 in an effort to make Kindle a blockbuster hit.

What started as the planet's biggest bookstore has rapidly become the planet's biggest anything store. The firm's main Web site offers millions of books, music, and movies (which still account for the majority of the firm's sales), not to mention auto parts, toys, electronics, home furnishings, apparel, health and beauty aids, prescription drugs, and groceries. Customers can also download books, games, MP3s, and films to their computers. In addition to Kindle, Amazon provides other products and services too, such as self-publishing, online advertising, and a Web store platform. The firm is capitalizing on a huge consumer shift toward online shopping during a recession.

Some states are strapped for cash and are forcing retailers to collect taxes on online sales. New York passed an Internet sales tax law in 2008. North Carolina, Hawaii, California, Maryland, Minnesota, and Tennessee are close to passing similar laws. Amazon is fighting these laws. Amazon collects sales tax only in the state of Washington, where it has offices and ware-houses. In mid-2009, Amazon ended business relationships with marketing affiliates in North Carolina, Rhode Island, and Hawaii to avoid collecting sales tax in the state. A *marketing affiliate* can be defined as a business that gets a sales commission by featuring links to outside e-commerce sites on their own Web site. There are mounting tensions between online retailers and cash-strapped states across the country. Amazon contends that it is unconstitutional to require sellers with no physical presence in a state to collect sales tax on sales to buyers in that state.

Source: Based on Geoffrey Fowler, "Amazon's Sales Surge, Bucking Retail Slump," *Wall Street Journal* (January 30, 2009): B1; Yukari Iwatani Kane and Dan Gallagher, "Amazon Gets in Used-Game Business," *Wall Street Journal* (March 6, 2009): B5.

The Nature of an Internal Audit

All organizations have strengths and weaknesses in the functional areas of business. No enterprise is equally strong or weak in all areas. Maytag, for example, is known for excellent production and product design, whereas Procter & Gamble is known for superb marketing. Internal strengths/weaknesses, coupled with external opportunities/threats and a clear statement of mission, provide the basis for establishing objectives and strategies. Objectives and strategies are established with the intention of capitalizing upon internal strengths and overcoming weaknesses. The internal-audit part of the strategic-management process is illustrated in Figure 4-1.

Key Internal Forces

It is not possible in a strategic-management text to review in depth all the material presented in courses such as marketing, finance, accounting, management, management information systems, and production/operations; there are many subareas within these functions, such as customer service, warranties, advertising, packaging, and pricing under marketing.

For different types of organizations, such as hospitals, universities, and government agencies, the functional business areas, of course, differ. In a hospital, for example, functional areas may include cardiology, hematology, nursing, maintenance, physician support, and receivables. Functional areas of a university can include athletic programs, placement services, housing, fund-raising, academic research, counseling, and intramural programs. Within large organizations, each division has certain strengths and weaknesses.

A firm's strengths that cannot be easily matched or imitated by competitors are called *distinctive competencies.* Building competitive advantages involves taking advantage of distinctive competencies. For example, 3M exploits its distinctive competence in research and development by producing a wide range of innovative products. Strategies are designed in part to improve on a firm's weaknesses, turning them into strengths—and maybe even into distinctive competencies.

Figure 4-2 illustrates that all firms should continually strive to improve on their weaknesses, turning them into strengths, and ultimately developing distinctive competencies that can provide the firm with competitive advantages over rival firms.

The Process of Performing an Internal Audit

The process of performing an *internal audit* closely parallels the process of performing an external audit. Representative managers and employees from throughout the firm need to be involved in determining a firm's strengths and weaknesses. The internal audit requires gathering and assimilating information about the firm's management, marketing, finance/accounting, production/operations, research and development (R&D), and management information systems operations. Key factors should be prioritized as described in Chapter 3 so that the firm's most important strengths and weaknesses can be determined collectively.

Compared to the external audit, the process of performing an internal audit provides more opportunity for participants to understand how their jobs, departments, and divisions

FIGURE 4-1

A Comprehensive Strategic-Management Model

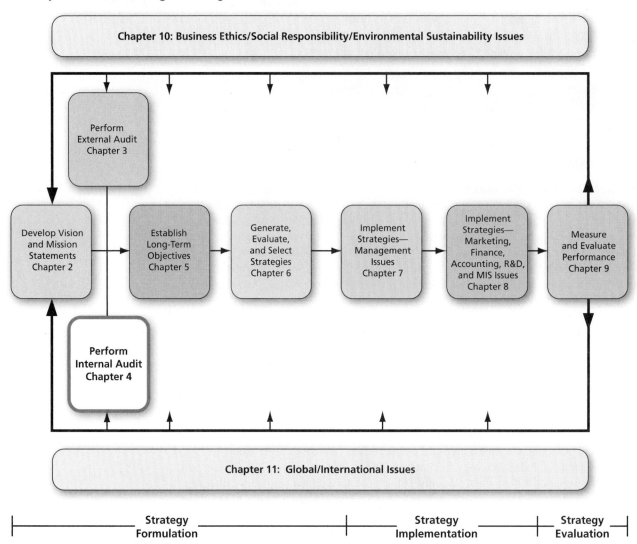

Source: Fred R. David, "How Companies Define Their Mission," *Long Range Planning* 22, no. 3 (June 1988): 40.

fit into the whole organization. This is a great benefit because managers and employees perform better when they understand how their work affects other areas and activities of the firm. For example, when marketing and manufacturing managers jointly discuss issues related to internal strengths and weaknesses, they gain a better appreciation of the issues, problems, concerns, and needs of all the functional areas. In organizations that do not use strategic management, marketing, finance, and manufacturing managers often do not interact with each other in significant ways. Performing an internal audit thus is an excellent vehicle or forum for improving the process of communication in the organization. *Communication* may be the most important word in management.

FIGURE 4-2

The Process of Gaining Competitive Advantage in a Firm

Weaknesses ⇒ Strengths ⇒ Distinctive Competencies ⇒ Competitive Advantage

Performing an internal audit requires gathering, assimilating, and evaluating information about the firm's operations. Critical success factors, consisting of both strengths and weaknesses, can be identified and prioritized in the manner discussed in Chapter 3. According to William King, a task force of managers from different units of the organization, supported by staff, should be charged with determining the 10 to 20 most important strengths and weaknesses that should influence the future of the organization. He says:

> The development of conclusions on the 10 to 20 most important organizational strengths and weaknesses can be, as any experienced manager knows, a difficult task, when it involves managers representing various organizational interests and points of view. Developing a 20-page list of strengths and weaknesses could be accomplished relatively easily, but a list of the 10 to 15 most important ones involves significant analysis and negotiation. This is true because of the judgments that are required and the impact which such a list will inevitably have as it is used in the formulation, implementation, and evaluation of strategies.[1]

Strategic management is a highly interactive process that requires effective coordination among management, marketing, finance/accounting, production/operations, R&D, and management information systems managers. Although the strategic-management process is overseen by strategists, success requires that managers and employees from all functional areas work together to provide ideas and information. Financial managers, for example, may need to restrict the number of feasible options available to operations managers, or R&D managers may develop products for which marketing managers need to set higher objectives. A key to organizational success is effective coordination and understanding among managers from all functional business areas. Through involvement in performing an internal strategic-management audit, managers from different departments and divisions of the firm come to understand the nature and effect of decisions in other functional business areas in their firm. Knowledge of these relationships is critical for effectively establishing objectives and strategies.

A failure to recognize and understand relationships among the functional areas of business can be detrimental to strategic management, and the number of those relationships that must be managed increases dramatically with a firm's size, diversity, geographic dispersion, and the number of products or services offered. Governmental and nonprofit enterprises traditionally have not placed sufficient emphasis on relationships among the business functions. Some firms place too great an emphasis on one function at the expense of others. Ansoff explained:

> During the first fifty years, successful firms focused their energies on optimizing the performance of one of the principal functions: production/operations, R&D, or marketing. Today, due to the growing complexity and dynamism of the environment, success increasingly depends on a judicious combination of several functional influences. This transition from a single function focus to a multifunction focus is essential for successful strategic management.[2]

Financial ratio analysis exemplifies the complexity of relationships among the functional areas of business. A declining return on investment or profit margin ratio could be the result of ineffective marketing, poor management policies, research and development errors, or a weak management information system. The effectiveness of strategy formulation, implementation, and evaluation activities hinges upon a clear understanding of how major business functions affect one another. For strategies to succeed, a coordinated effort among all the functional areas of business is needed. In the case of planning, George wrote:

> We may conceptually separate planning for the purpose of theoretical discussion and analysis, but in practice, neither is it a distinct entity nor is it capable of being separated. The planning function is mixed with all other business functions and, like ink once mixed with water, it cannot be set apart. It is spread throughout and is a part of the whole of managing an organization.[3]

The Resource-Based View (RBV)

Some researchers emphasize the importance of the internal audit part of the strategic-management process by comparing it to the external audit. Robert Grant concluded that the internal audit is more important, saying:

> In a world where customer preferences are volatile, the identity of customers is changing, and the technologies for serving customer requirements are continually evolving, an externally focused orientation does not provide a secure foundation for formulating long-term strategy. When the external environment is in a state of flux, the firm's own resources and capabilities may be a much more stable basis on which to define its identity. Hence, a definition of a business in terms of what it is capable of doing may offer a more durable basis for strategy than a definition based upon the needs which the business seeks to satisfy.[4]

The *Resource-Based View (RBV)* approach to competitive advantage contends that internal resources are more important for a firm than external factors in achieving and sustaining competitive advantage. In contrast to the I/O theory presented in the previous chapter, proponents of the RBV view contend that organizational performance will primarily be determined by internal resources that can be grouped into three all-encompassing categories: physical resources, human resources, and organizational resources.[5] Physical resources include all plant and equipment, location, technology, raw materials, machines; human resources include all employees, training, experience, intelligence, knowledge, skills, abilities; and organizational resources include firm structure, planning processes, information systems, patents, trademarks, copyrights, databases, and so on. RBV theory asserts that resources are actually what helps a firm exploit opportunities and neutralize threats.

The basic premise of the RBV is that the mix, type, amount, and nature of a firm's internal resources should be considered first and foremost in devising strategies that can lead to sustainable competitive advantage. Managing strategically according to the RBV involves developing and exploiting a firm's unique resources and capabilities, and continually maintaining and strengthening those resources. The theory asserts that it is advantageous for a firm to pursue a strategy that is not currently being implemented by any competing firm. When other firms are unable to duplicate a particular strategy, then the focal firm has a sustainable competitive advantage, according to RBV theorists.

For a resource to be valuable, it must be either (1) rare, (2) hard to imitate, or (3) not easily substitutable. Often called *empirical indicators,* these three characteristics of resources enable a firm to implement strategies that improve its efficiency and effectiveness and lead to a sustainable competitive advantage. The more a resource(s) is rare, nonimitable, and nonsubstitutable, the stronger a firm's competitive advantage will be and the longer it will last.

Rare resources are resources that other competing firms do not possess. If many firms have the same resource, then those firms will likely implement similar strategies, thus giving no one firm a sustainable competitive advantage. This is not to say that resources that are common are not valuable; they do indeed aid the firm in its chance for economic prosperity. However, to sustain a competitive advantage, it is more advantageous if the resource(s) is also rare.

It is also important that these same resources be difficult to imitate. If firms cannot easily gain the resources, say RBV theorists, then those resources will lead to a competitive advantage more so than resources easily imitable. Even if a firm employs resources that are rare, a sustainable competitive advantage may be achieved only if other firms cannot easily obtain these resources.

The third empirical indicator that can make resources a source of competitive advantage is substitutability. Borrowing from Porter's Five-Forces Model, to the degree that there are no viable substitutes, a firm will be able to sustain its competitive advantage. However, even if a competing firm cannot perfectly imitate a firm's resource, it can still obtain a sustainable competitive advantage of its own by obtaining resource substitutes.

The RBV has continued to grow in popularity and continues to seek a better understanding of the relationship between resources and sustained competitive advantage in strategic management. However, as alluded to in Chapter 3, one cannot say with any degree of certainty that either external or internal factors will always or even consistently be more important in seeking competitive advantage. Understanding both external and internal factors, and more importantly, understanding the relationships among them, will be the key to effective strategy formulation (discussed in Chapter 6). Because both external and internal factors continually change, strategists seek to identify and take advantage of positive changes and buffer against negative changes in a continuing effort to gain and sustain a firm's competitive advantage. This is the essence and challenge of strategic management, and oftentimes survival of the firm hinges on this work.

Integrating Strategy and Culture

Relationships among a firm's functional business activities perhaps can be exemplified best by focusing on organizational culture, an internal phenomenon that permeates all departments and divisions of an organization. *Organizational culture* can be defined as "a pattern of behavior that has been developed by an organization as it learns to cope with its problem of external adaptation and internal integration, and that has worked well enough to be considered valid and to be taught to new members as the correct way to perceive, think, and feel."[6] This definition emphasizes the importance of matching external with internal factors in making strategic decisions.

Organizational culture captures the subtle, elusive, and largely unconscious forces that shape a workplace. Remarkably resistant to change, culture can represent a major strength or weakness for the firm. It can be an underlying reason for strengths or weaknesses in any of the major business functions.

Defined in Table 4-1, *cultural products* include values, beliefs, rites, rituals, ceremonies, myths, stories, legends, sagas, language, metaphors, symbols, heroes, and heroines. These products or dimensions are levers that strategists can use to influence and direct strategy formulation, implementation, and evaluation activities. An organization's culture compares to an individual's personality in the sense that no two organizations have the same culture and no two individuals have the same personality. Both culture and personality are enduring and can be warm, aggressive, friendly, open, innovative, conservative, liberal, harsh, or likable.

At Google, the culture is very informal. Employees are encouraged to wander the halls on employee-sponsored scooters and brainstorm on public whiteboards provided everywhere.

TABLE 4-1   Example Cultural Products Defined

Rites	Planned sets of activities that consolidate various forms of cultural expressions into one event.
Ceremonial	Several rites connected together.
Ritual	A standardized set of behaviors used to manage anxieties.
Myth	A narrative of imagined events, usually not supported by facts.
Saga	A historical narrative describing the unique accomplishments of a group and its leaders.
Legend	A handed-down narrative of some wonderful event, usually not supported by facts.
Story	A narrative usually based on true events.
Folktale	A fictional story.
Symbol	Any object, act, event, quality, or relation used to convey meaning.
Language	The manner in which members of a group communicate.
Metaphors	Shorthand of words used to capture a vision or to reinforce old or new values
Values	Life-directing attitudes that serve as behavioral guidelines
Belief	An understanding of a particular phenomenon
Heroes/Heroines	Individuals greatly respected.

Source: Based on H. M. Trice and J. M. Beyer, "Studying Organizational Cultures through Rites and Ceremonials," *Academy of Management Review* 9, no. 4 (October 1984): 655.

In contrast, the culture at Procter & Gamble (P&G) is so rigid that employees jokingly call themselves "Proctoids." Despite this difference, the two companies are swapping employees and participating in each other's staff training sessions. Why? Because P&G spends more money on advertising than any other company and Google desires more of P&G's $8.7 billion annual advertising expenses; P&G has come to realize that the next generation of laundry-detergent, toilet-paper, and skin-cream customers now spend more time online than watching TV. Consumers age 18 to 27 say they use the Internet nearly 13 hours a week, compared to 10 hours of TV, according to market-data firm Forrester Research.[7]

Dimensions of organizational culture permeate all the functional areas of business. It is something of an art to uncover the basic values and beliefs that are deeply buried in an organization's rich collection of stories, language, heroes, and rituals, but cultural products can represent both important strengths and weaknesses. Culture is an aspect of an organization that can no longer be taken for granted in performing an internal strategic-management audit because culture and strategy must work together.

Table 4-2 provides some example (possible) aspects of an organization's culture. Note you could ask employees/managers to rate the degree that the dimension characterizes the firm. When one firm acquires another firm, integrating the two cultures can be important. For example, in Table 4-2, one firm may score mostly 1's and the other firm may score mostly 5's, which would present a challenging strategic problem.

The strategic-management process takes place largely within a particular organization's culture. Lorsch found that executives in successful companies are emotionally committed to the firm's culture, but he concluded that culture can inhibit strategic management in two basic ways. First, managers frequently miss the significance of changing external conditions because they are blinded by strongly held beliefs. Second, when a particular culture has been effective in the past, the natural response is to stick with it in the future, even during times of major strategic change.[8] An organization's culture must support the collective commitment of its people to a common purpose. It must foster competence and enthusiasm among managers and employees.

Organizational culture significantly affects business decisions and thus must be evaluated during an internal strategic-management audit. If strategies can capitalize on cultural strengths, such as a strong work ethic or highly ethical beliefs, then management often can swiftly and easily implement changes. However, if the firm's culture is not supportive, strategic changes may be ineffective or even counterproductive. A firm's culture can become antagonistic to new strategies, with the result being confusion and disorientation.

TABLE 4-2 Fifteen Example (Possible) Aspects of an Organization's Culture

Dimension	Degree				
1. Strong work ethic; arrive early and leave late	1	2	3	4	5
2. High ethical beliefs; clear code of business ethics followed	1	2	3	4	5
3. Formal dress; shirt and tie expected	1	2	3	4	5
4. Informal dress; many casual dress days	1	2	3	4	5
5. Socialize together outside of work	1	2	3	4	5
6. Do not question supervisor's decision	1	2	3	4	5
7. Encourage whistle-blowing	1	2	3	4	5
8. Be health conscious; have a wellness program	1	2	3	4	5
9. Allow substantial "working from home"	1	2	3	4	5
10. Encourage creativity/innovation/openmindness	1	2	3	4	5
11. Support women and minorities; no glass ceiling	1	2	3	4	5
12. Be highly socially responsible; be philanthropic	1	2	3	4	5
13. Have numerous meetings	1	2	3	4	5
14. Have a participative management style	1	2	3	4	5
15. Preserve the natural environment; have a sustainability program	1	2	3	4	5

An organization's culture should infuse individuals with enthusiasm for implementing strategies. Allarie and Firsirotu emphasized the need to understand culture:

> Culture provides an explanation for the insuperable difficulties a firm encounters when it attempts to shift its strategic direction. Not only has the "right" culture become the essence and foundation of corporate excellence, it is also claimed that success or failure of reforms hinges on management's sagacity and ability to change the firm's driving culture in time and in time with required changes in strategies.[9]

The potential value of organizational culture has not been realized fully in the study of strategic management. Ignoring the effect that culture can have on relationships among the functional areas of business can result in barriers to communication, lack of coordination, and an inability to adapt to changing conditions. Some tension between culture and a firm's strategy is inevitable, but the tension should be monitored so that it does not reach a point at which relationships are severed and the culture becomes antagonistic. The resulting disarray among members of the organization would disrupt strategy formulation, implementation, and evaluation. In contrast, a supportive organizational culture can make managing much easier.

Internal strengths and weaknesses associated with a firm's culture sometimes are overlooked because of the interfunctional nature of this phenomenon. It is important, therefore, for strategists to understand their firm as a sociocultural system. Success is often determined by linkages between a firm's culture and strategies. The challenge of strategic management today is to bring about the changes in organizational culture and individual mind-sets that are needed to support the formulation, implementation, and evaluation of strategies.

Management

The *functions of management* consist of five basic activities: planning, organizing, motivating, staffing, and controlling. An overview of these activities is provided in Table 4-3.

TABLE 4-3 The Basic Functions of Management

Function	Description	Stage of Strategic-Management Process When Most Important
Planning	Planning consists of all those managerial activities related to preparing for the future. Specific tasks include forecasting, establishing objectives, devising strategies, developing policies, and setting goals.	Strategy Formulation
Organizing	Organizing includes all those managerial activities that result in a structure of task and authority relationships. Specific areas include organizational design, job specialization, job descriptions, job specifications, span of control, unity of command, coordination, job design, and job analysis.	Strategy Implementation
Motivating	Motivating involves efforts directed toward shaping human behavior. Specific topics include leadership, communication, work groups, behavior modification, delegation of authority, job enrichment, job satisfaction, needs fulfillment, organizational change, employee morale, and managerial morale.	Strategy Implementation
Staffing	Staffing activities are centered on personnel or human resource management. Included are wage and salary administration, employee benefits, interviewing, hiring, firing, training, management development, employee safety, affirmative action, equal employment opportunity, union relations, career development, personnel research, discipline policies, grievance procedures, and public relations.	Strategy Implementation
Controlling	Controlling refers to all those managerial activities directed toward ensuring that actual results are consistent with planned results. Key areas of concern include quality control, financial control, sales control, inventory control, expense control, analysis of variances, rewards, and sanctions.	Strategy Evaluation

Planning

The only thing certain about the future of any organization is change, and *planning* is the essential bridge between the present and the future that increases the likelihood of achieving desired results. Planning is the process by which one determines whether to attempt a task, works out the most effective way of reaching desired objectives, and prepares to overcome unexpected difficulties with adequate resources. Planning is the start of the process by which an individual or business may turn empty dreams into achievements. Planning enables one to avoid the trap of working extremely hard but achieving little.

Planning is an up-front investment in success. Planning helps a firm achieve maximum effect from a given effort. Planning enables a firm to take into account relevant factors and focus on the critical ones. Planning helps ensure that the firm can be prepared for all reasonable eventualities and for all changes that will be needed. Planning enables a firm to gather the resources needed and carry out tasks in the most efficient way possible. Planning enables a firm to conserve its own resources, avoid wasting ecological resources, make a fair profit, and be seen as an effective, useful firm. Planning enables a firm to identify precisely what is to be achieved and to detail precisely the who, what, when, where, why, and how needed to achieve desired objectives. Planning enables a firm to assess whether the effort, costs, and implications associated with achieving desired objectives are warranted.[10] Planning is the cornerstone of effective strategy formulation. But even though it is considered the foundation of management, it is commonly the task that managers neglect most. Planning is essential for successful strategy implementation and strategy evaluation, largely because organizing, motivating, staffing, and controlling activities depend upon good planning.

The process of planning must involve managers and employees throughout an organization. The time horizon for planning decreases from two to five years for top-level to less than six months for lower-level managers. The important point is that all managers do planning and should involve subordinates in the process to facilitate employee understanding and commitment.

Planning can have a positive impact on organizational and individual performance. Planning allows an organization to identify and take advantage of external opportunities as well as minimize the impact of external threats. Planning is more than extrapolating from the past and present into the future. It also includes developing a mission, forecasting future events and trends, establishing objectives, and choosing strategies to pursue.

An organization can develop synergy through planning. *Synergy* exists when everyone pulls together as a team that knows what it wants to achieve; synergy is the $2 + 2 = 5$ effect. By establishing and communicating clear objectives, employees and managers can work together toward desired results. Synergy can result in powerful competitive advantages. The strategic-management process itself is aimed at creating synergy in an organization.

Planning allows a firm to adapt to changing markets and thus to shape its own destiny. Strategic management can be viewed as a formal planning process that allows an organization to pursue proactive rather than reactive strategies. Successful organizations strive to control their own futures rather than merely react to external forces and events as they occur. Historically, organisms and organizations that have not adapted to changing conditions have become extinct. Swift adaptation is needed today more than ever because changes in markets, economies, and competitors worldwide are accelerating. Many firms did not adapt to the global recession of late and went out of business.

Organizing

The purpose of *organizing* is to achieve coordinated effort by defining task and authority relationships. Organizing means determining who does what and who reports to whom. There are countless examples in history of well-organized enterprises successfully competing against—and in some cases defeating—much stronger but less-organized firms. A well-organized firm generally has motivated managers and employees who are committed to seeing the organization succeed. Resources are allocated more effectively and used more efficiently in a well-organized firm than in a disorganized firm.

The organizing function of management can be viewed as consisting of three sequential activities: breaking down tasks into jobs (work specialization), combining jobs to form departments (departmentalization), and delegating authority. Breaking down tasks into jobs requires the development of job descriptions and job specifications. These tools clarify for both managers and employees what particular jobs entail. In *The Wealth of Nations,* published in 1776, Adam Smith cited the advantages of work specialization in the manufacture of pins:

> One man draws the wire, another straightens it, a third cuts it, a fourth points it, a fifth grinds it at the top for receiving the head. Ten men working in this manner can produce 48,000 pins in a single day, but if they had all wrought separately and independently, each might at best produce twenty pins in a day.[11]

Combining jobs to form departments results in an organizational structure, span of control, and a chain of command. Changes in strategy often require changes in structure because positions may be created, deleted, or merged. Organizational structure dictates how resources are allocated and how objectives are established in a firm. Allocating resources and establishing objectives geographically, for example, is much different from doing so by product or customer.

The most common forms of departmentalization are functional, divisional, strategic business unit, and matrix. These types of structure are discussed further in Chapter 7.

Delegating authority is an important organizing activity, as evidenced in the old saying "You can tell how good a manager is by observing how his or her department functions when he or she isn't there." Employees today are more educated and more capable of participating in organizational decision making than ever before. In most cases, they expect to be delegated authority and responsibility and to be held accountable for results. Delegation of authority is embedded in the strategic-management process.

Motivating

Motivating can be defined as the process of influencing people to accomplish specific objectives.[12] Motivation explains why some people work hard and others do not. Objectives, strategies, and policies have little chance of succeeding if employees and managers are not motivated to implement strategies once they are formulated. The motivating function of management includes at least four major components: leadership, group dynamics, communication, and organizational change.

When managers and employees of a firm strive to achieve high levels of productivity, this indicates that the firm's strategists are good leaders. Good leaders establish rapport with subordinates, empathize with their needs and concerns, set a good example, and are trustworthy and fair. Leadership includes developing a vision of the firm's future and inspiring people to work hard to achieve that vision. Kirkpatrick and Locke reported that certain traits also characterize effective leaders: knowledge of the business, cognitive ability, self-confidence, honesty, integrity, and drive.[13]

Research suggests that democratic behavior on the part of leaders results in more positive attitudes toward change and higher productivity than does autocratic behavior. Drucker said:

> Leadership is not a magnetic personality. That can just as well be demagoguery. It is not "making friends and influencing people." That is flattery. Leadership is the lifting of a person's vision to higher sights, the raising of a person's performance to a higher standard, the building of a person's personality beyond its normal limitations.[14]

Group dynamics play a major role in employee morale and satisfaction. Informal groups or coalitions form in every organization. The norms of coalitions can range from being very positive to very negative toward management. It is important, therefore, that strategists identify the composition and nature of informal groups in an organization to facilitate strategy formulation, implementation, and evaluation. Leaders of informal groups are especially important in formulating and implementing strategy changes.

Communication, perhaps the most important word in management, is a major component in motivation. An organization's system of communication determines whether strategies can be implemented successfully. Good two-way communication is vital for gaining support for departmental and divisional objectives and policies. Top-down communication can encourage bottom-up communication. The strategic-management process becomes a lot easier when subordinates are encouraged to discuss their concerns, reveal their problems, provide recommendations, and give suggestions. A primary reason for instituting strategic management is to build and support effective communication networks throughout the firm.

> The manager of tomorrow must be able to get his people to commit themselves to the business, whether they are machine operators or junior vice-presidents. The key issue will be empowerment, a term whose strength suggests the need to get beyond merely sharing a little information and a bit of decision making.[15]

Staffing

The management function of *staffing,* also called *personnel management* or *human resource management,* includes activities such as recruiting, interviewing, testing, selecting, orienting, training, developing, caring for, evaluating, rewarding, disciplining, promoting, transferring, demoting, and dismissing employees, as well as managing union relations.

Staffing activities play a major role in strategy-implementation efforts, and for this reason, human resource managers are becoming more actively involved in the strategic-management process. It is important to identify strengths and weaknesses in the staffing area.

The complexity and importance of human resource activities have increased to such a degree that all but the smallest organizations now need a full-time human resource manager. Numerous court cases that directly affect staffing activities are decided each day. Organizations and individuals can be penalized severely for not following federal, state, and local laws and guidelines related to staffing. Line managers simply cannot stay abreast of all the legal developments and requirements regarding staffing. The human resources department coordinates staffing decisions in the firm so that an organization as a whole meets legal requirements. This department also provides needed consistency in administering company rules, wages, policies, and employee benefits as well as collective bargaining with unions.

Human resource management is particularly challenging for international companies. For example, the inability of spouses and children to adapt to new surroundings can be a staffing problem in overseas transfers. The problems include premature returns, job performance slumps, resignations, discharges, low morale, marital discord, and general discontent. Firms such as Ford Motor and ExxonMobil screen and interview spouses and children before assigning persons to overseas positions. 3M Corporation introduces children to peers in the target country and offers spouses educational benefits.

Controlling

The *controlling* function of management includes all of those activities undertaken to ensure that actual operations conform to planned operations. All managers in an organization have controlling responsibilities, such as conducting performance evaluations and taking necessary action to minimize inefficiencies. The controlling function of management is particularly important for effective strategy evaluation. Controlling consists of four basic steps:

1. Establishing performance standards
2. Measuring individual and organizational performance
3. Comparing actual performance to planned performance standards
4. Taking corrective actions

Measuring individual performance is often conducted ineffectively or not at all in organizations. Some reasons for this shortcoming are that evaluations can create confrontations that most managers prefer to avoid, can take more time than most managers are willing to give, and can require skills that many managers lack. No single approach to measuring individual performance is without limitations. For this reason, an organization should examine various methods, such as the graphic rating scale, the behaviorally anchored rating scale, and the critical incident method, and then develop or select a performance-appraisal approach that best suits the firm's needs. Increasingly, firms are striving to link organizational performance with managers' and employees' pay. This topic is discussed further in Chapter 7.

Management Audit Checklist of Questions

The following checklist of questions can help determine specific strengths and weaknesses in the functional area of business. An answer of *no* to any question could indicate a potential weakness, although the strategic significance and implications of negative answers, of course, will vary by organization, industry, and severity of the weakness. Positive or yes answers to the checklist questions suggest potential areas of strength.

1. Does the firm use strategic-management concepts?
2. Are company objectives and goals measurable and well communicated?
3. Do managers at all hierarchical levels plan effectively?
4. Do managers delegate authority well?
5. Is the organization's structure appropriate?
6. Are job descriptions and job specifications clear?
7. Is employee morale high?
8. Are employee turnover and absenteeism low?
9. Are organizational reward and control mechanisms effective?

Marketing

Marketing can be described as the process of defining, anticipating, creating, and fulfilling customers' needs and wants for products and services. There are seven basic *functions of marketing:* (1) customer analysis, (2) selling products/services, (3) product and service planning, (4) pricing, (5) distribution, (6) marketing research, and (7) opportunity analysis.[16] Understanding these functions helps strategists identify and evaluate marketing strengths and weaknesses.

Customer Analysis

Customer analysis—the examination and evaluation of consumer needs, desires, and wants—involves administering customer surveys, analyzing consumer information, evaluating market positioning strategies, developing customer profiles, and determining optimal market segmentation strategies. The information generated by customer analysis can be essential in developing an effective mission statement. Customer profiles can reveal the demographic characteristics of an organization's customers. Buyers, sellers, distributors, salespeople, managers, wholesalers, retailers, suppliers, and creditors can all participate in gathering information to successfully identify customers' needs and wants. Successful organizations continually monitor present and potential customers' buying patterns.

Selling Products/Services

Successful strategy implementation generally rests upon the ability of an organization to sell some product or service. *Selling* includes many marketing activities, such as advertising, sales promotion, publicity, personal selling, sales force management, customer relations, and dealer relations. These activities are especially critical when a firm pursues a market penetration strategy. The effectiveness of various selling tools for consumer and industrial products varies. Personal selling is most important for industrial goods companies, and advertising is most important for consumer goods companies.

U.S. advertising expenditures are expected to fall 6.2 percent in 2009 to $161.8 billion.[17] One aspect of ads in a recession is that they generally take more direct aim at competitors, and this marketing practice is holding true in our bad economic times. Nick Brien at Mediabrands says, "Ads have to get combative in bad times. It's a dog fight, and it's about getting leaner and meaner." Marketers in 2009 also say ads will be less lavish and glamorous

TABLE 4-4   Desirable Characteristics of Ads in a Global Economic Recession

1. Take direct aim at competitors, so leaner, meaner, and to the point.
2. Be less lavish and glamorous, requiring less production dollars to develop.
3. Be short and sweet, mostly 10- and 15-second ads rather than 30+ seconds.
4. "Make you feel good" or "put you in a good mood" because (a) ads can be more easily avoided than ever and (b) people are experiencing hard times and seek comfort.
5. Be more pervasive such as on buses, elevators, cell phones, and trucks.
6. Appear less on Web sites as banner ads become the new junk mail.
7. Red will overtake the color orange as the most popular ad color.
8. More than ever emphasize low price and value versus rivals.
9. More than ever emphasize how the product/service will make your life better.

Source: Based on Suzanne Vranica, "Ads to Go Leaner, Meaner in '09," *Wall Street Journal* (January 5, 2009): B8.

in a recession. Table 4-4 lists specific characteristics of ads forthcoming in late 2009 and 2010 in response to the economic hard times people nationwide and worldwide are facing. Total U.S. online advertising sending is expected to decline 0.3 percent to $36.9 billion in 2009, after growing 8.5 percent in 2008.

A 30-second advertisement on the Super Bowl in 2009 was $3 million. The NBC network airing the Super Bowl took in $206 million of ad revenue from the broadcast as just over 95 million people watched the Pittsburgh Steelers defeat the Arizona Cardinals in Super Bowl XLIII. The most watched television show in history was the 1983 season finale of *M*A*S*H*, which drew 106 million viewers.

Visa in 2009 launched a $140 million advertising campaign that includes print, TV, outdoor, and Internet ads designed to persuade consumers that debit cards "are more convenient, safer, and secure than cash or checks."

Pharmaceutical companies on average reduced their spending on consumer advertising of prescription drugs by 8 percent in 2008 to $4.4 billion. This was the first annual decrease since 1997 in their efforts to get patients to request a particular medicine from their doctor.

Determining organizational strengths and weaknesses in the selling function of marketing is an important part of performing an internal strategic-management audit. With regard to advertising products and services on the Internet, a new trend is to base advertising rates exclusively on sales rates. This new accountability contrasts sharply with traditional broadcast and print advertising, which bases rates on the number of persons expected to see a given advertisement. The new cost-per-sale online advertising rates are possible because any Web site can monitor which user clicks on which advertisement and then can record whether that consumer actually buys the product. If there are no sales, then the advertisement is free.

Product and Service Planning

Product and service planning includes activities such as test marketing; product and brand positioning; devising warranties; packaging; determining product options, features, style, and quality; deleting old products; and providing for customer service. Product and service planning is particularly important when a company is pursuing product development or diversification.

One of the most effective product and service planning techniques is *test marketing*. Test markets allow an organization to test alternative marketing plans and to forecast future sales of new products. In conducting a test market project, an organization must decide how many cities to include, which cities to include, how long to run the test, what information to collect during the test, and what action to take after the test has been completed. Test marketing is used more frequently by consumer goods companies than by industrial goods companies. Test marketing can allow an organization to avoid substantial losses by revealing weak products and ineffective marketing approaches before large-scale production begins. Starbucks is currently test marketing selling beer and wine in its stores to boost its "after 5 PM" sales.

Pricing

Five major stakeholders affect *pricing* decisions: consumers, governments, suppliers, distributors, and competitors. Sometimes an organization will pursue a forward integration strategy primarily to gain better control over prices charged to consumers. Governments can impose constraints on price fixing, price discrimination, minimum prices, unit pricing, price advertising, and price controls. For example, the Robinson-Patman Act prohibits manufacturers and wholesalers from discriminating in price among channel member purchasers (suppliers and distributors) if competition is injured.

Competing organizations must be careful not to coordinate discounts, credit terms, or condition of sale; not to discuss prices, markups, and costs at trade association meetings; and not to arrange to issue new price lists on the same date, to rotate low bids on contracts, or to uniformly restrict production to maintain high prices. Strategists should view price from both a short-run and a long-run perspective, because competitors can copy price changes with relative ease. Often a dominant firm will aggressively match all price cuts by competitors.

With regard to pricing, as the value of the dollar increases, U.S. multinational companies have a choice. They can raise prices in the local currency of a foreign country or risk losing sales and market share. Alternatively, multinational firms can keep prices steady and face reduced profit when their export revenue is reported in the United States in dollars.

Intense price competition, created by the global economic recession, coupled with Internet price-comparative shopping has reduced profit margins to bare minimum levels for most companies. For example, airline tickets, rental car prices, hotel room rates, and computer prices are lower today than they have been in many years.

In response to the economic recession, the family-dining chain Denny's did something that no family-dining chain had ever done before: give away breakfast from 6 AM until 2 PM on February 8, 2009, at all of its restaurants in the United States. More than 2 million people took advantage of the free breakfast at all but two of Denny's 1,550 restaurants nationwide. The entire promotion, including food, labor, and airing an ad on the Super Bowl the Sunday before, cost Denny's about $5 million. However, the firm reaped tons of positive public relations as well as $50 million of free news coverage nationwide and greatly increased customer loyalty. "People love free stuff when money's tight," says Dan Ariely, a business professor at Duke University. Other firms recently set a price of zero on their products, including McDonald's, Starbucks, Dunkin' Donuts, and Panera Bread. Denny's CEO Nelson Marchioli says that Denny's did better than break even on the free breakfast day, and it may do this promotion again.[18]

Distribution

Distribution includes warehousing, distribution channels, distribution coverage, retail site locations, sales territories, inventory levels and location, transportation carriers, wholesaling, and retailing. Most producers today do not sell their goods directly to consumers. Various marketing entities act as intermediaries; they bear a variety of names such as wholesalers, retailers, brokers, facilitators, agents, vendors—or simply distributors.

Distribution becomes especially important when a firm is striving to implement a market development or forward integration strategy. Some of the most complex and challenging decisions facing a firm concern product distribution. Intermediaries flourish in our economy because many producers lack the financial resources and expertise to carry out direct marketing. Manufacturers who could afford to sell directly to the public often can gain greater returns by expanding and improving their manufacturing operations.

Successful organizations identify and evaluate alternative ways to reach their ultimate market. Possible approaches vary from direct selling to using just one or many wholesalers and retailers. Strengths and weaknesses of each channel alternative should be determined according to economic, control, and adaptive criteria. Organizations should consider the costs and benefits of various wholesaling and retailing options. They must consider the need to motivate and control channel members and the need to adapt to changes in the future. Once a marketing channel is chosen, an organization usually must adhere to it for an extended period of time.

Marketing Research

Marketing research is the systematic gathering, recording, and analyzing of data about problems relating to the marketing of goods and services. Marketing research can uncover critical strengths and weaknesses, and marketing researchers employ numerous scales, instruments, procedures, concepts, and techniques to gather information. Marketing research activities support all of the major business functions of an organization. Organizations that possess excellent marketing research skills have a definite strength in pursuing generic strategies.

> The President of PepsiCo said, "Looking at the competition is the company's best form of market research. The majority of our strategic successes are ideas that we borrow from the marketplace, usually from a small regional or local competitor. In each case, we spot a promising new idea, improve on it, and then out-execute our competitor."[19]

Cost/Benefit Analysis

The seventh function of marketing is *cost/benefit analysis,* which involves assessing the costs, benefits, and risks associated with marketing decisions. Three steps are required to perform a cost/benefit analysis: (1) compute the total costs associated with a decision, (2) estimate the total benefits from the decision, and (3) compare the total costs with the total benefits. When expected benefits exceed total costs, an opportunity becomes more attractive. Sometimes the variables included in a cost/benefit analysis cannot be quantified or even measured, but usually reasonable estimates can be made to allow the analysis to be performed. One key factor to be considered is risk. Cost/benefit analysis should also be performed when a company is evaluating alternative ways to be socially responsible.

Marketing Audit Checklist of Questions

The following questions about marketing must be examined in strategic planning:

1. Are markets segmented effectively?
2. Is the organization positioned well among competitors?
3. Has the firm's market share been increasing?
4. Are present channels of distribution reliable and cost effective?
5. Does the firm have an effective sales organization?
6. Does the firm conduct market research?
7. Are product quality and customer service good?
8. Are the firm's products and services priced appropriately?
9. Does the firm have an effective promotion, advertising, and publicity strategy?
10. Are marketing, planning, and budgeting effective?
11. Do the firm's marketing managers have adequate experience and training?
12. Is the firm's Internet presence excellent as compared to rivals?

Finance/Accounting

Financial condition is often considered the single best measure of a firm's competitive position and overall attractiveness to investors. Determining an organization's financial strengths and weaknesses is essential to effectively formulating strategies. A firm's liquidity, leverage, working capital, profitability, asset utilization, cash flow, and equity can eliminate some strategies as being feasible alternatives. Financial factors often alter existing strategies and change implementation plans.

**TABLE 4-5   Excellent Web Sites to Obtain
Information on Companies,
Including Financial Ratios**

http://marketwatch.multexinvestor.com

http://moneycentral.msn.com

http://finance.yahoo.com

www.clearstation.com

https://us.etrade.com/e/t/invest/markets

www.hoovers.com

Especially good Web sites from which to obtain financial information about firms are provided in Table 4-5.

Finance/Accounting Functions

According to James Van Horne, the *functions of finance/accounting* comprise three decisions: the investment decision, the financing decision, and the dividend decision.[20] Financial ratio analysis is the most widely used method for determining an organization's strengths and weaknesses in the investment, financing, and dividend areas. Because the functional areas of business are so closely related, financial ratios can signal strengths or weaknesses in management, marketing, production, research and development, and management information systems activities. It is important to note here that financial ratios are equally applicable in for-profit and nonprofit organizations. Even though nonprofit organizations obviously would not have return-on-investment or earnings-per-share ratios, they would routinely monitor many other special ratios. For example, a church would monitor the ratio of dollar contributions to number of members, while a zoo would monitor dollar food sales to number of visitors. A university would monitor number of students divided by number of professors. Therefore, be creative when performing ratio analysis for nonprofit organizations because they strive to be financially sound just as for-profit firms do.

The *investment decision,* also called *capital budgeting,* is the allocation and reallocation of capital and resources to projects, products, assets, and divisions of an organization. Once strategies are formulated, capital budgeting decisions are required to successfully implement strategies. The *financing decision* determines the best capital structure for the firm and includes examining various methods by which the firm can raise capital (for example, by issuing stock, increasing debt, selling assets, or using a combination of these approaches). The financing decision must consider both short-term and long-term needs for working capital. Two key financial ratios that indicate whether a firm's financing decisions have been effective are the debt-to-equity ratio and the debt-to-total-assets ratio.

Dividend decisions concern issues such as the percentage of earnings paid to stockholders, the stability of dividends paid over time, and the repurchase or issuance of stock. Dividend decisions determine the amount of funds that are retained in a firm compared to the amount paid out to stockholders. Three financial ratios that are helpful in evaluating a firm's dividend decisions are the earnings-per-share ratio, the dividends-per-share ratio, and the price-earnings ratio. The benefits of paying dividends to investors must be balanced against the benefits of internally retaining funds, and there is no set formula on how to balance this trade-off. For the reasons listed here, dividends are sometimes paid out even when funds could be better reinvested in the business or when the firm has to obtain outside sources of capital:

1. Paying cash dividends is customary. Failure to do so could be thought of as a stigma. A dividend change is considered a signal about the future.
2. Dividends represent a sales point for investment bankers. Some institutional investors can buy only dividend-paying stocks.
3. Shareholders often demand dividends, even in companies with great opportunities for reinvesting all available funds.
4. A myth exists that paying dividends will result in a higher stock price.

More than 10 percent of S&P 500 companies cut their dividend payout in 2009. The record number of dividend cuts and dividend suspensions by companies continues. A total of 68 S&P 500 companies cut $40.61 billion in dividend payout money in 2008, but most of these cuts were among banks and brokerage firms. Stock prices for firms fell faster and farther in 2008 than did dividend payouts. Among all U.S. publicly held companies, about 225 increased their dividend payout in 2008.

Based in Stockholm, Sweden, telecom-equipment maker Ericsson recently cut its dividend to 1.85 kronor a share, down from 2.50 kronor the year before. The firm also laid off 5,000 employees in 2009 as its net income declined. Seagate Technology Inc. recently cut its quarterly dividend by 75 percent as part of a restructuring and strengthening of its balance sheet to cope with falling company demand. Seagate in 2009 laid off 2,950 employees and reduced the salaries of its top officers by as much as 25 percent.

Sherwin-Williams has a long-standing policy of paying dividends equal to 30 percent of the prior year's earnings. The firm followed through on this policy in 2008, paying $1.40 per share. The maker of paint and other coatings expects to maintain that policy again in 2009. Sherwin-Williams closed 80 of its 3,300 stores in 2008 and has a strong relationship with Wal-Mart Stores.

The world's largest steelmaker, ArcelorMittal, recently cut its 2009 dividend by 50 percent to 75 cents, reversing its pledge in 2008 to maintain a $1.50 dividend. Based in Luxembourg, ArcelorMittal has been incurring quarterly billion-dollar losses in earnings.

The New York Times Company's board of directors suspended the firm's dividend payments 100 percent in early 2009 to save about $34.5 million annually. The company is also trying to sell part of its 52-story headquarters building to raise cash. Times Company joins a growing list of media companies that have totally suspended their dividends, including E.W. Scripps Company, Media General Inc., and McClatchy Company.

In April 2009, IBM boosted its quarterly dividend 10 percent and added $3 billion to its stock-buyout program. This announcement came soon after IBM lost out to Oracle in its did to acquire Sun Microsystems Corp.

J.P. Morgan in 2009 cut its dividend by 87 percent to 5 cents per share, saving the firm $5 billion annually. Investors were surprised at the drastic cut because J.P. Morgan was regarded as one of the healthiest U.S. banks at the time. The firm's stock rose 6 percent on the news to $20.64 per share.

Wells Fargo in 2009 cut its dividend payout by 85 percent to 5 cents per share. This move came just two months after the firm purchased troubled rival Wachovia Corp. for $12.68 billion. Wells Fargo had paid the third largest dividend in the S&P 500 Index, behind AT&T and Exxon Mobil.

Oracle is doing great in the global economic recession. The company issued its first dividend ever in 2009 and posted a 2 percent revenue increase for its third quarter of fiscal 2009. Based in Redwood Shores, California, the business-software maker has $8.2 billion in cash and generates about $8 billion in cash a year.[21] Historically, tech companies have not issued dividends, and the few tech companies that do pay dividends, such as Microsoft and Intel, have not cut the payouts and continue to stockpile large reserves of cash.

Basic Types of Financial Ratios

Financial ratios are computed from an organization's income statement and balance sheet. Computing financial ratios is like taking a picture because the results reflect a situation at just one point in time. Comparing ratios over time and to industry averages is more likely to result in meaningful statistics that can be used to identify and evaluate strengths and weaknesses. Trend analysis, illustrated in Figure 4-3, is a useful technique that incorporates both the time and industry average dimensions of financial ratios. Note that the dotted lines reveal projected ratios. Some Web sites, such as those provided in Table 4-5, calculate financial ratios and provide data with charts.

Table 4-6 provides a summary of key financial ratios showing how each ratio is calculated and what each ratio measures. However, all the ratios are not significant for all industries and companies. For example, accounts receivable turnover and average collection

FIGURE 4-3

A Financial Ratio Trend Analysis

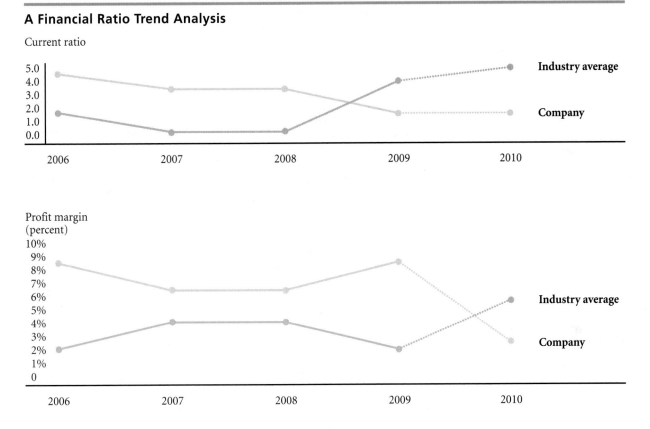

period are not very meaningful to a company that primarily does a cash receipts business. Key financial ratios can be classified into the following five types:

1. ***Liquidity ratios*** measure a firm's ability to meet maturing short-term obligations.
   Current ratio
   Quick (or acid-test) ratio

2. ***Leverage ratios*** measure the extent to which a firm has been financed by debt.
   Debt-to-total-assets ratio
   Debt-to-equity ratio
   Long-term debt-to-equity ratio
   Times-interest-earned (or coverage) ratio

3. ***Activity ratios*** measure how effectively a firm is using its resources.
   Inventory turnover
   Fixed assets turnover
   Total assets turnover
   Accounts receivable turnover
   Average collection period

4. ***Profitability ratios*** measure management's overall effectiveness as shown by the returns generated on sales and investment.
   Gross profit margin
   Operating profit margin
   Net profit margin
   Return on total assets (ROA)
   Return on stockholders' equity (ROE)
   Earnings per share (EPS)
   Price-earnings ratio

TABLE 4-6   **A Summary of Key Financial Ratios**

Ratio	How Calculated	What It Measures
Liquidity Ratios		
Current Ratio	$$\frac{\text{Current assets}}{\text{Current liabilities}}$$	The extent to which a firm can meet its short-term obligations
Quick Ratio	$$\frac{\text{Current assets minus inventory}}{\text{Current liabilities}}$$	The extent to which a firm can meet its short-term obligations without relying upon the sale of its inventories
Leverage Ratios		
Debt-to-Total-Assets Ratio	$$\frac{\text{Total debt}}{\text{Total assets}}$$	The percentage of total funds that are provided by creditors
Debt-to-Equity Ratio	$$\frac{\text{Total debt}}{\text{Total stockholders' equity}}$$	The percentage of total funds provided by creditors versus by owners
Long-Term Debt-to-Equity Ratio	$$\frac{\text{Long-term debt}}{\text{Total stockholders' equity}}$$	The balance between debt and equity in a firm's long-term capital structure
Times-Interest-Earned Ratio	$$\frac{\text{Profits before interest and taxes}}{\text{Total interest charges}}$$	The extent to which earnings can decline without the firm becoming unable to meet its annual interest costs
Activity Ratios		
Inventory Turnover	$$\frac{\text{Sales}}{\text{Inventory of finished goods}}$$	Whether a firm holds excessive stocks of inventories and whether a firm is slowly selling its inventories compared to the industry average
Fixed Assets Turnover	$$\frac{\text{Sales}}{\text{Fixed assets}}$$	Sales productivity and plant and equipment utilization
Total Assets Turnover	$$\frac{\text{Sales}}{\text{Total assets}}$$	Whether a firm is generating a sufficient volume of business for the size of its asset investment
Accounts Receivable Turnover	$$\frac{\text{Annual credit sales}}{\text{Accounts receivable}}$$	The average length of time it takes a firm to collect credit sales (in percentage terms)
Average Collection Period	$$\frac{\text{Accounts receivable}}{\text{Total credit sales/365 days}}$$	The average length of time it takes a firm to collect on credit sales (in days)
Profitability Ratios		
Gross Profit Margin	$$\frac{\text{Sales minus cost of goods sold}}{\text{Sales}}$$	The total margin available to cover operating expenses and yield a profit
Operating Profit Margin	$$\frac{\text{Earnings before interest and taxes (EBIT)}}{\text{Sales}}$$	Profitability without concern for taxes and interest
Net Profit Margin	$$\frac{\text{Net income}}{\text{Sales}}$$	After-tax profits per dollar of sales
Return on Total Assets (ROA)	$$\frac{\text{Net income}}{\text{Total assets}}$$	After-tax profits per dollar of assets; this ratio is also called return on investment (ROI)
Return on Stockholders' Equity (ROE)	$$\frac{\text{Net income}}{\text{Total stockholders' equity}}$$	After-tax profits per dollar of stockholders' investment in the firm

(continued)

TABLE 4-6   A Summary of Key Financial Ratios—continued

Ratio	How Calculated	What It Measures
Profitability Ratios		
Earnings Per Share (EPS)	$\dfrac{\text{Net income}}{\text{Number of shares of common stock outstanding}}$	Earnings available to the owners of common stock
Price-Earnings Ratio	$\dfrac{\text{Market price per share}}{\text{Earnings per share}}$	Attractiveness of firm on equity markets
Growth Ratios		
Sales	Annual percentage growth in total sales	Firm's growth rate in sales
Net Income	Annual percentage growth in profits	Firm's growth rate in profits
Earnings Per Share	Annual percentage growth in EPS	Firm's growth rate in EPS
Dividends Per Share	Annual percentage growth in dividends per share	Firm's growth rate in dividends per share

5. ***Growth ratios*** measure the firm's ability to maintain its economic position in the growth of the economy and industry.
    Sales
    Net income
    Earnings per share
    Dividends per share

Financial ratio analysis must go beyond the actual calculation and interpretation of ratios. The analysis should be conducted on three separate fronts:

1. ***How has each ratio changed over time?*** This information provides a means of evaluating historical trends. It is important to note whether each ratio has been historically increasing, decreasing, or nearly constant. For example, a 10 percent profit margin could be bad if the trend has been down 20 percent each of the last three years. But a 10 percent profit margin could be excellent if the trend has been up, up, up. Therefore, calculate the percentage change in each ratio from one year to the next to assess historical financial performance on that dimension. Identify and examine large percent changes in a financial ratio from one year to the next.

2. ***How does each ratio compare to industry norms?*** A firm's inventory turnover ratio may appear impressive at first glance but may pale when compared to industry standards or norms. Industries can differ dramatically on certain ratios. For example grocery companies, such as Kroger, have a high inventory turnover whereas automobile dealerships have a lower turnover. Therefore, comparison of a firm's ratios within its particular industry can be essential in determining strength/weakness.

3. ***How does each ratio compare with key competitors?*** Oftentimes competition is more intense between several competitors in a given industry or location than across all rival firms in the industry. When this is true, financial ratio analysis should include comparison to those key competitors. For example, if a firm's profitability ratio is trending up over time and compares favorably to the industry average, but it is trending down relative to its leading competitor, there may be reason for concern.

Financial ratio analysis is not without some limitations. First of all, financial ratios are based on accounting data, and firms differ in their treatment of such items as depreciation, inventory valuation, research and development expenditures, pension plan costs, mergers, and taxes. Also, seasonal factors can influence comparative ratios. Therefore, conformity to industry composite ratios does not establish with certainty that a firm is performing normally or that it is well managed. Likewise, departures from industry averages do not always indicate that a firm is doing especially well or badly. For example, a high inventory turnover ratio could indicate efficient inventory management and a strong working capital position, but it also could indicate a serious inventory shortage and a weak working capital position.

FIGURE 4-4

A Before and After Breakeven Chart When Prices Are Lowered

It is important to recognize that a firm's financial condition depends not only on the functions of finance, but also on many other factors that include (1) management, marketing, management production/operations, research and development, and management information systems decisions; (2) actions by competitors, suppliers, distributors, creditors, customers, and shareholders; and (3) economic, social, cultural, demographic, environmental, political, governmental, legal, and technological trends.

In a global economic recession when consumers are price sensitive, many firms are having to lower prices to compete. As a firm lowers prices, its *breakeven (BE) point* in terms of units sold increases, as illustrated in Figure 4-4. The breakeven point can be defined as the quantity of units that a firm must sell in order for its total revenues (TR) to equal its total costs (TC). Note that the before and after chart in Figure 4-4 reveals that the Total Revenue (TR) line rotates to the right with a decrease in Price, thus increasing the Quantity (Q) that must be sold just to break even. Increasing the breakeven point is thus a huge drawback of lowering prices. Of course when rivals are lowering prices, a firm may have to lower prices anyway to compete. However, the breakeven concept should be kept in mind because it is so important, especially in recessionary times.

Notice in Figure 4-5 that increasing Fixed Costs (FC) also raises a firm's breakeven quantity. Note the before and after chart in Figure 4-5 reveals that adding fixed costs such as more stores or more plants as part of a strategic plan raises the Total Cost (TC) line, which makes the intersection of the Total Cost (TC) and Total Revenue (TR) lines at a point farther down the Quantity axis. Increasing a firm's fixed costs (FC) thus significantly raises the quantity of goods that must be sold to break even. This is not just theory for the sake of theory. Firms with less fixed costs, such as Apple and Amazon.com, have lower breakeven points, which give them a decided advantage in harsh economic times. Figure 4-5 reveals that adding *fixed costs (FC)*, such as plant, equipment, stores, advertising, and land, may be detrimental whenever there is doubt that significantly more units can be sold to offset those expenditures.

FIGURE 4-5

A Before and After Breakeven Chart When Fixed Costs Are Increased

FIGURE 4-6

A Before and After Breakeven Chart When Prices Are Lowered and Fixed Costs Are Increased

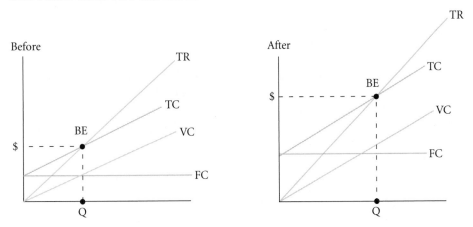

In a global economic recession especially, firms must be cognizant of the fact that lowering prices and adding fixed costs could be a catastrophic double whammy because the firm's breakeven quantity needed to be sold is increased dramatically. Figure 4-6 illustrates this double whammy. Note how far the breakeven point shifts with both a price decrease and an increase in fixed costs. If a firm does not break even, then it will of course incur losses, and losses are not good, especially sustained losses.

Finally, note in Figure 4-4, 4-5, and 4-6 that *Variable Costs (VC)* such as labor and materials when increased have the effect of raising the breakeven point too. Raising Variable Costs is reflected by the Variable Cost line shifting left or becoming steeper. When the Total Revenue (TR) line remains constant, the effect of increasing Variable Costs is to increase Total Costs, which increases the point at which Total Revenue = Total Costs (TC) = Breakeven (BE).

Suffice it to say here that various strategies can have dramatically beneficial or harmful effects on the firm's financial condition due to the concept of breakeven analysis.

Finance/Accounting Audit Checklist

The following finance/accounting questions, like the similar questions about marketing and management earlier, should be examined:

1. Where is the firm financially strong and weak as indicated by financial ratio analyses?
2. Can the firm raise needed short-term capital?
3. Can the firm raise needed long-term capital through debt and/or equity?
4. Does the firm have sufficient working capital?
5. Are capital budgeting procedures effective?
6. Are dividend payout policies reasonable?
7. Does the firm have good relations with its investors and stockholders?
8. Are the firm's financial managers experienced and well trained?
9. Is the firm's debt situation excellent?

Production/Operations

The *production/operations function* of a business consists of all those activities that transform inputs into goods and services. Production/operations management deals with inputs, transformations, and outputs that vary across industries and markets. A manufacturing operation transforms or converts inputs such as raw materials, labor, capital, machines, and facilities into finished goods and services. As indicated in Table 4-7, Roger Schroeder suggested that production/operations management comprises five functions or decision areas: process, capacity, inventory, workforce, and quality.

TABLE 4-7 The Basic Functions (Decisions) Within Production/Operations

Decision Areas	Example Decisions
1. Process	These decisions include choice of technology, facility layout, process flow analysis, facility location, line balancing, process control, and transportation analysis. Distances from raw materials to production sites to customers are a major consideration.
2. Capacity	These decisions include forecasting, facilities planning, aggregate planning, scheduling, capacity planning, and queuing analysis. Capacity utilization is a major consideration.
3. Inventory	These decisions involve managing the level of raw materials, work-in-process, and finished goods, especially considering what to order, when to order, how much to order, and materials handling.
4. Workforce	These decisions involve managing the skilled, unskilled, clerical, and managerial employees by caring for job design, work measurement, job enrichment, work standards, and motivation techniques.
5. Quality	These decisions are aimed at ensuring that high-quality goods and services are produced by caring for quality control, sampling, testing, quality assurance, and cost control.

Source: Adapted from R. Schroeder, *Operations Management* (New York: McGraw-Hill, 1981): 12.

Most automakers require a 30-day notice to build vehicles, but Toyota Motor fills a buyer's new car order in just 5 days. Honda Motor was considered the industry's fastest producer, filling orders in 15 days. Automakers have for years operated under just-in-time inventory systems, but Toyota's 360 suppliers are linked to the company via computers on a virtual assembly line. The new Toyota production system was developed in the company's Cambridge, Ontario, plant and now applies to its Solara, Camry, Corolla, and Tacoma vehicles.

Production/operations activities often represent the largest part of an organization's human and capital assets. In most industries, the major costs of producing a product or service are incurred within operations, so production/operations can have great value as a competitive weapon in a company's overall strategy. Strengths and weaknesses in the five functions of production can mean the success or failure of an enterprise.

Many production/operations managers are finding that cross-training of employees can help their firms respond faster to changing markets. Cross-training of workers can increase efficiency, quality, productivity, and job satisfaction. For example, at General Motors' Detroit gear and axle plant, costs related to product defects were reduced 400 percent in two years as a result of cross-training workers. A shortage of qualified labor in the United States is another reason cross-training is becoming a common management practice.

Singapore rivals Hong Kong as an attractive site for locating production facilities in Southeast Asia. Singapore is a city-state near Malaysia. An island nation of about 4 million, Singapore is changing from an economy built on trade and services to one built on information technology. A large-scale program in computer education for older (over age 26) residents is very popular. Singapore children receive outstanding computer training in schools. All government services are computerized nicely. Singapore lures multinational businesses with great tax breaks, world-class infrastructure, excellent courts that efficiently handle business disputes, exceptionally low tariffs, large land giveaways, impressive industrial parks, excellent port facilities, and a government very receptive to and cooperative with foreign businesses. Foreign firms now account for 70 percent of manufacturing output in Singapore.

In terms of ship container traffic processed annually, Singapore has the largest and busiest seaport in the world, followed by Hong Kong, Shanghai, Los Angeles, Busan (South Korea), Rotterdam, Hamburg, New York, and Tokyo. The Singapore seaport is five times the size of the New York City seaport.[22]

There is much reason for concern that many organizations have not taken sufficient account of the capabilities and limitations of the production/operations function in formulating strategies. Scholars contend that this neglect has had unfavorable consequences on corporate performance in America. As shown in Table 4-8, James Dilworth outlined implications of several types of strategic decisions that a company might make.

TABLE 4-8   Implications of Various Strategies on Production/Operations

Various Strategies	Implications
1. Low-cost provider	Creates high barriers to entry
	Creates larger market
	Requires longer production runs and fewer product changes
2. A high-quality provider	Requires more quality-assurance efforts
	Requires more expensive equipment
	Requires highly skilled workers and higher wages
3. Provide great customer service	Requires more service people, service parts, and equipment
	Requires rapid response to customer needs or changes in customer tastes
	Requires a higher inventory investment
4. Be the first to introduce new products	Has higher research and development costs
	Has high retraining and tooling costs
5. Become highly automated	Requires high capital investment
	Reduces flexibility
	May affect labor relations
	Makes maintenance more crucial
6. Minimize layoffs	Serves the security needs of employees and may develop employee loyalty
	Helps to attract and retain highly skilled employees

Source: Adapted from J. Dilworth, *Production and Operations Management: Manufacturing and Nonmanufacturing,* 2nd ed. Copyright © 1983 by Random House, Inc. Reprinted by permission of Random House, Inc.

Production/Operations Audit Checklist

Questions such as the following should be examined:

1. Are supplies of raw materials, parts, and subassemblies reliable and reasonable?
2. Are facilities, equipment, machinery, and offices in good condition?
3. Are inventory-control policies and procedures effective?
4. Are quality-control policies and procedures effective?
5. Are facilities, resources, and markets strategically located?
6. Does the firm have technological competencies?

Research and Development

The fifth major area of internal operations that should be examined for specific strengths and weaknesses is *research and development (R&D)*. Many firms today conduct no R&D, and yet many other companies depend on successful R&D activities for survival. Firms pursuing a product development strategy especially need to have a strong R&D orientation.

Organizations invest in R&D because they believe that such an investment will lead to a superior product or service and will give them competitive advantages. Research and development expenditures are directed at developing new products before competitors do, at improving product quality, or at improving manufacturing processes to reduce costs.

Effective management of the R&D function requires a strategic and operational partnership between R&D and the other vital business functions. A spirit of partnership and mutual trust between general and R&D managers is evident in the best-managed firms today. Managers in these firms jointly explore; assess; and decide the what, when, where, why, and how much of R&D. Priorities, costs, benefits, risks, and rewards associated with R&D activities are discussed openly and shared. The overall mission of R&D thus has become broad-based, including supporting existing businesses, helping launch new businesses, developing new products, improving product quality, improving manufacturing efficiency, and deepening or broadening the company's technological capabilities.[23]

The best-managed firms today seek to organize R&D activities in a way that breaks the isolation of R&D from the rest of the company and promotes a spirit of partnership between R&D managers and other managers in the firm. R&D decisions and plans must be integrated and coordinated across departments and divisions by having the departments share experiences and information. The strategic-management process facilitates this cross-functional approach to managing the R&D function.

Based in Sunnyvale, California, Juniper Networks spends about 20 percent of its revenues or $800 million annually on R&D. However, the company is struggling with falling demand for its products in a global recession. But rather than cutting R&D expenditures, the firm is cutting other expenses. About 70 percent of Juniper's revenues come from Internet routers for phone and cable companies. Juniper's annual R&D budget has not dropped since the company went public in 1999. Rival Cisco Systems spends 13 percent of its revenues on R&D. Motorola is slashing its R&D budget. Qualcomm Inc. is holding its R&D spending flat in 2009.

Although R&D is the lifeblood of pharmaceutical firms, Valeant Pharmaceuticals International recently cut its R&D budget by 50 percent to make acquisitions and buy back its own stock. Lead director Robert Ingram at Valeant says, "R&D is a high-risk bet, and the fact is we fail more often than we succeed." France's Sanofi-Aventis SA also recently cut its R&D spending, but for most pharmaceutical firms cutting such expenses is still taboo.

Internal and External R&D

Cost distributions among R&D activities vary by company and industry, but total R&D costs generally do not exceed manufacturing and marketing start-up costs. Four approaches to determining R&D budget allocations commonly are used: (1) financing as many project proposals as possible, (2) using a percentage-of-sales method, (3) budgeting about the same amount that competitors spend for R&D, or (4) deciding how many successful new products are needed and working backward to estimate the required R&D investment.

R&D in organizations can take two basic forms: (1) internal R&D, in which an organization operates its own R&D department, and/or (2) contract R&D, in which a firm hires independent researchers or independent agencies to develop specific products. Many companies use both approaches to develop new products. A widely used approach for obtaining outside R&D assistance is to pursue a joint venture with another firm. R&D strengths (capabilities) and weaknesses (limitations) play a major role in strategy formulation and strategy implementation.

Most firms have no choice but to continually develop new and improved products because of changing consumer needs and tastes, new technologies, shortened product life cycles, and increased domestic and foreign competition. A shortage of ideas for new products, increased global competition, increased market segmentation, strong special-interest groups, and increased government regulations are several factors making the successful development of new products more and more difficult, costly, and risky. In the pharmaceutical industry, for example, only one out of every few thousand drugs created in the laboratory ends up on pharmacists' shelves. Scarpello, Boulton, and Hofer emphasized that different strategies require different R&D capabilities:

> The focus of R&D efforts can vary greatly depending on a firm's competitive strategy. Some corporations attempt to be market leaders and innovators of new products, while others are satisfied to be market followers and developers of currently available products. The basic skills required to support these strategies will vary, depending on whether R&D becomes the driving force behind competitive strategy. In cases where new product introduction is the driving force for strategy, R&D activities must be extensive. The R&D unit must then be able to

TABLE 4-9   R&D Spending at Ten Sample Companies, 2008 Fourth Quarter ($Billion)

Company	Fourth Quarter R&D Spending
Microsoft	$2.29
Johnson & Johnson	2.11
IBM	1.53
Intel	1.28
Boeing	0.96
Google	0.73
Hewlett-Packard	0.73
Caterpillar	0.51
DuPont	0.34
Yahoo	0.28

Source: Based on Justin Scheck and Paul Glader, "R&D Spending Holds Steady in Slump," *Wall Street Journal* (April 6, 2009): A1; and Company *Form 10-K* Reports.

advance scientific and technological knowledge, exploit that knowledge, and manage the risks associated with ideas, products, services, and production requirements.[24]

Many U.S. companies are concerned about emerging from the recession with obsolete products, so their spending on R&D is holding steady even as their revenues fall. Intel, for example, is spending $5.4 billion on R&D in 2009, down slightly from 2008. 3M laid off 4,700 employees in 2008 and early 2009 and cut capital expenditures 30 percent in 2009, but its R&D spending increased slightly in 2009. Corning Inc. recently devised a strategy it called "rings of defense" against the economic downturn; R&D was placed in the innermost ring, making it among the last things to be cut. Then Corning soon cut its spending on marketing and administration by 31 percent, but R&D spending was unchanged. The company spent $627 million on R&D both in 2008 and in 2009.

Table 4-9 lists R&D spending at some U.S. companies in the fourth quarter of 2008 alone.

Research and Development Audit

Questions such as the following should be asked in performing an R&D audit:

1. Does the firm have R&D facilities? Are they adequate?
2. If outside R&D firms are used, are they cost-effective?
3. Are the organization's R&D personnel well qualified?
4. Are R&D resources allocated effectively?
5. Are management information and computer systems adequate?
6. Is communication between R&D and other organizational units effective?
7. Are present products technologically competitive?

Management Information Systems

Information ties all business functions together and provides the basis for all managerial decisions. It is the cornerstone of all organizations. Information represents a major source of competitive management advantage or disadvantage. Assessing a firm's internal strengths and weaknesses in information systems is a critical dimension of performing an internal audit. The company motto of Mitsui, a large Japanese trading company, is

"Information is the lifeblood of the company." A satellite network connects Mitsui's 200 worldwide offices.

A management information system's purpose is to improve the performance of an enterprise by improving the quality of managerial decisions. An effective information system thus collects, codes, stores, synthesizes, and presents information in such a manner that it answers important operating and strategic questions. The heart of an information system is a database containing the kinds of records and data important to managers.

A *management information system* receives raw material from both the external and internal evaluation of an organization. It gathers data about marketing, finance, production, and personnel matters internally, and social, cultural, demographic, environmental, economic, political, governmental, legal, technological, and competitive factors externally. Data are integrated in ways needed to support managerial decision making.

There is a logical flow of material in a computer information system, whereby data are input to the system and transformed into output. Outputs include computer printouts, written reports, tables, charts, graphs, checks, purchase orders, invoices, inventory records, payroll accounts, and a variety of other documents. Payoffs from alternative strategies can be calculated and estimated. *Data* become *information* only when they are evaluated, filtered, condensed, analyzed, and organized for a specific purpose, problem, individual, or time.

Because organizations are becoming more complex, decentralized, and globally dispersed, the function of information systems is growing in importance. Spurring this advance is the falling cost and increasing power of computers. There are costs and benefits associated with obtaining and evaluating information, just as with equipment and land. Like equipment, information can become obsolete and may need to be purged from the system. An effective information system is like a library, collecting, categorizing, and filing data for use by managers throughout the organization. Information systems are a major strategic resource, monitoring internal and external issues and trends, identifying competitive threats, and assisting in the implementation, evaluation, and control of strategy.

We are truly in an information age. Firms whose information-system skills are weak are at a competitive disadvantage. In contrast, strengths in information systems allow firms to establish distinctive competencies in other areas. Low-cost manufacturing and good customer service, for example, can depend on a good information system.

Strategic-Planning Software

Some strategic decision support systems, however, are too sophisticated, expensive, or restrictive to be used easily by managers in a firm. This is unfortunate because the strategic-management process must be a people process to be successful. People make the difference! Strategic-planning software should thus be simple and unsophisticated. Simplicity allows wide participation among managers in a firm and participation is essential for effective strategy implementation.

One strategic-planning software product that parallels this text and offers managers and executives a simple yet effective approach for developing organizational strategies is CheckMATE (www.checkmateplan.com). This personal computer software performs planning analyses and generates strategies a firm could pursue. CheckMATE incorporates the most modern strategic-planning techniques. No previous experience with computers or knowledge of strategic planning is required of the user. CheckMATE thus promotes communication, understanding, creativity, and forward thinking among users.

CheckMATE is not a spreadsheet program or database; it is an expert system that carries a firm through strategy formulation and implementation. A major strength of CheckMATE strategic-planning software is its simplicity and participative approach. The user is asked appropriate questions, responses are recorded, information is assimilated, and results are printed. Individuals can independently work through the software, and then the program will develop joint recommendations for the firm.

An individual license for CheckMATE costs $295. More information about CheckMATE can be obtained at www.checkmateplan.com or 910–579–5744 (phone).

The Web site www.strategyclub.com has become a leader in the world in providing strategic planning software, products, and services. This Web site provides the strategic Management Club Online as well as excellent economical software both for students and for business persons worldwide.

Management Information Systems Audit

Questions such as the following should be asked when conducting this audit:

1. Do all managers in the firm use the information system to make decisions?
2. Is there a chief information officer or director of information systems position in the firm?
3. Are data in the information system updated regularly?
4. Do managers from all functional areas of the firm contribute input to the information system?
5. Are there effective passwords for entry into the firm's information system?
6. Are strategists of the firm familiar with the information systems of rival firms?
7. Is the information system user-friendly?
8. Do all users of the information system understand the competitive advantages that information can provide firms?
9. Are computer training workshops provided for users of the information system?
10. Is the firm's information system continually being improved in content and user-friendliness?

Value Chain Analysis (VCA)

According to Porter, the business of a firm can best be described as a *value chain,* in which total revenues minus total costs of all activities undertaken to develop and market a product or service yields value. All firms in a given industry have a similar value chain, which includes activities such as obtaining raw materials, designing products, building manufacturing facilities, developing cooperative agreements, and providing customer service. A firm will be profitable as long as total revenues exceed the total costs incurred in creating and delivering the product or service. Firms should strive to understand not only their own value chain operations but also their competitors', suppliers', and distributors' value chains.

Value chain analysis (VCA) refers to the process whereby a firm determines the costs associated with organizational activities from purchasing raw materials to manufacturing product(s) to marketing those products. VCA aims to identify where low-cost advantages or disadvantages exist anywhere along the value chain from raw material to customer service activities. VCA can enable a firm to better identify its own strengths and weaknesses, especially as compared to competitors' value chain analyses and their own data examined over time.

Substantial judgment may be required in performing a VCA because different items along the value chain may impact other items positively or negatively, so there exist complex interrelationships. For example, exceptional customer service may be especially expensive yet may reduce the costs of returns and increase revenues. Cost and price differences among rival firms can have their origins in activities performed by suppliers, distributors, creditors, or even shareholders. Despite the complexity of VCA, the initial step in implementing this procedure is to divide a firm's operations into specific activities or business processes. Then the analyst attempts to attach a cost to each discrete activity, and the costs could be in terms of both time and money. Finally, the analyst converts the cost data into information by looking for competitive cost strengths and weaknesses that may yield competitive advantage or disadvantage. Conducting a VCA is supportive of the RBV's examination of a firm's assets and capabilities as sources of distinctive competence.

When a major competitor or new market entrant offers products or services at very low prices, this may be because that firm has substantially lower value chain costs or perhaps the rival firm is just waging a desperate attempt to gain sales or market share. Thus value chain analysis can be critically important for a firm in monitoring whether its prices and costs are competitive. An example value chain is illustrated in Figure 4-7. There can be more than a hundred particular value-creating activities associated with the business of producing and marketing a product or service, and each one of the activities can represent a competitive advantage or disadvantage for the firm. The combined costs of all the various activities in a company's value chain define the firm's cost of doing business. Firms should determine where cost advantages and disadvantages in their value chain occur *relative to the value chain of rival firms.*

Value chains differ immensely across industries and firms. Whereas a paper products company, such as Stone Container, would include on its value chain timber farming, logging, pulp mills, and papermaking, a computer company such as Hewlett-Packard would include programming, peripherals, software, hardware, and laptops. A motel would include food, housekeeping, check-in and check-out operations, Web site, reservations system, and so on. However all firms should use value chain analysis to develop and nurture a core competence and convert this competence into a distinctive competence. A *core competence* is a value chain activity that a firm performs especially well. When a core competence evolves into a major competitive advantage, then it is called a *distinctive competence.* Figure 4-8 illustrates this process.

More and more companies are using VCA to gain and sustain competitive advantage by being especially efficient and effective along various parts of the value chain. For example, Wal-Mart has built powerful value advantages by focusing on exceptionally tight inventory control, volume purchasing of products, and offering exemplary customer service. Computer companies in contrast compete aggressively along the distribution end of the value chain. Of course, price competitiveness is a key component of effectiveness among both mass retailers and computer firms.

Benchmarking

Benchmarking is an analytical tool used to determine whether a firm's value chain activities are competitive compared to rivals and thus conducive to winning in the marketplace. Benchmarking entails measuring costs of value chain activities across an industry to determine "best practices" among competing firms for the purpose of duplicating or improving upon those best practices. Benchmarking enables a firm to take action to improve its competitiveness by identifying (and improving upon) value chain activities where rival firms have comparative advantages in cost, service, reputation, or operation.

The hardest part of benchmarking can be gaining access to other firms' value chain activities with associated costs. Typical sources of benchmarking information, however, include published reports, trade publications, suppliers, distributors, customers, partners, creditors, shareholders, lobbyists, and willing rival firms. Some rival firms share benchmarking data. However, the International Benchmarking Clearinghouse provides guidelines to help ensure that restraint of trade, price fixing, bid rigging, bribery, and other improper business conduct do not arise between participating firms.

Due to the popularity of benchmarking today, numerous consulting firms such as Accenture, AT Kearney, Best Practices Benchmarking & Consulting, as well as the Strategic Planning Institute's Council on Benchmarking, gather benchmarking data, conduct benchmarking studies, and distribute benchmark information without identifying the sources.

FIGURE 4-7

An Example Value Chain for a Typical Manufacturing Firm

Supplier Costs ———— ———
     Raw materials ————
     Fuel ————
     Energy ————
     Transportation ————
     Truck drivers ————
     Truck maintenance ————
     Component parts ————
     Inspection ————
     Storing ————
     Warehouse ————
Production Costs ———— ———
     Inventory system ————
     Receiving ————
     Plant layout ————
     Maintenance ————
     Plant location ————
     Computer ————
     R&D ————
     Cost accounting ————
Distribution Costs ———— ———
     Loading ————
     Shipping ————
     Budgeting ————
     Personnel ————
     Internet ————
     Trucking ————
     Railroads ————
     Fuel ————
     Maintenance ————
Sales and Marketing Costs ————
     Salespersons ————
     Web site ————
     Internet ————
     Publicity ————
     Promotion ————
     Advertising ————
     Transportation ————
     Food and lodging ————
Customer Service Costs ———— ———
     Postage ————
     Phone ————
     Internet ————
     Warranty ———— ———
Management Costs ————
     Human resources ————
     Administration ————
     Employee benefits ————
     Labor relations ————
     Managers ————
     Employees ————
     Finance and legal ————

FIGURE 4-8

Transforming Value Chain Activities into Sustained Competitive Advantage

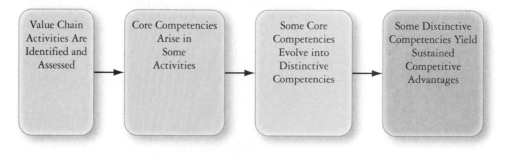

The Internal Factor Evaluation (IFE) Matrix

A summary step in conducting an internal strategic-management audit is to construct an *Internal Factor Evaluation (IFE) Matrix.* This strategy-formulation tool summarizes and evaluates the major strengths and weaknesses in the functional areas of a business, and it also provides a basis for identifying and evaluating relationships among those areas. Intuitive judgments are required in developing an IFE Matrix, so the appearance of a scientific approach should not be interpreted to mean this is an all-powerful technique. A thorough understanding of the factors included is more important than the actual numbers. Similar to the EFE Matrix and Competitive Profile Matrix described in Chapter 3, an IFE Matrix can be developed in five steps:

1. List key internal factors as identified in the internal-audit process. Use a total of from 10 to 20 internal factors, including both strengths and weaknesses. List strengths first and then weaknesses. Be as specific as possible, using percentages, ratios, and comparative numbers. Recall that Edward Deming said, "In God we trust. Everyone else bring data."
2. Assign a weight that ranges from 0.0 (not important) to 1.0 (all-important) to each factor. The weight assigned to a given factor indicates the relative importance of the factor to being successful in the firm's industry. Regardless of whether a key factor is an internal strength or weakness, factors considered to have the greatest effect on organizational performance should be assigned the highest weights. The sum of all weights must equal 1.0.
3. Assign a 1-to-4 rating to each factor to indicate whether that factor represents a major weakness (rating = 1), a minor weakness (rating = 2), a minor strength (rating = 3), or a major strength (rating = 4). Note that strengths must receive a 3 or 4 rating and weaknesses must receive a 1 or 2 rating. Ratings are thus company-based, whereas the weights in step 2 are industry-based.
4. Multiply each factor's weight by its rating to determine a weighted score for each variable.
5. Sum the weighted scores for each variable to determine the total weighted score for the organization.

Regardless of how many factors are included in an IFE Matrix, the total weighted score can range from a low of 1.0 to a high of 4.0, with the average score being 2.5. Total weighted scores well below 2.5 characterize organizations that are weak internally, whereas scores significantly above 2.5 indicate a strong internal position. Like the EFE Matrix, an IFE Matrix should include from 10 to 20 key factors. The number of factors has no effect upon the range of total weighted scores because the weights always sum to 1.0.

When a key internal factor is both a strength and a weakness, the factor should be included twice in the IFE Matrix, and a weight and rating should be assigned to each statement. For example, the Playboy logo both helps and hurts Playboy Enterprises; the logo

TABLE 4.10   A Sample Internal Factor Evaluation Matrix for a Retail Computer Store

Key Internal Factors	Weight	Rating	Weighted Score
Strengths			
1. Inventory turnover increased from 5.8 to 6.7	0.05	3	0.15
2. Average customer purchase increased from $97 to $128	0.07	4	0.28
3. Employee morale is excellent	0.10	3	0.30
4. In-store promotions resulted in 20 percent increase in sales	0.05	3	0.15
5. Newspaper advertising expenditures increased 10 percent	0.02	3	0.06
6. Revenues from repair/service segment of store up 16 percent	0.15	3	0.45
7. In-store technical support personnel have MIS college degrees	0.05	4	0.20
8. Store's debt-to-total assets ratio declined to 34 percent	0.03	3	0.09
9. Revenues per employee up 19 percent	0.02	3	0.06
Weaknesses			
1. Revenues from software segment of store down 12 percent	0.10	2	0.20
2. Location of store negatively impacted by new Highway 34	0.15	2	0.30
3. Carpet and paint in store somewhat in disrepair	0.02	1	0.02
4. Bathroom in store needs refurbishing	0.02	1	0.02
5. Revenues from businesses down 8 percent	0.04	1	0.04
6. Store has no Web site	0.05	2	0.10
7. Supplier on-time delivery increased to 2.4 days	0.03	1	0.03
8. Often customers have to wait to check out	0.05	1	0.05
Total	**1.00**		**2.50**

attracts customers to *Playboy* magazine, but it keeps the Playboy cable channel out of many markets. Be as quantitative as possible when stating factors. Use monetary amounts, percentages, numbers, and ratios to the extent possible.

An example of an IFE Matrix is provided in Table 4-10 for a retail computer store. Note that the two most important factors to be successful in the retail computer store business are "revenues from repair/service in the store" and "location of the store." Also note that the store is doing best on "average customer purchase amount" and "in-store technical support." The store is having major problems with its carpet, bathroom, paint, and checkout procedures. Note also that the matrix contains substantial quantitative data rather than vague statements; this is excellent. Overall, this store receives a 2.5 total weighted score, which on a 1-to-4 scale is exactly average/halfway, indicating there is definitely room for improvement in store operations, strategies, policies, and procedures.

The IFE Matrix provides important information for strategy formulation. For example, this retail computer store might want to hire another checkout person and repair its carpet, paint, and bathroom problems. Also, the store may want to increase advertising for its repair/services, because that is a really important (weight 0.15) factor to being successful in this business.

In multidivisional firms, each autonomous division or strategic business unit should construct an IFE Matrix. Divisional matrices then can be integrated to develop an overall corporate IFE Matrix.

Conclusion

Management, marketing, finance/accounting, production/operations, research and development, and management information systems represent the core operations of most businesses. A strategic-management audit of a firm's internal operations is vital to organizational health. Many companies still prefer to be judged solely on their bottom-line performance. However, an increasing number of successful organizations are using the internal audit to gain competitive advantages over rival firms.

Systematic methodologies for performing strength-weakness assessments are not well developed in the strategic-management literature, but it is clear that strategists must identify and evaluate internal strengths and weaknesses in order to effectively formulate and choose among alternative strategies. The EFE Matrix, Competitive Profile Matrix, IFE Matrix, and clear statements of vision and mission provide the basic information needed to successfully formulate competitive strategies. The process of performing an internal audit represents an opportunity for managers and employees throughout the organization to participate in determining the future of the firm. Involvement in the process can energize and mobilize managers and employees.

We invite you to visit the David page on the Prentice Hall Companion Web site at http://www.pearsonhighered.com/david/ for this chapter's review quiz.

Key Terms and Concepts

Activity Ratios (p. 109)
Benchmarking (p. 120)
Breakeven Point (p. 112)
Capital Budgeting (p. 107)
Communication (p. 94)
Controlling (p. 102)
Core Competence (p. 120)
Cost/Benefit Analysis (p. 106)
Cultural Products (p. 97)
Customer Analysis (p. 103)
Data (p. 118)
Distinctive Competencies (p. 93)
Distribution (p. 105)
Dividend Decisions (p. 107)
Empirical Indicators (p. 96)
Financial Ratio Analysis (p. 95)
Fixed Costs (p. 112)
Financing Decision (p. 107)
Functions of Finance/Accounting (p. 107)
Functions of Management (p. 99)
Functions of Marketing (p. 103)
Growth Ratios (p. 111)
Human Resource Management (p. 102)
Information (p. 118)
Internal Audit (p. 93)

Internal Factor Evaluation (IFE)
   Matrix (p. 122)
Investment Decision (p. 107)
Leverage Ratios (p. 109)
Liquidity Ratios (p. 109)
Management Information System (p. 118)
Marketing Affiliate (p. 93)
Marketing Research (p. 106)
Motivating (p. 101)
Organizational Culture (p. 97)
Organizing (p. 100)
Personnel Management (p. 102)
Planning (p. 100)
Pricing (p. 105)
Product and Service Planning (p. 104)
Production/Operations Function (p. 113)
Profitability Ratios (p. 109)
Research and Development (R&D) (p. 115)
Resource-Based View (RBV) (p. 96)
Selling (p. 103)
Staffing (p. 102)
Synergy (p. 100)
Test Marketing (p. 104)
Value Chain Analysis (VCA) (p. 119)
Variable Costs (p. 113)

Issues for Review and Discussion

1. List three firms you are familiar with and give a distinctive competence for each firm.
2. Give some key reasons why prioritizing strengths and weaknesses is essential.
3. Why may it be easier in performing an internal assessment to develop a list of 80 strengths/weaknesses than to decide on the top 20 to use in formulating strategies?
4. Think of an organization you are very familiar with. Lit three resources of that entity that are empirical indicators.
5. Think of an organization you are very familiar with. Rate that entity's organizational culture on the 15 example dimensions listed in Table 4-2.

6. If you and a partner were going to visit a foreign country where you have never been before, how much planning would you do ahead of time? What benefit would you expect that planning to provide?

7. Even though planning is considered the foundation of management, why do you think it is commonly the task that managers neglect most?

8. Are you more organized than the person sitting beside you in class? If not, what problems could that present in terms of your performance and rank in the class? How analogous is this situation to rival companies?

9. List the three ways that financial ratios should be compared/utilized. Which of the three comparisons do you feel is most important? Why?

10. Illustrate how value chain activities can become core competencies and eventually distinctive competencies. Give an example for an organization you are familiar with.

11. In an IFEM, would it be advantageous to list your strengths, and then your weaknesses, in order of increasing "weight"? Why?

12. In an IFEM, a critic may say there is no significant different between a "weight" of 0.08 and 0.06. How would you respond?

13. List six desirable characteristics of advertisements in recessionary times.

14. Why are so many firms cutting their dividend payout amounts?

15. When someone says dividends paid are double taxed, what are they referring to?

16. Draw a breakeven chart to illustrate a drop in labor costs.

17. Draw a breakeven chart to illustrate an increase in advertising expenses.

18. Draw a breakeven chart to illustrate closing stores.

19. Draw a breakeven chart to illustrate lowering price.

20. Explain why prioritizing the relative importance of strengths and weaknesses in an IFE Matrix is an important strategic-management activity.

21. How can delegation of authority contribute to effective strategic management?

22. Diagram a formal organizational chart that reflects the following positions: a president, 2 executive officers, 4 middle managers, and 18 lower-level managers. Now, diagram three overlapping and hypothetical informal group structures. How can this information be helpful to a strategist in formulating and implementing strategy?

23. Which of the three basic functions of finance/accounting do you feel is most important in a small electronics manufacturing concern? Justify your position.

24. Do you think aggregate R&D expenditures for U.S. firms will increase or decrease next year? Why?

25. Explain how you would motivate managers and employees to implement a major new strategy.

26. Why do you think production/operations managers often are not directly involved in strategy-formulation activities? Why can this be a major organizational weakness?

27. Give two examples of staffing strengths and two examples of staffing weaknesses of an organization with which you are familiar.

28. Would you ever pay out dividends when your firm's annual net profit is negative? Why? What effect could this have on a firm's strategies?

29. If a firm has zero debt in its capital structure, is that always an organizational strength? Why or why not?

30. Describe the production/operations system in a police department.

31. After conducting an internal audit, a firm discovers a total of 100 strengths and 100 weaknesses. What procedures then could be used to determine the most important of these? Why is it important to reduce the total number of key factors?

32. Why do you believe cultural products affect all the functions of business?

33. Do you think cultural products affect strategy formulation, implementation, or evaluation the most? Why?

34. Identify cultural products at your college or university. Do these products, viewed collectively or separately, represent a strength or weakness for the organization?

35. Describe the management information system at your college or university.

36. Explain the difference between data and information in terms of each being useful to strategists.

37. What are the most important characteristics of an effective management information system?

38. Do you agree or disagree with the RBV theorists that internal resources are more important for a firm than external factors in achieving and sustaining competitive advantage? Explain your and their position.

39. Define and discuss "empirical indicators."

40. Define and discuss the "spam" problem in the United States.
41. Define and explain value chain analysis (VCA).
42. List five financial ratios that may be used by your university to monitor operations.
43. Explain benchmarking.

Notes

1. Reprinted by permission of the publisher from "Integrating Strength–Weakness Analysis into Strategic Planning," by William King, *Journal of Business Research* 2, no. 4: p. 481. Copyright 1983 by Elsevier Science Publishing Co., Inc.

2. Igor Ansoff, "Strategic Management of Technology" *Journal of Business Strategy* 7, no. 3 (Winter 1987): 38.

3. Claude George Jr., *The History of Management Thought*, 2nd ed. (Upper Saddle River, NJ: Prentice-Hall, 1972): 174.

4. Robert Grant, "The Resource-Based Theory of Competitive Advantage: Implications for Strategy Formulation," *California Management Review* (Spring 1991): 116.

5. J. B. Barney, "Firm Resources and Sustained Competitive Advantage," *Journal of Management* 17 (1991): 99–120; J. B. Barney, "The Resource-Based Theory of the Firm," *Organizational Science* 7 (1996): 469; J. B. Barney, "Is the Resource-Based 'View' a Useful Perspective for Strategic Management Research? Yes." *Academy of Management Review* 26, no. 1 (2001): 41–56.

6. Edgar Schein, *Organizational Culture and Leadership* (San Francisco: Jossey-Bass, 1985): 9.

7. Ellen Byron, "A New Odd Couple: Google, P&G Swap Workers to Spur Innovation," *Wall Street Journal* (November 19, 2008): A1.

8. John Lorsch, "Managing Culture: The Invisible Barrier to Strategic Change," *California Management Review* 28, no. 2 (1986): 95–109.

9. Y. Allarie and M. Firsirotu, "How to Implement Radical Strategies in Large Organizations," *Sloan Management Review* (Spring 1985): 19.

10. www.mindtools.com/plfailpl.html.

11. Adam Smith, *The Wealth of Nations* (New York: Modern Library, 1937): 3–4.

12. Richard Daft, *Management*, 3rd ed. (Orlando, FL: Dryden Press, 1993): 512.

13. Shelley Kirkpatrick and Edwin Locke, "Leadership: Do Traits Matter?" *Academy of Management Executive* 5, no. 2 (May 1991): 48.

14. Peter Drucker, *Management Tasks, Responsibilities, and Practice* (New York: Harper & Row, 1973): 463.

15. Brian Dumaine, "What the Leaders of Tomorrow See," *Fortune* (July 3, 1989): 51.

16. J. Evans and B. Bergman, *Marketing* (New York: Macmillan, 1982): 17.

17. Suzanne Vranica, "Ads to Go Leaner, Meaner in '09," *Wall Street Journal* (January 5, 2009): B8.

18. Bruce Horowitz, "2 Million Enjoy Free Breakfast at Denny's," *USA Today* (February 4, 2009): 1B, 2B.

19. Quoted in Robert Waterman, Jr., "The Renewal Factor," *BusinessWeek* (September 14, 1987): 108.

20. J. Van Horne, *Financial Management and Policy* (Upper Saddle River, N.J.: Prentice-Hall, 1974): 10.

21. Ben Worthen, "Oracle to Pay First Dividend," *Wall Street Journal* (March 19, 2009): B1.

22. Kevin Klowden, "The Quiet Revolution in Transportation," *Wall Street Journal* (April 24, 2007): A14.

23. Philip Rousebl, Kamal Saad, and Tamara Erickson, "The Evolution of Third Generation R&D," *Planning Review* 19, no. 2 (March–April 1991): 18–26.

24. Vida Scarpello, William Boulton, and Charles Hofer, "Reintegrating R&D into Business Strategy," *Journal of Business Strategy* 6, no. 4 (Spring 1986): 50–51.

Current Readings

Aggarwal, Vikas, and David Hsu. "Modes of Cooperative R&D Commercialization by Start-Ups." *Strategic Management Journal* (August 2009): 835–864.

Amit, Raphael, and Christoph Zott. "The Fit Between Product Market Strategy and Business Model: Implications for Firm Performance." *Strategic Management Journal* 29, no. 1 (January 2008): 1.

Cannella, Albert A., Jr., Ho-Uk Lee, and Jong-Hun Park. "Top Management Team Functional Background Diversity and Firm Performance: Examining the Roles of Team Member Relocation and Environmental Uncertainty." *The Academy of Management Journal* 51, no. 4 (August 2008): 768.

Gandossy, Robert, and Robin Guarnieri. "Can You Measure Leadership?" *MIT Sloan Management Review* 50, no. 1 (Fall 2008): 65.

Favaro, Ken, Tim Romberger, and David Meer. "Five Rules for Retailing in a Recession." *Harvard Business Review* (April 2009): 64–73.

Fine, Leslie. "The Bottom Line: Marketing and Firm Performance." *Business Horizons* (May–June 2009): 209–214.

Garnier, Jean-Pierre. "Rebuilding the R&D Engine in Big Pharma." *Harvard Business Review* (May 2008): 68.

Montgomery, Cynthia A. "Putting Leadership Back into Strategy." *Harvard Business Review* (January 2008): 54.

Noble, Charles H., and Rajiv K. Sinha. "The Adoption of Radical Manufacturing Technologies and Firm Survival." *Strategic Management Journal* 29, no. 9 (September 2008): 943.

Sims, Henry Jr., Samer Faraj, and Seokhwa Yun. "When Should a Leader Be Directive or Empowering? How to Develop Your Own Situational Theory of Leadership." *Business Horizons* (March–April 2009): 105–108.

Quelch, John A., and Katherine E. Jocz. "How to Market in a Downturn." *Harvard Business Review* (April 2009): 52–63.

Wind, Yoram (Jerry). "A Plan to Invent the Marketing We Need Today." *MIT Sloan Management Review* 49, no. 4 (Summer 2008): 21.

ASSURANCE OF LEARNING EXERCISES

Assurance of Learning Exercise 4A

Performing a Financial Ratio Analysis for McDonald's Corporation (MCD)

Purpose

Financial ratio analysis is one of the best techniques for identifying and evaluating internal strengths and weaknesses. Potential investors and current shareholders look closely at firms' financial ratios, making detailed comparisons to industry averages and to previous periods of time. Financial ratio analyses provide vital input information for developing an IFE Matrix.

Instructions

Step 1   On a separate sheet of paper, number from 1 to 20. Referring to McDonald's income statement and balance sheet (pp. 31–32), calculate 20 financial ratios for 2008 for the company. Use Table 4-7 as a reference.

Step 2   In a second column, indicate whether you consider each ratio to be a strength, a weakness, or a neutral factor for McDonald's.

Step 3   Go to the Web sites in Table 4-6 that calculate McDonald's financial ratios, without your having to pay a subscription (fee) for the service. Make a copy of the ratio information provided and record the source. Report this research to your classmates and your professor.

Assurance of Learning Exercise 4B

Constructing an IFE Matrix for McDonald's Corporation

Purpose

This exercise will give you experience in developing an IFE Matrix. Identifying and prioritizing factors to include in an IFE Matrix fosters communication among functional and divisional managers. Preparing an IFE Matrix allows human resource, marketing, production/operations, finance/accounting, R&D, and management information systems managers to articulate their concerns and thoughts regarding the business condition of the firm. This results in an improved collective understanding of the business.

Instructions

Step 1   Join with two other individuals to form a three-person team. Develop a team IFE Matrix for McDonald's.

Step 2   Compare your team's IFE Matrix to other teams' IFE Matrices. Discuss any major differences.

Step 3   What strategies do you think would allow McDonald's to capitalize on its major strengths? What strategies would allow McDonald's to improve upon its major weaknesses?

Assurance of Learning Exercise 4C

Constructing an IFE Matrix for My University

Purpose

This exercise gives you the opportunity to evaluate your university's major strengths and weaknesses. As will become clearer in the next chapter, an organization's strategies are largely based upon striving to take advantage of strengths and improving upon weaknesses.

Instructions

Step 1   Join with two other individuals to form a three-person team. Develop a team IFE Matrix for your university. You may use the strengths/weaknesses determined in Assurance of Learning Exercise 1D.

Step 2   Go to the board and diagram your team's IFE Matrix.

Step 3   Compare your team's IFE Matrix to other teams' IFE Matrices. Discuss any major differences.

Step 4   What strategies do you think would allow your university to capitalize on its major strengths? What strategies would allow your university to improve upon its major weaknesses?

CHAPTER 5
Strategies in Action

Assurance of Learning Exercises

Source: Shutterstock/Photosito

"Notable Quotes"

"Alice said, 'Would you please tell me which way to go from here?' The cat said, 'That depends on where you want to get to.' "

—Lewis Carroll

"Tomorrow always arrives. It is always different. And even the mightiest company is in trouble if it has not worked on the future. Being surprised by what happens is a risk that even the largest and richest company cannot afford, and even the smallest business need not run."

—Peter Drucker

"Planning. Doing things today to make us better tomorrow. Because the future belongs to those who make the hard decisions today."

—Eaton Corporation

"One big problem with American business is that when it gets into trouble, it redoubles its effort. It's like digging for gold. If you dig down twenty feet and haven't found it, one of the strategies you could use is to dig twice as deep. But if the gold is twenty feet to the side, you could dig a long time and not find it."

—Edward De Bono

"Even if you're on the right track, you'll get run over if you just sit there."

—Will Rogers

"Strategies for taking the hill won't necessarily hold it."
—Amar Bhide

"The early bird may get the worm, but the second mouse gets the cheese."

—Unknown

Assurance of Learning Exercise 5E
Developing Alternative Strategies for My University

Assurance of Learning Exercise 5F
Lessons in Doing Business Globally

Hundreds of companies today, including Sears, IBM, Searle, and Hewlett-Packard, have embraced strategic planning fully in their quest for higher revenues and profits. Kent Nelson, former chair of UPS, explains why his company has created a new strategic-planning department: "Because we're making bigger bets on investments in technology, we can't afford to spend a whole lot of money in one direction and then find out five years later it was the wrong direction."[1]

This chapter brings strategic management to life with many contemporary examples. Sixteen types of strategies are defined and exemplified, including Michael Porter's generic strategies: cost leadership, differentiation, and focus. Guidelines are presented for determining when it is most appropriate to pursue different types of strategies. An overview of strategic management in nonprofit organizations, governmental agencies, and small firms is provided.

Doing Great in a Weak Economy. How?

Volkswagen AG

While most automobile companies talk about bankruptcy, merger, collapse, and liquidation, Volkswagen AG is posting solid earnings. Based in Wolfsburg, Germany, and Europe's biggest automaker by sales, Volkswagen (VW) managed the global economic recession well by focusing on emerging markets such as China and Brazil and continually reducing costs. VW is the leading auto firm in China, not Toyota or Nissan. VW's market share in Western Europe rose to 20 percent in 2009 from 17.9 percent a year ago. While shrinking demand for new cars in major markets and high raw-material costs, and unfavorable exchange rates have reduced earnings of most European automakers, VW anticipated these conditions through excellent strategic planning and continues to take market share from rival firms worldwide.

The German truck maker and engineering company MAN AG is VW's largest single shareholder at 30 percent, and its business too has been good. MAN's third quarter of 2008 saw profit jump 34 percent, lifted by strong sales of trucks, diesel engines, and turbo machinery. VW is currently spending $1 billion to build a new plant in Chattanooga, Tennessee, for the production of a midsize sedan in 2011 with initial capacity of 150,000 cars annually. VW's plans for 2018 include increasing its U.S. market share from 2 percent to 6 percent by selling 800,000 vehicles annually in the United States. By 2018, VW also plans to export

125,000 vehicles from North America to Europe. VW's plans include large expansions at its Puebla, Mexico, plant.

While most auto companies are cutting expenses, VW is increasing is 2009 U.S. marketing budget by 15 percent in its Audi AG luxury division. The Audi ads even ran during the 2009 Super Bowl.

For all of 2008, VW's net profit rose 15 percent to 4.75 billion euros and revenues rose 4.5 percent to 114 billion. VW expects flat or even slight declines in 2009 but some of its competitors are incurring billion dollar losses.

VW has cars named for climate patterns, insects, and small mammals. Along with the New Beetle, VW's annual production of 6 million cars, trucks, and vans includes such models such as Passat (trade wind), Jetta (jet stream), Rabbit, and Fox. VW also owns several luxury carmakers, including AUDI, Lamborghini, Bentley, and Bugatti. Other VW makes include SEAT (family cars, Spain) and SKODA (family cars, the Czech Republic). VW operates plants in Africa, the Americas, Asia/Pacific, and Europe. VW holds 68 percent of the voting rights in Swedish truck maker Scania and about 30 percent of MAN AG. VW also offers consumer financing.

VW is acquiring Porsche Automobil Holding SE and merging their auto brands into VW. Based in Stuttgart, Germany, Porsche already owns 51 percent of VW but has weakened in 2009 after taking on $12 billion in new debt.

VW is in talks with China's BYD Co. to build hybrid and electric vehicles powered by lithium batteries. Based in Shenzhen, BYD will supply VW with the battery technology. This will be the first automotive partner for BYD, which is one of the world's largest suppliers of cell phone batteries.

VW is building a new assembly plant in Indonesia for $47 million about 1 hour east of Jakarta, the capital. This plant will assemble the Touran and employ about 3,000 persons. Toyota already has a manufacturing plant in Indonesia and dominates that market. Currently many VW vehicles are imported into Indonesia, thus being subject to a 200 percent tariff.

VW reported 2nd quarter 2009 earnings of $397 million; the Audi division was the biggest contributor to the gains.

Source: Based on Christoph Rauwald, "VW Earnings Buck Auto-Industry Trend," *Wall Street Journal* (October 31, 2008): B3; Christoph Rauwald, "Volkswagen to Raise Output by 2018," *Wall Street Journal* (April 28, 2009): B3.

Long-Term Objectives

Long-term objectives represent the results expected from pursuing certain strategies. Strategies represent the actions to be taken to accomplish long-term objectives. The time frame for objectives and strategies should be consistent, usually from two to five years.

The Nature of Long-Term Objectives

Objectives should be quantitative, measurable, realistic, understandable, challenging, hierarchical, obtainable, and congruent among organizational units. Each objective should also be associated with a timeline. Objectives are commonly stated in terms such as growth in assets, growth in sales, profitability, market share, degree and nature of diversification, degree and nature of vertical integration, earnings per share, and social responsibility. Clearly established objectives offer many benefits. They provide direction, allow synergy, aid in evaluation, establish priorities, reduce uncertainty, minimize conflicts, stimulate exertion, and aid in both the allocation of resources and the design of jobs. Objectives provide a basis for consistent decision making by managers whose values and attitudes differ. Objectives serve as standards by which individuals, groups, departments, divisions, and entire organizations can be evaluated.

Long-term objectives are needed at the corporate, divisional, and functional levels of an organization. They are an important measure of managerial performance. Many practitioners and academicians attribute a significant part of U.S. industry's competitive decline to the short-term, rather than long-, strategy orientation of managers in the United States. Arthur D. Little argues that bonuses or merit pay for managers today must be based to a greater extent on long-term objectives and strategies. A general framework for relating objectives to performance evaluation is provided in Table 5-1. A particular organization could tailor these guidelines to meet its own needs, but incentives should be attached to both long-term and annual objectives.

Without long-term objectives, an organization would drift aimlessly toward some unknown end. It is hard to imagine an organization or individual being successful without clear objectives (see Tables 5-2 and 5-3). Success only rarely occurs by accident; rather, it is the result of hard work directed toward achieving certain objectives.

TABLE 5-1   Varying Performance Measures by Organizational Level

Organizational Level	Basis for Annual Bonus or Merit Pay
Corporate	75% based on long-term objectives
	25% based on annual objectives
Division	50% based on long-term objectives
	50% based on annual objectives
Function	25% based on long-term objectives
	75% based on annual objectives

TABLE 5-2   The Desired Characteristics of Objectives

1. Quantitative
2. Measurable
3. Realistic
4. Understandable
5. Challenging
6. Hierarchical
7. Obtainable
8. Congruent across departments

TABLE 5-3   The Benefits of Having Clear Objectives

1. Provide direction by revealing expectations
2. Allow synergy
3. Aid in evaluation by serving as standards
4. Establish priorities
5. Reduce uncertainty
6. Minimize conflicts
7. Stimulate exertion
8. Aid in allocation of resources
9. Aid in design of jobs
10. Provide basis for consistent decision making

Financial versus Strategic Objectives

Two types of objectives are especially common in organizations: financial and strategic objectives. Financial objectives include those associated with growth in revenues, growth in earnings, higher dividends, larger profit margins, greater return on investment, higher earnings per share, a rising stock price, improved cash flow, and so on; while strategic objectives include things such as a larger market share, quicker on-time delivery than rivals, shorter design-to-market times than rivals, lower costs than rivals, higher product quality than rivals, wider geographic coverage than rivals, achieving technological leadership, consistently getting new or improved products to market ahead of rivals, and so on.

Although financial objectives are especially important in firms, oftentimes there is a trade-off between financial and strategic objectives such that crucial decisions have to be made. For example, a firm can do certain things to maximize short-term financial objectives that would harm long-term strategic objectives. To improve financial position in the short run through higher prices may, for example, jeopardize long-term market share. The dangers associated with trading off long-term strategic objectives with near-term bottom-line performance are especially severe if competitors relentlessly pursue increased market share at the expense of short-term profitability. And there are other trade-offs between financial and strategic objectives, related to riskiness of actions, concern for business ethics, need to preserve the natural environment, and social responsibility issues. Both financial and strategic objectives should include both annual and long-term performance targets. Ultimately, the best way to sustain competitive advantage over the long run is to relentlessly pursue strategic objectives that strengthen a firm's business position over rivals. Financial objectives can best be met by focusing first and foremost on achievement of strategic objectives that improve a firm's competitiveness and market strength.

Not Managing by Objectives

An unidentified educator once said, "If you think education is expensive, try ignorance." The idea behind this saying also applies to establishing objectives. Strategists should avoid the following alternative ways to "not managing by objectives."

- *Managing by Extrapolation*—adheres to the principle "If it ain't broke, don't fix it." The idea is to keep on doing about the same things in the same ways because things are going well.
- *Managing by Crisis*—based on the belief that the true measure of a really good strategist is the ability to solve problems. Because there are plenty of crises and problems to go around for every person and every organization, strategists ought to bring their time and creative energy to bear on solving the most pressing problems of the day. Managing by crisis is actually a form of reacting rather than acting and of letting events dictate the what and when of management decisions.
- *Managing by Subjectives*—built on the idea that there is no general plan for which way to go and what to do; just do the best you can to accomplish what you think should be done. In short, "Do your own thing, the best way you know how" (sometimes referred to as *the mystery approach to decision making* because subordinates are left to figure out what is happening and why).
- *Managing by Hope*—based on the fact that the future is laden with great uncertainty and that if we try and do not succeed, then we hope our second (or third) attempt will succeed. Decisions are predicated on the hope that they will work and the good times are just around the corner, especially if luck and good fortune are on our side![2]

The Balanced Scorecard

Developed in 1993 by Harvard Business School professors Robert Kaplan and David Norton, and refined continually through today, the Balanced Scorecard is a strategy evaluation and control technique.[3] *Balanced Scorecard* derives its name from the perceived need of firms to "balance" financial measures that are oftentimes used exclusively in strategy evaluation and control with nonfinancial measures such as product quality and customer service. An effective Balanced Scorecard contains a carefully chosen combination of strategic and financial objectives tailored to the company's business. As a tool to manage and evaluate strategy, the Balanced Scorecard is currently in use at Sears, United Parcel Service, 3M Corporation, Heinz, and hundreds of other firms. For example, 3M Corporation has a financial objective to achieve annual growth in earnings per share of 10 percent or better, as well as a strategic objective to have at least 30 percent of sales come from products introduced in the past four years. The overall aim of the Balanced Scorecard is to "balance" shareholder objectives with customer and operational objectives. Obviously, these sets of objectives interrelate and many even conflict. For example, customers want low price and high service, which may conflict with shareholders' desire for a high return on their investment. The Balanced Scorecard concept is consistent with the notions of continuous improvement in management (CIM) and total quality management (TQM).

Although the Balanced Scorecard concept is covered in more detail in Chapter 9 as it relates to evaluating strategies, note here that firms should establish objectives and evaluate strategies on items other than financial measures. This is the basic tenet of the Balanced Scorecard. Financial measures and ratios are vitally important. However, of equal importance are factors such as customer service, employee morale, product quality, pollution abatement, business ethics, social responsibility, community involvement, and other such items. In conjunction with financial measures, these "softer" factors comprise an integral part of both the objective-setting process and the strategy-evaluation process. These factors can vary by organization, but such items, along with financial measures, comprise the essence of a Balanced Scorecard. A Balanced Scorecard for a firm is simply a listing of all key objectives to work toward, along with an associated time dimension of when each objective is to be accomplished, as well as a primary responsibility or contact person, department, or division for each objective.

Types of Strategies

The model illustrated in Figure 5-1 provides a conceptual basis for applying strategic management. Defined and exemplified in Table 5-4, alternative strategies that an enterprise could pursue can be categorized into 11 actions: forward integration, backward

FIGURE 5-1

A Comprehensive Strategic-Management Model

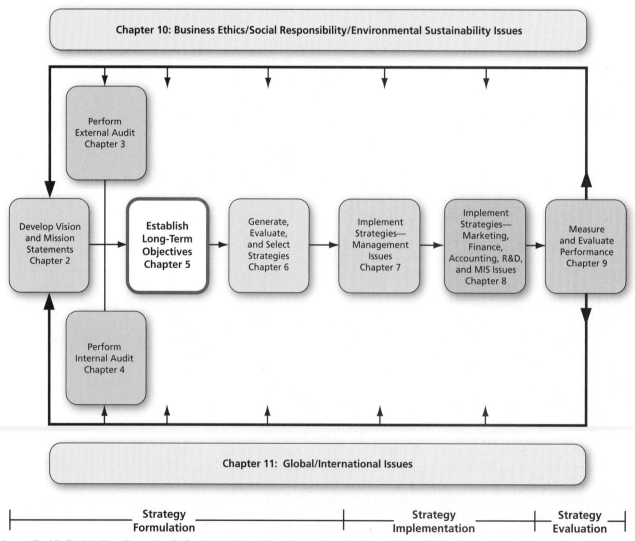

Source: Fred R. David, "How Companies Define Their Mission," *Long Range Planning* 22, no. 3 (June 1988): 40.

TABLE 5-4   Alternative Strategies Defined and Exemplified

Strategy	Definition	2009 Examples
Forward Integration	Gaining ownership or increased control over distributors or retailers	PepsiCo launched a hostile takeover of Pepsi Bottling Group after its $4.2 billion offer was rejected
Backward Integration	Seeking ownership or increased control of a firm's suppliers	Chinese carmaker Geely Automobile Holdings Ltd. purchased Australian car-parts maker Drivetrain Systems International Pty. Ltd.
Horizontal Integration	Seeking ownership or increased control over competitors	Pfizer acquires Wyeth; both are huge drug companies
Market Penetration	Seeking increased market share for present products or services in present markets through greater marketing efforts	Coke spending millions on its new slogan "Open Happiness"
Market Development	Introducing present products or services into new geographic area	Time Warner purchased 31 percent of Central European Media Enterprises Ltd. in order to expand into Romania, Czech Republic, Ukraine, and Bulgaria
Product Development	Seeking increased sales by improving present products or services or developing new ones	News Corp.'s book publisher HarperCollins began producing audio books for download, such as Jeff Jarvis's "What Would Google Do?"
Related Diversification	Adding new but related products or services	Sprint Nextel Corp. diversified from the cell phone business by partnering with Garmin Ltd. to deliver wireless Internet services into GPS machines
Unrelated Diversification	Adding new, unrelated products or services	Cisco Systems Inc. entered the camcorder business by acquiring Pure Digital Technology
Retrenchment	Regrouping through cost and asset reduction to reverse declining sales and profit	The world's largest steelmaker, ArcelorMittal, shut down half of its plants and laid off thousands of employees even amid worker protests worldwide
Divestiture	Selling a division or part of an organization	The British airport firm BAA Ltd. divested three UK airports
Liquidation	Selling all of a company's assets, in parts, for their tangible worth	Michigan newspapers such as the *Ann Arbor News, Detroit Free Press,* and *Detroit News* liquidated hard-copy operations

integration, horizontal integration, market penetration, market development, product development, related diversification, unrelated diversification, retrenchment, divestiture, and liquidation. Each alternative strategy has countless variations. For example, market penetration can include adding salespersons, increasing advertising expenditures, couponing, and using similar actions to increase market share in a given geographic area.

Many, if not most, organizations simultaneously pursue a combination of two or more strategies, but a *combination strategy* can be exceptionally risky if carried too far. No organization can afford to pursue all the strategies that might benefit the firm. Difficult decisions must be made. Priority must be established. Organizations, like individuals, have limited resources. Both organizations and individuals must choose among alternative strategies and avoid excessive indebtedness.

Hansen and Smith explain that strategic planning involves "choices that risk resources" and "trade-offs that sacrifice opportunity." In other words, if you have a strategy to go north, then you must buy snowshoes and warm jackets (spend resources) and forgo the opportunity of "faster population growth in southern states." You cannot have a strategy to go north and then take a step east, south, or west "just to be on the safe side." Firms spend resources and focus on a finite number of opportunities in pursuing strategies to achieve an uncertain outcome in the future. Strategic planning is much more than a roll of the dice; it is a wager based on predictions and hypotheses that are continually tested and refined by knowledge, research, experience, and learning. Survival of the firm itself may hinge on your strategic plan.[4]

Organizations cannot do too many things well because resources and talents get spread thin and competitors gain advantage. In large diversified companies, a combination strategy is commonly employed when different divisions pursue different strategies. Also, organizations struggling to survive may simultaneously employ a combination of several defensive strategies, such as divestiture, liquidation, and retrenchment.

Levels of Strategies

Strategy making is not just a task for top executives. As discussed in Chapter 1, middle- and lower-level managers too must be involved in the strategic-planning process to the extent possible. In large firms, there are actually four levels of strategies: corporate, divisional, functional, and operational—as illustrated in Figure 5-2. However, in small firms, there are actually three levels of strategies: company, functional, and operational.

In large firms, the persons primarily responsible for having effective strategies at the various levels include the CEO at the corporate level; the president or executive vice president at the divisional level; the respective chief finance officer (CFO), chief information officer (CIO), human resource manager (HRM), chief marketing officer (CMO), and so on, at the functional level; and the plant manager, regional sales manager, and so on, at the operational level. In small firms, the persons primarily responsible for having effective strategies at the various levels include the business owner or president at the company level and then the same range of persons at the lower two levels, as with a large firm.

It is important to note that all persons responsible for strategic planning at the various levels ideally participate and understand the strategies at the other organizational levels to help ensure coordination, facilitation, and commitment while avoiding inconsistency, inefficiency, and miscommunication. Plant managers, for example, need to understand and be supportive of the overall corporate strategic plan (game plan) while the president and the CEO need to be knowledgeable of strategies being employed in various sales territories and manufacturing plants.

FIGURE 5-2

Levels of Strategies with Persons Most Responsible

Large Company

Small Company

Integration Strategies

Forward integration, backward integration, and horizontal integration are sometimes collectively referred to as *vertical integration* strategies. Vertical integration strategies allow a firm to gain control over distributors, suppliers, and/or competitors.

Forward Integration

Forward integration involves gaining ownership or increased control over distributors or retailers. Increasing numbers of manufacturers (suppliers) today are pursuing a forward integration strategy by establishing Web sites to directly sell products to consumers. This strategy is causing turmoil in some industries. For example, Microsoft is opening its own retail stores, a forward integration strategy similar to rival Apple Inc., which currently has more than 200 stores around the world. Microsoft wants to learn firsthand about what consumers want and how they buy. CompUSA Inc. recently closed most of its retail stores, and neither Hewlett-Packard nor IBM have retail stores. Some Microsoft shareholders are concerned that the company's plans to open stores will irk existing retail partners such as Best Buy.

Automobile dealers have for many years pursued forward integration, perhaps too much. Ford has almost 4,000 dealers compared to Toyota, which has fewer than 2,000 U.S. dealers. That means the average Toyota dealer sold, for example, 1,628 vehicles in 2007 compared to 236 vehicles for Ford dealers. GM, Ford, and Chrysler are all reducing their number of dealers dramatically.

The Canadian company Research in Motion (RIM) opened its first online store for BlackBerry applications in April 2009. RIM is looking to tap a market for software made popular by Apple and its iPhone. BlackBerry users can download the new RIM storefront from the main RIM Web site, but then they need to buy applications using PayPal.

An effective means of implementing forward integration is *franchising*. Approximately 2,000 companies in about 50 different industries in the United States use franchising to distribute their products or services. Businesses can expand rapidly by franchising because costs and opportunities are spread among many individuals. Total sales by franchises in the United States are annually about $1 trillion.

In today's credit crunch reduced availability of financing, franchiser firms are more and more breaking tradition and helping franchisees out with liquidity needs. For example, RE/MAX International will finance 50 percent of its initial $25,000 franchise fee. Coverall Cleaning Concepts lends up to $6,800 of its initial franchise fee. Persons interested in becoming franchisees should go onto franchising blogs, such as Bleu MauMau, Franchise-Chat, Franchise Pundit, Rush On Business, Unhappy Franchisee, and WikidFranchise.org. These sites offer inside news, advice, and comments by people already owning franchise businesses.

However, a growing trend is for franchisees, who for example may operate 10 franchised restaurants, stores, or whatever, to buy out their part of the business from their franchiser (corporate owner). There is a growing rift between franchisees and franchisers as the segment often outperforms the parent. For example, McDonald's today owns less than 23 percent of its 32,000 restaurants, down from 26 percent in 2006. Restaurant chains are increasingly being pressured to own fewer of their locations. McDonald's sold 1,600 of its Latin America and Caribbean restaurants to Woods Staton, a former McDonald's executive. Companies such as McDonald's are using proceeds from the sale of company stores/restaurants to franchisees to buy back company stock, pay higher dividends, and make other investments to benefit shareholders.

These six guidelines indicate when forward integration may be an especially effective strategy:[5]

- When an organization's present distributors are especially expensive, or unreliable, or incapable of meeting the firm's distribution needs.
- When the availability of quality distributors is so limited as to offer a competitive advantage to those firms that integrate forward.
- When an organization competes in an industry that is growing and is expected to continue to grow markedly; this is a factor because forward integration reduces an organization's ability to diversify if its basic industry falters.

- When an organization has both the capital and human resources needed to manage the new business of distributing its own products.
- When the advantages of stable production are particularly high; this is a consideration because an organization can increase the predictability of the demand for its output through forward integration.
- When present distributors or retailers have high profit margins; this situation suggests that a company profitably could distribute its own products and price them more competitively by integrating forward.

Backward Integration

Both manufacturers and retailers purchase needed materials from suppliers. *Backward integration* is a strategy of seeking ownership or increased control of a firm's suppliers. This strategy can be especially appropriate when a firm's current suppliers are unreliable, too costly, or cannot meet the firm's needs.

When you buy a box of Pampers diapers at Wal-Mart, a scanner at the store's checkout counter instantly zaps an order to Procter & Gamble Company. In contrast, in most hospitals, reordering supplies is a logistical nightmare. Inefficiency caused by lack of control of suppliers in the health-care industry, however, is rapidly changing as many giant health-care purchasers, such as the U.S. Defense Department and Columbia/HCA Healthcare Corporation, move to require electronic bar codes on every supply item purchased. This allows instant tracking and recording without invoices and paperwork. Of the estimated $83 billion spent annually on hospital supplies, industry reports indicate that $11 billion can be eliminated through more effective backward integration.

In a major strategic shift to design its own computer chips, Apple Inc. in 2009 began a backward integration strategy to shield Apple technology from rival firms. Apple envisions soon to produce its own internally developed chips for its iPhone and iPod Touch devices. Online job postings from Apple describe dozens of chip-related positions. Apple's new strategy also is aimed at sharing fewer details about Apple technology plans with external chip suppliers. This new backward integration strategy marks a break from a long-term trend among most big electronics companies to outsource the development of chips and other components to external suppliers.

Some industries in the United States, such as the automotive and aluminum industries, are reducing their historical pursuit of backward integration. Instead of owning their suppliers, companies negotiate with several outside suppliers. Ford and Chrysler buy over half of their component parts from outside suppliers such as TRW, Eaton, General Electric, and Johnson Controls. *De-integration* makes sense in industries that have global sources of supply. Companies today shop around, play one seller against another, and go with the best deal. Global competition is also spurring firms to reduce their number of suppliers and to demand higher levels of service and quality from those they keep. Although traditionally relying on many suppliers to ensure uninterrupted supplies and low prices, American firms now are following the lead of Japanese firms, which have far fewer suppliers and closer, long-term relationships with those few. "Keeping track of so many suppliers is onerous," says Mark Shimelonis, formerly of Xerox.

Seven guidelines for when backward integration may be an especially effective strategy are:[6]

- When an organization's present suppliers are especially expensive, or unreliable, or incapable of meeting the firm's needs for parts, components, assemblies, or raw materials.
- When the number of suppliers is small and the number of competitors is large.
- When an organization competes in an industry that is growing rapidly; this is a factor because integrative-type strategies (forward, backward, and horizontal) reduce an organization's ability to diversify in a declining industry.
- When an organization has both capital and human resources to manage the new business of supplying its own raw materials.

- When the advantages of stable prices are particularly important; this is a factor because an organization can stabilize the cost of its raw materials and the associated price of its product(s) through backward integration.
- When present supplies have high profit margins, which suggests that the business of supplying products or services in the given industry is a worthwhile venture.
- When an organization needs to quickly acquire a needed resource.

Horizontal Integration

Horizontal integration refers to a strategy of seeking ownership of or increased control over a firm's competitors. One of the most significant trends in strategic management today is the increased use of horizontal integration as a growth strategy. Mergers, acquisitions, and takeovers among competitors allow for increased economies of scale and enhanced transfer of resources and competencies. Kenneth Davidson makes the following observation about horizontal integration:

> The trend towards horizontal integration seems to reflect strategists' misgivings about their ability to operate many unrelated businesses. Mergers between direct competitors are more likely to create efficiencies than mergers between unrelated businesses, both because there is a greater potential for eliminating duplicate facilities and because the management of the acquiring firm is more likely to understand the business of the target.[7]

These five guidelines indicate when horizontal integration may be an especially effective strategy:[8]

- When an organization can gain monopolistic characteristics in a particular area or region without being challenged by the federal government for "tending substantially" to reduce competition.
- When an organization competes in a growing industry.
- When increased economies of scale provide major competitive advantages.
- When an organization has both the capital and human talent needed to successfully manage an expanded organization.
- When competitors are faltering due to a lack of managerial expertise or a need for particular resources that an organization possesses; note that horizontal integration would not be appropriate if competitors are doing poorly, because in that case overall industry sales are declining.

Intensive Strategies

Market penetration, market development, and product development are sometimes referred to as *intensive strategies* because they require intensive efforts if a firm's competitive position with existing products is to improve.

Market Penetration

A *market penetration* strategy seeks to increase market share for present products or services in present markets through greater marketing efforts. This strategy is widely used alone and in combination with other strategies. Market penetration includes increasing the number of salespersons, increasing advertising expenditures, offering extensive sales promotion items, or increasing publicity efforts. As indicated in Table 5-4, Coke in 2009/2010 spent millions on its new advertising slogan, "Open Happiness," which replaced "The Coke Side of Life."

These five guidelines indicate when market penetration may be an especially effective strategy:[9]

- When current markets are not saturated with a particular product or service.
- When the usage rate of present customers could be increased significantly.

- When the market shares of major competitors have been declining while total industry sales have been increasing.
- When the correlation between dollar sales and dollar marketing expenditures historically has been high.
- When increased economies of scale provide major competitive advantages.

Market Development

Market development involves introducing present products or services into new geographic areas. For example, Retailers such as Wal-Mart Stores, Carrefour SA, and Tesco PLC are expanding further into China in 2009/2010 even in a world of slumping sales. Tesco is opening fewer stores in Britain to divert capital expenditures to China. French hypermarket chain Carrefour is opening 28 stores in China in 2009, up from 22 in 2008. Wal-Mart opened 30 stores in China in 2008 and plans to nearly double that number in 2009. Wal-Mart had roughly 250 stores in China at year-end 2009. Housing goods giant Ikea plans to build two more stores in China in 2009 to have eight stores total. All of these market development strategies come in the face of a slowing Chinese economy and faltering consumer confidence among Chinese consumers.

Delta Air Lines in 2009 began serving 15 new international destinations as part of a strategy by the Atlanta-based carrier to derive more traffic from international routes. This market development strategy is being implemented largely by deploying its recently acquired Northwest Airlines big jets from unprofitable domestic routes to global routes, especially into Asia, where Delta previously had only a few routes.

PepsiCo Inc. is spending $1 billion in China from 2009 to 2012 to build more plants, specifically in western and interior areas of China. Also in China, PepsiCo is developing products tailored to Chinese consumers, building a larger sales force, and expanding research and development efforts. China is Pepsi's second-largest beverage market by volume, behind the United States. Pepsi owns Lay's potato chips and in China sells the chips with Beijing duck flavor. Pepsi has 41 percent share of the potato chip market in China. Pepsi's new market development strategy is aimed primarily at rival Coke, which dominates Pepsi in the carbonated-soft-drink sector in China; Coke has a 51.9 percent share of the market to Pepsi's 32.6 percent.

Yum! Brands Inc., the parent company of Pizza Hut, KFC, and Taco Bell, recently said it would open 500 new KFC restaurants in China in 2009. In addition to these stores, Yum Brands is opening 900 other restaurants outside the United States in 2009. Yum Brands' most profitable brand has been Taco Bell, so the company plans to open these restaurants in both Spain and India in 2009. Taco Bell's target market is young consumers ages 16 to 24. The company's new strategic plan includes selling many if not most of its stores worldwide to existing franchisees or new investors.

These six guidelines indicate when market development may be an especially effective strategy:[10]

- When new channels of distribution are available that are reliable, inexpensive, and of good quality.
- When an organization is very successful at what it does.
- When new untapped or unsaturated markets exist.
- When an organization has the needed capital and human resources to manage expanded operations.
- When an organization has excess production capacity.
- When an organization's basic industry is rapidly becoming global in scope.

Product Development

Product development is a strategy that seeks increased sales by improving or modifying present products or services. Product development usually entails large research and development expenditures. Google's new Chrome OS operating system illuminates years of monies spent on product development. Google expects Chrome OS to overtake Microsoft Windows by 2015.

These five guidelines indicate when product development may be an especially effective strategy to pursue:[11]

- When an organization has successful products that are in the maturity stage of the product life cycle; the idea here is to attract satisfied customers to try new (improved) products as a result of their positive experience with the organization's present products or services.
- When an organization competes in an industry that is characterized by rapid technological developments.
- When major competitors offer better-quality products at comparable prices.
- When an organization competes in a high-growth industry.
- When an organization has especially strong research and development capabilities.

Diversification Strategies

There are two general types of *diversification strategies*: related and unrelated. Businesses are said to be *related* when their value chains posses competitively valuable cross-business strategic fits; businesses are said to be *unrelated* when their value chains are so dissimilar that no competitively valuable cross-business relationships exist.[12] Most companies favor related diversification strategies in order to capitalize on synergies as follows:

- Transferring competitively valuable expertise, technological know-how, or other capabilities from one business to another.
- Combining the related activities of separate businesses into a single operation to achieve lower costs.
- Exploiting common use of a well-known brand name.
- Cross-business collaboration to create competitively valuable resource strengths and capabilities.[13]

Diversification strategies are becoming less popular as organizations are finding it more difficult to manage diverse business activities. In the 1960s and 1970s, the trend was to diversify so as not to be dependent on any single industry, but the 1980s saw a general reversal of that thinking. Diversification is now on the retreat. Michael Porter, of the Harvard Business School, says, "Management found it couldn't manage the beast." Hence businesses are selling, or closing, less profitable divisions to focus on core businesses.

The greatest risk of being in a single industry is having all of the firm's eggs in one basket. Although many firms are successful operating in a single industry, new technologies, new products, or fast-shifting buyer preferences can decimate a particular business. For example, digital cameras are decimating the film and film processing industry, and cell phones have permanently altered the long-distance telephone calling industry.

Diversification must do more than simply spread business risk across different industries, however, because shareholders could accomplish this by simply purchasing equity in different firms across different industries or by investing in mutual funds. Diversification makes sense only to the extent the strategy adds more to shareholder value than what shareholders could accomplish acting individually. Thus, the chosen industry for diversification must be attractive enough to yield consistently high returns on investment and offer potential across the operating divisions for synergies greater than those entities could achieve alone.

A few companies today, however, pride themselves on being conglomerates, from small firms such as Pentair Inc., and Blount International to huge companies such as Textron, Allied Signal, Emerson Electric, General Electric, Viacom, and Samsung. Conglomerates prove that focus and diversity are not always mutually exclusive.

Many strategists contend that firms should "stick to the knitting" and not stray too far from the firms' basic areas of competence. However, diversification is still sometimes an appropriate strategy, especially when the company is competing in an unattractive industry. For example, United Technologies is diversifying away from its core aviation business due to the slumping airline industry. United Technologies now owns British electronic-security company Chubb PLC, as well as Otis Elevator Company and Carrier air conditioning to reduce its dependence on the volatile airline industry. United Technologies also owns UTC Fire & Security, Pratt & Whitney, Hamilton Sundstrand, and Sikorsky Black Hawk Helicopters. However, almost of all of the company's divisions expect a drop in sales in 2009, and so the firm is laying off thousands of employees. Only the Sikorsky division is expected to be profitable in 2009.

Hamish Maxwell, Philip Morris's former CEO, says, "We want to become a consumer-products company." Diversification makes sense for Philip Morris because cigarette consumption is declining, product liability suits are a risk, and some investors reject tobacco stocks on principle.

Related Diversification

Google's stated strategy is to organize all the world's information into searchable form, diversifying the firm beyond its roots as a Web search engine that sells advertising. The maker of jam, peanut butter, and Crisco oils, J. M. Smuckers Co. recently completed the acquisition of Procter & Gamble's Folger's coffee business for $2.65 billion, which nearly doubled Smuckers's annual sales. Smuckers continues to strive to acquire related food and consumer brand businesses as it pursues related diversification.

When Merck & Co. acquired rival Schering-Plough Corp for $41.1 billion in 2009, that acquisition brought to Merck three new, related businesses. The three new areas of business are biotech, consumer health, and animal health. In addition, the acquisition brought to Merck an expanded presence in Brazil, China, and other emerging markets.

Based in Baltimore, the sports apparel maker Under Armour pursued related diversification in 2009 when it introduced athletic "running" shoes for the first time. This strategy broadened Under Armour's appeal from boys and young men to women, older consumers, and more casual athletes. The athletic footwear business is dominated by Nike and Adidas, but Under Armour uses sophisticated design software, new manufacturing techniques, the latest in material engineering, and robust information technology systems to produce all its products. Under Armour's 2009 sales are expected to increase 20 percent to $900 million.

In a related diversification move in 2009, Tyson Foods entered the dog food business, selling refrigerated pet food targeted to consumers who give their pets everything from clothes and car seats to cemetery graves. Prior to this move by Tyson, meatpacking companies has been content to sell scraps such as chicken fat and by-products to makers of canned and dry pet food. Scott Morris of Freshpet Company in Secaucus, New Jersey, says this move by Tyson will change the fact that "pet food today looks the same as it did 30 years ago."

Six guidelines for when related diversification may be an effective strategy are as follows.[14]

- When an organization competes in a no-growth or a slow-growth industry.
- When adding new, but related, products would significantly enhance the sales of current products.
- When new, but related, products could be offered at highly competitive prices.
- When new, but related, products have seasonal sales levels that counterbalance an organization's existing peaks and valleys.
- When an organization's products are currently in the declining stage of the product's life cycle.
- When an organization has a strong management team.

Unrelated Diversification

An unrelated diversification strategy favors capitalizing on a portfolio of businesses that are capable of delivering excellent financial performance in their respective industries, rather than striving to capitalize on value chain strategic fits among the businesses. Firms that employ unrelated diversification continually search across different industries for companies that can be acquired for a deal and yet have potential to provide a high return on investment. Pursuing unrelated diversification entails being on the hunt to acquire companies whose assets are undervalued, or companies that are financially distressed, or companies that have high growth prospects but are short on investment capital. An obvious drawback of unrelated diversification is that the parent firm must have an excellent top management team that plans, organizes, motivates, delegates, and controls effectively. It is much more difficult to manage businesses in many industries than in a single industry. However, some firms are successful pursuing unrelated diversification, such as Walt Disney, which owns ABC, and General Electric, which owns NBC.

Many more firms have failed at unrelated diversification than have succeeded due to immense management challenges. However, unrelated diversification can be good, as it is for Cendant Corp., which owns the real-estate firm Century 21, the car-rental agency Avis, the travel-booking sites Orbitz and Flairview Travel, and the hotel brands Days Inn and Howard Johnson.

In what can be considered an unrelated diversification strategy, Dell Inc. recently began producing smart phones, which are similar to Apple's iPhone and Research in Motion's Web browsing phones. Dell has continued to lose market share with a 13.7 percent share of the personal computer, down from 14.6 percent.

San Diego–based Qualcomm Inc. recently diversified beyond cell phones into desktop hardware. The company's strategy is to bring Web access to places in the world that have cell phone networks but do not have Internet access because it is impractical or unaffordable. Qualcomm is test marketing its new device called Kayak. The company expects Intel to be its main competitor in this new product area.

IBM in 2009 entered the water management business with the creation of new desalination-membrane technology that removes arsenic and boron salts from contaminated groundwater. The company expects to license the technology rather than build desalination plants itself. But IBM has begun installing systems of water sensors and software to monitor water pipes, reservoirs, rivers, and harbors. It is all part of IBM's 2009 Big Green Innovations Initiative. The firm has always been known as Big Blue.

Cisco Systems diversified in 2009 by jumping into the fiercely competitive computer server market, placing it in direct competition for the first time with its longtime partners Hewlett-Packard and IBM. Before this strategic move, Cisco was primarily in the router and switch business, which directs Internet traffic. This new Cisco strategy highlights the fact that data centers are becoming a new battleground as large customers manage Internet traffic and energy costs escalate. Michael Corrado at IBM says it is not unusual for tech companies to be both partners and competitors. However, HP's Jim Ganthier says, "HP is delivering today what Cisco is promising tomorrow."[15]

French aerospace manufacturer Safran SA recently diversified further away from jet propulsion into maintenance and service operations by buying 81 percent of General Electric Company's Homeland Protection division for $580 million in cash. This new division of Safran focuses on explosive and narcotics detection. GE and Safran have worked together for more than 30 years, including a joint venture that produces the CFM commercial-jet engine.

Ten guidelines for when unrelated diversification may be an especially effective strategy are:[16]

- When revenues derived from an organization's current products or services would increase significantly by adding the new, unrelated products.
- When an organization competes in a highly competitive and/or a no-growth industry, as indicated by low industry profit margins and returns.
- When an organization's present channels of distribution can be used to market the new products to current customers.
- When the new products have countercyclical sales patterns compared to an organization's present products.
- When an organization's basic industry is experiencing declining annual sales and profits.
- When an organization has the capital and managerial talent needed to compete successfully in a new industry.
- When an organization has the opportunity to purchase an unrelated business that is an attractive investment opportunity.

- When there exists financial synergy between the acquired and acquiring firm. (Note that a key difference between related and unrelated diversification is that the former should be based on some commonality in markets, products, or technology, whereas the latter should be based more on profit considerations.)
- When existing markets for an organization's present products are saturated.
- When antitrust action could be charged against an organization that historically has concentrated on a single industry.

Defensive Strategies

In addition to integrative, intensive, and diversification strategies, organizations also could pursue retrenchment, divestiture, or liquidation.

Retrenchment

Retrenchment occurs when an organization regroups through cost and asset reduction to reverse declining sales and profits. Sometimes called a *turnaround* or *reorganizational strategy,* retrenchment is designed to fortify an organization's basic distinctive competence. During retrenchment, strategists work with limited resources and face pressure from shareholders, employees, and the media. Retrenchment can entail selling off land and buildings to raise needed cash, pruning product lines, closing marginal businesses, closing obsolete factories, automating processes, reducing the number of employees, and instituting expense control systems.

Smithfield Foods, the world's largest pork processor, is closing 6 of its 40 plants, laying off 1,800 employees, and cutting production by 10 percent in 2009 in efforts to stop the liquidity drain on the firm. The retrenchment moves are expected to save the firm $55 million in 2010 and $125 million in 2011. Pork is the world's most consumed meat by volume.[17]

Starbucks has launched a massive retrenchment strategy in efforts to save the company. CEO Howard Schultz says Starbucks will soon close 300 underperforming, company-operated stores worldwide, including 200 in the United States. These closing are on top of 600 recent Starbucks closings in the United States and 61 closings in Australia. However, the firm plans to open 140 stores in the United States in 2009 and open 170 stores outside the United States. Starbucks plans to cut 700 corporate and nonretail positions globally. In addition, as part of Starbucks's strategy to survive the global recession, the company will enter the value-meal race to combat McDonald's new McCafe coffee bars, which are spreading nationally and likely soon globally.

Pursing a heavy retrenchment strategy to survive, Citigroup recently announced that it is cutting 52,000 more jobs. This is the largest corporate layoff announcement since 1993, when IBM cut 60,000 jobs. Citigroup had already cut 23,000 jobs in 2008 as its stock price fell 70 percent in that year alone.

Tokyo-based Sony Corp. is cutting 8,000 jobs and closing 6 of its 57 factories by March 2010 as prices of televisions fall and consumer spending in general declines. Sony has also been hurt by falling demand for digital cameras and the sharp rise in the yen against major currencies, which has cut into profits by reducing its overseas revenue when converted back into the Japanese currency.

Most banks are pursuing retrenchment. A total of 25 banks failed in 2008, including 16 with less than $1 billion in assets. The three largest bank failures by size in 2008 were Washington Mutual in Seattle, Washington, IndyMac Bank in Pasadena, California, and Downey Savings and Loan Association in Newport Beach, California.

Macy's Inc. in 2009 eliminated 7,000 jobs among its 840 department stores and cut its dividend by 62 percent. The firm also ended merit pay increases for executives and slashed its 2009 capital-spending budget by $150 million to about $450 million, down from the planned amount of $1 billion. Also as part of its retrenchment strategy, Macy's bought back $950 million in debt. Macy's expects sales to be down about 8 percent on average per store in 2009. The company is merging its four divisions under one person and discounting its merchandise substantially.

The largest U.S. chemical company by revenue is Dow Chemical Company, and Dow is pursuing an aggressive retrenchment strategy. Dow recently closed 20 plants, put on idle 180 more plants, and laid off more than 5,000 employees.

In some cases, *bankruptcy* can be an effective type of retrenchment strategy. Bankruptcy can allow a firm to avoid major debt obligations and to void union contracts. There are five major types of bankruptcy: Chapter 7, Chapter 9, Chapter 11, Chapter 12, and Chapter 13.

Chapter 7 bankruptcy is a liquidation procedure used only when a corporation sees no hope of being able to operate successfully or to obtain the necessary creditor agreement. All the organization's assets are sold in parts for their tangible worth.

Chapter 9 bankruptcy applies to municipalities. A municipality that successfully declared bankruptcy is Camden, New Jersey, the state's poorest city and the fifth-poorest city in the United States. A crime-ridden city of 87,000, Camden received $62.5 million in state aid and has withdrawn its bankruptcy petition. Between 1980 and 2000, only 18 U.S. cities declared bankruptcy. Some states do not allow municipalities to declare bankruptcy.

Chapter 11 bankruptcy allows organizations to reorganize and come back after filing a petition for protection.

Chapter 12 bankruptcy was created by the Family Farmer Bankruptcy Act of 1986. This law became effective in 1987 and provides special relief to family farmers with debt equal to or less than $1.5 million.

Chapter 13 bankruptcy is a reorganization plan similar to Chapter 11, but it is available only to small businesses owned by individuals with unsecured debts of less than $100,000 and secured debts of less than $350,000. The Chapter 13 debtor is allowed to operate the business while a plan is being developed to provide for the successful operation of the business in the future.

More than 60 percent of Fortune 500 companies are incorporated in Wilmington, Delaware, so this city has recently become known as the "bankruptcy capital of the world." More than half of all large U.S. firms that declared bankruptcy in recent years have done so in Wilmington. Personal bankruptcy filings in the United States exceeded 1 million for the first time ever in 2008, coming on the heels of 822,590 and 617,660 filings in 2008 and 2007, respectively.

Telecom-equipment maker Nortel Networks filed for Chapter 11 bankruptcy in 2009 as its heavy debt load would not withstand falling demand. Rival firm Cisco Systems, Alcatel SA of France, Nokia Corp., and Avaya Inc. are sure to benefit from Nortel's demise. Nortel has been plagued by accounting restatements, price cutting, falling demand, and high interest payments.

Instead of emerging from bankruptcy, Nortel Networks is considering selling its two divisions: wireless equipment and telecom systems for offices. Potential buyers such as Avaya Inc. and Siemensw AG and Gores Group LLC and even Cisco Systems are in talks with Nortel.

Pilgrim's Pride, the largest chicken company in the United States, recently declared bankruptcy. Large debt, high feed costs, and lower prices for broilers have crushed the company's operations, especially in the United States. The company's Mexican operations were not included in the bankruptcy filing.

Tribune Company, which owns eight daily major newspapers, including the *Los Angeles Times* and *Chicago Tribune*, as well as the Chicago Cubs baseball team, recently declared bankruptcy. Tribune is the nation's second largest newspaper chain, but also owns quite a few television stations.

The year 2008 was especially tough for many financial firms, retailers, restaurants, and other companies. It was so rough that a record number of firms declared bankruptcy. Table 5-5 describes some well-known firms that recently declared Chapter 11 bankruptcy.

Five guidelines for when retrenchment may be an especially effective strategy to pursue are as follows:[18]

- When an organization has a clearly distinctive competence but has failed consistently to meet its objectives and goals over time.
- When an organization is one of the weaker competitors in a given industry.
- When an organization is plagued by inefficiency, low profitability, poor employee morale, and pressure from stockholders to improve performance.

TABLE 5-5   Companies That Recently Declared Chapter 11 Bankruptcy

Tribune Company—This media conglomerate that owns the *Chicago Tribune*, the *Los Angeles Times*, the Chicago Cubs, and Wrigley Field recently declared bankruptcy.

Advantage—This car rental company filed for bankruptcy in December 2008 as cash-strapped consumers do less traveling during a slumping economy. Advantage is closing about 40 percent of its U.S. retail locations.

Bally Total Fitness—For the second time in two years, this gym operator filed for bankruptcy protection in December 2008. The company operates nearly 350 facilities nationwide.

Pilgrim's Pride—U.S. meat makers' profits have shrunk in the wake of high feed prices and excessive debt. In December 2008, Pilgrim's Pride, the largest U.S. chicken producer, filed for Chapter 11 bankruptcy protection.

Hawaiian Telcom Communications Inc.—The largest telephone company on the Hawaiian Islands, this firm filed for Chapter 11 bankruptcy protection in December 2008. The company cited increased competition, economic volatility, and its failure to meet capital expenditure needs.

Circuit City—This electronics retailer recently closed 155 of its more than 700 stores and declared Chapter 11 bankruptcy.

Mattress Discounters—Following $2.9 million in losses in 2008 in the New England market, the firm closed 48 stores and filed for Chapter 11 protection.

Washington Mutual—This huge firm recently filed for bankruptcy protection after selling its banking operations to JPMorgan Chase. It was the biggest bank failure in U.S. history at the time.

Mrs. Fields Famous Brands LLC—The company was founded by housewife Debbi Fields in the late 1970s. Her famous homemade cookies quickly grew in popularity. The company filed for bankruptcy protection.

Tropicana Entertainment—The casino company declared Chapter 11 recently when its New Jersey casino license was revoked. The company has operated in the hotel/hospitality industry for more than 35 years.

Polaroid—Founded in 1937 by Edwin Land, the Massachusetts-based company was most famous for its instant film cameras. Polaroid ceased making cameras in 2007 and announced it will stop selling film in 2009. In December 2008, Polaroid filed for Chapter 11 bankruptcy protection.

- When an organization has failed to capitalize on external opportunities, minimize external threats, take advantage of internal strengths, and overcome internal weaknesses over time; that is, when the organization's strategic managers have failed (and possibly will be replaced by more competent individuals).
- When an organization has grown so large so quickly that major internal reorganization is needed.

Divestiture

Selling a division or part of an organization is called *divestiture*. Divestiture often is used to raise capital for further strategic acquisitions or investments. Divestiture can be part of an overall retrenchment strategy to rid an organization of businesses that are unprofitable, that require too much capital, or that do not fit well with the firm's other activities. Divestiture has also become a popular strategy for firms to focus on their core businesses and become less diversified. For example, to raise cash, Motorola in 2009 divested its Good Technology mobile e-mail division to Visto Corporation. Both Good Technology and Visto Corp. lag behind market leader Research in Motion Ltd. maker of BlackBerry devices. Motorola has fallen from being the number two maker of cell phones to number 5.

Ailing Lehman Brothers Holdings divested its venture-capital division in 2009 as the firm shed assets to raise cash and pay creditors. The acquiring firm, HarbourVEst Partners LLC, changed the name of the Lehman division to Tenaya Capital.

Cadbury PLC recently sold its Australian drinks business to Asahi Breweries Ltd. of Japan for $811.9 million. Asahi is Japan's largest beer brewer by market share. Just prior to this divestiture, Cadbury had divested its Dr Pepper Snapple business to a private-equity consortium. Table 5-6 gives a few more recent divestitures.

Historically firms have divested their unwanted or poorly performing divisions, but the global recession has witnessed firms simply closing such operations. For example, Home Depot is shutting down its Expo home-design stores; defense and aerospace manufacturer Textron Corp is closing groups that financed real estate deals; Pioneer Corp. will

TABLE 5-6 Recent Divestitures

Parent Company	Part Being Divested	Acquiring Company
Volkswagen AG	Brazilian truck and bus operations	MAN AG
Toni & Guy	TIGI Hair-care schools and products	Unilever
Reliant Energy	Electricity sales	NRG Energy
E-Bay	Skype (upcoming)	
CV Anheuser-Busch InBev	Beer operations in Romania, Serbia, Bulgaria, Czech Republic, and Hungary	CVC Capital Partners

soon stop making televisions; Praxair Inc. is closing some of its service-related businesses outside the United States; even Google recently halted efforts to sell advertising on radio stations and in newspapers. Saks, the luxury clothing chain, recently closed 16 of its 18 bridal salons, leaving open only its departments in Manhattan and Beverly Hills.

Six guidelines for when divestiture may be an especially effective strategy to pursue follow:[19]

- When an organization has pursued a retrenchment strategy and failed to accomplish needed improvements.
- When a division needs more resources to be competitive than the company can provide.
- When a division is responsible for an organization's overall poor performance.
- When a division is a misfit with the rest of an organization; this can result from radically different markets, customers, managers, employees, values, or needs.
- When a large amount of cash is needed quickly and cannot be obtained reasonably from other sources.
- When government antitrust action threatens an organization.

Liquidation

Selling all of a company's assets, in parts, for their tangible worth is called *liquidation*. Liquidation is a recognition of defeat and consequently can be an emotionally difficult strategy. However, it may be better to cease operating than to continue losing large sums of money. For example, despite four years in development and two years in construction, the Hard Rock Park in Myrtle Beach, South Carolina, liquidated in 2009 just nine months after it opened. The park had been called the world's first rock 'n' roll theme park and the single-largest tourism investment in South Carolina history. From its opening in April 2008 to its closing six months later, the park generated only $20 million in ticket sales, way below its $24 million in annual interest payments due. The park drew far fewer than the projected 30,000 people a day. Bad planning and being too highly leveraged crushed this business very quickly.

In contrast, Disney's Shanghai, China–based Disneyland Park is still on schedule to open in 2010 as Disney downplays global economic distress and pitches the park as creating 50,000 new jobs amid a cooling Chinese economy. The Hong Kong Disneyland Park has struggled for the three years it has been in existence, and many analysts criticize Disney's overall strategy in China.

Based in Knoxville, Tennessee, Goody's Family Clothing liquidated all its 282 stores in 2009 and all 10,000 of its employees lost their jobs. The moderately priced clothing retailer had been operating under Chapter 11 bankruptcy during 2008 but was unable to restructure terms with its creditors. Intense price competition among rival firms coupled with falling consumer demand and being highly leveraged combined to crush this well-known firm in the Southeast.

Woolworths Group PLC recently launched a liquidation sale at all its stores that virtually ended its 99-year-old British retail icon. This British company is not related to the U.S. and Australian companies with similar names. Woolworths Group PLC has 815 stores and about 30,000 employees. Woolies, as the British call this company, began in Britain in 1909 when Frank Woolworth opened the first store in Liverpool, England.

KB Toys Inc. recently said it would liquidate its 400 mall-based and outlet stores. Hundreds of retailers have liquidated, including Linens 'n Things and Mervyn's. One of the largest retailers of Western wear in the United States is BTWW Retail L.P., and that company too is liquidating its 95 stores. Perhaps the most well-known American retailers that liquidated in 2009 was 60-year-old appliance and electronics chain, Circuit City, which closed all of its remaining 567 stores and laid off all of its remaining 34,000 employees. Nearly every major U.S. retailer that has sought to reorganize under bankruptcy-court protection in the last two years has eventually liquidated due to lack of buyers or financing. Circuit City's disappearance is expected to benefit Best Buy and the world's largest retailer, Wal-Mart Stores. Just prior to Circuit City's liquidation, the firm owed more than $1 billion to more than 100,000 creditors, including owing $118.8 million to Hewlett-Packard and $115.9 million to Samsung.

Perhaps the most well-known European firm that liquidated in 2009 was Waterford Wedgwood PLC in Ireland. This maker of Waterford Crystal as well as the Wedgwood and Royal Doulton china patterns was founded in 1759 and had 7,700 employees in the United Kingdom, Ireland, Indonesia, and elsewhere. This company was heavily laden with debt, and when consumer spending on expensive dinnerware declined drastically in 2008, the firm was brought to its knees.

The Lynchburg, Virginia–based Peanut Corporation of American filed for Chapter 7 liquidation in early 2009 after the national salmonella outbreak attributed to the firm crippled the business. The salmonella outbreak had been traced to the company's plant in Blakely, Georgia. Companies that file Chapter 7 sell their assets and distribute the proceeds to creditors.

Several retailers that officially completed their Chapter 7 liquidations in 2009 were Goody's, Whitehall Jewelers, and Circuit City. Table 5-7 describes firms that recently liquidated.

Thousands of small businesses in the United States liquidate annually without ever making the news. It is tough to start and successfully operate a small business. In China and Russia, thousands of government-owned businesses liquidate annually as those countries try to privatize and consolidate industries.

TABLE 5-7 Companies That Recently Liquidated, Declaring Chapter 7 Bankruptcy

Aloha Airlines—After more than 60 years of service to and within Hawaii, the firm made its last passenger flight on March 31, 2008. The company liquidated after bankruptcy protection did not work for it.

Sharper Image Corporation—The company recently liquidated, citing declining sales, three straight years of losses, and litigation involving its Ionic Breeze air purifiers.

DayJet Corporation—The Boca Raton, Florida–based small startup airline, which intended to shuttle busy business travelers between regional airports, recently grounded its planes and liquidated.

Tweeter—The home electronics retailer filed for Chapter 7 liquidation and is selling all merchandise in all its stores.

IMetromedia Restaurant Group—The parent company of Bennigan's and Steak & Ale restaurant chains, the firm recently filed for Chapter 7 bankruptcy protection and closed all 150 of its company-owned stores.

IndyMac Bank—The Office of Thrift Supervision shut down this bank recently after it succumbed to the pressures of tighter credit, tumbling home prices, and rising foreclosures. Control of its assets was transferred to the Federal Deposit Insurance Corp. as IndyMac filed for bankruptcy protection.

Skybus Airlines—This discount airline known for $10 fares and à la carte extras abruptly liquidated recently. The airline had made 74 daily flights to 15 U.S. cities. The shutdown affected about 350 employees in Columbus, Ohio, and 100 in Greensboro, North Carolina.

Whitehall Jewelers—Founded in 1895, the Chicago-based jeweler had about 375 retail locations in 39 states. Following a bankruptcy filing in June 2008, the firm recently closed all its locations.

Amabassadair—The Indianapolis-based airline was founded in 1973, but the unexpected loss of a major contract for its military charter business forced the airline into bankruptcy and then the firm ceased operations.

Domain Home Furniture—The 27-store Norwood, Massachusetts–based chain was founded in 1985. For two decades, Domain Home was a mainstay of the Northeast's high-end furniture market known for quality furniture and other home decor products. The company recently declared bankruptcy and closed all stores.

These three guidelines indicate when liquidation may be an especially effective strategy to pursue:[20]

- When an organization has pursued both a retrenchment strategy and a divestitute strategy, and neither has been successful.
- When an organization's only alternative is bankruptcy. Liquidation represents an orderly and planned means of obtaining the greatest possible cash for an organization's assets. A company can legally declare bankruptcy first and then liquidate various divisions to raise needed capital.
- When the stockholders of a firm can minimize their losses by selling the organization's assets.

Michael Porter's Five Generic Strategies

Probably the three most widely read books on competitive analysis in the 1980s were Michael Porter's *Competitive Strategy* (Free Press, 1980), *Competitive Advantage* (Free Press, 1985), and *Competitive Advantage of Nations* (Free Press, 1989). According to Porter, strategies allow organizations to gain competitive advantage from three different bases: cost leadership, differentiation, and focus. Porter calls these bases *generic strategies.* *Cost leadership* emphasizes producing standardized products at a very low per-unit cost for consumers who are price-sensitive. Two alternative types of cost leadership strategies can be defined. Type 1 is a *low-cost* strategy that offers products or services to a wide range of customers at the lowest price available on the market. Type 2 is a *best-value* strategy that offers products or services to a wide range of customers at the best price-value available on the market; the best-value strategy aims to offer customers a range of products or services at the lowest price available compared to a rival's products with similar attributes. Both Type 1 and Type 2 strategies target a large market.

Porter's Type 3 generic strategy is *differentiation,* a strategy aimed at producing products and services considered unique industrywide and directed at consumers who are relatively price-insensitive.

Focus means producing products and services that fulfill the needs of small groups of consumers. Two alternative types of focus strategies are Type 4 and Type 5. Type 4 is a *low-cost focus* strategy that offers products or services to a small range (niche group) of customers at the lowest price available on the market. Examples of firms that use the Type 4 strategy include Jiffy Lube International and Pizza Hut, as well as local used car dealers and hot dog restaurants. Type 5 is a *best-value focus* strategy that offers products or services to a small range of customers at the best price-value available on the market. Sometimes called "focused differentiation," the best-value focus strategy aims to offer a niche group of customers products or services that meet their tastes and requirements better than rivals' products do. Both Type 4 and Type 5 focus strategies target a small market. However, the difference is that Type 4 strategies offer products services to a niche group at the lowest price, whereas Type 5 offers products/services to a niche group at higher prices but loaded with features so the offerings are perceived as the best value. Examples of firms that use the Type 5 strategy include Cannondale (top-of-the-line mountain bikes), Maytag (washing machines), and Lone Star Restaurants (steak house), as well as bed-and-breakfast inns and local retail boutiques.

Porter's five strategies imply different organizational arrangements, control procedures, and incentive systems. Larger firms with greater access to resources typically compete on a cost leadership and/or differentiation basis, whereas smaller firms often compete on a focus basis. Porter's five generic strategies are illustrated in Figure 5-3. Note that a differentiation strategy (Type 3) can be pursued with either a small target market or a large target market. However, it is not effective to pursue a cost leadership strategy in a small market because profits margins are generally too small. Likewise, it is not effective to pursue a focus strategy in a large market because economies of scale would generally favor a low-cost or best-value cost leaderships strategy to gain and/or sustain competitive advantage.

FIGURE 5-3

Porter's Five Generic Strategies

Type 1: Cost Leadership—Low Cost
Type 2: Cost Leadership—Best Value
Type 3: Differentiation
Type 4: Focus—Low Cost
Type 5: Focus—Best Value

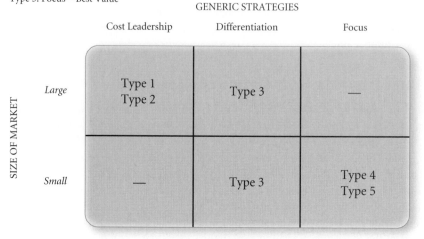

GENERIC STRATEGIES

	Cost Leadership	Differentiation	Focus
Large	Type 1 Type 2	Type 3	—
Small	—	Type 3	Type 4 Type 5

SIZE OF MARKET

Source: Based on Michael E. Porter, *Competitive Strategy: Techniques for Analyzing Industries and Competitors* (New York: Free Press, 1980): 35–40.

Porter stresses the need for strategists to perform cost-benefit analyses to evaluate "sharing opportunities" among a firm's existing and potential business units. Sharing activities and resources enhances competitive advantage by lowering costs or increasing differentiation. In addition to prompting sharing, Porter stresses the need for firms to effectively "transfer" skills and expertise among autonomous business units to gain competitive advantage. Depending on factors such as type of industry, size of firm, and nature of competition, various strategies could yield advantages in cost leadership, differentiation, and focus.

Cost Leadership Strategies (Type 1 and Type 2)

A primary reason for pursuing forward, backward, and horizontal integration strategies is to gain low-cost or best-value cost leadership benefits. But cost leadership generally must be pursued in conjunction with differentiation. A number of cost elements affect the relative attractiveness of generic strategies, including economies or diseconomies of scale achieved, learning and experience curve effects, the percentage of capacity utilization achieved, and linkages with suppliers and distributors. Other cost elements to consider in choosing among alternative strategies include the potential for sharing costs and knowledge within the organization, R&D costs associated with new product development or modification of existing products, labor costs, tax rates, energy costs, and shipping costs.

Striving to be the low-cost producer in an industry can be especially effective when the market is composed of many price-sensitive buyers, when there are few ways to achieve product differentiation, when buyers do not care much about differences from brand to brand, or when there are a large number of buyers with significant bargaining power. The basic idea is to underprice competitors and thereby gain market share and sales, entirely driving some competitors out of the market. Companies employing a low-cost (Type 1) or best-value (Type 2) cost leadership strategy must achieve their competitive advantage in ways that are difficult for competitors to copy or match. If rivals find it relatively easy or inexpensive to imitate the leader's cost leadership methods, the leaders' advantage will not last long enough to yield a valuable edge in the marketplace. Recall that for a resource to be valuable, it must be either rare, hard to imitate, or not easily substitutable. To employ a cost leadership strategy successfully, a firm must ensure that its total costs across its overall value chain are lower than competitors' total costs. There are two ways to accomplish this:[21]

1. Perform value chain activities more efficiently than rivals and control the factors that drive the costs of value chain activities. Such activities could include altering the plant layout, mastering newly introduced technologies, using common parts or components in different products, simplifying product design, finding ways to operate close to full capacity year-round, and so on.
2. Revamp the firm's overall value chain to eliminate or bypass some cost-producing activities. Such activities could include securing new suppliers or distributors, selling products online, relocating manufacturing facilities, avoiding the use of union labor, and so on.

When employing a cost leadership strategy, a firm must be careful not to use such aggressive price cuts that their own profits are low or nonexistent. Constantly be mindful of cost-saving technological breakthroughs or any other value chain advancements that could erode or destroy the firm's competitive advantage. A Type 1 or Type 2 cost leadership strategy can be especially effective under the following conditions:[22]

1. When price competition among rival sellers is especially vigorous.
2. When the products of rival sellers are essentially identical and supplies are readily available from any of several eager sellers.
3. When there are few ways to achieve product differentiation that have value to buyers.
4. When most buyers use the product in the same ways.
5. When buyers incur low costs in switching their purchases from one seller to another.
6. When buyers are large and have significant power to bargain down prices.
7. When industry newcomers use introductory low prices to attract buyers and build a customer base.

A successful cost leadership strategy usually permeates the entire firm, as evidenced by high efficiency, low overhead, limited perks, intolerance of waste, intensive screening of budget requests, wide spans of control, rewards linked to cost containment, and broad employee participation in cost control efforts. Some risks of pursuing cost leadership are that competitors may imitate the strategy, thus driving overall industry profits down; that technological breakthroughs in the industry may make the strategy ineffective; or that buyer interest may swing to other differentiating features besides price. Several example firms that are well known for their low-cost leadership strategies are Wal-Mart, BIC, McDonald's, Black & Decker, Lincoln Electric, and Briggs & Stratton.

Differentiation Strategies (Type 3)

Different strategies offer different degrees of differentiation. Differentiation does not guarantee competitive advantage, especially if standard products sufficiently meet customer needs or if rapid imitation by competitors is possible. Durable products protected by barriers to quick copying by competitors are best. Successful differentiation can mean greater product flexibility, greater compatibility, lower costs, improved service, less maintenance, greater convenience, or more features. Product development is an example of a strategy that offers the advantages of differentiation.

A differentiation strategy should be pursued only after a careful study of buyers' needs and preferences to determine the feasibility of incorporating one or more differentiating features into a unique product that features the desired attributes. A successful differentiation strategy allows a firm to charge a higher price for its product and to gain customer loyalty because consumers may become strongly attached to the differentiation features. Special features that differentiate one's product can include superior service, spare parts availability, engineering design, product performance, useful life, gas mileage, or ease of use.

A risk of pursuing a differentiation strategy is that the unique product may not be valued highly enough by customers to justify the higher price. When this happens, a cost leadership strategy easily will defeat a differentiation strategy. Another risk of pursuing a differentiation strategy is that competitors may quickly develop ways to copy the differentiating features. Firms thus must find durable sources of uniqueness that cannot be imitated quickly or cheaply by rival firms.

Common organizational requirements for a successful differentiation strategy include strong coordination among the R&D and marketing functions and substantial amenities to attract scientists and creative people. Firms can pursue a differentiation (Type 3) strategy based on many different competitive aspects. For example, Mountain Dew and root beer have a unique taste; Lowe's, Home Depot, and Wal-Mart offer wide selection and one-stop shopping; Dell Computer and FedEx offer superior service; BMW and Porsche offer engineering design and performance; IBM and Hewlett-Packard offer a wide range of products; and E*Trade and Ameritrade offer Internet convenience. Differentiation opportunities exist or can potentially be developed anywhere along the firm's value chain, including supply chain activities, product R&D activities, production and technological activities, manufacturing activities, human resource management activities, distribution activities, or marketing activities.

The most effective differentiation bases are those that are hard or expensive for rivals to duplicate. Competitors are continually trying to imitate, duplicate, and outperform rivals along any differentiation variable that has yielded competitive advantage. For example, when U.S. Airways cut its prices, Delta quickly followed suit. When Caterpillar instituted its quick-delivery-of-spare-parts policy, John Deere soon followed suit. To the extent that differentiating attributes are tough for rivals to copy, a differentiation strategy will be especially effective, but the sources of uniqueness must be time-consuming, cost prohibitive, and simply too burdensome for rivals to match. A firm, therefore, must be careful when employing a differentiation (Type 3) strategy. Buyers will not pay the higher differentiation price unless their perceived value exceeds the price they are paying.[23] Based on such matters as attractive packaging, extensive advertising, quality of sales presentations, quality of Web site, list of customers, professionalism, size of the firm, and/or profitability of the company, perceived value may be more important to customers than actual value.

A Type 3 differentiation strategy can be especially effective under the following conditions:[24]

1. When there are many ways to differentiate the product or service and many buyers perceive these differences as having value.
2. When buyer needs and uses are diverse.
3. When few rival firms are following a similar differentiation approach.
4. When technological change is fast paced and competition revolves around rapidly evolving product features.

Focus Strategies (Type 4 and Type 5)

A successful focus strategy depends on an industry segment that is of sufficient size, has good growth potential, and is not crucial to the success of other major competitors. Strategies such as market penetration and market development offer substantial focusing advantages. Midsize and large firms can effectively pursue focus-based strategies only in conjunction with differentiation or cost leadership–based strategies. All firms in essence follow a differentiated strategy. Because only one firm can differentiate itself with the lowest cost, the remaining firms in the industry must find other ways to differentiate their products.

Focus strategies are most effective when consumers have distinctive preferences or requirements and when rival firms are not attempting to specialize in the same target segment. Sara Lee Corp. is pursuing a focus strategy as it is trying to divest of its European household and personal-care business so the firm can focus on its core food and beverage business. The company is asking about $2 billion for its household business. Sara Lee sells Jimmy Dean sausages and Ball Park Franks and a mix of coffee and baked goods. Possible bidders for its household business are Unilever PLC, Johnson & Johnson, and Colgate-Palmolive.

Risks of pursuing a focus strategy include the possibility that numerous competitors will recognize the successful focus strategy and copy it or that consumer preferences will drift toward the product attributes desired by the market as a whole. An organization using a focus strategy may concentrate on a particular group of customers, geographic markets, or on particular product-line segments to serve a well-defined but narrow market better than competitors who serve a broader market.

A low-cost (Type 4) or best-value (Type 5) focus strategy can be especially attractive under the following conditions:[25]

1. When the target market niche is large, profitable, and growing.
2. When industry leaders do not consider the niche to be crucial to their own success.
3. When industry leaders consider it too costly or difficult to meet the specialized needs of the target market niche while taking care of their mainstream customers.
4. When the industry has many different niches and segments, thereby allowing a focuser to pick a competitively attractive niche suited to its own resources.
5. When few, if any, other rivals are attempting to specialize in the same target segment.

Strategies for Competing in Turbulent, High-Velocity Markets

The world is changing more and more rapidly, and consequently industries and firms themselves are changing faster than ever. Some industries are changing so fast that researchers call them *turbulent, high-velocity markets,* such as telecommunications, medical, biotechnology, pharmaceuticals, computer hardware, software, and virtually all Internet-based industries. High-velocity change is clearly becoming more and more the rule rather than the exception, even in such industries as toys, phones, banking, defense, publishing, and communication.

Meeting the challenge of high-velocity change presents the firm with a choice of whether to react, anticipate, or lead the market in terms of its own strategies. To primarily react to changes in the industry would be a defensive strategy used to counter, for example, unexpected shifts in buyer tastes and technological breakthroughs. The react-to-change strategy would not be as effective as the anticipate-change strategy, which would entail devising and following through with plans for dealing with the expected changes. However, firms ideally strive to be in a position to lead the changes in high-velocity markets, whereby they pioneer new and better technologies and products and set industry standards. Being the leader or pioneer of change in a high-velocity market is an aggressive, offensive strategy that includes rushing next-generation products to market ahead of rivals and being continually proactive in shaping the market to one's own benefit. Although a lead-change strategy is best whenever the firm has the resources to pursue this approach, on occasion even the strongest firms in turbulent industries have to employ the react-to-the-market strategy and the anticipate-the-market strategy.

An example firm, Hewlett-Packard, pursued a lead-change strategy in 2009 in the computer industry, a turbulent, high-velocity market, when the firm introduced glossy, touch-sensitive screens, called TouchSmart desktops. HP is pushing these screens in commercial settings, such as their sale of 50 of these machines to Chicago's O'Hare International Airport.

Means for Achieving Strategies

Cooperation Among Competitors

Strategies that stress cooperation among competitors are being used more. For collaboration between competitors to succeed, both firms must contribute something distinctive, such as technology, distribution, basic research, or manufacturing capacity. But a major risk is that unintended transfers of important skills or technology may occur at organizational levels below where the deal was signed.[26] Information not covered in the formal agreement often gets traded in the day-to-day interactions and dealings of engineers, marketers, and product developers. Firms often give away too much information to rival firms when operating under cooperative agreements! Tighter formal agreements are needed.

Perhaps the best example of rival firms in an industry forming alliances to compete against each other is the airline industry. Today there are three major alliances. With the addition of Continental Airlines, the Star Alliance has 25 airlines such as Air Canada, Spanair, United, and Singapore Airlines; the OneWorld Alliance has 10 airlines such as American, British Air, and LanChile; and finally, SkyTeam Alliance has 15 airlines such as Air France, Delta, and Korean Air. Firms are moving to compete as groups within alliances more and more as it becomes increasingly difficult to survive alone in some industries.

The idea of joining forces with a competitor is not easily accepted by Americans, who often view cooperation and partnerships with skepticism and suspicion. Indeed, joint ventures and cooperative arrangements among competitors demand a certain amount of trust if companies are to combat paranoia about whether one firm will injure the other. However, multinational firms are becoming more globally cooperative, and increasing numbers of domestic firms are joining forces with competitive foreign firms to reap mutual benefits. Kathryn Harrigan at Columbia University says, "Within a decade, most companies will be members of teams that compete against each other." Once major rivals, Google's YouTube and Vivendi SA's Universal Music Group have formed a partnership called Vevo to provide a new music-video service. Google provides the technology and Universal Music provides the content, and both firms share the revenues. The two firms now operate the stand-alone site Vevo.com.

U.S. companies often enter alliances primarily to avoid investments, being more interested in reducing the costs and risks of entering new businesses or markets than in acquiring new skills. In contrast, *learning from the partner* is a major reason why Asian and European firms enter into cooperative agreements. U.S. firms, too, should place learning high on the list of reasons to be cooperative with competitors. U.S. companies often form alliances with Asian firms to gain an understanding of their manufacturing excellence, but Asian competence in this area is not easily transferable. Manufacturing excellence is a complex system that includes employee training and involvement, integration with suppliers, statistical process controls, value engineering, and design. In contrast, U.S. know-how in technology and related areas can be imitated more easily. U.S. firms thus need to be careful not to give away more intelligence than they receive in cooperative agreements with rival Asian firms.

Joint Venture/Partnering

Joint venture is a popular strategy that occurs when two or more companies form a temporary partnership or consortium for the purpose of capitalizing on some opportunity. Often, the two or more sponsoring firms form a separate organization and have shared equity ownership in the new entity. Other types of *cooperative arrangements* include research and development partnerships, cross-distribution agreements, cross-licensing agreements, cross-manufacturing agreements, and joint-bidding consortia. Once bitter rivals, Nokia Corp. and Qualcomm recently formed a cooperative agreement to develop next-generation cell phones for North America to hit the market in mid-2010. Based in Finland, Nokia has roughly 40 percent of the global cell phone market but has lagged behind in North America.

Nokia is also in discussion with Facebook Inc. to form a partnership that would embed parts of the social network into some Nokia phones. Contact information stored in Facebook, for example, could be integrated with the phone's address book. On the phone, when users look up a contact they can see whether their Facebook friends are logged on, send them messages, and post comments on their profile pages. Facebook is also in discussion with Palm Inc. and Motorola Inc. to form other partnerships to integrate Facebook features into cell phones. Facebook has fewer U.S. users than MySpace but has eclipsed MySpace in U.S. visitors from mobile phones. MySpace is owned by News Corporation, which also owns Dow Jones, publisher of the *Wall Street Journal*.

Microsoft, based in Redmond, Washington, and Yahoo, based in Sunnyvale, California, recently resumed talks about search and advertising partnerships as many firms are doing the same—shifting their focus from acquisitions to partnerships.

Joint ventures and cooperative arrangements are being used increasingly because they allow companies to improve communications and networking, to globalize operations, and to minimize risk. Joint ventures and partnerships are often used to pursue an opportunity that is too complex, uneconomical, or risky for a single firm to pursue alone. Such business creations also are used when achieving and sustaining competitive advantage when an industry requires a broader range of competencies and know-how than any one firm can marshal. Kathryn Rudie Harrigan, professor of strategic management at Columbia University, summarizes the trend toward increased joint venturing:

> In today's global business environment of scarce resources, rapid rates of technological change, and rising capital requirements, the important question is no longer "Shall we form a joint venture?" Now the question is "Which joint ventures and cooperative arrangements are most appropriate for our needs and expectations?" followed by "How do we manage these ventures most effectively?"[27]

In a global market tied together by the Internet, joint ventures, and partnerships, alliances are proving to be a more effective way to enhance corporate growth than mergers and acquisitions.[28] Strategic partnering takes many forms, including outsourcing, information sharing, joint marketing, and joint research and development. Many companies, such as Eli Lilly, now host partnership training classes for their managers and partners. There are today more than 10,000 joint ventures formed annually, more than all mergers and acquisitions. There are countless examples of successful strategic alliances, such as Internet coverage.

A major reason why firms are using partnering as a means to achieve strategies is globalization. Wal-Mart's successful joint venture with Mexico's Cifra is indicative of how a domestic firm can benefit immensely by partnering with a foreign company to gain substantial presence in that new country. Technology also is a major reason behind the need to form strategic alliances, with the Internet linking widely dispersed partners. The Internet paved the way and legitimized the need for alliances to serve as the primary means for corporate growth.

Evidence is mounting that firms should use partnering as a means for achieving strategies. However, the sad fact is that most U.S. firms in many industries—such as financial services, forest products, metals, and retailing—still operate in a merger or acquire mode to obtain growth. Partnering is not yet taught at most business schools and is often viewed within companies as a financial issue rather than a strategic issue. However, partnering has become a core competency, a strategic issue of such importance that top management involvement initially and throughout the life of an alliance is vital.[29]

Joint ventures among once rival firms are commonly being used to pursue strategies ranging from retrenchment to market development.

Although ventures and partnerships are preferred over mergers as a means for achieving strategies, certainly they are not all successful. The good news is that joint ventures and partnerships are less risky for companies than mergers, but the bad news is that many alliances fail. *Forbes* has reported that about 30 percent of all joint ventures and partnership alliances are outright failures, while another 17 percent have limited success and then dissipate due to problems.[30] There are countless examples of failed joint ventures. A few common problems that cause joint ventures to fail are as follows:

1. Managers who must collaborate daily in operating the venture are not involved in forming or shaping the venture.
2. The venture may benefit the partnering companies but may not benefit customers, who then complain about poorer service or criticize the companies in other ways.
3. The venture may not be supported equally by both partners. If supported unequally, problems arise.
4. The venture may begin to compete more with one of the partners than the other.[31]

Six guidelines for when a joint venture may be an especially effective means for pursuing strategies are:[32]

- When a privately owned organization is forming a joint venture with a publicly owned organization; there are some advantages to being privately held, such as closed ownership; there are some advantages of being publicly held, such as access to stock issuances as a source of capital. Sometimes, the unique advantages of being privately and publicly held can be synergistically combined in a joint venture.

- When a domestic organization is forming a joint venture with a foreign company; a joint venture can provide a domestic company with the opportunity for obtaining local management in a foreign country, thereby reducing risks such as expropriation and harassment by host country officials.
- When the distinct competencies of two or more firms complement each other especially well.
- When some project is potentially very profitable but requires overwhelming resources and risks.
- When two or more smaller firms have trouble competing with a large firm.
- When there exists a need to quickly introduce a new technology.

Merger/Acquisition

Merger and acquisition are two commonly used ways to pursue strategies. A *merger* occurs when two organizations of about equal size unite to form one enterprise. An *acquisition* occurs when a large organization purchases (acquires) a smaller firm, or vice versa. When a merger or acquisition is not desired by both parties, it can be called a *takeover* or *hostile takeover*. In contrast, if the acquisition is desired by both firms, it is termed a *friendly merger*. Most mergers are friendly.

There were numerous examples in 2009 of hostile takeover attempts. For example, Swiss drug company Roche Holding AG in 2009 launched an $86.50-a-share hostile takeover for the 44.2 percent of Genentech Inc. that it did not already own. Genentech's board of directors strongly urged shareholders not to accept the Roche Holding offer, saying that Roche's $40 billion offer was inadequate. Genentech's board said the firm was worth $112 per share at the time. A few weeks later, Roche increased its bid to $93 per share.

Headquartered near each other in California, Emulex Corp. in May 2009 rejected a hostile takeover bid from Broadcom Corp. even though the Broadcom offer represented a 40 percent premium over the Emulex current stock price. Emulex installed a "poison pill" in January 2009 as protection against hostile takeover offers. Both companies produce and sell networking equipment that connect servers in data centers.

As stock prices have plunged in many companies, their rivals with cash are eyeing them as takeover candidates. Fertilizer producer Agrium recently offered to buy rival Deerfield, Illinois–based CF Industries Holdings for $3.6 billion, which created a three-way hostile takeover battle because CF at the time had a hostile takeover offer on the table to acquire Terra Industries.

Private-equity-led buyouts, which accounted for 15 percent of all merger and acquisition in 2007, fell to 6 percent of the total in 2008. That smaller percentage is likely to remain in place in 2009 as big cross-border deals are unlikely in the near term. Private-equity investing in tech companies fell almost 80 percent in 2008 to $26.3 billion as sources of debt financing became scarce.

Private-equity firms such as Blackstone Group Inc. and Kohlberg Kravis Roberts & Co. that led the massive acquisition trend in 2006–2007 are still around, but they operate much more carefully now. Such firms are trying today to purchase the agricultural-sciences division (Agro Sciences) of Dow Chemical. Dow needs cash to complete its own acquisition of Rohm & Haas Co. Agro Sciences should be worth between $7 and $10 billion. A rival Swiss firm named Syngenta AG also is interested in acquiring Agro Sciences.

For all of 2008, global merger and acquisition volume fell 29 percent to $3.06 trillion, which was on par with 2005. Big deals in 2008 included Mars Inc.'s $23 billion acquisition of Wm. Wrigley Jr. Co., InBev NV's $52 billion purchase of Anheuser-Busch, and HP's $13.2 billion acquisition of EDS.

In a stock deal that created the nation's largest home builder, Pulte Homes recently acquired Centex Corp. for $1.3 billion. This merger signaled a bottom in the housing market, which had dropped so drastically in the United States in 2008 and early 2009.

Cross-border merger and acquisition (M&A) deals by companies in major nations fell 26 percent in the United States in 2008 versus 2007, as compared to a fall of 15 percent in France, and a fall of 67 percent in the United Kingdom.[33]

Firms with cash such as Marubeni and Itochu in Japan are on the hunt for super deals outside of Japan. Cross-border M&A deals in Japan grew 231 percent in 2008 and grew 101 percent in China. Japanese companies in total spent $77.8 billion in 2008 on acquisitions outside Japan, more than triple the amount spent in 2007. "Hard times often come hand in hand with opportunities," said Teruo Asada, president and chief executive of the 150-year-old Marubeni Corporation in Japan.

According to Strategas Research Partners, 168 of 419 nonfinancial firms in the S&P 500 have at least $1 billion in cash apiece, and 16 have more than $10 billion each.[34] Exxon/Mobil has $32 billion in cash, Cisco Systems has $29.5 billion, and Apple has $25.6 billion.

The largest business software firm in the world, Oracle Corp. is another cash-rich firm acquiring other firms, having completed 12 acquisition in the last 12 months. A few of the firms acquired by Oracle recently are mValent, Tacit Software, Primavera Systems, Advanced Visual Tech, ClearApp, Skywire Software, AdminServer, and Empirix. Many companies with high-quality products have turned into desperate sellers amid the worst recession in a generation. Oracle dominates the market for industrial-strength databases that companies rely on the organize everything from inventories to payrolls.

White knight is a term that refers to a firm that agrees to acquire another firm when that other firm is facing a hostile takeover by some company. For example, in 2009, Palo Alto, California–based CV Thereapeutics Inc., a heart-drug maker, was fighting a hostile takeover bid by Japan's Astellas Pharma. Then CVT struck a friendly deal to be acquired by Forest City, California–based Gilead Sciences at a higher price of $1.4 billion in cash. Gilead is known for its HIV drugs, so its move into the heart-drug business surprised many analysts.

Not all mergers are effective and successful. Pricewaterhouse Coopers LLP recently researched mergers and found that the average acquirer's stock was 3.7 percent lower than its industry peer group a year later. *BusinessWeek* and the *Wall Street Journal* studied mergers and concluded that about half produced negative returns to shareholders. Warren Buffett once said in a speech that "too-high purchase price for the stock of an excellent company can undo the effects of a subsequent decade of favorable business developments." Research suggests that perhaps 20 percent of all mergers and acquisitions are successful, approximately 60 percent produce disappointing results, and the last 20 percent are clear failures.[35] So a merger between two firms can yield great benefits, but the price and reasoning must be right. Some key reasons why many mergers and acquisitions fail are provided in Table 5-8.

Among mergers, acquisitions, and takeovers in recent years, same-industry combinations have predominated. A general market consolidation is occurring in many industries, especially banking, insurance, defense, and health care, but also in pharmaceuticals, food, airlines, accounting, publishing, computers, retailing, financial services, and biotechnology. For example, SXR Uranium One Inc. purchased rival uranium miner UrAsia Energy Ltd., creating the world's second-largest uranium company after Cameco

TABLE 5-8 Key Reasons Why Many Mergers and Acquisitions Fail

- Integration difficulties
- Inadequate evaluation of target
- Large or extraordinary debt
- Inability to achieve synergy
- Too much diversification
- Managers overly focused on acquisitions
- Too large an acquisition
- Difficult to integrate different organizational cultures
- Reduced employee morale due to layoffs and relocations

TABLE 5-9   Some Large Mergers Completed Globally in 2009

Acquiring Firm	Acquired Firm	Price (in $Billions)
InBev	Anheuser-Busch Cos.	52.000
Bank of America Corp.	Merrill Lynch & Co.	50.0
Wells Fargo & Co.	Wachovia Corp.	15.1
Delta Air Lines	Northwest Airlines Corp.	2.600
AT&T	Centennial Communications	0.937
Johnson & Johnson	Mentor Corp.	1.070
King Pharmaceuticals Inc.	Alpharma Inc.	1.600
CenturyTel	Embark	5.000

Corp. Similarly, Tenaris SA, based in Luxembourg and the world's biggest maker of steel tubes used in oil exploration and production, recently acquired rival Hydril Company, based in Houston, Texas.

Table 5-9 shows some mergers and acquisitions completed in 2009. There are many potential benefits of merging with or acquiring another firm, as indicated in Table 5-10.

Johnson & Johnson's (J&J) recent acquisition of Mentor for $1.07 billion was a hefty 92 percent premium over Mentor's closing price before the deal was announced, but was 23 percent below another widely used evaluation method that was number of shares outstanding times the target firm's 52-week stock price high. Many companies are being forced to sell under duress, so firms with a lot of cash such as J&J and Apple can pick up deals of a lifetime these days. J&J had $14 billion in cash on hand in 2009 when it purchased Omrix Pharmaceuticals for $438 million. Then the largest health-care company in the world, J&J purchased Mentor for $1.07 billion in cash. Bristol-Myers Squibb's CEO James Cornelius recently said that company is looking to do six or seven additional acquisitions or partnerships with the $9 billion in cash it has on hand to bolster its drug pipeline.

The volume of mergers completed annually worldwide is growing dramatically and exceeds $1 trillion. There are annually more than 10,000 mergers in the United States that total more than $700 billion. The proliferation of mergers is fueled by companies' drive for market share, efficiency, and pricing power, as well as by globalization, the need for greater economies of scale, reduced regulation and antitrust concerns, the Internet, and e-commerce.

A *leveraged buyout* (LBO) occurs when a corporation's shareholders are bought (hence *buyout*) by the company's management and other private investors using borrowed funds (hence *leverage*).[36] Besides trying to avoid a hostile takeover, other reasons for initiating an LBO are senior management decisions that particular divisions do not fit into an overall corporate strategy or must be sold to raise cash, or receipt of an attractive offering price. An LBO takes a corporation private.

TABLE 5-10   Potential Benefits of Merging with or Acquiring Another Firm

- To provide improved capacity utilization
- To make better use of the existing sales force
- To reduce managerial staff
- To gain economies of scale
- To smooth out seasonal trends in sales
- To gain access to new suppliers, distributors, customers, products, and creditors
- To gain new technology
- To reduce tax obligations

First Mover Advantages

First mover advantages refer to the benefits a firm may achieve by entering a new market or developing a new product or service prior to rival firms.[37] As indicated in Table 5-11, some advantages of being a first mover include securing access to rare resources, gaining new knowledge of key factors and issues, and carving out market share and a position that is easy to defend and costly for rival firms to overtake. First mover advantages are analogous to taking the high ground first, which puts one in an excellent strategic position to launch aggressive campaigns and to defend territory. Being the first mover can be especially wise when such actions (1) build a firm's image and reputation with buyers, (2) produce cost advantages over rivals in terms of new technologies, new components, new distribution channels, and so on, (3) create strongly loyal customers, and (4) make imitation or duplication by a rival hard or unlikely.[38]

To sustain the competitive advantage gained by being the first mover, such a firm also needs to be a fast learner. There would, however, be risks associated with being the first mover, such as unexpected and unanticipated problems and costs that occur from being the first firm doing business in the new market. Therefore, being a slow mover (also called *fast follower* or *late mover*) can be effective when a firm can easily copy or imitate the lead firm's products or services. If technology is advancing rapidly, slow movers can often leapfrog a first mover's products with improved second-generation products. However, slow movers often are relegated to relying on the first mover being a slow mover and making strategic and tactical mistakes. This situation does not occur often, so first mover advantages clearly offset the first mover disadvantages most of the time. Apple Inc. has always been a good example of a first mover firm.

Strategic-management research indicates that first mover advantages tend to be greatest when competitors are roughly the same size and possess similar resources. If competitors are not similar in size, then larger competitors can wait while others make initial investments and mistakes, and then respond with greater effectiveness and resources.

Outsourcing

Business-process outsourcing (BPO) is a rapidly growing new business that involves companies taking over the functional operations, such as human resources, information systems, payroll, accounting, customer service, and even marketing of other firms. Companies are choosing to outsource their functional operations more and more for several reasons: (1) it is less expensive, (2) it allows the firm to focus on its core businesses, and (3) it enables the firm to provide better services. Other advantages of outsourcing are that the strategy (1) allows the firm to align itself with "best-in-world" suppliers who focus on performing the special task, (2) provides the firm flexibility should customer needs shift unexpectedly, and (3) allows the firm to concentrate on other internal value chain activities critical to sustaining competitive advantage. BPO is a means for achieving strategies that are similar to partnering and joint venturing. The worldwide BPO market exceeds $173 billion.

Many firms, such as Dearborn, Michigan–based Visteon Corp. and J. P. Morgan Chase & Co., outsource their computer operations to IBM, which competes with firms such as Electronic Data Systems and Computer Sciences Corp. in the computer outsourcing

---

TABLE 5-11   Benefits of a Firm Being the First Mover

1. Secure access and commitments to rare resources
2. Gain new knowledge of critical success factors and issues
3. Gain market share and position in the best locations
4. Establish and secure long-term relationships with customers, suppliers, distributors, and investors
5. Gain customer loyalty and commitments

business. 3M Corp. is outsourcing all of its manufacturing operations to Flextronics International Ltd. of Singapore or Jabil Circuit in Florida. 3M is also outsourcing all design and manufacturing of low-end standardized volume products by building a new design center in Taiwan.

U.S. and European companies for more than a decade have been outsourcing their manufacturing, tech support, and back-office work, but most insisted on keeping research and development activities in-house. However, an ever-growing number of firms today are outsourcing their product design to Asian developers. China and India are becoming increasingly important suppliers of intellectual property. For companies that include Hewlett-Packard, PalmOne, Dell, Sony, Apple, Kodak, Motorola, Nokia, Ericsson, Lucent, Cisco, and Nortel, the design of personal computers and cameras is mostly outsourced to China and India.

Companies pay about $68 billion in outsourcing operations to other firms, but the details of what work to outsource, to whom, where, and for how much can challenge even the biggest, most sophisticated companies.[39] And some outsourcing deals do not work out, such as the J.P. Morgan Chase deal with IBM and Dow Chemical's deal with Electronic Data Systems. Both outsourcing deals were abandoned after several years. Lehman Brothers Holdings and Dell Inc. both recently reversed decisions to move customer call centers to India after a customer rebellion. India has become a booming place for outsourcing. Sprint Nextel Corp. in 2009 outsourced management of its cellular network to Swedish firm Telefon A.B. L.M. Ericsson, which transferred about 6,000 jobs from the United States to Sweden. Based in Overland Park, Kansas, Sprint sees network outsourcing as a way to free up resources to focus on areas like product development, marketing, and strategic partnerships. Ericsson, as well as Alcatel-Lucent SA and Nokia-Siemens Networks, have been aggressively courting service contracts to make up for declining prices of telecom equipment.

Strategic Management in Nonprofit and Governmental Organizations

The strategic-management process is being used effectively by countless nonprofit and governmental organizations, such as the Girl Scouts, Boy Scouts, the Red Cross, chambers of commerce, educational institutions, medical institutions, public utilities, libraries, government agencies, and churches. The nonprofit sector, surprisingly, is by far America's largest employer. Many nonprofit and governmental organizations outperform private firms and corporations on innovativeness, motivation, productivity, and strategic management. For many nonprofit examples of strategic planning in practice, click on Strategic Planning Links found at the www.strategyclub.com Web site.

Compared to for-profit firms, nonprofit and governmental organizations may be totally dependent on outside financing. Especially for these organizations, strategic management provides an excellent vehicle for developing and justifying requests for needed financial support.

Educational Institutions

Educational institutions are more frequently using strategic-management techniques and concepts. Richard Cyert, former president of Carnegie Mellon University, said, "I believe we do a far better job of strategic management than any company I know." Population shifts nationally from the Northeast and Midwest to the Southeast and West are but one factor causing trauma for educational institutions that have not planned for changing enrollments. Ivy League schools in the Northeast are recruiting more heavily in the Southeast and West. This trend represents a significant change in the competitive climate for attracting the best high school graduates each year.

Online college degrees are becoming common and represent a threat to traditional colleges and universities. "You can put the kids to bed and go to law school," says Andrew Rosen, chief operating officer of Kaplan Education Centers, a subsidiary of the Washington Post Company.

Medical Organizations

The $200 billion U.S. hospital industry is experiencing declining margins, excess capacity, bureaucratic overburdening, poorly planned and executed diversification strategies, soaring health care costs, reduced federal support, and high administrator turnover. The seriousness of this problem is accented by a 20 percent annual decline in use by inpatients nationwide. Declining occupancy rates, deregulation, and accelerating growth of health maintenance organizations, preferred provider organizations, urgent care centers, outpatient surgery centers, diagnostic centers, specialized clinics, and group practices are other major threats facing hospitals today. Many private and state-supported medical institutions are in financial trouble as a result of traditionally taking a reactive rather than a proactive approach in dealing with their industry.

Hospitals—originally intended to be warehouses for people dying of tuberculosis, smallpox, cancer, pneumonia, and infectious diseases—are creating new strategies today as advances in the diagnosis and treatment of chronic diseases are undercutting that earlier mission. Hospitals are beginning to bring services to the patient as much as bringing the patient to the hospital; health care is more and more being concentrated in the home and in the residential community, not on the hospital campus. Chronic care will require day-treatment facilities, electronic monitoring at home, user-friendly ambulatory services, decentralized service networks, and laboratory testing. A successful hospital strategy for the future will require renewed and deepened collaboration with physicians, who are central to hospitals' well-being, and a reallocation of resources from acute to chronic care in home and community settings.

Current strategies being pursued by many hospitals include creating home health services, establishing nursing homes, and forming rehabilitation centers. Backward integration strategies that some hospitals are pursuing include acquiring ambulance services, waste disposal services, and diagnostic services. Millions of persons annually research medical ailments online, which is causing a dramatic shift in the balance of power between doctor, patient, and hospitals. The number of persons using the Internet to obtain medical information is skyrocketing. A motivated patient using the Internet can gain knowledge on a particular subject far beyond his or her doctor's knowledge, because no person can keep up with the results and implications of billions of dollars' worth of medical research reported weekly. Patients today often walk into the doctor's office with a file folder of the latest articles detailing research and treatment options for their ailments.

Governmental Agencies and Departments

Federal, state, county, and municipal agencies and departments, such as police departments, chambers of commerce, forestry associations, and health departments, are responsible for formulating, implementing, and evaluating strategies that use taxpayers' dollars in the most cost-effective way to provide services and programs. Strategic-management concepts are generally required and thus widely used to enable governmental organizations to be more effective and efficient. For a list of government agency strategic plans, click on Strategic Planning Links found at the www.strategyclub.com Web site, and scroll down through the government sites.

Strategists in governmental organizations operate with less strategic autonomy than their counterparts in private firms. Public enterprises generally cannot diversify into unrelated businesses or merge with other firms. Governmental strategists usually enjoy little freedom in altering the organizations' missions or redirecting objectives. Legislators and politicians often have direct or indirect control over major decisions and resources. Strategic issues get discussed and debated in the media and legislatures. Issues become politicized, resulting in fewer strategic choice alternatives. There is now more predictability in the management of public sector enterprises.

Government agencies and departments are finding that their employees get excited about the opportunity to participate in the strategic-management process and thereby have an effect on the organization's mission, objectives, strategies, and policies. In addition, government agencies are using a strategic-management approach to develop and substantiate formal requests for additional funding.

Strategic Management in Small Firms

The reason why "becoming your own boss" has become a national obsession is that entrepreneurs are America's role models. Almost everyone wants to own a business—from teens and college students, who are signing up for entrepreneurial courses in record numbers, to those over age 65, who are forming more companies every year.

As hundreds of thousands of people have been laid off from work in the last two years, many of these individuals have started small businesses. The *Wall Street Journal* recently provided a 10-page article on how to be a successful entrepreneur.[40] Not only laid off employees but also college graduates are seeking more and more to open their own businesses. As of April 15, 2009, the Small Business Administration had approved more than $1.5 billion in Recovery Act loans and supported more than $2 billion in lending to small businesses. "I was not envisioning myself as an entrepreneur when I began the MBA program at Northwestern University, but this is part of the journey," said student Tiffany Urrechaga. "It's kind of a blessing that I didn't get a job because I was able to reshift my thinking."[41]

Strategic management is vital for large firms' success, but what about small firms? The strategic-management process is just as vital for small companies. From their inception, all organizations have a strategy, even if the strategy just evolves from day-to-day operations. Even if conducted informally or by a single owner/entrepreneur, the strategic-management process can significantly enhance small firms' growth and prosperity. Because an ever-increasing number of men and women in the United States are starting their own businesses, more individuals are becoming strategists. Widespread corporate layoffs have contributed to an explosion in small businesses and new ideas.

Numerous magazine and journal articles have focused on applying strategic-management concepts to small businesses. A major conclusion of these articles is that a lack of strategic-management knowledge is a serious obstacle for many small business owners. Other problems often encountered in applying strategic-management concepts to small businesses are a lack of both sufficient capital to exploit external opportunities and a day-to-day cognitive frame of reference. Research also indicates that strategic management in small firms is more informal than in large firms, but small firms that engage in strategic management outperform those that do not.

Conclusion

The main appeal of any managerial approach is the expectation that it will enhance organizational performance. This is especially true of strategic management. Through involvement in strategic-management activities, managers and employees achieve a better understanding of an organization's priorities and operations. Strategic management allows organizations to be efficient, but more important, it allows them to be effective. Although strategic management does not guarantee organizational success, the process allows proactive rather than reactive decision making. Strategic management may represent a radical change in philosophy for some organizations, so strategists must be trained to anticipate and constructively respond to questions and issues as they arise. The 16 strategies discussed in this chapter can represent a new beginning for many firms, especially if managers and employees in the organization understand and support the plan for action.

We invite you to visit the David page on the Prentice Hall Companion Web site at http://www.pearsonhighered.com/david/ for this chapter's review quiz.

Key Terms and Concepts

Acquisition (p. 158)

Backward Integration (p. 140)

Balanced Scorecard (p. 135)

Bankruptcy (p. 147)

Business-Processing Outsourcing (BPO) (p. 161)

Combination Strategy (p. 137)

Cooperative Arrangements (p. 156)

Cost Leadership (p. 151)

De-integration (p. 140)
Differentiation (p. 151)
Diversification Strategies (p. 143)
Divestiture (p. 148)
First Mover Advantages (p. 161)
Focus (p. 151)
Forward Integration (p. 139)
Franchising (p. 139)
Friendly Merger (p. 158)
Generic Strategies (p. 151)
Horizontal Integration (p. 141)
Hostile Takeover (p. 158)
Integration Strategies (p. 139)
Intensive Strategies (p. 141)
Joint Venture (p. 156)

Leveraged Buyout (p. 160)
Liquidation (p. 149)
Long-Term Objectives (p. 133)
Market Development (p. 142)
Market Penetration (p. 141)
Merger (p. 158)
Product Development (p. 142)
Related Diversification (p. 144)
Retrenchment (p. 146)
Takeover (p. 158)
Turbulent, High-Velocity Markets (p. 155)
Unrelated Diversification (p. 144)
Vertical Integration (p. 139)
White Knight (p. 159)

Issues for Review and Discussion

1. In order of importance, list six "characteristics of objectives."
2. In order of importance, list six "benefits of objectives."
3. Called de-integration, there appears to be a growing trend for firms to become less forward integrated. Discuss why.
4. Called de-integration, there appears to be a growing trend for firms to become less backward integrated. Discuss why.
5. If a company has $1 million to spend on a new strategy and is considering market development versus product development, what determining factors would be most important to consider?
6. What conditions, externally and internally, would be desired/necessary for a firm to diversify?
7. Discuss "nationalization versus bankruptcy" for large American icon firms such as General Motors, AIG, and Citigroup. Which strategy is best for (1) the company and (2) the U.S. economy? Discuss.
8. Could a firm simultaneously pursue focus, differentiation, and cost leadership? Should firms do that? Discuss.
9. There is a growing trend of increased collaboration among competitors. List the benefits and drawbacks of this practice.
10. List four major benefits of forming a joint venture to achieve desired objectives.
11. List six major benefits of acquiring another firm to achieve desired objectives.
12. List five reasons why many merger/acquisitions historically have failed.
13. Can you think of any reasons why not-for-profit firms would benefit less from doing strategic planning than for-profit companies?
14. Discuss how important it is for a college football or basketball team to have a good game plan for the big rival game this coming weekend. How much time and effort do you feel the coaching staff puts into developing that game plan? Why is such time and effort essential?
15. Why are more than 60 percent of Fortune 500 firms headquartered in Wilmington, Delaware?
16. Define and give a hypothetical example of a "white knight" in the fast-food industry.
17. How does strategy formulation differ for a small versus a large organization? How does it differ for a for-profit versus a nonprofit organization?
18. Give recent examples of market penetration, market development, and product development.
19. Give recent examples of forward integration, backward integration, and horizontal integration.
20. Give recent examples of related and unrelated diversification.
21. Give recent examples of joint venture, retrenchment, divestiture, and liquidation.
22. Do you think hostile takeovers are unethical? Why or why not?
23. What are the major advantages and disadvantages of diversification?
24. What are the major advantages and disadvantages of an integrative strategy?
25. How does strategic management differ in for-profit and nonprofit organizations?
26. Why is it not advisable to pursue too many strategies at once?

27. Consumers can purchase tennis shoes, food, cars, boats, and insurance on the Internet. Are there any products today than cannot be purchased online? What is the implication for traditional retailers?
28. What are the pros and cons of a firm merging with a rival firm?
29. Visit the CheckMATE strategic-planning software Web site at www.checkmateplan.com, and discuss the benefits offered.
30. Compare and contrast financial objectives with strategic objectives. Which type is more important in your opinion? Why?
31. Diagram a two-division organizational chart that includes a CEO, COO, CIO, CSO, CFO, CMO, HRM, R&D, and two division presidents. *Hint:* Division presidents report to the COO.
32. How do the levels of strategy differ in a large firm versus a small firm?
33. List 11 types of strategies. Give a hypothetical example of each strategy listed.
34. Discuss the nature of as well as the pros and cons of a "friendly merger" versus "hostile takeover" in acquiring another firm. Give an example of each.
35. Define and explain "first mover advantages."
36. Define and explain "outsourcing."
37. Discuss the business of offering a BBA or MBA degree online.
38. What strategies are best for turbulent, high-velocity markets?

Notes

1. John Byrne, "Strategic Planning—It's Back," *BusinessWeek* (August 26, 1996): 46.
2. Steven C. Brandt, *Strategic Planning in Emerging Companies* (Reading, MA: Addison-Wesley, 1981). Reprinted with permission of the publisher.
3. R. Kaplan and D. Norton, "Putting the Balanced Scorecard to Work," *Harvard Business Review* (September–October, 1993): 147.
4. F. Hansen and M. Smith, "Crisis in Corporate America: The Role of Strategy," *Business Horizons* (January–February 2003): 9.
5. Adapted from F. R. David, "How Do We Choose Among Alternative Growth Strategies?" *Managerial Planning* 33, no. 4 (January–February 1985): 14–17, 22.
6. Ibid.
7. Kenneth Davidson, "Do Megamergers Make Sense?" *Journal of Business Strategy* 7, no. 3 (Winter 1987): 45.
8. Op. cit., David.
9. Ibid.
10. Op. cit., David.
11. Ibid.
12. Arthur Thompson Jr., A. J. Strickland III, and John Gamble. *Crafting and Executing Strategy: Text and Readings* (New York: McGraw-Hill/Irwin, 2005): 241.
13. Michael E. Porter, *Competitive Strategy: Techniques for Analyzing Industries and Competitors* (New York: Free Press, 1980): 53–57, 318–319.
14. Sheila Muto, "Seeing a Boost, Hospitals Turn to Retail Stores," *Wall Street Journal* (November 7, 2001): B1, B8.
15. Jon Swartz, "Cisco Gets into Computer Server Market," *Wall Street Journal* (March 17, 2009): 4B.
16. Op. cit., David.
17. Doug Cameron, "Smithfield to Close Six Plants, Shed Jobs," *Wall Street Journal* (February 18, 2009): B3.
18. Op. cit., David.
19. Ibid.
20. Ibid.
21. Michael Porter, *Competitive Advantage* (New York: Free Press, 1985): 97. Also, Arthur Thompson Jr., A. J. Strickland III, and John Gamble, *Crafting and Executing Strategy: Text and Readings* (New York: McGraw-Hill/Irwin, 2005): 117.
22. Arthur Thompson Jr., A. J. Strickland III, and John Gamble, *Crafting and Executing Strategy: Text and Readings* (New York: McGraw-Hill/Irwin, 2005): 125–126.
23. Porter, *Competitive Advantage,* pp. 160–162.
24. Thompson, Strickland, and Gamble, pp. 129–130.
25. Ibid., 134.
26. Gary Hamel, Yves Doz, and C. K. Prahalad, "Collaborate with Your Competitors—and Win," *Harvard Business Review* 67, no. 1 (January–February 1989): 133.
27. Kathryn Rudie Harrigan, "Joint Ventures: Linking for a Leap Forward," *Planning Review* 14, no. 4 (July–August 1986): 10.
28. Matthew Schifrin, "Partner or Perish," *Forbes* (May 21, 2001): 26.
29. Ibid., p. 28.
30. Nikhil Hutheesing, "Marital Blisters," *Forbes* (May 21, 2001): 32.
31. Ibid., p. 32.
32. Steven Rattner, "Mergers: Windfalls or Pitfalls?" *Wall Street Journal* (October 11, 1999): A22; Nikhil Deogun, "Merger Wave Spurs More Stock Wipeouts," *Wall Street Journal* (November 29, 1999): C1.
33. Yuka Hayashi, "Japanese Firms, Flush with Cash, Step Up Deals," *Wall Street Journal* (January 6, 2009): B1.
34. Jason Zweig, "Corporate-Cash Umbrellas: Too Big for This Storm? *Wall Street Journal* (March 14–15, 2009): B1.
35. J. A. Schmidt, "Business Perspective on Mergers and Acquisitions," in J. A. Schmidt, ed., *Making Mergers Work,* Alexandria, VA: Society for Human Resource Management, (2002): 23–46.
36. Joel Millman, "Mexican Mergers/Acquisitions Triple from 2001," *Wall Street Journal* (December 27, 2002): A2.

37. Robert Davis, "Net Empowering Patients," *USA Today* (July 14, 1999): 1A.

38. M. J. Gannon, K. G. Smith, and C. Grimm, "An Organizational Information-Processing Profile of First Movers," *Journal of Business Research* 25 (1992): 231–241; M. B. Lieberman and D. B. Montgomery, "First Mover Advantages," *Strategic Management Journal* 9 (Summer 1988): 41–58.

39. Scott Thurm, "Behind Outsourcing: Promise and Pitfalls," *Wall Street Journal* (February 26, 2007): B3.

40. Kelly Spors, "So, You Want to Be an Entrepreneur," *Wall Street Journal* (February 28, 2009): R1.

41. Kim Thai and Laura Petrecca, "Today's MBA Graduates Create Their Own Jobs," *USA Today* (April 27, 2009): 7B.

Current Readings

Barkema, Harry G., and Mario Schijven. "How Do Firms Learn to Make Acquisitions? A Review of Past Research and an Agenda for the Future." *Journal of Management* 34, no. 3 (June 2008): 594.

Bowen, Harry P., and Margarethe Wiersema. "Corporate Diversification: The Impact of Foreign Competition, Industry Globalization, and Product Diversification." *Strategic Management Journal* 29, no. 2 (February 2008): 115.

Dalton, Catherine. "Strategic Alliances: There Are Battles and There Is the War." *Business Horizons* 52, no. 2 (March–April 2009): 105–108.

De Fontenay, Catherine C., and Joshua S. Gans. "A Bargaining Perspective on Strategic Outsourcing and Supply Competition." *Strategic Management Journal* 29, no. 8 (August 2008): 819.

Doving, Erik, and Paul N. Gooderham. "Dynamic Capabilities as Antecedents of the Scope of Related Diversification: The Case of Small Firm Accountancy Practices." *Strategic Management Journal* 29, no. 8 (August 2008): 841.

Dykes, Bernadine Johnson, Jerayr (John), Haleblian, and Gerry M. McNamara. "The Performance Implications of Participating in an Acquisition Wave: Early Mover Advantages, Bandwagon Effects, and in the Moderating Influence of Industry Characteristics and Acquirer Tactics." *The Academy of Management Journal* 51, no. 1 (February 2008): 113.

Garrette, Bernard, Xavier Castaner, and Pierre Dussauge. "Horizontal Alliances as an Alternative to Autonomous Production: Product Expansion Mode Choice in the Worldwide Aircraft Industry." *Strategic Management Journal* (August 2009): 885–894.

Hagiu, Andrei, and David B. Yoffie. "What's Your Google Strategy?" *Harvard Business Review* (April 2009): 74–83.

Haleblian, Jerayr, Cynthia Devers, Gerry McNamara, Mason Carpenter, and Robert Davison. "Taking Stock of What We Know About Mergers and Acquisitions: A Review and Research Agenda." *Journal of Management* (June 2009): 469–502.

Harding, David, Michael C. Mankins, and Rolf-Magnus Weddigen. "How the Best Divest." *Harvard Business Review* (October 2008): 92.

Hult, Tomas M., David J. Ketchen, David Meyer, and William Rebarick. "Best Value Supply Chains: A Key Competitive Weapon for the 21st Century." *Business Horizons* 51, no. 3 (May–June 2008): 235.

Kim, Jay, and Sydney Finkelstein. "The Effects of Strategic and Market Complementarity on Acquisition Performance: Evidence from the U.S. Commercial Banking Industry." *Strategic Management Journal* (June 2009): 617–646.

King, Brian L. "Strategizing at Leading Venture Capital Firms: Of Planning, Opportunism and Deliberate Emergence." *Long Range Planning* 41, no. 3 (June 2008): 345.

Kumar, Nirmalya. "How Emerging Giants Are Rewriting the Rules of M&A." *Harvard Business Review* (May 2009): 115–125.

Luo, Yadong. "Procedural Fairness and Interfirm Cooperation in Strategic Alliances." *Strategic Management Journal* 29, no. 1 (January 2008): 27.

Luo, Yadong. "Structuring Interorganizational Cooperation: The Role of Economic Integration in Strategic Alliances." *Strategic Management Journal* 29 (June 2008): 617.

Meyer, Christine Benedichte. "Value Leakages in Mergers and Acquisitions: Why They Occur and How They Can Be Addressed." *Long Range Planning* 41, no 2 (April 2008): 197.

Ozcan, Pinar, and Kathleen Eisenhardt. "Origin of Alliance Portfolios: Entrepreneurs, Network Strategies, and Firm Performance." *Academy of Management Journal* (April 2009): 246–279.

Pearce, John A., II, and Keith D. Robbins. "Strategic Transformation as the Essential Last Step in the Process of Business Turnaround." *Business Horizons* 51, no. 2 (March–April 2008): 121.

Shah, Reshma H., and Vanitha Swaminathan. "Factors Influencing Partner Selection in Strategic Alliances: The Moderating Role of Alliance Context." *Strategic Management Journal* 29, no. 5 (May 2008): 471.

Shanley, Mark, and Xiaoli Yin. "Industry Determinants of the 'Merger versus Alliance' Decision." *The Academy of Management Review* 33, no. 2 (April 2008): 473.

Slater, Stanley F., Robert A. Weigand, and Thomas J. Zwirlein. "The Business Case for Commitment to Diversity." *Business Horizons* 51, no. 3 (May–June 2008): 201.

ASSURANCE OF LEARNING EXERCISES

Assurance of Learning Exercise 5A

What Strategies Should McDonald's Pursue in 2011–2013?

Purpose

In performing strategic management case analysis, you can find information about the respective company's actual and planned strategies. Comparing what is planned versus *what you recommend* is an important part of case analysis. Do not recommend what the firm actually plans, unless in-depth analysis of the situation reveals those strategies to be best among all feasible alternatives. This exercise gives you experience conducting library and Internet research to determine what McDonald's should do in 2011–2013.

Instructions

Step 1	Look up McDonald's (MCD) and Burger King Holdings (BKC) using the Web sites provided in Table 4-5. Find some recent articles about firms in this industry. Scan Moody's, Dun & Bradstreet, and Standard & Poor's publications for information.
Step 2	Summarize your findings in a three-page report entitled "Strategies Being Pursued by McDonald's in 2010."

Assurance of Learning Exercise 5B

Examining Strategy Articles

Purpose

Strategy articles can be found weekly in journals, magazines, and newspapers. By reading and studying strategy articles, you can gain a better understanding of the strategic-management process. Several of the best journals in which to find corporate strategy articles are *Advanced Management Journal, Business Horizons, Long Range Planning, Journal of Business Strategy,* and *Strategic Management Journal.* These journals are devoted to reporting the results of empirical research in management. They apply strategic-management concepts to specific organizations and industries. They introduce new strategic-management techniques and provide short case studies on selected firms.

Other good journals in which to find strategic-management articles are *Harvard Business Review, Sloan Management Review, California Management Review, Academy of Management Review, Academy of Management Journal, Academy of Management Executive, Journal of Management,* and *Journal of Small Business Management.*

In addition to journals, many magazines regularly publish articles that focus on business strategies. Several of the best magazines in which to find applied strategy articles are *Dun's Business Month, Fortune, Forbes, BusinessWeek, Inc.,* and *Industry Week.* Newspapers such as *USA Today, Wall Street Journal, New York Times,* and *Barrons* cover strategy events when they occur—for example, a joint venture announcement, a bankruptcy declaration, a new advertising campaign start, acquisition of a company, divestiture of a division, a chief executive officer's hiring or firing, or a hostile takeover attempt.

In combination, journal, magazine, and newspaper articles can make the strategic-management course more exciting. They allow current strategies of for-profit and nonprofit organizations to be identified and studied.

Instructions

Step 1 Go to your college library and find a recent journal article that focuses on a strategic-management topic. Select your article from one of the journals listed previously, not from a magazine. Copy the article and bring it to class.

Step 2 Give a 3-minute oral report summarizing the most important information in your article. Include comments giving your personal reaction to the article. Pass your article around in class.

Assurance of Learning Exercise 5C

Classifying Some Year 2009 Strategies

Purpose

This exercise can improve your understanding of various strategies by giving you experience classifying strategies. This skill will help you use the strategy-formulation tools presented later. Consider the following 8 actual year-2009 strategies by various firms:

1. Microsoft developed a new videocamera for its Xbox 360 console that allowed players to control games with the movement of their bodies, rather than by holding a plastic wand in their hands, as required with Nintendo's popular Wii game console.
2. Wells Fargo and Bank of America began to "tweet"—post messages of 140 characters or less on Twitter.com, so customers could see product features. Banks are also putting marketing videos on YouTube.
3. The United Kingdom's huge telecom firm, BT Group PLC, cut 15,000 more jobs on top of the 15,000 the prior year.
4. Japanese electronics maker Panasonic Corp. acquired Osaka, Japan-based Sanyo Electric Company.
5. News Corp. sold off many of its television stations.
6. More than 1,000 Chrysler dealers closed their doors and ceased doing business.
7. Germany's Metro AG, the world's fourth-largest retailer after Wal-Mart, Carrefour SA, and Home Depot, is expanding aggressively into China.
8. Time Warner plans to spin off or sell all or part of AOL.

Instructions

Step 1 On a separate sheet of paper, number from 1 to 8. These numbers correspond to the strategies described.

Step 2 What type of strategy best describes the 8 actions cited? Indicate your answers.

Step 3 Exchange papers with a classmate, and grade each other's paper as your instructor gives the right answers.

Assurance of Learning Exercise 5D

How Risky Are Various Alternative Strategies?

Purpose

This exercise focuses on how risky various alternative strategies are for organizations to pursue. Different degrees of risk are based largely on varying degrees of *externality*, defined as movement away from present business into new markets and products. In general, the greater the degree of externality, the greater the probability of loss resulting from unexpected events. High-risk strategies generally are less attractive than low-risk strategies.

Instructions

Step 1 On a separate sheet of paper, number vertically from 1 to 10. Think of 1 as "most risky," 2 as "next most risky," and so forth to 10, "least risky."

Step 2 Write the following strategies beside the appropriate number to indicate how risky you believe the strategy is to pursue: horizontal integration, related diversification, liquidation, forward integration, backward integration, product development, market development, market penetration, retrenchment, and unrelated diversification.

Step 3   Grade your paper as your instructor gives you the right answers and supporting rationale. Each correct answer is worth 10 points.

Assurance of Learning Exercise 5E

Developing Alternative Strategies for My University

Purpose

It is important for representatives from all areas of a college or university to identify and discuss alternative strategies that could benefit faculty, students, alumni, staff, and other constituencies. As you complete this exercise, notice the learning and understanding that occurs as people express differences of opinion. Recall that *the process of planning is more important than the document.*

Instructions

Step 1   Recall or locate the external opportunity/threat and internal strength/weakness factors that you identified as part of Exercise 1B. If you did not do that exercise, discuss now as a class important external and internal factors facing your college or university.

Step 2   Identify and put on the chalkboard alternative strategies that you feel could benefit your college or university. Your proposed actions should allow the institution to capitalize on particular strengths, improve upon certain weaknesses, avoid external threats, and/or take advantage of particular external opportunities. List 10 possible strategies on the board. Number the strategies as they are written on the board.

Step 3   On a separate sheet of paper, number from 1 to 10. Everyone in class individually should rate the strategies identified, using a 1 to 3 scale, where 1 = *I do not support implementation*, 2 = *I am neutral about implementation*, and 3 = *I strongly support implementation*. In rating the strategies, recognize that your institution cannot do everything desired or potentially beneficial.

Step 4   Go to the board and record your ratings in a row beside the respective strategies. Everyone in class should do this, going to the board perhaps by rows in the class.

Step 5   Sum the ratings for each strategy so that a prioritized list of recommended strategies is obtained. This prioritized list reflects the collective wisdom of your class. Strategies with the highest score are deemed best.

Step 6   Discuss how this process could enable organizations to achieve understanding and commitment from individuals.

Step 7   Share your class results with a university administrator, and ask for comments regarding the process and top strategies recommended.

Assurance of Learning Exercise 5F

Lessons in Doing Business Globally

Purpose

The purpose of this exercise is to discover some important lessons learned by local businesses that do business internationally.

Instructions

Contact several local business leaders by phone. Find at least three firms that engage in international or export operations. Visit the owner or manager of each business in person. Ask the businessperson to give you several important lessons that his or her firm has learned in globally doing business. Record the lessons on paper, and report your findings to the class.

CHAPTER 6
Strategy Analysis and Choice

CHAPTER OBJECTIVES

After studying this chapter, you should be able to do the following:

1. Describe a three-stage framework for choosing among alternative strategies.

2. Explain how to develop a SWOT Matrix, SPACE Matrix, BCG Matrix, IE Matrix, and QSPM.

3. Identify important behavioral, political, ethical, and social responsibility considerations in strategy analysis and choice.

4. Discuss the role of intuition in strategic analysis and choice.

5. Discuss the role of organizational culture in strategic analysis and choice.

6. Discuss the role of a board of directors in choosing among alternative strategies.

Assurance of Learning Exercises

Assurance of Learning Exercise 6A

Developing a SWOT Matrix for McDonald's

Assurance of Learning Exercise 6B

Developing a SPACE Matrix for McDonald's

Assurance of Learning Exercise 6C

Developing a BCG Matrix for McDonald's

Assurance of Learning Exercise 6D

Developing a QSPM for McDonald's

Assurance of Learning Exercise 6E

Formulating Individual Strategies

Source: Shutterstock

"Notable Quotes"

"Strategic management is not a box of tricks or a bundle of techniques. It is analytical thinking and commitment of resources to action. But quantification alone is not planning. Some of the most important issues in strategic management cannot be quantified at all."

—Peter Drucker

"Objectives are not commands; they are commitments. They do not determine the future; they are the means to mobilize resources and energies of an organization for the making of the future."

—Peter Drucker

"Life is full of lousy options."

—General P. X. Kelley

"When a crisis forces choosing among alternatives, most people will choose the worst possible one."

—Rudin's Law

"Strategy isn't something you can nail together in slapdash fashion by sitting around a conference table."

—Terry Haller

"Planning is often doomed before it ever starts, either because too much is expected of it or because not enough is put into it."

—T. J. Cartwright

"Whether it's broke or not, fix it—make it better. Not just products, but the whole company if necessary."

—Bill Saporito

Assurance of Learning Exercise 6F

The Mach Test

Assurance of Learning Exercise 6G

Developing a BCG Matrix for My University

Assurance of Learning Exercise 6H

The Role of Boards of Directors

Assurance of Learning Exercise 6I

Locating Companies in a Grand Strategy Matrix

Strategy analysis and choice largely involve making subjective decisions based on objective information. This chapter introduces important concepts that can help strategists generate feasible alternatives, evaluate those alternatives, and choose a specific course of action. Behavioral aspects of strategy formulation are described, including politics, culture, ethics, and social responsibility considerations. Modern tools for formulating strategies are described, and the appropriate role of a board of directors is discussed.

Doing Great in a Weak Economy. How?

Apple

When most firms were struggling in 2008, Apple increased its revenues from $24.0 billion in 2007 to $32.4 billion in 2008. Apple's net income was $4.4 billion in 2008, up from $3.5 billion the prior year—wonderfully impressive in a global slump. *Fortune* magazine in 2009 rated Apple as their number-one "Most Admired Company in the World" in terms of their management and performance. That's right, number one out of millions of companies around the world.

In the global recession, technology purchases were deemed disposable or discretionary for most businesses and individuals. New orders for both business and consumer tech products plummeted, and technology firms shed workers rapidly. This led to massive layoffs in the computer industry and related industries. The meltdown permeated all the way down the supply chain to chip makers, hard drive makers, peripheral makers, software vendors, and other segments. Hewlett-Packard recently cut 24,600 employees and Dell laid off 8,900. Microsoft recently cut its travel budget 20 percent and laid off 5,000 employees.

Amid recession and faltering rivals, Apple is doing great. Brisk sales of iPods, iPhones, and laptops are yielding higher and higher revenues and profits every quarter. Legendary CEO Steve Jobs and his colleagues are implementing a great strategic plan. Apple has no manufacturing plants but does have retail stores. Apple continues to amaze the world with its new, innovative products, being one of the best examples of a "first mover" firm in developing new products. Apple has very loyal customers and has about $25.6

billion in cash on their balance sheet to go along with zero long-term debt.

Based in Cupertino, California, Apple has not cut prices of computers much at all during the recession, even as competitors have slashed prices dramatically.

On June 9, 2009, Apple did however lower the price of its entry-level iPhone by 50 percent to $99 and rolled out a next-generation model named iPhone 3GS which is faster than existing models and can capture videos. Apple by mid-2009 had sold over 20 million iPhones and reported in July 2009 that the company was unable to supply enough iPhones and Macintosh computers to meet demand. Apple sold 5.2 million iPhones in the quarter ending that month, more than 7 times what it sold the same quarter the prior year. Shipments of Macintosh computers that quarter were up 4 percent to 2.6 million. For the first 7 months of 2009, Apple's stock rose 80 percent compared to the Nasdaq Composite being up 25 percent.

Apple has aggressive new plans to design its own computer chips in order (1) obtain better chips for its unique products, and (2) share fewer details about its technology with external chip manufacturers.

Source: Based on Byron Acohido and Matt Krantz, "Even Tech Stalwarts Hit Hard," *USA Today* (January 23, 2009): B1, B2; Geoff Colvin, "The World's Most Admired Companies," *Fortune* (March 16, 2009): 76–86.

The Nature of Strategy Analysis and Choice

As indicated by Figure 6-1, this chapter focuses on generating and evaluating alternative strategies, as well as selecting strategies to pursue. Strategy analysis and choice seek to determine alternative courses of action that could best enable the firm to achieve its mission and objectives. The firm's present strategies, objectives, and mission, coupled with the external and internal audit information, provide a basis for generating and evaluating feasible alternative strategies.

Unless a desperate situation confronts the firm, alternative strategies will likely represent incremental steps that move the firm from its present position to a desired future position. Alternative strategies do not come out of the wild blue yonder; they are derived from the firm's vision, mission, objectives, external audit, and internal audit; they are consistent with, or build on, past strategies that have worked well.

The Process of Generating and Selecting Strategies

Strategists never consider all feasible alternatives that could benefit the firm because there are an infinite number of possible actions and an infinite number of ways to implement those actions. Therefore, a manageable set of the most attractive alternative strategies must be developed. The advantages, disadvantages, trade-offs, costs, and benefits of these strategies should be determined. This section discusses the process that many firms use to determine an appropriate set of alternative strategies.

Identifying and evaluating alternative strategies should involve many of the managers and employees who earlier assembled the organizational vision and mission statements, performed the external audit, and conducted the internal audit. Representatives from each department and division of the firm should be included in this process, as was the case in previous strategy-formulation activities. Recall that involvement provides the best opportunity for managers and employees to gain an understanding of what the firm is doing and why and to become committed to helping the firm accomplish its objectives.

All participants in the strategy analysis and choice activity should have the firm's external and internal audit information by their sides. This information, coupled with the firm's mission statement, will help participants crystallize in their own minds particular strategies that they believe could benefit the firm most. Creativity should be encouraged in this thought process.

Alternative strategies proposed by participants should be considered and discussed in a meeting or series of meetings. Proposed strategies should be listed in writing. When all feasible strategies identified by participants are given and understood, the strategies should be ranked in order of attractiveness by all participants, with 1 = should not be implemented, 2 = possibly should be implemented, 3 = probably should be implemented, and 4 = definitely should be implemented. This process will result in a prioritized list of best strategies that reflects the collective wisdom of the group.

FIGURE 6-1

A Comprehensive Strategic-Management Model

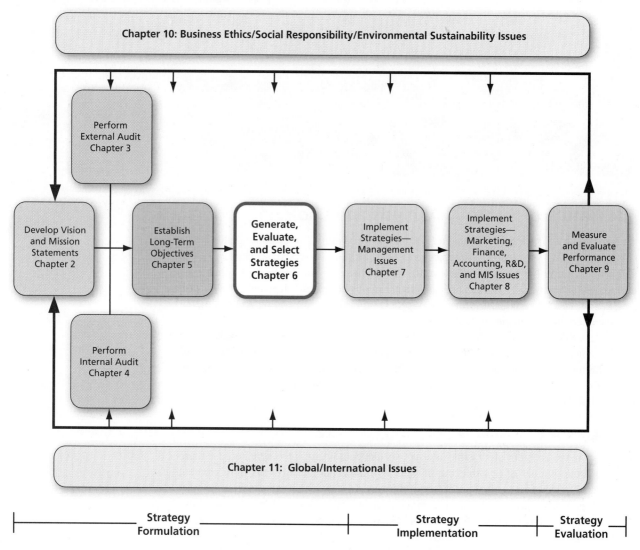

Source: Fred R. David, "How Companies Define Their Mission," *Long Range Planning* 22, no. 3 (June 1988): 40.

A Comprehensive Strategy-Formulation Framework

Important strategy-formulation techniques can be integrated into a three-stage decision-making framework, as shown in Figure 6-2. The tools presented in this framework are applicable to all sizes and types of organizations and can help strategists identify, evaluate, and select strategies.

Stage 1 of the formulation framework consists of the EFE Matrix, the IFE Matrix, and the Competitive Profile Matrix (CPM). Called the *Input Stage,* Stage 1 summarizes the basic input information needed to formulate strategies. Stage 2, called the *Matching Stage,* focuses upon generating feasible alternative strategies by aligning key external and internal factors. Stage 2 techniques include the Strengths-Weaknesses-Opportunities-Threats (SWOT) Matrix, the Strategic Position and Action Evaluation (SPACE) Matrix, the Boston Consulting Group (BCG) Matrix, the Internal-External (IE) Matrix, and the Grand Strategy Matrix. Stage 3, called the *Decision Stage,* involves a single technique, the Quantitative Strategic Planning Matrix (QSPM). A QSPM uses input information from Stage 1 to objectively evaluate feasible alternative strategies identified in Stage 2. A QSPM reveals the relative attractiveness of alternative strategies and thus provides objective basis for selecting specific strategies.

FIGURE 6-2

The Strategy-Formulation Analytical Framework

STAGE 1: THE INPUT STAGE		
External Factor Evaluation (EFE) Matrix	Competitive Profile Matrix (CPM)	Internal Factor Evaluation (IFE) Matrix

STAGE 2: THE MATCHING STAGE				
Strengths-Weaknesses-Opportunities-Threats (SWOT) Matrix	Strategic Position and Action Evaluation (SPACE) Matrix	Boston Consulting Group (BCG) Matrix	Internal-External (IE) Matrix	Grand Strategy Matrix

STAGE 3: THE DECISION STAGE

Quantitative Strategic Planning Matrix (QSPM)

All nine techniques included in the *strategy-formulation framework* require the integration of intuition and analysis. Autonomous divisions in an organization commonly use strategy-formulation techniques to develop strategies and objectives. Divisional analyses provide a basis for identifying, evaluating, and selecting among alternative corporate-level strategies.

Strategists themselves, not analytic tools, are always responsible and accountable for strategic decisions. Lenz emphasized that the shift from a words-oriented to a numbers-oriented planning process can give rise to a false sense of certainty; it can reduce dialogue, discussion, and argument as a means for exploring understandings, testing assumptions, and fostering organizational learning.[1] Strategists, therefore, must be wary of this possibility and use analytical tools to facilitate, rather than to diminish, communication. Without objective information and analysis, personal biases, politics, emotions, personalities, and *halo error* (the tendency to put too much weight on a single factor) unfortunately may play a dominant role in the strategy-formulation process.

The Input Stage

Procedures for developing an EFE Matrix, an IFE Matrix, and a CPM were presented in Chapters 3 and 4. The information derived from these three matrices provides basic input information for the matching and decision stage matrices described later in this chapter.

The input tools require strategists to quantify subjectivity during early stages of the strategy-formulation process. Making small decisions in the input matrices regarding the relative importance of external and internal factors allows strategists to more effectively generate and evaluate alternative strategies. Good intuitive judgment is always needed in determining appropriate weights and ratings.

The Matching Stage

Strategy is sometimes defined as the match an organization makes between its internal resources and skills and the opportunities and risks created by its external factors.[2] The matching stage of the strategy-formulation framework consists of five techniques that can be used in any sequence: the SWOT Matrix, the SPACE Matrix, the BCG Matrix, the IE Matrix, and the Grand Strategy Matrix. These tools rely upon information derived from the input stage to match external opportunities and threats with internal strengths and weaknesses. *Matching* external and internal critical success factors is the key to effectively generating feasible alternative strategies. For example, a firm with excess working capital (an internal strength) could take advantage of the cell phone industry's

TABLE 6-1 Matching Key External and Internal Factors to Formulate Alternative Strategies

Key Internal Factor	Key External Factor	Resultant Strategy
Excess working capital (an internal strength)	+ 20 percent annual growth in the cell phone industry (an external opportunity)	= Acquire Cellfone, Inc.
Insufficient capacity (an internal weakness)	+ Exit of two major foreign competitors from the industry (an external opportunity)	= Pursue horizontal integration by buying competitors' facilities
Strong R&D expertise (an internal strength)	+ Decreasing numbers of younger adults (an external threat)	= Develop new products for older adults
Poor employee morale (an internal weakness)	+ Rising healthcare costs (an external threat)	= Develop a new wellness program

20 percent annual growth rate (an external opportunity) by acquiring Cellfone, Inc., a firm in the cell phone industry. This example portrays simple one-to-one matching. In most situations, external and internal relationships are more complex, and the matching requires multiple alignments for each strategy generated. The basic concept of matching is illustrated in Table 6-1.

Any organization, whether military, product-oriented, service-oriented, governmental, or even athletic, must develop and execute good strategies to win. A good offense without a good defense, or vice versa, usually leads to defeat. Developing strategies that use strengths to capitalize on opportunities could be considered an offense, whereas strategies designed to improve upon weaknesses while avoiding threats could be termed defensive. Every organization has some external opportunities and threats and internal strengths and weaknesses that can be aligned to formulate feasible alternative strategies.

The Strengths-Weaknesses-Opportunities-Threats (SWOT) Matrix

The *Strengths-Weaknesses-Opportunities-Threats (SWOT) Matrix* is an important matching tool that helps managers develop four types of strategies: SO (strengths-opportunities) Strategies, WO (weaknesses-opportunities) Strategies, ST (strengths-threats) Strategies, and WT (weaknesses-threats) Strategies.[3] Matching key external and internal factors is the most difficult part of developing a SWOT Matrix and requires good judgment—and there is no one best set of matches. Note in Table 6-1 that the first, second, third, and fourth strategies are SO, WO, ST, and WT strategies, respectively.

SO Strategies use a firm's internal strengths to take advantage of external opportunities. All managers would like their organizations to be in a position in which internal strengths can be used to take advantage of external trends and events. Organizations generally will pursue WO, ST, or WT strategies to get into a situation in which they can apply SO Strategies. When a firm has major weaknesses, it will strive to overcome them and make them strengths. When an organization faces major threats, it will seek to avoid them to concentrate on opportunities.

WO Strategies aim at improving internal weaknesses by taking advantage of external opportunities. Sometimes key external opportunities exist, but a firm has internal weaknesses that prevent it from exploiting those opportunities. For example, there may be a high demand for electronic devices to control the amount and timing of fuel injection in automobile engines (opportunity), but a certain auto parts manufacturer may lack the technology required for producing these devices (weakness). One possible WO Strategy would be to acquire this technology by forming a joint venture with a firm having competency in this area. An alternative WO Strategy would be to hire and train people with the required technical capabilities.

ST Strategies use a firm's strengths to avoid or reduce the impact of external threats. This does not mean that a strong organization should always meet threats in the external environment head-on. An example of ST Strategy occurred when Texas Instruments used an excellent legal department (a strength) to collect nearly $700 million in damages and royalties from nine Japanese and Korean firms that infringed on patents for semiconductor memory chips (threat).

Rival firms that copy ideas, innovations, and patented products are a major threat in many industries. This is still a major problem for U.S. firms selling products in China.

WT Strategies are defensive tactics directed at reducing internal weakness and avoiding external threats. An organization faced with numerous external threats and internal weaknesses may indeed be in a precarious position. In fact, such a firm may have to fight for its survival, merge, retrench, declare bankruptcy, or choose liquidation.

A schematic representation of the SWOT Matrix is provided in Figure 6-3. Note that a SWOT Matrix is composed of nine cells. As shown, there are four key factor cells, four strategy cells, and one cell that is always left blank (the upper-left cell). The four strategy cells, labeled *SO, WO, ST,* and *WT,* are developed after completing four key factor cells, labeled *S, W, O,* and *T.* There are eight steps involved in constructing a SWOT Matrix:

1. List the firm's key external opportunities.
2. List the firm's key external threats.
3. List the firm's key internal strengths.
4. List the firm's key internal weaknesses.
5. Match internal strengths with external opportunities, and record the resultant SO Strategies in the appropriate cell.
6. Match internal weaknesses with external opportunities, and record the resultant WO Strategies.
7. Match internal strengths with external threats, and record the resultant ST Strategies.
8. Match internal weaknesses with external threats, and record the resultant WT Strategies.

Some important aspects of a SWOT Matrix are evidenced in Figure 6-3. For example, note that both the internal/external factors and the SO/ST/WO/WT Strategies are stated in quantitative terms to the extent possible. This is important. For example, regarding the second SO #2 and ST #1 strategies, if the analyst just said, "Add new repair/service persons," the reader might think that 20 new repair/service persons are needed. Actually only two are needed. Always *be specific* to the extent possible in stating factors and strategies.

It is also important to include the "S1, O2" type notation after each strategy in a SWOT Matrix. This notation reveals the rationale for each alternative strategy. Strategies do not rise out of the blue. Note in Figure 6-3 how this notation reveals the internal/external factors that were matched to formulate desirable strategies. For example, note that this retail computer store business may need to "purchase land to build new store" because a new Highway 34 will make its location less desirable. The notation (W2, O2) and (S8, T3) in Figure 6-3 exemplifies this matching process.

The purpose of each Stage 2 matching tool is to generate feasible alternative strategies, not to select or determine which strategies are best. Not all of the strategies developed in the SWOT Matrix, therefore, will be selected for implementation.

The strategy-formulation guidelines provided in Chapter 5 can enhance the process of matching key external and internal factors. For example, when an organization has both the capital and human resources needed to distribute its own products (internal strength) and distributors are unreliable, costly, or incapable of meeting the firm's needs (external threat), forward integration can be an attractive ST Strategy. When a firm has excess production capacity (internal weakness) and its basic industry is experiencing declining annual sales and profits (external threat), related diversification can be an effective WT Strategy.

Although the SWOT matrix is widely used in strategic planning, the analysis does have some limitations.[4] First, SWOT does not show how to achieve a competitive advantage, so it must not be an end in itself. The matrix should be the starting point for a discussion on how proposed strategies could be implemented as well as cost-benefit considerations that ultimately could lead to competitive advantage. Second, SWOT is a static assessment (or snapshot) in time. A SWOT matrix can be like studying a single frame of a motion picture where you see the lead characters and the setting but have no clue as to the plot. As circumstances, capabilities, threats, and strategies change, the dynamics of a competitive

FIGURE 6-3

A SWOT Matrix for a Retail Computer Store

	Strengths	Weaknesses
	1. Inventory turnover up 5.8 to 6.7	1. Software revenues in store down 12%
	2. Average customer purchase up $97 to $128	2. Location of store hurt by new Hwy 34
	3. Employee morale is excellent	3. Carpet and paint in store in disrepair
	4. In-store promotions = 20% increase in sales	4. Bathroom in store needs refurbishing
	5. Newspaper advertising expenditures down 10%	5. Total store revenues down 8%
	6. Revenues from repair/service in-store up 16%	6. Store has no Web site
	7. In-store technical support persons have MIS degrees	7. Supplier on-time-delivery up to 2.4 days
	8. Store's debt-to-total assets ratio down 34%	8. Customer checkout process too slow
		9. Revenues per employee up 19%
Opportunities	**SO Strategies**	**WO Strategies**
1. Population of city growing 10%	1. Add 4 new in-store promotions monthly (S4,O3)	1. Purchase land to build new store (W2, O2)
2. Rival computer store opening 1 mile away	2. Add 2 new repair/service persons (S6, O5)	2. Install new carpet/paint/bath (W3, W4, O1)
3. Vehicle traffic passing store up 12%	3. Send flyer to all seniors over age 55 (S5, O5)	3. Up Web site services by 50% (W6, O7, O8)
4. Vendors average six new products/yr		4. Launch mailout to all Realtors in city (W5, O7)
5. Senior citizen use of computers up 8%		
6. Small business growth in area up 10%		
7. Desire for Web sites up 18% by Realtors		
8. Desire for Web sites up 12% by small firms		
Threats	**ST Strategies**	**WT Strategies**
1. Best Buy opening new store in 1yr nearby	1. Hire two more repair persons and market these new services (S6, S7, T1)	1. Hire 2 new cashiers (W8, T1, T4)
2. Local university offers computer repair	2. Purchase land to build new store (S8, T3)	2. Install new carpet/paint/ bath (W3, W4, T1)
3. New bypass Hwy 34 in 1 yr will divert traffic	3. Raise out-of-store service calls from $60 to $80 (S6, T5)	
4. New mall being built nearby		
5. Gas prices up 14%		
6. Vendors raising prices 8%		

environment may not be revealed in a single matrix. Third, SWOT analysis may lead the firm to overemphasize a single internal or external factor in formulating strategies. There are interrelationships among the key internal and external factors that SWOT does not reveal that may be important in devising strategies.

The Strategic Position and Action Evaluation (SPACE) Matrix

The *Strategic Position and Action Evaluation (SPACE) Matrix,* another important Stage 2 matching tool, is illustrated in Figure 6-4. Its four-quadrant framework indicates whether aggressive, conservative, defensive, or competitive strategies are most appropriate for a given organization. The axes of the SPACE Matrix represent two internal dimensions (*financial position [FP]* and *competitive position [CP]*) and two external dimensions (*stability position [SP]* and *industry position [IP]*). These four factors are perhaps the most important determinants of an organization's overall strategic position.[5]

Depending on the type of organization, numerous variables could make up each of the dimensions represented on the axes of the SPACE Matrix. Factors that were included earlier in the firm's EFE and IFE Matrices should be considered in developing a SPACE Matrix. Other variables commonly included are given in Table 6-2. For example, return on investment, leverage, liquidity, working capital, and cash flow are commonly considered to be determining factors of an organization's financial strength. Like the SWOT Matrix, the SPACE Matrix should be both tailored to the particular organization being studied and based on factual information as much as possible.

FIGURE 6-4

The SPACE Matrix

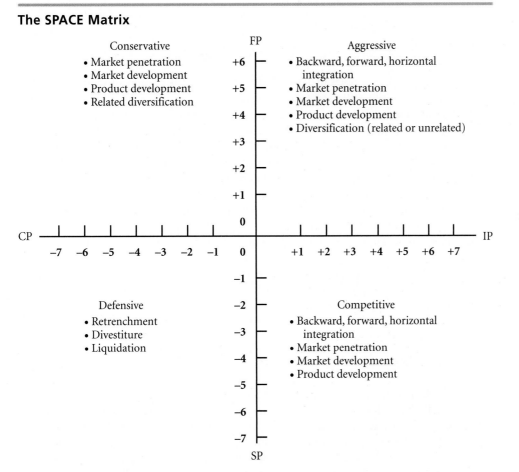

Source: Adapted from H. Rowe, R. Mason, and K. Dickel, *Strategic Management and Business Policy: A Methodological Approach* (Reading, MA: Addison-Wesley Publishing Co. Inc., © 1982): 155.

TABLE 6-2   Example Factors That Make Up the SPACE Matrix Axes

Internal Strategic Position	External Strategic Position
Financial Position (FP)	*Stability Position (SP)*
Return on investment	Technological changes
Leverage	Rate of inflation
Liquidity	Demand variability
Working capital	Price range of competing products
Cash flow	Barriers to entry into market
Inventory turnover	Competitive pressure
Earnings per share	Ease of exit from market
Price earnings ratio	Price elasticity of demand
	Risk involved in business
Competitive Position (CP)	*Industry Position (IP)*
Market share	Growth potential
Product quality	Profit potential
Product life cycle	Financial stability
Customer loyalty	Extent leveraged
Capacity utilization	Resource utilization
Technological know-how	Ease of entry into market
Control over suppliers and distributors	Productivity, capacity utilization

Source: Adapted from H. Rowe, R. Mason, and K. Dickel, *Strategic Management and Business Policy: A Methodological Approach* (Reading, MA: Addison-Wesley Publishing Co. Inc., © 1982): 155–156.

The steps required to develop a SPACE Matrix are as follows:

1.   Select a set of variables to define financial position (FP), competitive position (CP), stability position (SP), and industry position (IP).
2.   Assign a numerical value ranging from +1 (worst) to +7 (best) to each of the variables that make up the FP and IP dimensions. Assign a numerical value ranging from −1 (best) to −7 (worst) to each of the variables that make up the SP and CP dimensions. On the FP and CP axes, make comparison to competitors. On the IP and SP axes, make comparison to other industries.
3.   Compute an average score for FP, CP, IP, and SP by summing the values given to the variables of each dimension and then by dividing by the number of variables included in the respective dimension.
4.   Plot the average scores for FP, IP, SP, and CP on the appropriate axis in the SPACE Matrix.
5.   Add the two scores on the *x*-axis and plot the resultant point on *X*. Add the two scores on the *y*-axis and plot the resultant point on *Y*. Plot the intersection of the new *xy* point.
6.   Draw a *directional vector* from the origin of the SPACE Matrix through the new intersection point. This vector reveals the type of strategies recommended for the organization: aggressive, competitive, defensive, or conservative.

Some examples of strategy profiles that can emerge from a SPACE analysis are shown in Figure 6-5. The directional vector associated with each profile suggests the type of strategies to pursue: aggressive, conservative, defensive, or competitive. When a firm's directional vector is located in the *aggressive quadrant* (upper-right quadrant) of the SPACE Matrix, an organization is in an excellent position to use its internal strengths to (1) take advantage of external opportunities, (2) overcome internal weaknesses, and (3) avoid external threats. Therefore, market penetration, market development, product development, backward integration, forward integration, horizontal integration, or diversification, can be feasible, depending on the specific circumstances that face the firm.

FIGURE 6-5

Example Strategy Profiles

Aggressive Profiles

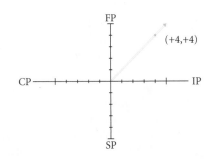

A financially strong firm that has achieved major competitive advantages in a growing and stable industry

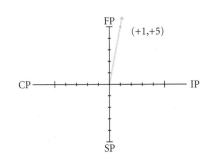

A firm whose financial strength is a dominating factor in the industry

Conservative Profiles

A firm that has achieved financial strength in a stable industry that is not growing; the firm has few competitive advantages

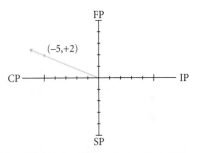

A firm that suffers from major competitive disadvantages in an industry that is technologically stable but declining in sales

Competitive Profiles

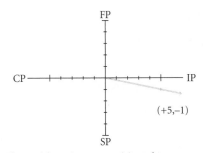

A firm with major competitive advantages in a high-growth industry

An organization that is competing fairly well in an unstable industry

Defensive Profiles

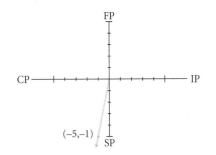

A firm that has a very weak competitive position in a negative growth, stable industry

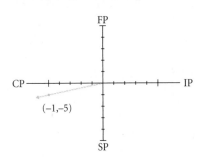

A financially troubled firm in a very unstable industry

Source: Adapted from H. Rowe, R. Mason, and K. Dickel, *Strategic Management and Business Policy: A Methodological Approach* (Reading, MA: Addison-Wesley Publishing Co. Inc., © 1982): 155.

When a particular company is known, the analyst must be much more specific in terms of implied strategies. For example, instead of saying market penetration is a recommended strategy when your vector goes in the Conservative quadrant, say that adding 34 new stores in India is a recommended strategy. This is a very important point for students doing case analyses because a particular company is generally known, and terms such as *market development* are too vague to use. That term could refer to adding a manufacturing plant in Thailand or Mexico or South Africa—*so students—Be specific to the extent possible regarding implications of all the matrices presented in Chapter 6.*

The directional vector may appear in the *conservative quadrant* (upper-left quadrant) of the SPACE Matrix, which implies staying close to the firm's basic competencies and not taking excessive risks. Conservative strategies most often include market penetration, market development, product development, and related diversification. The directional vector may be located in the lower-left or *defensive quadrant* of the SPACE Matrix, which suggests that the firm should focus on rectifying internal weaknesses and avoiding external threats. Defensive strategies include retrenchment, divestiture, liquidation, and related diversification. Finally, the directional vector may be located in the lower-right or *competitive quadrant* of the SPACE Matrix, indicating competitive strategies. Competitive strategies include backward, forward, and horizontal integration; market penetration; market development and product development.

A SPACE Matrix analysis for a bank is provided in Table 6-3. Note that competitive type strategies are recommended.

TABLE 6-3   A SPACE Matrix for a Bank

Financial Position (FP)	Ratings
The bank's primary capital ratio is 7.23 percent, which is 1.23 percentage points over the generally required ratio of 6 percent.	1.0
The bank's return on assets is negative 0.77, compared to a bank industry average ratio of positive 0.70.	1.0
The bank's net income was $183 million, down 9 percent from a year earlier.	3.0
The bank's revenues increased 7 percent to $3.46 billion.	4.0
	9.0

Industry Position (IP)	
Deregulation provides geographic and product freedom.	4.0
Deregulation increases competition in the banking industry.	2.0
Pennsylvania's interstate banking law allows the bank to acquire other banks in New Jersey, Ohio, Kentucky, the District of Columbia, and West Virginia.	4.0
	10.0

Stability Position (SP)	
Less-developed countries are experiencing high inflation and political instability.	−4.0
Headquartered in Pittsburgh, the bank historically has been heavily dependent on the steel, oil, and gas industries. These industries are depressed.	−5.0
Banking deregulation has created instability throughout the industry.	−4.0
	−13.0

Competitive Position (CP)	
The bank provides data processing services for more than 450 institutions in 38 states.	−2.0
Superregional banks, international banks, and nonbanks are becoming increasingly competitive.	−5.0
The bank has a large customer base.	−2.0
	−9.0

Conclusion

SP Average is −13.0 ÷ 3 = −4.33   IP Average is +10.0 ÷ 3 = 3.33

CP Average is −9.0 ÷ 3 = −3.00   FP Average is +9.0 ÷ 4 = 2.25

Directional Vector Coordinates: x-axis: −3.00 + (+3.33) = +0.33

y-axis: −4.33 + (+2.25) = −2.08

The bank should pursue Competitive Strategies.

The Boston Consulting Group (BCG) Matrix

Autonomous divisions (or profit centers) of an organization make up what is called a *business portfolio*. When a firm's divisions compete in different industries, a separate strategy often must be developed for each business. The *Boston Consulting Group (BCG) Matrix* and the *Internal-External (IE) Matrix* are designed specifically to enhance a multidivisional firm's efforts to formulate strategies. (BCG is a private management consulting firm based in Boston. BCG employs about 4,300 consultants worldwide.)

In a *Form 10K* or *Annual Report*, some companies do not disclose financial information by segment, so a BCG portfolio analysis is not possible by external entities. Reasons to disclose by-division financial information in the author's view, however, more than offset the reasons not to disclose, as indicated in Table 6-4.

The BCG Matrix graphically portrays differences among divisions in terms of relative market share position and industry growth rate. The BCG Matrix allows a multidivisional organization to manage its portfolio of businesses by examining the relative market share position and the industry growth rate of each division relative to all other divisions in the organization. *Relative market share position* is defined as the ratio of a division's own market share (or revenues) in a particular industry to the market share (or revenues) held by the largest rival firm in that industry. Note in Table 6-5 that other variables can be in this analysis besides revenues. Relative market share position for Heineken could also be determined by dividing Heineken's revenues by the leader Corona Extra's revenues.

Relative market share position is given on the *x*-axis of the BCG Matrix. The midpoint on the *x*-axis usually is set at .50, corresponding to a division that has half the market share of the leading firm in the industry. The *y*-axis represents the industry growth rate in sales, measured in percentage terms. The growth rate percentages on the *y*-axis could range from −20 to +20 percent, with 0.0 being the midpoint. The average annual increase in revenues for several leading firms in the industry would be a good estimate of the value. Also, various sources such as the S&P Industry Survey would provide this value. These numerical ranges on the *x*- and *y*-axes are often used, but other numerical values could be established as deemed appropriate for particular organizations, such as −10 to +10 percent.

The basic BCG Matrix appears in Figure 6-6. Each circle represents a separate division. The size of the circle corresponds to the proportion of corporate revenue generated by that business unit, and the pie slice indicates the proportion of corporate profits generated by that division. Divisions located in Quadrant I of the BCG Matrix are called "Question Marks," those located in Quadrant II are called "Stars," those located in Quadrant III are called "Cash Cows," and those divisions located in Quadrant IV are called "Dogs."

- *Question Marks*—Divisions in Quadrant I have a low relative market share position, yet they compete in a high-growth industry. Generally these firms' cash needs are

TABLE 6-4   Reasons to (or Not to) Disclose Financial Information by Segment (by Division)

Reasons to Disclose	Reasons Not to Disclose
1. Transparency is a good thing in today's world of Sarbanes-Oxley	1. Can become free competitive information for rival firms
2. Investors will better understand the firm, which can lead to greater support	2. Can hide performance failures
3. Managers/employees will better understand the firm, which should lead to greater commitment	3. Can reduce rivalry among segments
4. Disclosure enhances the communication process both within the firm and with outsiders	

TABLE 6-5 Market Share Data for Selected Industries in 2009

U.S. Top Five Airlines by Number of Passengers Boarded in 2008 (in millions; estimate)	
Southwest	7.5
American	5.0
Delta	4.5
United	4.0
US Airways	3.5
U.S. Top Five Imported Beers in 2008 (in millions of barrels imported)	
Corona Extra	8.0
Heineken	5.0
Modelo Especial	2.0
Tecate	1.5
Guinness	1.0

Source: Based on David Kesmodel, "U.S. Beer Imports Lose Their Fizz," *Wall Street Journal* (February 20, 2009): B5; S&P Industry Surveys and Company *Form 10-K* Reports.

high and their cash generation is low. These businesses are called *Question Marks* because the organization must decide whether to strengthen them by pursuing an intensive strategy (market penetration, market development, or product development) or to sell them.

- *Stars*—Quadrant II businesses (*Stars*) represent the organization's best long-run opportunities for growth and profitability. Divisions with a high relative market share and a high industry growth rate should receive substantial investment to maintain or strengthen their dominant positions. Forward, backward, and horizontal integration; market penetration; market development; and product development are appropriate strategies for these divisions to consider, as indicated in Figure 6-6.

- *Cash Cows*—Divisions positioned in Quadrant III have a high relative market share position but compete in a low-growth industry. Called *Cash Cows* because they generate cash in excess of their needs, they are often milked. Many of today's Cash

FIGURE 6-6

The BCG Matrix

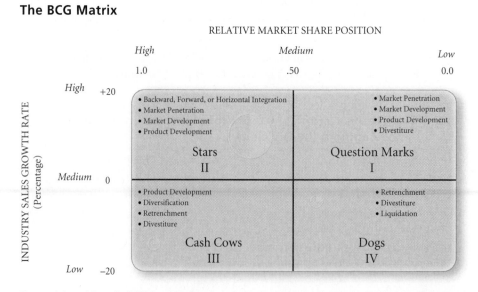

Source: Adapted from the BCG Portfolio Matrix from the Product Portfolio Matrix, © 1970, The Boston Consulting Group.

Cows were yesterday's Stars. Cash Cow divisions should be managed to maintain their strong position for as long as possible. Product development or diversification may be attractive strategies for strong Cash Cows. However, as a Cash Cow division becomes weak, retrenchment or divestiture can become more appropriate.

- ***Dogs***—Quadrant IV divisions of the organization have a low relative market share position and compete in a slow- or no-market-growth industry; they are *Dogs* in the firm's portfolio. Because of their weak internal and external position, these businesses are often liquidated, divested, or trimmed down through retrenchment. When a division first becomes a Dog, retrenchment can be the best strategy to pursue because many Dogs have bounced back, after strenuous asset and cost reduction, to become viable, profitable divisions.

The major benefit of the BCG Matrix is that it draws attention to the cash flow, investment characteristics, and needs of an organization's various divisions. The divisions of many firms evolve over time: Dogs become Question Marks, Question Marks become Stars, Stars become Cash Cows, and Cash Cows become Dogs in an ongoing counterclockwise motion. Less frequently, Stars become Question Marks, Question Marks become Dogs, Dogs become Cash Cows, and Cash Cows become Stars (in a clockwise motion). In some organizations, no cyclical motion is apparent. Over time, organizations should strive to achieve a portfolio of divisions that are Stars.

An example BCG Matrix is provided in Figure 6-7, which illustrates an organization composed of five divisions with annual sales ranging from $5,000 to $60,000. Division 1 has the greatest sales volume, so the circle representing that division is the largest one in the matrix. The circle corresponding to Division 5 is the smallest because its sales volume ($5,000) is least among all the divisions. The pie slices within the circles reveal the percent of corporate profits contributed by each division. As shown, Division 1 contributes the highest profit percentage, 39 percent. Notice in the diagram that Division 1 is considered a Star, Division 2 is a Question Mark, Division 3 is also a Question Mark, Division 4 is a Cash Cow, and Division 5 is a Dog.

FIGURE 6-7

An Example BCG Matrix

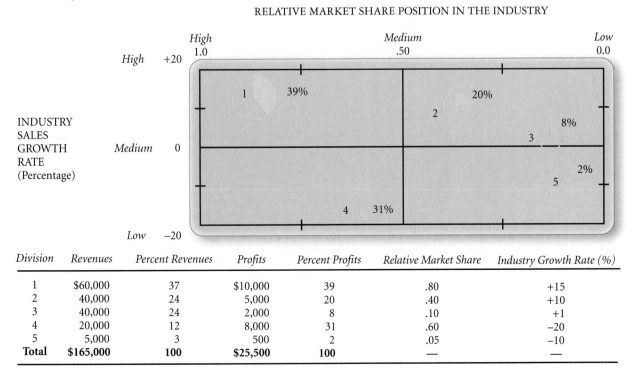

Division	Revenues	Percent Revenues	Profits	Percent Profits	Relative Market Share	Industry Growth Rate (%)
1	$60,000	37	$10,000	39	.80	+15
2	40,000	24	5,000	20	.40	+10
3	40,000	24	2,000	8	.10	+1
4	20,000	12	8,000	31	.60	−20
5	5,000	3	500	2	.05	−10
Total	**$165,000**	**100**	**$25,500**	**100**	—	—

The BCG Matrix, like all analytical techniques, has some limitations. For example, viewing every business as either a Star, Cash Cow, Dog, or Question Mark is an oversimplification; many businesses fall right in the middle of the BCG Matrix and thus are not easily classified. Furthermore, the BCG Matrix does not reflect whether or not various divisions or their industries are growing over time; that is, the matrix has no temporal qualities, but rather it is a snapshot of an organization at a given point in time. Finally, other variables besides relative market share position and industry growth rate in sales, such as size of the market and competitive advantages, are important in making strategic decisions about various divisions.

An example BCG Matrix is provided in Figure 6-8. Note in Figure 6-8 that Division 5 had an operating loss of $188 million. Take note how the percent profit column is still calculated because oftentimes a firm will have a division that incurs a loss for a year. In terms of the pie slice in circle 5 of the diagram, note that it is a *different color* from the positive profit segments in the other circles.

The Internal-External (IE) Matrix

The *Internal-External (IE) Matrix* positions an organization's various divisions in a nine-cell display, illustrated in Figure 6-9. The IE Matrix is similar to the BCG Matrix in that both tools involve plotting organization divisions in a schematic diagram; this is why they are both called "portfolio matrices." Also, the size of each circle represents the percentage sales contribution of each division, and pie slices reveal the percentage profit contribution of each division in both the BCG and IE Matrix.

But there are some important differences between the BCG Matrix and the IE Matrix. First, the axes are different. Also, the IE Matrix requires more information about the divisions than the BCG Matrix. Furthermore, the strategic implications of each matrix are different. For these reasons, strategists in multidivisional firms often develop both the BCG Matrix and the IE Matrix in formulating alternative strategies. A common practice is to develop a BCG Matrix and an IE Matrix for the present and then develop projected matrices to reflect expectations of the future. This before-and-after analysis forecasts the expected effect of strategic decisions on an organization's portfolio of divisions.

FIGURE 6-8

An Example BCG Matrix

RELATIVE MARKET SHARE POSITION (RMSP)

Division	$ Sales (millions)	% Sales	$ Profits (millions)	% Profits	RMSP	IG Rate %
1.	$5,139	51.5	$799	68.0	0.8	10
2.	2,556	25.6	400	39.0	0.4	05
3.	1,749	17.5	12	1.2	0.2	00
4.	493	4.9	4	0.1	0.5	−05
5.	42	0.5	−188	(18.3)	.02	−10
Total	**$9,979**	**100.0**	**$1,027**	**100.0**		

FIGURE 6-9

The Internal–External (IE) Matrix

Source: Adapted. The IE Matrix was developed from the General Electric (GE) Business Screen Matrix. For a description of the GE Matrix see Michael Allen, "Diagramming GE's Planning for What's WATT," in R. Allio and M. Pennington, eds., *Corporate Planning: Techniques and Applications* (New York: AMACOM, 1979).

The IE Matrix is based on two key dimensions: the IFE total weighted scores on the *x*-axis and the EFE total weighted scores on the *y*-axis. Recall that each division of an organization should construct an IFE Matrix and an EFE Matrix for its part of the organization. The total weighted scores derived from the divisions allow construction of the corporate-level IE Matrix. On the *x*-axis of the IE Matrix, an IFE total weighted score of 1.0 to 1.99 represents a weak internal position; a score of 2.0 to 2.99 is considered average; and a score of 3.0 to 4.0 is strong. Similarly, on the *y*-axis, an EFE total weighted score of 1.0 to 1.99 is considered low; a score of 2.0 to 2.99 is medium; and a score of 3.0 to 4.0 is high.

The IE Matrix can be divided into three major regions that have different strategy implications. First, the prescription for divisions that fall into cells I, II, or IV can be described as *grow and build*. Intensive (market penetration, market development, and product development) or integrative (backward integration, forward integration, and horizontal integration) strategies can be most appropriate for these divisions. Second, divisions that fall into cells III, V, or VII can be managed best with *hold and maintain* strategies; market penetration and product development are two commonly employed strategies for these types of divisions. Third, a common prescription for divisions that fall into cells VI, VIII, or IX is *harvest or divest*. Successful organizations are able to achieve a portfolio of businesses positioned in or around cell I in the IE Matrix.

An example of a completed IE Matrix is given in Figure 6-10, which depicts an organization composed of four divisions. As indicated by the positioning of the circles, *grow and build* strategies are appropriate for Division 1, Division 2, and Division 3. Division 4 is a candidate for *harvest or divest*. Division 2 contributes the greatest percentage of company sales and thus is represented by the largest circle. Division 1 contributes the greatest proportion of total profits; it has the largest-percentage pie slice.

As indicated in Figure 6-11, the IE Matrix has five product segments. Note that Division #1 has the largest revenues (as indicated by the largest circle) and the largest profits (as indicated by the largest pie slice) in the matrix. It is common for organizations to

FIGURE 6-10

An Example IE Matrix

THE IFE TOTAL WEIGHTED SCORES

Division	Sales	Percent Sales	Profits	Percent Profits	IFE Scores	EFE Scores
1	$100	25.0	10	50	3.6	3.2
2	200	50.0	5	25	2.1	3.5
3	50	12.5	4	20	3.1	2.1
4	50	12.5	1	5	1.8	2.5
Total	**400**	**100.0**	**20**	**100**		

FIGURE 6-11

The IE Matrix

THE IFE TOTAL WEIGHTED SCORES

Grow and Build

Segments	$ Revenue	% Revenue	$ Profit	% Profit	EFE Scores	IFE Scores
1.	$7,868	71.5%	$3,000	59%	2.5	3
2.	1,241	11.3%	1,000	19%	2	2
3.	1,578	14.3%	800	16%	3	3
4.	90	0.8%	100	2%	2.5	2.5
5.	223	2.1%	200	4%	3	2
Total	**$11,000**	**100%**	**$5,100**	**100%**	—	—

develop both geographic and product-based IE Matrices to more effectively formulate strategies and allocate resources among divisions. In addition, firms often prepare an IE (or BCG) Matrix for competitors. Furthermore, firms will often prepare "before and after" IE (or BCG) Matrices to reveal the situation at present versus the expected situation after one year. This latter idea minimizes the limitation of these matrices being a "snapshot in time." In performing case analysis, feel free to estimate the IFE and EFE scores for the various divisions based upon your research into the company and industry—rather than preparing a separate IE Matrix for each division.

The Grand Strategy Matrix

In addition to the SWOT Matrix, SPACE Matrix, BCG Matrix, and IE Matrix, the *Grand Strategy Matrix* has become a popular tool for formulating alternative strategies. All organizations can be positioned in one of the Grand Strategy Matrix's four strategy quadrants. A firm's divisions likewise could be positioned. As illustrated in Figure 6-12, the Grand Strategy Matrix is based on two evaluative dimensions: competitive position and market (industry) growth. Any industry whose annual growth in sales exceeds 5 percent could be considered to have rapid growth. Appropriate strategies for an organization to consider are listed in sequential order of attractiveness in each quadrant of the matrix.

Firms located in Quadrant I of the Grand Strategy Matrix are in an excellent strategic position. For these firms, continued concentration on current markets (market penetration and market development) and products (product development) is an appropriate strategy. It is unwise for a Quadrant I firm to shift notably from its established competitive advantages. When a Quadrant I organization has excessive resources, then backward, forward, or horizontal integration may be effective strategies. When a Quadrant I firm is too heavily committed to a single product, then related diversification may reduce the risks associated with a narrow product line. Quadrant I firms can afford to take advantage of external opportunities in several areas. They can take risks aggressively when necessary.

FIGURE 6-12

The Grand Strategy Matrix

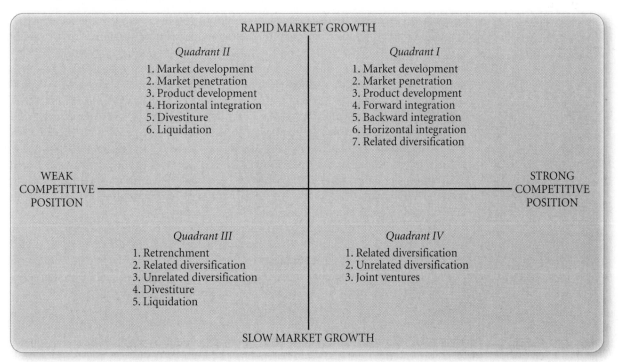

Source: Adapted from Roland Christensen, Norman Berg, and Malcolm Salter, *Policy Formulation and Administration* (Homewood, IL: Richard D. Irwin, 1976): 16–18.

Firms positioned in Quadrant II need to evaluate their present approach to the market-place seriously. Although their industry is growing, they are unable to compete effectively, and they need to determine why the firm's current approach is ineffective and how the company can best change to improve its competitiveness. Because Quadrant II firms are in a rapid-market-growth industry, an intensive strategy (as opposed to integrative or diversification) is usually the first option that should be considered. However, if the firm is lacking a distinctive competence or competitive advantage, then horizontal integration is often a desirable alternative. As a last resort, divestiture or liquidation should be considered. Divestiture can provide funds needed to acquire other businesses or buy back shares of stock.

Quadrant III organizations compete in slow-growth industries and have weak competitive positions. These firms must make some drastic changes quickly to avoid further decline and possible liquidation. Extensive cost and asset reduction (retrenchment) should be pursued first. An alternative strategy is to shift resources away from the current business into different areas (diversify). If all else fails, the final options for Quadrant III businesses are divestiture or liquidation.

Finally, Quadrant IV businesses have a strong competitive position but are in a slow-growth industry. These firms have the strength to launch diversified programs into more promising growth areas: Quadrant IV firms have characteristically high cash-flow levels and limited internal growth needs and often can pursue related or unrelated diversification successfully. Quadrant IV firms also may pursue joint ventures.

The Decision Stage

Analysis and intuition provide a basis for making strategy-formulation decisions. The matching techniques just discussed reveal feasible alternative strategies. Many of these strategies will likely have been proposed by managers and employees participating in the strategy analysis and choice activity. Any additional strategies resulting from the matching analyses could be discussed and added to the list of feasible alternative options. As indicated earlier in this chapter, participants could rate these strategies on a 1 to 4 scale so that a prioritized list of the best strategies could be achieved.

The Quantitative Strategic Planning Matrix (QSPM)

Other than ranking strategies to achieve the prioritized list, there is only one analytical technique in the literature designed to determine the relative attractiveness of feasible alternative actions. This technique is the *Quantitative Strategic Planning Matrix (QSPM)*, which comprises Stage 3 of the strategy-formulation analytical framework.[6] This technique objectively indicates which alternative strategies are best. The QSPM uses input from Stage 1 analyses and matching results from Stage 2 analyses to decide objectively among alternative strategies. That is, the EFE Matrix, IFE Matrix, and Competitive Profile Matrix that make up Stage 1, coupled with the SWOT Matrix, SPACE Matrix, BCG Matrix, IE Matrix, and Grand Strategy Matrix that make up Stage 2, provide the needed information for setting up the QSPM (Stage 3). The QSPM is a tool that allows strategists to evaluate alternative strategies objectively, based on previously identified external and internal critical success factors. Like other strategy-formulation analytical tools, the QSPM requires good intuitive judgment.

The basic format of the QSPM is illustrated in Table 6-6. Note that the left column of a QSPM consists of key external and internal factors (from Stage 1), and the top row consists of feasible alternative strategies (from Stage 2). Specifically, the left column of a QSPM consists of information obtained directly from the EFE Matrix and IFE Matrix. In a column adjacent to the critical success factors, the respective weights received by each factor in the EFE Matrix and the IFE Matrix are recorded.

The top row of a QSPM consists of alternative strategies derived from the SWOT Matrix, SPACE Matrix, BCG Matrix, IE Matrix, and Grand Strategy Matrix. These matching tools usually generate similar feasible alternatives. However, not every strategy suggested by the matching techniques has to be evaluated in a QSPM. Strategists should use good intuitive judgment in selecting strategies to include in a QSPM.

TABLE 6-6   The Quantitative Strategic Planning Matrix—QSPM

Key Factors	Weight	Strategy 1	Strategy 2	Strategy 3
		Strategic Alternatives		
Key External Factors				
Economy				
Political/Legal/Governmental				
Social/Cultural/Demographic/Environmental				
Technological				
Competitive				
Key Internal Factors				
Management				
Marketing				
Finance/Accounting				
Production/Operations				
Research and Development				
Management Information Systems				

Conceptually, the QSPM determines the relative attractiveness of various strategies based on the extent to which key external and internal critical success factors are capitalized upon or improved. The relative attractiveness of each strategy within a set of alternatives is computed by determining the cumulative impact of each external and internal critical success factor. Any number of sets of alternative strategies can be included in the QSPM, and any number of strategies can make up a given set, but only strategies within a given set are evaluated relative to each other. For example, one set of strategies may include diversification, whereas another set may include issuing stock and selling a division to raise needed capital. These two sets of strategies are totally different, and the QSPM evaluates strategies only within sets. Note in Table 6-6 that three strategies are included, and they make up just one set.

A QSPM for a retail computer store is provided in Table 6-7. This example illustrates all the components of the QSPM: Strategic Alternatives, Key Factors, Weights, Attractiveness Scores (AS), Total Attractiveness Scores (TAS), and the Sum Total Attractiveness Score. The three new terms just introduced—(1) Attractiveness Scores, (2) Total Attractiveness Scores, and (3) the Sum Total Attractiveness Score—are defined and explained as the six steps required to develop a QSPM are discussed:

Step 1   *Make a list of the firm's key external opportunities/threats and internal strengths/weaknesses in the left column of the QSPM.* This information should be taken directly from the EFE Matrix and IFE Matrix. A minimum of 10 external key success factors and 10 internal key success factors should be included in the QSPM.

Step 2   *Assign weights to each key external and internal factor.* These weights are identical to those in the EFE Matrix and the IFE Matrix. The weights are presented in a straight column just to the right of the external and internal critical success factors.

Step 3   *Examine the Stage 2 (matching) matrices, and identify alternative strategies that the organization should consider implementing.* Record these strategies in the top row of the QSPM. Group the strategies into mutually exclusive sets if possible.

Step 4   *Determine the Attractiveness Scores (AS)* defined as numerical values that indicate the relative attractiveness of each strategy in a given set of alternatives. *Attractiveness Scores (AS)* are determined by examining each key external or internal factor, one at a time, and asking the question "Does this factor affect the choice of strategies being made?" If the answer to this question is yes, then the strategies should be compared relative to that key factor. Specifically, Attractiveness Scores should be assigned to each strategy to indicate the relative attractiveness of one strategy over others, considering the particular factor. The range for Attractiveness Scores is 1 = not attractive, 2 = somewhat attractive, 3 = reasonably attractive, and

TABLE 6-7   **A QSPM for a Retail Computer Store**

		STRATEGIC ALTERNATIVES			
		1		2	
		Buy New Land and Build New Larger Store		Fully Renovate Existing Store	
Key Factors	Weight	AS	TAS	AS	TAS
Opportunities					
1. Population of city growing 10%	0.10	4	0.40	2	0.20
2. Rival computer store opening 1 mile away	0.10	2	0.20	4	0.40
3. Vehicle traffic passing store up 12%	0.08	1	0.08	4	0.32
4. Vendors average six new products/year	0.05	—		—	
5. Senior citizen use of computers up 8%	0.05	—		—	
6. Small business growth in area up 10%	0.10	—		—	
7. Desire for Web sites up 18% by Realtors	0.06	—		—	
8. Desire for Web sites up 12% by small firms	0.06	—		—	
Threats					
1. Best Buy opening new store nearby in 1 year	0.15	4	0.60	3	0.45
2. Local university offers computer repair	0.08	—		—	
3. New bypass for Hwy 34 in 1 year will divert traffic	0.12	4	0.48	1	0.12
4. New mall being built nearby	0.08	2	0.16	4	0.32
5. Gas prices up 14%	0.04	—		—	
6. Vendors raising prices 8%	0.03	—		—	
	1.00				
Strengths					
1. Inventory turnover increased from 5.8 to 6.7	0.05	—		—	
2. Average customer purchase increased from $97 to $128	0.07	2	0.14	4	0.28
3. Employee morale is excellent	0.10	—		—	
4. In-store promotions resulted in 20% increase in sales	0.05	—		—	
5. Newspaper advertising expenditures increased 10%	0.02	—		—	
6. Revenues from repair/service segment of store up 16%	0.15	4	0.60	3	0.45
7. In-store technical support personnel have MIS college degrees	0.05	—		—	
8. Store's debt-to-total assets ratio declined to 34%	0.03	4	0.12	2	0.06
9. Revenues per employee up 19%	0.02	—		—	
Weaknesses					
1. Revenues from software segment of store down 12%	0.10	—		—	
2. Location of store negatively impacted by new Hwy 34	0.15	4	0.60	1	0.15
3. Carpet and paint in store somewhat in disrepair	0.02	1	0.02	4	0.08
4. Bathroom in store needs refurbishing	0.02	1	0.02	4	0.08
5. Revenues from businesses down 8%	0.04	3	0.12	4	0.16
6. Store has no Web site	0.05	—		—	
7. Supplier on-time delivery increased to 2.4 days	0.03	—		—	
8. Often customers have to wait to check out	0.05	2	0.10	4	0.20
Total	1.00		4.36		3.27

4 = highly attractive. By attractive, we mean the extent that one strategy, compared to others, enables the firm to either capitalize on the strength, improve on the weakness, exploit the opportunity, or avoid the threat. Work row by row in developing a QSPM. If the answer to the previous question is *no,* indicating that the respective key factor has no effect upon the specific choice being made, then do not assign Attractiveness Scores to the strategies in that set. Use a dash to indicate that the key factor does not affect the choice being made. *Note:* If you assign an AS score to one strategy, then assign AS score(s) to the other. In other words, if one strategy receives a dash, then all others must receive a dash in a given row.

Step 5   *Compute the Total Attractiveness Scores. Total Attractiveness Scores (TAS)* are defined as the product of multiplying the weights (Step 2) by the Attractiveness Scores (Step 4) in each row. The Total Attractiveness Scores indicate the relative attractiveness of each alternative strategy, considering only the impact of the adjacent external or internal critical success factor. The higher the Total Attractiveness Score, the more attractive the strategic alternative (considering only the adjacent critical success factor).

Step 6   *Compute the Sum Total Attractiveness Score.* Add Total Attractiveness Scores in each strategy column of the QSPM. The *Sum Total Attractiveness Scores (STAS)* reveal which strategy is most attractive in each set of alternatives. Higher scores indicate more attractive strategies, considering all the relevant external and internal factors that could affect the strategic decisions. The magnitude of the difference between the Sum Total Attractiveness Scores in a given set of strategic alternatives indicates the relative desirability of one strategy over another.

In Table 6-7, two alternative strategies—(1) buy new land and build new larger store and (2) fully renovate existing store—are being considered by a computer retail store. Note by sum total attractiveness scores of 4.63 versus 3.27 that the analysis indicates the business should buy new land and build a new larger store. Note the use of dashes to indicate which factors do not affect the strategy choice being considered. If a particular factor affects one strategy but not the other, it affects the choice being made, so attractiveness scores should be recorded for both strategies. Never rate one strategy and not the other. Note also in Table 6-7 that there are no double 1's, 2's, 3's, or 4's in a row. Never duplicate scores in a row. Never work column by column; always prepare a QSPM working row by row. If you have more than one strategy in the QSPM, then let the AS scores range from 1 to "the number of strategies being evaluated." This will enable you to have a different AS score for each strategy. These are all important guidelines to follow in developing a QSPM. In actual practice, the store did purchase the new land and build a new store; the business also did some minor refurbishing until the new store was operational.

There should be a rationale for each AS score assigned. Note in Table 6-7 in the first row that the "city population growing 10 percent annually" opportunity could be capitalized on best by strategy 1, "building the new, larger store," so an AS score of 4 was assigned to Strategy 1. AS scores, therefore, are not mere guesses; they should be rational, defensible, and reasonable.

Avoid giving each strategy the same AS score. Note in Table 6-7 that dashes are inserted all the way across the row when used. Also note that double 4's, or double 3's, or double 2's, or double 1's are never in a given row. Again work row by row, not column by column. These are important guidelines to follow in constructing a QSPM.

Positive Features and Limitations of the QSPM

A positive feature of the QSPM is that sets of strategies can be examined sequentially or simultaneously. For example, corporate-level strategies could be evaluated first, followed by division-level strategies, and then function-level strategies. There is no limit to the number of strategies that can be evaluated or the number of sets of strategies that can be examined at once using the QSPM.

Another positive feature of the QSPM is that it requires strategists to integrate pertinent external and internal factors into the decision process. Developing a QSPM makes it less likely that key factors will be overlooked or weighted inappropriately. A QSPM draws attention to important relationships that affect strategy decisions.

Although developing a QSPM requires a number of subjective decisions, making small decisions along the way enhances the probability that the final strategic decisions will be best for the organization. A QSPM can be adapted for use by small and large for-profit and nonprofit organizations so can be applied to virtually any type of organization. A QSPM can especially enhance strategic choice in multinational firms because many key factors and strategies can be considered at once. It also has been applied successfully by a number of small businesses.[7]

The QSPM is not without some limitations. First, it always requires intuitive judgments and educated assumptions. The ratings and attractiveness scores require judgmental decisions, even though they should be based on objective information. Discussion among strategists, managers, and employees throughout the strategy-formulation process, including development of a QSPM, is constructive and improves strategic decisions. Constructive discussion during strategy analysis and choice may arise because of genuine differences of interpretation of information and varying opinions. Another limitation of the QSPM is that it can be only as good as the prerequisite information and matching analyses upon which it is based.

Cultural Aspects of Strategy Choice

All organizations have a culture. *Culture* includes the set of shared values, beliefs, attitudes, customs, norms, personalities, heroes, and heroines that describe a firm. Culture is the unique way an organization does business. It is the human dimension that creates solidarity and meaning, and it inspires commitment and productivity in an organization when strategy changes are made. All human beings have a basic need to make sense of the world, to feel in control, and to make meaning. When events threaten meaning, individuals react defensively. Managers and employees may even sabotage new strategies in an effort to recapture the status quo.

It is beneficial to view strategic management from a cultural perspective because success often rests upon the degree of support that strategies receive from a firm's culture. If a firm's strategies are supported by cultural products such as values, beliefs, rites, rituals, ceremonies, stories, symbols, language, heroes, and heroines, then managers often can implement changes swiftly and easily. However, if a supportive culture does not exist and is not cultivated, then strategy changes may be ineffective or even counterproductive. A firm's culture can become antagonistic to new strategies, and the result of that antagonism may be confusion and disarray.

Strategies that require fewer cultural changes may be more attractive because extensive changes can take considerable time and effort. Whenever two firms merge, it becomes especially important to evaluate and consider culture-strategy linkages.

Culture provides an explanation for the difficulties a firm encounters when it attempts to shift its strategic direction, as the following statement explains:

> Not only has the "right" corporate culture become the essence and foundation of corporate excellence, but success or failure of needed corporate reforms hinges on management's sagacity and ability to change the firm's driving culture in time and in tune with required changes in strategies.[8]

The Politics of Strategy Choice

All organizations are political. Unless managed, political maneuvering consumes valuable time, subverts organizational objectives, diverts human energy, and results in the loss of some valuable employees. Sometimes political biases and personal preferences get unduly embedded in strategy choice decisions. Internal politics affect the choice of strategies in all organizations. The hierarchy of command in an organization, combined with the career aspirations of different people and the need to allocate scarce resources, guarantees the formation of coalitions of individuals who strive to take care of themselves first and the organization second, third, or fourth. Coalitions of individuals often form around key strategy issues that face an enterprise. A major responsibility of strategists is to guide the development of coalitions, to nurture an overall team concept, and to gain the support of key individuals and groups of individuals.

In the absence of objective analyses, strategy decisions too often are based on the politics of the moment. With development of improved strategy-formation tools, political factors become less important in making strategic decisions. In the absence of objectivity, political factors sometimes dictate strategies, and this is unfortunate. Managing political relationships is an integral part of building enthusiasm and esprit de corps in an organization.

A classic study of strategic management in nine large corporations examined the political tactics of successful and unsuccessful strategists.[9] Successful strategists were found to let weakly supported ideas and proposals die through inaction and to establish additional hurdles or tests for strongly supported ideas considered unacceptable but not openly opposed. Successful strategists kept a low political profile on unacceptable proposals and strived to let most negative decisions come from subordinates or a group consensus, thereby reserving their personal vetoes for big issues and crucial moments. Successful strategists did a lot of chatting and informal questioning to stay abreast of how things were progressing and to know when to intervene. They led strategy but did not dictate it. They gave few orders, announced few decisions, depended heavily on informal questioning, and sought to probe and clarify until a consensus emerged.

Successful strategists generously and visibly rewarded key thrusts that succeeded. They assigned responsibility for major new thrusts to *champions,* the individuals most strongly identified with the idea or product and whose futures were linked to its success. They stayed alert to the symbolic impact of their own actions and statements so as not to send false signals that could stimulate movements in unwanted directions.

Successful strategists ensured that all major power bases within an organization were represented in, or had access to, top management. They interjected new faces and new views into considerations of major changes. This is important because new employees and managers generally have more enthusiasm and drive than employees who have been with the firm a long time. New employees do not see the world the same old way; nor do they act as screens against changes. Successful strategists minimized their own political exposure on highly controversial issues and in circumstances in which major opposition from key power centers was likely. In combination, these findings provide a basis for managing political relationships in an organization.

Because strategies must be effective in the marketplace and capable of gaining internal commitment, the following tactics used by politicians for centuries can aid strategists:

- *Equifinality*—It is often possible to achieve similar results using different means or paths. Strategists should recognize that achieving a successful outcome is more important than imposing the method of achieving it. It may be possible to generate new alternatives that give equal results but with far greater potential for gaining commitment.
- *Satisfying*—Achieving satisfactory results with an acceptable strategy is far better than failing to achieve optimal results with an unpopular strategy.
- *Generalization*—Shifting focus from specific issues to more general ones may increase strategists' options for gaining organizational commitment.
- *Focus on Higher-Order Issues*—By raising an issue to a higher level, many short-term interests can be postponed in favor of long-term interests. For instance, by focusing on issues of survival, the airline and automotive industries were able to persuade unions to make concessions on wage increases.
- *Provide Political Access on Important Issues*—Strategy and policy decisions with significant negative consequences for middle managers will motivate intervention behavior from them. If middle managers do not have an opportunity to take a position on such decisions in appropriate political forums, they are capable of successfully resisting the decisions after they are made. Providing such political access provides strategists with information that otherwise might not be available and that could be useful in managing intervention behavior.[10]

Governance Issues

A "director," according to Webster's Dictionary, is "one of a group of persons entrusted with the overall direction of a corporate enterprise." A *board of directors* is a group of individuals who are elected by the ownership of a corporation to have oversight and guidance over management and who look out for shareholders' interests. The act of oversight and direction is referred to as *governance*. The National Association of Corporate Directors defines governance as "the characteristic of ensuring that long-term strategic objectives and plans are established and that the proper management structure is in place to achieve those objectives, while at the same time making sure that the structure functions to maintain the corporation's integrity, reputation, and responsibility to its various constituencies." This broad scope of responsibility for the board shows how boards are being held accountable for the entire performance of the firm. In the Worldcom, Tyco, and Enron bankruptcies and scandals, the firms' boards of directors were sued by shareholders for mismanaging their interests. New accounting rules in the United States and Europe now enhance corporate-governance codes and require much more extensive financial disclosure among publicly held firms. The roles and duties of a board of directors can be divided into four broad categories, as indicated in Table 6-8.

The recession and credit crunch of 2008–2009 prompted shareholders to become more wary of boards of directors. Shareholders of hundreds of firms are demanding that their boards do a better job of governing corporate America.[11] New compensation policies are needed as well as direct shareholder involvement in some director activities. For

TABLE 6-8   Board of Director Duties and Responsibilities

1. CONTROL AND OVERSIGHT OVER MANAGEMENT
    a. Select the Chief Executive Officer (CEO).
    b. Sanction the CEO's team.
    c. Provide the CEO with a forum.
    d. Ensure managerial competency.
    e. Evaluate management's performance.
    f. Set management's salary levels, including fringe benefits.
    g. Guarantee managerial integrity through continuous auditing.
    h. Chart the corporate course.
    i. Devise and revise policies to be implemented by management.

2. ADHERENCE TO LEGAL PRESCRIPTIONS
    a. Keep abreast of new laws.
    b. Ensure the entire organization fulfills legal prescriptions.
    c. Pass bylaws and related resolutions.
    d. Select new directors.
    e. Approve capital budgets.
    f. Authorize borrowing, new stock issues, bonds, and so on.

3. CONSIDERATION OF STAKEHOLDERS' INTERESTS
    a. Monitor product quality.
    b. Facilitate upward progression in employee quality of work life.
    c. Review labor policies and practices.
    d. Improve the customer climate.
    e. Keep community relations at the highest level.
    f. Use influence to better governmental, professional association, and educational contacts.
    g. Maintain good public image.

4. ADVANCEMENT OF STOCKHOLDERS' RIGHTS
    a. Preserve stockholders' equity.
    b. Stimulate corporate growth so that the firm will survive and flourish.
    c. Guard against equity dilution.
    d. Ensure equitable stockholder representation.
    e. Inform stockholders through letters, reports, and meetings.
    f. Declare proper dividends.
    g. Guarantee corporate survival.

example, boards could require CEOs to groom possible replacements from inside the firm because exorbitant compensation is most often paid to new CEOs coming from outside the firm.

Shareholders are also upset at boards for allowing CEOs to receive huge end-of-year bonuses when the firm's stock price drops drastically during the year.[12] For example, Chesapeake Energy Corp. and its board of directors are under fire from shareholders for paying Chairman and CEO Aubrey McClendon $112 million in 2008 as the firm's stock price plummeted. Investor Jeffrey Bronchick wrote in a letter to the Chesapeake board that the CEO's compensation was a "near perfect illustration of the complete collapse of appropriate corporate governance."

Until recently, boards of directors did most of their work sitting around polished wooden tables. However, Hewlett-Packard's directors, among many others, now log on to their own special board Web site twice a week and conduct business based on extensive confidential briefing information posted there by the firm's top management team. Then the board members meet face to face and fully informed every two months to discuss the biggest issues facing the firm. Even the decision of whether to locate operations in countries with low corporate tax rates would be reviewed by a board of directors.

Today, boards of directors are composed mostly of outsiders who are becoming more involved in organizations' strategic management. The trend in the United States is toward much greater board member accountability with smaller boards, now averaging 12 members rather than 18 as they did a few years ago. *BusinessWeek* recently evaluated the boards of most large U.S. companies and provided the following "principles of good governance":

1. No more than two directors are current or former company executives.
2. No directors do business with the company or accept consulting or legal fees from the firm.
3. The audit, compensation, and nominating committees are made up solely of outside directors.
4. Each director owns a large equity stake in the company, excluding stock options.
5. At least one outside director has extensive experience in the company's core business and at least one has been CEO of an equivalent-size company.
6. Fully employed directors sit on no more than four boards and retirees sit on no more than seven.
7. Each director attends at least 75 percent of all meetings.
8. The board meets regularly without management present and evaluates its own performance annually.
9. The audit committee meets at least four times a year.
10. The board is frugal on executive pay, diligent in CEO succession oversight responsibilities, and prompt to act when trouble arises.
11. The CEO is not also the chairperson of the board.
12. Shareholders have considerable power and information to choose and replace directors.
13. Stock options are considered a corporate expense.
14. There are no interlocking directorships (where a director or CEO sits on another director's board).[13]

Being a member of a board of directors today requires much more time, is much more difficult, and requires much more technical knowledge and financial commitment than in the past. Jeff Sonnerfeld, associate dean of the Yale School of Management, says, "Boards of directors are now rolling up their sleeves and becoming much more closely involved with management decision making." Since the Enron and Worldcom scandals, company CEOs and boards are required to personally certify financial statements; company loans to company executives and directors are illegal; and there is faster reporting of insider stock transactions.

Just as directors are beginning to place more emphasis on staying informed about an organization's health and operations, they are also taking a more active role in ensuring that publicly issued documents are accurate representations of a firm's status. It is becoming widely recognized that a board of directors has legal responsibilities to stockholders and society for all company activities, for corporate performance, and for ensuring that a firm has an effective strategy. Failure to accept responsibility for auditing or evaluating a firm's strategy is considered a serious breach of a director's duties. Stockholders, government agencies, and customers are filing legal suits against directors for fraud, omissions, inaccurate disclosures, lack of due diligence, and culpable ignorance about a firm's operations with increasing frequency. Liability insurance for directors has become exceptionally expensive and has caused numerous directors to resign.

The Sarbanes-Oxley Act resulted in scores of boardroom overhauls among publicly traded companies. The jobs of chief executive and chairman are now held by separate persons, and board audit committees must now have at least one financial expert as a member. Board audit committees now meet 10 or more times per year, rather than 3 or 4 times as they did prior to the act. The act put an end to the "country club" atmosphere of most boards and has shifted power from CEOs to directors. Although aimed at public companies, the act has also had a similar impact on privately owned companies.[14]

In Sweden, a new law has recently been passed requiring 25 percent female representation in boardrooms. The Norwegian government has passed a similar law that requires 40 percent of corporate director seats to go to women. In the United States, women currently hold about 13 percent of board seats at S&P 500 firms and 10 percent at S&P 1,500 firms. The Investor Responsibility Research Center in Washington, D.C. reports that minorities hold just 8.8 percent of board seats of S&P 1,500 companies. Progressive firms realize that women and minorities ask different questions and make different suggestions in boardrooms than white men, which is helpful because women and minorities comprise much of the consumer base everywhere.

A direct response of increased pressure on directors to stay informed and execute their responsibilities is that audit committees are becoming commonplace. A board of directors should conduct an annual strategy audit in much the same fashion that it reviews the annual financial audit. In performing such an audit, a board could work jointly with operating management and/or seek outside counsel. Boards should play a role beyond that of performing a strategic audit. They should provide greater input and advice in the strategy-formulation process to ensure that strategists are providing for the long-term needs of the firm. This is being done through the formation of three particular board committees: nominating committees to propose candidates for the board and senior officers of the firm; compensation committees to evaluate the performance of top executives and determine the terms and conditions of their employment; and audit committees to give board-level attention to company accounting and financial policies and performance.

Conclusion

The essence of strategy formulation is an assessment of whether an organization is doing the right things and how it can be more effective in what it does. Every organization should be wary of becoming a prisoner of its own strategy, because even the best strategies become obsolete sooner or later. Regular reappraisal of strategy helps management avoid complacency. Objectives and strategies should be consciously developed and coordinated and should not merely evolve out of day-to-day operating decisions.

An organization with no sense of direction and no coherent strategy precipitates its own demise. When an organization does not know where it wants to go, it usually ends up some place it does not want to be. Every organization needs to consciously establish and communicate clear objectives and strategies.

Modern strategy-formulation tools and concepts are described in this chapter and integrated into a practical three-stage framework. Tools such as the SWOT Matrix, SPACE Matrix, BCG Matrix, IE Matrix, and QSPM can significantly enhance the quality of strategic decisions, but they should never be used to dictate the choice of strategies. Behavioral, cultural, and political aspects of strategy generation and selection are always important to consider and manage. Because of increased legal pressure from outside groups, boards of directors are assuming a more active role in strategy analysis and choice. This is a positive trend for organizations.

We invite you to visit the David page on the Prentice Hall Companion Web site at http://www.pearsonhighered.com/david/ for this chapter's review quiz.

Key Terms and Concepts

Aggressive Quadrant (p. 182)
Attractiveness Scores (AS) (p. 193)
Board of Directors (p. 198)
Boston Consulting Group (BCG) Matrix (p. 184)
Business Portfolio (p. 184)
Cash Cows (p. 186)
Champions (p. 197)
Competitive Position (CP) (p. 181)
Competitive Quadrant (p. 184)
Conservative Quadrant (p. 184)
Culture (p. 196)
Decision Stage (p. 176)
Defensive Quadrant (p. 184)
Directional Vector (p. 182)
Dogs (p. 187)
Equifinality (p.197)
Financial Position (FP) (p. 181)
Governance (p. 198)
Grand Strategy Matrix (p. 191)
Halo Error (p. 177)
Industry Position (IP) (p. 181)

Input Stage (p. 176)
Internal-External (IE) Matrix (p. 184)
Matching (p. 177)
Matching Stage (p. 176)
Quantitative Strategic Planning Matrix (QSPM) (p. 192)
Question Marks (p. 186)
Relative Market Share Position (p. 184)
SO Strategies (p. 178)
Stability Position (SP) (p. 181)
Stars (p. 186)
Strategic Position and Action Evaluation (SPACE) Matrix (p. 181)
Strategy-Formulation Framework (p. 177)
Strengths-Weaknesses Opportunities-Threats (SWOT) Matrix (p. 178)
ST Strategies (p. 178)
Sum Total Attractiveness Scores (STAS) (p. 195)
Total Attractiveness Scores (TAS) (p. 195)
WO Strategies (p. 178)
WT Strategies (p. 179)

Issues for Review and Discussion

1. Many multidivisional firms do not report revenues or profits by division or segment in their *Form 10K* or *Annual Report*. What are the pros and cons of this management practice? Discuss.
2. Define halo error. How can halo error inhibit selecting the best strategies to pursue?
3. List six drawbacks of using only subjective information in formulating strategies.
4. For a firm that you know well, give an example SO Strategy, showing how an internal strength can be matched with an external opportunity to formulate a strategy.
5. For a firm that you know well, give an example WT Strategy, showing how an internal weakness can be matched with an external threat to formulate a strategy.
6. List three limitations of the SWOT matrix and analysis.
7. For the following three firms using the given factors, calculate a reasonable Stability Position (SP) coordinate to go on their SPACE Matrix axis, given what you know about the nature of those industries.

Factors	Winnebago	Apple	U.S. Postal Service
Barriers to entry into market			
Seasonal nature of business			
Technological changes			
SP Score			

8. Would the angle or degrees of the vector in a SPACE Matrix be important in generating alternative strategies? Explain.

9. On the Competitive Position (CP) axis of a SPACE Matrix, what level of capacity utilization would be necessary for you to give the firm a negative 1? Negative 7? Why?

10. If a firm has weak financial position and competes in an unstable industry, in which quadrant will the SPACE vector lie?

11. Describe a situation where the SPACE analysis would have no vector. In other words, describe a situation where the SPACE analysis coordinate would be (0,0). What should an analyst do in this situation?

12. Develop a BCG Matrix for your university. Because your college does not generate profits, what would be a good surrogate for the pie slice values? How many circles do you have and how large are they? Explain.

13. In a BCG Matrix, would the Question Mark quadrant or the Cash Cow quadrant be more desirable? Explain.

14. Would a BCG Matrix and analysis be worth performing if you do not know the profits of each segment? Why?

15. What major limitations of the BCG Matrix does the IE Matrix overcome?

16. In an IE Matrix, do you believe it is more advantageous for a division to be located in quadrant II or IV? Why?

17. Develop a $2 \times 2 \times 2$ QSPM for an organization of your choice (i.e., two strengths, two weaknesses, two opportunities, two threats, and two strategies). Follow all the QSPM guidelines presented in the chapter.

18. Give an example of "equifinality" as defined in the chapter.

19. Do you believe the reasons to disclose by-segment financial information offset the reasons not to disclose by-segment financial information? Explain why or why not.

20. How would application of the strategy-formulation framework differ from a small to a large organization?

21. What types of strategies would you recommend for an organization that achieves total weighted scores of 3.6 on the IFE and 1.2 on the EFE Matrix?

22. Given the following information, develop a SPACE Matrix for the XYZ Corporation: FP = +2; SP = −6; CP = −2; IP = +4.

23. Given the information in the following table, develop a BCG Matrix and an IE Matrix:

Divisions	1	2	3
Profits	$10	$15	$25
Sales	$100	$50	$100
Relative Market Share	0.2	0.5	0.8
Industry Growth Rate	+.20	+.10	−.10
IFE Total Weighted Scores	1.6	3.1	2.2
EFE Total Weighted Scores	2.5	1.8	3.3

24. Explain the steps involved in developing a QSPM.

25. How would you develop a set of objectives for your school or business?

26. What do you think is the appropriate role of a board of directors in strategic management? Why?

27. Discuss the limitations of various strategy-formulation analytical techniques.

28. Explain why cultural factors should be an important consideration in analyzing and choosing among alternative strategies.

29. How are the SWOT Matrix, SPACE Matrix, BCG Matrix, IE Matrix, and Grand Strategy Matrix similar? How are they different?

30. How would for-profit and nonprofit organizations differ in their applications of the strategy-formulation framework?

31. Develop a SPACE Matrix for a company that is weak financially and is a weak competitor. The industry for this company is pretty stable, but the industry's projected growth in revenues and profits is not good. Label all axes and quadrants.

32. List four limitations of a BCG Matrix.

33. Make up an example to show clearly and completely that you can develop an IE Matrix for a three-division company, where each division has $10, $20, and $40 in revenues and $2, $4, and $1 in profits. State other assumptions needed. Label axes and quadrants.

34. What procedures could be necessary if the SPACE vector falls right on the axis between the Competitive and Defensive quadrants?

35. In a BCG Matrix or the Grand Strategy Matrix, what would you consider to be a rapid market (or industry) growth rate?

36. What are the pros and cons of a company (and country) participating in a Sustainability Report?

37. How does the Sarbanes-Oxley Act of 2002 impact boards of directors?

38. Rank *BusinessWeek*'s "principles of good governance" from 1 to 14 (1 being most important and 14 least important) to reveal your assessment of these new rules.
39. Why is it important to work row by row instead of column by column in preparing a QSPM?
40. Why should one avoid putting double 4's in a row in preparing a QSPM?
41. Envision a QSPM with no weight column. Would that still be a useful analysis? Why or why not? What do you lose by deleting the weight column?
42. Prepare a BCG Matrix for a two-division firm with sales of $5 and $8 versus profits of $3 and $1, respectively. State assumptions for the RMSP and IGR axes to enable you to construct the diagram.
43. Consider developing a before-and-after BCG or IE Matrix to reveal the expected results of your proposed strategies. What limitation of the analysis would this procedure overcome somewhat?
44. If a firm has the leading market share in its industry, where on the BCG Matrix would the circle lie?
45. If a firm competes in a very unstable industry, such as telecommunications, where on the SP axis of the SPACE Matrix would you plot the appropriate point?
46. Why do you think the SWOT Matrix is the most widely used of all strategy matrices?
47. The strategy templates described at the www.strategyclub.com Web site have templates for all of the Chapter 6 matrices. How could those templates be useful in preparing an example BCG or IE Matrix?

Notes

1. R. T. Lenz, "Managing the Evolution of the Strategic Planning Process," *Business Horizons* 30, no. 1 (January–February 1987): 37.
2. Robert Grant, "The Resource-Based Theory of Competitive Advantage: Implications for Strategy Formulation," *California Management Review* (Spring 1991): 114.
3. Heinz Weihrich, "The TOWS Matrix: A Tool for Situational Analysis," *Long Range Planning* 15, no. 2 (April 1982): 61. Note: Although Dr. Weihrich first modified SWOT analysis to form the TOWS matrix, the acronym SWOT is much more widely used than TOWS in practice.
4. Greg, Dess, G. T. Lumpkin, and Alan Eisner, *Strategic Management: Text and Cases* (New York: McGraw-Hill/Irwin, 2006): 72.
5. Adapted from H. Rowe, R. Mason, and K. Dickel, *Strategic Management and Business Policy: A Methodological Approach* (Reading, MA: Addison-Wesley, 1982): 155–156.
6. Fred David, "The Strategic Planning Matrix—A Quantitative Approach," *Long Range Planning* 19, no. 5 (October 1986): 102; Andre Gib and Robert Margulies, "Making Competitive Intelligence Relevant to the User," *Planning Review* 19, no. 3 (May–June 1991): 21.
7. Fred David, "Computer-Assisted Strategic Planning in Small Businesses," *Journal of Systems Management* 36, no. 7 (July 1985): 24–34.
8. Y. Allarie and M. Firsirotu, "How to Implement Radical Strategies in Large Organizations," *Sloan Management Review* 26, no. 3 (Spring 1985): 19. Another excellent article is P. Shrivastava, "Integrating Strategy Formulation with Organizational Culture," *Journal of Business Strategy* 5, no. 3 (Winter 1985): 103–111.
9. James Brian Quinn, *Strategies for Changes: Logical Incrementalism* (Homewood, IL: Richard D. Irwin, 1980): 128–145. These political tactics are listed in A. Thompson and A. Strickland, *Strategic Management: Concepts and Cases* (Plano, TX: Business Publications, 1984): 261.
10. William Guth and Ian MacMillan, "Strategy Implementation Versus Middle Management Self-Interest," *Strategic Management Journal* 7, no. 4 (July–August 1986): 321.
11. Joann Lublin, "Corporate Directors' Group Gives Repair Plan to Boards," *Wall Street Journal* (March 24, 2009): B4.
12. Phred Dvorak, "Poor Year Doesn't Stop CEO Bonuses," *Wall Street Journal* (March 18, 2009): B1.
13. Louis Lavelle, "The Best and Worst Boards," *BusinessWeek* (October 7, 2002): 104–110.
14. Matt Murray, "Private Companies Also Feel Pressure to Clean Up Acts," *Wall Street Journal* (July 22, 2003): B1.

Current Readings

Angwin, Duncan, Sotirios, Paroutis, and Sarah Mitson. "Connecting Up Strategy: Are Senior Strategy Directors a Missing Link?" *California Management Review* (Spring 2009): 49–73.
Berdrow, Iris, Hsing-Er Lin, Edward F. McDonough, and Michael H. Zack. "The Threefold Path to Strategy: Adding Knowledge and Innovation Positions to the Mix." *MIT Sloan Management Review* 50, no. 1 (Fall 2008): 53.
Capron, Laurence, and Mauro Guillen. "National Corporate Governance Institutions and Post-Acquisition Target Reorganization." *Strategic Management Journal* (August 2008): 803–833.

Dahling, Jason, Brian Whitaker, and Paul Levy. "The Development and Validation of a New Machiavellianism Scale." *Journal of Management* (March 2009): 219–257.

Makadok, Richard, and Russell Coff. "Both Market and Hierarchy: An Incentive-System Theory of Hybrid Governance." *Academy of Management Review* (April 2009): 297–319.

Dalton, Catherine M. "From the Battlefield to the Boardroom." *Business Horizons* 51, no. 2 (March–April 2008): 79.

Dalton, Dan R., and Catherine M. Dalton. "Corporate Governance in the Post Sarbanes-Oxley Period: Compensation Disclosure and Analysis (CD&A)." *Business Horizons* 51, no. 2 (March–April 2008): 85.

Douglas, Thomas J., William Q. Judge, and Ali M. Kutan. "Institutional Antecedents of Corporate Governance Legitimacy." *Journal of Management* 34, no. 4 (August 2008): 765.

Graebner, Melissa E., Michael L. McDonald, and James D. Westphal, "What Do They Know? The Effects of Outside Director Acquisition Experience on Firm Acquisition. Performance." *Strategic Management Journal* 29, no. 11 (November 2008): 1155.

Khanna, Poonam, Michael L. McDonald, and James D. Westphal. "Getting Them to Think Outside the Circle: Corporate Governance, CEOs' External Advice Networks, and Firm Performance." *The Academy of Management Journal* 51, no. 3 (June 2008): 453.

Koka, Balaji R., and John E. Prescott. "Designing Alliance Networks: The Influence of Network Position, Environmental Change, and Strategy on Firm Performance." *Strategic Management Journal* 29, no. 6 (June 2008): 639.

Kroll, Mark, Bruce A. Walters, and Peter Wright. "Board Vigilance, Director Experience, and Corporate Outcomes." *Strategic Management Journal* 29, no. 4 (April 2008): 363.

MacMilan, Ian C., and Larry Selden. "The Incumbent's Advantage." *Harvard Business Review* (October 2008): 111.

Nayak, Ajit. "Enhancing the Innovation Performance of Firms by Balancing Cohesiveness and Bridging Ties." *Long Range Planning* 41, no. 4 (August 2008): 420.

Zhang, Yan, and Nandini Rajagopalan. "Corporate Governance Reforms in China and India: Challenges and Opportunities." *Business Horizons* 51, no. 1 (January–February 2008): 55.

ASSURANCE OF LEARNING EXERCISES

Assurance of Learning Exercise 6A

Developing a SWOT Matrix for McDonald's

Purpose

The most widely used strategy-formulation technique among U.S. firms is the SWOT Matrix. This exercise requires the development of a SWOT Matrix for McDonald's. Matching key external and internal factors in a SWOT Matrix requires good intuitive and conceptual skills. You will improve with practice in developing a SWOT Matrix.

Instructions

Recall from Experiential Exercise 1A that you already may have determined McDonald's external opportunities/threats and internal strengths/weaknesses. This information could be used to complete this exercise. Follow the steps outlined as follows:

Step 1   On a separate sheet of paper, construct a large nine-cell diagram that will represent your SWOT Matrix. Appropriately label the cells.

Step 2   Appropriately record McDonald's opportunities/threats and strengths/weaknesses in your diagram.

Step 3   Match external and internal factors to generate feasible alternative strategies for McDonald's. Record SO, WO, ST, and WT strategies in the appropriate cells of the SWOT Matrix. Use the proper notation to indicate the rationale for the strategies. You do not necessarily have to have strategies in all four strategy cells.

Step 4   Compare your SWOT Matrix to another student's SWOT Matrix. Discuss any major differences.

Assurance of Learning Exercise 6B

Developing a SPACE Matrix for McDonald's

Purpose

Should McDonald's pursue aggressive, conservative, competitive, or defensive strategies? Develop a SPACE Matrix for McDonald's to answer this question. Elaborate on the strategic implications of your directional vector. Be specific in terms of strategies that could benefit McDonald's.

Instructions

Step 1   Join with two other people in class and develop a joint SPACE Matrix for McDonald's.

Step 2   Diagram your SPACE Matrix on the board. Compare your matrix with other team's matrices.

Step 3   Discuss the implications of your SPACE Matrix.

Assurance of Learning Exercise 6C

Developing a BCG Matrix for McDonald's

Purpose

Portfolio matrices are widely used by multidivisional organizations to help identify and select strategies to pursue. A BCG analysis identifies particular divisions that should receive fewer resources than others. It may identify some divisions that need to be divested. This exercise can give you practice developing a BCG Matrix.

Instructions

Step 1   Place the following five column headings at the top of a separate sheet of paper: Divisions, Revenues, Profits, Relative Market Share Position, Industry Growth Rate. Down the far left of your page, list MCD's geographic divisions. Now turn back to the Cohesion Case and find information to fill in all the cells in your data table from page 30.

Step 2   Complete a BCG Matrix for McDonald's.

Step 3   Compare your BCG Matrix to other students' matrices. Discuss any major differences.

Assurance of Learning Exercise 6D

Developing a QSPM for McDonald's

Purpose

This exercise can give you practice developing a Quantitative Strategic Planning Matrix to determine the relative attractiveness of various strategic alternatives.

Instructions

Step 1   Join with two other students in class to develop a joint QSPM for McDonald's.

Step 2   Go to the blackboard and record your strategies and their Sum Total Attractiveness Score. Compare your team's strategies and Sum Total Attractiveness Score to those of other teams. Be sure not to assign the same AS score in a given row. Recall that dashes should be inserted all the way across a given row when used.

Step 3   Discuss any major differences.

Assurance of Learning Exercise 6E

Formulating Individual Strategies

Purpose

Individuals and organizations are alike in many ways. Each has competitors, and each should plan for the future. Every individual and organization faces some external opportunities and threats and has some internal strengths and weaknesses. Both individuals and organizations establish objectives and allocate resources. These and other similarities make it possible for individuals to use many strategic-management concepts and tools. This exercise is designed to demonstrate how the SWOT Matrix can be used by individuals to plan their futures. As one nears completion of a college degree and begins interviewing for jobs, planning can be particularly important.

Instructions

On a separate sheet of paper, construct a SWOT Matrix. Include what you consider to be your major external opportunities, your major external threats, your major strengths, and your major weaknesses. An internal weakness may be a low grade point average. An external opportunity may be that your university offers a graduate program that interests you. Match key external and internal factors by recording in the appropriate cell of the matrix alternative strategies or actions that would allow you to capitalize upon your strengths, overcome your weaknesses, take advantage of your external opportunities, and minimize the impact of external threats. Be sure to use the appropriate matching notation in the strategy cells of the matrix. Because every individual (and organization) is unique, there is no one right answer to this exercise.

Assurance of Learning Exercise 6F

The Mach Test

Purpose

The purpose of this exercise is to enhance your understanding and awareness of the impact that behavioral and political factors can have on strategy analysis and choice.

Instructions

Step 1   On a separate sheet of paper, number from 1 to 10. For each of the 10 statements given as follows, record a *1, 2, 3, 4,* or *5* to indicate your attitude,

where

1 = I disagree a lot.
2 = I disagree a little.
3 = My attitude is neutral.
4 = I agree a little.
5 = I agree a lot.

1. The best way to handle people is to tell them what they want to hear.
2. When you ask someone to do something for you, it is best to give the real reason for wanting it, rather than a reason that might carry more weight.
3. Anyone who completely trusts anyone else is asking for trouble.
4. It is hard to get ahead without cutting corners here and there.
5. It is safest to assume that all people have a vicious streak, and it will come out when they are given a chance.
6. One should take action only when it is morally right.
7. Most people are basically good and kind.
8. There is no excuse for lying to someone else.
9. Most people forget more easily the death of their father than the loss of their property.
10. Generally speaking, people won't work hard unless they're forced to do so.

Step 2   Add up the numbers you recorded beside statements 1, 3, 4, 5, 9, and 10. This sum is Subtotal One. For the other four statements, reverse the numbers you recorded, so a *5* becomes a *1, 4* becomes *2, 2* becomes *4, 1* becomes *5,* and *3* remains *3.* Then add those four numbers to get Subtotal Two. Finally, add Subtotal One and Subtotal Two to get your Final Score.

Your Final Score

Your Final Score is your Machiavellian Score. Machiavellian principles are defined in a dictionary as "manipulative, dishonest, deceiving, and favoring political expediency over morality." These tactics are not desirable, are not ethical, and are not recommended in the strategic-management process! You may, however, encounter some highly Machiavellian individuals in your career, so beware. It is important for strategists not to manipulate others in the pursuit of organizational objectives. Individuals today recognize and resent manipulative tactics more than ever before. J. R. Ewing (on *Dallas,* a television show in the 1980s) was a good example of someone who was a high Mach (score over 30). The National Opinion Research Center used this short quiz in a random sample of U.S. adults and found the national average Final Score to be 25.[1] The higher your score, the more Machiavellian (manipulative) you tend to be. The following scale is descriptive of individual scores on this test:

- Below 16: Never uses manipulation as a tool.
- 16 to 20: Rarely uses manipulation as a tool.
- 21 to 25: Sometimes uses manipulation as a tool.
- 26 to 30: Often uses manipulation as a tool.
- Over 30: Always uses manipulation as a tool.

Test Development

The Mach (Machiavellian) test was developed by Dr. Richard Christie, whose research suggests the following tendencies:

1. Men generally are more Machiavellian than women.
2. There is no significant difference between high Machs and low Machs on measures of intelligence or ability.
3. Although high Machs are detached from others, they are detached in a pathological sense.
4. Machiavellian scores are not statistically related to authoritarian values.
5. High Machs tend to be in professions that emphasize the control and manipulation of individuals—for example, law, psychiatry, and behavioral science.
6. Machiavellianism is not significantly related to major demographic characteristics such as educational level or marital status.
7. High Machs tend to come from a city or have urban backgrounds.
8. Older adults tend to have lower Mach scores than younger adults.[2]

A classic book on power relationships, *The Prince,* was written by Niccolo Machiavelli. Several excerpts from *The Prince* follow:

Men must either be cajoled or crushed, for they will revenge themselves for slight wrongs, while for grave ones they cannot. The injury therefore that you do to a man should be such that you need not fear his revenge.

We must bear in mind . . . that there is nothing more difficult and dangerous, or more doubtful of success, than an attempt to introduce a new order of things in any state. The innovator has for enemies all those who derived advantages from the old order of things, while those who expect to be benefitted by the new institution will be but lukewarm defenders.

A wise prince, therefore, will steadily pursue such a course that the citizens of his state will always and under all circumstances feel the need for his authority, and will therefore always prove faithful to him.

A prince should seem to be merciful, faithful, humane, religious, and upright, and should even be so in reality, but he should have his mind so trained that, when occasion requires it, he may know how to change to the opposite.[3]

Notes

1. Richard Christie and Florence Geis, *Studies in Machiavellianism* (Orlando, FL: Academic Press, 1970). Material in this exercise adapted with permission of the authors and the Academic Press.
2. Ibid., 82–83.
3. Niccolo Machiavelli, *The Prince* (New York: The Washington Press, 1963).

Assurance of Learning Exercise 6G

Developing a BCG Matrix for My University

Purpose

Developing a BCG Matrix for many nonprofit organizations, including colleges and universities, is a useful exercise. Of course, there are no profits for each division or department—and in some cases no revenues. However, you can be creative in performing a BCG Matrix. For example, the pie slice in the circles can represent the number of majors receiving jobs upon graduation, the number of faculty teaching in that area, or some other variable that you believe is important to consider. The size of the circles can represent the number of students majoring in particular departments or areas.

Instructions

Step 1   On a separate sheet of paper, develop a BCG Matrix for your university. Include all academic schools, departments, or colleges.
Step 2   Diagram your BCG Matrix on the blackboard.
Step 3   Discuss differences among the BCG Matrices on the board.

Assurance of Learning Exercise 6H

The Role of Boards of Directors

Purpose

This exercise will give you a better understanding of the role of boards of directors in formulating, implementing, and evaluating strategies.

Instructions

Identify a person in your community who serves on a board of directors. Make an appointment to interview that person, and seek answers to the following questions. Summarize your findings in a five-minute oral report to the class.

- On what board are you a member?
- How often does the board meet?
- How long have you served on the board?
- What role does the board play in this company?

- How has the role of the board changed in recent years?
- What changes would you like to see in the role of the board?
- To what extent do you prepare for the board meeting?
- To what extent are you involved in strategic management of the firm?

Assurance of Learning Exercise 6I

Locating Companies in a Grand Strategy Matrix

Purpose

The Grand Strategy Matrix is a popular tool for formulating alternative strategies. All organizations can be positioned in one of the Grand Strategy Matrix's four strategy quadrants. The divisions of a firm likewise could be positioned. The Grand Strategy Matrix is based on two evaluative dimensions: competitive position and market growth. Appropriate strategies for an organization to consider are listed in sequential order of attractiveness in each quadrant of the matrix. This exercise gives you experience using a Grand Strategy Matrix.

Instructions

Using the year-end 2008 financial information provided, prepare a Grand Strategy Matrix on a separate sheet of paper. Write the respective company names in the appropriate quadrant of the matrix. Based on this analysis, what strategies are recommended for each company?

Company	Company Sales/ Profit Growth (%)	Industry	Industry Sales/ Profit Growth (%)
Boeing	−8 / −34	Aerospace/defense	+7 / +13
DuPont	+4 / −33	Chemicals	+7 / −23
Wal-Mart	+7 / +5	General merchandise	−3 / −44
Sears Holdings	−8 / −94	General merchandise	−3 / −44
Black & Decker	−7 / −43	Home equipment	−9 / −111
TIAA-CREF	+7 / +7	Insurance	−1 / −178
Nucor	+43 / +24	Metals	−16 / −24
Allegheny	−3 / −24	Metals	−16 / −24

CHAPTER 7
Implementing Strategies: Management and Operations Issues

CHAPTER OBJECTIVES

After studying this chapter, you should be able to do the following:

1. Explain why strategy implementation is more difficult than strategy formulation.

2. Discuss the importance of annual objectives and policies in achieving organizational commitment for strategies to be implemented.

3. Explain why organizational structure is so important in strategy implementation.

4. Compare and contrast restructuring and reengineering.

5. Describe the relationships between production/operations and strategy implementation.

6. Explain how a firm can effectively link performance and pay to strategies.

7. Discuss employee stock ownership plans (ESOPs) as a strategic-management concept.

8. Describe how to modify an organizational culture to support new strategies.

9. Discuss the culture in Mexico and Japan.

10. Describe the glass ceiling in the United States.

Assurance of Learning Exercises

Assurance of Learning Exercise 7A
Revising McDonald's Organizational Chart

Assurance of Learning Exercise 7B
Do Organizations Really Establish Objectives?

Assurance of Learning Exercise 7C
Understanding My University's Culture

Source: Shutterstock, Photographer Feng Yu

"Notable Quotes"

"You want your people to run the business as if it were their own."

—**William Fulmer**

"Poor Ike; when he was a general, he gave an order and it was carried out. Now, he's going to sit in that office and give an order and not a damn thing is going to happen."

—**Harry Truman**

"Changing your pay plan is a big risk, but not changing it could be a bigger one."

—**Nancy Perry**

"Objectives can be compared to a compass bearing by which a ship navigates. A compass bearing is firm, but in actual navigation, a ship may veer off its course for many miles. Without a compass bearing, a ship would neither find its port nor be able to estimate the time required to get there."

—**Peter Drucker**

"The best game plan in the world never blocked or tackled anybody."

—**Vince Lombardi**

"Pretend that every single person you meet has a sign around his or her neck that says, 'Make me feel important.' "

—**Mary Kay Ash**

The strategic-management process does not end when the firm decides what strategy or strategies to pursue. There must be a translation of strategic thought into strategic action. This translation is much easier if managers and employees of the firm understand the business, feel a part of the company, and through involvement in strategy-formulation activities have become committed to helping the organization succeed. Without understanding and commitment, strategy-implementation efforts face major problems.

Implementing strategy affects an organization from top to bottom; it affects all the functional and divisional areas of a business. It is beyond the purpose and scope of this text to examine all of the business administration concepts and tools important in strategy implementation. This chapter focuses on management issues most central to implementing strategies in 2010–2011 and Chapter 8 focuses on marketing, finance/accounting, R&D, and management information systems issues.

Even the most technically perfect strategic plan will serve little purpose if it is not implemented. Many organizations tend to spend an inordinate amount of time, money, and effort on developing the strategic plan, treating the means and circumstances under which it will be implemented as afterthoughts! Change comes through implementation and evaluation, not through the plan. A technically imperfect plan that is implemented well will achieve more than the perfect plan that never gets off the paper on which it is typed.[1]

Doing Great in a Weak Economy. How?

Google

When most firms were struggling in 2008, Google increased its revenues and profits such that *Fortune* magazine in 2009 rated Google as their fourth "Most Admired Company in the World" in terms of their management and performance. Based in Mountain View, California, Google's first quarter of 2009 revenues grew 6.2 percent to $5.51 billion, followed by $5.52 billion the second quarter. These results widened Google's lead in overall searches and online advertising market share. Google owns both YouTube and DoubleClick.

Google in 2009 began selling books online. This related diversification strategy led Google to digitize close to 10 million books by year's end. Google cofounder Sergey Brin recently said, "Call me weird, but I think there are a lot of advantages to reading books online. Today's monitors have great resolution and you don't have to wait on the book to arrive once ordered."

Google does not charge people to use its search engine. Instead of charging what the market will bear as

most firms do, Google charges as little as they can bear. Thus Google obtains networks of people, millions of people, which strengthens its competitive position.

Google's founders, Larry Page and Sergey Brin, each have nearly 30 percent voting control of the firm and have established a golden rule that permeates Google's internal culture. The rule is to "Don't be evil," and this operating policy encourages all employees to challenge all managers on decisions—to make sure the decisions are true to the firm's mission. Another internal rule at Google is to "Give up control," which means giving up control to outsiders to reap the benefits of their input. This latter rule is done through beta launches of any new software, product, or service they do. Google's philosophy is that "Low prices are good, but free is better" because they want every customer they can get.

Google stock in July 2009 rose above $400 per share as the company prepares to launch its own operating system for computers, a direct assault on the business of software giant Microsoft. Google's strategic plan is to attack Microsoft in nearly all of its businesses, including browsers, where Google has 1.8 percent market share versus Microsoft's 66 percent, smartphone operating systems (Google 1.6% versus Microsoft 10%), office suites (Google 0.04% versus Microsoft 94%), and Web searches (Google 65% versus Microsoft 8%).

Google's Chrome OS operating system will require users to be connected to the Internet, unlike Microsoft's operating systems. CEO Eric Schmidt at Google has been on a mission for the last several years, according to analysts, to capture Microsoft's market share. The Google strategy is accelerating a shift in the personal computer (PC) industry to become more like the cell phone industry whereby customers pay monthly service fees for use of hardware and software.

Google's Chrome will be free to all computer makers such as Hewlett-Packard who historically have pre-installed Microsoft's operating system for a fee to consumers. Microsoft released its new Microsoft Windows 2010 in the fall 2009 and believes that the learning curve for any consumer to switch away to Google's operating system will not be worth the effort. Google.com is the most visited Web site in the world and even in 2009 offered its own online word processing, spreadsheet, and presentation programs free – called Google Docs. The Google strategy is a huge bet that online programs can eventually overtake and crush desktop software.

Due to its dominance in the Internet search and advertising business, Google is coming under increasing scrutiny from the U.S. Justice Department regarding possible antitrust infringement. The pending Microsoft/Yahoo merger may negate that Google vulnerability. Google obtains about 95 percent of its revenues from online advertising.

Source: Based on Jeff Jarvis, "How the Google Model Could Help Detroit," *Business Week* (February 9, 2009): 33–36; Geoff Colvin, "The World's Most Admired Companies," *Fortune* (March 16, 2009): 76–86.

The Nature of Strategy Implementation

The strategy-implementation stage of strategic management is revealed in Figure 7-1. Successful strategy formulation does not guarantee successful strategy implementation. It is always more difficult to do something (strategy implementation) than to say you are going to do it (strategy formulation)! Although inextricably linked, strategy implementation is fundamentally different from strategy formulation. Strategy formulation and implementation can be contrasted in the following ways:

- Strategy formulation is positioning forces before the action.
- Strategy implementation is managing forces during the action.
- Strategy formulation focuses on effectiveness.
- Strategy implementation focuses on efficiency.
- Strategy formulation is primarily an intellectual process.
- Strategy implementation is primarily an operational process.
- Strategy formulation requires good intuitive and analytical skills.
- Strategy implementation requires special motivation and leadership skills.
- Strategy formulation requires coordination among a few individuals.
- Strategy implementation requires coordination among many individuals.

Strategy-formulation concepts and tools do not differ greatly for small, large, for-profit, or nonprofit organizations. However, strategy implementation varies substantially among different types and sizes of organizations. Implementing strategies requires such actions as altering sales territories, adding new departments, closing facilities, hiring new employees, changing an organization's pricing strategy, developing financial budgets, developing new employee benefits, establishing cost-control procedures, changing advertising strategies, building new facilities, training new employees, transferring managers among

FIGURE 7-1

Comprehensive Strategic-Management Model

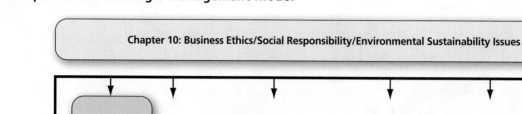

Source: Fred R. David, "How Companies Define Their Mission," *Long Range Planning* 22, no. 3 (June 1988): 40.

divisions, and building a better management information system. These types of activities obviously differ greatly between manufacturing, service, and governmental organizations.

Management Perspectives

In all but the smallest organizations, the transition from strategy formulation to strategy implementation requires a shift in responsibility from strategists to divisional and functional managers. Implementation problems can arise because of this shift in responsibility, especially if strategy-formulation decisions come as a surprise to middle- and lower-level managers. Managers and employees are motivated more by perceived self-interests than by organizational interests, unless the two coincide. Therefore, it is essential that divisional and functional managers be involved as much as possible in strategy-formulation activities. Of equal importance, strategists should be involved as much as possible in strategy-implementation activities.

As indicated in Table 7-1, management issues central to strategy implementation include establishing annual objectives, devising policies, allocating resources, altering an existing organizational structure, restructuring and reengineering, revising reward and incentive plans, minimizing resistance to change, matching managers with strategy, developing a strategy-supportive culture, adapting production/operations processes, developing an effective human

**TABLE 7-1   Some Management Issues Central
                to Strategy Implementation**

Establish annual objectives

Devise policies

Allocate resources

Alter an existing organizational structure

Restructure and reengineer

Revise reward and incentive plans

Minimize resistance to change

Match managers with strategy

Develop a strategy-supportive culture

Adapt production/operations processes

Develop an effective human resources function

Downsize and furlough as needed

Link performance and pay to strategies

resources function, and, if necessary, downsizing. Management changes are necessarily more extensive when strategies to be implemented move a firm in a major new direction.

Managers and employees throughout an organization should participate early and directly in strategy-implementation decisions. Their role in strategy implementation should build upon prior involvement in strategy-formulation activities. Strategists' genuine personal commitment to implementation is a necessary and powerful motivational force for managers and employees. Too often, strategists are too busy to actively support strategy-implementation efforts, and their lack of interest can be detrimental to organizational success. The rationale for objectives and strategies should be understood and clearly communicated throughout an organization. Major competitors' accomplishments, products, plans, actions, and performance should be apparent to all organizational members. Major external opportunities and threats should be clear, and managers' and employees' questions should be answered. Top-down flow of communication is essential for developing bottom-up support.

Firms need to develop a competitor focus at all hierarchical levels by gathering and widely distributing competitive intelligence; every employee should be able to benchmark her or his efforts against best-in-class competitors so that the challenge becomes personal. For example, Starbucks Corp. in 2009–2010 is instituting "lean production/operations" at its 11,000 U.S. stores. This system eliminates idle employee time and unnecessary employee motions, such as walking, reaching, and bending. Starbucks says 30 percent of employees' time is motion and the company wants to reduce that. They say "motion and work are two different things."

Annual Objectives

Establishing annual objectives is a decentralized activity that directly involves all managers in an organization. Active participation in establishing annual objectives can lead to acceptance and commitment. *Annual objectives* are essential for strategy implementation because they (1) represent the basis for allocating resources; (2) are a primary mechanism for evaluating managers; (3) are the major instrument for monitoring progress toward achieving long-term objectives; and (4) establish organizational, divisional, and departmental priorities. Considerable time and effort should be devoted to ensuring that annual objectives are well conceived, consistent with long-term objectives, and supportive of strategies to be implemented. Approving, revising, or rejecting annual objectives is much more than a rubber-stamp activity. The purpose of annual objectives can be summarized as follows:

Annual objectives serve as guidelines for action, directing and channeling efforts and activities of organization members. They provide a source of legitimacy in an enterprise by justifying activities to stakeholders. They serve as standards of performance.

They serve as an important source of employee motivation and identification. They give incentives for managers and employees to perform. They provide a basis for organizational design.[2]

Clearly stated and communicated objectives are critical to success in all types and sizes of firms. Annual objectives, stated in terms of profitability, growth, and market share by business segment, geographic area, customer groups, and product, are common in organizations. Figure 7-2 illustrates how the Stamus Company could establish annual objectives based on long-term objectives. Table 7-2 reveals associated revenue figures that correspond to the objectives outlined in Figure 7-2. Note that, according to plan, the

FIGURE 7-2

The Stamus Company's Hierarchy of Aims

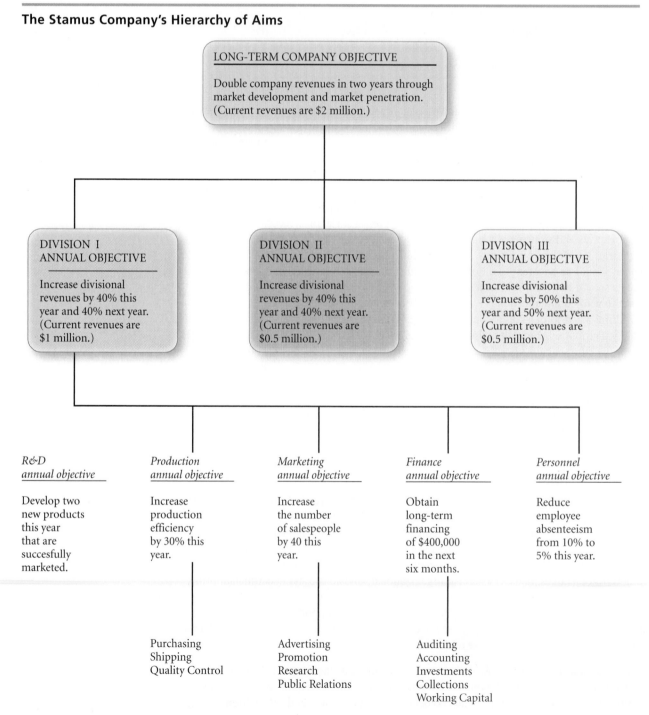

TABLE 7-2 **The Stamus Company's Revenue Expectations (in $Millions)**

	2010	2011	2012
Division I Revenues	1.0	1.400	1.960
Division II Revenues	0.5	0.700	0.980
Division III Revenues	0.5	0.750	1.125
Total Company Revenues	**2.0**	**2.850**	**4.065**

Stamus Company will slightly exceed its long-term objective of doubling company revenues between 2010 and 2012.

Figure 7-2 also reflects how a hierarchy of annual objectives can be established based on an organization's structure. Objectives should be consistent across hierarchical levels and form a network of supportive aims. *Horizontal consistency of objectives* is as important as *vertical consistency of objectives.* For instance, it would not be effective for manufacturing to achieve more than its annual objective of units produced if marketing could not sell the additional units.

Annual objectives should be measurable, consistent, reasonable, challenging, clear, communicated throughout the organization, characterized by an appropriate time dimension, and accompanied by commensurate rewards and sanctions. Too often, objectives are stated in generalities, with little operational usefulness. Annual objectives, such as "to improve communication" or "to improve performance," are not clear, specific, or measurable. Objectives should state quantity, quality, cost, and time—and also be verifiable. Terms and phrases such as *maximize, minimize, as soon as possible*, and *adequate* should be avoided.

Annual objectives should be compatible with employees' and managers' values and should be supported by clearly stated policies. More of something is not always better. Improved quality or reduced cost may, for example, be more important than quantity. It is important to tie rewards and sanctions to annual objectives so that employees and managers understand that achieving objectives is critical to successful strategy implementation. Clear annual objectives do not guarantee successful strategy implementation, but they do increase the likelihood that personal and organizational aims can be accomplished. Overemphasis on achieving objectives can result in undesirable conduct, such as faking the numbers, distorting the records, and letting objectives become ends in themselves. Managers must be alert to these potential problems.

Policies

Changes in a firm's strategic direction do not occur automatically. On a day-to-day basis, policies are needed to make a strategy work. Policies facilitate solving recurring problems and guide the implementation of strategy. Broadly defined, *policy* refers to specific guidelines, methods, procedures, rules, forms, and administrative practices established to support and encourage work toward stated goals. Policies are instruments for strategy implementation. Policies set boundaries, constraints, and limits on the kinds of administrative actions that can be taken to reward and sanction behavior; they clarify what can and cannot be done in pursuit of an organization's objectives. For example, Carnival's *Paradise* ship has a no smoking policy anywhere, anytime aboard ship. It is the first cruise ship to ban smoking comprehensively. Another example of corporate policy relates to surfing the Web while at work. About 40 percent of companies today do not have a formal policy preventing employees from surfing the Internet, but software is being marketed now that allows firms to monitor how, when, where, and how long various employees use the Internet at work.

Policies let both employees and managers know what is expected of them, thereby increasing the likelihood that strategies will be implemented successfully. They provide a basis for management control, allow coordination across organizational units, and reduce the amount of time managers spend making decisions. Policies also clarify what work is to be done and by whom. They promote delegation of decision making to appropriate managerial levels where various problems usually arise. Many organizations have a policy manual that serves to guide and direct behavior. Wal-Mart has a policy that it calls the "10 Foot" Rule, whereby customers can find assistance within 10 feet of anywhere in the store. This is a welcomed policy in Japan, where Wal-Mart is trying to gain a foothold; 58 percent of all retailers in Japan are mom-and-pop stores and consumers historically have had to pay "top yen" rather than "discounted prices" for merchandise.

Policies can apply to all divisions and departments (for example, "We are an equal opportunity employer"). Some policies apply to a single department ("Employees in this department must take at least one training and development course each year"). Whatever their scope and form, policies serve as a mechanism for implementing strategies and obtaining objectives. Policies should be stated in writing whenever possible. They represent the means for carrying out strategic decisions. Examples of policies that support a company strategy, a divisional objective, and a departmental objective are given in Table 7-3.

Some example issues that may require a management policy are provided in Table 7-4.

TABLE 7-3 A Hierarchy of Policies

Company Strategy

Acquire a chain of retail stores to meet our sales growth and profitability objectives.

Supporting Policies

1. "All stores will be open from 8 A.M. to 8 P.M. Monday through Saturday." (This policy could increase retail sales if stores currently are open only 40 hours a week.)

2. "All stores must submit a Monthly Control Data Report." (This policy could reduce expense-to-sales ratios.)

3. "All stores must support company advertising by contributing 5 percent of their total monthly revenues for this purpose." (This policy could allow the company to establish a national reputation.)

4. "All stores must adhere to the uniform pricing guidelines set forth in the Company Handbook." (This policy could help assure customers that the company offers a consistent product in terms of price and quality in all its stores.)

Divisional Objective

Increase the division's revenues from $10 million in 2009 to $15 million in 2010.

Supporting Policies

1. "Beginning in January 2010, each one of this division's salespersons must file a weekly activity report that includes the number of calls made, the number of miles traveled, the number of units sold, the dollar volume sold, and the number of new accounts opened." (This policy could ensure that salespersons do not place too great an emphasis in certain areas.)

2. "Beginning in January 2010, this division will return to its employees 5 percent of its gross revenues in the form of a Christmas bonus." (This policy could increase employee productivity.)

3. "Beginning in January 2010, inventory levels carried in warehouses will be decreased by 30 percent in accordance with a just-in-time (JIT) manufacturing approach." (This policy could reduce production expenses and thus free funds for increased marketing efforts.)

Production Department Objective

Increase production from 20,000 units in 2009 to 30,000 units in 2010.

Supporting Policies

1. "Beginning in January 2010, employees will have the option of working up to 20 hours of overtime per week." (This policy could minimize the need to hire additional employees.)

2. "Beginning in January 2010, perfect attendance awards in the amount of $100 will be given to all employees who do not miss a workday in a given year." (This policy could decrease absenteeism and increase productivity.)

3. "Beginning in January 2010, new equipment must be leased rather than purchased." (This policy could reduce tax liabilities and thus allow more funds to be invested in modernizing production processes.)

TABLE 7-4   Some Issues That May Require a Management Policy

- To offer extensive or limited management development workshops and seminars
- To centralize or decentralize employee-training activities
- To recruit through employment agencies, college campuses, and/or newspapers
- To promote from within or to hire from the outside
- To promote on the basis of merit or on the basis of seniority
- To tie executive compensation to long-term and/or annual objectives
- To offer numerous or few employee benefits
- To negotiate directly or indirectly with labor unions
- To delegate authority for large expenditures or to centrally retain this authority
- To allow much, some, or no overtime work
- To establish a high- or low-safety stock of inventory
- To use one or more suppliers
- To buy, lease, or rent new production equipment
- To greatly or somewhat stress quality control
- To establish many or only a few production standards
- To operate one, two, or three shifts
- To discourage using insider information for personal gain
- To discourage sexual harassment
- To discourage smoking at work
- To discourage insider trading
- To discourage moonlighting

Resource Allocation

Resource allocation is a central management activity that allows for strategy execution. In organizations that do not use a strategic-management approach to decision making, resource allocation is often based on political or personal factors. Strategic management enables resources to be allocated according to priorities established by annual objectives.

Nothing could be more detrimental to strategic management and to organizational success than for resources to be allocated in ways not consistent with priorities indicated by approved annual objectives.

All organizations have at least four types of resources that can be used to achieve desired objectives: financial resources, physical resources, human resources, and technological resources. Allocating resources to particular divisions and departments does not mean that strategies will be successfully implemented. A number of factors commonly prohibit effective resource allocation, including an overprotection of resources, too great an emphasis on short-run financial criteria, organizational politics, vague strategy targets, a reluctance to take risks, and a lack of sufficient knowledge.

Below the corporate level, there often exists an absence of systematic thinking about resources allocated and strategies of the firm. Yavitz and Newman explain why:

> Managers normally have many more tasks than they can do. Managers must allocate time and resources among these tasks. Pressure builds up. Expenses are too high. The CEO wants a good financial report for the third quarter. Strategy formulation and implementation activities often get deferred. Today's problems soak up available energies and resources. Scrambled accounts and budgets fail to reveal the shift in allocation away from strategic needs to currently squeaking wheels.[3]

The real value of any resource allocation program lies in the resulting accomplishment of an organization's objectives. Effective resource allocation does not guarantee successful strategy implementation because programs, personnel, controls, and commitment must breathe life into the resources provided. Strategic management itself is sometimes referred to as a "resource allocation process."

TABLE 7-5   Some Management Trade-Off Decisions Required in Strategy Implementation

To emphasize short-term profits or long-term growth

To emphasize profit margin or market share

To emphasize market development or market penetration

To lay off or furlough

To seek growth or stability

To take high risk or low risk

To be more socially responsible or more profitable

To outsource jobs or pay more to keep jobs at home

To acquire externally or to build internally

To restructure or reengineer

To use leverage or equity to raise funds

To use part-time or full-time employees

Managing Conflict

Interdependency of objectives and competition for limited resources often leads to conflict. *Conflict* can be defined as a disagreement between two or more parties on one or more issues. Establishing annual objectives can lead to conflict because individuals have different expectations and perceptions, schedules create pressure, personalities are incompatible, and misunderstandings between line managers (such as production supervisors) and staff managers (such as human resource specialists) occur. For example, a collection manager's objective of reducing bad debts by 50 percent in a given year may conflict with a divisional objective to increase sales by 20 percent.

Establishing objectives can lead to conflict because managers and strategists must make trade-offs, such as whether to emphasize short-term profits or long-term growth, profit margin or market share, market penetration or market development, growth or stability, high risk or low risk, and social responsiveness or profit maximization. Trade-offs are necessary because no firm has sufficient resources pursue all strategies to would benefit the firm. Table 7-5 reveals some important management trade-off decisions required in strategy implementation.

Conflict is unavoidable in organizations, so it is important that conflict be managed and resolved before dysfunctional consequences affect organizational performance. Conflict is not always bad. An absence of conflict can signal indifference and apathy. Conflict can serve to energize opposing groups into action and may help managers identify problems.

Various approaches for managing and resolving conflict can be classified into three categories: avoidance, defusion, and confrontation. *Avoidance* includes such actions as ignoring the problem in hopes that the conflict will resolve itself or physically separating the conflicting individuals (or groups). *Defusion* can include playing down differences between conflicting parties while accentuating similarities and common interests, compromising so that there is neither a clear winner nor loser, resorting to majority rule, appealing to a higher authority, or redesigning present positions. *Confrontation* is exemplified by exchanging members of conflicting parties so that each can gain an appreciation of the other's point of view or holding a meeting at which conflicting parties present their views and work through their differences.

Matching Structure with Strategy

Changes in strategy often require changes in the way an organization is structured for two major reasons. First, structure largely dictates how objectives and policies will be established. For example, objectives and policies established under a geographic organizational structure are couched in geographic terms. Objectives and policies are stated largely in terms of products in an organization whose structure is based on product groups. The structural format for developing objectives and policies can significantly impact all other strategy-implementation activities.

The second major reason why changes in strategy often require changes in structure is that structure dictates how resources will be allocated. If an organization's structure is based on customer groups, then resources will be allocated in that manner. Similarly, if an organization's structure is set up along functional business lines, then resources are allocated by functional areas. Unless new or revised strategies place emphasis in the same areas as old strategies, structural reorientation commonly becomes a part of strategy implementation.

Changes in strategy lead to changes in organizational structure. Structure should be designed to facilitate the strategic pursuit of a firm and, therefore, follow strategy. Without a strategy or reasons for being (mission), companies find it difficult to design an effective structure. Chandler found a particular structure sequence to be repeated often as organizations grow and change strategy over time; this sequence is depicted in Figure 7-3.

There is no one optimal organizational design or structure for a given strategy or type of organization. What is appropriate for one organization may not be appropriate for a similar firm, although successful firms in a given industry do tend to organize themselves in a similar way. For example, consumer goods companies tend to emulate the divisional structure-by-product form of organization. Small firms tend to be functionally structured (centralized). Medium-sized firms tend to be divisionally structured (decentralized). Large firms tend to use a strategic business unit (SBU) or matrix structure. As organizations grow, their structures generally change from simple to complex as a result of concatenation, or the linking together of several basic strategies.

Numerous external and internal forces affect an organization; no firm could change its structure in response to every one of these forces, because to do so would lead to chaos. However, when a firm changes its strategy, the existing organizational structure may become ineffective. As indicated in Table 7-6, symptoms of an ineffective organizational structure include too many levels of management, too many meetings attended by too many people, too much attention being directed toward solving interdepartmental conflicts, too large a span of control, and too many unachieved objectives. Changes in structure can facilitate strategy-implementation efforts, but changes in structure should not be expected to make a bad strategy good, to make bad managers good, or to make bad products sell.

Structure undeniably can and does influence strategy. Strategies formulated must be workable, so if a certain new strategy required massive structural changes it would not be an attractive choice. In this way, structure can shape the choice of strategies. But a more important concern is determining what types of structural changes are needed to implement new

FIGURE 7-3

Chandler's Strategy-Structure Relationship

Source: Adapted from Alfred Chandler, *Strategy and Structure* (Cambridge, MA: MIT Press, 1962).

TABLE 7-6 Symptoms of an Ineffective Organizational Structure

1. Too many levels of management
2. Too many meetings attended by too many people
3. Too much attention being directed toward solving interdepartmental conflicts
4. Too large a span of control
5. Too many unachieved objectives
6. Declining corporate or business performance
7. Losing ground to rival firms
8. Revenue and/or earnings divided by number of employees and/or number of managers is low compared to rival firms

strategies and how these changes can best be accomplished. We examine this issue by focusing on seven basic types of organizational structure: functional, divisional by geographic area, divisional by product, divisional by customer, divisional process, strategic business unit (SBU), and matrix.

The Functional Structure

The most widely used structure is the functional or centralized type because this structure is the simplest and least expensive of the seven alternatives. A *functional structure* groups tasks and activities by business function, such as production/operations, marketing, finance/accounting, research and development, and management information systems. A university may structure its activities by major functions that include academic affairs, student services, alumni relations, athletics, maintenance, and accounting. Besides being simple and inexpensive, a functional structure also promotes specialization of labor, encourages efficient use of managerial and technical talent, minimizes the need for an elaborate control system, and allows rapid decision making.

Some disadvantages of a functional structure are that it forces accountability to the top, minimizes career development opportunities, and is sometimes characterized by low employee morale, line/staff conflicts, poor delegation of authority, and inadequate planning for products and markets.

A functional structure often leads to short-term and narrow thinking that may undermine what is best for the firm as a whole. For example, the research and development department may strive to overdesign products and components to achieve technical elegance, while manufacturing may argue for low-frills products that can be mass produced more easily. Thus, communication is often not as good in a functional structure. Schein gives an example of a communication problem in a functional structure:

> The word "marketing" will mean product development to the engineer, studying customers through market research to the product manager, merchandising to the salesperson, and constant change in design to the manufacturing manager. Then when these managers try to work together, they often attribute disagreements to personalities and fail to notice the deeper, shared assumptions that vary and dictate how each function thinks.[4]

Most large companies have abandoned the functional structure in favor of decentralization and improved accountability. However, two large firms that still successfully use a functional structure are Nucor Steel, based in Charlotte, North Carolina, and Sharp, the $17 billion consumer electronics firm.

Table 7-7 summarizes the advantages and disadvantages of a functional organizational structure.

The Divisional Structure

The *divisional* or *decentralized structure* is the second most common type used by U.S. businesses. As a small organization grows, it has more difficulty managing different products and services in different markets. Some form of divisional structure generally

TABLE 7-7   Advantages and Disadvantages of a Functional Organizational Structure

Advantages	Disadvantages
1. Simple and inexpensive	1. Accountability forced to the top
2. Capitalizes on specialization of business activities such as marketing and finance	2. Delegation of authority and responsibility not encouraged
3. Minimizes need for elaborate control system	3. Minimizes career development
	4. Low employee/manager morale
4. Allows for rapid decision making	5. Inadequate planning for products and markets
	6. Leads to short-term, narrow thinking
	7. Leads to communication problems

becomes necessary to motivate employees, control operations, and compete successfully in diverse locations. The divisional structure can be organized in one of four ways: *by geographic area, by product* or *service, by customer,* or *by process.* With a divisional structure, functional activities are performed both centrally and in each separate division.

Cisco Systems recently discarded its divisional structure by customer and reorganized into a functional structure. CEO John Chambers replaced the three-customer structure based on big businesses, small businesses, and telecoms, and now the company has centralized its engineering and marketing units so that they focus on technologies such as wireless networks. Chambers says the goal was to eliminate duplication, but the change should not be viewed as a shift in strategy. Chambers's span of control in the new structure is reduced from 15 to 12 managers reporting directly to him. He continues to operate Cisco without a chief operating officer or a number-two executive.

Sun Microsystems recently reduced the number of its business units from seven to four. Kodak recently reduced its number of business units from seven by-customer divisions to five by-product divisions. As consumption patterns become increasingly similar worldwide, a by-product structure is becoming more effective than a by-customer or a by-geographic type divisional structure. In the restructuring, Kodak eliminated its global operations division and distributed those responsibilities across the new by-product divisions.

A divisional structure has some clear advantages. First and perhaps foremost, accountability is clear. That is, divisional managers can be held responsible for sales and profit levels. Because a divisional structure is based on extensive delegation of authority, managers and employees can easily see the results of their good or bad performances. As a result, employee morale is generally higher in a divisional structure than it is in a centralized structure. Other advantages of the divisional design are that it creates career development opportunities for managers, allows local control of situations, leads to a competitive climate within an organization, and allows new businesses and products to be added easily.

The divisional design is not without some limitations, however. Perhaps the most important limitation is that a divisional structure is costly, for a number of reasons. First, each division requires functional specialists who must be paid. Second, there exists some duplication of staff services, facilities, and personnel; for instance, functional specialists are also needed centrally (at headquarters) to coordinate divisional activities. Third, managers must be well qualified because the divisional design forces delegation of authority; better-qualified individuals require higher salaries. A divisional structure can also be costly because it requires an elaborate, headquarters-driven control system. Fourth, competition between divisions may become so intense that it is dysfunctional and leads to limited sharing of ideas and resources for the common good of the firm. Table 7-8 summarizes the advantages and disadvantages of divisional organizational structure.

TABLE 7-8 **Advantages and Disadvantages of a Divisional Organizational Structure**

Advantages	Disadvantages
1. Accountability is clear	1. Can be costly
2. Allows local control of local situations	2. Duplication of functional activities
3. Creates career development chances	3. Requires a skilled management force
4. Promotes delegation of authority	4. Requires an elaborate control system
5. Leads to competitive climate internally	5. Competition among divisions can become so intense as to be dysfunctional
6. Allows easy adding of new products or regions	6. Can lead to limited sharing of ideas and resources
7. Allows strict control and attention to products, customers, and/or regions	7. Some regions/products/customers may receive special treatment

Ghoshal and Bartlett, two leading scholars in strategic management, note the following:

As their label clearly warns, divisions divide. The divisional model fragments companies' resources; it creates vertical communication channels that insulate business units and prevents them from sharing their strengths with one another. Consequently, the whole of the corporation is often less than the sum of its parts. A final limitation of the divisional design is that certain regions, products, or customers may sometimes receive special treatment, and it may be difficult to maintain consistent, companywide practices. Nonetheless, for most large organizations and many small firms, the advantages of a divisional structure more than offset the potential limitations.[5]

A *divisional structure by geographic area* is appropriate for organizations whose strategies need to be tailored to fit the particular needs and characteristics of customers in different geographic areas. This type of structure can be most appropriate for organizations that have similar branch facilities located in widely dispersed areas. A divisional structure by geographic area allows local participation in decision making and improved coordination within a region. Hershey Foods is an example of a company organized using the divisional by geographic region type of structure. Hershey's divisions are United States, Canada, Mexico, Brazil, and Other. Analysts contend that this type of structure may not be best for Hershey because consumption patterns for candy are quite similar worldwide. An alternative—and perhaps better—type of structure for Hershey would be divisional by product because the company produces and sells three types of products worldwide: (1) chocolate, (2) nonchocolate, and (3) grocery.

The *divisional structure by product (or services)* is most effective for implementing strategies when specific products or services need special emphasis. Also, this type of structure is widely used when an organization offers only a few products or services or when an organization's products or services differ substantially. The divisional structure allows strict control over and attention to product lines, but it may also require a more skilled management force and reduced top management control. General Motors, DuPont, and Procter & Gamble use a divisional structure by product to implement strategies. Huffy, the largest bicycle company in the world, is another firm that is highly decentralized based on a divisional-by-product structure. Based in Ohio, Huffy's divisions are the Bicycle division, the Gerry Baby Products division, the Huffy Sports division, YLC Enterprises, and Washington Inventory Service. Harry Shaw, Huffy's chairman, believes decentralization is one of the keys to Huffy's success.

Eastman Chemical established a new by-product divisional organizational structure. The company's two new divisions, Eastman Company and Voridian Company, focus on chemicals and polymers, respectively. The Eastman division focuses on coatings, adhesives, inks, and plastics, whereas the Voridian division focuses on fibers, polyethylene, and other polymers. Microsoft recently reorganized the whole corporation into three large divisions-by-product. Headed by a president, the new divisions are (1) platform products and services, (2) business, and (3) entertainment and devices. The Swiss electrical-engineering company ABB Ltd. recently scrapped its two core divisions, (1) power technologies and (2) automation technologies, and replaced them with five new divisions: (1) power products, (2) power systems, (3) automation products, (4) process automation, and (5) robotics.

When a few major customers are of paramount importance and many different services are provided to these customers, then a *divisional structure by customer* can be the most effective way to implement strategies. This structure allows an organization to cater effectively to the requirements of clearly defined customer groups. For example, book publishing companies often organize their activities around customer groups, such as colleges, secondary schools, and private commercial schools. Some airline companies have two major customer divisions: passengers and freight or cargo services.

Merrill Lynch is organized into separate divisions that cater to different groups of customers, including wealthy individuals, institutional investors, and small corporations. Motorola's semiconductor chip division is also organized divisionally by customer, having three separate segments that sell to (1) the automotive and industrial market, (2) the mobile phone market, and (3) the data-networking market. The automotive and industrial segment is doing well, but the other two segments are faltering, which is a reason why Motorola is trying to divest its semiconductor operations.

A *divisional structure by process* is similar to a functional structure, because activities are organized according to the way work is actually performed. However, a key difference between these two designs is that functional departments are not accountable for profits or revenues, whereas divisional process departments are evaluated on these criteria. An example of a divisional structure by process is a manufacturing business organized into six divisions: electrical work, glass cutting, welding, grinding, painting, and foundry work. In this case, all operations related to these specific processes would be grouped under the separate divisions. Each process (division) would be responsible for generating revenues and profits. The divisional structure by process can be particularly effective in achieving objectives when distinct production processes represent the thrust of competitiveness in an industry.

The Strategic Business Unit (SBU) Structure

As the number, size, and diversity of divisions in an organization increase, controlling and evaluating divisional operations become increasingly difficult for strategists. Increases in sales often are not accompanied by similar increases in profitability. The span of control becomes too large at top levels of the firm. For example, in a large conglomerate organization composed of 90 divisions, such as ConAgra, the chief executive officer could have difficulty even remembering the first names of divisional presidents. In multidivisional organizations, an SBU structure can greatly facilitate strategy-implementation efforts. ConAgra has put its many divisions into three primary SBUs: (1) food service (restaurants), (2) retail (grocery stores), and (3) agricultural products.

The SBU structure groups similar divisions into strategic business units and delegates authority and responsibility for each unit to a senior executive who reports directly to the chief executive officer. This change in structure can facilitate strategy implementation by improving coordination between similar divisions and channeling accountability to distinct business units. In a 100-division conglomerate, the divisions could perhaps be regrouped into 10 SBUs according to certain common characteristics, such as competing in the same industry, being located in the same area, or having the same customers.

Two disadvantages of an SBU structure are that it requires an additional layer of management, which increases salary expenses. Also, the role of the group vice president is often ambiguous. However, these limitations often do not outweigh the advantages of improved coordination and accountability. Another advantage of the SBU structure is that it makes the tasks of planning and control by the corporate office more manageable.

Citigroup in 2009 reorganized the whole company into two SBUs: (1) Citigroup, which includes the retail bank, the corporate and investment bank, the private bank, and global transaction services; and (2) Citi Holdings, which includes Citi's asset management and consumer finance segments, CitiMortgage, CitiFinancial, and the joint brokerage operations with Morgan Stanley. Citigroup's CEO, Vikram Pandit, says the restructuring will allow the company to reduce operating costs and to divest (spin off) Citi Holdings.

The huge computer firm Dell Inc., reorganized in 2009 into two SBUs. One SBU is Consumer Products and the other is Commercial. As part of its reorganization, Dell deleted the geographic divisions within its Consumer Products segment. However within its Commercial segment, there are now three worldwide units: (1) large enterprise, (2) public sector, and (3) small and midsize businesses. Dell is also closing a manufacturing facility in Austin, Texas, and laying off more employees as the company struggles to compete. Computer prices and demand are falling as competition increases. Atlantic Richfield Fairchild Industries, and Honeywell International are examples of firms that successfully use an SBU-type structure.

As illustrated in Figure 7-4, Sonoco Products Corporation, based in Hartsville, South Carolina, utilizes an SBU organizational structure. Note that Sonoco's SBUs—Industrial Products and Consumer Products—each have four autonomous divisions that have their own sales, manufacturing, R&D, finance, HRM, and MIS functions.

The Matrix Structure

A *matrix structure* is the most complex of all designs because it depends upon both vertical and horizontal flows of authority and communication (hence the term *matrix*). In contrast, functional and divisional structures depend primarily on vertical flows of authority and communication. A matrix structure can result in higher overhead because it creates more management positions. Other disadvantages of a matrix structure that contribute to overall complexity include dual lines of budget authority (a violation of the unity-of-command principle), dual sources of reward and punishment, shared authority, dual reporting channels, and a need for an extensive and effective communication system.

Despite its complexity, the matrix structure is widely used in many industries, including construction, health care, research, and defense. As indicated in Table 7-9, some advantages of a matrix structure are that project objectives are clear, there are many channels of communication, workers can see the visible results of their work, and shutting down a project can be accomplished relatively easily. Another advantage of a matrix structure is that it facilitates the use of specialized personnel, equipment, and facilities. Functional resources are shared in a matrix structure, rather than duplicated as in a divisional structure. Individuals with a high degree of expertise can divide their time as needed among projects, and they in turn develop their own skills and competencies more than in other structures. Walt Disney Corp. relies on a matrix structure.

FIGURE 7-4

Sonoco Products' SBU Organizational Chart

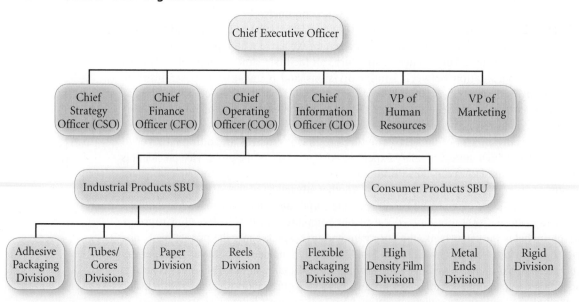

TABLE 7-9   Advantages and Disadvantages of a Matrix Structure

Advantages	Disadvantages
1. Project objectives are clear	1. Requires excellent vertical and horizontal flows of communication
2. Employees can clearly see results of their work	2. Costly because creates more manager positions
3. Shutting down a project is easily accomplished	3. Violates unity of command principle
4. Facilitates uses of special equipment/ personnel/facilities	4. Creates dual lines of budget authority
5. Functional resources are shared instead of duplicated as in a divisional structure	5. Creates dual sources of reward/punishment
	6. Creates shared authority and reporting
	7. Requires mutual trust and understanding

A typical matrix structure is illustrated in Figure 7-5. Note that the letters (A through Z4) refer to managers. For example, if you were manager A, you would be responsible for financial aspects of Project 1, and you would have two bosses: the Project 1 Manager on site and the CFO off site.

For a matrix structure to be effective, organizations need participative planning, training, clear mutual understanding of roles and responsibilities, excellent internal communication, and mutual trust and confidence. The matrix structure is being used more

FIGURE 7-5

An Example Matrix Structure

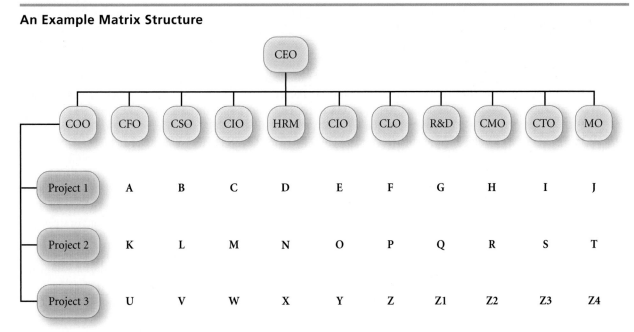

Notes: Titles spelled out as follows.

Chief Executive Officer (CEO)
Chief Finance Officer (CFO)
Chief Strategy Officer (CSO)
Chief Information Officer (CIO)
Human Resources Manager (HRM)
Chief Operating Officer (COO)
Chief Legal Officer (CLO)
Research & Development Officer (R&D)
Chief Marketing Officer (CMO)
Chief Technology Officer (CTO)
Competitive Intelligence Officer (CIO)
Maintenance Officer (MO)

frequently by U.S. businesses because firms are pursuing strategies that add new products, customer groups, and technology to their range of activities. Out of these changes are coming product managers, functional managers, and geographic-area managers, all of whom have important strategic responsibilities. When several variables, such as product, customer, technology, geography, functional area, and line of business, have roughly equal strategic priorities, a matrix organization can be an effective structural form.

Some Do's and Don'ts in Developing Organizational Charts

Students analyzing strategic management cases are often asked to revise and develop a firm's organizational structure. This section provides some basic guidelines for this endeavor. There are some basic do's and don'ts in regard to devising or constructing organizational charts, especially for midsize to large firms. First of all, reserve the title CEO for the top executive of the firm. Don't use the title "president" for the top person; use it for the division top managers if there are divisions within the firm. Also, do not use the title "president" for functional business executives. They should have the title "chief," or "vice president," or "manager," or "officer," such as "Chief Information Officer," or "VP of Human Resources." Further, do not recommend a dual title (such as "CEO and president") for just one executive. The chairman of the board and CEO of Bristol-Myers Squibb, Peter Dolan, recently gave up his title as chairman. However, Pfizer's CEO, Jeffrey Kindler, recently added chairman of the board to his title when he succeeded Hank McKinnell as chairman of Pfizer's board. And Comverse Technology recently named Andre Dahan as its president, chief executive officer, and board director. Actually, "chairperson" is much better than "chairman" for this title.

A significant movement began among corporate America in mid-2009 to split the chairperson of the board and the CEO positions in publicly held companies.[6] The movement includes asking the New York Stock Exchange and Nasdaq to adopt listing rules that would require separate positions. About 37 percent of companies in the S&P 500 stock index have separate positions, up from 22 percent in 2002, but this still leaves plenty of room for improvement. Among European and Asian companies, the split in these two positions is much more common. For example, 79 percent of British companies split the positions, and all German and Dutch companies split the position.

Directly below the CEO, it is best to have a COO (chief operating officer) with any division presidents reporting directly to the COO. On the same level as the COO and also reporting to the CEO, draw in your functional business executives, such as a CFO (chief financial officer), VP of human resources, a CSO (chief strategy officer), a CIO (chief information officer), a CMO (chief marketing Officer), a VP of R&D, a VP of legal affairs, an investment relations officer, maintenance officer, and so on. Note in Figure 7-6 that these positions are labeled and placed appropriately. Note that a controller and/or treasurer would normally report to the CFO.

In developing an organizational chart, avoid having a particular person reporting to more than one person above in the chain of command. This would violate the unity-of-command principle of management that "every employee should have just one boss." Also, do not have the CFO, CIO, CSO, human resource officer, or other functional positions report to the COO. All these positions report directly to the CEO.

A key consideration in devising an organizational structure concerns the divisions. Note whether the divisions (if any) of a firm presently are established based upon geography, customer, product, or process. If the firm's organizational chart is not available, you often can devise a chart based on the titles of executives. An important case analysis activity is for you to decide how the divisions of a firm should be organized for maximum effectiveness. Even if the firm presently has no divisions, determine whether the firm would operate better with divisions. In other words, which type of divisional breakdown do you (or your group or team) feel would be best for the firm in allocating resources, establishing objectives, and devising compensation incentives? This important strategic decision faces many midsize and large firms (and teams of students analyzing a strategic-management case). As consumption patterns become more and more similar worldwide, the divisional-by-product form of structure is increasingly the most effective. Be mindful that all firms

FIGURE 7-6

Typical Top Managers of a Large Firm

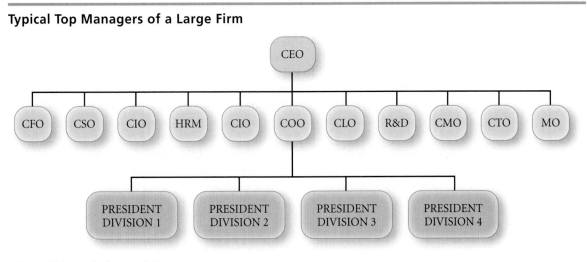

Notes: Titles spelled out as follows.

Chief Executive Officer (CEO)
Chief Finance Officer (CFO)
Chief Strategy Officer (CSO)
Chief Information Officer (CIO)
Human Resources Manager (HRM)
Chief Operating Officer (COO)
Chief Legal Officer (CLO)
Research & Development Officer (R&D)
Chief Marketing Officer (CMO)
Chief Technology Officer (CTO)
Competitive Intelligence Officer (CIO)
Maintenance Officer (MO)

have functional staff below their top executive and often readily provide this information, so be wary of concluding prematurely that a particular firm utilizes a functional structure. If you see the word "president" in the titles of executives, coupled with financial-reporting segments, such as by product or geographic region, then the firm is divisionally structured.

If the firm is large with numerous divisions, decide whether an SBU type of structure would be more appropriate to reduce the span of control reporting to the COO. Note in Figure 7-4 that the Sonoco Products' strategic business units (SBUs) are based on product groupings. An alternative SBU structure would have been to base the division groupings on location. One never knows for sure if a proposed or actual structure is indeed most effective for a particular firm. Note from Chandler's strategy-structure relationship (p. 221) illustrated previously in this chapter that declining financial performance signals a need for altering the structure.

Restructuring, Reengineering, and E-Engineering

Restructuring and reengineering are becoming commonplace on the corporate landscape across the United States and Europe. *Restructuring*—also called *downsizing, rightsizing,* or *delayering*—involves reducing the size of the firm in terms of number of employees, number of divisions or units, and number of hierarchical levels in the firm's organizational structure. This reduction in size is intended to improve both efficiency and effectiveness. Restructuring is concerned primarily with shareholder well-being rather than employee well-being.

Recessionary economic conditions have forced many European companies to downsize, laying off managers and employees. This was almost unheard of prior to the mid-1990s because European labor unions and laws required lengthy negotiations or huge severance checks before workers could be terminated. In contrast to the United States, labor union executives of large European firms sit on most boards of directors.

Job security in European companies is slowly moving toward a U.S. scenario, in which firms lay off almost at will. From banks in Milan to factories in Mannheim, European employers are starting to show people the door in an effort to streamline operations, increase efficiency, and compete against already slim and trim U.S. firms. Massive U.S.-style layoffs are still rare in Europe, but unemployment rates throughout the continent are rising quite rapidly. European firms still prefer to downsize by attrition and retirement rather than by blanket layoffs because of culture, laws, and unions.

In contrast, *reengineering* is concerned more with employee and customer well-being than shareholder well-being. Reengineering—also called process management, process innovation, or process redesign—involves reconfiguring or redesigning work, jobs, and processes for the purpose of improving cost, quality, service, and speed. Reengineering does not usually affect the organizational structure or chart, nor does it imply job loss or employee layoffs. Whereas restructuring is concerned with eliminating or establishing, shrinking or enlarging, and moving organizational departments and divisions, the focus of reengineering is changing the way work is actually carried out.

Reengineering is characterized by many tactical (short-term, business-function-specific) decisions, whereas restructuring is characterized by strategic (long-term, affecting all business functions) decisions. Developed by Motorola in 1986 and made famous by CEO Jack Welch at General Electric and more recently by Robert Nardelli, former CEO of Home Depot, *Six Sigma* is a quality-boosting process improvement technique that entails training several key persons in the firm in the techniques to monitor, measure, and improve processes and eliminate defects. Six Sigma has been widely applied across industries from retailing to financial services. CEO Dave Cote at Honeywell and CEO Jeff Immelt at General Electric spurred acceptance of Six Sigma, which aims to improve work processes and eliminate waste by training "select" employees who are given judo titles such as Master Black Belts, Black Belts, and Green Belts.

Six Sigma was criticized in a 2007 *Wall Street Journal* article that cited many example firms whose stock price fell for a number of years after adoption of Six Sigma. The technique's reliance on the special group of trained employees is problematic and its use within retail firms such as Home Depot has not been as successful as in manufacturing firms.[7]

Restructuring

Firms often employ restructuring when various ratios appear out of line with competitors as determined through benchmarking exercises. Recall that *benchmarking* simply involves comparing a firm against the best firms in the industry on a wide variety of performance-related criteria. Some benchmarking ratios commonly used in rationalizing the need for restructuring are headcount-to-sales-volume, or corporate-staff-to-operating-employees, or span-of-control figures.

The primary benefit sought from restructuring is cost reduction. For some highly bureaucratic firms, restructuring can actually rescue the firm from global competition and demise. But the downside of restructuring can be reduced employee commitment, creativity, and innovation that accompanies the uncertainty and trauma associated with pending and actual employee layoffs. In 2009, Walt Disney merged its ABC television network with its ABC Studios television production as part of a restructuring to cope with declining advertising and shrinking viewership. Disney also is laying off employees and offering buyouts to more than 600 executives. The Disney restructuring is paralleled by rival General Electric Company's merger of its NBC Network with its Universal Media Studios, which is also a bid to cut costs. Ad revenues at the four largest television networks in the United States fell 3 percent in 2009.

Another downside of restructuring is that many people today do not aspire to become managers, and many present-day managers are trying to get off the management track.[8] Sentiment against joining management ranks is higher today than ever. About 80 percent of employees say they want nothing to do with management, a major shift from just a decade ago when 60 to 70 percent hoped to become managers. Managing others historically led to enhanced career mobility, financial rewards, and executive perks; but in today's global, more competitive, restructured arena, managerial jobs demand more hours and headaches with fewer financial rewards. Managers today manage more people spread over different locations, travel more, manage diverse functions, and are change agents even when they have nothing to do with the creation of the plan or disagree with its approach. *Employers today are looking for people who can do things, not for people who make other people do things.* Restructuring in many firms has made a manager's job an invisible, thankless role. More workers today are self-managed, entrepreneurs, interpreneurs, or team-managed. Managers today need to be counselors, motivators, financial advisors, and psychologists. They also run the risk of becoming technologically behind in their areas of expertise. "Dilbert" cartoons commonly portray managers as enemies or as morons.

Reengineering

The argument for a firm engaging in reengineering usually goes as follows: Many companies historically have been organized vertically by business function. This arrangement has led over time to managers' and employees' mind-sets being defined by their particular functions rather than by overall customer service, product quality, or corporate performance. The logic is that all firms tend to bureaucratize over time. As routines become entrenched, turf becomes delineated and defended, and politics takes precedence over performance. Walls that exist in the physical workplace can be reflections of "mental" walls.

In reengineering, a firm uses information technology to break down functional barriers and create a work system based on business processes, products, or outputs rather than on functions or inputs. Cornerstones of reengineering are decentralization, reciprocal interdependence, and information sharing. A firm that exemplifies complete information sharing is Springfield Remanufacturing Corporation, which provides to all employees a weekly income statement of the firm, as well as extensive information on other companies' performances.

The *Wall Street Journal* noted that reengineering today must go beyond knocking down internal walls that keep parts of a company from cooperating effectively; it must also knock down the external walls that prohibit or discourage cooperation with other firms—even rival firms.[9] A maker of disposable diapers echoes this need differently when it says that to be successful "cooperation at the firm must stretch from stump to rump."

Hewlett-Packard is a good example of a company that has knocked down the external barriers to cooperation and practices modern reengineering. The HP of today shares its forecasts with all of its supply-chain partners and shares other critical information with its distributors and other stakeholders. HP does all the buying of resin for its many manufacturers, giving it a volume discount of up to 5 percent. HP has established many alliances and cooperative agreements of the kind discussed in Chapter 5.

A benefit of reengineering is that it offers employees the opportunity to see more clearly how their particular jobs affect the final product or service being marketed by the firm. However, reengineering can also raise manager and employee anxiety, which, unless calmed, can lead to corporate trauma.

Linking Performance and Pay to Strategies

Caterpillar Inc. is slashing its executive compensation by roughly 50 percent in 2009 and cutting pay for senior managers by up to 35 percent. Wages of other Caterpillar managers and employees are being lowered 15 percent. The company is cutting 20,000 more jobs amid a global slowdown in construction. Caterpillar's sales for 2009 are projected to be $40 billion, down sharply from $51.32 billion in 2008.

CEOs at Japanese companies with more than $10 billion in annual revenues are paid about $1.3 million annually, including bonuses and stock options.[10] This compares to an average CEO pay among European firms of $6 million and an average among U.S. firms of $12 million. As firms acquire other firms in other countries, these pay differences can cause resentment and even turmoil. Larger pay packages of American CEOs are socially less acceptable in many other countries. For example, in Japan, seniority rather than performance has been the key factor in determining pay, and harmony among managers is emphasized over individual excellence.

How can an organization's reward system be more closely linked to strategic performance? How can decisions on salary increases, promotions, merit pay, and bonuses be more closely aligned to support the long-term strategic objectives of the organization? There are no widely accepted answers to these questions, but a dual bonus system based on both annual objectives and long-term objectives is becoming common. The percentage of a manager's annual bonus attributable to short-term versus long-term results should vary by hierarchical level in the organization. A chief executive officer's annual bonus could, for example, be determined on a 75 percent short-term and 25 percent long-term basis. It is important that bonuses not be based solely on short-term results because such a system ignores long-term company strategies and objectives.

Wal-Mart Stores recently revamped its bonus program for hourly employees as the firm began paying bonuses based on sales, profit, and inventory performance at individual stores on a quarterly, rather than annual, basis. The average full-time employee at Wal-Mart in the United States is paid $10.51 per hour, but this is significantly below the $17.46 average paid to Costco Wholesale Corp. employees.[11]

One aspect of the deepening global recession is that companies are instituting policies to allow their shareholders to vote on executive compensation policies. A "say-on-pay" policy was installed at 14 large companies in 2008–2009. Aflac was the first U.S. corporation to voluntarily give shareholders an advisory vote on executive compensation. Aflac did this back in 2007. Apple did this in 2008, as did H&R Block. Several companies that instituted say-on-pay policies in 2009 were Ingersoll-Rand, Verizon, and Motorola. In 2010 and 2011, Occidental Petroleum and Hewlett-Packard are expected to institute such policies. These new policies underscore how the financial crisis and shareholder outrage about top executive pay has affected compensation practice. None of the shareholder votes are binding on the companies, however, at least not so far. The U.S. House of Representatives recently passed a bill to formalize this shareholder tactic, which is gaining steam across the country as a means to combat exorbitant executive pay.

In an effort to cut costs and increase productivity, more and more Japanese companies are switching from seniority-based pay to performance-based approaches. Toyota has switched to a full merit system for 20,000 of its 70,000 white-collar workers. Fujitsu, Sony, Matsushita Electric Industrial, and Kao also have switched to merit pay systems. This switching is hurting morale at some Japanese companies, which have trained workers for decades to cooperate rather than to compete and to work in groups rather than individually.

Richard Brown, CEO of Electronic Data Systems (EDS), once said,

> You have to start with an appraisal system that gives genuine feedback and differentiates performance. Some call it ranking people. That seems a little harsh. But you can't have a manager checking a box that says you're either stupendous, magnificent, very good, good, or average. Concise, constructive feedback is the fuel workers use to get better. A company that doesn't differentiate performance risks losing its best people.[12]

Profit sharing is another widely used form of incentive compensation. More than 30 percent of U.S. companies have profit sharing plans, but critics emphasize that too many factors affect profits for this to be a good criterion. Taxes, pricing, or an acquisition would wipe out profits, for example. Also, firms try to minimize profits in a sense to reduce taxes.

Still another criterion widely used to link performance and pay to strategies is gain sharing. *Gain sharing* requires employees or departments to establish performance targets; if actual results exceed objectives, all members get bonuses. More than 26 percent of U.S. companies use some form of gain sharing; about 75 percent of gain sharing plans have been adopted since 1980. Carrier, a subsidiary of United Technologies, has had excellent success with gain sharing in its six plants in Syracuse, New York; Firestone's tire plant in Wilson, North Carolina, has experienced similar success with gain sharing.

Criteria such as sales, profit, production efficiency, quality, and safety could also serve as bases for an effective *bonus system*. If an organization meets certain understood, agreed-upon profit objectives, every member of the enterprise should share in the harvest. A bonus system can be an effective tool for motivating individuals to support strategy-implementation efforts. BankAmerica, for example, recently overhauled its incentive system to link pay to sales of the bank's most profitable products and services. Branch managers receive a base salary plus a bonus based both on the number of new customers and on sales of bank products. Every employee in each branch is also eligible for a bonus if the branch exceeds its goals. Thomas Peterson, a top BankAmerica executive, says, "We want to make people responsible for meeting their goals, so we pay incentives on sales, not on controlling costs or on being sure the parking lot is swept."

Five tests are often used to determine whether a performance-pay plan will benefit an organization:

1. ***Does the plan capture attention?*** Are people talking more about their activities and taking pride in early successes under the plan?
2. ***Do employees understand the plan?*** Can participants explain how it works and what they need to do to earn the incentive?
3. ***Is the plan improving communication?*** Do employees know more than they used to about the company's mission, plans, and objectives?
4. ***Does the plan pay out when it should?*** Are incentives being paid for desired results—and being withheld when objectives are not met?
5. ***Is the company or unit performing better?*** Are profits up? Has market share grown? Have gains resulted in part from the incentives?[13]

In addition to a dual bonus system, a combination of reward strategy incentives, such as salary raises, stock options, fringe benefits, promotions, praise, recognition, criticism, fear, increased job autonomy, and awards, can be used to encourage managers and employees to push hard for successful strategic implementation. The range of options for getting people, departments, and divisions to actively support strategy-implementation activities in a particular organization is almost limitless. Merck, for example, recently gave each of its 37,000 employees a 10-year option to buy 100 shares of Merck stock at a set price of $127. Steven Darien, Merck's vice president of human resources, says, "We needed to find ways to get everyone in the workforce on board in terms of our goals and objectives. Company executives will begin meeting with all Merck workers to explore ways in which employees can contribute more."

Many countries worldwide are curbing executive pay in the wake of a global financial crisis. For example, the German cabinet recently imposed a $650,000 annual salary cap on banks that receive any government-backed capital injections. The German cabinet also imposed a ban on bank executive bonuses, stock options, and severance payments through 2012. Companies worldwide that participate in government bailouts or capital infusions are increasingly being constrained in executive compensation. The U.S. House of Representatives and Senate members severely criticized the CEOs of Ford, GM, and Chrysler for being paid so much in the face of failing companies.

There is rising public resentment over executive pay, and there are government restrictions on compensation. Based in Thousand Oaks, California, Amgen recently directed all shareholders to a 10-item questionnaire asking them what they think about the firm's compensation plan. Schering-Plough Corp. was going to use a similar survey just as it agreed to be acquired by Merck & Co. Home Depot now meets with shareholders regularly to hear their concerns. In April 2009, Royal Bank of Scotland Group PLC voted 9-to-1 against the bank's 2008 compensation package.

Executive pay declined slightly in 2008 and is expected to decrease somewhat substantially in 2009 as pressure for shareholders and government subsidy constraints lower payouts. The five CEOs who in 2008 received the highest compensation in a recent survey are Sanjay Jha at Motorola ($104 million), Ray Irani at Occidental Petroleum ($49.9 million), Robert Iger at Walt Disney ($49.7 million), Vikram Pandit at Citigroup ($38.2 million), and Louis Camilleri at Philip Morris ($36.4 million).[14]

Managing Resistance to Change

No organization or individual can escape change. But the thought of change raises anxieties because people fear economic loss, inconvenience, uncertainty, and a break in normal social patterns. Almost any change in structure, technology, people, or strategies has the potential to disrupt comfortable interaction patterns. For this reason, people resist change. The strategic-management process itself can impose major changes on individuals and processes. Reorienting an organization to get people to think and act strategically is not an easy task.

Resistance to change can be considered the single greatest threat to successful strategy implementation. Resistance regularly occurs in organizations in the form of sabotaging production machines, absenteeism, filing unfounded grievances, and an unwillingness to cooperate. People often resist strategy implementation because they do not understand what is happening or why changes are taking place. In that case, employees may simply need accurate information. Successful strategy implementation hinges upon managers' ability to develop an organizational climate conducive to change. Change must be viewed as an opportunity rather than as a threat by managers and employees.

Resistance to change can emerge at any stage or level of the strategy-implementation process. Although there are various approaches for implementing changes, three commonly used strategies are a force change strategy, an educative change strategy, and a rational or self-interest change strategy. A *force change strategy* involves giving orders and enforcing those orders; this strategy has the advantage of being fast, but it is plagued by low commitment and high resistance. The *educative change strategy* is one that presents information to convince people of the need for change; the disadvantage of an educative change strategy is that implementation becomes slow and difficult. However, this type of strategy evokes greater commitment and less resistance than does the force change strategy. Finally, a *rational* or *self-interest change strategy* is one that attempts to convince individuals that the change is to their personal advantage. When this appeal is successful, strategy implementation can be relatively easy. However, implementation changes are seldom to everyone's advantage.

The rational change strategy is the most desirable, so this approach is examined a bit further. Managers can improve the likelihood of successfully implementing change by carefully designing change efforts. Jack Duncan described a rational or self-interest change strategy as consisting of four steps. First, employees are invited to participate in the process of change and in the details of transition; participation allows everyone to give opinions, to feel a part of the change process, and to identify their own self-interests regarding the recommended change. Second, some motivation or incentive to change is required; self-interest can be the most important motivator. Third, communication is needed so that people can understand the purpose for the changes. Giving and receiving feedback is the fourth step: everyone enjoys knowing how things are going and how much progress is being made.[15]

Because of diverse external and internal forces, change is a fact of life in organizations. The rate, speed, magnitude, and direction of changes vary over time by industry and organization. Strategists should strive to create a work environment in which change is recognized as necessary and beneficial so that individuals can more easily adapt to change. Adopting a strategic-management approach to decision making can itself require major changes in the philosophy and operations of a firm.

Strategists can take a number of positive actions to minimize managers' and employees' resistance to change. For example, individuals who will be affected by a change should be involved in the decision to make the change and in decisions about how to implement the change. Strategists should anticipate changes and develop and offer training and development workshops so that managers and employees can adapt to those changes. They also need to effectively communicate the need for changes. The strategic-management process can be described as a process of managing change.

Organizational change should be viewed today as a continuous process rather than as a project or event. The most successful organizations today continuously adapt to changes in the competitive environment, which themselves continue to change at an accelerating rate. It is not sufficient today to simply react to change. Managers need to anticipate change and ideally be the creator of change. Viewing change as a continuous process is in stark contrast to an old management doctrine regarding change, which was to unfreeze behavior, change the behavior, and then refreeze the new behavior. The new "continuous organizational change" philosophy should mirror the popular "continuous quality improvement philosophy."

Creating a Strategy-Supportive Culture

Strategists should strive to preserve, emphasize, and build upon aspects of an existing *culture* that support proposed new strategies. Aspects of an existing culture that are antagonistic to a proposed strategy should be identified and changed. Substantial research indicates that new strategies are often market-driven and dictated by competitive forces. For this reason, changing a firm's culture to fit a new strategy is usually more effective than changing a strategy to fit an existing culture. As indicated in Table 7-10, numerous techniques are available to alter an organization's culture, including recruitment, training, transfer, promotion, restructure of an organization's design, role modeling, positive reinforcement, and mentoring.

Schein indicated that the following elements are most useful in linking culture to strategy:

1. Formal statements of organizational philosophy, charters, creeds, materials used for recruitment and selection, and socialization
2. Designing of physical spaces, facades, buildings
3. Deliberate role modeling, teaching, and coaching by leaders
4. Explicit reward and status system, promotion criteria
5. Stories, legends, myths, and parables about key people and events

TABLE 7-10   Ways and Means for Altering an Organization's Culture

1. Recruitment
2. Training
3. Transfer
4. Promotion
5. Restructuring
6. Reengineering
7. Role modeling
8. Positive reinforcement
9. Mentoring
10. Revising vision and/or mission
11. Redesigning physical spaces/facades
12. Altering reward system
13. Altering organizational policies/procedures/practices

6. What leaders pay attention to, measure, and control
7. Leader reactions to critical incidents and organizational crises
8. How the organization is designed and structured
9. Organizational systems and procedures
10. Criteria used for recruitment, selection, promotion, leveling off, retirement, and "excommunication" of people[16]

In the personal and religious side of life, the impact of loss and change is easy to see.[17] Memories of loss and change often haunt individuals and organizations for years. Ibsen wrote, "Rob the average man of his life illusion and you rob him of his happiness at the same stroke."[18] When attachments to a culture are severed in an organization's attempt to change direction, employees and managers often experience deep feelings of grief. This phenomenon commonly occurs when external conditions dictate the need for a new strategy. Managers and employees often struggle to find meaning in a situation that changed many years before. Some people find comfort in memories; others find solace in the present. Weak linkages between strategic management and organizational culture can jeopardize performance and success. Deal and Kennedy emphasized that making strategic changes in an organization always threatens a culture:

> People form strong attachments to heroes, legends, the rituals of daily life, the hoopla of extravaganza and ceremonies, and all the symbols of the workplace. Change strips relationships and leaves employees confused, insecure, and often angry. Unless something can be done to provide support for transitions from old to new, the force of a culture can neutralize and emasculate strategy changes.[19]

Production/Operations Concerns When Implementing Strategies

Production/operations capabilities, limitations, and policies can significantly enhance or inhibit the attainment of objectives. Production processes typically constitute more than 70 percent of a firm's total assets. A major part of the strategy-implementation process takes place at the production site. Production-related decisions on plant size, plant location, product design, choice of equipment, kind of tooling, size of inventory, inventory control, quality control, cost control, use of standards, job specialization, employee training, equipment and resource utilization, shipping and packaging, and technological innovation can have a dramatic impact on the success or failure of strategy-implementation efforts.

Examples of adjustments in production systems that could be required to implement various strategies are provided in Table 7-11 for both for-profit and nonprofit organizations. For instance, note that when a bank formulates and selects a strategy to add 10 new branches, a production-related implementation concern is site location. The largest bicycle company in the United States, Huffy, recently ended its own production of bikes and now contracts out those services to Asian and Mexican manufacturers. Huffy focuses instead on

TABLE 7-11   Production Management and Strategy Implementation

Type of Organization	Strategy Being Implemented	Production System Adjustments
Hospital	Adding a cancer center (Product Development)	Purchase specialized equipment and add specialized people.
Bank	Adding 10 new branches (Market Development)	Perform site location analysis.
Beer brewery	Purchasing a barley farm operation (Backward Integration)	Revise the inventory control system.
Steel manufacturer	Acquiring a fast-food chain (Unrelated Diversification)	Improve the quality control system.
Computer company	Purchasing a retail distribution chain (Forward Integration)	Alter the shipping, packaging, and transportation systems.

the design, marketing, and distribution of bikes, but it no longer produces bikes itself. The Dayton, Ohio, company closed its plants in Ohio, Missouri, and Mississippi.

Just-in-time (JIT) production approaches have withstood the test of time. JIT significantly reduces the costs of implementing strategies. With JIT, parts and materials are delivered to a production site just as they are needed, rather than being stockpiled as a hedge against later deliveries. Harley-Davidson reports that at one plant alone, JIT freed $22 million previously tied up in inventory and greatly reduced reorder lead time.

Factors that should be studied before locating production facilities include the availability of major resources, the prevailing wage rates in the area, transportation costs related to shipping and receiving, the location of major markets, political risks in the area or country, and the availability of trainable employees.

For high-technology companies, production costs may not be as important as production flexibility because major product changes can be needed often. Industries such as biogenetics and plastics rely on production systems that must be flexible enough to allow frequent changes and the rapid introduction of new products. An article in the *Harvard Business Review* explained why some organizations get into trouble:

> They too slowly realize that a change in product strategy alters the tasks of a production system. These tasks, which can be stated in terms of requirements for cost, product flexibility, volume flexibility, product performance, and product consistency, determine which manufacturing policies are appropriate. As strategies shift over time, so must production policies covering the location and scale of manufacturing facilities, the choice of manufacturing process, the degree of vertical integration of each manufacturing facility, the use of R&D units, the control of the production system, and the licensing of technology.[20]

A common management practice, cross-training of employees, can facilitate strategy implementation and can yield many benefits. Employees gain a better understanding of the whole business and can contribute better ideas in planning sessions. Cross-training employees can, however, thrust managers into roles that emphasize counseling and coaching over directing and enforcing and can necessitate substantial investments in training and incentives.

Human Resource Concerns When Implementing Strategies

More and more companies are instituting furloughs to cut costs as an alternative to laying off employees. *Furloughs* are temporary layoffs and even white-collar managers are being given furloughs, once confined to blue-collar workers. A few organizations furloughing professional workers in 2009 included Gulfstream Aerospace, Media General, Gannett, the University of Maryland, Clemson University, and Spansion. Recent research shows that 11 percent of larger U.S. companies implemented furloughs during the global economic recession.[21] Winnebago Industries, for example, required all salaried employees to take a week-long furlough, which saved the company $850,000. The Port of Seattle saved $2.9 million by furloughing all of its 800 nonunion workers, mostly professionals, for two weeks. Table 7-12 lists ways that companies today are reducing labor costs to stay financially sound.

The job of human resource manager is changing rapidly as companies continue to downsize and reorganize. Strategic responsibilities of the human resource manager include assessing the staffing needs and costs for alternative strategies proposed during strategy formulation and developing a staffing plan for effectively implementing strategies. This plan must consider how best to manage spiraling health care insurance costs. Employers' health coverage expenses consume an average 26 percent of firms' net profits, even though most companies now require employees to pay part of their health insurance premiums. The plan must also include how to motivate employees and managers during a time when layoffs are common and workloads are high.

TABLE 7-12   Labor Cost-Saving Tactics

Salary freeze

Hiring freeze

Salary reductions

Reduce employee benefits

Raise employee contribution to health-care premiums

Reduce employee 401(k)/403(b) match

Reduce employee workweek

Mandatory furlough

Voluntary furlough

Hire temporary instead of full-time employees

Hire contract employees instead of full-time employees

Volunteer buyouts (Walt Disney is doing this)

Halt production for 3 days a week (Toyota Motor is doing this)

Layoffs

Early retirement

Reducing/eliminating bonuses

Source: Based on Dana Mattioli, "Employers Make Cuts Despite Belief Upturn Is Near," *Wall Street Journal* (April 23, 2009): B4.

The human resource department must develop performance incentives that clearly link performance and pay to strategies. The process of empowering managers and employees through their involvement in strategic-management activities yields the greatest benefits when all organizational members understand clearly how they will benefit personally if the firm does well. Linking company and personal benefits is a major new strategic responsibility of human resource managers. Other new responsibilities for human resource managers may include establishing and administering an *employee stock ownership plan (ESOP)*, instituting an effective child-care policy, and providing leadership for managers and employees in a way that allows them to balance work and family.

A well-designed strategic-management system can fail if insufficient attention is given to the human resource dimension. Human resource problems that arise when businesses implement strategies can usually be traced to one of three causes: (1) disruption of social and political structures, (2) failure to match individuals' aptitudes with implementation tasks, and (3) inadequate top management support for implementation activities.[22]

Strategy implementation poses a threat to many managers and employees in an organization. New power and status relationships are anticipated and realized. New formal and informal groups' values, beliefs, and priorities may be largely unknown. Managers and employees may become engaged in resistance behavior as their roles, prerogatives, and power in the firm change. Disruption of social and political structures that accompany strategy execution must be anticipated and considered during strategy formulation and managed during strategy implementation.

A concern in matching managers with strategy is that jobs have specific and relatively static responsibilities, although people are dynamic in their personal development. Commonly used methods that match managers with strategies to be implemented include transferring managers, developing leadership workshops, offering career development activities, promotions, job enlargement, and job enrichment.

A number of other guidelines can help ensure that human relationships facilitate rather than disrupt strategy-implementation efforts. Specifically, managers should do a lot of chatting and informal questioning to stay abreast of how things are progressing and to know when to intervene. Managers can build support for strategy-implementation efforts by giving few orders, announcing few decisions, depending heavily on informal questioning, and seeking to probe and clarify until a consensus emerges. Key thrusts that succeed should be rewarded generously and visibly.

It is surprising that so often during strategy formulation, individual values, skills, and abilities needed for successful strategy implementation are not considered. It is rare that a firm selecting new strategies or significantly altering existing strategies possesses the right line and staff personnel in the right positions for successful strategy implementation. The need to match individual aptitudes with strategy-implementation tasks should be considered in strategy choice.

Inadequate support from strategists for implementation activities often undermines organizational success. Chief executive officers, small business owners, and government agency heads must be personally committed to strategy implementation and express this commitment in highly visible ways. Strategists' formal statements about the importance of strategic management must be consistent with actual support and rewards given for activities completed and objectives reached. Otherwise, stress created by inconsistency can cause uncertainty among managers and employees at all levels.

Perhaps the best method for preventing and overcoming human resource problems in strategic management is to actively involve as many managers and employees as possible in the process. Although time consuming, this approach builds understanding, trust, commitment, and ownership and reduces resentment and hostility. The true potential of strategy formulation and implementation resides in people.

Employee Stock Ownership Plans (ESOPs)

An *ESOP* is a tax-qualified, defined-contribution, employee-benefit plan whereby employees purchase stock of the company through borrowed money or cash contributions. ESOPs empower employees to work as owners; this is a primary reason why the number of ESOPs have grown dramatically to more than 10,000 firms covering more than 10 million employees. ESOPs now control more than $600 billion in corporate stock in the United States.

Besides reducing worker alienation and stimulating productivity, ESOPs allow firms other benefits, such as substantial tax savings. Principal, interest, and dividend payments on ESOP-funded debt are tax deductible. Banks lend money to ESOPs at interest rates below prime. This money can be repaid in pretax dollars, lowering the debt service as much as 30 percent in some cases. "The ownership culture really makes a difference, when management is a facilitator, not a dictator," says Corey Rosen, executive director of the National Center for Employee Ownership. Fifteen employee-owned companies are listed in Table 7-13.

TABLE 7-13   Fifteen Example ESOP Firms

Firm	Headquarters Location
Publix Supermarkets	Florida
Science Applications	California
Lifetouch	Minnesota
John Lewis Partnership	United Kingdom
Mondragon Cooperative	Spain
Houchens Industries	Kentucky
Amsted Industries	Illinois
Mast General Store	North Carolina
HDR, Inc.	Nebraska
Yoke's Fresh Market	Washington
SPARTA, Inc.	California
Hy-Vee	Iowa
Bi-Mart	Washington
Ferrellgas Partners	Kansas

Source: Based on Edward Iwata, "ESOPs Can Offer Both Upsides, Drawbacks," *USA Today* (April 3, 2007): 2B.

If an ESOP owns more than 50 percent of the firm, those who lend money to the ESOP are taxed on only 50 percent of the income received on the loans. ESOPs are not for every firm, however, because the initial legal, accounting, actuarial, and appraisal fees to set up an ESOP are about $50,000 for a small or midsized firm, with annual administration expenses of about $15,000. Analysts say ESOPs also do not work well in firms that have fluctuating payrolls and profits. Human resource managers in many firms conduct preliminary research to determine the desirability of an ESOP, and then they facilitate its establishment and administration if benefits outweigh the costs.

Wyatt Cafeterias, a southwestern United States operator of 120 cafeterias, also adopted the ESOP concept to prevent a hostile takeover. Employee productivity at Wyatt greatly increased since the ESOP began, as illustrated in the following quote:

> The key employee in our entire organization is the person serving the customer on the cafeteria line. In the past, because of high employee turnover and entry-level wages for many line jobs, these employees received far less attention and recognition than managers. We now tell the tea cart server, "You own the place. Don't wait for the manager to tell you how to do your job better or how to provide better service. You take care of it." Sure, we're looking for productivity increases, but since we began pushing decisions down to the level of people who deal directly with customers, we've discovered an awesome side effect—suddenly the work crews have this "happy to be here" attitude that the customers really love.[23]

Balancing Work Life and Home Life

Work/family strategies have become so popular among companies today that the strategies now represent a competitive advantage for those firms that offer such benefits as elder care assistance, flexible scheduling, job sharing, adoption benefits, an on-site summer camp, employee help lines, pet care, and even lawn service referrals. New corporate titles such as work/life coordinator and director of diversity are becoming common.

Working Mother magazine annually published its listing of "The 100 Best Companies for Working Mothers" (www.workingmother.com). Three especially important variables used in the ranking were availability of flextime, advancement opportunities, and equitable distribution of benefits among companies. Other important criteria are compressed weeks, telecommuting, job sharing, childcare facilities, maternity leave for both parents, mentoring, career development, and promotion for women. *Working Mother's* top eight best companies for working women in 2009 are provided in Table 7-14. *Working Mother* also conducts extensive research to determine the best U.S. firms for women of color.

Human resource managers need to foster a more effective balancing of professional and private lives because nearly 60 million people in the United States are now part of two-career families. A corporate objective to become more lean and mean must today

TABLE 7-14   A Few Excellent Workplaces for Women

1. Abbott—An elaborate child care center at headquarters serves 670 infants, toddlers, and pre-schoolers; employees can visit their children during the day.

2. Allstate Insurance—Child care centers are abundant: all employees have access to discounted child care.

3. American Express—Flex scheduling and tuition reimbursement enable most employees to continue their education.

4. Citi—Telecommuting for employees makes caring for family a priority.

5. Fannie Mae—Reimburses tuition-related expenses up to $10,000 per child; provides four weeks of paid maternity leave.

6. IBM—Work/life balance is an integral part of the IBM culture.

7. Johnson & Johnson—Nearly all employees say you never have to choose between family and work at J&J.

8. Merck & Company—Flextime and tuition reimbursement are available to nearly all Merck employees.

Source: Based on 2009 Web site, http://www.workingmother.com/web?service=direct/1/ViewArticlePage/dlinkFullArticle&sp=1780&sp=94.

include consideration for the fact that a good home life contributes immensely to a good work life.

The work/family issue is no longer just a women's issue. Some specific measures that firms are taking to address this issue are providing spouse relocation assistance as an employee benefit; providing company resources for family recreational and educational use; establishing employee country clubs, such as those at IBM and Bethlehem Steel; and creating family/work interaction opportunities. A study by Joseph Pleck of Wheaton College found that in companies that do not offer paternity leave for fathers as a benefit, most men take short, informal paternity leaves anyway by combining vacation time and sick days.

Some organizations have developed family days, when family members are invited into the workplace, taken on plant or office tours, dined by management, and given a chance to see exactly what other family members do each day. Family days are inexpensive and increase the employee's pride in working for the organization. Flexible working hours during the week are another human resource response to the need for individuals to balance work life and home life. The work/family topic is being made part of the agenda at meetings and thus is being discussed in many organizations.

Only 2.6 percent of Fortune 500 firms have a woman CEO. However, recent studies have found that companies with more female executives and directors outperform other firms.[24] Judy Rosener at the University of California, Irvine, says, "Brain scans prove that men and women think differently, so companies with a mix of male and female executives will outperform competitors that rely on leadership of a single sex." It is not that women are better than men, Rosener says. It is the mix of thinking styles that is key to management effectiveness.

During the first week of 2009, Ellen Kullman replaced Chad Holliday as CEO of DuPont, which brought to 13 the number of female CEOs running the 500 largest public firms in the United States. Thirteen is a record number, but only one more than the total for the prior year. Lynn Elsenhans became CEO of Sunoco in 2008. In 2008, two Fortune 500 women CEOs departed: Meg Whitman at eBay and Paula Reynolds at Safeco.

USA Today tracks the performance of women CEOs versus male CEOs, and their research shows virtually no difference in the two groups.[25] The year 2008 saw the S&P 500 stocks fall 38.5 percent, its worst year since 1937. The stock of firms that year with women CEOs fell 42.7 percent, but some firms run by women CEOs did much better, such as Kraft Foods, down only 18 percent under Irene Rosenfeld. Two firms doing great under woman CEOs are Avon under Andrea Jung and Reynolds American under Susan Ivey. Those stocks are up 65.4 percent and 20.8 percent, respectively, since those women became CEO. Table 7-15 gives the 13 Fortune 500 Women CEOs in 2009.

TABLE 7-15   Fortune 500 Women CEOs in 2009

CEO	Company	Fortune 500 Rank
Angela Braly	WellPoint	33
Patricia Woertz	Archer Daniels Midland	52
Lynn Elsenhans	Sunoco	56
Indra Nooyi	PepsiCo	59
Irene Rosenfeld	Kraft Foods	63
Carol Meyrowitz	TJX	132
Mary Sammons	Rite Aid	142
Anne Mulcahy	Xerox	144
Brenda Barnes	Sara Lee	203
Andrea Jung	Avon Products	265
Susan Ivey	Reynolds American	290
Christina Gold	Western Union	473

There is great room for improvement in removing the *glass ceiling* domestically, especially considering that women make up 47 percent of the U.S. labor force. *Glass ceiling* refers to the invisible barrier in many firms that bars women and minorities from top-level management positions. The United States leads the world in promoting women and minorities into mid- and top-level managerial positions in business.

Boeing's firing of CEO Harry Stonecipher for having an extramarital affair raised public awareness of office romance. However, just 12 percent of 391 companies surveyed by the American Management Association have written guidelines on office dating.[26] The fact of the matter is that most employers in the United States turn a blind eye to marital cheating. Some employers, such as Southwest Airlines, which employs more than 1,000 married couples, explicitly allow consensual office relationships. Research suggests that more men than women engage in extramarital affairs at work, roughly 22 percent to 15 percent; however, the percentage of women having extramarital affairs is increasing steadily, whereas the percentage of men having affairs with co-workers is holding steady.[27] If an affair is disrupting your work, then "the first step is to go to the offending person privately and try to resolve the matter. If that fails, then go to the human-resources manager seeking assistance."[28] Filing a discrimination lawsuit based on the affair is recommended only as a last resort because courts generally rule that co-workers' injuries are not pervasive enough to warrant any damages.

Benefits of a Diverse Workforce

Toyota has committed almost $8 billion over 10 years to diversify its workforce and to use more minority suppliers. Hundreds of other firms, such as Ford Motor Company and Coca-Cola, are also striving to become more diversified in their workforces. TJX Companies, the parent of 1,500 T. J. Maxx and Marshall's stores, has reaped great benefits and is an exemplary company in terms of diversity.

An organization can perhaps be most effective when its workforce mirrors the diversity of its customers. For global companies, this goal can be optimistic, but it is a worthwhile goal.

Corporate Wellness Programs

A recent *BusinessWeek* cover story article details how firms are striving to lower the accelerating costs of employees' health-care insurance premiums.[29] Many firms such as Scotts Miracle-Gro Company (based in Marysville, Ohio), IBM, and Microsoft are implementing wellness programs, requiring employees to get healthier or pay higher insurance premiums. Employees that do get healthier win bonuses, free trips, and pay lower premiums; nonconforming employees pay higher premiums and receive no "healthy" benefits. Wellness of employees has become a strategic issue for many firms. Most firms require a health examination as a part of an employment application, and healthiness is more and more becoming a hiring factor. Michael Porter, coauthor of *Redefining Health Care*, says, "We have this notion that you can gorge on hot dogs, be in a pie-eating contest, and drink every day, and society will take care of you. We can't afford to let individuals drive up company costs because they're not willing to address their own health problems."

Slightly more than 60 percent of companies with 10,000 or more employees had a wellness program in 2008, up from 47 percent in 2005.[30] Among firms with wellness programs, the average cost per employee was $7,173. However, in the weak economy of late, companies are cutting back on their wellness programs. Many employees say they are so stressed about work and finances they have little time to eat right and exercise. PepsiCo in 2008 introduced a $600 surcharge for all its employees that smoke; the company has a smoking-cessation program. PepsiCo's smoking quit rate among employees increased to 34 percent in 2008 versus 20 percent in 2007.

Wellness programs provide counseling to employees and seek lifestyle changes to achieve healthier living. For example, trans fats are a major cause of heart disease. Near elimination of trans fats in one's diet will reduce one's risk for heart attack by as much as 19 percent, according to a recent article. New York City now requires restaurants to inform

TABLE 7-16 **The Key to Staying Healthy, Living to 100, and Being a "Well" Employee**

1. Eat nutritiously—eat a variety of fruits and vegetables daily because they have ingredients that the body uses to repair and strengthen itself.

2. Stay hydrated—drink plenty of water to aid the body in eliminating toxins and to enable body organs to function efficiently; the body is mostly water.

3. Get plenty of rest—the body repairs itself during rest, so get at least seven hours of sleep nightly, preferably eight hours.

4. Get plenty of exercise—exercise vigorously at least 30 minutes daily so the body can release toxins and strengthen vital organs.

5. Reduce stress—the body's immune system is weakened when one is under stress, making the body vulnerable to many ailments, so keep stress to a minimum.

6. Do not smoke—smoking kills, no doubt about it anymore.

7. Take vitamin supplements—consult your physician, but because it is difficult for diet alone to supply all the nutrients and vitamins needed, supplements can be helpful in achieving good health and longevity.

Source: Based on Lauren Etter, "Trans Fats: Will They Get Shelved?" *Wall Street Journal* (December 8, 2006): A6; Joel Fuhrman, MD, *Eat to Live* (Boston: Little, Brown, 2003).

customers about levels of trans fat being served in prepared foods. Chicago is considering a similar ban on trans fats. Denmark in 2003 became the first country to strictly regulate trans fats.

Restaurant chains are only slowly reducing trans fat levels in served foods because (1) trans fat oils make fried foods crispier, (2) trans fats give baked goods a longer shelf life, (3) trans fat oils can be used multiple times compared to other cooking oils, and (4) trans fat oils taste better. Three restaurant chains have switched to oils free of trans fat—Chili's, Ruby Tuesday, and Wendy's—but some chains still may use trans fat oils, including Kentucky Fried Chicken, McDonald's, Dunkin' Donuts, Taco Bell, and Burger King. Marriott International in February 2007 eliminated trans fats from the food it serves at its 2,300 North American hotels, becoming the first big hotel chain to do so, although the 18-hotel Lowes luxury chain is close behind. Marriott's change includes its Renaissance, Courtyard, and Residence Inn brands.

Saturated fats are also bad, so one should avoid eating too much red meat and dairy products, which are high in saturated fats. Seven key lifestyle habits listed in Table 7-16 may significantly improve health and longevity.

Conclusion

Successful strategy formulation does not at all guarantee successful strategy implementation. Although inextricably interdependent, strategy formulation and strategy implementation are characteristically different. In a single word, strategy implementation means *change*. It is widely agreed that "the real work begins after strategies are formulated." Successful strategy implementation requires the support of, as well as discipline and hard work from, motivated managers and employees. It is sometimes frightening to think that a single individual can irreparably sabotage strategy-implementation efforts.

Formulating the right strategies is not enough, because managers and employees must be motivated to implement those strategies. Management issues considered central to strategy implementation include matching organizational structure with strategy, linking performance and pay to strategies, creating an organizational climate conducive to change, managing political relationships, creating a strategy-supportive culture, adapting production/ operations processes, and managing human resources. Establishing annual objectives, devising policies, and allocating resources are central strategy-implementation activities common to all organizations. Depending on the size and type of the organization, other management issues could be equally important to successful strategy implementation.

We invite you to visit the David page on the Prentice Hall Companion Web site at http://www.pearsonhighered.com/david/ for this chapter's review quiz.

Key Terms and Concepts

Annual Objectives (p. 215)
Avoidance (p. 220)
Benchmarking (p. 230)
Bonus System (p. 233)
Conflict (p. 220)
Confrontation (p. 220)
Culture (p. 235)
Decentralized Structure (p. 222)
Defusion (p. 220)
Delayering (p. 229)
Divisional Structure by Geographic Area, Product, Customer, or Process (p. 224)
Downsizing (p. 229)
Educative Change Strategy (p. 234)
Employee Stock Ownership Plans (ESOP) (p. 238)
Establishing Annual Objectives (p. 215)
Force Change Strategy (p. 234)
Functional Structure (p. 222)

Furloughs (p. 237)
Gain Sharing (p. 232)
Glass Ceiling (p. 242)
Horizontal Consistency of Objectives (p. 217)
Just-in-Time (JIT) (p. 237)
Matrix Structure (p. 226)
Policy (p. 217)
Profit Sharing (p. 232)
Rational Change Strategy (p. 234)
Reengineering (p. 230)
Resistance to Change (p. 234)
Resource Allocation (p. 219)
Restructuring (p. 229)
Rightsizing (p. 229)
Self-Interest Change Strategy (p. 234)
Six Sigma (p. 230)
Strategic Business Unit (SBU) Structure (p. 225)
Vertical Consistency of Objectives (p. 217)

Issues for Review and Discussion

1. List the five labor cost-saving activities that you believe would be most effective for (1) Best Buy, (2) your university, and (3) the U.S. Postal Service. Give a rationale for each company.
2. Define and give an example of furloughs as they could apply to your business school.
3. The chapter says strategy formulation focuses on effectiveness, whereas strategy implementation focuses on efficiency. Which is more important, effectiveness or efficiency? Give an example of each concept.
4. In stating objectives, why should terms such as *increase, minimize, maximize, as soon as possible, adequate,* and *decrease* be avoided?
5. What are four types of resources that all organizations have? List them in order of importance for your university or business school.
6. Considering avoidance, defusion, confrontation, which method of conflict resolution do you prefer most? Why? Which do you prefer least? Why?
7. Explain why Chandler's strategy-structure relationship commonly exists among firms.
8. If you owned and opened three restaurants after you graduated, would you operate from a functional or divisional structure? Why?
9. Explain how to choose between a divisional-by-product and a divisional-by-region organizational structure.
10. Think of a company that would operate best in your opinion by a division-by-services organizational structure. Explain your reasoning.
11. What are the two major disadvantages of an SBU-type organizational structure? What are the two major advantages? At what point in a firm's growth do you feel the advantages offset the disadvantages? Explain.
12. In order of importance in your opinion, list six advantages of a matrix organizational structure.
13. Why should division head persons have the title president rather than vice president?
14. Is Six Sigma more a restructuring or reengineering management technique? Why?
15. Compare and contrast profit sharing with gain sharing as employee performance incentives.
16. List three resistance to change strategies. Give an example when you would use each method or approach.
17. In order of importance in your opinion, list six techniques or activities widely used to alter an organization's culture.

18. What are the benefits of establishing an ESOP in a company?
19. List reasons why is it important for an organization not to have a "glass ceiling."
20. Allocating resources can be a political and an ad hoc activity in firms that do not use strategic management. Why is this true? Does adopting strategic management ensure easy resource allocation? Why?
21. Compare strategy formulation with strategy implementation in terms of each being an art or a science.
22. Describe the relationship between annual objectives and policies.
23. Identify a long-term objective and two supporting annual objectives for a familiar organization.
24. Identify and discuss three policies that apply to your present strategic-management class.
25. Explain the following statement: Horizontal consistency of goals is as important as vertical consistency.
26. Describe several reasons why conflict may occur during objective-setting activities.
27. In your opinion, what approaches to conflict resolution would be best for resolving a disagreement between a personnel manager and a sales manager over the firing of a particular salesperson? Why?
28. Describe the organizational culture of your college or university.
29. Explain why organizational structure is so important in strategy implementation.
30. In your opinion, how many separate divisions could an organization reasonably have without using an SBU-type organizational structure? Why?
31. Would you recommend a divisional structure by geographic area, product, customer, or process for a medium-sized bank in your local area? Why?
32. What are the advantages and disadvantages of decentralizing the wage and salary functions of an organization? How could this be accomplished?
33. Consider a college organization with which you are familiar. How did management issues affect strategy implementation in that organization?
34. As production manager of a local newspaper, what problems would you anticipate in implementing a strategy to increase the average number of pages in the paper by 40 percent?
35. Do you believe expenditures for child care or fitness facilities are warranted from a cost-benefit perspective? Why or why not?
36. Explain why successful strategy implementation often hinges on whether the strategy-formulation process empowers managers and employees.
37. Discuss the glass ceiling in the United States, giving your ideas and suggestions.
38. Discuss three ways discussed in this book for linking performance and pay to strategies.
39. List the different types of organizational structure. Diagram what you think is the most complex of these structures and label your chart clearly.
40. List the advantages and disadvantages of a functional versus a divisional organizational structure.
41. Discuss recent trends in women and minorities becoming top executives in the United States.
42. Discuss recent trends in firms downsizing family-friendly programs.
43. Research the latest developments in the class-action lawsuit involving women managers versus Wal-Mart Stores and report your findings to the class.
44. List seven guidelines to follow in developing an organizational chart.

Notes

1. Dale McConkey, "Planning in a Changing Environment," *Business Horizons* (September–October 1988): 66.
2. A. G. Bedeian and W. F. Glueck, *Management,* 3rd ed. (Chicago: The Dryden Press, 1983): 212.
3. Boris Yavitz and William Newman, *Strategy in Action: The Execution, Politics, and Payoff of Business Planning* (New York: The Free Press, 1982): 195.
4. E. H. Schein. "Three Cultures of Management: The Key to Organizational Learning," *Sloan Management Review* 38, 1 (1996): 9–20.
5. S. Ghoshal and C. A. Bartlett, "Changing the Role of Management: Beyond Structure to Processes." *Harvard Business Review* 73, 1 (1995): 88.
6. Joann Lublin, "Chairman-CEO Split Gains Allies," *Wall Street Journal* (March 30, 2009): B4.
7. Karen Richardson, "The 'Six Sigma' Factor for Home Depot," *Wall Street Journal* (January 4, 2007): C3.
8. "Want to Be a Manager? Many People Say No, Calling Job Miserable," *Wall Street Journal* (April 4, 1997): 1; Stephanie Armour, "Management Loses Its Allure," *USA Today* (October 10, 1997): 1B.

9. Paul Carroll, "No More Business as Usual, Please. Time to Try Something Different," *Wall Street Journal* (October 23, 2001): A24.

10. Yuka Hayashi and Phred Dvorak, "Japanese Wrestle with CEO Pay as They Go Global," *Wall Street Journal* (November 28, 2008): B1.

11. Kris Maher and Kris Hudson, "Wal-Mart to Sweeten Bonus Plans for Staff," *Wall Street Journal* (March 22, 2007): A11.

12. Richard Brown, "Outsider CEO: Inspiring Change with Force and Grace," *USA Today* (July 19, 1999): 3B.

13. Yavitz and Newman, 58.

14. Phred Dvorak, "Executive Salaries May Fall More Sharply in 2009," *Wall Street Journal* (April 3, 2009): B4.

15. Jack Duncan, *Management* (New York: Random House, 1983): 381–390.

16. E. H. Schein, "The Role of the Founder in Creating Organizational Culture," *Organizational Dynamics* (Summer 1983): 13–28.

17. T. Deal and A. Kennedy, "Culture: A New Look Through Old Lenses," *Journal of Applied Behavioral Science* 19, no. 4 (1983): 498–504.

18. H. Ibsen, "The Wild Duck," in O. G. Brochett and L. Brochett (eds.), *Plays for the Theater* (New York: Holt, Rinehart & Winston, 1967); R. Pascale, "The Paradox of 'Corporate Culture': Reconciling Ourselves to Socialization," *California Management Review* 28, no. 2 (1985): 26, 37–40.

19. T. Deal and A. Kennedy, *Corporate Cultures: The Rites and Rituals of Corporate Life* (Reading, MA: Addison-Wesley, 1982): 256.

20. Robert Stobaugh and Piero Telesio, "Match Manufacturing Policies and Product Strategy," *Harvard Business Review* 61, no. 2 (March–April 1983): 113.

21. Dana Magttioli and Sara Murray, "Employers Hit Salaried Staff with Furloughs," *Wall Street Journal* (February 24, 2009): D1; Laura Petrecca, "More Companies Turn to Furloughs to Save Money, Jobs," *USA Today* (March 5, 2009): B1.

22. R. T. Lenz and Marjorie Lyles, "Managing Human Resource Problems in Strategy Planning Systems," *Journal of Business Strategy* 60, no. 4 (Spring 1986): 58.

23. J. Warren Henry, "ESOPs with Productivity Payoffs," *Journal of Business Strategy* (July–August 1989): 33.

24. Del Jones, "Women Slowly Gain on Corporate America," *USA Today* (January 2, 2009): 6B.

25. Ibid.

26. Sue Shellenbarger, "Employers Often Ignore Office Affairs, Leaving Co-workers in Difficult Spot," *Wall Street Journal* (March 10, 2005): D1.

27. Ibid.

28. Ibid.

29. Michelle Conlin, "Get Healthy—or Else," *BusinessWeek* (February 26, 2007): 58–69.

30. Laura Petrecca, "Companies Re-Evaluate Wellness Programs," *USA Today* (June 17, 2009): 3B.

Current Readings

Barkema, Harry G., and Mario Schijven. "Toward Unlocking the Full Potential of Acquisitions: The Role of Organizational Restructuring." *Academy of Management Journal* 51, no. 4 (August 2008): 696.

Bennett, Nathan, and Stephen A. Miles. "6 Steps to (Re) Building a Top Management Team." *MIT Sloan Management Review* 50, no. 1 (Fall 2008): 60.

Bergh, Donald D., and Elizabeth Lim. "Learning How to Restructure: Absorptive Capacity and Improvisational Views of Restructuring Actions and Performance." *Strategic Management Journal* 29, no. 6 (June 2008): 593.

Berrone, Pascual, and Luis Gomez-Mejia. "Environmental Performance and Executive Compensation: An Integrated Agency-Institutional Perspective." *Academy of Management Journal* (February 2009): 103–126.

Boeker, Warren, and Frank T. Rothaermel. "Old Technology Meets New Technology: Complementarities, Similarities, and Alliance Formation." *Strategic Management Journal* 29, no. 1 (January 2008): 47.

Brandes, Pamela, Maria Goranova, and Steven Hall. "Navigating Shareholder Influence: Compensation Plans and the Shareholder Approval Process." *Academy of Management Perspectives* 22, no. 1 (February 2008): 41.

Brush, Candida G., and Elizabeth J. Gatewood. "Women Growing Businesses: Clearing the Hurdles." *Business Horizons* 51, no. 3 (May–June 2008): 175.

Canales, J. Ignacio, and Joaquim Vila. "Can Strategic Planning Make Strategy More Relevant and Build Commitment Over Time? The Case of RACC." *Long Range Planning* 41, no. 3 (June 2008): 273.

Conyon, Martin J., Simon I. Peck, and Graham Sadler. "Compensation Consultants and Executive Pay: Evidence from the United States and the United Kingdom." *Academy of Management Perspectives* (February 2009): 43–55.

Crittenden, Victoria L., and William F. Crittenden. "Building a Capable Organization: The Eight Levers of Strategy Implementation." *Business Horizons* 51, no. 4 (July–August 2008): 301.

D'Amelio, Angelo, Jeffrey D. Ford, and Laurie W. Ford. "Resistance to Change: The Rest of the Story." *Academy of Management Review* 33, no. 2 (April 2008): 362.

Ford, Jeffrey D., and Laurie W. Ford. "Decoding Resistance to Change." *Harvard Business Review* (April 2009): 99–104.

Heugens, Pursey, and Michel Lander. "Structure! Agency!: A Meta-Analysis of Institutional Theories of Organization." *Academy of Management Journal* (February 2009): 87–102.

Humphreys, John, and Hal Langford. "Managing a Corporate Culture 'Slide.'" *MIT Sloan Management Review* 49, no. 3 (Spring 2008): 25.

Kaplan, Robert S., and David P. Norton. "Mastering the Management System." *Harvard Business Review* (January 2008): 62.

Kaplan, Steven N. "CEO Compensation: Are U.S. CEOs Overpaid?" *Academy of Management Perspectives* 22, no. 2 (May 2008): 5.

Lam, Kevin, Ji Li, Shirley X.Y. Liu, and James J. M. Sun. "Strategic Human Resource Management, Institutionalization, and Employment Modes: An Empirical Study in China." *Strategic Management Journal* 29, no. 3 (March 2008): 337.

Lawler, Edward E. III. "Why Are We Losing All Our Good People?" *Harvard Business Review* (June 2008): 41.

Love, Geoffrey, and Matthew Kraatz. "Character, Conformity, or the Bottom Line? How and Why Downsizing Affected Corporate Reputation." *Academy of Management Journal* (April 2009): 314–335.

Miller, Susan, David Hickson, and David Wilson. "From Strategy to Action: Involvement and Influence in Top Level Decisions." *Long Range Planning* 41, no. 6 (December 2008): 606–628.

O'Leary-Kelly, Anne, Lynn Bowes-Sperry, Collette, Bates, and Emily Lean. "Sexual Harassment at Work: A Decade (Plus) of Progress." *Journal of Management* (June 2009): 503–538.

Remus, Ilies, Kelly Wilson, and David Wagner. "The Spillover of Daily Job Satisfaction onto Employees Family Lives: The Facilitating Role of Work-Family Integration." *Academy of Management Journal* (February 2009): 87–102

Sutton, Robert. "How to Be a Good Boss in a Bad Economy." *Harvard Business Review* (June 2009): 42–53.

Veloso, Francisco M., and Claudio Wolter. "The Effects of Innovation on Vertical Structure: Perspectives on Transaction Costs and Competences." *Academy of Management Review* (July 2008): 586.

Watkins, Michael. "Picking the Right Transition Strategy." *Harvard Business Review* (January 2009): 46–53.

ASSURANCE OF LEARNING EXERCISES

Assurance of Learning Exercise 7A

Revising McDonald's Organizational Chart

Purpose

Developing and altering organizational charts is an important skill for strategists to possess. This exercise can improve your skill in altering an organization's hierarchical structure in response to new strategies being formulated.

Instructions

Step 1 Turn to the McDonald's Cohesion Case (p. 29) and review the organizational chart. On a separate sheet of paper, answer the following questions:

1. What type of organizational chart is illustrated for McDonald's?
2. What improvements could you recommend for the McDonald's organizational chart? Give your reasoning for each suggestion.
3. What aspects of McDonald's chart do you especially like?
4. What type of organizational chart do you believe would best suit McDonald's? Why?

Assurance of Learning Exercise 7B

Do Organizations Really Establish Objectives?

Purpose

Objectives provide direction, allow synergy, aid in evaluation, establish priorities, reduce uncertainty, minimize conflicts, stimulate exertion, and aid in both the allocation of resources and the design of jobs. This exercise will enhance your understanding of how organizations use or misuse objectives.

Instructions

Step 1 Join with one other person in class to form a two-person team.

Step 2 Contact by telephone the owner or manager of an organization in your city or town. Request a 30-minute personal interview or meeting with that person for the purpose of discussing "business objectives." During your meeting, seek answers to the following questions:

1. Do you believe it is important for a business to establish and clearly communicate long-term and annual objectives? Why or why not?
2. Does your organization establish objectives? If yes, what type and how many? How are the objectives communicated to individuals? Are your firm's objectives in written form or simply communicated orally?
3. To what extent are managers and employees involved in the process of establishing objectives?
4. How often are your business objectives revised and by what process?

Step 3 Take good notes during the interview. Let one person be the note taker and one person do most of the talking. Have your notes typed up and ready to turn in to your professor.

Step 4 Prepare a 5-minute oral presentation for the class, reporting the results of your interview. Turn in your typed report.

Assurance of Learning Exercise 7C

Understanding My University's Culture

Purpose

It is something of an art to uncover the basic values and beliefs that are buried deeply in an organization's rich collection of stories, language, heroes, heroines, and rituals, yet culture can be the most important factor in implementing strategies.

Instructions

Step 1   On a separate sheet of paper, list the following terms: hero/heroine, belief, metaphor, language, value, symbol, story, legend, saga, folktale, myth, ceremony, rite, and ritual.

Step 2   For your college or university, give examples of each term. If necessary, speak with faculty, staff, alumni, administration, or fellow students of the institution to identify examples of each term.

Step 3   Report your findings to the class. Tell the class how you feel regarding cultural products being consciously used to help implement strategies.

CHAPTER 8

Implementing Strategies: Marketing, Finance/Accounting, R&D, and MIS Issues

CHAPTER OBJECTIVES

After studying this chapter, you should be able to do the following:

1. Explain market segmentation and product positioning as strategy-implementation tools.

2. Discuss procedures for determining the worth of a business.

3. Explain why projected financial statement analysis is a central strategy-implementation tool.

4. Explain how to evaluate the attractiveness of debt versus stock as a source of capital to implement strategies.

5. Discuss the nature and role of research and development in strategy implementation.

6. Explain how management information systems can determine the success of strategy-implementation efforts.

Assurance of Learning Exercises

Assurance of Learning Exercise 8A
Developing a Product-Positioning Map for McDonald's

Assurance of Learning Exercise 8B
Performing an EPS/EBIT Analysis for McDonald's

Assurance of Learning Exercise 8C
Preparing Projected Financial Statements for McDonald's

Assurance of Learning Exercise 8D
Determining the Cash Value of McDonald's

Source: Shutterstock/AJT

"Notable Quotes"

"The greatest strategy is doomed if it's implemented badly."

—**Bernard Reimann**

"There is no 'perfect' strategic decision. One always has to pay a price. One always has to balance conflicting objectives, conflicting opinions, and conflicting priorities. The best strategic decision is only an approximation—and a risk."

—**Peter Drucker**

"The real question isn't how well you're doing today against your own history, but how you're doing against your competitors."

—**Donald Kress**

"As market windows open and close more quickly, it is important that R&D be tied more closely to corporate strategy."

—**William Spenser**

"Most of the time, strategists should not be formulating strategy at all; they should be getting on with implementing strategies they already have."

—**Henry Mintzberg**

"It is human nature to make decisions based on emotion, rather than on fact. But nothing could be more illogical."

—**Toshiba Corporation**

"No business can do everything. Even if it has the money, it will never have enough good people. It has to set priorities. The worst thing to do is a little bit of everything. This makes sure that nothing is being accomplished. It is better to pick the wrong priority than none at all."

—**Peter Drucker**

Assurance of Learning Exercise 8E
Developing a Product-Positioning Map for My University

Assurance of Learning Exercise 8F
Do Banks Require Projected Financial Statements?

Strategies have no chance of being implemented successfully in organizations that do not market goods and services well, in firms that cannot raise needed working capital, in firms that produce technologically inferior products, or in firms that have a weak information system. This chapter examines marketing, finance/accounting, R&D, and management information systems (MIS) issues that are central to effective strategy implementation. Special topics include market segmentation, market positioning, evaluating the worth of a business, determining to what extent debt and/or stock should be used as a source of capital, developing projected financial statements, contracting R&D outside the firm, and creating an information support system. Manager and employee involvement and participation are essential for success in marketing, finance/accounting, R&D, and MIS activities.

The Nature of Strategy Implementation

The quarterback can call the best play possible in the huddle, but that does not mean the play will go for a touchdown. The team may even lose yardage unless the play is executed (implemented) well. Less than 10 percent of strategies formulated are successfully implemented! There are many reasons for this low success rate, including failing to appropriately segment markets, paying too much for a new acquisition, and falling behind competitors in R&D. Johnson & Johnson implements strategies well.

Strategy implementation directly affects the lives of plant managers, division managers, department managers, sales managers, product managers, project managers, personnel managers, staff managers, supervisors, and all employees. In some situations, individuals may not have participated in the strategy-formulation process at all and may not appreciate, understand, or even accept the work and thought that went into strategy formulation. There may even be foot dragging or resistance on their part. Managers and employees who do not understand the business and are not committed to the business may attempt to sabotage strategy-implementation efforts in hopes that the organization will return to its old ways. The strategy-implementation stage of the strategic-management process is highlighted in Figure 8-1.

Doing Great in a Weak Economy. How?

Johnson & Johnson (J&J)

Founded in 1886 and based in New Brunswick, New Jersey, J&J produces a wide variety of health-care products, ranging from baby powder to Listerine to joint replacement parts to pharmaceutical drugs. J&J is a gigantic well-managed company that pays the fifth highest dividend amount annually of any firm in the world.

Among all the corporations in the world, *Fortune* magazine rated J&J as number 5 on their 2009 "Most Admired Companies" list. J&J's revenues for 2008 increased from $61 billion to $63 billion when most firms endured revenue decreases. Also for calendar 2008, J&J's

net income increased to $12.9 billion from $10.5 billion when most firms experienced dramatic losses.

J&J's CEO, Bill Weldon, says, "Our Credo, laid out by Robert Wood Johnson in 1943, still governs J&J. Our Credo really sets our priorities. And our first priority is to the people who use our products—to make sure we're supplying them with quality products," he says. J&J applicants must read the credo before being hired, and Weldon says that anyone transitioning into a leadership position in the company spends two days with him, J&J's HR boss, and general counsel talking about how the credo "has shaped our organization and decisions" over 66 years.

If you get sick, you likely will begin using J&J products. The diversified giant operates in three segments through more than 250 operating companies located in some 60 countries. The J&J Pharmaceuticals division makes drugs (including schizophrenia medication Risperdal and psoriasis drug Remicade) for an array of ailments, such as neurological conditions, blood disorders, autoimmune diseases, and pain. J&J's Medical Devices and Diagnostics division offers surgical equipment, monitoring devices, orthopedic

products, and contact lenses, among other items. The consumer segment makes over-the-counter drugs and products for skin and hair care, oral care, first aid, and women's health.

In mid-2009, J&J agreed to acquire the small cancer drug-developer Cougar Biotechnology for about $894 million in cash. Cougar has an excellent drug for late stage prostate cancer. J&J's purchase price of $43 a share was a 16 percent premium over Cougar's closing stock price.

J&J reported second quarter 2009 net income of $3.21 billion and sales of $15.24 billion. During that quarter, sales of J&J's Remicade treatment for rheumatoid arthritis rose 24 percent to $1.1 billion. In July 2009, the company acquired a minority stake in Elan Corporation, which makes Alzheimer's drugs.

Source: Based on Geoff Colvin, "The World's Most Admired Companies," *Fortune* (March 16, 2009): 76–86; Jessica Shambora, "Most Admired Companies Know Their Values," *CNN Money* (March 5, 2009).

Current Marketing Issues

Countless marketing variables affect the success or failure of strategy implementation, and the scope of this text does not allow us to address all those issues. Some examples of marketing decisions that may require policies are as follows:

1. To use exclusive dealerships or multiple channels of distribution
2. To use heavy, light, or no TV advertising
3. To limit (or not) the share of business done with a single customer
4. To be a price leader or a price follower
5. To offer a complete or limited warranty
6. To reward salespeople based on straight salary, straight commission, or a combination salary/commission
7. To advertise online or not

A marketing issue of increasing concern to consumers today is the extent to which companies can track individuals' movements on the Internet—and even be able to identify an individual by name and e-mail address. Individuals' wanderings on the Internet are no longer anonymous, as many persons still believe. Marketing companies such as DoubleClick, Flycast, AdKnowledge, AdForce, and Real Media have sophisticated methods to identify who you are and your particular interests.[1] If you are especially concerned about being tracked, visit the www.networkadvertising.org Web site, which gives details about how marketers today are identifying you and your buying habits.

Marketing of late has become more about building a two-way relationship with consumers than just informing consumers about a product or service. Marketers today must get their customers involved in their company Web site and solicit suggestions from customers in terms of product development, customer service, and ideas. The online community is much quicker, cheaper, and effective than traditional focus groups and surveys.

Companies and organizations should encourage their employees to create *wikis*—Web sites that allows users to add, delete, and edit content regarding frequently asked questions

FIGURE 8-1

A Comprehensive Strategic-Management Model

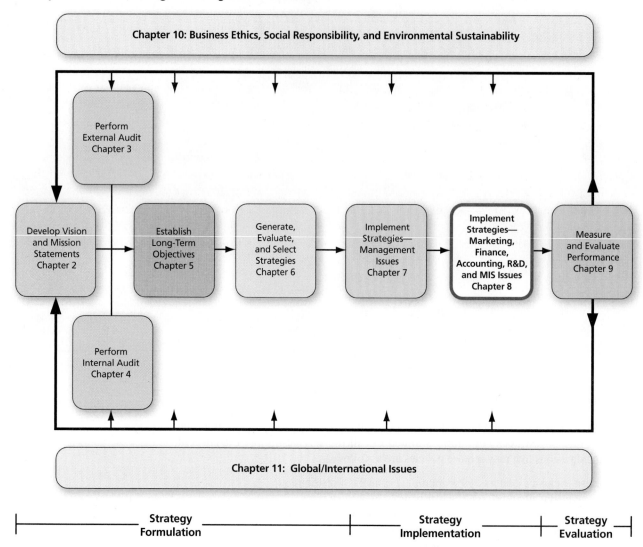

Source: Fred R. David, "How Companies Define Their Mission," *Long Range Planning* 22, no. 3 (June 1988): 40.

and information across the firm's whole value chain of activities. The most common wiki is Wikipedia, but think of wikis as user-generated content. Know that anyone can change the content in a wiki but the group and other editors can change the content or changes that you submit.

Firms should provide incentives to consumers to share their thoughts, opinions, and experiences on the company Web site. Encourage consumers to network among themselves on topics of their choosing on the company Web site. So the company Web site must not be all about the company—it must be all about the customer too. Perhaps offer points or discounts for customers who provide ideas and suggestions. This practice will not only encourage participation but will allow both the company and other customers to interact with "experts."

New Principles of Marketing

Today a business or organization's Web site must provide clear and simple instructions for customers to set up a blog and/or contribute to a wiki. Customers trust each others' opinions more than a company's marketing pitch, and the more they talk freely, the more the firm can learn how to improve its product, service, and marketing. Marketers today monitor blogs daily to determine, evaluate, and influence opinions being formed by customers. Customers must not feel like they are a captive audience for advertising at a firm's Web site. Table 8-1 provides new principles of marketing according to Parise, Guinan, and Weinberg.[2]

Wells Fargo and Bank of America in 2009 began to *tweet* customers, meaning they posted messages of 140 characters or less on Twitter.com to describe features of bank products. Some banks are placing marketing videos on YouTube. Discover Financial, American Express, and Citigroup all now have Facebook or MySpace pages. UMB Financial of Kansas City, Missouri, tweets about everything from the bank's financial stability to the industry's prospects. Steve Furman, Discover's director of e-commerce, says the appeal of social networking is that it provides "pure, instant" communication with customers.[3]

When the big three U.S. automakers were asking lawmakers for bailout funding, all three firms launched extensive Internet marketing campaigns to garner support for their requests and plans for the future. Ford's online marketing campaign was anchored by the Web site www.TheFordStory.com. In addition to a new Web site of its own, Chrysler launched a new marketing YouTube Channel named Grab Democracy and also posted ad information to its blog. GM employed similar marketing tactics to drive visitors to its main Web site. Once any controversial topic arises in a company or industry, millions of people are out there googling, yahooing, aoling, youtubing, facebooking, and myspacing to find out more information in order to form their own opinions and preferences.[4]

Although the exponential increase in social networking and business online has created huge opportunities for marketers, it also has produced some severe threats. Perhaps the greatest threat is that any king of negative publicity travels fast online. For example, Dr Pepper recently suffered immensely when an attorney for the rock band Guns N' Roses accused the company of not following through on giving every American a soft drink if they released their album *Chinese Democracy*. Other examples abound, such as Motrin ads that lightheartedly talked about Mom's back pain from holding babies in slings, and Burger King's Whopper Virgin campaign, which featured a taste test of a Whopper versus a McDonald's Big Mac in remote areas of the world. Even Taco Bell suffered from its ads that featured asking 50 Cent (aka Curtis Jackson) if he would change his name to 79 Cent or 89 Cent for a day in exchange for a $10,000 donation to charity. Seemingly minor ethical and questionable actions can catapult these days into huge public relations problems for companies as a result of the monumental online social and business communications. For example, Domino's, the nation's largest pizza delivery chain, spent a month in 2009 trying to dispel the video on YouTube and Facebook showing two of its employees doing gross things to a Domino's sub sandwich, including passing gas on salami.[5]

In increasing numbers, people living in underdeveloped and poor nations around the world have cell phones but no computers, so the Internet is rapidly moving to cell phone

TABLE 8-1   The New Principles of Marketing

1. Don't just talk at consumers—work with them throughout the marketing process.
2. Give consumers a reason to participate.
3. Listen to—and join—the conversation outside your company's Web site.
4. Resist the temptation to sell, sell, sell. Instead attract, attract, attract.
5. Don't control online conversations; let it flow freely.
6. Find a "marketing technologist," a person who has three excellent skill sets (marketing, technology, and social interaction).
7. Embrace instant messaging and chatting.

Source: Based on Salvatore Parise, Patricia Guinan, and Bruce Weinberg, "The Secrets of Marketing in a Web 2.0 World," *Wall Street Journal* (December 15, 2008): R1.

platforms. This is opening up even larger markets to online marketing. People in remote parts of Indonesia, Egypt, and Russia represent the fastest growing customer base for Opera Software ASA, a Norwegian maker of Internet browsers for mobile devices. Actually, persons who cannot afford computers live everywhere in every country, and many of these persons will soon be on the Internet on their cell phones. Cell phones are rapidly becoming used for data transfer, not just for phone calls. Companies such as Nokia, AT&T, Purple Labs SA of France, Japan's Access, Vodafone Group PLC, Siemens AG, Research in Motion, and Apple are spurring this transition by developing new and improved Web-capable mobile products every day.[6]

Advertising Media

Recent research by Forrester Research reveals that people ages 18 to 27 spend more time weekly on the Internet than watching television, listening to the radio, or watching DVDs or VHS tapes. Table 8-2 reveals why companies are rapidly coming to the realization that social networking sites and video sites are better means of reaching their customers than spending so many marketing dollars on traditional yellow pages or television, magazine, radio, or newspaper ads. Note the time that people spend on the Internet. And it is not just the time. Television viewers are passive viewers of ads, whereas Internet users take an active role in choosing what to look at—so customers on the Internet are tougher for marketers to reach.[7]

New companies such as Autonet Mobile based in San Francisco are selling new technology equipment for cars so the front passenger may conduct an iChat video conference while persons in the back each have a laptop and watch a YouTube video or download music or wirelessly transfer pictures from a digital camera. Everyone in the vehicle can be online except, of course, the driver. This technology is now available for installation in nearly all cars and is accelerating the movement from hard media to Web-based media. With this technology also, when the vehicle drives into a new location, you may instantly download information on shows, museums, hotels, and other attractions around you.

Growth of Internet advertising is expected to decline from a 16 percent increase in 2008 to a 5 percent increase in 2009. With this slowdown, companies are changing the restrictions they previously imposed on the categories and formats of advertising. For example, marketers are more and more allowed to create bigger, more intrusive ads that take up more space on the Web page. And Web sites are allowing lengthier ads to run before short video clips play. And blogs are creating more content that doubles also as an ad. Companies are also waiving minimum ad purchases. Companies are redesigning their Web sites to be much more interactive and are building new sponsorship programs and

TABLE 8-2 **Average Amount of Time That 18- to 27-Year-Olds Spend Weekly on Various Media (in hours)**

Media	Hours
On the Internet	High-13.0
Watching television	
On their cell phone	↓
Listening to the Radio	Medium-7.0
Watching DVDs or VHSs	
Playing video games	↓
Reading magazines	Low-1.0

Source: Based on Ellen Byron, "A New Odd Couple: Google, P&G Swap Workers to Spur Innovation," *Wall Street Journal* (November 19, 2008): A1.

other enticements on their sites. Editorial content and advertising content are increasingly being mixed on blogs.

In 2009–2011, consumers will act rationally. JC Penney CEO Mike Ullman says, "Consumers now shop for what they 'need' and less for what they 'want.' And they don't need much." Essentials, such as food, health-care products, and beauty aids are selling, but even in those industries, consumers are shifting to less costly brands and stores. There is a need for marketers to convince consumers that their brand will make life easier or better. Consumers now often wait until prices are slashed 75 percent or more to buy. Consumers today are very cautious about how they spend their money. Gone are the days when retailers could convince consumers to buy something they do not need.

JC Penney is among many firms that today have revamped their marketing to be more digital related. Penney's is segmenting its e-mail databases according to customers' shopping behaviors and then sending out relevant messages. Penney's corporate director of brand communications recently said, "Tailoring the e-mail insures that our customers are receiving timely, relevant information."

Expectations for total U.S. advertising spending in 2009 may decline anywhere from 6.2 percent to 3 percent to about $160 billion as the fallout from global financial crises continues to cut into ad spending.[8] Global ad spending is expected to decline about 0.5 percent. One bright spot, however, is online advertising expenditures that are expected to increase 5 percent in 2009 following a 16 percent increase in 2008. Companies are shifting ad dollars from newspaper, magazine, and radio to online media.

Purpose-Based Marketing

The global marketing chief at Procter & Gamble, Jim Stengel, recently started his own LLC business to try to persuade companies that the best way to sell in a weak economy is to "show customers how they can improve their lives" with your product or service. Stengel calls this "*purpose-based marketing,*" and hundreds of firms have now adopted this approach successfully. He says there is need in an ad to build trust and an emotional connection to the customer in order to differentiate your product or service.[9]

In a weak economy when consumers are more interested in buying cheaper brands, Stengel acknowledges that ads must promote price, but he says ads must also show the intrinsic value of the product or service to be cost effective. Stengel contends that ads should do both: promote low price and build emotional equity through "purpose-based appeal."

The Coca-Cola Company is leading the way to another new kind of selling in a weak economy. CEO Muhtar Kent at Coke says marketing today must "employ optimism." That is why Coca-Cola launched a new global ad campaign in 2009 appealing to consumers' longing for comfort and optimism. The new campaign features the new slogan "Open Happiness," which replaced Coke's prior popular slogan of three years, "The Coke Side of Life." The Coke CEO says marketers must use feel-good messages to counter the fallout from the economic crisis. Firms must today project to customers that their products or services offer a beacon of comfort and optimism. Coke's cola volume declined 4.0 percent in the United States in 2008. Coke Classic's U.S. volume fell about 16 percent from 1998 through 2007 as customers switched to bottled water, enhanced teas, and other alternative drinks.[10]

Market Segmentation

Two variables are of central importance to strategy implementation: *market segmentation* and *product positioning*. Market segmentation and product positioning rank as marketing's most important contributions to strategic management.

Market segmentation is widely used in implementing strategies, especially for small and specialized firms. Market segmentation can be defined as the subdividing of a market into distinct subsets of customers according to needs and buying habits.

TABLE 8-3 **The Marketing Mix Component Variables**

Product	Place	Promotion	Price
Quality	Distribution channels	Advertising	Level
Features and options	Distribution coverage	Personal selling	Discounts and allowances
	Outlet location	Sales promotion	
Style	Sales territories	Publicity	Payment terms
Brand name	Inventory levels and locations		
Packaging			
Product line	Transportation carriers		
Warranty			
Service level			
Other services			

Source: From E. Jerome McCarthy, *Basic Marketing: A Managerial Approach,* 9th ed. (Homewood, IL: Richard D. Irwin, Inc., 1987): 37–44. Used with permission.

Market segmentation is an important variable in strategy implementation for at least three major reasons. First, strategies such as market development, product development, market penetration, and diversification require increased sales through new markets and products. To implement these strategies successfully, new or improved market-segmentation approaches are required. Second, market segmentation allows a firm to operate with limited resources because mass production, mass distribution, and mass advertising are not required. Market segmentation enables a small firm to compete successfully with a large firm by maximizing per-unit profits and per-segment sales. Finally, market segmentation decisions directly affect *marketing mix variables*: product, place, promotion, and price, as indicated in Table 8-3. For example, SnackWells, a pioneer in reduced-fat snacks, has shifted its advertising emphasis from low-fat to great taste as part of its new market-segmentation strategy.

Perhaps the most dramatic new market-segmentation strategy is the targeting of regional tastes. Firms from McDonald's to General Motors are increasingly modifying their products to meet different regional preferences within the United States. Campbell's has a spicier version of its nacho cheese soup for the Southwest, and Burger King offers breakfast burritos in New Mexico but not in South Carolina. Geographic and demographic bases for segmenting markets are the most commonly employed, as illustrated in Table 8-4.

Evaluating potential market segments requires strategists to determine the characteristics and needs of consumers, to analyze consumer similarities and differences, and to develop consumer group profiles. Segmenting consumer markets is generally much simpler and easier than segmenting industrial markets, because industrial products, such as electronic circuits and forklifts, have multiple applications and appeal to diverse customer groups.

Segmentation is a key to matching supply and demand, which is one of the thorniest problems in customer service. Segmentation often reveals that large, random fluctuations in demand actually consist of several small, predictable, and manageable patterns. Matching supply and demand allows factories to produce desirable levels without extra shifts, overtime, and subcontracting. Matching supply and demand also minimizes the number and severity of stock-outs. The demand for hotel rooms, for example, can be dependent on foreign tourists, businesspersons, and vacationers. Focusing separately on these three market segments, however, can allow hotel firms to more effectively predict overall supply and demand.

Banks now are segmenting markets to increase effectiveness. "You're dead in the water if you aren't segmenting the market," says Anne Moore, president of a bank consulting firm in Atlanta. The Internet makes market segmentation easier today because consumers naturally form "communities" on the Web.

TABLE 8-4   Alternative Bases for Market Segmentation

Variable	Typical Breakdowns
	Geographic
Region	Pacific, Mountain, West North Central, West South Central, East North Central, East South Central, South Atlantic, Middle Atlantic, New England
County Size	A, B, C, D
City Size	Under 5,000; 5,000–20,000; 20,001–50,000; 50,001–100,000; 100,001–250,000; 250,001–500,000; 500,001–1,000,000; 1,000,001–4,000,000; 4,000,001 or over
Density	Urban, suburban, rural
Climate	Northern, southern
	Demographic
Age	Under 6, 6–11, 12–19, 20–34, 35–49, 50–64, 65+
Gender	Male, female
Family Size	1–2, 3–4, 5+
Family Life Cycle	Young, single; young, married, no children; young, married, youngest child under 6; young, married, youngest child 6 or over; older, married, with children; older, married, no children under 18; older, single; other
Income	Under $10,000; $10,001–$15,000; $15,001–$20,000; $20,001–$30,000; $30,001–$50,000; $50,001–$70,000; $70,001–$100,000; over $100,000
Occupation	Professional and technical; managers, officials, and proprietors; clerical and sales; craftspeople; foremen; operatives; farmers; retirees; students; housewives; unemployed
Education	Grade school or less; some high school; high school graduate; some college; college graduate
Religion	Catholic, Protestant, Jewish, Islamic, other
Race	White, Asian, Hispanic, African American
Nationality	American, British, French, German, Scandinavian, Italian, Latin American, Middle Eastern, Japanese
	Psychographic
Social Class	Lower lowers, upper lowers, lower middles, upper middles, lower uppers, upper uppers
Personality	Compulsive, gregarious, authoritarian, ambitious
	Behavioral
Use Occasion	Regular occasion, special occasion
Benefits Sought	Quality, service, economy
User Status	Nonuser, ex-user, potential user, first-time user, regular user
Usage Rate	Light user, medium user, heavy user
Loyalty Status	None, medium, strong, absolute
Readiness Stage	Unaware, aware, informed, interested, desirous, intending to buy
Attitude Toward Product	Enthusiastic, positive, indifferent, negative, hostile

Source: Adapted from Philip Kotler, *Marketing Management: Analysis, Planning and Control,* © 1984: 256. Adapted by permission of Prentice-Hall, Inc., Upper Saddle River, New Jersey.

Does the Internet Make Market Segmentation Easier?

Yes. The segments of people whom marketers want to reach online are much more precisely defined than the segments of people reached through traditional forms of media, such as television, radio, and magazines. For example, Quepasa.com is widely visited by Hispanics. Marketers aiming to reach college students, who are notoriously difficult to reach via traditional media, focus on sites such as collegeclub.com and studentadvantage.com. The gay and lesbian population, which is estimated to comprise about 5 percent of the U.S. population, has always been difficult to reach via traditional media but now can be focused on at sites such as gay.com. Marketers can reach persons interested in specific topics, such as travel or fishing, by placing banners on related Web sites.

People all over the world are congregating into virtual communities on the Web by becoming members/customers/visitors of Web sites that focus on an endless range of topics. People in essence segment themselves by nature of the Web sites that comprise their "favorite places," and many of these Web sites sell information regarding their "visitors." Businesses and groups of individuals all over the world pool their purchasing power in Web sites to get volume discounts.

Product Positioning

After markets have been segmented so that the firm can target particular customer groups, the next step is to find out what customers want and expect. This takes analysis and research. A severe mistake is to assume the firm knows what customers want and expect. Countless research studies reveal large differences between how customers define service and rank the importance of different service activities and how producers view services. Many firms have become successful by filling the gap between what customers and producers see as good service. What the customer believes is good service is paramount, not what the producer believes service should be.

Identifying target customers to focus marketing efforts on sets the stage for deciding how to meet the needs and wants of particular consumer groups. Product positioning is widely used for this purpose. Positioning entails developing schematic representations that reflect how your products or services compare to competitors' on dimensions most important to success in the industry. The following steps are required in product positioning:

1. Select key criteria that effectively differentiate products or services in the industry.
2. Diagram a two-dimensional product-positioning map with specified criteria on each axis.
3. Plot major competitors' products or services in the resultant four-quadrant matrix.
4. Identify areas in the positioning map where the company's products or services could be most competitive in the given target market. Look for vacant areas (niches).
5. Develop a marketing plan to position the company's products or services appropriately.

Because just two criteria can be examined on a single product-positioning map, multiple maps are often developed to assess various approaches to strategy implementation. *Multidimensional scaling* could be used to examine three or more criteria simultaneously, but this technique requires computer assistance and is beyond the scope of this text. Some examples of product-positioning maps are illustrated in Figure 8-2.

Some rules for using product positioning as a strategy-implementation tool are the following:

1. Look for the hole or *vacant niche*. The best strategic opportunity might be an unserved segment.
2. Don't serve two segments with the same strategy. Usually, a strategy successful with one segment cannot be directly transferred to another segment.
3. Don't position yourself in the middle of the map. The middle usually means a strategy that is not clearly perceived to have any distinguishing characteristics. This rule can vary with the number of competitors. For example, when there are only two competitors, as in U.S. presidential elections, the middle becomes the preferred strategic position.[11]

An effective product-positioning strategy meets two criteria: (1) it uniquely distinguishes a company from the competition, and (2) it leads customers to expect slightly less service than a company can deliver. Firms should not create expectations that exceed the service the firm can or will deliver. Network Equipment Technology is an example of a company that keeps customer expectations slightly below perceived performance. This is a constant challenge for marketers. Firms need to inform customers about what to expect and then exceed the promise. Underpromise and then overdeliver is the key!

FIGURE 8-2

Examples of Product-Positioning Maps

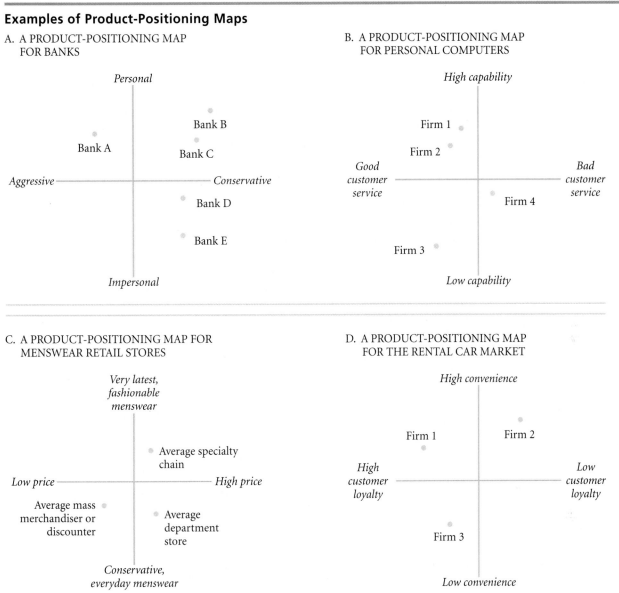

A. A PRODUCT-POSITIONING MAP FOR BANKS

B. A PRODUCT-POSITIONING MAP FOR PERSONAL COMPUTERS

C. A PRODUCT-POSITIONING MAP FOR MENSWEAR RETAIL STORES

D. A PRODUCT-POSITIONING MAP FOR THE RENTAL CAR MARKET

Finance/Accounting Issues

In this section, we examine several finance/accounting concepts considered to be central to strategy implementation: acquiring needed capital, developing projected financial statements, preparing financial budgets, and evaluating the worth of a business. Some examples of decisions that may require finance/accounting policies are these:

1. To raise capital with short-term debt, long-term debt, preferred stock, or common stock
2. To lease or buy fixed assets
3. To determine an appropriate dividend payout ratio
4. To use LIFO (Last-in, First-out), FIFO (First-in, First-out), or a market-value accounting approach
5. To extend the time of accounts receivable
6. To establish a certain percentage discount on accounts within a specified period of time
7. To determine the amount of cash that should be kept on hand

Acquiring Capital to Implement Strategies

Successful strategy implementation often requires additional capital. Besides net profit from operations and the sale of assets, two basic sources of capital for an organization are debt and equity. Determining an appropriate mix of debt and equity in a firm's capital structure can be vital to successful strategy implementation. An *Earnings Per Share/Earnings Before Interest and Taxes (EPS/EBIT) analysis* is the most widely used technique for determining whether debt, stock, or a combination of debt and stock is the best alternative for raising capital to implement strategies. This technique involves an examination of the impact that debt versus stock financing has on earnings per share under various assumptions as to EBIT.

Theoretically, an enterprise should have enough debt in its capital structure to boost its return on investment by applying debt to products and projects earning more than the cost of the debt. In low earning periods, too much debt in the capital structure of an organization can endanger stockholders' returns and jeopardize company survival. Fixed debt obligations generally must be met, regardless of circumstances. This does not mean that stock issuances are always better than debt for raising capital. Some special concerns with stock issuances are dilution of ownership, effect on stock price, and the need to share future earnings with all new shareholders.

Without going into detail on other institutional and legal issues related to the debt versus stock decision, EPS/EBIT may be best explained by working through an example. Let's say the Brown Company needs to raise $1 million to finance implementation of a market-development strategy. The company's common stock currently sells for $50 per share, and 100,000 shares are outstanding. The prime interest rate is 10 percent, and the company's tax rate is 50 percent. The company's earnings before interest and taxes next year are expected to be $2 million if a recession occurs, $4 million if the economy stays as is, and $8 million if the economy significantly improves. EPS/EBIT analysis can be used to determine if all stock, all debt, or some combination of stock and debt is the best capital financing alternative. The EPS/EBIT analysis for this example is provided in Table 8-5.

As indicated by the EPS values of 9.5, 19.50, and 39.50 in Table 8-5, debt is the best financing alternative for the Brown Company if a recession, boom, or normal year is expected. An EPS/EBIT chart can be constructed to determine the break-even point, where one financing alternative becomes more attractive than another. Figure 8-3 indicates that issuing common stock is the least attractive financing alternative for the Brown Company.

EPS/EBIT analysis is a valuable tool for making the capital financing decisions needed to implement strategies, but several considerations should be made whenever using this technique. First, profit levels may be higher for stock or debt alternatives when EPS

TABLE 8-5 EPS/EBIT Analysis for the Brown Company (in millions)

	Common Stock Financing			Debt Financing			Combination Financing		
	Recession	*Normal*	*Boom*	*Recession*	*Normal*	*Boom*	*Recession*	*Normal*	*Boom*
EBIT	$2.0	$ 4.0	$ 8.0	$2.0	$ 4.0	$ 8.0	$2.0	$ 4.0	$ 8.0
Interest[a]	0	0	0	.10	.10	.10	.05	.05	.05
EBT	2.0	4.0	8.0	1.9	3.9	7.9	1.95	3.95	7.95
Taxes	1.0	2.0	4.0	.95	1.95	3.95	.975	1.975	3.975
EAT	1.0	2.0	4.0	.95	1.95	3.95	.975	1.975	3.975
#Shares[b]	.12	.12	.12	.10	.10	.10	.11	.11	.11
EPS[c]	8.33	16.66	33.33	9.5	19.50	39.50	8.86	17.95	36.14

[a]The annual interest charge on $1 million at 10% is $100,000 and on $0.5 million is $50,000. **This row is in $, not %.**

[b]To raise all of the needed $1 million with stock, 20,000 new shares must be issued, raising the total to 120,000 shares outstanding. To raise one-half of the needed $1 million with stock, 10,000 new shares must be issued, raising the total to 110,000 shares outstanding.

[c]EPS = Earnings After Taxes (EAT) divided by shares (number of shares outstanding).

FIGURE 8-3

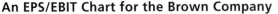

An EPS/EBIT Chart for the Brown Company

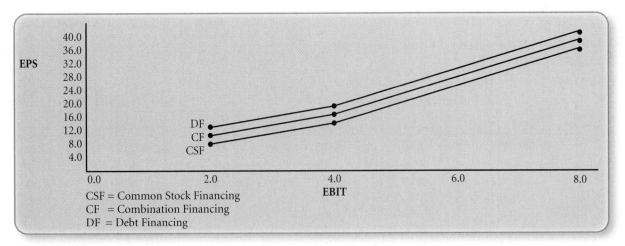

CSF = Common Stock Financing
CF = Combination Financing
DF = Debt Financing

levels are lower. For example, looking only at the earnings after taxes (EAT) values in Table 8-5, you can see that the common stock option is the best alternative, regardless of economic conditions. If the Brown Company's mission includes strict profit maximization, as opposed to the maximization of stockholders' wealth or some other criterion, then stock rather than debt is the best choice of financing.

Another consideration when using EPS/EBIT analysis is flexibility. As an organization's capital structure changes, so does its flexibility for considering future capital needs. Using all debt or all stock to raise capital in the present may impose fixed obligations, restrictive covenants, or other constraints that could severely reduce a firm's ability to raise additional capital in the future. Control is also a concern. When additional stock is issued to finance strategy implementation, ownership and control of the enterprise are diluted. This can be a serious concern in today's business environment of hostile takeovers, mergers, and acquisitions.

Dilution of ownership can be an overriding concern in closely held corporations in which stock issuances affect the decision-making power of majority stockholders. For example, the Smucker family owns 30 percent of the stock in Smucker's, a well-known jam and jelly company. When Smucker's acquired Dickson Family, Inc., the company used mostly debt rather than stock in order not to dilute the family ownership.

When using EPS/EBIT analysis, timing in relation to movements of stock prices, interest rates, and bond prices becomes important. In times of depressed stock prices, debt may prove to be the most suitable alternative from both a cost and a demand standpoint. However, when cost of capital (interest rates) is high, stock issuances become more attractive.

Tables 8-6 and 8-7 provide EPS/EBIT analyses for two companies—Gateway and Boeing. Notice in those analyses that the combination stock/debt options vary from 30/70 to 70/30. Any number of combinations could be explored. However, sometimes in preparing the EPS/EBIT graphs, the lines will intersect, thus revealing break-even points at which one financing alternative becomes more or less attractive than another. The slope of these lines will be determined by a combination of factors including stock price, interest rate, number of shares, and amount of capital needed. Also, it should be noted here that the best financing alternatives are indicated by the highest EPS values. In Tables 8-6 and 8-7, note that the tax rates for the companies vary considerably and should be computed from the respective income statements by dividing taxes paid by income before taxes.

In Table 8-6, the higher EPS values indicate that Gateway should use stock to raise capital in recession or normal economic conditions but should use debt financing under boom conditions. Stock is the best alternative for Gateway under all three conditions if

TABLE 8-6   EPS/EBIT Analysis for Gateway (M = In Millions)

Amount Needed: $1,000 M

EBIT Range: − $500 M to + $100 M to + $500 M

Interest Rate: 5%

Tax Rate: 0% (because the firm has been incurring a loss annually)

Stock Price: $6.00

# of Shares Outstanding: 371 M

	Common Stock Financing			Debt Financing		
	Recession	*Normal*	*Boom*	*Recession*	*Normal*	*Boom*
EBIT	(500.00)	100.00	500.00	(500.00)	100.00	500.00
Interest	0.00	0.00	0.00	50.00	50.00	50.00
EBT	(500.00)	100.00	500.00	(550.00)	50.00	450.00
Taxes	0.00	0.00	0.00	0.00	0.00	0.00
EAT	(500.00)	100.00	500.00	(550.00)	50.00	450.00
#Shares	537.67	537.67	537.67	371.00	371.00	371.00
EPS	**(0.93)**	**0.19**	**0.93**	**(1.48)**	**0.13**	**1.21**

	70 Percent Stock—30 Percent Debt			70 Percent Debt—30 Percent Stock		
	Recession	*Normal*	*Boom*	*Recession*	*Normal*	*Boom*
EBIT	(500.00)	100.00	500.00	(500.00)	100.00	500.00
Interest	15.00	15.00	15.00	35.00	35.00	35.00
EBT	(515.00)	85.00	485.00	(535.00)	65.00	465.00
Taxes	0.00	0.00	0.00	0.00	0.00	0.00
EAT	(515.00)	85.00	485.00	(535.00)	65.00	465.00
#Shares	487.67	487.67	487.67	421.00	421.00	421.00
EPS	**(1.06)**	**0.17**	**0.99**	**(1.27)**	**0.15**	**1.10**

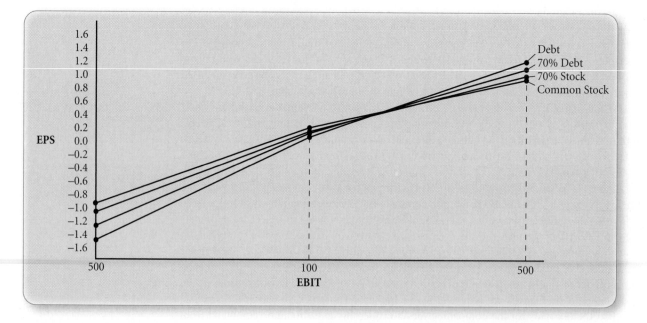

Conclusion: Gateway should use common stock to raise capital in recession or normal economic conditions but should use debt financing under boom conditions. Note that stock is the best alternative under all three conditions according to EAT (profit maximization), but EPS (maximize shareholders' wealth) is the better ratio to make this decision.

TABLE 8-7   EPS/EBIT Analysis for Boeing (M = In Millions)

Amount Needed: $10,000 M

Interest Rate: 5%

Tax Rate: 7%

Stock Price: $53.00

# of Shares Outstanding: 826 M

	Common Stock Financing			Debt Financing		
	Recession	*Normal*	*Boom*	*Recession*	*Normal*	*Boom*
EBIT	1,000.00	2,500.00	5,000.00	1,000.00	2,500.00	5,000.00
Interest	0.00	0.00	0.00	500.00	500.00	500.00
EBT	1,000.00	2,500.00	5,000.00	500.00	2,000.00	4,500.00
Taxes	70.00	175.00	350.00	35.00	140.00	315.00
EAT	930.00	2,325.00	4,650.00	465.00	1,860.00	4,185.00
# Shares	1,014.68	1,014.68	1,014.68	826.00	826.00	826.00
EPS	**0.92**	**2.29**	**4.58**	**0.56**	**2.25**	**5.07**

	70% Stock—30% Debt			70% Debt—30% Stock		
	Recession	*Normal*	*Boom*	*Recession*	*Normal*	*Boom*
EBIT	1,000.00	2,500.00	5,000.00	1,000.00	2,500.00	5,000.00
Interest	150.00	150.00	150.00	350.00	350.00	350.00
EBT	850.00	2,350.00	4,850.00	650.00	2,150.00	4,650.00
Taxes	59.50	164.50	339.50	45.50	150.50	325.50
EAT	790.50	2,185.50	4,510.50	604.50	1,999.50	4,324.50
# Shares	958.08	958.08	958.08	882.60	882.60	882.60
EPS	**0.83**	**2.28**	**4.71**	**0.68**	**2.27**	**4.90**

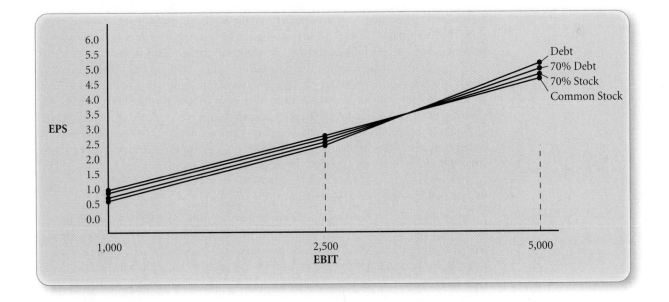

Conclusion: Boeing should use common stock to raise capital in recession (see 0.92) or normal (see 2.29) economic conditions but should use debt financing under boom conditions (see 5.07). Note that a dividends row is absent from this analysis. The more shares outstanding, the more dividends to be paid (if the firm pays dividends), which would lower the common stock EPS values.

EAT (profit maximization) were the decision criteria, but EPS (maximize shareholders' wealth) is the better ratio to make this decision. Firms can do many things in the short run to maximize profits, so investors and creditors consider maximizing shareholders' wealth to be the better criteria for making financing decisions.

In Table 8-7, note that Boeing should use stock to raise capital in recession (see 0.92) or normal (see 2.29) economic conditions but should use debt financing under boom conditions (see 5.07). Let's calculate here the number of shares figure of 1014.68 given under Boeing's stock alternative. Divide $10,000 M funds needed by the stock price of $53 = 188.68 M new shares to be issued + the 826 M shares outstanding already = 1014.68 M shares under the stock scenario. Along the final row, EPS is the number of shares outstanding divided by EAT in all columns.

Note in Table 8-6 and Table 8-7 that a dividends row is absent from both the Gateway and Boeing analyses. The more shares outstanding, the more dividends to be paid (if the firm indeed pays dividends). Paying dividends lowers EAT, which lowers the stock EPS values whenever this aspect is included. To consider dividends in an EPS/EBIT analysis, simply insert another row for "Dividends" right below the "EAT" row and then insert an "Earnings After Taxes and Dividends" row. Considering dividends would make the analysis more robust.

Note in both the Gateway and Boeing graphs, there is a break-even point between the normal and boom range of EBIT where the debt option overtakes the 70% Debt/30% Stock option as the best financing alternative. A break-even point is where two lines cross each other. A break-even point is the EBIT level where various financing alternative represented by lines crossing are equally attractive in terms of EPS. Both the Gateway and Boeing graphs indicate that EPS values are highest for the 100 percent debt option at high EBIT levels. The two graphs also reveal that the EPS values for 100 percent debt increase faster than the other financing options as EBIT levels increase beyond the break-even point. At low levels of EBIT however, both the Gateway and Boeing graphs indicate that 100 percent stock is the best financing alternative because the EPS values are highest.

New Source of Funding

Credit unions were not involved in the subprime-loan market, so many of them are flush with cash and are making loans, especially to small businesses. Deposits to credit unions were also up when many investors abandoned the stock market. Roughly 27 percent of the 8,147 U.S. credit unions offer business loans.[12] The amount of businesses loans was up 18 percent in 2008 to $33 billion, and the average loan size was $215,000.

Many credit unions want to give more business loans, but the 1998 federal law (Credit Union Membership Access Act) caps the amount of business loans credit unions can have at 12.25 percent of their assets. Credit unions are trying to get this law changed, but of course banks are lobbying hard to have the law remain in place. Credit unions are chartered as nonprofit cooperative institutions owned by their members. Thus credit unions are tax-exempt organizations. Bankers argue that allowing credit unions to give more business loans would give them an unfair competitive advantage over traditional banks.

Projected Financial Statements

Projected financial statement analysis is a central strategy-implementation technique because it allows an organization to examine the expected results of various actions and approaches. This type of analysis can be used to forecast the impact of various implementation decisions (for example, to increase promotion expenditures by 50 percent to support a market-development strategy, to increase salaries by 25 percent to support a market-penetration strategy, to increase research and development expenditures by 70 percent to support product development, or to sell $1 million of common stock to raise capital for diversification). Nearly all financial institutions require at least three years of projected financial statements whenever a business seeks capital. A projected income statement and balance sheet allow an organization to compute projected financial ratios under various strategy-implementation scenarios. When compared to prior years and to industry averages, financial ratios provide valuable insights into the feasibility of various strategy-implementation approaches.

Primarily as a result of the Enron collapse and accounting scandal and the ensuing Sarbanes-Oxley Act, companies today are being much more diligent in preparing projected financial statements to "reasonably rather than too optimistically" project future expenses and earnings. There is much more care not to mislead shareholders and other constituencies.[13]

A 2011 projected income statement and a balance sheet for the Litten Company are provided in Table 8-8. The projected statements for Litten are based on five assumptions: (1) The company needs to raise $45 million to finance expansion into foreign markets; (2) $30 million of this total will be raised through increased debt and $15 million through common stock; (3) sales are expected to increase 50 percent; (4) three new facilities, costing a total of $30 million, will be constructed in foreign markets; and (5) land for the new facilities is already owned by the company. Note in Table 8-8 that Litten's

TABLE 8-8 A Projected Income Statement and Balance Sheet for the Litten Company (in millions)

	Prior Year 2010	Projected Year 2011	Remarks
PROJECTED INCOME STATEMENT			
Sales	$100	$150.00	50% increase
Cost of Goods Sold	70	105.00	70% of sales
Gross Margin	30	45.00	
Selling Expense	10	15.00	10% of sales
Administrative Expense	5	7.50	5% of sales
Earnings Before Interest and Taxes	15	22.50	
Interest	3	3.00	
Earnings Before Taxes	12	19.50	
Taxes	6	9.75	50% rate
Net Income	**6**	**9.75**	
Dividends	2	5.00	
Retained Earnings	4	4.75	
PROJECTED BALANCE SHEET			
Assets			
Cash	5	7.75	Plug figure
Accounts Receivable	2	4.00	100% increase
Inventory	20	45.00	
Total Current Assets	27	56.75	
Land	15	15.00	
Plant and Equipment	50	80.00	Add three new plants at $10 million each
Less Depreciation	10	20.00	
Net Plant and Equipment	40	60.00	
Total Fixed Assets	55	75.00	
Total Assets	**82**	**131.75**	
Liabilities			
Accounts Payable	10	10.00	
Notes Payable	10	10.00	
Total Current Liabilities	20	20.00	
Long-term Debt	40	70.00	Borrowed $30 million
Additional Paid-in-Capital	20	35.00	Issued 100,000 shares at $150 each
Retained Earnings	2	6.75	$2 + $4.75
Total Liabilities and Net Worth	**82**	**131.75**	

strategies and their implementation are expected to result in a sales increase from $100 million to $150 million and in a net increase in income from $6 million to $9.75 million in the forecasted year.

There are six steps in performing projected financial analysis:

1. Prepare the projected income statement before the balance sheet. Start by forecasting sales as accurately as possible. Be careful not to blindly push historical percentages into the future with regard to revenue (sales) increases. Be mindful of what the firm did to achieve those past sales increases, which may not be appropriate for the future unless the firm takes similar or analogous actions (such as opening a similar number of stores, for example). If dealing with a manufacturing firm, also be mindful that if the firm is operating at 100 percent capacity running three eight-hour shifts per day, then probably new manufacturing facilities (land, plant, and equipment) will be needed to increase sales further.

2. Use the percentage-of-sales method to project cost of goods sold (CGS) and the expense items in the income statement. For example, if CGS is 70 percent of sales in the prior year (as it is in Table 8-8), then use that same percentage to calculate CGS in the future year—unless there is a reason to use a different percentage. Items such as interest, dividends, and taxes must be treated independently and cannot be forecasted using the percentage-of-sales method.

3. Calculate the projected net income.

4. Subtract from the net income any dividends to be paid for that year. This remaining net income is retained earnings (RE). Bring this retained earnings amount for that year ($NI - DIV = RE$) over to the balance sheet by adding it to the prior year's RE shown on the balance sheet. In other words, every year a firm adds its RE for that particular year (from the income statement) to its historical RE total on the balance sheet. Therefore, the RE amount on the balance sheet is a cumulative number rather than money available for strategy implementation! Note that RE is the first projected balance sheet item to be entered. Due to this accounting procedure in developing projected financial statements, the RE amount on the balance sheet is usually a large number. However, it also can be a low or even negative number if the firm has been incurring losses. The only way for RE to decrease from one year to the next on the balance sheet is (1) if the firm incurred an earnings loss that year or (2) the firm had positive net income for the year but paid out dividends more than the net income. Be mindful that RE is the key link between a projected income statement and balance sheet, so be careful to make this calculation correctly.

5. Project the balance sheet items, beginning with retained earnings and then forecasting stockholders' equity, long-term liabilities, current liabilities, total liabilities, total assets, fixed assets, and current assets (in that order). Use the cash account as the plug figure—that is, use the cash account to make the assets total the liabilities and net worth. Then make appropriate adjustments. For example, if the cash needed to balance the statements is too small (or too large), make appropriate changes to borrow more (or less) money than planned.

6. List comments (remarks) on the projected statements. Any time a significant change is made in an item from a prior year to the projected year, an explanation (remark) should be provided. Remarks are essential because otherwise pro formas are meaningless.

Projected Financial Statement Analysis for Mattel, Inc.

Because so many strategic management students have limited experience developing projected financial statements, let's apply the steps outlined on the previous pages to Mattel, the huge toy company headquartered in El Segundo, California. Mattel designs, manufactures, and markets toy products from fashion dolls to children's books. The company Web site is www.mattel.com. Mattel's recent income statements and balance sheets are provided in Table 8-9 and Table 8-10 respectively.

TABLE 8-9   Mattel's Actual Income Statements (in thousands)

	2006	2005	2004
Total Revenue	$5,650,156	5,179,016	5,102,786
Cost of Revenue	3,038,363	2,806,148	2,692,061
Gross Profit	2,611,793	2,372,868	2,410,725
Operating Expenses			
Research Development	-	-	-
Selling General and Administrative	1,882,975	1,708,339	1,679,908
Non-Recurring	-	-	-
Others	-	-	-
Total Operating Expenses	-	-	-
Operating Income or Loss	728,818	664,529	730,817
Income from Continuing Operations			
Total Other Income/Expenses Net	34,791	64,010	43,201
Earnings Before Interest and Taxes	763,609	728,539	774,018
Interest Expense	79,853	76,490	77,764
Income Before Tax	683,756	652,049	696,254
Income Tax Expense	90,829	235,030	123,531
Minority Interest	-	-	-
Net Income from Continuing Ops	592,927	417,019	572,723
Non-Recurring Events			
Discontinued Operations	-	-	-
Extraordinary Items	-	-	-
Effect of Accounting Changes	-	-	-
Other Items	-	-	-
Net Income	592,927	417,019	572,723
Preferred Stock and Other Adjustments	-	-	-
Net Income Applicable to Common Shares	$592,927	$417,019	$572,723

In Tables 8-11 and 8-12, Mattel's projected income statements and balance sheets respectively for 2007, 2008, and 2009 are provided based on the firm pursuing the following strategies:

1. The company desires to build 20 Mattel stores annually at a cost of $1 million each.
2. The company plans to develop new toy products at an annual cost of $10 million.
3. The company plans to increase its advertising/promotion expenditures 30 percent over three years, at a cost of $30 million ($10 million per year).
4. The company plans to buy back $100 million of its own stock (called Treasury stock) annually for the next three years.
5. The company expects revenues to increase 10 percent annually with the above strategies. Mattel can handle this increase with existing production facilities.
6. Dividend payout will be increased from 57 percent of net income to 60 percent.
7. To finance the $380 million total cost for the above strategies, Mattel plans to use long-term debt for $150 million ($50 million per year for three years) and $230 million by issuing stock ($77 million per year for three years).

The Mattel projected financial statements were prepared using the six steps outlined on prior pages and the above seven strategy statements. Note the cash account is used as the plug figure, and it is too high, so Mattel could reduce this number and concurrently reduce a liability and/or equity account the same amount to keep the statement in balance. Rarely is the cash account perfect on the first pass through, so adjustments are needed and made. However, these adjustments are *not* made on the projected statements given in

TABLE 8-10   Mattel's Actual Balance Sheets (in thousands)

	2006	2005	2004
Assets			
Current Assets			
Cash and Cash Equivalents	$1,205,552	997,734	1,156,835
Short-Term Investments	-	-	-
Net Receivables	943,813	760,643	759,033
Inventory	383,149	376,897	418,633
Other Current Assets	317,624	277,226	302,649
Total Current Assets	2,850,138	2,412,500	2,637,150
Long-Term Investments	-	-	-
Property, Plant, and Equipment	536,749	547,104	586,526
Goodwill	845,324	718,069	735,680
Intangible Assets	70,593	20,422	22,926
Accumulated Amortization	-	-	-
Other Assets	149,912	178,304	201,836
Deferred Long-Term Asset Charges	503,168	495,914	572,374
Total Assets	$4,955,884	4,372,313	4,756,492
Liabilities			
Current Liabilities			
Accounts Payable	$1,518,234	1,245,191	1,303,822
Short/Current Long-Term Debt	64,286	217,994	423,349
Other Current Liabilities	-	-	-
Total Current Liabilities	1,582,520	1,463,185	1,727,171
Long-Term Debt	635,714	525,000	400,000
Other Liabilities	304,676	282,395	243,509
Deferred Long-Term Liability Charges	-	-	-
Minority Interest	-	-	-
Negative Goodwill	-	-	-
Total Liabilities	2,522,910	2,270,580	2,370,680
Stockholders' Equity			
Misc. Stocks, Options, Warrants	-	-	-
Redeemable Preferred Stock	-	-	-
Preferred Stock	-	-	-
Common Stock	441,369	441,369	441,369
Retained Earnings	1,652,140	1,314,068	1,093,288
Treasury Stock	(996,981)	(935,711)	(473,349)
Capital Surplus	1,613,307	1,589,281	1,594,332
Other Stockholders' Equity	(276,861)	(307,274)	(269,828)
Total Stockholders' Equity	2,432,974	2,101,733	2,385,812
Total Liabilities and SE	$4,955,884	4,372,313	4,756,492

Tables 8-11 and 8-12, so that the seven strategy statements above can be more readily seen on respective rows. Note the author's comments on Tables 8-11 and 8-12 that help explain changes in the numbers.

The U.S. Securities and Exchange Commission (SEC) conducts fraud investigations if projected numbers are misleading or if they omit information that's important to investors. Projected statements must conform with generally accepted accounting principles (GAAP) and must not be designed to hide poor expected results. The

TABLE 8-11   Mattel's Projected Income Statements (in thousands)

	2009	2008	2007	Author Comment
Total Revenue	$7,520,357	6,836,688	6,215,171	up 10% annually
Cost of Revenue	4,060,992	3,691,811	3,356,192	remains 54%
Gross Profit	3,459,365	3,144,877	2,858,979	subtraction
Operating Expenses				
Research Development	10,000	10,000	10,000	total $30M new
Selling General and Administrative	2,491,717	2,256,107	2,051,006	remains 33% + $10 M annually
Non-Recurring	-	-	-	
Others	-	-	-	
Total Operating Expenses	-	-	-	
Operating Income or Loss	957,648	878,770	797,973	subtraction
Income from Continuing Operations				
Total Other Income/Expenses Net	34,791	34,791	34,791	keep it the same
Earnings Before Interest and Taxes	992,439	913,561	832,764	addition
Interest Expense	97,823	91,423	85,442	up 7%; LTD up 7%
Income Before Tax	894,616	822,138	737,322	
Income Tax Expense	90,829	90,829	90,829	keep it the same
Minority Interest	-	-	-	
Net Income from Continuing Ops	803,787	731,309	646,493	subtraction
Discontinued Operations	-	-	-	
Extraordinary Items	-	-	-	
Effect of Accounting Changes	-	-	-	
Other Items	-	-	-	
Net Income	803,787	731,309	646,493	
Preferred Stock and Other Adjustments	-	-	-	
Net Income Applicable to Common Shares	$803,787	731,309	646,493	

Sarbanes-Oxley Act requires CEOs and CFOs of corporations to personally sign their firms' financial statements attesting to their accuracy. These executives could thus be held personally liable for misleading or inaccurate statements. The collapse of the Arthur Andersen accounting firm, along with its client Enron, fostered a "zero tolerance" policy among auditors and shareholders with regard to a firm's financial statements. But plenty of firms still "inflate" their financial projections and call them "pro formas," so investors, shareholders, and other stakeholders must still be wary of different companies' financial projections.[14]

On financial statements, different companies use different terms for various items, such as *revenues* or *sales* used for the same item by different companies. For net income, many firms use the term *earnings*, and many others use the term *profits*.

Financial Budgets

A *financial budget* is a document that details how funds will be obtained and spent for a specified period of time. Annual budgets are most common, although the period of time for a budget can range from one day to more than 10 years. Fundamentally, financial budgeting is a method for specifying what must be done to complete strategy implementation successfully. Financial budgeting should not be thought of as a tool for limiting expenditures but rather as a method for obtaining the most productive and profitable use of an organization's resources. Financial budgets can be viewed as the planned allocation of a firm's resources based on forecasts of the future.

There are almost as many different types of financial budgets as there are types of organizations. Some common types of budgets include cash budgets, operating budgets, sales budgets, profit budgets, factory budgets, capital budgets, expense budgets, divisional

TABLE 8-12 Mattel's Projected Balance Sheets (in thousands)

	2009	2008	2007	Author Comment
Assets				
Current Assets				
Cash and Cash Equivalents	$3,232,406	2,972,664	2,570,635	too high, could reduce this and pay off some LTD to keep balance
Short-Term Investments	-	-	-	
Net Receivables	943,813	760,643	759,033	
Inventory	509,969	463,609	421,463	up 10% annually
Other Current Assets	317,624	317,624	317,624	keep it the same
Total Current Assets				
Long-Term Investments	-	-	-	
Property, Plant, and Equipment	596,749	576,749	556,749	up $20M annually
Goodwill	845,324	845,324	845,324	keep it the same
Intangible Assets	70,593	70,593	70,593	keep it the same
Accumulated Amortization	-	-	-	
Other Assets	149,912	149,912	149,912	keep it the same
Deferred Long-Term Asset Charges	503,168	503,168	503,168	keep it the same
Total Assets	7,169,558	6,660,286	6,194,501	
Liabilities				
Current Liabilities				
Accounts Payable	1,518,234	1,518,234	1,518,234	keep it the same
Short/Current Long-Term Debt	64,286	64,286	64,286	keep it the same
Other Current Liabilities	-	-	-	
Total Current Liabilities	1,582,520	1,582,520	1,582,520	
Long-Term Debt	785,714	735,714	685,714	up $50M annually
Other Liabilities	304,676	304,676	304,676	keep it the same
Deferred Long-Term Liability Charges	-	-	-	
Minority Interest	-	-	-	
Negative Goodwill	-	-	-	
Total Liabilities	2,672,910	2,622,910	2,572,910	
Stockholders' Equity				
Misc. Stocks, Options, Warrants	-	-	-	
Redeemable Preferred Stock	-	-	-	
Preferred Stock	-	-	-	
Common Stock	441,369	441,369	441,369	keep it the same
Retained Earnings	2,961,092	2,478,820	2,040,035	60% of NI = div
Treasury Stock	(1,296,981)	(1,196,981)	(1,096,981)	up $100M annually
Capital Surplus	2,114,307	2,037,307	1,960,307	up $77M annually
Other Stockholders' Equity	(276,861)	(276,861)	(276,861)	keep it the same
Total Stockholders' Equity	4,496,648	4,037,376	3,621,591	addition
Total Liabilities and SE	$7,169,558	6,660,286	6,194,501	addition

budgets, variable budgets, flexible budgets, and fixed budgets. When an organization is experiencing financial difficulties, budgets are especially important in guiding strategy implementation.

Perhaps the most common type of financial budget is the *cash budget*. The Financial Accounting Standards Board (FASB) has mandated that every publicly held company in the United States must issue an annual cash-flow statement in addition to the usual financial reports. The statement includes all receipts and disbursements of cash in operations, investments, and financing. It supplements the Statement on Changes in Financial Position formerly included in the annual reports of all publicly held companies. A cash budget for the year 2011 for the Toddler Toy Company is provided in Table 8-13. Note that Toddler is not expecting to have surplus cash until November 2011.

Financial budgets have some limitations. First, budgetary programs can become so detailed that they are cumbersome and overly expensive. Overbudgeting or underbudgeting can cause problems. Second, financial budgets can become a substitute for objectives. A budget is a tool and not an end in itself. Third, budgets can hide inefficiencies if based solely on precedent rather than on periodic evaluation of circumstances and standards. Finally, budgets are sometimes used as instruments of tyranny that result in frustration, resentment, absenteeism, and high turnover. To minimize the effect of this last concern, managers should increase the participation of subordinates in preparing budgets.

Evaluating the Worth of a Business

Evaluating the worth of a business is central to strategy implementation because integrative, intensive, and diversification strategies are often implemented by acquiring other firms. Other strategies, such as retrenchment and divestiture, may result in the sale of a division of an organization or of the firm itself. Thousands of transactions occur each year in which businesses are bought or sold in the United States. In all these cases, it is necessary to establish the financial worth or cash value of a business to successfully implement strategies.

All the various methods for determining a business's worth can be grouped into three main approaches: what a firm owns, what a firm earns, or what a firm will bring in the market. But it is important to realize that valuation is not an exact science. The valuation of a firm's worth is based on financial facts, but common sense and intuitive judgment must enter into the process. It is difficult to assign a monetary value to some factors—such as a loyal customer base, a history of growth, legal suits pending,

TABLE 8-13 Six-Month Cash Budget for the Toddler Toy Company in 2011

Cash Budget (in thousands)	July	Aug.	Sept.	Oct.	Nov.	Dec.	Jan.
Receipts							
Collections	$12,000	$21,000	$31,000	$35,000	$22,000	$18,000	$11,000
Payments							
Purchases	14,000	21,000	28,000	14,000	14,000	7,000	
Wages and Salaries	1,500	2,000	2,500	1,500	1,500	1,000	
Rent	500	500	500	500	500	500	
Other Expenses	200	300	400	200	—	100	
Taxes	—	8,000	—	—	—	—	
Payment on Machine	—	—	10,000	—	—	—	
Total Payments	$16,200	$31,800	$41,400	$16,200	$16,000	$8,600	
Net Cash Gain (Loss) During Month	−4,200	−10,800	−10,400	18,800	6,000	9,400	
Cash at Start of Month if No Borrowing Is Done	6,000	1,800	−9,000	−19,400	−600	5,400	
Cumulative Cash (Cash at start plus gains or minus losses)	1,800	−9,000	−19,400	−600	5,400	14,800	
Less Desired Level of Cash	−5,000	−5,000	−5,000	−5,000	−5,000	−5,000	
Total Loans Outstanding to Maintain $5,000 Cash Balance	$3,200	$14,000	$24,400	$5,600	—	—	
Surplus Cash	—	—	—	—	400	9,800	

dedicated employees, a favorable lease, a bad credit rating, or good patents—that may not be reflected in a firm's financial statements. Also, different valuation methods will yield different totals for a firm's worth, and no prescribed approach is best for a certain situation. Evaluating the worth of a business truly requires both qualitative and quantitative skills.

The first approach in evaluating the worth of a business is determining its net worth or stockholders' equity. Net worth represents the sum of common stock, additional paid-in capital, and retained earnings. After calculating net worth, add or subtract an appropriate amount for goodwill, overvalued or undervalued assets, and intangibles. Whereas intangibles include copyrights, patents, and trademarks, goodwill arises only if a firm acquires another firm and pays more than the book value for that firm.

It should be noted that Financial Accounting Standards Board (FASB) Rule 142 requires companies to admit once a year if the premiums they paid for acquisitions, called goodwill, were a waste of money. Goodwill is not a good thing to have on a balance sheet. Note in Table 8-14 that Mattel's goodwill of $815 million as a percent of its total assets ($4,675 million) is 17.4 percent, which is extremely high compared to Nordstrom's goodwill of $53 million as a percentage of its total assets ($5,661 million), 0.94 percent. Pfizer's goodwill to total assets percentage also is high at 19.3 percent.

At year-end 2008, Mattel, Nordstrom, and Pfizer had $815 million, $53 million, and $21,464 billion in goodwill, respectively, on their balance sheets. Most creditors and investors feel that goodwill indeed should be added to the stockholders' equity in calculating worth of a business, but some feel it should be subtracted, and still others feel it should not be included at all. Perhaps whether you are buying or selling the business may determine whether you negotiate to add or subtract goodwill in the analysis. Goodwill is sometimes listed as intangibles on the balance sheet, but technically intangibles refers to patents, trademarks, and copyrights, rather than the value a firm paid over book value for an acquisition, which is goodwill. If a firm paid less than book value for an acquisition, that could be called negative goodwill—which is a line item on Mattel's balance sheets.

The second approach to measuring the value of a firm grows out of the belief that the worth of any business should be based largely on the future benefits its owners may derive through net profits. A conservative rule of thumb is to establish a business's worth as five times the firm's current annual profit. A five-year average profit level could also be used.

TABLE 8-14   Company Worth Analysis for Mattel, Nordstrom, and Pfizer (year-end 2008, in $millions, except stock price and EPS)

Input Data	Mattel	Nordstrom	Pfizer
Shareholders' Equity	$2,117	$1,210	$57,556
Net Income (NI)	379	401	8,104
Stock Price	15	10	15
EPS	1.03	1.83	1.19
# of Shares Outstanding	358	215	6,750
Goodwill + Intangibles	815	53	21,464
Total Assets	235	0	17,721
Company Worth Analyses			
1. Shareholders' Equity + Goodwill + Intangibles	$3,167	$1,263	$ 96,741
2. Net Income × 5	1,895	2,005	40,520
3. (Stock Price/EPS) × NI	5,519	2,191	102,151
4. # of Shares Out × Stock Price	5,340	2,150	101,250
5. Four Method Average	3,988	1,902	76,049
$Goodwill/$Total Assets	17.4%	0.94%	19.3%

When using the approach, remember that firms normally suppress earnings in their financial statements to minimize taxes.

The third approach is called the *price-earnings ratio method.* To use this method, divide the market price of the firm's common stock by the annual earnings per share and multiply this number by the firm's average net income for the past five years.

The fourth method can be called the *outstanding shares method.* To use this method, simply multiply the number of shares outstanding by the market price per share and add a premium. The premium is simply a per-share dollar amount that a person or firm is willing to pay to control (acquire) the other company. A pharmaceutical company based in Tokyo, Astellas Pharma Inc., recently launched an unsolicited takeover of biotechnology company CV Therapeutics Inc., based in Palo Alto, California. Astellas offered $16 a share, or nearly $1 billion, which represented a 41 percent premium over CV's closing stock price of $11.35 on the Nasdaq stock market. The CEO of Astellas said, "We are disappointed that CV's board of directors has rejected outright what we believe is a very compelling all-cash proposal that would deliver stockholders significant immediate value that we believe far exceeds what CV can achieve as a stand-alone company."

Business evaluations are becoming routine in many situations. Businesses have many strategy-implementation reasons for determining their worth in addition to preparing to be sold or to buy other companies. Employee plans, taxes, retirement packages, mergers, acquisitions, expansion plans, banking relationships, death of a principal, divorce, partnership agreements, and IRS audits are other reasons for a periodic valuation. It is just good business to have a reasonable understanding of what your firm is worth. This knowledge protects the interests of all parties involved

Table 8-14 provides the cash value analyses for three companies—Mattel, Nordstrom, and Pfizer—for year-end 2008. Notice that there is significant variation among the four methods used to determine cash value. For example, the worth of the toy company Mattel ranged from $1,895 billion to $5,519 billion. Obviously, if you were selling your company, you would seek the larger values, while if purchasing a company you would seek the lower values. In practice, substantial negotiation takes place in reaching a final compromise (or averaged) amount. Also recognize that if a firm's net income is negative, theoretically the approaches involving that figure would result in a negative number, implying that the firm would pay you to acquire them. Of course, you obtain all of the firm's debt and liabilities in an acquisition, so theoretically this would be possible.

Deciding Whether to Go Public

Going public means selling off a percentage of your company to others in order to raise capital; consequently, it dilutes the owners' control of the firm. Going public is not recommended for companies with less than $10 million in sales because the initial costs can be too high for the firm to generate sufficient cash flow to make going public worthwhile. One dollar in four is the average total cost paid to lawyers, accountants, and underwriters when an initial stock issuance is under $1 million; 1 dollar in 20 will go to cover these costs for issuances over $20 million.

In addition to initial costs involved with a stock offering, there are costs and obligations associated with reporting and management in a publicly held firm. For firms with more than $10 million in sales, going public can provide major advantages: It can allow the firm to raise capital to develop new products, build plants, expand, grow, and market products and services more effectively.

Research and Development (R&D) Issues

Research and development (R&D) personnel can play an integral part in strategy implementation. These individuals are generally charged with developing new products and improving old products in a way that will allow effective strategy implementation.

R&D employees and managers perform tasks that include transferring complex technology, adjusting processes to local raw materials, adapting processes to local markets, and altering products to particular tastes and specifications. Strategies such as product development, market penetration, and related diversification require that new products be successfully developed and that old products be significantly improved. But the level of management support for R&D is often constrained by resource availability.

Technological improvements that affect consumer and industrial products and services shorten product life cycles. Companies in virtually every industry are relying on the development of new products and services to fuel profitability and growth.[15] Surveys suggest that the most successful organizations use an R&D strategy that ties external opportunities to internal strengths and is linked with objectives. Well-formulated R&D policies match market opportunities with internal capabilities. R&D policies can enhance strategy implementation efforts to:

1. Emphasize product or process improvements.
2. Stress basic or applied research.
3. Be leaders or followers in R&D.
4. Develop robotics or manual-type processes.
5. Spend a high, average, or low amount of money on R&D.
6. Perform R&D within the firm or to contract R&D to outside firms.
7. Use university researchers or private-sector researchers.

Pfizer Inc. has only a few new drugs in its pipeline to show for its $7.5 billion R&D budget, so the firm is laying off 5,000 to 8,000 of its researchers and scientists in labs around the world. Cash-strapped consumers are filling fewer prescriptions and are turning more and more to generic drugs. Pfizer is bracing for the 2011 expiration of its patent on cholesterol fighter Lipitor, the world's top-selling drug that alone accounts for a quarter of Pfizer's roughly $48 billion in annual revenue. Pfizer's $7.5 billion R&D budget is the largest of any drug maker. The firm recently scrapped two drugs nearly ready to go to market—insulin spray Exubera and a Lipitor successor drug—after spending billions to develop them. Research areas that Pfizer is exiting include anemia, bone health, gastrointestinal disorders, obesity, liver disease, osteoarthritis, and peripheral artery disease.

There must be effective interactions between R&D departments and other functional departments in implementing different types of generic business strategies. Conflicts between marketing, finance/accounting, R&D, and information systems departments can be minimized with clear policies and objectives. Table 8-15 gives some examples of R&D activities that could be required for successful implementation of various strategies. Many U.S. utility, energy, and automotive companies are employing their research and development departments to determine how the firm can effectively reduce its gas emissions.

TABLE 8-15 Research and Development Involvement in Selected Strategy-Implementation Situations

Type of Organization	Strategy Being Implemented	R&D Activity
Pharmaceutical company	Product development	Test the effects of a new drug on different subgroups.
Boat manufacturer	Related diversification	Test the performance of various keel designs under various conditions.
Plastic container manufacturer	Market penetration	Develop a biodegradable container.
Electronics company	Market development	Develop a telecommunications system in a foreign country.

Many firms wrestle with the decision to acquire R&D expertise from external firms or to develop R&D expertise internally. The following guidelines can be used to help make this decision:

1. If the rate of technical progress is slow, the rate of market growth is moderate, and there are significant barriers to possible new entrants, then in-house R&D is the preferred solution. The reason is that R&D, if successful, will result in a temporary product or process monopoly that the company can exploit.

2. If technology is changing rapidly and the market is growing slowly, then a major effort in R&D may be very risky, because it may lead to the development of an ultimately obsolete technology or one for which there is no market.

3. If technology is changing slowly but the market is growing quickly, there generally is not enough time for in-house development. The prescribed approach is to obtain R&D expertise on an exclusive or nonexclusive basis from an outside firm.

4. If both technical progress and market growth are fast, R&D expertise should be obtained through acquisition of a well-established firm in the industry.[16]

There are at least three major R&D approaches for implementing strategies. The first strategy is to be the first firm to market new technological products. This is a glamorous and exciting strategy but also a dangerous one. Firms such as 3M and General Electric have been successful with this approach, but many other pioneering firms have fallen, with rival firms seizing the initiative.

A second R&D approach is to be an innovative imitator of successful products, thus minimizing the risks and costs of start-up. This approach entails allowing a pioneer firm to develop the first version of the new product and to demonstrate that a market exists. Then, laggard firms develop a similar product. This strategy requires excellent R&D personnel and an excellent marketing department.

A third R&D strategy is to be a low-cost producer by mass-producing products similar to but less expensive than products recently introduced. As a new product is accepted by customers, price becomes increasingly important in the buying decision. Also, mass marketing replaces personal selling as the dominant selling strategy. This R&D strategy, requires substantial investment in plant and equipment but fewer expenditures in R&D than the two approaches described previously.

R&D activities among U.S. firms need to be more closely aligned to business objectives. There needs to be expanded communication between R&D managers and strategists. Corporations are experimenting with various methods to achieve this improved communication climate, including different roles and reporting arrangements for managers and new methods to reduce the time it takes research ideas to become reality.

Perhaps the most current trend in R&D management has been lifting the veil of secrecy whereby firms, even major competitors, are joining forces to develop new products. Collaboration is on the rise due to new competitive pressures, rising research costs, increasing regulatory issues, and accelerated product development schedules. Companies not only are working more closely with each other on R&D, but they are also turning to consortia at universities for their R&D needs. More than 600 research consortia are now in operation in the United States. Lifting of R&D secrecy among many firms through collaboration has allowed the marketing of new technologies and products even before they are available for sale. For example, some firms are collaborating on the efficient design of solar panels to power homes and businesses.

Management Information Systems (MIS) Issues

Firms that gather, assimilate, and evaluate external and internal information most effectively are gaining competitive advantages over other firms. Having an effective *management information system (MIS)* may be the most important factor in differentiating successful from unsuccessful firms. The process of strategic management is facilitated immensely in firms that have an effective information system.

Information collection, retrieval, and storage can be used to create competitive advantages in ways such as cross-selling to customers, monitoring suppliers, keeping managers and employees informed, coordinating activities among divisions, and managing funds. Like inventory and human resources, information is now recognized as a valuable organizational asset that can be controlled and managed. Firms that implement strategies using the best information will reap competitive advantages in the twenty-first century.

A good information system can allow a firm to reduce costs. For example, online orders from salespersons to production facilities can shorten materials ordering time and reduce inventory costs. Direct communications between suppliers, manufacturers, marketers, and customers can link together elements of the value chain as though they were one organization. Improved quality and service often result from an improved information system.

Firms must increasingly be concerned about computer hackers and take specific measures to secure and safeguard corporate communications, files, orders, and business conducted over the Internet. Thousands of companies today are plagued by computer hackers who include disgruntled employees, competitors, bored teens, sociopaths, thieves, spies, and hired agents. Computer vulnerability is a giant, expensive headache.

Dun & Bradstreet is an example company that has an excellent information system. Every D&B customer and client in the world has a separate nine-digit number. The database of information associated with each number has become so widely used that it is like a business Social Security number. D&B reaps great competitive advantages from its information system.

In many firms, information technology is doing away with the workplace and allowing employees to work at home or anywhere, anytime. The mobile concept of work allows employees to work the traditional 9-to-5 workday across any of the 24 time zones around the globe. Affordable desktop videoconferencing software allows employees to "beam in" whenever needed. Any manager or employee who travels a lot away from the office is a good candidate for working at home rather than in an office provided by the firm. Salespersons or consultants are good examples, but any person whose job largely involves talking to others or handling information could easily operate at home with the proper computer system and software.

Many people see the officeless office trend as leading to a resurgence of family togetherness in U.S. society. Even the design of homes may change from having large open areas to having more private small areas conducive to getting work done.[17]

Conclusion

Successful strategy implementation depends on cooperation among all functional and divisional managers in an organization. Marketing departments are commonly charged with implementing strategies that require significant increases in sales revenues in new areas and with new or improved products. Finance and accounting managers must devise effective strategy-implementation approaches at low cost and minimum risk to that firm. R&D managers have to transfer complex technologies or develop new technologies to successfully implement strategies. Information systems managers are being called upon more and more to provide leadership and training for all individuals in the firm. The nature and role of marketing, finance/accounting, R&D, and management information systems activities, coupled with the management activities described in Chapter 7, largely determine organizational success.

We invite you to visit the David page on the Prentice Hall Companion Web site at http://www.pearsonhighered.com/david for this chapter's review quiz.

Key Terms and Concepts

Cash Budget (p. 272)
EPS/EBIT Analysis (p. 262)
Financial Budget (p. 271)
Management Information System (MIS) (p. 277)
Market Segmentation (p. 257)
Marketing Mix Variables (p. 258)
Multidimensional Scaling (p. 260)
Outstanding Shares Method (p. 275)

Price-Earnings Ratio Method (p. 275)
Product Positioning (p. 257)
Projected Financial Statement Analysis (p. 266)
Purpose-Based Marketing (p. 257)
Research and Development (R&D) (p. 275)
Tweet (p. 255)
Vacant Niche (p. 260)
Wikis (p. 253)

Issues for Review and Discussion

1. Review a company's Web site that you are familiar with. Discuss the extent to which that organization has instituted the new principles of marketing according to Parise, Guinan, and Weinberg.
2. For companies in general, identify and discuss three opportunities and three threats associated with social networking activities on the Internet.
3. Do you agree or disagree with the following statement? "Television viewers are passive viewers of ads, whereas Internet users take an active role in choosing what to look at— so customers on the Internet are tougher for marketers to reach." Explain your reasoning.
4. How important or relevant do you believe "purpose-based marketing" is for organizations today?
5. Why is it essential for organizations to segment markets and target particular groups of consumers?
6. Explain how and why the Internet makes market segmentation easier.
7. A product-positioning rule given in the chapter is that "When there are only two competitors, the middle becomes the preferred strategic position." Illustrate this for the cruise ship industry, where two firms, Carnival and Royal Caribbean, dominate. Illustrate this for the commercial airliner building industry, where Boeing and Airbus dominate.
8. How could/would dividends affect an EPS/EBIT analysis? Would it be correct to refer to "earnings after taxes, interest, and dividends" as retained earnings for a given year?
9. In performing an EPS/EBIT analysis, where does the first row (EBIT) numbers come from?
10. In performing an EPS/EBIT analysis, where does the tax rate percentage come from?
11. For the Litten Company in Table 8-8, what would the Retained Earnings value have to have been in 2009 on the balance sheet, given that the 2010 NI-DIV value was $4?
12. Show algebraically that the price earnings ratio formula is identical to the number of shares outstanding times stock price formula. Why are the values obtained from these two methods sometimes different?
13. In accounting terms, distinguish between intangibles and goodwill on a balance sheet. Why do these two items generally stay the same on projected financial statements?
14. What are the three major R&D approaches to implementing strategies? Which approach would you prefer as owner of a small software company? Why?
15. Suppose your company has just acquired a firm that produces battery-operated lawn mowers, and strategists want to implement a market-penetration strategy. How would you segment the market for this product? Justify your answer.
16. Explain how you would estimate the total worth of a business.
17. Diagram and label clearly a product-positioning map that includes six fast-food restaurant chains.
18. Explain why EPS/EBIT analysis is a central strategy-implementation technique.
19. How would the R&D role in strategy implementation differ in small versus large organizations?
20. Discuss the limitations of EPS/EBIT analysis.
21. Explain how marketing, finance/accounting, R&D, and management information systems managers' involvement in strategy formulation can enhance strategy implementation.
22. Consider the following statement: "Retained earnings on the balance sheet are not monies available to finance strategy implementation." Is it true or false? Explain.
23. Explain why projected financial statement analysis is considered both a strategy-formulation and a strategy-implementation tool.

24. Describe some marketing, finance/accounting, R&D, and management information systems activities that a small restaurant chain might undertake to expand into a neighboring state.
25. What effect is e-commerce having on firms' efforts to segment markets?
26. How has the Sarbanes-Oxley Act of 2002 changed CEOs' and CFOs' handling of financial statements?
27. To what extent have you been exposed to natural environment issues in your business courses? Which course has provided the most coverage? What percentage of your business courses provided no coverage? Comment.
28. Complete the following EPS/EBIT analysis for a company whose stock price is $20, interest rate on funds is 5 percent, tax rate is 20 percent, number of shares outstanding is 500 million, and EBIT range is $100 million to $300 million. The firm needs to raise $200 million in capital. Use the accompanying table to complete the work.
29. Under what conditions would retained earnings on the balance sheet decrease from one year to the next?
30. In your own words, list all the steps in developing projected financial statements.
31. Based on the financial statements provided for McDonald's (pp. 31–32), how much dividends in dollars did McDonald's pay in 2007? In 2008?
32. Based on the financial statements provided in this chapter for the Litten Company, calculate the value of this company if you know that its stock price is $20 and it has 1 million shares outstanding. Calculate four different ways and average.
33. Why should you be careful not to use historical percentages blindly in developing projected financial statements?
34. In developing projected financial statements, what should you do if the $ amount you must put in the cash account (to make the statement balance) is far more (or less) than desired?
35. Why is it both important and necessary to segment markets and target groups of customers, rather than market to all possible consumers?
36. In full detail, explain the following EPS/EBIT chart.

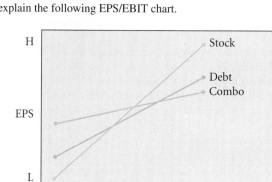

	100% Common Stock	100% Debt Financing	20% Debt-80%Stock
EBIT			
Interest			
EBT			
Taxes			
EAT			
# Shares			
EPS			

Notes

1. Leslie Miller and Elizabeth Weise, "E-Privacy—FTC Studies 'Profiling' by Web Sites," *USA Today* (November 8, 1999): 1A, 2A.
2. Salvatore Parise, Patricia Guinan, and Bruce Weinberg, "The Secrets of Marketing in a Web 2.0 World," *Wall Street Journal* (December 15, 2008): R1.
3. Kathy Chu and Kim Thai, "Banks Jump on Twitter Wagon," *USA Today* (May 12, 2009): B1.
4. Emily Steel, "Car Makers Take Case to the Web," *Wall Street Journal* (December 5, 2006): B7; Salvatore Parise, Patricia Guinan, and Bruce Weinberg, "The Secrets of Marketing in a Web 2.0 World," *Wall Street Journal* (December 15, 2008): R1.

5. Laura Petrecca, "Negative PR Travels Fast Online," *USA Today*, December 8, 2008; Emily Steel, "MySpace Weds the Wider Web," *Wall Street Journal* (December 9, 2008): B5; Bruce Horowitz, "Domino's Nightmare Holds Lessons for Marketers," *Wall Street Journal* (April 16, 2009): 3B.

6. Tom Wright, "Poor Nations Go Online on Cell Phones," *Wall Street Journal* (December 5, 2008): B8.

7. Ellen Byron, "A New Odd Couple: Google, P&G Swap Workers to Spur Innovation," *Wall Street Journal* (November 19, 2008): A1.

8. Emily Steel, "Ad-Spending Forecasts Are Glum," *Wall Street Journal* (December 8, 2008): B5.

9. Susanne Vranica, "Veteran Marketer Promotes a New Kind of Selling," *Wall Street Journal* (October 31, 2008): B4.

10. Betsy McKay and Suzanne Vranica, "Coca-Cola Ads Will Employ Optimism to Sell Coke," *Wall Street Journal* (January 14, 2009): B6.

11. Ralph Biggadike, "The Contributions of Marketing to Strategic Management," *Academy of Management Review* 6, no. 4 (October 1981): 627.

12. Jilian Mincer, "Small Businesses Find a New Source of Funding," *Wall Street Journal* (March 3, 2009): B7.

13. Phyllis Plitch, "Companies in Many Sectors Give Earnings a Pro Forma Makeover, Survey Finds," *Wall Street Journal* (January 22, 2002): A4.

14. Michael Rapoport, "Pro Forma Is a Hard Habit to Break," *Wall Street Journal* (September 18, 2003): B3A.

15. Amy Merrick, "U.S. Research Spending to Rise Only 3.2 Percent," *Wall Street Journal* (December 28, 2001): A2.

16. Pier Abetti, "Technology: A Key Strategic Resource," *Management Review* 78, no. 2 (February 1989): 38.

17. Adapted from Edward Baig, "Welcome to the Officeless Office," *BusinessWeek* (June 26, 1995).

Current Readings

Balmer, John M., Helen Stuart, and Stephen A. Greyser. "Aligning Identity and Strategy: Corporate Branding at British Airways in the Late 20th Century." *California Management Review* (Spring 2009): 6–23.

Bartol, Kathryn M., Dmitry M. Khanin, Michael D. Pfarrer, Ken G. Smith, and Xiaomeng Zhang. "CEOs on the Edge: Earnings Manipulation and Stock-Based Incentive Misalignment." *The Academy of Management Journal* 51, no. 2 (April 2008): 241.

Choi, Jaepil, and Heli Wang. "Stakeholder Relations and the Persistence of Corporate Financial Performance." *Strategic Management Journal* (August 2009): 895–907.

Fernando, Chitru S., and Mark P. Sharfman. "Environmental Risk Management and the Cost of Capital." *Strategic Management Journal* 29, no. 6 (June 2008): 569.

Finkbeiner, Carl, Dominique M. Hanssens, and Daniel Thorpe. "Marketing When Customer Equity Matters." *Harvard Business Review* (May 2008): 117.

Harrington, Richard J., and Anthony K. Tjan. "Transforming Strategy One Customer at a Time." *Harvard Business Review* (March 2008): 62.

Kumar, Minu, and Charles H. Noble. "Using Product Design Strategically to Create Deeper Consumer Connections." *Business Horizons* 51, no. 5 (September–October 2008): 441.

Levitas, Edward, and Ann McFadyen. "Managing Liquidity in Research-Intensive Firms: Signaling and Cash Flow Effects of Patents and Alliance Activities." *Strategic Management Journal* (June 2009): 659–678.

Morgan, Neil, Douglas Vorhies, and Charlotte Mason. "Market Orientation, Marketing Capabilities and Firm Performance." *Strategic Management Journal* (August 2009): 909–920.

Chowdhury, Shamaud, and Eric Wang. "Institutional Activism Types and CEO Compensation: A Time-Series Analysis of Large Canadian Corporations." *Journal of Management* (February 2009): 5–38.

ASSURANCE OF LEARNING EXERCISES

Assurance of Learning Exercise 8A

Developing a Product-Positioning Map for McDonald's

Purpose

Organizations continually monitor how their products and services are positioned relative to competitors. This information is especially useful for marketing managers but is also used by other managers and strategists.

Instructions

Step 1   On a separate sheet of paper, develop a product-positioning map for McDonald's, Wendy's, Burger King, and Hardee's. Include in your diagram.

Step 2   At the chalkboard, diagram your product-positioning map.

Step 3   Compare your product-positioning map with those diagrammed by other students. Discuss any major differences.

Assurance of Learning Exercise 8B

Performing an EPS/EBIT Analysis for McDonald's

Purpose

An EPS/EBIT analysis is one of the most widely used techniques for determining the extent that debt and/or stock should be used to finance strategies to be implemented. This exercise can give you practice performing EPS/EBIT analysis.

Instructions (1-1-10 Data)

Let's say McDonald's needs to raise $1 billion to expand into Africa. Determine whether McDonald's should have used all debt, all stock, or a 50-50 combination of debt and stock to finance this market-development strategy. Assume a 38 percent tax rate, 5 percent interest rate, McDonald's stock price of $50 per share, and an annual dividend of $0.30 per share of common stock. The EBIT range for 2010 is between $6.332 billion and $9 billion. A total of 1 billion shares of common stock are outstanding. Develop an EPS/EBIT chart to reflect your analysis.

Assurance of Learning Exercise 8C

Preparing Projected Financial Statements for McDonald's

Purpose

This exercise is designed to give you experience preparing projected financial statements. Pro forma analysis is a central strategy-implementation technique because it allows managers to anticipate and evaluate the expected results of various strategy-implementation approaches.

Instructions

Step 1   Work with a classmate. Develop a 2008 projected income statement and balance sheet for McDonald's. Assume that McDonald's plans to raise $900 million in 2010 to begin serving Africa and plans to obtain 50 percent financing from a bank and 50 percent financing from a stock issuance. Make other assumptions as needed, and state them clearly in written form.

Step 2   Compute McDonald's current ratio, debt-to-equity ratio, and return-on-investment ratio for 2008 and 2009. How do your 2010 projected ratios compare to the 2008 and 2009 ratios? Why is it important to make this comparison? Use http://finance.yahoo.com to obtain 2009 financial statements.

Step 3   Bring your projected statements to class, and discuss any problems or questions you encountered.

Step 4   Compare your projected statements to the statements of other students. What major differences exist between your analysis and the work of other students?

Assurance of Learning Exercise 8D

Determining the Cash Value of McDonald's

Purpose

It is simply good business practice to periodically determine the financial worth or cash value of your company. This exercise gives you practice determining the total worth of a company using several methods. Use year-end 2008 data as given in the Cohesion Case on pages 31–32.

Instructions

Step 1   Calculate the financial worth of McDonald's based on four methods: (1) the net worth or stockholders' equity, (2) the future value of McDonald's earnings, (3) the price-earnings ratio, and (4) the outstanding shares method.

Step 2   In a dollar amount, how much is McDonald's worth?

Step 3   Compare your analyses and conclusions with those of other students.

Assurance of Learning Exercise 8E

Developing a Product-Positioning Map for My University

Purpose

The purpose of this exercise is to give you practice developing product-positioning maps. Nonprofit organizations, such as universities, are increasingly using product-positioning maps to determine effective ways to implement strategies.

Instructions

Step 1   Join with two other people in class to form a group of three.

Step 2   Jointly prepare a product-positioning map that includes your institution and four other colleges or universities in your state.

Step 3   At the chalkboard, diagram your product-positioning map.

Step 4   Discuss differences among the maps diagrammed on the board.

Assurance of Learning Exercise 8F

Do Banks Require Projected Financial Statements?

Purpose

The purpose of this exercise is to explore the practical importance and use of projected financial statements in the banking business.

Instructions

Contact two local bankers by phone and seek answers to the questions that follow. Record the answers you receive, and report your findings to the class.

1. Does your bank require projected financial statements as part of a business loan application?
2. How does your bank use projected financial statements when they are part of a business loan application?
3. What special advice do you give potential business borrowers in preparing projected financial statements?

CHAPTER 9
Strategy Review, Evaluation, and Control

CHAPTER OBJECTIVES

After studying this chapter, you should be able to do the following:

1. Describe a practical framework for evaluating strategies.

2. Explain why strategy evaluation is complex, sensitive, and yet essential for organizational success.

3. Discuss the importance of contingency planning in strategy evaluation.

4. Discuss the role of auditing in strategy evaluation.

5. Explain how computers can aid in evaluating strategies.

6. Discuss the Balanced Scorecard.

7. Discuss three twenty-first-century challenges in strategic management.

Assurance of Learning Exercises

Assurance of Learning Exercise 9A
Preparing a Strategy-Evaluation Report for McDonald's

Assurance of Learning Exercise 9B
Evaluating My University's Strategies

Source: Shutterstock/Diego Cervo

"Notable Quotes"

"Complicated controls do not work. They confuse. They misdirect attention from what is to be controlled to the mechanics and methodology of the control."

—Seymour Tilles

"Although Plan A may be selected as the most realistic . . . the other major alternatives should not be forgotten. They may well serve as contingency plans."

—Dale McConkey

"Organizations are most vulnerable when they are at the peak of their success."

—R. T. Lenz

"Strategy evaluation must make it as easy as possible for managers to revise their plans and reach quick agreement on the changes."

—Dale McConkey

"While strategy is a word that is usually associated with the future, its link to the past is no less central. Life is lived forward but understood backward. Managers may live strategy in the future, but they understand it through the past."

—Henry Mintzberg

"Unless strategy evaluation is performed seriously and systematically, and unless strategists are willing to act on the results, energy will be used up defending yesterday. No one will have the time, resources, or will to work on exploiting today, let alone to work on making tomorrow."

—Peter Drucker

"Executives, consultants, and B-school professors all agree that strategic planning is now the single most important management issue and will remain so for the next five years. Strategy has become a part of the main agenda at lots of organizations today. Strategic planning is back with a vengeance."

—John Byrne

"Planners should not plan, but serve as facilitators, catalysts, inquirers, educators, and synthesizers to guide the planning process effectively."

—A. Hax and N. Majluf

Doing Great in a Weak Economy. How?

Family Dollar Stores

Founded in 1959 by the father of CEO Howard Levine, Family Dollar Stores (FDO) is doing great in the ongoing recession as cash-strapped consumers hunt for bargains. The company's second-quarter 2009 results exceeded expectations: Sales were up 8.7 percent from last year to $2 billion. Pro-forma earnings are expected to be between 59 and 61 cents per share, safely ahead of the consensus estimate of 50 cents. Family Dollar's same-store sales, a key retail metric, were up 6.4 percent the second quarter of 2009. FDO's fiscal 2009 3rd quarter earnings increased another 36 percent.

Family Dollar's earnings held up well throughout the global recession, beating estimates in each of the last four quarters. The company was one of three S&P 500 companies to have a rising stock price in 2008. For fiscal 2008, FDO's sales increased from $6.8 billion to $6.9 billion. The company's net income for 2008 was $233 million.

The nation's number two dollar store (behind Dollar General), Family Dollar targets women shopping for a family that earns less than $30,000 a year. Family Dollar operates about 6,600 stores in some 45 states and the District of Columbia. Consumables (food, health and beauty aids, and household products) account for about 60 percent of sales; the stores also sell apparel, shoes, and linens. Family Dollar emphasizes neighborhood stores near its low- and middle-income customers in rural and urban areas. Most merchandise is less than $10.

The best formulated and best implemented strategies become obsolete as a firm's external and internal environments change. It is essential, therefore, that strategists systematically review, evaluate, and control the execution of strategies. This chapter presents a framework that can guide managers' efforts to evaluate strategic-management activities, to make sure they are working, and to make timely changes. Management information systems being used to evaluate strategies are discussed. Guidelines are presented for formulating, implementing, and evaluating strategies. Family Dollar Stores evaluates strategies well.

The Nature of Strategy Evaluation

The strategic-management process results in decisions that can have significant, long-lasting consequences. Erroneous strategic decisions can inflict severe penalties and can be exceedingly difficult, if not impossible, to reverse. Most strategists agree, therefore, that strategy evaluation is vital to an organization's well-being; timely evaluations can alert management to problems or potential problems before a situation becomes critical. Strategy evaluation includes three basic activities: (1) examining the underlying bases of a firm's strategy, (2) comparing expected results with actual results, and (3) taking corrective actions to ensure that performance conforms to plans. The strategy-evaluation stage of the strategic-management process is illustrated in Figure 9-1.

FIGURE 9-1

A Comprehensive Strategic-Management Model

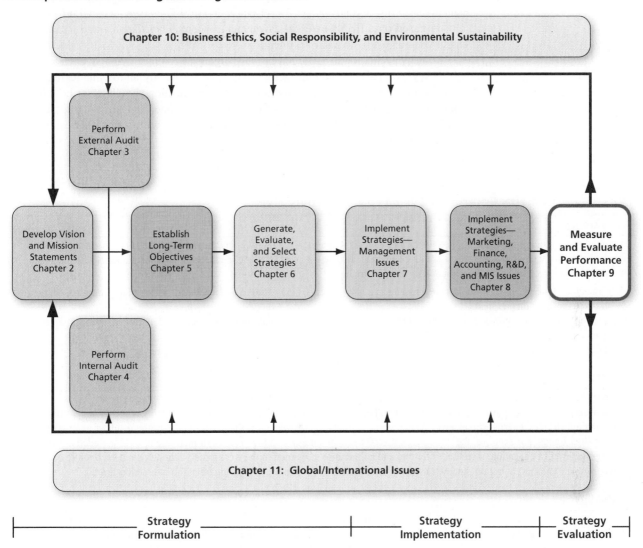

Source: Fred R. David, "How Companies Define Their Mission," *Long Range Planning* 22, no. 3 (June 1988): 40.

Adequate and timely feedback is the cornerstone of effective strategy evaluation. Strategy evaluation can be no better than the information on which it is based. Too much pres sure from top managers may result in lower managers contriving numbers they think will be satisfactory.

Strategy evaluation can be a complex and sensitive undertaking. Too much emphasis on evaluating strategies may be expensive and counterproductive. No one likes to be evaluated too closely! The more managers attempt to evaluate the behavior of others, the less control they have. Yet too little or no evaluation can create even worse problems. Strategy evaluation is essential to ensure that stated objectives are being achieved.

In many organizations, strategy evaluation is simply an appraisal of how well an organization has performed. Have the firm's assets increased? Has there been an increase in profitability? Have sales increased? Have productivity levels increased? Have profit margin, return on investment, and earnings-per-share ratios increased? Some firms argue that their strategy must have been correct if the answers to these types of questions are affirmative. Well, the strategy or strategies may have been correct, but this type of reasoning can be misleading because strategy evaluation must have both a long-run and short-run focus. Strategies often do not affect short-term operating results until it is too late to make needed changes.

It is impossible to demonstrate conclusively that a particular strategy is optimal or even to guarantee that it will work. One can, however, evaluate it for critical flaws. Richard Rumelt offered four criteria that could be used to evaluate a strategy: consistency, consonance, feasibility, and advantage. Described in Table 9-1, *consonance* and *advantage* are mostly based on a firm's external assessment, whereas *consistency* and *feasibility* are largely based on an internal assessment.

Strategy evaluation is important because organizations face dynamic environments in which key external and internal factors often change quickly and dramatically. Success today is no guarantee of success tomorrow! An organization should never be lulled into complacency with success. Countless firms have thrived one year only to struggle for survival the following year. Organizational trouble can come swiftly, as further evidenced by the examples described in Table 9-2.

TABLE 9-1 Rumelt's Criteria for Evaluating Strategies

Consistency

A strategy should not present inconsistent goals and policies. Organizational conflict and interdepartmental bickering are often symptoms of managerial disorder, but these problems may also be a sign of strategic inconsistency. Three guidelines help determine if organizational problems are due to inconsistencies in strategy:

- If managerial problems continue despite changes in personnel and if they tend to be issue-based rather than people-based, then strategies may be inconsistent.
- If success for one organizational department means, or is interpreted to mean, failure for another department, then strategies may be inconsistent.
- If policy problems and issues continue to be brought to the top for resolution, then strategies may be inconsistent.

Consonance

Consonance refers to the need for strategists to examine *sets of trends*, as well as individual trends, in evaluating strategies. A strategy must represent an adaptive response to the external environment and to the critical changes occurring within it. One difficulty in matching a firm's key internal and external factors in the formulation of strategy is that most trends are the result of interactions among other trends. For example, the day-care explosion came about as a combined result of many trends that included a rise in the average level of education, increased inflation, and an increase in women in the workforce. Although single economic or demographic trends might appear steady for many years, there are waves of change going on at the interaction level.

Feasibility

A strategy must neither overtax available resources nor create unsolvable subproblems. The final broad test of strategy is its feasibility; that is, can the strategy be attempted within the physical, human, and financial resources of the enterprise? The financial resources of a business are the easiest to quantify and are normally the first limitation against which strategy is evaluated. It is sometimes forgotten, however, that innovative approaches to financing are often possible. Devices, such as captive subsidiaries, sale-leaseback arrangements, and tying plant mortgages to long-term contracts, have all been used effectively to help win key positions in suddenly expanding industries. A less quantifiable, but actually more rigid, limitation on strategic choice is that imposed by individual and organizational capabilities. In evaluating a strategy, it is important to examine whether an organization has demonstrated in the past that it possesses the abilities, competencies, skills, and talents needed to carry out a given strategy.

Advantage

A strategy must provide for the creation and/or maintenance of a competitive advantage in a selected area of activity. Competitive advantages normally are the result of superiority in one of three areas: (1) resources, (2) skills, or (3) position. The idea that the positioning of one's resources can enhance their combined effectiveness is familiar to military theorists, chess players, and diplomats. Position can also play a crucial role in an organization's strategy. Once gained, a good position is defensible—meaning that it is so costly to capture that rivals are deterred from full-scale attacks. Positional advantage tends to be self-sustaining as long as the key internal and environmental factors that underlie it remain stable. This is why entrenched firms can be almost impossible to unseat, even if their raw skill levels are only average. Although not all positional advantages are associated with size, it is true that larger organizations tend to operate in markets and use procedures that turn their size into advantage, while smaller firms seek product/market positions that exploit other types of advantage. The principal characteristic of good position is that it permits the firm to obtain advantage from policies that would not similarly benefit rivals without the same position. Therefore, in evaluating strategy, organizations should examine the nature of positional advantages associated with a given strategy.

Source: Adapted from Richard Rumelt, "The Evaluation of Business Strategy," in W. F. Glueck (ed.), *Business Policy and Strategic Management* (New York: McGraw-Hill, 1980): 359–367. Used with permission.

TABLE 9-2   Examples of Organizational Demise

A. Some Large Companies That Experienced a Large Drop in Revenues in 2008 vs. 2007		B. Some Large Companies That Experienced a Large Drop in Profits in 2008 vs. 2007	
Molson Coors Brewing	−23%	UAL	−1,427%
Citigroup	−29%	Sonic Automotive	−818%
Morgan Stanley	−29%	Citigroup	−865%
Goldman Sachs Group	−39%	CBS	−1,036%
Fannie Mae	−48%	Rite Aid	−4,122%
Freddie Mac	−71%	Pilgrim's Pride	−2,224%
Weyerhaeuser	−32%	Centex	−1,090%
Centex	−41%	Harrah's Entertainment	−939%
Pulte Homes	−32%	American International Group	−1,701%
Massachusetts Mutual Life	−26%	Gannett	−730%
Allstate	−20%	OfficeMax	−899%
American International Group	−90%	Brunswick	−806%
Hartford Financial	−64%	Brightpoint	−822%
Atria Group	−58%	Owens Corning	−974%

Strategy evaluation is becoming increasingly difficult with the passage of time, for many reasons. Domestic and world economies were more stable in years past, product life cycles were longer, product development cycles were longer, technological advancement was slower, change occurred less frequently, there were fewer competitors, foreign companies were weak, and there were more regulated industries. Other reasons why strategy evaluation is more difficult today include the following trends:

1.   A dramatic increase in the environment's complexity
2.   The increasing difficulty of predicting the future with accuracy
3.   The increasing number of variables
4.   The rapid rate of obsolescence of even the best plans
5.   The increase in the number of both domestic and world events affecting organizations
6.   The decreasing time span for which planning can be done with any degree of certainty[1]

A fundamental problem facing managers today is how to control employees effectively in light of modern organizational demands for greater flexibility, innovation, creativity, and initiative from employees.[2] How can managers today ensure that empowered employees acting in an entrepreneurial manner do not put the well-being of the business at risk? Recall that Kidder, Peabody & Company lost $350 million when one of its traders allegedly booked fictitious profits; Sears, Roebuck and Company took a $60 million charge against earnings after admitting that its automobile service businesses were performing unnecessary repairs. The costs to companies such as these in terms of damaged reputations, fines, missed opportunities, and diversion of management's attention are enormous.

When empowered employees are held accountable for and pressured to achieve specific goals and are given wide latitude in their actions to achieve them, there can be dysfunctional behavior. For example, Nordstrom, the upscale fashion retailer known for outstanding customer service, was subjected to lawsuits and fines when employees underreported hours worked in order to increase their sales per hour—the company's primary performance criterion. Nordstrom's customer service and earnings were enhanced until the misconduct was reported, at which time severe penalties were levied against the firm.

The Process of Evaluating Strategies

Strategy evaluation is necessary for all sizes and kinds of organizations. Strategy evaluation should initiate managerial questioning of expectations and assumptions, should trigger a review of objectives and values, and should stimulate creativity in generating alternatives and formulating criteria of evaluation.[3] Regardless of the size of the organization, a certain amount of *management by wandering around* at all levels is essential to effective strategy evaluation. Strategy-evaluation activities should be performed on a continuing basis, rather than at the end of specified periods of time or just after problems occur. Waiting until the end of the year, for example, could result in a firm closing the barn door after the horses have already escaped.

Evaluating strategies on a continuous rather than on a periodic basis allows benchmarks of progress to be established and more effectively monitored. Some strategies take years to implement; consequently, associated results may not become apparent for years. Successful strategies combine patience with a willingness to promptly take corrective actions when necessary. There always comes a time when corrective actions are needed in an organization! Centuries ago, a writer (perhaps Solomon) made the following observations about change:

> There is a time for everything,
> A time to be born and a time to die,
> A time to plant and a time to uproot,
> A time to kill and a time to heal,
> A time to tear down and a time to build,
> A time to weep and a time to laugh,
> A time to mourn and a time to dance,
> A time to scatter stones and a time to gather them,
> A time to embrace and a time to refrain,
> A time to search and a time to give up,
> A time to keep and a time to throw away,
> A time to tear and a time to mend,
> A time to be silent and a time to speak,
> A time to love and a time to hate,
> A time for war and a time for peace.[4]

Managers and employees of the firm should be continually aware of progress being made toward achieving the firm's objectives. As critical success factors change, organizational members should be involved in determining appropriate corrective actions. If assumptions and expectations deviate significantly from forecasts, then the firm should renew strategy-formulation activities, perhaps sooner than planned. In strategy evaluation, like strategy formulation and strategy implementation, people make the difference. Through involvement in the process of evaluating strategies, managers and employees become committed to keeping the firm moving steadily toward achieving objectives.

A Strategy-Evaluation Framework

Table 9-3 summarizes strategy-evaluation activities in terms of key questions that should be addressed, alternative answers to those questions, and appropriate actions for an organization to take. Notice that corrective actions are almost always needed except when (1) external and internal factors have not significantly changed and (2) the firm is progressing satisfactorily toward achieving stated objectives. Relationships among strategy-evaluation activities are illustrated in Figure 9-2.

Reviewing Bases of Strategy

As shown in Figure 9-2, *reviewing the underlying bases of an organization's strategy* could be approached by developing a revised EFE Matrix and IFE Matrix. A *revised IFE Matrix* should focus on changes in the organization's management, marketing, finance/accounting,

TABLE 9-3   A Strategy-Evaluation Assessment Matrix

Have Major Changes Occurred in the Firm Internal Strategic Position?	Have Major Changes Occurred in the Firm External Strategic Position?	Has the Firm Progressed Satisfactorily Toward Achieving Its Stated Objectives?	Result
No	No	No	Take corrective actions
Yes	Yes	Yes	Take corrective actions
Yes	Yes	No	Take corrective actions
Yes	No	Yes	Take corrective actions
Yes	No	No	Take corrective actions
No	Yes	Yes	Take corrective actions
No	Yes	No	Take corrective actions
No	No	Yes	Continue present strategic course

production/operations, R&D, and management information systems strengths and weaknesses. A *revised EFE Matrix* should indicate how effective a firm's strategies have been in response to key opportunities and threats. This analysis could also address such questions as the following:

1. How have competitors reacted to our strategies?
2. How have competitors' strategies changed?
3. Have major competitors' strengths and weaknesses changed?
4. Why are competitors making certain strategic changes?
5. Why are some competitors' strategies more successful than others?
6. How satisfied are our competitors with their present market positions and profitability?
7. How far can our major competitors be pushed before retaliating?
8. How could we more effectively cooperate with our competitors?

Numerous external and internal factors can prevent firms from achieving long-term and annual objectives. Externally, actions by competitors, changes in demand, changes in technology, economic changes, demographic shifts, and governmental actions may prevent objectives from being accomplished. Internally, ineffective strategies may have been chosen or implementation activities may have been poor. Objectives may have been too optimistic. Thus, failure to achieve objectives may not be the result of unsatisfactory work by managers and employees. All organizational members need to know this to encourage their support for strategy-evaluation activities. Organizations desperately need to know as soon as possible when their strategies are not effective. Sometimes managers and employees on the front lines discover this well before strategists.

External opportunities and threats and internal strengths and weaknesses that represent the bases of current strategies should continually be monitored for change. It is not really a question of whether these factors will change but rather when they will change and in what ways. Here are some key questions to address in evaluating strategies:

1. Are our internal strengths still strengths?
2. Have we added other internal strengths? If so, what are they?
3. Are our internal weaknesses still weaknesses?
4. Do we now have other internal weaknesses? If so, what are they?
5. Are our external opportunities still opportunities?
6. Are there now other external opportunities? If so, what are they?
7. Are our external threats still threats?
8. Are there now other external threats? If so, what are they?
9. Are we vulnerable to a hostile takeover?

FIGURE 9-2

A Strategy-Evaluation Framework

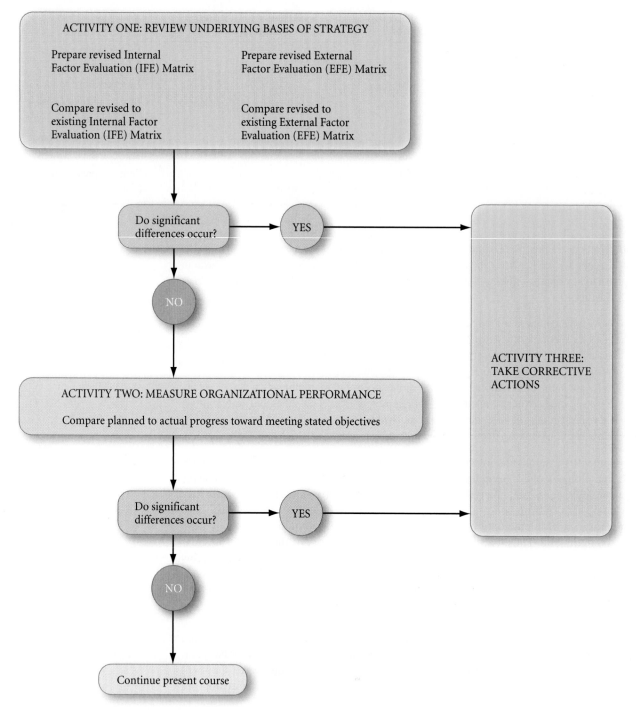

Measuring Organizational Performance

Another important strategy-evaluation activity is *measuring organizational performance*. This activity includes comparing expected results to actual results, investigating deviations from plans, evaluating individual performance, and examining progress being made toward meeting stated objectives. Both long-term and annual objectives are commonly used in this process. Criteria for evaluating strategies should be measurable and easily verifiable. Criteria that predict results may be more important than those that reveal what already has happened. For example, rather than simply being informed that sales in the last quarter were 20 percent under what was expected, strategists need to know that sales in the next quarter may be 20 percent below standard unless some action is taken to counter the trend. Really effective control requires accurate forecasting.

Failure to make satisfactory progress toward accomplishing long-term or annual objectives signals a need for corrective actions. Many factors, such as unreasonable policies, unexpected turns in the economy, unreliable suppliers or distributors, or ineffective strategies, can result in unsatisfactory progress toward meeting objectives. Problems can result from ineffectiveness (not doing the right things) or inefficiency (poorly doing the right things).

Many variables can and should be included in measuring organizational performance. As indicated in Table 9-4, typically a favorable or unfavorable variance is recorded monthly, quarterly, and annually, and resultant actions needed are then determined.

Determining which objectives are most important in the evaluation of strategies can be difficult. Strategy evaluation is based on both quantitative and qualitative criteria. Selecting the exact set of criteria for evaluating strategies depends on a particular organization's size, industry, strategies, and management philosophy. An organization pursuing a retrenchment strategy, for example, could have an entirely different set of evaluative criteria from an organization pursuing a market-development strategy. Quantitative criteria commonly used to evaluate strategies are financial ratios, which strategists use to make three critical comparisons: (1) comparing the firm's performance over different time periods, (2) comparing the firm's performance to competitors', and (3) comparing the firm's performance to industry averages. Some key financial ratios that are particularly useful as criteria for strategy evaluation are as follows:

1. Return on investment (ROI)
2. Return on equity (ROE)
3. Profit margin
4. Market share
5. Debt to equity
6. Earnings per share
7. Sales growth
8. Asset growth

TABLE 9-4   A Sample Framework for Measuring Organizational Performance

Factor	Actual Result	Expected Result	Variance	Action Needed
Corporate Revenues				
Corporate Profits				
Corporate ROI				
Region 1 Revenues				
Region 1 Profits				
Region 1 ROI				
Region 2 Revenues				
Region 2 Profits				
Region 2 ROI				
Product 1 Revenues				
Product 1 Profits				
Product 1 ROI				
Product 2 Revenues				
Product 2 Profits				
Product 2 ROI				

But some potential problems are associated with using quantitative criteria for evaluating strategies. First, most quantitative criteria are geared to annual objectives rather than long-term objectives. Also, different accounting methods can provide different results on many quantitative criteria. Third, intuitive judgments are almost always involved in deriving quantitative criteria. For these and other reasons, qualitative criteria are also important in evaluating strategies. Human factors such as high absenteeism and turnover rates, poor production quality and quantity rates, or low employee satisfaction can be underlying causes of declining performance. Marketing, finance/accounting, R&D, or management information systems factors can also cause financial problems.

Some additional key questions that reveal the need for qualitative or intuitive judgments in strategy evaluation are as follows:

1. How good is the firm's balance of investments between high-risk and low-risk projects?
2. How good is the firm's balance of investments between long-term and short-term projects?
3. How good is the firm's balance of investments between slow-growing markets and fast-growing markets?
4. How good is the firm's balance of investments among different divisions?
5. To what extent are the firm's alternative strategies socially responsible?
6. What are the relationships among the firm's key internal and external strategic factors?
7. How are major competitors likely to respond to particular strategies?

Taking Corrective Actions

The final strategy-evaluation activity, *taking corrective actions,* requires making changes to competitively reposition a firm for the future. As indicated in Table 9-5, examples of changes that may be needed are altering an organization's structure, replacing one or more key individuals, selling a division, or revising a business mission. Other changes could include establishing or revising objectives, devising new policies, issuing stock to raise capital, adding additional salespersons, differently allocating resources, or developing new performance incentives. Taking corrective actions does not necessarily mean that existing strategies will be abandoned or even that new strategies must be formulated.

The probabilities and possibilities for incorrect or inappropriate actions increase geometrically with an arithmetic increase in personnel. Any person directing an overall undertaking must check on the actions of the participants as well as the results that they have achieved. If either the actions or results do not comply with preconceived or planned achievements, then corrective actions are needed.[5]

TABLE 9-5 Corrective Actions Possibly Needed to Correct Unfavorable Variances

1. Alter the firm's structure
2. Replace one or more key individuals
3. Divest a division
4. Alter the firm's vision and/or mission
5. Revise objectives
6. Alter strategies
7. Devise new policies
8. Install new performance incentives
9. Raise capital with stock or debt
10. Add or terminate salespersons, employees, or managers
11. Allocate resources differently
12. Outsource (or rein in) business functions

No organization can survive as an island; no organization can escape change. Taking corrective actions is necessary to keep an organization on track toward achieving stated objectives. In his thought-provoking books *Future Shock* and *The Third Wave,* Alvin Toffler argued that business environments are becoming so dynamic and complex that they threaten people and organizations with *future shock,* which occurs when the nature, types, and speed of changes overpower an individual's or organization's ability and capacity to adapt. Strategy evaluation enhances an organization's ability to adapt successfully to changing circumstances.

Taking corrective actions raises employees' and managers' anxieties. Research suggests that participation in strategy-evaluation activities is one of the best ways to overcome individuals' resistance to change. According to Erez and Kanfer, individuals accept change best when they have a cognitive understanding of the changes, a sense of control over the situation, and an awareness that necessary actions are going to be taken to implement the changes.[6]

Strategy evaluation can lead to strategy-formulation changes, strategy-implementation changes, both formulation and implementation changes, or no changes at all. Strategists cannot escape having to revise strategies and implementation approaches sooner or later. Hussey and Langham offered the following insight on taking corrective actions:

> Resistance to change is often emotionally based and not easily overcome by rational argument. Resistance may be based on such feelings as loss of status, implied criticism of present competence, fear of failure in the new situation, annoyance at not being consulted, lack of understanding of the need for change, or insecurity in changing from well-known and fixed methods. It is necessary, therefore, to overcome such resistance by creating situations of participation and full explanation when changes are envisaged.[7]

Corrective actions should place an organization in a better position to capitalize upon internal strengths; to take advantage of key external opportunities; to avoid, reduce, or mitigate external threats; and to improve internal weaknesses. Corrective actions should have a proper time horizon and an appropriate amount of risk. They should be internally consistent and socially responsible. Perhaps most important, corrective actions strengthen an organization's competitive position in its basic industry. Continuous strategy evaluation keeps strategists close to the pulse of an organization and provides information needed for an effective strategic-management system. Carter Bayles described the benefits of strategy evaluation as follows:

> Evaluation activities may renew confidence in the current business strategy or point to the need for actions to correct some weaknesses, such as erosion of product superiority or technological edge. In many cases, the benefits of strategy evaluation are much more far-reaching, for the outcome of the process may be a fundamentally new strategy that will lead, even in a business that is already turning a respectable profit, to substantially increased earnings. It is this possibility that justifies strategy evaluation, for the payoff can be very large.[8]

The Balanced Scorecard

Introduced earlier in the Chapter 5 discussion of objectives, the Balanced Scorecard is an important strategy-evaluation tool. It is a process that allows firms to evaluate strategies from four perspectives: financial performance, customer knowledge, internal business processes, and learning and growth. The *Balanced Scorecard* analysis requires that firms seek answers to the following questions and utilize that information, in conjunction with financial measures, to adequately and more effectively evaluate strategies being implemented:

1. How well is the firm continually improving and creating value along measures such as innovation, technological leadership, product quality, operational process efficiencies, and so on?

2. How well is the firm sustaining and even improving upon its core competencies and competitive advantages?

3. How satisfied are the firm's customers?

A sample Balanced Scorecard is provided in Table 9-6. Notice that the firm examines six key issues in evaluating its strategies: (1) Customers, (2) Managers/Employees, (3) Operations/Processes, (4) Community/Social Responsibility, (5) Business Ethics/Natural Environment, and (6) Financial. The basic form of a Balanced Scorecard may differ for different organizations. The Balanced Scorecard approach to strategy evaluation aims to balance long-term with short-term concerns, to balance financial with nonfinancial concerns, and to balance internal with external concerns. It can be an excellent management tool, and it is used successfully today by Chemical Bank, Exxon/Mobil Corporation, CIGNA Property and Casualty Insurance, and numerous other firms. The Balanced Scorecard would be constructed differently, that is, adapted, to particular firms in various industries with the underlying theme or thrust being the same, which is to evaluate the firm's strategies based upon both key quantitative and qualitative measures.

TABLE 9-6   An Example Balanced Scorecard

Area of Objectives	Measure or Target	Time Expectation	Primary Responsibility
Customers			
1.			
2.			
3.			
4.			
Managers/Employees			
1.			
2.			
3.			
4.			
Operations/Processes			
1.			
2.			
3.			
4.			
Community/Social Responsibility			
1.			
2.			
3.			
4.			
Business Ethics/Natural Environment			
1.			
2.			
3.			
4.			
Financial			
1.			
2.			
3.			
4.			

Published Sources of Strategy-Evaluation Information

A number of publications are helpful in evaluating a firm's strategies. For example, *Fortune* annually identifies and evaluates the Fortune 1,000 (the largest manufacturers) and the Fortune 50 (the largest retailers, transportation companies, utilities, banks, insurance companies, and diversified financial corporations in the United States). *Fortune* ranks the best and worst performers on various factors, such as return on investment, sales volume, and profitability. In its March issue each year, *Fortune* publishes its strategy-evaluation research in an article entitled "America's Most Admired Companies." Eight key attributes serve as evaluative criteria: people management; innovativeness; quality of products or services; financial soundness; social responsibility; use of corporate assets; long-term investment; and quality of management. In October of each year, *Fortune* publishes additional strategy-evaluation research in an article entitled "The World's Most Admired Companies." *Fortune's* 2009 evaluation in Table 9-7 reveals the firms most admired (best managed) in their industry. The most admired company in the world in 2009 was Nike, followed by Anheuser-Busch, Nestle, and Procter & Gamble.[9]

Another excellent evaluation of corporations in America, "The Annual Report on American Industry," is published annually in the January issue of *Forbes*. It provides a detailed and comprehensive evaluation of hundreds of U.S. companies in many different industries. *BusinessWeek*, *Industry Week*, and *Dun's Business Month* also periodically publish detailed evaluations of U.S. businesses and industries. Although published sources of strategy-evaluation information focus primarily on large, publicly held businesses, the comparative ratios and related information are widely used to evaluate small businesses and privately owned firms as well.

TABLE 9-7   The Most Admired Company in Various Industries (2009)

Industry	The Most Admired Company
Apparel	Nike
Beverages	Anheuser-Busch
Consumer food products	Nestle
Soaps and cosmetics	Procter & Gamble
Credit card services	Visa
Insurance	Berkshire Hathaway
Megabanks	Bank of America
Forest and paper products	International Paper
Pharmaceuticals	Johnson & Johnson
Petroleum refining	Exxon Mobil
Electronics	General Electric
Food services	McDonald's
Railroads	Union Pacific
Motor vehicles	BMW
Industrial and farm equipment	Caterpillar
Airlines	Continental Airlines
Aerospace and defense	United Technologies
Metals	Alcoa

Source: Based on Adam Lashinsky, "The World's Most Admired Companies," *Fortune* (March 16, 2009): 81–91.

Characteristics of an Effective Evaluation System

Strategy evaluation must meet several basic requirements to be effective. First, strategy-evaluation activities must be economical; too much information can be just as bad as too little information; and too many controls can do more harm than good. Strategy-evaluation activities also should be meaningful; they should specifically relate to a firm's objectives. They should provide managers with useful information about tasks over which they have control and influence. Strategy-evaluation activities should provide timely information; on occasion and in some areas, managers may daily need information. For example, when a firm has diversified by acquiring another firm, evaluative information may be needed frequently. However, in an R&D department, daily or even weekly evaluative information could be dysfunctional. Approximate information that is timely is generally more desirable as a basis for strategy evaluation than accurate information that does not depict the present. Frequent measurement and rapid reporting may frustrate control rather than give better control. The time dimension of control must coincide with the time span of the event being measured.

Strategy evaluation should be designed to provide a true picture of what is happening. For example, in a severe economic downturn, productivity and profitability ratios may drop alarmingly, although employees and managers are actually working harder. Strategy evaluations should fairly portray this type of situation. Information derived from the strategy-evaluation process should facilitate action and should be directed to those individuals in the organization who need to take action based on it. Managers commonly ignore evaluative reports that are provided only for informational purposes; not all managers need to receive all reports. Controls need to be action-oriented rather than information-oriented.

The strategy-evaluation process should not dominate decisions; it should foster mutual understanding, trust, and common sense. No department should fail to cooperate with another in evaluating strategies. Strategy evaluations should be simple, not too cumbersome, and not too restrictive. Complex strategy-evaluation systems often confuse people and accomplish little. The test of an effective evaluation system is its usefulness, not its complexity.

Large organizations require a more elaborate and detailed strategy-evaluation system because it is more difficult to coordinate efforts among different divisions and functional areas. Managers in small companies often communicate daily with each other and their employees and do not need extensive evaluative reporting systems. Familiarity with local environments usually makes gathering and evaluating information much easier for small organizations than for large businesses. But the key to an effective strategy-evaluation system may be the ability to convince participants that failure to accomplish certain objectives within a prescribed time is not necessarily a reflection of their performance.

There is no one ideal strategy-evaluation system. The unique characteristics of an organization, including its size, management style, purpose, problems, and strengths, can determine a strategy-evaluation and control system's final design. Robert Waterman offered the following observation about successful organizations' strategy-evaluation and control systems:

> Successful companies treat facts as friends and controls as liberating. Morgan Guaranty and Wells Fargo not only survive but thrive in the troubled waters of bank deregulation, because their strategy evaluation and control systems are sound, their risk is contained, and they know themselves and the competitive situation so well. Successful companies have a voracious hunger for facts. They see information where others see only data. They love comparisons, rankings, anything that removes decision making from the realm of mere opinion. Successful companies maintain tight, accurate financial controls. Their people don't regard controls as an imposition of autocracy but as the benign checks and balances that allow them to be creative and free.[10]

Contingency Planning

A basic premise of good strategic management is that firms plan ways to deal with unfavorable and favorable events before they occur. Too many organizations prepare contingency plans just for unfavorable events; this is a mistake, because both minimizing threats and capitalizing on opportunities can improve a firm's competitive position.

Regardless of how carefully strategies are formulated, implemented, and evaluated, unforeseen events, such as strikes, boycotts, natural disasters, arrival of foreign competitors, and government actions, can make a strategy obsolete. To minimize the impact of potential threats, organizations should develop contingency plans as part of their strategy-evaluation process. *Contingency plans* can be defined as alternative plans that can be put into effect if certain key events do not occur as expected. Only high-priority areas require the insurance of contingency plans. Strategists cannot and should not try to cover all bases by planning for all possible contingencies. But in any case, contingency plans should be as simple as possible.

Some contingency plans commonly established by firms include the following:

1. If a major competitor withdraws from particular markets as intelligence reports indicate, what actions should our firm take?
2. If our sales objectives are not reached, what actions should our firm take to avoid profit losses?
3. If demand for our new product exceeds plans, what actions should our firm take to meet the higher demand?
4. If certain disasters occur—such as loss of computer capabilities; a hostile takeover attempt; loss of patent protection; or destruction of manufacturing facilities because of earthquakes, tornadoes or hurricanes—what actions should our firm take?
5. If a new technological advancement makes our new product obsolete sooner than expected, what actions should our firm take?

Too many organizations discard alternative strategies not selected for implementation although the work devoted to analyzing these options would render valuable information. Alternative strategies not selected for implementation can serve as contingency plans in case the strategy or strategies selected do not work. U.S. companies and governments are increasingly considering nuclear-generated electricity as the most efficient means of power generation. Many contingency plans certainly call for nuclear power rather than for coal- and gas-derived electricity.

When strategy-evaluation activities reveal the need for a major change quickly, an appropriate contingency plan can be executed in a timely way. Contingency plans can promote a strategist's ability to respond quickly to key changes in the internal and external bases of an organization's current strategy. For example, if underlying assumptions about the economy turn out to be wrong and contingency plans are ready, then managers can make appropriate changes promptly.

In some cases, external or internal conditions present unexpected opportunities. When such opportunities occur, contingency plans could allow an organization to quickly capitalize on them. Linneman and Chandran reported that contingency planning gave users, such as DuPont, Dow Chemical, Consolidated Foods, and Emerson Electric, three major benefits: (1) It permitted quick response to change, (2) it prevented panic in crisis situations, and (3) it made managers more adaptable by encouraging them to appreciate just how variable the future can be. They suggested that effective contingency planning involves a seven-step process:

1. Identify both beneficial and unfavorable events that could possibly derail the strategy or strategies.
2. Specify trigger points. Calculate about when contingent events are likely to occur.
3. Assess the impact of each contingent event. Estimate the potential benefit or harm of each contingent event.
4. Develop contingency plans. Be sure that contingency plans are compatible with current strategy and are economically feasible.

5. Assess the counterimpact of each contingency plan. That is, estimate how much each contingency plan will capitalize on or cancel out its associated contingent event. Doing this will quantify the potential value of each contingency plan.

6. Determine early warning signals for key contingent events. Monitor the early warning signals.

7. For contingent events with reliable early warning signals, develop advance action plans to take advantage of the available lead time.[11]

Auditing

A frequently used tool in strategy evaluation is the audit. *Auditing* is defined by the American Accounting Association (AAA) as "a systematic process of objectively obtaining and evaluating evidence regarding assertions about economic actions and events to ascertain the degree of correspondence between these assertions and established criteria, and communicating the results to interested users."[12]

Auditors examine the financial statement of firms to determine whether they have been prepared according to generally accepted accounting principles (GAAP) and whether they fairly represent the activities of the firm. Independent auditors use a set of standards called *generally accepted auditing standards* (GAAS). Public accounting firms often have a consulting arm that provides strategy-evaluation services. The SEC in late 2009 charged General Electric with accounting fraud, specifically for inflating its earnings and revenues in prior years. GE has agreed to pay $50 million to settle the charges. (Students—when preparing projected financial statements as described in Chapter 8, do not inflate the numbers.)

The new era of international financial reporting standards (IFRS) appears unstoppable, and businesses need to go ahead and get ready to use IFRS. Many U.S. companies now report their finances using both the old generally accepted accounting standards (GAAP) and the new IFRS. "If companies don't prepare, if they don't start three years in advance," warns business professor Donna Street at the University of Dayton, "they're going to be in big trouble." GAAP standards comprised 25,000 pages, whereas IFRS comprises only 5,000 pages, so in that sense IFRS is less cumbersome.

This accounting switch from GAAP to IFRS in the United States is going to cost businesses millions of dollars in fees and upgraded software systems and training. U.S. CPAs need to study global accounting principles intensely, and business schools should go ahead and begin teaching students the new accounting standards.

All companies have the option to use the IFRS procedures in 2011, and then all companies are required to use IFRS in 2014, unless that timetable is changed. The U.S. Chamber of Commerce supports the change, saying it will lead to much more cross-border commerce and will help the United States compete in the world economy. Already the European Union and 113 nations have adopted or soon plan to use international rules, including Australia, China, India, Mexico, and Canada. So the United States likely will also adopt IFRS rules on schedule, but this switch could unleash a legal and regulatory nightmare. The United States lags the rest of the world in global accounting. But a few U.S. multinational firms already use IFRS for their foreign subsidiaries, such as United Technologies (UT). UT derives more than 60 percent of its revenues from abroad and is already training its entire staff to use IFRS. UT has redone its 2007 through 2009 financial statements in the IFRS format.

Movement to IFRS from GAAP encompasses a company's entire operations, including auditing, oversight, cash management, taxes, technology, software, investing, acquiring, merging, importing, exporting, pension planning, and partnering. Switching from GAAP to IFRS is also likely to be plagued by gaping differences in business customs, financial regulations, tax laws, politics, and other factors. One critic of the upcoming switch is Charles Niemeier of the Public Company Accounting Oversight Board, who says the switch "has the potential to be a Tower of Babel," costing firms millions when they do not even have thousands to spend.

Others say the switch will help U.S. companies raise capital abroad and do business with firms abroad. Perhaps the biggest upside of the switch is that IFRS rules are more streamlined and less complex than GAAP. Lenovo, the China-based technology firm that bought IBM's personal computer business, is a big advocate of IFRS. Lenovo's view is that they desire to be a world company rather than a U.S. or Chinese company, so the faster the switch to IFRS, the better for them. The bottom line is that IFRS is coming to the United States, sooner than later, so we all need to gear up for this switch as soon as possible.[13]

Twenty-First-Century Challenges in Strategic Management

Three particular challenges or decisions that face all strategists today are (1) deciding whether the process should be more an art or a science, (2) deciding whether strategies should be visible or hidden from stakeholders, and (3) deciding whether the process should be more top-down or bottom-up in their firm.[14]

The Art or Science Issue

This textbook is consistent with most of the strategy literature in advocating that strategic management be viewed more as a science than an art. This perspective contends that firms need to systematically assess their external and internal environments, conduct research, carefully evaluate the pros and cons of various alternatives, perform analyses, and then decide upon a particular course of action. In contrast, Mintzberg's notion of "crafting" strategies embodies the artistic model, which suggests that strategic decision making be based primarily on holistic thinking, intuition, creativity, and imagination.[15] Mintzberg and his followers reject strategies that result from objective analysis, preferring instead subjective imagination. "Strategy scientists" reject strategies that emerge from emotion, hunch, creativity, and politics. Proponents of the artistic view often consider strategic planning exercises to be time poorly spent. The Mintzberg philosophy insists on informality, whereas strategy scientists (and this text) insist on more formality. Mintzberg refers to strategic planning as an "emergent" process whereas strategy scientists use the term "deliberate" process.[16]

The answer to the art versus science question is one that strategists must decide for themselves, and certainly the two approaches are not mutually exclusive. In deciding which approach is more effective, however, consider that the business world today has become increasingly complex and more intensely competitive. There is less room for error in strategic planning. Recall that Chapter 1 discussed the importance of intuition and experience and subjectivity in strategic planning, and even the weights and ratings discussed in Chapters 3, 4, and 6 certainly require good judgment. But the idea of deciding on strategies for any firm without thorough research and analysis, at least in the mind of this writer, is unwise. Certainly, in smaller firms there can be more informality in the process compared to larger firms, but even for smaller firms, a wealth of competitive information is available on the Internet and elsewhere and should be collected, assimilated, and evaluated before deciding on a course of action upon which survival of the firm may hinge. The livelihood of countless employees and shareholders may hinge on the effectiveness of strategies selected. Too much is at stake to be less than thorough in formulating strategies. It is not wise for a strategist to rely too heavily on gut feeling and opinion instead of research data, competitive intelligence, and analysis in formulating strategies.

The Visible or Hidden Issue

An interesting aspect of any competitive analysis discussion is whether strategies themselves should be secret or open within firms. The Chinese warrior Sun Tzu and military leaders today strive to keep strategies secret, as war is based on deception. However, for a business organization, secrecy may not be best. Keeping strategies secret from employees and stakeholders at large could severely inhibit employee and stakeholder communication, understanding, and commitment and also forgo valuable input that these persons could have regarding formulation and/or implementation of that strategy. Thus strategists in a particular firm must decide for themselves whether the risk of rival firms easily knowing and exploiting a firm's strategies is worth the benefit of improved employee and stakeholder motivation and input. Most executives agree that some strategic information should remain confidential to top managers, and that steps should be taken to ensure that such information is not disseminated beyond the inner circle. For a firm that you may own or manage, would you advocate openness or secrecy in regard to strategies being formulated and implemented?

There are certainly good reasons to keep the strategy process and strategies themselves visible and open rather than hidden and secret. There are also good reasons to keep strategies hidden from all but top-level executives. Strategists must decide for themselves what is best for their firms. This text comes down largely on the side of being visible and open, but certainly this may not be best for all strategists and all firms. As pointed out in Chapter 1, Sun Tzu argued that all war is based on deception and that the best maneuvers are those not easily predicted by rivals. Business and war are analogous.

Some reasons to be completely open with the strategy process and resultant decisions are these:

1. Managers, employees, and other stakeholders can readily contribute to the process. They often have excellent ideas. Secrecy would forgo many excellent ideas.
2. Investors, creditors, and other stakeholders have greater basis for supporting a firm when they know what the firm is doing and where the firm is going.
3. Visibility promotes democracy, whereas secrecy promotes autocracy. Domestic firms and most foreign firms prefer democracy over autocracy as a management style.
4. Participation and openness enhance understanding, commitment, and communication within the firm.

Reasons why some firms prefer to conduct strategic planning in secret and keep strategies hidden from all but the highest-level executives are as follows:

1. Free dissemination of a firm's strategies may easily translate into competitive intelligence for rival firms who could exploit the firm given that information.
2. Secrecy limits criticism, second guessing, and hindsight.
3. Participants in a visible strategy process become more attractive to rival firms who may lure them away.
4. Secrecy limits rival firms from imitating or duplicating the firm's strategies and undermining the firm.

The obvious benefits of the visible versus hidden extremes suggest that a working balance must be sought between the apparent contradictions. Parnell says that in a perfect world all key individuals both inside and outside the firm should be involved in strategic planning, but in practice particularly sensitive and confidential information should always remain strictly confidential to top managers.[17] This balancing act is difficult but essential for survival of the firm.

The Top-Down or Bottom-Up Approach

Proponents of the top-down approach contend that top executives are the only persons in the firm with the collective experience, acumen, and fiduciary responsibility to make key strategy decisions. In contrast, bottom-up advocates argue that lower- and middle-level managers and employees who will be implementing the strategies need to be actively involved in the process of formulating the strategies to ensure their support and commitment. Recent strategy research and this textbook emphasize the bottom-up approach, but earlier work by Schendel and Hofer stressed the need for firms to rely on perceptions of their top managers in strategic planning.[18] Strategists must reach a working balance of the two approaches in a manner deemed best for their firms at a particular time, while cognizant of the fact that current research supports the bottom-up approach, at least among U.S. firms. Increased education and diversity of the workforce at all levels are reasons why middle- and lower-level managers—and even nonmanagers—should be invited to participate in the firm's strategic planning process, at least to the extent that they are willing and able to contribute.

Conclusion

This chapter presents a strategy-evaluation framework that can facilitate accomplishment of annual and long-term objectives. Effective strategy evaluation allows an organization to capitalize on internal strengths as they develop, to exploit external opportunities as they emerge, to recognize and defend against threats, and to mitigate internal weaknesses before they become detrimental.

Strategists in successful organizations take the time to formulate, implement, and then evaluate strategies deliberately and systematically. Good strategists move their organization forward with purpose and direction, continually evaluating and improving the firm's external and internal strategic positions. Strategy evaluation allows an organization to shape its own future rather than allowing it to be constantly shaped by remote forces that have little or no vested interest in the well-being of the enterprise.

Although not a guarantee for success, strategic management allows organizations to make effective long-term decisions, to execute those decisions efficiently, and to take corrective actions as needed to ensure success. Computer networks and the Internet help to coordinate strategic-management activities and to ensure that decisions are based on good information. The Checkmate Strategic Planning Software is especially good in this regard (www.checkmateplan.com). A key to effective strategy evaluation and to successful strategic management is an integration of intuition and analysis:

> A potentially fatal problem is the tendency for analytical and intuitive issues to polarize. This polarization leads to strategy evaluation that is dominated by either analysis or intuition, or to strategy evaluation that is discontinuous, with a lack of coordination among analytical and intuitive issues.[19]

Strategists in successful organizations realize that strategic management is first and foremost a people process. It is an excellent vehicle for fostering organizational communication. People are what make the difference in organizations.

The real key to effective strategic management is to accept the premise that the planning process is more important than the written plan, that the manager is continuously planning and does not stop planning when the written plan is finished. The written plan is only a snapshot as of the moment it is approved. If the manager is not planning on a continuous basis—planning, measuring, and revising—the written plan can become obsolete the day it is finished. This obsolescence becomes more of a certainty as the increasingly rapid rate of change makes the business environment more uncertain.[20]

We invite you to visit the David page on the Prentice Hall Companion Web site at http://www.pearsonhighered.com/david for this chapter's review quiz.

Key Terms and Concepts

Advantage (p. 288)	**GAAS, GAAP, and IFRS** (p. 300)
Auditing (p. 300)	**Management by Wandering Around** (p. 290)
Balanced Scorecard (p. 295)	**Measuring Organizational Performance** (p. 292)
Consistency (p. 288)	**Reviewing the Underlying Bases of an Organization's**
Consonance (p. 288)	**Strategy** (p. 290)
Contingency Plans (p. 299)	**Revised EFE Matrix** (p. 291)
Feasibility (p. 288)	**Revised IFE Matrix** (p. 290)
Future Shock (p. 295)	**Taking Corrective Actions** (p. 294)

Issues for Review and Discussion

1. Discuss the nature and implications of the upcoming accounting switch from GAAP to IFRS in the United States.
2. Ask an accounting professor at your college or university the following question and report back to the class: "To what extent would my learning the IFRS standards on my own give me competitive advantage in the job market?"
3. Give an example of "consonance" other than the one provided by Rumelt in the chapter.
4. Evaluating strategies on a continuous rather than a periodic basis is desired. Discuss the pros and cons of this statement.
5. How often should an organization's vision/mission be changed in light of strategy evaluation activities?
6. Compare Mintzberg's notion of "crafting" strategies with this textbook's notion of "gathering and assimilating information" to formulate strategies.
7. Why has strategy evaluation become so important in business today?
8. BellSouth Services is considering putting divisional EFE and IFE matrices online for continual updating. How would this affect strategy evaluation?
9. What types of quantitative and qualitative criteria do you think Ellen Kullman, CEO of DuPont, uses to evaluate the company's strategy?
10. As owner of a local, independent supermarket, explain how you would evaluate the firm's strategy.
11. Under what conditions are corrective actions not required in the strategy-evaluation process?
12. Identify types of organizations that may need to evaluate strategy more frequently than others. Justify your choices.
13. As executive director of the state forestry commission, in what way and how frequently would you evaluate the organization's strategies?
14. Identify some key financial ratios that would be important in evaluating a bank's strategy.
15. As owner of a chain of hardware stores, describe how you would approach contingency planning.
16. Strategy evaluation allows an organization to take a proactive stance toward shaping its own future. Discuss the meaning of this statement.
17. Explain and discuss the Balanced Scorecard.
18. Why is the Balanced Scorecard an important topic both in devising objectives and in evaluating strategies?
19. Develop a Balanced Scorecard for a local fast-food restaurant.
20. Do you believe strategic management should be more visible or hidden as a process in a firm? Explain.
21. Do you feel strategic management should be more a top-down or bottom-up process in a firm? Explain.
22. Do you believe strategic management is more an art or a science? Explain.

Notes

1. Dale McConkey, "Planning in a Changing Environment," *Business Horizons* (September–October 1988): 64.
2. Robert Simons, "Control in an Age of Empowerment," *Harvard Business Review* (March–April 1995): 80.
3. Dale Zand, "Reviewing the Policy Process," *California Management Review* 21, no. 1 (Fall 1978): 37.
4. Eccles. 3: 1–8.
5. Claude George Jr., *The History of Management Thought* (Upper Saddle River, New Jersey: Prentice Hall, 1968): 165–166.
6. M. Erez and F. Kanfer, "The Role of Goal Acceptance in Goal Setting and Task Performance," *Academy of Management Review* 8, no. 3 (July 1983): 457.
7. D. Hussey and M. Langham, *Corporate Planning: The Human Factor* (Oxford, England: Pergamon Press, 1979): 138.
8. Carter Bayles, "Strategic Control: The President's Paradox," *Business Horizons* 20, no. 4 (August 1977): 18.
9. Adam Lashinsky, "The World's Most Admired Companies," *Fortune* (March 16, 2009): 81–91.
10. Robert Waterman, Jr., "How the Best Get Better," *BusinessWeek* (September 14, 1987): 105.
11. Robert Linneman and Rajan Chandran, "Contingency Planning: A Key to Swift Managerial Action in the Uncertain Tomorrow," *Managerial Planning* 29, no. 4 (January–February 1981): 23–27.

12. American Accounting Association, *Report of Committee on Basic Auditing Concepts* (1971): 15–74.
13. Edward Iwata, "Will Going Global Extend to Accounting?" *USA Today* (January 6, 2009): B1.
14. John Parnell, "Five Critical Challenges in Strategy Making," *SAM Advanced Management Journal* 68, no. 2 (Spring 2003): 15–22.
15. Henry Mintzberg, "Crafting Strategy," *Harvard Business Review* (July–August 1987): 66–75.
16. Henry Mintzberg and J. Waters, "Of Strategies, Deliberate and Emergent," *Strategic Management Journal* 6, no. 2: 257–272.
17. Parnell, 15–22.
18. D. E. Schendel and C. W. Hofer (Eds.), *Strategic Management* (Boston: Little, Brown, 1979).
19. Michael McGinnis, "The Key to Strategic Planning: Integrating Analysis and Intuition," *Sloan Management Review* 26, no. 1 (Fall 1984): 49.
20. McConkey, 72.

Current Readings

Franken, Arnoud, Chris Edwards, and Rob Lambert, "Executing Strategic Change: Understanding the Critical Management Elements That Lead to Success." *California Management Review* (Spring 2009): 49–73.

Giraudeau, Martin. "The Drafts of Strategy: Opening Up Plans and Their Uses." *Long Range Planning* 41, no. 3 (June 2008): 291.

Hall, Joseph, and Eric Johnson. "When Should a Process Be Art, Not Science?" *Harvard Business Review* (March 2009): 58–65.

Jarzablowski, Paula. "Shaping Strategy as a Structuration Process." *The Academy of Management Journal* 51, no. 4 (August 2008): 621.

Li, Jing, Changhui Zhou, and Edward Zajac. "Control, Collaboration, and Productivity in International Joint Ventures: Theory and Evidence." *Strategic Management Journal* (August 2009): 865–884.

McFarland, Keith R. "Should You Build Strategy Like You Build Software?" *MIT Sloan Management Review* 49, no. 3 (Spring 2008): 69.

Neilson, Gary L., Karla L. Martin, and Elizabeth Powers. "The Secrets to Successful Strategy Execution." *Harvard Business Review* (June 2008): 60.

Pieter de Man, Ard, and Nadine Roijakkers. "Alliance Governance: Balancing Control and Trust in Dealing with Risk." *Long Range Planning* (February 2009): 75–95.

ASSURANCE OF LEARNING EXERCISES

Assurance of Learning Exercise 9A

Preparing a Strategy-Evaluation Report for McDonald's Corp.

Purpose

This exercise can give you experience locating strategy-evaluation information. Use of the Internet coupled with published sources of information can significantly enhance the strategy-evaluation process. Performance information on competitors, for example, can help put into perspective a firm's own performance.

Instructions

Step 1   Visit http://marketwatch.multexinvestor.com, http://moneycentral.msn.com, http://finance. yahoo.com, www.clearstation.com to locate strategy-evaluation information on competitors. Read some recent articles that discuss the fast-food restaurant business.

Step 2   Summarize your research findings by preparing a strategy-evaluation report for your instructor. Include in your report a summary of McDonald's strategies and performance in 2010 and a summary of your conclusions regarding the effectiveness of McDonald's strategies.

Step 3   Based on your analysis, do you feel that McDonald's is pursuing effective strategies? What recommendations would you offer to McDonald's chief executive officer?

Assurance of Learning Exercise 9B

Evaluating My University's Strategies

Purpose

An important part of evaluating strategies is determining the nature and extent of changes in an organization's external opportunities/threats and internal strengths/weaknesses. Changes in these underlying critical success factors can indicate a need to change or modify the firm's strategies.

Instructions

As a class, discuss positive and negative changes in your university's external and internal factors during your college career. Begin by listing on the board new or emerging opportunities and threats. Then identify strengths and weaknesses that have changed significantly during your college career. In light of the external and internal changes that were identified, discuss whether your university's strategies need modifying. Are there any new strategies that you would recommend? Make a list to recommend to your department chair, dean, president, or chancellor.

CHAPTER 10

Business Ethics/ Social Responsibility/ Environmental Sustainability

CHAPTER OBJECTIVES

After studying this chapter, you should be able to do the following:

1. Explain why good ethics is good business in strategic management.

2. Explain how firms can best ensure that their code of business ethics guides decision making instead of being ignored.

3. Explain why whistle-blowing is important to encourage in a firm.

4. Discuss the nature and role of corporate sustainability reports.

5. Discuss specific ways that firms can be good stewards of the natural environment.

6. Explain ISO 14000 and 14001.

Assurance of Learning Exercises

Assurance of Learning Exercise 10A
Does McDonald's Have a Code of Business Ethics?

Assurance of Learning Exercise 10B
The Ethics of Spying on Competitors

Assurance of Learning Exercise 10C
Who Prepares a Sustainability Report?

Source: Ivan Cholakov Gostock

"Notable Quotes"

"If business is not based on ethical grounds, it is of no benefit to society and will, like all other unethical combinations, pass into oblivion."

—C. Max Killan

"Good ethics is good business."

"Do unto others as you would have them do unto you."

"Be joyful when you do things to conserve, preserve, and enhance the natural environment."

Doing Great in a Weak Economy. How?

Walt Disney

When most firms were struggling in 2008, Walt Disney increased its revenues from $35 billion in 2007 to $37 billion in 2008 with net income of $4.4 billion. *Fortune* magazine in 2009 rated Walt Disney their 13th "Most Admired Company in the World" in terms of management and performance.

Walt Disney is cutting carbon emissions from fuels by half by 2012, and ultimately will emit zero greenhouse gas emissions at its office and retail complexes, theme parks, and cruise lines. Disney's long-term goal is to cut to zero the amount of waste it sends to landfills, which totaled nearly 300,000 tons in 2006, much of it from construction, through diverting some to recycling centers, composting, and buying more postconsumer recycled materials. Beth Stevens, senior vice president of environmental affairs, said Disney has "not put a definite time horizon" on taking emissions to zero and may have to rely in part on technology that is still under development to reach that goal. "We set those (goals) because they were very aspirational," Stevens said. "We thought it was important . . . to communicate a sense of commitment." The environmental plan was released in 2009 in its "corporate responsibility" report.

"Current scientific conclusions indicate that urgent reductions in greenhouse gas emissions are required to avert accelerated climate change," the report said. "A successful response to these challenges demands fundamental changes in the way society, including businesses, use natural resources, and Disney is no exception." Disney works with Conservation International on emissions reduction targets, and it plans to have a third party monitor its progress through annual audits. By 2013, Disney plans to reduce its electricity consumption by 10 percent compared with its 2006 baseline.

The world's number two media conglomerate (behind Time Warner) has extensive assets in movies,

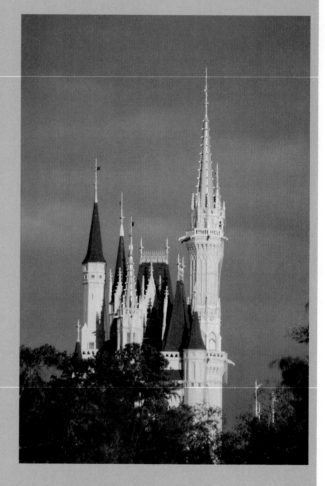

music, publishing, television, and theme parks. Walt Disney's TV holdings include the ABC television network and 10 broadcast stations, as well as cable networks including ABC Family, A&E Television Networks (37 percent owned), and ESPN (80 percent). Walt Disney Studios produces films through such imprints as Walt Disney Pictures, Touchstone, Pixar, and Miramax. Walt Disney Parks and Resorts is one of the top theme park operators in the world, anchored by its popular Walt Disney World and Disneyland resorts. In

May 2009, Disney formed a partnership with Hulu.com to stream ABC's full-episode television programming online as well as many of titles for Disney's television and movie library. In July, Disney announced it would fund a 50/50, $452 million expansion of Disneyland Park in Hong Kong with that city's government.

Source: Geoff Colvin, "The World's Most Admired Companies," *Fortune* (March 16, 2009): 76–86; http://www.reuters.com/article/marketsNews/idAFN0939621220090310?rpc=44.

Although the three sections of this chapter (Business Ethics, Social Responsibility, and Sustainability) are distinct, the topics are quite related. Many people, for example, consider it unethical for a firm to be socially irresponsible. *Social responsibility* refers to actions an organization takes beyond what is legally required to protect or enhance the well-being of living things. *Sustainability* refers to the extent that an organization's operations and actions protect, mend, and preserve rather than harm or destroy the natural environment. Polluting the environment, for example, is unethical, irresponsible, and in many cases illegal. Business ethics, social responsibility, and sustainability issues therefore are interrelated and impact all areas of the comprehensive strategic-management model, as illustrated in Figure 10.1 on page 312.

A sample company that adheres to the highest ethical standards and that has excelled during the recent weak economy is Walt Disney. Disney in March 2009 published an elaborate corporate social responsibility/business ethics/sustainability report that can be found online at http://disney.go.com/crreport/home.html. In that report, the Disney CEO says:

Our Corporate Responsibility team has developed a cohesive strategy for the company with that in mind, incorporating existing outreach, safety, nutrition, environmental and labor programs and working with executives across Disney, ABC and ESPN to coordinate and strengthen our company-wide efforts. They've organized our approach around five broad areas—Children & Family, Content & Products, Environment, Community and Workplaces—with the goal of further embedding corporate responsibility into Disney's business DNA, making sure it continues to be taken into consideration in decisions big and small.[1]

Business Ethics

Good ethics is good business. Bad ethics can derail even the best strategic plans. This chapter provides an overview of the importance of business ethics in strategic management. *Business ethics* can be defined as principles of conduct within organizations that guide decision making and behavior. Good business ethics is a prerequisite for good strategic management; good ethics is just good business!

A rising tide of consciousness about the importance of business ethics is sweeping the United States and the rest of the world. Strategists such as CEOs and business owners are the individuals primarily responsible for ensuring that high ethical principles are espoused and practiced in an organization. All strategy formulation, implementation, and evaluation decisions have ethical ramifications.

Newspapers and business magazines daily report legal and moral breaches of ethical conduct by both public and private organizations. Being unethical can be very expensive. For example, some of the largest payouts for class-action legal fraud suits ever were against Enron ($7.16 billion), WorldCom ($6.16 billion), Cendant ($3.53 billion), Tyco ($2.98 billion), AOL Time Warner ($2.5 billion), Nortel Networks ($2.47 billion), and Royal Ahold ($1.09 billion). A company named Coast IRB LLC in Colorado recently was forced to close after the Food and Drug Administration (FDA) discovered in a sting operation that the firm conducted a fake medical study. Coast is one of many firms paid

FIGURE 10.1

A Comprehensive Strategic-Management Model

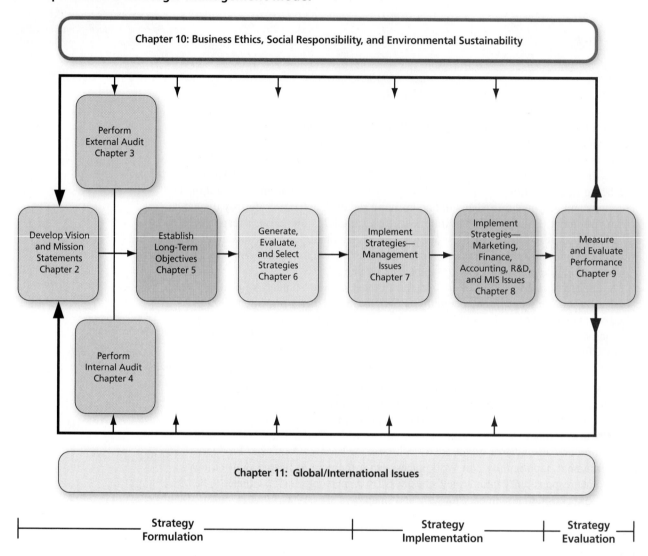

Source: Fred R. David, "How Companies Define Their Mission," *Long Range Planning* 22, no. 3 (June 1988): 40.

by pharmaceutical firms to oversee clinical trials and independently ensure that patient safety is protected.

Other business actions considered to be unethical include misleading advertising or labeling, causing environmental harm, poor product or service safety, padding expense accounts, insider trading, dumping banned or flawed products in foreign markets, not providing equal opportunities for women and minorities, overpricing, moving jobs overseas, and sexual harassment.

Code of Business Ethics

A new wave of ethics issues related to product safety, employee health, sexual harassment, AIDS in the workplace, smoking, acid rain, affirmative action, waste disposal, foreign business practices, cover-ups, takeover tactics, conflicts of interest, employee privacy, inappropriate gifts, and security of company records has accentuated the need for strategists to develop a clear code of business ethics. Internet fraud, hacking into company computers, spreading viruses, and identity theft are other unethical activities that plague every sector of online commerce.

United Technologies has a 21-page code of ethics and a vice president of business ethics. Baxter Travenol Laboratories, IBM, Caterpillar Tractor, Chemical Bank, ExxonMobil, Dow Corning, and Celanese are firms that have formal codes of business ethics. A *code of business ethics* is a document that provides behavioral guidelines that cover daily activities and decisions within an organization.

Merely having a code of ethics, however, is not sufficient to ensure ethical business behavior. A code of ethics can be viewed as a public relations gimmick, a set of platitudes, or window dressing. To ensure that the code is read, understood, believed, and remembered, periodic ethics workshops are needed to sensitize people to workplace circumstances in which ethics issues may arise.[2] If employees see examples of punishment for violating the code as well as rewards for upholding the code, this reinforces the importance of a firm's code of ethics. The Web site www.ethicsweb.ca/codes provides guidelines on how to write an effective code of ethics.

An Ethics Culture

An ethics "culture" needs to permeate organizations! To help create an ethics culture, Citicorp developed a business ethics board game that is played by thousands of employees worldwide. Called "The Word Ethic," this game asks players business ethics questions, such as how do you deal with a customer who offers you football tickets in exchange for a new, backdated IRA? Diana Robertson at the Wharton School of Business believes the game is effective because it is interactive. Many organizations have developed a code-of-conduct manual outlining ethical expectations and giving examples of situations that commonly arise in their businesses.

Harris Corporation and other firms warn managers and employees that failing to report an ethical violation by others could bring discharge. The Securities and Exchange Commission (SEC) recently strengthened its whistle-blowing policies, virtually mandating that anyone seeing unethical activity report such behavior. *Whistle-blowing* refers to policies that require employees to report any unethical violations they discover or see in the firm.

An unidentified whistle-blower in 2009 filed a lawsuit against Amgen Inc., accusing the biotechnology company of illegal marketing of its blockbuster drugs Enbrel and Aranesp. The drug company Wyeth co-markets Enbrel with Amgen, and was named as a defendant too, along with wholesale drug distributor AmerisourceBergen Corp., online health-information provider WebMD Health Corp., and others. The federal whistle-blower law protects the identity of the plaintiff. In the drug industry, such suits are often filed by former employees.

One reason strategists' salaries are high is that they must take the moral risks of the firm. Strategists are responsible for developing, communicating, and enforcing the code of business ethics for their organizations. Although primary responsibility for ensuring ethical behavior rests with a firm's strategists, an integral part of the responsibility of all managers is to provide ethics leadership by constant example and demonstration. Managers hold positions that enable them to influence and educate many people. This makes managers responsible for developing and implementing ethical decision making. Gellerman and Drucker, respectively, offer some good advice for managers:

All managers risk giving too much because of what their companies demand from them. But the same superiors, who keep pressing you to do more, or to do it better, or faster, or less expensively, will turn on you should you cross that fuzzy line between right and wrong. They will blame you for exceeding instructions or for ignoring their warnings. The smartest managers already know that the best answer to the question "How far is too far?" is don't try to find out.[3]

A man (or woman) might know too little, perform poorly, lack judgment and ability, and yet not do too much damage as a manager. But if that person lacks character and integrity—no matter how knowledgeable, how brilliant, how successful—he destroys. He destroys people, the most valuable resource of the enterprise. He destroys spirit. And he destroys performance. This is particularly true of the people at the head of an enterprise. For the spirit of an organization is created from the top. If an organization is great in spirit, it is because the spirit of its top people is great. If it decays, it does so because the top rots. As the proverb has it, "Trees die from the top." No one should ever become a strategist unless he or she is willing to have his or her character serve as the model for subordinates.[4]

No society anywhere in the world can compete very long or successfully with people stealing from one another or not trusting one another, with every bit of information requiring notarized confirmation, with every disagreement ending up in litigation, or with government having to regulate businesses to keep them honest. Being unethical is a recipe for headaches, inefficiency, and waste. History has proven that the greater the trust and confidence of people in the ethics of an institution or society, the greater its economic strength. Business relationships are built mostly on mutual trust and reputation. Short-term decisions based on greed and questionable ethics will preclude the necessary self-respect to gain the trust of others. More and more firms believe that ethics training and an ethics culture create strategic advantage.

Ethics training programs should include messages from the CEO or owner of the business emphasizing ethical business practices, the development and discussion of codes of ethics, and procedures for discussing and reporting unethical behavior. Firms can align ethical and strategic decision making by incorporating ethical considerations into long-term planning, by integrating ethical decision making into the performance appraisal process, by encouraging whistle-blowing or the reporting of unethical practices, and by monitoring departmental and corporate performance regarding ethical issues.

Bribes

Bribery is defined by *Black's Law Dictionary* as the offering, giving, receiving, or soliciting of any item of value to influence the actions of an official or other person in discharge of a public or legal duty. A *bribe* is a gift bestowed to influence a recipient's conduct. The gift may be any money, good, right in action, property, preferment, privilege, emolument, object of value, advantage, or merely a promise or undertaking to induce or influence the action, vote, or influence of a person in an official or public capacity. Bribery is a crime in most countries of the world, including the United States.[5]

Siemens AG, the large German engineering firm, recently was fined $800 million for routinely offering bribes to various companies around the world to win overseas contracts. The U.S. Justice Department and the SEC brought suit against Siemens under the U.S. Foreign Corruptions Act. The Siemens fine was 20 times larger than any previous bribery penalty. The SEC claimed that Siemens made at least 4,283 bribe payments totaling $1.4 billion between 2001 and 2007. These bribes allegedly were paid to government officials in 10 countries.

Paying bribes is considered both illegal and unethical in the United States, but in some foreign countries, paying bribes and kickbacks is acceptable. Tipping is even considered bribery in some countries. Important antibribery and extortion initiatives are advocated by many organizations, including the World Bank, the International Monetary Fund, the European Union, the Council of Europe, the Organization of American States, the Pacific Basin Economic Council, the Global Coalition for Africa, and the United Nations.

The U.S. Justice Department in mid-2009 increased its prosecutions of alleged acts of foreign bribery. Businesses have to be much more careful these days. For years, taking business associates to lavish dinners and giving them expensive holiday gifts and even outright cash may be expected in many countries, such as South Korea and China, but there is now stepped-up enforcement of bribery laws. Kellogg Brown and Root (KBR) and Halliburton recently paid $579 million for bribing officials in Nigeria.

Love Affairs at Work

A recent *Wall Street Journal* article recapped current American standards regarding boss-subordinate love affairs at work.[6] Only 5 percent of all firms sampled had no restrictions on such relationships; 80 percent of firms have policies that prohibit relationships between a supervisor and a subordinate. Only 4 percent of firms strictly prohibited such relationships, but 39 percent of firms had policies that required individuals to inform their supervisors whenever a romantic relationship begins with a coworker. Only 24 percent of firms required the two persons to be in different departments.

In Europe, romantic relationships at work are largely viewed as private matters and most firms have no policies on the practice. However, European firms are increasingly adopting explicit, American-style sexual harassment laws. The U.S. military strictly bans officers from dating or having sexual relationships with enlistees. At the World Bank, sexual relations between a supervisor and an employee are considered "a de facto conflict of interest which must be resolved to avoid favoritism." World Bank president Paul Wolfowitz recently was forced to resign due to a relationship he had with a bank staff person.

The United Nations (UN) in mid-2009 was struggling with its own sexual-harassment complaints as many women employees say the organization's current system for handling complaints is arbitrary, unfair, and mired in bureaucracy. Sexual harassment cases at the UN can take years to adjudicate, and accusers have no access to investigative reports. The UN plans to "soon" make changes to its internal justice system for handling harassment complaints; the UN aspires to protect human rights around the world.

Social Responsibility

Some strategists agree with Ralph Nader, who proclaims that organizations have tremendous social obligations. Nader points out, for example, that Exxon/Mobil has more assets than most countries, and because of this such firms have an obligation to help society cure its many ills. Other people, however, agree with the economist Milton Friedman, who asserts that organizations have no obligation to do any more for society than is legally required. Friedman may contend that it is irresponsible for a firm to give monies to charity.

Do you agree more with Nader or Friedman? Surely we can all agree that the first social responsibility of any business must be to make enough profit to cover the costs of the future because if this is not achieved, no other social responsibility can be met. Indeed, no social need can be met by the firm if the firm fails.

Strategists should examine social problems in terms of potential costs and benefits to the firm, and focus on social issues that could benefit the firm most. For example, should a firm avoid laying off employees so as to protect the employees' livelihood, when that decision may force the firm to liquidate?

Social Policy

The term *social policy* embraces managerial philosophy and thinking at the highest level of the firm, which is why the topic is covered in this textbook. Social policy concerns what responsibilities the firm has to employees, consumers, environmentalists, minorities, communities, shareholders, and other groups. After decades of debate, many firms still struggle to determine appropriate social policies.

The impact of society on business and vice versa is becoming more pronounced each year. Corporate social policy should be designed and articulated during strategy formulation, set and administered during strategy implementation, and reaffirmed or changed during strategy evaluation.[7]

In 2009, the most admired companies for social responsibility according to *Fortune* magazine were as follows:

1. Anheuser-Busch
2. Marriott International
3. Integrys Energy Group
4. Walt Disney
5. Herman Miller
6. Edison
7. Starbucks
8. Steelcase

9. Union Pacific
10. Fortune Brands[8]

From a social responsibility perspective, these were the least admired companies in 2009:

1. Circuit City Stores
2. Family Dollar Stores
3. Dillard's
4. Sears Holdings
5. Tribune
6. Hon Hai Precision Industry
7. Fiat
8. PEMEX
9. Surgutneftegas
10. Huawei Technologies[9]

Firms should strive to engage in social activities that have economic benefits. Merck & Co. once developed the drug ivermectin for treating river blindness, a disease caused by a fly-borne parasitic worm endemic in poor tropical areas of Africa, the Middle East, and Latin America. In an unprecedented gesture that reflected its corporate commitment to social responsibility, Merck then made ivermectin available at no cost to medical personnel throughout the world. Merck's action highlights the dilemma of orphan drugs, which offer pharmaceutical companies no economic incentive for profitable development and distribution. Merck did however garner substantial goodwill among its stakeholders for its actions.

Social Policies on Retirement

Some countries around the world are facing severe workforce shortages associated with their aging populations. The percentage of persons age 65 or older exceeds 20 percent in Japan, Italy, and Germany—and will reach 20 percent in 2018 in France. In 2036, the percentage of persons age 65 or older will reach 20 percent in the United States and China. Unlike the United States, Japan is reluctant to rely on large-scale immigration to bolster its workforce. Instead, Japan provides incentives for its elderly to work until ages 65 to 75. Western European countries are doing the opposite, providing incentives for its elderly to retire at ages 55 to 60. The International Labor Organization says 71 percent of Japanese men ages 60 to 64 work, compared to 57 percent of American men and just 17 percent of French men in the same age group.

Sachiko Ichioka, a typical 67-year-old man in Japan, says, "I want to work as long as I'm healthy. The extra money means I can go on trips, and I'm not a burden on my children." Better diet and health care have raised Japan's life expectancy now to 82, the highest in the world. Japanese women are having on average only 1.28 children compared to 2.04 in the United States. Keeping the elderly at work, coupled with reversing the old-fashioned trend of keeping women at home, are Japan's two key remedies for sustaining its workforce in factories and businesses. This prescription for dealing with problems associated with an aging society should be considered by many countries around the world. The Japanese government is phasing in a shift from age 60 to age 65 as the date when a person may begin receiving a pension, and premiums paid by Japanese employees are rising while payouts are falling. Unlike the United States, Japan has no law against discrimination based on age.

Japan's huge national debt, 175 percent of gross domestic product (GDP) compared to 65 percent for the United States, is difficult to lower with a falling population because Japan has fewer taxpaying workers. Worker productivity increases in Japan are not able to offset declines in number of workers, thus resulting in a decline in overall economic production. Like many countries, Japan does not view immigration as a good way to solve this problem.

Japan's shrinking workforce has become such a concern that the government just recently allowed an unspecified number of Indonesian and Filipino nurses and caregivers to work in Japan for two years. The number of working-age Japanese—those between ages 15 and 64—is projected to shrink to 70 million by 2030, from 82 million in 2009. Using foreign workers is known as *gaikokujin roudousha* in Japanese. Many Filipinos have recently been hired now to work in agriculture and factories throughout Japan.

The percentage of foreign workers to the total population is 20 percent in the United States, nearly 10 percent in Germany, 5 percent in the United Kingdom, and less than 1 percent in Japan. But most Japanese now acknowledge that this percentage must move upward, and perhaps quickly, for their nation's economy to prosper.[10]

Environmental Sustainability

The strategies of both companies and countries are increasingly scrutinized and evaluated from a nautral environment perspective. Companies such as Wal-Mart now monitor not only the price its vendors offer for products, but also how those products are made in terms of environmental practices. A growing number of business schools offer separate courses and even a concentration in environmental management.

Businesses must not exploit and decimate the natural environment. Mark Starik at George Washington University says, "Halting and reversing worldwide ecological destruction and deterioration is a strategic issue that needs immediate and substantive attention by all businesses and managers. According to the International Standards Organization (ISO), the word *environment* is defined as "surroundings in which an organization operates, including air, water, land, natural resources, flora, fauna, humans, and their interrelation." This chapter illustrates how many firms are gaining competitive advantage by being good stewards of the natural environment.

Employees, consumers, governments, and society are especially resentful of firms that harm rather than protect the natural environment. Conversely people today are especially appreciative of firms that conduct operations in a way that mends, conserves, and preserves the natural environment. Consumer interest in businesses preserving nature's ecological balance and fostering a clean, healthy environment is high.

No business wants a reputation as being a polluter. A bad sustainability record will hurt the firm in the market, jeopardize its standing in the community, and invite scrutiny by regulators, investors, and environmentalists. Governments increasingly require businesses to behave responsibly and require, for example, that businesses publicly report the pollutants and wastes their facilities produce.

In terms of megawatts of wind power generated by various states in the United States, Iowa's 2,791 recently overtook California's 2,517, but Texas's 7,118 megawatts dwarfs all other states. Minnesota also is making substantial progress in wind power generation. New Jersey recently outfitted 200,000 utility poles with solar panels, which made it the nation's second-largest producer of solar energy behind California. New Jersey is also adding solar panels to corporate rooftops. The state's $514 million solar program will double its solar capacity to 160 megawatts by 2013. The state's goal is to obtain 3 percent of its electricity from the sun and 12 percent from offshore wind by 2020.

What Is a Sustainability Report?

Wal-Mart Stores is one among many companies today that annually provides a sustainability report that reveals how the firm's operations impact the natural environment. This document discloses to shareholders information about Wal-Mart's firm's labor practices, product sourcing, energy efficiency, environmental impact, and business ethics practices.

It is good business for a business to provide a sustainability report annually to the public. With 60,000 suppliers and over $350 billion in annual sales, Wal-Mart works with its suppliers to make sure they provide such reports. Wal-Mart monitors not only prices its vendors' offer for products, but also the vendors' social-responsibility and environmental practices. Many firms use the Wal-Mart sustainability report as a benchmark, guideline, and model to follow in preparing their own report.

The Global Reporting Initiative recently issued a set of detailed reporting guidelines specifying what information should go into sustainability reports. The proxy advisory firm Institutional Shareholder Services reports that an increasing number of shareholder groups are pushing firms to provide sustainability information annually.

Wal-Mart also now encourages and expects its 1.35 million U.S. employees to adopt what it calls Personal Sustainability Projects, which include such measures as organizing weight-loss or smoking-cessation support groups, biking to work, or starting recycling programs. Employee wellness can be a part of sustainability.

Wal-Mart is installing solar panels on its stores in California and Hawaii, providing as much as 30 percent of the power in some stores. Wal-Mart may go national with solar power if this test works well. Also moving to solar energy is department-store chain Kohl's Corp., which is converting 64 of its 80 California stores to using solar power. There are big subsidies for solar installations in some states.

Home Depot, the world's second largest retailer behind Wal-Mart, recently more than doubled its offering of environmentally friendly products such as all-natural insect repellent. Home Depot has made it much easier for consumers to find its organic products by using special labels similar to Timberland's (the outdoor company) Green Index tags. Another huge retailer, Target, now offers more than 500 choices of organic certified food and has 18 buildings in California alone powered only by solar energy. The largest solar power plant in North America is the one in Nevada that powers Nellis Air Force Base outside Las Vegas.[11]

Managers and employees of firms must be careful not to become scapegoats blamed for company environmental wrongdoings. Harming the natural environment can be unethical, illegal, and costly. When organizations today face criminal charges for polluting the environment, they increasingly turn on their managers and employees to win leniency. Employee firings and demotions are becoming common in pollution-related legal suits. Managers were fired at Darling International, Inc., and Niagara Mohawk Power Corporation for being indirectly responsible for their firms polluting water. Managers and employees today must be careful not to ignore, conceal, or disregard a pollution problem, or they may find themselves personally liable.

Lack of Standards Changing

A few years ago, firms could get away with placing "green" terminology on their products and labels using such terms as *organic*, *green*, *safe*, *earth-friendly*, *nontoxic*, and/or *natural* because there were no legal or generally accepted definitions. Today, however, such terms as these carry much more specific connotations and expectations. Uniform standards defining environmentally responsible company actions are rapidly being incorporated into our legal landscape. It has become more and more difficult for firms to make "green" claims when their actions are not substantive, comprehensive, or even true. Lack of standards once made consumers cynical about corporate environmental claims, but those claims today are increasingly being challenged in courts. Joel Makower says, "One of the main reasons to truly become a green firm is for your employees. They're the first group that needs assurance than any claims you make hold water."[12]

Around the world, political and corporate leaders now realize that the "business green" topic will not go away and in fact is gaining ground rapidly. Strategically, companies more than ever must demonstrate to their customers and stakeholders that their green efforts are substantive and set the firm apart from competitors. A firm's performance facts and figures must back up their rhetoric and be consistent with sustainability standards.

Obama Regulations

The Obama administration is imposing strict regulations requiring firms to conserve energy. Federal government buildings are being refitted with energy-efficient improvements. Alternative-energy firms are busy with new customers every day as the federal stimulus package includes adding alternative-energy infrastructure. Venture capitalists and lenders are funding new "clean technology" business start-ups, including solar power, wind power, biofuels, and insulation firms. Such firms are boosting marketing efforts, expanding geographically, and hiring more staff. Venture capital investments in clean technology companies totaled $8.4 billion in 2008, up nearly 40 percent from 2007.

A wide variety of firms are participating in this clean energy growth business, such as Seattle-based Verdiem Corporation. That firm sells software that provides centralized control over power consumption, such as remotely turning off computer monitors left on overnight.[13] General Electric plans to achieve $20 billion in sales by 2011 in eco-friendly technologies that include cleaner coal-fired power plants, a diesel-and-electric hybrid loco-motive, and agricultural silicon that cuts the amount of water and pesticide used in spray-ing fields. This is double GE's sales today in "green" products. GE has a goal to improve its energy efficiency by 30 percent between 2005 and 2012.

The Environmental Protection Agency recently reported that U.S. citizens and organizations annually spend more than about $200 billion on pollution abatement. Environmental concerns touch all aspects of a business's operations, including workplace risk exposures, packaging, waste reduction, energy use, alternative fuels, environmental cost accounting, and recycling practices.

Managing Environmental Affairs in the Firm

The ecological challenge facing all organizations requires managers to formulate strategies that preserve and conserve natural resources and control pollution. Special natural environ-ment issues include ozone depletion, global warming, depletion of rain forests, destruction of animal habitats, protecting endangered species, developing biodegradable products and packages, waste management, clean air, clean water, erosion, destruction of natural resources, and pollution control. Firms increasingly are developing green product lines that are biodegradable and/or are made from recycled products. Green products sell well.

Managing as if "health of the planet" matters requires an understanding of how international trade, competitiveness, and global resources are connected. Managing envi-ronmental affairs can no longer be simply a technical function performed by specialists in a firm; more emphasis must be placed on developing an environmental perspective among all employees and managers of the firm. Many companies are moving environmental affairs from the staff side of the organization to the line side, thus making the corporate environmental group report directly to the chief operating officer. Firms that manage envi-ronmental affairs will enhance relations with consumers, regulators, vendors, and other industry players, substantially improving their prospects of success.

Environmental strategies could include developing or acquiring green businesses, divesting or altering environment-damaging businesses, striving to become a low-cost pro-ducer through waste minimization and energy conservation, and pursuing a differentiation strategy through green-product features. In addition, firms could include an environmental representative on their board of directors, conduct regular envrionmental audits, imple-ment bonuses for favorable environmental results, become involved in environmental issues and programs, incorporate environmental values in mission statements, establish environmentally oriented objectives, acquire environmental skills, and provide environ-mental training programs for company employees and managers.

Should Students Receive Environmental Training?

The *Wall Street Journal* reports that companies actively consider environmental training in employees they hire. A recent study reported that 77 percent of corporate recruiters said "it is important to hire students with an awareness of social and environmental responsibil-ity." According to Ford Motor Company's director of corporate governance, "We want students who will help us find solutions to societal challenges and we have trouble hiring students with such skills."

The Aspen Institute contends that most business schools currently do not, but should, incorporate environmental training in all facets of their core curriculum, not just in special elective courses. The institute reports that the University of Texas, the University of North Carolina, and the University of Michigan, among others, are at the cutting edge in provid-ing environmental coverage at their respective MBA levels. Companies favor hiring graduates from such universities.

Findings from research suggest that business schools at the undergraduate level are doing a poor job of educating students on environmental issues. Business students with limited knowledge on environmental issues may make poor decisions, so business schools should address environmental issues more in their curricula. Failure to do so could result in graduates making inappropriate business decisions in regard to the natural environment. Failing to provide adequate coverage of natural environment issues and decisions in their training could make those students less attractive to employers.[14]

Reasons Why Firms Should "Be Green"

Preserving the environment should be a permanent part of doing business for the following reasons:

1. Consumer demand for environmentally safe products and packages is high.
2. Public opinion demanding that firms conduct business in ways that preserve the natural environment is strong.
3. Environmental advocacy groups now have over 20 million Americans as members.
4. Federal and state environmental regulations are changing rapidly and becoming more complex.
5. More lenders are examining the environmental liabilities of businesses seeking loans.
6. Many consumers, suppliers, distributors, and investors shun doing business with environmentally weak firms.
7. Liability suits and fines against firms having environmental problems are on the rise.

Be Proactive, Not Reactive

More firms are becoming environmentally proactive—doing more than the bare minimum to develop and implement strategies that preserve the environment. The old undesirable alternative of being environmentally reactive—changing practices only when forced to do so by law or consumer pressure more often today leads to high cleanup costs, liability suits, reduced market share, reduced customer loyalty, and higher medical costs. In contrast, a proactive policy views environmental pressures as opportunities and includes such actions as developing green products and packages, conserving energy, reducing waste, recycling, and creating a corporate culture that is environmentally sensitive.

New required diesel technology has reduced emissions by up to 98 percent in all new big trucks, at an average cost increase of $12,000 per truck. "Clean air is not free," says Rich Moskowitz, who handles regulatory affairs for the American Trucking Association, which supports the transition.[15]

ISO 14000/14001 Certification

Based in Geneva, Switzerland, the International Organization for Standardization (ISO) is a network of the national standards institutes of 147 countries, one member per country. ISO is the world's largest developer of sustainability standards. Widely accepted all over the world, ISO standards are voluntary because ISO has no legal authority to enforce their implementation. ISO itself does not regulate or legislate.

Governmental agencies in various countries, such as the Environmental Protection Agency (EPA) in the United States, have adopted ISO standards as part of their regulatory framework, and the standards are the basis of much legislation. Adoptions are sovereign decisions by the regulatory authorities, governments, and/or companies concerned.

ISO 14000 refers to a series of voluntary standards in the environmental field. The ISO 14000 family of standards concerns the extent to which a firm minimizes harmful effects on the environment caused by its activities and continually monitors and improves its own environmental performance. Included in the ISO 14000 series are the ISO 14001 standards in fields such as environmental auditing, environmental performance evaluation, environmental labeling, and life-cycle assessment.

ISO 14001 is a set of standards adopted by thousands of firms worldwide to certify to their constituencies that they are conducting business in an environmentally friendly manner. ISO 14001 standards offer a universal technical standard for environmental compliance that more and more firms are requiring not only of themselves but also of their suppliers and distributors.

The ISO 14001 standard requires that a community or organization put in place and implement a series of practices and procedures that, when taken together, result in an *environmental management system* (EMS). ISO 14001 is not a technical standard and as such does not in any way replace technical requirements embodied in statutes or regulations. It also does not set prescribed standards of performance for organizations. Not being ISO 14001 certified can be a strategic disadvantage for towns, counties, and companies because people today expect organizations to minimize or, even better, to eliminate environmental harm they cause.[16] The major requirements of an EMS under ISO 14001 include the following:

- Show commitments to prevention of pollution, continual improvement in overall environmental performance, and compliance with all applicable statutory and regulatory requirements.
- Identify all aspects of the organization's activities, products, and services that could have a significant impact on the environment, including those that are not regulated.
- Set performance objectives and targets for the management system that link back to three policies: (1) prevention of pollution, (2) continual improvement, and (3) compliance.
- Meet environmental objectives that include training employees, establishing work instructions and practices, and establishing the actual metrics by which the objectives and targets will be measured.
- Conduct an audit operation of the EMS.
- Take corrective actions when deviations from the EMS occur.

Electric Car Networks Are Coming

In August 2009, President Obama announced $2.4 billion in funding for electric car manufacturing. Grants will go to 11 companies in Michigan and 7 in Indiana that are matching the funds.

The company Better Place is building a network of 250,000 electric car recharging stations in the San Francisco/Oakland Bay Area. Each station is about the size of a parking meter. The company has already built such networks in Denmark, Israel, and Australia. City officials in the Bay Area expect that region to lead the United States in electric cars in the near future. The stations are essential because most electric cars need recharging after about 40 miles. Better Place is also building about 200 stations in the Bay Area where electric car batteries can be switched out within 15 minutes, so no waiting is needed for recharging. Even with petroleum prices at low levels, expectations are for the United States and other countries to switch to electric cars quite aggressively over the next 10 years—for pollution minimization reasons and to take advantage of government incentives and eventual mandates.

General Motors and Chrysler are pouring money into developing electric plug-in vehicles. GM is expected to launch its Chevy Volt in late 2010 in the United States. Nissan Motor Co. and Toyota Motor Co. are also quickly developing electric cars.

The Chinese auto maker BYD Co. recently unveiled the country's first all-electric vehicle for mass market. The company's F3DM vehicle runs off batteries that can be charged from a regular electrical outlet. BYD plans to sell this car in the United States in 2010. BYD sold about 10,000 F3DMs in 2009 at a price of 150,000 yuan, or $22,000 each. BYD is headquartered in Shenzhen.

Hawaii is creating an electric car network for the islands that by 2012 is expected to wean the state from near-complete dependence on oil for its energy needs. The firm Better Place is creating 70,000 to 100,000 recharging points throughout the islands to support plug-in electric cars. Under the Hawaii Clean Energy Initiative, the state intends to cut its dependence on oil to 30 percent by 2030. Hawaiians pay very high electricity prices because costly oil is burned to produce power. Electric cars have a driving range of 40 miles between charges, which is suitable for Hawaii.[17]

AT&T Inc. in 2009 committed to spend $565 million over 10 years to replace its 7,100 passenger cars with 8,000 hybrid-electric and natural gas vans to perform its installation and repair activities. The company is paying on average 29 percent more for these vehicles than it would for gasoline-powered models, but this expense will be offset by lower fuel costs, less emissions, and enhanced public image. The AT&T strategy will reduce carbon emissions by 211,000 metric tons over 10 years. AT&T is working with natural gas providers to build up to 40 fueling stations across its operating region. There are only about 110,000 natural gas vehicles in the United States compared to over 10 million such vehicles worldwide. This bold move by AT&T expands on similar initiatives by United Parcel Service and PG&E.[18]

The March 2009 Copenhagen Meeting

More than 2,000 scientists convened together in Copenhagen in March 2009 and warned the world that global warming is worse than expected. They strongly encouraged companies and governments to "vigorously" implement all economic and technological tools available to cut emissions of heat-trapping greenhouse gases. By the end of this century, scientists warn, sea levels will rise at least 20 inches and possibly as much as 39 inches unless companies and governments implement policies to radically reduce greenhouse gas emissions.

The Kyoto Protocal expires in 2012, and the results of this March 2009 Copenhagen Meeting are expected to replace that agreement. Near-coastal areas worldwide will be under water by the end of this century if drastic actions are not implemented soon worldwide to curb greenhouse gas emissions from companies, cars, trucks, power-generating plants, and planes.

Table 10-1 reveals the impact that bad environmental policies have on two of nature's many ecosystems.

TABLE 10-1   Songbirds and Coral Reefs Need Help

Songbirds

Be a good steward of the natural environment to save our songbirds. Bluebirds are one of 76 songbird species in the United States that have dramatically declined in numbers in the last two decades. Not all birds are considered songbirds, and why birds sing is not clear. Some scientists say they sing when calling for mates or warning of danger, but many scientists now contend that birds sing for sheer pleasure. Songbirds include chickadees, orioles, swallows, mockingbirds, warblers, sparrows, vireos, and the wood thrush. "These birds are telling us there's a problem, something's out of balance in our environment," says Jeff Wells, bird conservation director for the National Audubon Society. Songbirds may be telling us that their air or water is too dirty or that we are destroying too much of their habitat. People collect Picasso paintings and save historic buildings. "Songbirds are part of our natural heritage. Why should we be willing to watch songbirds destroyed any more than allowing a great work of art to be destroyed?" asks Wells. Whatever message songbirds are singing to us today about their natural environment, the message is becoming less and less heard nationwide. Listen when you go outside today. Each of us as individuals, companies, states, and countries should do what we reasonably can to help improve the natural environment for songbirds.[19] A recent study concludes that 67 of the 800 bird species in the United States are endangered, and another 184 species are designated of "conservation concern." The birds of Hawaii are in the greatest peril.

Coral Reefs

Be a good steward of the natural environment to save our coral reefs. The ocean covers more than 71 percent of the earth. The destructive effect of commercial fishing on ocean habitats coupled with increasing pollution runoff into the ocean and global warming of the ocean have decimated fisheries, marine life, and coral reefs around the world. The unfortunate consequence of fishing over the last century has been overfishing, with the principal reasons being politics and greed. Trawl fishing with nets destroys coral reefs and has been compared to catching squirrels by cutting down forests because bottom nets scour and destroy vast areas of the ocean. The great proportion of marine life caught in a trawl is "by-catch" juvenile fish and other life that are killed and discarded. Warming of the ocean due to carbon dioxide emissions also kills thousands of acres of coral reefs annually. The total area of fully protected marine habitats in the United States is only about 50 square miles, compared to some 93 million acres of national wildlife refuges and national parks on the nation's land. A healthy ocean is vital to the economic and social future of the nation—and, indeed, all countries of the world. Everything we do on land ends up in the ocean, so we all must become better stewards of this last frontier on earth in order to sustain human survival and the quality of life.[20]

Conclusion

In a final analysis, ethical standards come out of history and heritage. Our predecessors have left us with an ethical foundation to build on. Even the legendary football coach Vince Lombardi knew that some things were worth more than winning, and he required his players to have three kinds of loyalty: to God, to their families, and to the Green Bay Packers, "in that order." Employees, customers, and shareholders have become less and less tolerant of business ethics violations in firms, and more and more appreciative of model ethical firms. Information sharing across the Internet increasingly reveals such model firms versus irresponsible firms.

Consumers across the country and around the world appreciate firms that do more than is legally required to be socially responsible. But staying in business while adhering to all laws and regulations must be a primary objective of any business. One of the best ways to be socially responsible is for the firm to proactively conserve and preserve the natural environment. For example, to develop a corporate sustainability report annually is not legally required, but such a report, based on concrete actions, goes a long way toward assuring stakeholders that the firm is worthy of their support. Business ethics, social responsibility, and environmental sustainability are interrelated and key strategic issues facing all organizations.

Key Terms and Concepts

Bribe (p. 314)
Bribery (p. 314)
Business Ethics (p. 311)
Code of Business Ethics (p. 313)
Environment (p. 317)
EMS (environmental management system) (p. 321)

ISO 14000 (p. 320)
ISO 14001 (p. 320)
Social policy (p. 315)
Social responsibility (p. 311)
Sustainability (p. 311)
Whistle-Blowing (p. 313)

Issues for Review and Discussion

1. If you owned a small business, would you develop a code of business conduct? If yes, what variables would you include? If no, how would you ensure that ethical business standards were being followed by your employees?
2. What do you feel is the relationship between personal ethics and business ethics? Are they or should they be the same?
3. How can firms best ensure that their code of business ethics ensure is read, understood, believed, remembered, and acted on, rather than ignored?
4. Why is it important *not* to view the concept of "whistle-blowing" as "tattle-telling" or "ratting" on another employee?
5. List six desired results of "ethics training programs" in terms of recommended business ethics policies/procedures in the firm.
6. Discuss bribery. Would actions such as politicians adding earmarks in legislation or pharmaceutical salespersons giving away drugs to physicians constitute bribery? Identify three business activities that would constitute bribery and three actions that would not.
7. How could a strategist's attitude toward social responsibility affect a firm's strategy? On a 1 to 10 scale ranging from Nader's view to Friedman's view, what is your attitude toward social responsibility?
8. How do social policies on retirement differ in various countries around the world?
9. Firms should formulate and implement strategies from an environmental perspective. List eight ways firms can do this.
10. Discuss the major requirements of an EMS under ISO 14001.

Notes

1. http://disney.go.com/crreport/home.html.
2. Joann Greco, "Privacy—Whose Right Is It Anyhow?" *Journal of Business Strategy* (January–February 2001): 32.
3. Saul Gellerman, "Why 'Good' Managers Make Bad Ethical Choices," *Harvard Business Review* 64, no. 4 (July–August 1986): 88.
4. Peter Drucker, *Management: Tasks, Responsibilities, and Practices* (New York: Harper & Row, 1974): 462, 463.
5. www.wikipedia.org.
6. Phred Dvorak, Bob Davis, and Louise Radnofsky, "Firms Confront Boss-Subordinate Love Affairs," *Wall Street Journal* (October 27, 2008): B5.
7. Archie Carroll and Frank Hoy, "Integrating Corporate Social Policy into Strategic Management," *Journal of Business Strategy* 4, no. 3 (Winter 1984): 57.
8. http://money.cnn.com/magazines/fortune/mostadmired/2009/best_worst/best4.html.
9. Ibid.
10. Sebastian Moffett, "Fat-Aging Japan Keeps Its Elders on the Job Longer," *Wall Street Journal* (June 15, 2005): A1, A8; Sebastian Moffett, "Japan Seeks More Efficiency as Population Drops," *Wall Street Journal* (December 12, 2006): A2; Yuka Hayashi, "Japan Turns to Foreign Workers Amid Labor Crunch," *Wall Street Journal* (November 30, 2006): A10; Yuka Hayashi and Sebastian Moffett, "Cautiously, an Aging Japan Warms to Foreign Workers," *Wall Street Journal* (May 25, 2007): A1, A12.
11. Antonie Boessenkool, "Activists Push More Firms on Social Responsibility," *Wall Street Journal* (January 31, 2007): B13; Kris Hudson, "Wal-Mart Wants Supplies, Workers to Join Green Effort," *Wall Street Journal* (February 2, 2007): A14; Jayne O'Donnell and Christine Dugas, "More Retailers Go for Green—The Eco Kind," *USA Today* (April 18, 2007): 3B.
12. Kerry Hannon, "Businesses' Green Opportunities Are Wide, But Complex," *USA Today* (January 2, 2009): 5B.
13. Simona Covel, "Alternative-Energy Companies Grow Even as Others Falter," *Wall Street Journal* (January 13, 209): B4.
14. R. Alsop, "Corporations Still Put Profits First, But Social Concerns Gain Ground," *Wall Street Journal* (2001): B14; Jane Kim, "Business Schools Take a Page from Kinder, Gentler Textbook," *Wall Street Journal* (October 22, 2003): B2C; Beth Gardner, "Business Schools Going Green," *Wall Street Journal* (June 6, 2007): B5A.
15. Forest Reinhardt, "Bringing the Environment Down to Earth," *Harvard Business Review* (July–August 1999): 149–158; Christine Rosen, "Environmental Strategy and Competitive Advantage," *California Management Review* 43, no. 3 (Spring 2001): 8–15; Chris Woodyard, "Cleaner Diesel Engine Rules Take Effect," *USA Today* (December 29, 2006): 1B.
16. Adapted from the www.iso14000.com Web site and the www.epa.gov Web site.
17. Jim Carlton, "Electric-Car Network Planned," *Wall Street Journal* (November 21, 2008): B2. Also, "BYD to Introduce China's First Electric Car," *Wall Street Journal* (December 15, 2008): B2. Rebecca Smith, "Hawaii Makes Big Bet on Electric Cars," *Wall Street Journal* (December 3, 2008): A2.
18. Amol Sharma, "AT&T Invests in Green Fleet," *Wall Street Journal* (March 12, 2009): B3.
19. Tom Brook, "Declining Numbers Mute Many Birds' Songs," *USA Today* (September 11, 2001): 4A.
20. John Ogden, "Maintaining Diversity in the Oceans," *Environment* (April 2001): 29–36.

Current Readings

Amram, Martha, and Nalin Kulatilaka. "The Invisible Green Hand: How Individual Decisions and Markets Can Reduce Greenhouse Gas Emissions." *California Management Review* (Winter 2009): 194–218.

Basu, Kunal, and Guido Palazzo. "Corporate Social Responsibility: A Process Model of Sensemaking." *The Academy of Management Review* 33, no. 1 (January 2008): 122.

Berrone, Pascual, and Luis Gomez-Mejia. "Environmental Performance and Executive Compensation: An Integrated Agency-Institutional Perspective." *Academy of Management Journal* 52, no. 1 (February 2009): 103–126.

Cochran, Phillip L., and Robert Neal. "Corporate Social Responsibility, Corporate Governance, and Financial Performance: Lessons from Finance." *Business Horizons* 51, no. 5 (September–October 2008): 535.

Hull, Clyde Eirkur, and Sandra Rothenburg. "Firm Performance: The Interactions of Corporate Social Performance with Innovation and Industry Differentiation." *Strategic Management Journal* 29, no. 7 (July 2008): 781.

Kacmar, Michele. "From the Editors: An Ethical Quiz." *Academy of Management Journal* (June 2009): 432–434.

Kaptein, Muel. "Developing a Measure of Unethical Behavior in the Workplace: A Stakeholder Perspective." *Journal of Management* 34, no.5 (October 2008): 978.

Karniker, Joy, and Margaret Williams. "Organizational Justice and Organizational Citizenship Behavior: A Mediated Multifoci Model." *Journal of Management* (February 2009): 112–135.

Kramer, Roderick. "Rethinking Trust." *Harvard Business Review* (June 2009): 68–78.

Lim, Elizabeth, Shobha Das, and Amit Das. "Diversification Strategy, Capital Structure, and the Asian Financial Crisis (1997–1998): Evidence from Singapore Firms." *Strategic Management Journal* (June 2009): 577–594.

Love, E. Geoffrey, and Matthew Kraatz. "Character, Conformity, or the Bottom Line? How and Why Downsizing Affected Corporate Reputation." *Academy of Management Journal* (April 2009): 314–335.

Peloza, John, and Loren Falkenberg. "The Role of Collaboration in Achieving Corporate Social Responsibility Objectives." *California Management Review* (Spring 2009): 95–113.

Puranam, Phanish, and Bart Vanneste. "Trust and Governance: Untangling a Tangled Web." *Academy of Management Review* (January 2009): 11–31.

Thurston, Ken. "The Green Conversation." *Harvard Business Review* (September 2008): 58.

Urbany, Joel E., Thomas J. Reynolds, and Joan M. Phillips. "How to Make Values Count in Everyday Decisions." *MIT Sloan Management Review* 49, no. 4 (Summer 2008): 75.

Webb, Justin, Laszlo Tihanyi, Duane Ireland, and David Sirmon. "You Say Illegal, I Say Legitimate: Entrepreneurship in the Informal Economy." *Academy of Management Review* (July 2009): 492–510.

ASSURANCE OF LEARNING EXERCISES

Assurance of Learning Exercise 10A

Does McDonald's Have a Code of Business Ethics?

Purpose

This exercise aims to familiarize you with corporate codes of business ethics. Go to Starbucks' Standards of Business Conduct found at their www.starbucks.com Web site and more particularly at the http://www.starbucks.com/aboutus/SoBC_FY09_eng.pdf Web page.

Then see the Code of Business Ethics for McDonald's Corporation or lack of one thereof. (At the time of this writing, the author could only find a social responsibility statement for McDonald's, and it was at the http://www.mcdonalds.com/usa/work/socialresp.html Web page.)

Instructions

Step 1   Go to the two Web sites just listed and print the Standards of Business Conduct information for (1) Starbucks Corp. and (2) McDonald's Corp. Read the two statements.

Step 2   On a separate sheet of paper, list three aspects that you like most and three aspects that you like least about (1) the Starbucks statement and (2) the McDonald's statement. In other words, compare the two statements. Conclude by indicating which statement of conduct you like best. Why do you think it is best?

Step 3   Explain why having a code of business ethics is not sufficient for ensuring ethical behavior in an organization. What other means are necessary to help ensure ethical behavior? Give the class an example of a breach of ethical conduct that you recall in your work experience.

Assurance of Learning Exercise 1B

The Ethics of Spying on Competitors

Purpose

This exercise gives you an opportunity to discuss in class ethical and legal issues related to methods being used by many companies to spy on competing firms. Gathering and using information about competitors is an area of strategic management that Japanese firms do more proficiently than American firms.

Instructions

On a separate sheet of paper, number from 1 to 18. For the 18 spying activities listed as follows, indicate whether or not you believe the activity is ethical or unethical and legal or illegal. Place either an *E* for ethical or *U* for unethical, and either an *L* for legal or an *I* for illegal for each activity. Compare your answers to those of your classmates and discuss any differences.

1. Buying competitors' garbage
2. Dissecting competitors' products
3. Taking competitors' plant tours anonymously
4. Counting tractor-trailer trucks leaving competitors' loading bays
5. Studying aerial photographs of competitors' facilities
6. Analyzing competitors' labor contracts
7. Analyzing competitors' help-wanted ads
8. Quizzing customers and buyers about the sales of competitors' products

9. Infiltrating customers' and competitors' business operations
10. Quizzing suppliers about competitors' level of manufacturing
11. Using customers to buy out phony bids
12. Encouraging key customers to reveal competitive information
13. Quizzing competitors' former employees
14. Interviewing consultants who may have worked with competitors
15. Hiring key managers away from competitors
16. Conducting phony job interviews to get competitors' employees to reveal information
17. Sending engineers to trade meetings to quiz competitors' technical employees
18. Quizzing potential employees who worked for or with competitors

Assurance of Learning Exercise 10C

Who Prepares a Sustainability Report?

Purpose

The purpose of this activity is to determine the nature and prevalence of Sustainability Reports among companies in your state.

Instructions

Contact by phone at least five different plant managers or owners of large businesses in your area. Seek answers to the following questions. Present your findings in a written report to your instructor.

1. Does your company prepare a Sustainability Report? If yes, please describe the nature and scope of the report.
2. Are environmental criteria included in the performance evaluation of managers? If yes, please specify the criteria.
3. Are environmental affairs more a technical function or a management function in your company?
4. Does your firm offer any environmental workshops for employees? If yes, please describe them.

CHAPTER 11
Global/International Issues

CHAPTER **OBJECTIVES**

After studying this chapter, you should be able to do the following:

1. Explain the advantages and disadvantages of entering global markets.

2. Discuss protectionism as it impacts the world economy.

3. Explain when and why a firm (or industry) may need to become more or less global in nature to compete.

4. Discuss the global challenge facing American firms.

5. Compare and contrast the culture in the United States with Mexico and Japan.

6. Describe how management style varies across Europe.

7. Discuss communication differences across countries.

Assurance of Learning Exercises

Assurance of Learning Exercise 11A
McDonald's Wants to Enter Africa. Help Them.

Assurance of Learning Exercise 11B
Does My University Recruit in Foreign Countries?

Assurance of Learning Exercise 11C
Assessing Differences in Culture Across Countries

Assurance of Learning Exercise 11D
How Well Traveled Are Business Students at Your University?

Source: John Sartin/Shutterstock

"Notable Quotes"

"Sad but true, U.S. businesspeople have the lowest foreign language proficiency of any major trading nation. U.S. business schools do not emphasize foreign languages, and students traditionally avoid them."
—Ronald Dulek

"America's economy has become much less American."

"In God we trust. All others bring data."
—Edward Deming

Doing Great in a Weak Economy. How?

Marriott International

Among all hotels, casinos, and resorts, Marriott International scored the highest on *Fortune's* "Most Admired Companies" both in 2007 and 2008. When most firms were struggling, Marriott made $362 million in net income on $12.88 billion in revenues, quite impressive for a hotel/motel firm in 2008. *Fortune* rated Marriott as their 13th overall "Most Admired Company in the World" in terms of their management and performance. Marriott is looking past the current slump in travel by planning to open 130 new hotels in the next four years. About half of the new hotels are targeted for emerging markets such as China, India, and the United Arab Emirates. The new hotels will add 32,000 rooms to Bethesda, Maryland–based Marriott's capacity of 560,000 rooms at 3,178 properties. Marriott declared a new stock dividend in August 2009.

Marriott is one of the world's leading hoteliers, with some 3,000 properties in more than 65 countries, including Renaissance Hotels and Marriott Hotels & Resorts, as well as Courtyard and Fairfield Inn. It also owns the Ritz-Carlton and time-share properties operated by Marriott Vacation Club International. Marriott additionally provides more than 2,000 rental units for corporate housing and manages 45 golf courses. The Marriott family, including CEO J. W. Marriott Jr., owns about 30 percent of the firm.

Marriott prefers to manage rather than own properties. The firm is planning to purchase some of the Greenbrier Hotel Corporation's assets, including its historic luxury White Sulphur Springs, West Virginia, resort. Then Marriott will sell that property to another hotel owner but maintain management rights to the property. Greenbrier entered Chapter 11 bankruptcy in 2009, which prompted Marriott to offer to acquire some of their assets.

Source: Based On Geoff Colvin, "The World's Most Admired Companies," *Fortune* (March 16, 2009): 76–86; Rachel Feintzeig and Kris Hudson, "Greenbrier Hotel Seeks Chapter 11, Plans to Sell to Marriott," *Wall Street Journal* (March 20, 2009): B3.

As illustrated in Figure 11-1, global considerations impact virtually all strategic decisions. The boundaries of countries no longer can define the limits of our imaginations. To see and appreciate the world from the perspective of others has become a matter of survival for businesses. The underpinnings of strategic management hinge on managers gaining an understanding of competitors, markets, prices, suppliers, distributors, governments, creditors, shareholders, and customers worldwide. The price and quality of a firm's products and services must be competitive on a worldwide basis, not just on a local basis. As indicated above, Marriott International is an example global business that performed outstandingly well during the recent global recession.

The World Trade Organization (WTO) in March 2009 issued the most pessimistic report on global trade in its 62-year history: that global trade would drop by 9 percent or more in 2009.[1] A world market has emerged from what previously was a multitude of

FIGURE 11-1

A Comprehensive Strategic-Management Mode

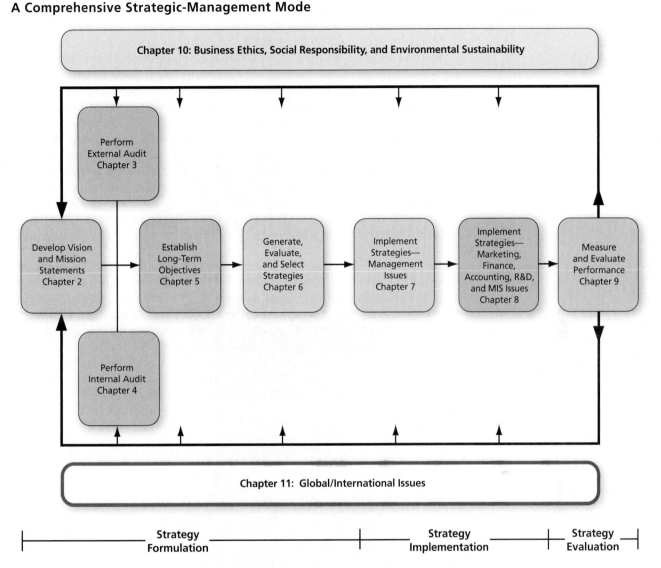

Source: Fred R. David, "How Companies Define Their Mission," *Long Range Planning* 22, no. 3 (June 1988): 40.

distinct national markets, and the climate for international business today is more favorable than in years past. Mass communication and high technology have created similar patterns of consumption in diverse cultures worldwide. This means that many companies may find it difficult to survive by relying solely on domestic markets.

It is not exaggeration that in an industry that is, or is rapidly becoming, global, the riskiest possible posture is to remain a domestic competitor. The domestic competitor will watch as more aggressive companies use this growth to capture economies of scale and learning. The domestic competitor will then be faced with an attack on domestic markets using different (and possibly superior) technology, product design, manufacturing, marketing approaches, and economies of scale.[2]

Multinational Organizations

Organizations that conduct business operations across national borders are called *international firms* or *multinational corporations*. The strategic-management process is conceptually the same for multinational firms as for purely domestic firms; however, the process is more complex for international firms due to more variables and relationships. The social, cultural, demographic, environmental, political, governmental, legal, technological, and competitive opportunities and threats that face a multinational corporation are almost limitless, and the number and complexity of these factors increase dramatically with the number of products produced and the number of geographic areas served.

More time and effort are required to identify and evaluate external trends and events in multinational corporations than in domestic corporations. Geographic distance, cultural and national differences, and variations in business practices often make communication between domestic headquarters and overseas operations difficult. Strategy implementation can be more difficult because different cultures have different norms, values, and work ethics.

Multinational corporations (MNCs) face unique and diverse risks, such as expropriation of assets, currency losses through exchange rate fluctuations, unfavorable foreign court interpretations of contracts and agreements, social/political disturbances, import/export restrictions, tariffs, and trade barriers. Strategists in MNCs are often confronted with the need to be globally competitive and nationally responsive at the same time. With the rise in world commerce, government and regulatory bodies are more closely monitoring foreign business practices. The U.S. Foreign Corrupt Practices Act, for example, monitors business practices in many areas.

Before entering international markets, firms should scan relevant journals and patent reports, seek the advice of academic and research organizations, participate in international trade fairs, form partnerships, and conduct extensive research to broaden their contacts and diminish the risk of doing business in new markets. Firms can also offset some risks of doing business internationally by obtaining insurance from the U.S. government's Overseas Private Investment Corporation (OPIC).

Philips Electronics NV is one of many firms moving into emerging markets. A few of Philips's acquisitions in the year 2008 alone were Medel in Italy, Meditronics in India, Alpha X-Ray Technologies in India, Dixtal Biomedica & Tecnologia in Brazil, Shenzhen Goldway Industrial in China, and VMI-Sistemes Medicos in Brazil.

Advantages and Disadvantages of International Operations

Firms have numerous reasons for formulating and implementing strategies that initiate, continue, or expand involvement in business operations across national borders. Perhaps the greatest advantage is that firms can gain new customers for their products and services, thus increasing revenues. Growth in revenues and profits is a common organizational objective and often an expectation of shareholders because it is a measure of organizational success.

Potential advantages to initiating, continuing, and/or expanding international operations are as follows:

1. Firms can gain new customers for their products.
2. Foreign operations can absorb excess capacity, reduce unit costs, and spread economic risks over a wider number of markets.
3. Foreign operations can allow firms to establish low-cost production facilities in locations close to raw materials and/or cheap labor.
4. Competitors in foreign markets may not exist, or competition may be less intense than in domestic markets.
5. Foreign operations may result in reduced tariffs, lower taxes, and favorable political treatment.
6. Joint ventures can enable firms to learn the technology, culture, and business practices of other people and to make contacts with potential customers, suppliers, creditors, and distributors in foreign countries.
7. Economies of scale can be achieved from operation in global rather than solely domestic markets. Larger-scale production and better efficiencies allow higher sales volumes and lower-price offerings.

8. A firm's power and prestige in domestic markets may be significantly enhanced if the firm competes globally. Enhanced prestige can translate into improved negotiating power among creditors, suppliers, distributors, and other important groups.

The availability, depth, and reliability of economic and marketing information in different countries vary extensively, as do industrial structures, business practices, and the number and nature of regional organizations. There are also numerous potential disadvantages of initiating, continuing, or expanding business across national borders, such as the following:

1. Foreign operations could be seized by nationalistic factions.
2. Firms confront different and often little-understood social, cultural, demographic, environmental, political, governmental, legal, technological, economic, and competitive forces when doing business internationally. These forces can make communication difficult in the firm.
3. Weaknesses of competitors in foreign lands are often overestimated, and strengths are often underestimated. Keeping informed about the number and nature of competitors is more difficult when doing business internationally.
4. Language, culture, and value systems differ among countries, which can create barriers to communication and problems managing people.
5. Gaining an understanding of regional organizations such as the European Economic Community, the Latin American Free Trade Area, the International Bank for Reconstruction and Development, and the International Finance Corporation is difficult but is often required in doing business internationally.
6. Dealing with two or more monetary systems can complicate international business operations.

The Global Challenge

Foreign competitors are battering U.S. firms in many industries. In its simplest sense, the global challenge faced by U.S. business is twofold: (1) how to gain and maintain exports to other nations and (2) how to defend domestic markets against imported goods. Few companies can afford to ignore the presence of international competition. Firms that seem insulated and comfortable today may be vulnerable tomorrow; for example, foreign banks do not yet compete or operate in most of the United States, but this too is changing.

America's economy is becoming much less American. A world economy and monetary system are emerging. Corporations in every corner of the globe are taking advantage of the opportunity to obtain customers globally. Markets are shifting rapidly and in many cases converging in tastes, trends, and prices. Innovative transport systems are accelerating the transfer of technology. Shifts in the nature and location of production systems, especially to China and India, are reducing the response time to changing market conditions.

More and more countries around the world are welcoming foreign investment and capital. As a result, labor markets have steadily become more international. East Asian countries are market leaders in labor-intensive industries, Brazil offers abundant natural resources and rapidly developing markets, and Germany offers skilled labor and technology. The drive to improve the efficiency of global business operations is leading to greater functional specialization. This is not limited to a search for the familiar low-cost labor in Latin America or Asia. Other considerations include the cost of energy, availability of resources, inflation rates, tax rates, and the nature of trade regulations.

Many countries became more protectionist during the recent global economic recession. *Protectionism* refers to countries imposing tariffs, taxes, and regulations on firms outside the country to favor their own companies and people. Most economists argue that protectionism harms the world economy because it inhibits trade among countries and invites retaliation.

When China joined the World Trade Organization in 2001, that country agreed to respect copyright protections and liberalize restrictions on the import and distribution of foreign-made goods. However, Chinese counterfeiters still can be criminally prosecuted for commercial piracy only when caught in possession of at least 500 counterfeit items.[3] In China, pirated goods such as Nike running shoes, new Hollywood movies on DVD, and Microsoft software can be purchased for a fraction of their actual prices on many streets. China still has substantial barriers to sales of authentic U.S.-made copyrighted products. Former U.S. Trade Representative Susan Schwab says, "This is more than a handbag here or a logo item there; it is often theft on a grand scale." China's counterfeit trade practices contribute to an annual bilateral trade deficit of about $250 billion with the United States. Chinese pirating of products is an external threat facing many firms.

Advancements in telecommunications are drawing countries, cultures, and organizations worldwide closer together. Foreign revenue as a percentage of total company revenues already exceeds 50 percent in hundreds of U.S. firms, including Exxon/Mobil, Gillette, Dow Chemical, Citicorp, Colgate-Palmolive, and Texaco.

A primary reason why most domestic firms are engaging in global operations is that growth in demand for goods and services outside the United States is considerably higher than inside. For example, the domestic food industry is growing just 3 percent per year, so Kraft Foods, the second largest food company in the world behind Nestle, is focusing on foreign acquisitions.

Shareholders and investors expect sustained growth in revenues from firms; satisfactory growth for many firms can only be achieved by capitalizing on demand outside the United States. Joint ventures and partnerships between domestic and foreign firms are becoming the rule rather than the exception!

Fully 95 percent of the world's population lives outside the United States, and this group is growing 70 percent faster than the U.S. population. The lineup of competitors in virtually all industries is global. General Motors, Ford, and Chrysler compete with Toyota and Hyundai. General Electric and Westinghouse battle Siemens and Mitsubishi. Caterpillar and John Deere compete with Komatsu. Goodyear battles Michelin, Bridgestone/Firestone, and Pirelli. Boeing competes with Airbus. Only a few U.S. industries—such as furniture, printing, retailing, consumer packaged goods, and retail banking—are not yet greatly challenged by foreign competitors. But many products and components in these industries too are now manufactured in foreign countries. International operations can be as simple as exporting a product to a single foreign country or as complex as operating manufacturing, distribution, and marketing facilities in many countries.

Globalization

Globalization is a process of doing business worldwide, so strategic decisions are made based on global profitability of the firm rather than just domestic considerations. A global strategy seeks to meet the needs of customers worldwide, with the highest value at the lowest cost. This may mean locating production in countries with the lowest labor costs or abundant natural resources, locating research and complex engineering centers where skilled scientists and engineers can be found, and locating marketing activities close to the markets to be served.

A *global strategy* includes designing, producing, and marketing products with global needs in mind, instead of considering individual countries alone. A global strategy integrates actions against competitors into a worldwide plan. Today, there are global buyers and sellers, and the instant transmission of money and information across continents.

It is clear that different industries become global for different reasons. The need to amortize massive R&D investments over many markets is a major reason why the aircraft manufacturing industry became global. Monitoring globalization in one's industry is an important strategic-management activity. Knowing how to use that information for one's competitive advantage is even more important. For example, firms may look around the world for the best technology and select one that has the most promise for the largest number of markets. When firms design a product, they design it to be marketable in as many countries as possible. When firms manufacture a product, they select the lowest-cost source, which may be Japan for semiconductors, Sri Lanka for textiles, Malaysia for simple electronics, and Europe for precision machinery.

A Weak Economy

A weak economy still plagues many countries around the world. The British pound reached a 23-year low against the U.S. dollar in January 2009. Two consecutive quarters of a decline in real gross domestic product is commonly used as a definition of a *recession*, and the last quarter of 2008 marked this occurrence in the United Kingdom. The speed and breadth at which the United Kingdom's economy shrunk makes economists think the UK recession could last through 2012. Like the U.S. government, the UK government has poured hundreds of billions of pounds into stimulus and financial bailout measures. Further interest rate cuts by the Bank of England are expected soon, although the bank's rates are already the lowest in the bank's 315-year history. The pound's fall has done little to boost exports. David Sandall, a businessman in Cheshire, Northern England, says, "It doesn't matter what the price of something is if your customer hasn't got the money." And that is the primary situation in the United Kingdom's two largest trading regions—Europe and the United States.

Unemployment rates are high across the United States and around the world. Consumer spending remains low and cautious while banks continue to be reluctant to loan money. Stock prices have rebounded, but many investors still have an appetite only for government securities. New corporate profit warnings and bankruptcies spell continued recession in many countries.

United States versus Foreign Business Cultures

To compete successfully in world markets, U.S. managers must obtain a better knowledge of historical, cultural, and religious forces that motivate and drive people in other countries. In Japan, for example, business relations operate within the context of *Wa,* which stresses group harmony and social cohesion. In China, business behavior revolves around *guanxi,* or personal relations. In South Korea, activities involve concern for *inhwa,* or harmony based on respect of hierarchical relationships, including obedience to authority.[4]

In Europe, it is generally true that the farther north on the continent, the more participatory the management style. Most European workers are unionized and enjoy more frequent vacations and holidays than U.S. workers. A 90-minute lunch break plus 20-minute morning and afternoon breaks are common in European firms. Guaranteed permanent employment is typically a part of employment contracts in Europe. In socialist countries such as France, Belgium, and the United Kingdom, the only grounds for immediate dismissal from work is a criminal offense. A six-month trial period at the beginning of employment is usually part of the contract with a European firm. Many Europeans resent pay-for-performance, commission salaries, and objective measurement and reward systems. This is true especially of workers in southern Europe. Many Europeans also find the notion of team spirit difficult to grasp because the unionized environment has dichotomized worker–management relations throughout Europe.

A weakness of some U.S. firms in competing with Pacific Rim firms is a lack of understanding of Asian cultures, including how Asians think and behave. Spoken Chinese, for example, has more in common with spoken English than with spoken Japanese or Korean. U.S. managers consistently put more weight on being friendly and liked, whereas Asian and European managers often exercise authority without this concern. Americans tend to use first names instantly in business dealings with foreigners, but foreigners find this presumptuous. In Japan, for example, first names are used only among family members and intimate friends; even longtime business associates and coworkers shy away from the use of first names. Table 11-1 lists other cultural differences or pitfalls that U.S. managers need to know about.

U.S. managers have a low tolerance for silence, whereas Asian managers view extended periods of silence as important for organizing and evaluating one's thoughts. U.S. managers are much more action oriented than their counterparts around the world; they rush to appointments, conferences, and meetings—and then feel the day has been productive. But for many foreign managers, resting, listening, meditating, and thinking is considered productive.

TABLE 11-1   Cultural Pitfalls That May Help You Be a Better Manager

- Waving is a serious insult in Greece and Nigeria, particularly if the hand is near someone's face.
- Making a "good-bye" wave in Europe can mean "No," but it means "Come here" in Peru.
- In China, last names are written first.
- A man named Carlos Lopez-Garcia should be addressed as Mr. Lopez in Latin America but as Mr. Garcia in Brazil.
- Breakfast meetings are considered uncivilized in most foreign countries.
- Latin Americans are on average 20 minutes late to business appointments.
- Direct eye contact is impolite in Japan.
- Don't cross your legs in any Arab or many Asian countries—it's rude to show the sole of your shoe.
- In Brazil, touching your thumb and first finger—an American "Okay" sign—is the equivalent of raising your middle finger.
- Nodding or tossing your head back in southern Italy, Malta, Greece, and Tunisia means "No." In India, this body motion means "Yes."
- Snapping your fingers is vulgar in France and Belgium.
- Folding your arms across your chest is a sign of annoyance in Finland.
- In China, leave some food on your plate to show that your host was so generous that you couldn't finish.
- Do not eat with your left hand when dining with clients from Malaysia or India.
- One form of communication works the same worldwide. It's the smile—so take that along wherever you go.

Sitting through a conference without talking is unproductive in the United States, but it is viewed as positive in Japan if one's silence helps preserve unity.

U.S. managers place greater emphasis on short-term results than foreign managers. In marketing, for example, Japanese managers strive to achieve "everlasting customers," whereas many Americans strive to make a onetime sale. Marketing managers in Japan see making a sale as the beginning, not the end, of the selling process. This is an important distinction. Japanese managers often criticize U.S. managers for worrying more about shareholders, whom they do not know, than employees, whom they do know. Americans refer to "hourly employees," whereas many Japanese companies still refer to "lifetime employees."

Rose Knotts recently summarized some important cultural differences between U.S. and foreign managers:[5]

1. Americans place an exceptionally high priority on time, viewing time as an asset. Many foreigners place more worth on relationships. This difference results in foreign managers often viewing U.S. managers as "more interested in business than people."

2. Personal touching and distance norms differ around the world. Americans generally stand about three feet from each other when carrying on business conversations, but Arabs and Africans stand about one foot apart. Touching another person with the left hand in business dealings is taboo in some countries. American managers need to learn the personal-space rules of foreign managers with whom they interact in business.

3. Family roles and relationships vary in different countries. For example, males are valued more than females in some cultures, and peer pressure, work situations, and business interactions reinforce this phenomenon.

4. Business and daily life in some societies are governed by religious factors. Prayer times, holidays, daily events, and dietary restrictions, for example, need to be respected by American managers not familiar with these practices in some countries.

5. Time spent with the family and the quality of relationships are more important in some cultures than the personal achievement and accomplishments espoused by the traditional U.S. manager.

6. Many cultures around the world value modesty, team spirit, collectivity, and patience much more than the competitiveness and individualism that are so important in the United States.

7. Punctuality is a valued personal trait when conducting business in the United States, but it is not revered in many of the world's societies. Eating habits also differ

dramatically across cultures. For example, belching is acceptable in some countries as evidence of satisfaction with the food that has been prepared. Chinese culture considers it good manners to sample a portion of each food served.

8. To prevent social blunders when meeting with managers from other lands, one must learn and respect the rules of etiquette of others. Sitting on a toilet seat is viewed as unsanitary in most countries, but not in the United States. Leaving food or drink after dining is considered impolite in some countries, but not in China. Bowing instead of shaking hands is customary in many countries. Some cultures view Americans as unsanitary for locating toilet and bathing facilities in the same area, whereas Americans view people of some cultures as unsanitary for not taking a bath or shower every day.

9. Americans often do business with individuals they do not know, unlike businesspersons in many other cultures. In Mexico and Japan, for example, an amicable relationship is often mandatory before conducting business.

In many countries, effective managers are those who are best at negotiating with government bureaucrats rather than those who inspire workers. Many U.S. managers are uncomfortable with nepotism and bribery, which are practiced in some countries. The United States has gained a reputation for defending women from sexual harassment and minorities from discrimination, but not all countries embrace the same values.

American managers in China have to be careful about how they arrange office furniture because Chinese workers believe in *feng shui,* the practice of harnessing natural forces. U.S. managers in Japan have to be careful about *nemaswashio,* whereby Japanese workers expect supervisors to alert them privately of changes rather than informing them in a meeting. Japanese managers have little appreciation for versatility, expecting all managers to be the same. In Japan, "If a nail sticks out, you hit it into the wall," says Brad Lashbrook, an international consultant for Wilson Learning.

Probably the biggest obstacle to the effectiveness of U.S. managers—or managers from any country working in another—is the fact that it is almost impossible to change the attitude of a foreign workforce. "The system drives you; you cannot fight the system or culture," says Bill Parker, president of Phillips Petroleum in Norway.

The Mexican Culture

Mexico is an authoritarian society in terms of schools, churches, businesses, and families. Employers seek workers who are agreeable, respectful, and obedient, rather than innovative, creative, and independent. Mexican workers tend to be activity oriented rather than problem solvers. When visitors walk into a Mexican business, they are impressed by the cordial, friendly atmosphere. This is almost always true because Mexicans desire harmony rather than conflict; desire for harmony is part of the social fabric in worker–manager relations. There is a much lower tolerance for adversarial relations or friction at work in Mexico as compared to the United States.

Mexican employers are paternalistic, providing workers with more than a paycheck, but in return they expect allegiance. Weekly food baskets, free meals, free bus service, and free day care are often part of compensation. The ideal working condition for a Mexican worker is the family model, with people all working together, doing their share, according to their designated roles. Mexican workers do not expect or desire a work environment in which self-expression and initiative are encouraged. Whereas U.S. business embodies individualism, achievement, competition, curiosity, pragmatism, informality, spontaneity, and doing more than expected on the job, Mexican businesses stress collectivism, continuity, cooperation, belongingness, formality, and doing exactly what you're told.

In Mexico, business associates rarely entertain each other at their homes, which are places reserved exclusively for close friends and family. Business meetings and entertaining are nearly always done at a restaurant. Preserving one's honor, saving face, and looking important are also exceptionally important in Mexico. This is why Mexicans do not accept criticism and change easily; many find it humiliating to acknowledge having made a mistake. A meeting among employees and managers in a business located in Mexico is a forum for giving orders and directions rather than for discussing problems or participating in decision making. Mexican workers want to be closely supervised, cared for, and corrected in a civil manner. Opinions expressed by employees are often regarded as back talk in Mexico. Mexican supervisors are viewed as weak if they explain the rationale for their orders to workers.

Mexicans do not feel compelled to follow rules that are not associated with a particular person in authority they work for or know well. Thus signs to wear earplugs or safety glasses, or attendance or seniority policies, and even one-way street signs are often ignored. Whereas Americans follow the rules, Mexicans often do not.

Life is slower in Mexico than in the United States. The first priority is often assigned to the last request, rather than to the first. Telephone systems break down. Banks may suddenly not have pesos. Phone repair can take a month. Electricity for an entire plant or town can be down for hours or even days. Business and government offices may open and close at odd hours. Buses and taxis may be hours off schedule. Meeting times for appointments are not rigid. Tardiness is common everywhere. Effectively doing business in Mexico requires knowledge of the Mexican way of life, culture, beliefs, and customs.

The Japanese Culture

The Japanese place great importance on group loyalty and consensus, a concept called *Wa*. Nearly all corporate activities in Japan encourage *Wa* among managers and employees. *Wa* requires that all members of a group agree and cooperate; this results in constant discussion and compromise. Japanese managers evaluate the potential attractiveness of alternative business decisions in terms of the long-term effect on the group's *Wa*. This is why silence, used for pondering alternatives, can be a plus in a formal Japanese meeting. Discussions potentially disruptive to *Wa* are generally conducted in very informal settings, such as at a bar, so as to minimize harm to the group's *Wa*. Entertaining is an important business activity in Japan because it strengthens *Wa*. Formal meetings are often conducted in informal settings. When confronted with disturbing questions or opinions, Japanese managers tend to remain silent, whereas Americans tend to respond directly, defending themselves through explanation and argument.

Most Japanese managers are reserved, quiet, distant, introspective, and other oriented, whereas most U.S. managers are talkative, insensitive, impulsive, direct, and individual oriented. Americans often perceive Japanese managers as wasting time and carrying on pointless conversations, whereas U.S. managers often use blunt criticism, ask prying questions, and make quick decisions. These kinds of cultural differences have disrupted many potentially productive Japanese–American business endeavors. Viewing the Japanese communication style as a prototype for all Asian cultures is a stereotype that must be avoided.

Communication Differences Across Countries

Americans increasingly interact with managers in other countries, so it is important to understand foreign business cultures. Americans often come across as intrusive, manipulative, and garrulous; this impression may reduce their effectiveness in communication. *Forbes* recently provided the following cultural hints from Charis Intercultural Training:

1. Italians, Germans, and French generally do not soften up executives with praise before they criticize. Americans do soften up folks, and this practice seems manipulative to Europeans.
2. Israelis are accustomed to fast-paced meetings and have little patience for American informality and small talk.
3. British executives often complain that American executives chatter too much. Informality, egalitarianism, and spontaneity from Americans in business settings jolt many foreigners.
4. Europeans feel they are being treated like children when asked to wear name tags by Americans.

5. Executives in India are used to interrupting one another. Thus, when American executives listen without asking for clarification or posing questions, they are viewed by Indians as not paying attention.

6. When negotiating orally with Malaysian or Japanese executives, it is appropriate to allow periodically for a time of silence. However, no pause is needed when negotiating in Israel.

7. Refrain from asking foreign managers questions such as "How was your weekend?" That is intrusive to foreigners, who tend to regard their business and private lives as totally separate.[6]

Americans have more freedom to control their own fates than do the Japanese. Life in the United States and life in Japan are very different; the United States offers more upward mobility to its people. This is a great strength of the United States, as indicated here:

> America is not like Japan and can never be. America's strength is the opposite: It opens its doors and brings the world's disorder in. It tolerates social change that would tear most other societies apart. This openness encourages Americans to adapt as individuals rather than as a group. Americans go west to California to get a new start; they move east to Manhattan to try to make the big time; they move to Vermont or to a farm to get close to the soil. They break away from their parents' religions or values or class; they rediscover their ethnicity. They go to night school; they change their names. [7]

Worldwide Tax Rates

The lowest corporate tax rates among developed countries reside in Europe, and European countries are lowering tax rates further to attract investment. The average corporate tax rate among European Union countries is 26 percent, compared with 30 percent in the Asia-Pacific region and 38 percent in the United States and Japan. Ireland and the former Soviet-bloc nations of Eastern Europe recently slashed corporate tax rates to nearly zero, attracting substantial investment. Germany cut its corporate tax rate from 39 percent in 2007 to just under 30 percent in 2008. Great Britain cut its corporate tax rate to 28 percent from 30 percent. France cut its rate from 34 percent to 27 percent in 2008.

Other factors besides the corporate tax rate obviously affect companies' decisions to locate plants and facilities. For example, the large and affluent market and efficient infrastructure in Germany and Britain attract companies, but the high labor costs and strict labor laws keep other companies away.

Ralph Gomory, president of the Alfred P. Sloan Foundation and a former top executive at IBM, warns of a growing divergence between the interests of U.S. corporations and interests of the U.S. government. Specifically, he says U.S. trade liberalization/globalization policies for the last two decades have encouraged corporations to seek the lowest-cost locations for their operations. The new 1,200-worker Intel semiconductor plant in Vietnam is just one example among thousands. Gomory says the United States must use the corporate income tax to *reward* companies that invest in jobs here, especially high-tech jobs, and must *penalize* companies that move facilities overseas. We must make it in the self-interest of companies to invest in America, Gomory says. Otherwise, living standards here will inevitably decline and America will severely weaken economically.[8]

Joint Ventures in India

The government of India is highly in debt, 80 percent of GDP, and is cutting expenses to curtail spending, so the gap between rich and poor is widening further. (The U.S. federal debt is about 65 percent of GDP.) But India's middle class is growing, so foreign firms continue to invest. Nissan Motor is building a factory in Chennai in conjunction with

Mahindra & Mahindra Ltd., India's largest maker of jeeps and tractors. The factory began operating in 2009.

Joint ventures remain mandatory for foreign companies doing business in India. Verizon Business India, a joint venture between Verizon and Videocon Group of Mumbai, is rapidly expanding its phone and Internet services in India to compete more fiercely with AT&T and other telecom companies. Almost 20 million new cell phone customers are added in India every quarter, about the same rate of increase as in China—compared with only about 2.8 million new cell phone customers added in the United States quarterly. India's Reliance Communications Ltd. is in a battle with Britain's Vodafone Group PLC for control of India's fourth-largest cellular service, Hutchison Essar. But Vodafone must find a local partner because Indian law restricts foreign firms to 74 percent ownership of any India-based firm.

Most joint ventures among firms in India and foreign firms fail. Of 25 major joint ventures between foreign and Indian companies between 1993 and 2003, only three survive today. The Indian government has eased the joint-venture restriction in the investment-banking industry, but not in other areas. Even Wal-Mart has an Indian partner, Bharti Enterprises Ltd. Heavy friction exists in virtually all joint-ventures in India. John Band, president of Zoom Cortex in Mumbai, says, "Anyone that gets into a joint venture in India should assume it will fail and should be comfortable with the terms of what happens when it does fail." [9]

Due to tourism growing 12 percent annually, hotel chains are scrambling to get established in India. Hilton Hotels just established a joint venture with New Delhi–based DLF Ltd. to develop 75 hotels in India in 2007–2010. Marriott, Four Seasons, and Carlson Companies are also establishing joint ventures in India and building hotels rapidly.

Conclusion

The population of the world has almost reached 7 billion persons. For centuries before Columbus reached America, and for centuries to come, businesses will search for new opportunities beyond their national boundaries. There has never been a more internationalized and economically competitive society than today's model. Some U.S. industries, such as automobiles, textiles, steel, and consumer electronics, are in complete disarray as a result of the international challenge.

Success in business increasingly depends on offering products and services that are competitive on a world basis, not just on a local basis. If the price and quality of a firm's products and services are not competitive with those available elsewhere in the world, the firm may soon face extinction. Global markets have become a reality in all but the most remote areas of the world. Certainly throughout the United States, even in small towns, firms feel the pressure of world competitors.

This chapter has provided some basic global information that can be essential to consider in developing a strategic plan for any organization. The advantages of engaging in international business may well offset the drawbacks for most firms. It is important in strategic planning to be effective, and the nature of global operations may be the key component in a plan's overall effectiveness.

Key Terms and Concepts

Feng Shui (p. 337)
Global Strategy (p. 334)
Globalization (p. 334)
Guanxi (p. 335)
International Firms (p. 331)
Inhwa (p. 335)

Multinational Corporations (p. 331)
Nemaswashio (p. 337)
Protectionism (p. 333)
Recession (p. 335)
Wa (p. 335)

Issues for Review and Discussion

1. Explain why consumption patterns are becoming similar worldwide. What are the strategic implications of this trend?
2. What are the advantages and disadvantages of beginning export operations in a foreign country?
3. What are the major differences between U.S. and multinational operations that affect strategic management?
4. Why is globalization of industries a common factor today?
5. Compare and contrast U.S. versus foreign cultures in terms of doing business.
6. List six reasons that strategic management is more complex in a multinational firm.
7. Do you feel that protectionism is good or bad for the world economy? Why?
8. Why are some industries more "global" than others? Discuss.
9. *Wa, guanxi,* and *inhwa* are important management terms in Japan, China, and South Korea, respectively. What would be analogous terms to describe American management practices?
10. Why do many Europeans find the notion of "team spirit" in a work environment difficult to grasp?
11. In China, *feng shui* is important in business, whereas in Japan, *nemaswashio* is important. What are analogous American terms and practices?
12. Describe the business culture in Mexico.
13. Describe the business culture in Japan.
14. Compare tax rates in the United States versus other countries. What impact could these differences have on "keeping jobs at home"?
15. Discuss requirements for doing business in India.

Notes

1. John Miller, "WTO Predicts Global Trade Will Slide 9% This Year," *Wall Street Journal* (March 24, 2009): A8.
2. Frederick Gluck, "Global Competition in the 1990s," *Journal of Business Strategy* (Spring 1983): 22–24.
3. David Lynch, "U.S. Complains to WTO on China," *USA Today* (April 10, 2007): B1.
4. Jon Alston, "Wa, Guanxi, and Inhwa: Managerial Principles in Japan, China and Korea," *Business Horizons* 32, no. 2 (March–April 1989): 26.
5. Rose Knotts, "Cross-Cultural Management: Transformations and Adaptations," *Business Horizons* (January–February 1989): 29–33.
6. Lalita Khosla, "You Say Tomato," *Forbes* (May 21, 2001): 36.
7. Stratford Sherman, "How to Beat the Japanese," *Fortune* (April 10, 1989): 145.

8. Marcus Walker, "Europe Competes for Investment with Lower Corporate Tax Rates," *Wall Street Journal* (April 17, 2007): A12.
9. Eric Bellman and P. R. Venkat, "India's Growth Raises Fears Rates May Rise," *Wall Street Journal* (February 8, 2007): A6; Dionne Searcey, "Verizon Targets Business in India," *Wall Street Journal* (February 6, 2007): A7; Peter Wonacott, "India Faces Dark Side of Its Boom," *Wall Street Journal* (February 27, 2007): A10; Amy Chozick, "Nissan Enters Venture to Build Indian Plant," *Wall Street Journal* (February 27, 2007): A4; Cassell Bryan and Eric Bellman, "Vodafone, Reliance Gear Up for Battle in India," *Wall Street Journal* (December 22, 2006): B4; Peter Wonacott and Eric Bellman, "Foreign Firms Find Rough Passage to India," *Wall Street Journal* (February 1, 2007): A6; Binny Sabharwal, "Hilton Expands in India as Market Demand Soars," *Wall Street Journal* (May 10, 2007): D6.

Current Readings

Brouthers, Keith D., Lance Eliot Brouthers, and Steve Werner. "Resource-Based Advantages in an International Context." *Journal of Management* 34, no. 2 (April 2008): 189.

Brown, John Seely, Lang Davison, and John Hagel III. "Shaping Strategy in a World of Constant Disruption." *Harvard Business Review* (October 2008): 80.

Butter, Den, A. G. Frank, and Kees A. Linse. "How Procurement Informs Strategy in the Era of Globalization." *MIT Sloan Management Review* 50, no. 1 (Fall 2008): 76.

Desia, Mihir, A. "The Finance Function in a Global Corporation." *Harvard Business Review* (July–August 2008): 108.

Feinberg, Susan, and Anil Gupta. "MNC Subsidiaries and County Risk: Internalization as a Safeguard Against Weak External Institutions." *Academy of Management Journal* (April 2009): 381–399.

Hitt, Michael A., and Xiaoming He. "Firm Strategies in a Changing Global Competitive Landscape." *Business Horizons* 51, no. 5 (September–October 2008): 363.

Inkpen, Andrew C. "Knowledge Transfer and International Joint Ventures: The Case of NUMMI and General Motors." *Strategic Management Journal* 29, no. 4 (April 2008): 447.

Karra, Neri, Nelson Phillips, and Paul Tracey. "Building the Born Global Firm Developing Entrepreneurial Capabilities for International New Venture Success." *Long Range Planning* 41, no. 4 (August 2008): 420.

Lee, Seung-Hyun, Jiatao Li, and Oded Shenkar. "Cultural Distance, Investment Flow, and Control in Cross-Border Cooperation." *Strategic Management Journal* 29, no. 10 (October 2008): 1117.

Nelson, Phillips, and Paul Tracey. "Institutional Theory and the MNC." *Academy of Management Review* (January 2009): 169–171.

Nill, Alexander, and Clifford Schultz II. "Global Software Piracy: Trends and Strategic Considerations." *Business Horizons* (May–June 2009): 289–298.

Peng, Mike W., Jeffery J. Reuer, and Tony W. Tong. "International Joint Ventures and the Value of Growth Options." *Academy of Management Journal* 51, no. 5 (October 2008): 1014.

Prashantham, Shameen, and Julian Birkinshaw. "Dancing with Gorillas: How Small Companies Can Partner Effectively with MNCs." *California Management Review* 51, no. 1 (Fall 2008): 6–23.

Ren, Hong, Barbara Gray, and Kwangho Kim. "Performance of International Joint Ventures: What Factors Really Make a Difference and How?" *Journal of Management* (June 2009): 805–832.

Strutton, David. "Horseshoes, Global Supply Chains, and an Emerging Chinese Threat: Creating Remedies One Idea at a Time." *Business Horizons* (January–February 2009): 31–43.

ASSURANCE OF LEARNING EXERCISES

Assurance of Learning Exercise 11A

McDonald's Wants to Enter Africa. Help Them.

Purpose

More and more companies every day decide to begin doing business in the forgotten continent—Africa. Research is necessary to determine the best strategy for being the first mover in many African countries (i.e., being the first competitor doing business in various countries).

Instructions

Step 1	Print off a map of Africa.
Step 2	Print off demographic data on 10 African countries.
Step 3	Gather competitive information regarding the presence of fast-food firms doing business in Africa.
Step 4	List in prioritized order eight countries that you would recommend for McDonald's entry. Country 1 is your best, and country 2 is your next best. Based on your research, indicate how many McDonald's restaurants you would recommend building over the next three years in each country. List in prioritized order three cities in each of your eight African countries where you believe McDonald's should build most of its restaurants.

Assurance of Learning Exercise 11B

Does My University Recruit in Foreign Countries?

Purpose

A competitive climate is emerging among colleges and universities around the world. Colleges and universities in Europe and Japan are increasingly recruiting U.S. students to offset declining enrollments. Foreign students already make up more than a third of the student body at many U.S. universities. The purpose of this exercise is to identify particular colleges and universities in foreign countries that recruit U.S. students.

Instructions

Step 1	Select a foreign country. Conduct research to determine the number and nature of colleges and universities in that country. What are the major educational institutions in that country? What programs are those institutions recognized for offering? What percentage of undergraduate and graduate students attending those institutions are U.S. citizens? Do these institutions actively recruit U.S. students? Are any of the schools of business at the various universities AACSB-International accredited?
Step 2	Prepare a report that summarizes your research findings. Present your report to the class.

Assurance of Learning Exercise 11C

Assessing Differences in Culture Across Countries

Purpose

Americans can be more effective in dealing with businesspeople from other countries if they have some awareness and understanding of differences in culture across countries. This is a fun exercise that provides information for your class regarding some of these key differences.

Instructions

Step 1 Identify four individuals who either grew up in a foreign country or who have lived in a foreign country for more than one year. Interview those four persons. Try to have four different countries represented. During each interview, develop a list of eight key differences between American style/custom and that particular country's style/custom in terms of various aspects of speaking, meetings, meals, relationships, friendships, and communication that could impact business dealings.

Step 2 Develop a 15-minute PowerPoint presentation for your class and give a talk summarizing your findings. Identify in your talk the persons you interviewed as well as the length of time those persons lived in the respective countries. Give your professor a hard copy of your PowerPoint presentation.

Assurance of Learning Exercise 11D

How Well Traveled Are Business Students at Your University?

Purpose

It would be interesting to know how traveled are students at your university and also how those students consider their travels to be helpful in becoming an effective businessperson. Generally speaking, the more one has traveled, especially outside the United States, the more tolerant, understanding, and appreciative one is for diversity. Many students even state on their resume the extent to which they have traveled, both across the United States and perhaps around the world.

Instructions

Administer the following survey to at least 30 business students, including your classmates in the strategic management course. Analyze the results. Give a 15-minute presentation to your class regarding your findings. Turn in a written report of your findings to your professor.

The Survey

1. How many states in the United States have you visited?
2. How many states in the United States have you lived for at least three months?
3. How many countries outside the United States have you visited?
4. List the countries outside the United States that you have visited.
5. How many countries outside the United States have you lived for at least three months?
6. List the countries outside the United States that you have lived for at least three months.
7. To what extent do you feel that traveling across the United States can make a person a more effective businessperson? Use a 1 to 10 scale, where 1 is "Cannot Make a Difference" and 10 is "Can Make a Tremendous Difference."
8. To what extent do you feel that visiting countries outside the United States can make a person a more effective business person? Use a 1 to 10 scale, where 1 is "Cannot Make a Difference" and 10 is "Can Make a Tremendous Difference."
9. To what extent do you feel that living in another country can make a person a more effective businessperson? Use a 1 to 10 scale, where 1 is "Cannot Make a Difference" and 10 is "Can Make a Tremendous Difference."
10. What three important ways so you feel that traveling or living outside the United States would be helpful to a person in being a more effective businessperson?

How to Prepare and Present a Case Analysis

CHAPTER OBJECTIVES

After studying this chapter, you should be able to do the following:

1. Describe the case method for learning strategic-management concepts.

2. Identify the steps in preparing a comprehensive written case analysis.

3. Describe how to give an effective oral case analysis presentation.

4. Discuss special tips for doing case analysis.

Assurance of Learning Exercises

Oral Presentation—Step 1
Introduction (2 minutes)

Oral Presentation—Step 2
Mission/Vision (4 minutes)

Oral Presentation—Step 3
Internal Assessment (8 minutes)

Oral Presentation—Step 4
External Assessment (8 minutes)

"Notable Quotes"

"Two heads are better than one."
—Unknown Author

"One reaction frequently heard is 'I don't have enough information.' In reality strategists never have enough information because some information is not available and some is too costly."
—William Glueck

"I keep six honest serving men. They taught me all I know. Their names are What, Why, When, How, Where, and Who."
—Rudyard Kipling

"Don't recommend anything you would not be prepared to do yourself if you were in the decision maker's shoes."
—A. J. Strickland III

"A picture is worth a thousand words."
—Unknown Author

Oral Presentation— Step 5
Strategy Formulation (14 minutes)

Oral Presentation— Step 6
Strategy Implementation (8 minutes)

Oral Presentation— Step 7
Strategy Evaluation (2 minutes)

Oral Presentation— Step 8
Conclusion (4 minutes)

The purpose of this section is to help you analyze strategic-management cases. Guidelines for preparing written and oral case analyses are given, and suggestions for preparing cases for class discussion are presented. Steps to follow in preparing case analyses are provided. Guidelines for making an oral presentation are described.

What Is a Strategic-Management Case?

A *strategic-management case* describes an organization's external and internal conditions and raises issues concerning the firm's mission, strategies, objectives, and policies. Most of the information in a business policy case is established fact, but some information may be opinions, judgments, and beliefs. Strategic-management cases are more comprehensive than those you may have studied in other courses. They generally include a description of related management, marketing, finance/accounting, production/operations, R&D, computer information systems, and natural environment issues. A strategic-management case puts the reader on the scene of the action by describing a firm's situation at some point in time. Strategic-management cases are written to give you practice applying strategic-management concepts. The case method for studying strategic management is often called *learning by doing*.

Guidelines for Preparing Case Analyses

The Need for Practicality

There is no such thing as a complete case, and no case ever gives you all the information you need to conduct analyses and make recommendations. Likewise, in the business world, strategists never have all the information they need to make decisions: information may be unavailable or too costly to obtain, or it may take too much time to obtain. So in preparing strategic-management cases, do what strategists do every day—make reasonable assumptions about unknowns, clearly state assumptions, perform appropriate analyses, and make decisions. *Be practical.* For example, in performing a projected financial analysis, make reasonable assumptions, appropriately state them, and proceed to show what impact your recommendations are expected to have on the organization's financial position. Avoid saying, "I don't have enough information." You can always supplement the information provided in a case with Internet and library research.

The Need for Justification

The most important part of analyzing cases is not what strategies you recommend but rather how you support your decisions and how you propose that they be implemented. There is no single best solution or one right answer to a case, so give ample justification for your recommendations. This is important. In the business world, strategists usually do not know if their decisions are right until resources have been allocated and consumed. Then it is often too late to reverse a decision. This cold fact accents the need for careful integration of intuition and analysis in preparing business policy case analyses.

The Need for Realism

Avoid recommending a course of action beyond an organization's means. *Be realistic.* No organization can possibly pursue all the strategies that could potentially benefit the firm. Estimate how much capital will be required to implement what you recommended. Determine whether debt, stock, or a combination of debt and stock could be used to obtain the capital. Make sure your recommendations are feasible. Do not prepare a case analysis that omits all arguments and information not supportive of your recommendations. Rather, present the major advantages and disadvantages of several feasible alternatives. Try not to exaggerate, stereotype, prejudge, or overdramatize. Strive to demonstrate that your interpretation of the evidence is reasonable and objective.

The Need for Specificity

Do not make broad generalizations such as "The company should pursue a market penetration strategy." Be specific by telling *what, why, when, how, where*, and *who*. Failure to use specifics is the single major shortcoming of most oral and written case analyses. For example, in an internal audit say, "The firm's current ratio fell from 2.2 in 2009 to 1.3 in 2010, and this is considered to be a major weakness," instead of "The firm's financial condition is bad." Rather than concluding from a Strategic Position and Action Evaluation (SPACE) Matrix that a firm should be defensive, be more specific, saying, "The firm should consider closing three plants, laying off 280 employees, and divesting itself of its chemical division, for a net savings of $20.2 million in 2010." Use ratios, percentages, numbers, and dollar estimates. Businesspeople dislike generalities and vagueness.

The Need for Originality

Do not necessarily recommend the course of action that the firm plans to take or actually undertook, even if those actions resulted in improved revenues and earnings. The aim of case analysis is for you to consider all the facts and information relevant to the organization at the time, to generate feasible alternative strategies, to choose among those alternatives, and to defend your recommendations. Put yourself back in time to the point when strategic decisions were being made by the firm's strategists. Based on the information available then, what would you have done? Support your position with charts, graphs, ratios, analyses, and the like—not a revelation from the library. You can become a good strategist by thinking through situations, making management assessments, and proposing plans yourself. *Be original*. Compare and contrast what you recommend versus what the company plans to do or did.

The Need to Contribute

Strategy formulation, implementation, and evaluation decisions are commonly made by a group of individuals rather than by a single person. Therefore, your professor may divide the class into three- or four-person teams and ask you to prepare written or oral case analyses. Members of a strategic-management team, in class or in the business world, differ on their aversion to risk, their concern for short-run versus long-run benefits, their attitudes toward social responsibility, and their views concerning globalization. There are no perfect people, so there are no perfect strategies. Be open-minded to others' views. *Be a good listener and a good contributor.*

Preparing a Case for Class Discussion

Your professor may ask you to prepare a case for class discussion. Preparing a case for class discussion means that you need to read the case before class, make notes regarding the organization's external opportunities/threats and internal strengths/weaknesses, perform appropriate analyses, and come to class prepared to offer and defend some specific recommendations.

The Case Method versus Lecture Approach

The case method of teaching is radically different from the traditional lecture approach, in which little or no preparation is needed by students before class. The *case method* involves a classroom situation in which students do most of the talking; your professor facilitates discussion by asking questions and encouraging student interaction regarding ideas, analyses, and recommendations. Be prepared for a discussion along the lines of "What would you do, why would you do it, when would you do it, and how would you do it?" Prepare answers to the following types of questions:

- What are the firm's most important external opportunities and threats?
- What are the organization's major strengths and weaknesses?
- How would you describe the organization's financial condition?

- What are the firm's existing strategies and objectives?
- Who are the firm's competitors, and what are their strategies?
- What objectives and strategies do you recommend for this organization? Explain your reasoning. How does what you recommend compare to what the company plans?
- How could the organization best implement what you recommend? What implementation problems do you envision? How could the firm avoid or solve those problems?

The Cross-Examination

Do not hesitate to take a stand on the issues and to support your position with objective analyses and outside research. Strive to apply strategic-management concepts and tools in preparing your case for class discussion. Seek defensible arguments and positions. Support opinions and judgments with facts, reasons, and evidence. Crunch the numbers before class! Be willing to describe your recommendations to the class without fear of disapproval. Respect the ideas of others, but be willing to go against the majority opinion when you can justify a better position.

Strategic management case analysis gives you the opportunity to learn more about yourself, your colleagues, strategic management, and the decision-making process in organizations. The rewards of this experience will depend on the effort you put forth, so do a good job. Discussing business policy cases in class is exciting and challenging. Expect views counter to those you present. Different students will place emphasis on different aspects of an organization's situation and submit different recommendations for scrutiny and rebuttal. Cross-examination discussions commonly arise, just as they occur in a real business organization. Avoid being a silent observer.

Preparing a Written Case Analysis

In addition to asking you to prepare a case for class discussion, your professor may ask you to prepare a written case analysis. Preparing a written case analysis is similar to preparing a case for class discussion, except written reports are generally more structured and more detailed. There is no ironclad procedure for preparing a written case analysis because cases differ in focus; the type, size, and complexity of the organizations being analyzed also vary.

When writing a strategic-management report or case analysis, avoid using jargon, vague or redundant words, acronyms, abbreviations, sexist language, and ethnic or racial slurs. And watch your spelling! Use short sentences and paragraphs and simple words and phrases. Use quite a few subheadings. Arrange issues and ideas from the most important to the least important. Arrange recommendations from the least controversial to the most controversial. Use the active voice rather than the passive voice for all verbs; for example, say "Our team recommends that the company diversify" rather than "It is recommended by our team to diversify." Use many examples to add specificity and clarity. Tables, figures, pie charts, bar charts, timelines, and other kinds of exhibits help communicate important points and ideas. Sometimes a picture *is* worth a thousand words.

The Executive Summary

Your professor may ask you to focus the written case analysis on a particular aspect of the strategic-management process, such as (1) to identify and evaluate the organization's existing mission, objectives, and strategies; or (2) to propose and defend specific recommendations for the company; or (3) to develop an industry analysis by describing the competitors, products, selling techniques, and market conditions in a given industry. These types of written reports are sometimes called *executive summaries*. An executive summary usually ranges from three to five pages of text in length, plus exhibits.

The Comprehensive Written Analysis

Your professor may ask you to prepare a *comprehensive written analysis*. This assignment requires you to apply the entire strategic-management process to the particular organization. When preparing a comprehensive written analysis, picture yourself as a consultant who has been asked by a company to conduct a study of its external and internal environment and to make specific recommendations for its future. Prepare exhibits to support your recommendations. Highlight exhibits with some discussion in the paper. Comprehensive written analyses are usually about 10 pages in length, plus exhibits.

Steps in Preparing a Comprehensive Written Analysis

In preparing a **written** case analysis, you could follow the steps outlined here, which correlate to the stages in the strategic-management process and the chapters in this text. (Note—The steps in presenting an **oral** case analysis are given on pages 356–358, are more detailed, and could be used here).

Step 1   Identify the firm's existing vision, mission, objectives, and strategies.

Step 2   Develop vision and mission statements for the organization.

Step 3   Identify the organization's external opportunities and threats.

Step 4   Construct a Competitive Profile Matrix (CPM).

Step 5   Construct an External Factor Evaluation (EFE) Matrix.

Step 6   Identify the organization's internal strengths and weaknesses.

Step 7   Construct an Internal Factor Evaluation (IFE) Matrix.

Step 8   Prepare a Strengths-Weaknesses-Opportunities-Threats (SWOT) Matrix, Strategic Position and Action Evaluation (SPACE) Matrix, Boston Consulting Group (BCG) Matrix, Internal-External (IE) Matrix, Grand Strategy Matrix, and Quantitative Strategic Planning Matrix (QSPM) as appropriate. Give advantages and disadvantages of alternative strategies.

Step 9   Recommend specific strategies and long-term objectives. Show how much your recommendations will cost. Clearly itemize these costs for each projected year. Compare your recommendations to actual strategies planned by the company.

Step 10   Specify how your recommendations can be implemented and what results you can expect. Prepare forecasted ratios and projected financial statements. Present a timetable or agenda for action.

Step 11   Recommend specific annual objectives and policies.

Step 12   Recommend procedures for strategy review and evaluation.

Making an Oral Presentation

Your professor may ask you to prepare a strategic-management case analysis, individually or as a group, and present your analysis to the class. Oral presentations are usually graded on two parts: content and delivery. *Content* refers to the quality, quantity, correctness, and appropriateness of analyses presented, including such dimensions as logical flow through the presentation, coverage of major issues, use of specifics, avoidance of generalities, absence of mistakes, and feasibility of recommendations. *Delivery* includes such dimensions as audience attentiveness, clarity of visual aids, appropriate dress, persuasiveness of arguments, tone of voice, eye contact, and posture. Great ideas are of no value unless others can be convinced of their merit through clear communication. The guidelines presented here can help you make an effective oral presentation.

Organizing the Presentation

Begin your presentation by introducing yourself and giving a clear outline of topics to be covered. If a team is presenting, specify the sequence of speakers and the areas each person will address. At the beginning of an oral presentation, try to capture your audience's interest and attention. You could do this by displaying some products made by the company, telling an interesting short story about the company, or sharing an experience you had that is related to the company, its products, or its services. You could develop or obtain a video to show at the beginning of class; you could visit a local distributor of the firm's products and tape a personal interview with the business owner or manager. A light or humorous introduction can be effective at the beginning of a presentation.

Be sure the setting of your presentation is well organized, with seats for attendees, flip charts, a transparency projector, and whatever else you plan to use. Arrive at the classroom at least 15 minutes early to organize the setting, and be sure your materials are ready to go. Make sure everyone can see your visual aids well.

Controlling Your Voice

An effective rate of speaking ranges from 100 to 125 words per minute. Practice your presentation aloud to determine if you are going too fast. Individuals commonly speak too fast when nervous. Breathe deeply before and during the presentation to help yourself slow down. Have a cup of water available; pausing to take a drink will wet your throat, give you time to collect your thoughts, control your nervousness, slow you down, and signal to the audience a change in topic.

Avoid a monotone by placing emphasis on different words or sentences. Speak loudly and clearly, but don't shout. Silence can be used effectively to break a monotone voice. Stop at the end of each sentence, rather than running sentences together with *and* or *uh*.

Managing Body Language

Be sure not to fold your arms, lean on the podium, put your hands in your pockets, or put your hands behind you. Keep a straight posture, with one foot slightly in front of the other. Do not turn your back to the audience; doing so is not only rude, but it also prevents your voice from projecting well. Avoid using too many hand gestures. On occasion, leave the podium or table and walk toward your audience, but do not walk around too much. Never block the audience's view of your visual aids.

Maintain good eye contact throughout the presentation. This is the best way to persuade your audience. There is nothing more reassuring to a speaker than to see members of the audience nod in agreement or smile. Try to look everyone in the eye at least once during your presentation, but focus more on individuals who look interested than on those who seem bored. To stay in touch with your audience, use humor and smiles as appropriate throughout your presentation. A presentation should never be dull!

Speaking from Notes

Be sure not to read to your audience because reading puts people to sleep. Perhaps worse than reading is merely reciting what you have memorized. Do not try to memorize anything. Rather, practice unobtrusively using notes. Make sure your notes are written clearly so you will not flounder when trying to read your own writing. Include only main ideas on your note cards. Keep note cards on a podium or table if possible so that you won't drop them or get them out of order; walking with note cards tends to be distracting.

Constructing Visual Aids

Make sure your visual aids are legible to individuals in the back of the room. Use color to highlight special items. Avoid putting complete sentences on visual aids; rather, use short phrases and then orally elaborate on issues as you make your presentation. Generally, there should be no more than four to six lines of text on each visual aid. Use clear headings and subheadings. Be careful about spelling and grammar; use a consistent style of lettering. Use masking tape or an easel for posters—do not hold posters in your hand. Transparencies and handouts are excellent aids; however, be careful not to use too many handouts or your audience may concentrate on them instead of you during the presentation.

Answering Questions

It is best to field questions at the end of your presentation, rather than during the presentation itself. Encourage questions, and take your time to respond to each one. Answering questions can be persuasive because it involves you with the audience. If a team is giving the presentation, the audience should direct questions to a specific person. During the question-and-answer period, be polite, confident, and courteous. Avoid verbose responses. Do not get defensive with your answers, even if a hostile or confrontational question is asked. Staying calm during potentially disruptive situations, such as a cross-examination, reflects self-confidence, maturity, poise, and command of the particular company and its industry. Stand up throughout the question-and-answer period.

Tips for Success in Case Analysis

Strategic-management students who have used this text over 12 editions offer you the following tips for success in doing case analysis. The tips are grouped into two basic sections: (1) Content Tips and (2) Process Tips. Content tips relate especially to the content of your case analysis, whereas the Process tips relate mostly to the process that you and your group mates undergo in preparing and delivering your case analysis/presentation.

Content Tips

1. Use the www.strategyclub.com Web site resources. The software described there is especially useful.
2. In preparing your external assessment, use the S&P Industry Survey material in your college library.
3. Go to the http://finance.yahoo.com or http://moneycentral.msn/investor/home.asp and enter your company's stock symbol.
4. View your case analysis and presentation as a product that must have some competitive factor to favorably differentiate it from the case analyses of other students.
5. Develop a mind-set of *why*, continually questioning your own and others' assumptions and assertions.
6. Because strategic management is a capstone course, seek the help of professors in other specialty areas when necessary.
7. Read your case frequently as work progresses so you don't overlook details.
8. At the end of each group session, assign each member of the group a task to be completed for the next meeting.
9. Become friends with the library and the Internet.
10. Be creative and innovative throughout the case analysis process.
11. A goal of case analysis is to improve your ability to think clearly in ambiguous and confusing situations; do not get frustrated that there is no single best answer.
12. Do not confuse symptoms with causes; do not develop conclusions and solutions prematurely; recognize that information may be misleading, conflicting, or wrong.
13. Work hard to develop the ability to formulate reasonable, consistent, and creative plans; put yourself in the strategist's position.
14. Develop confidence in using quantitative tools for analysis. They are not inherently difficult; it is just practice and familiarity you need.
15. Strive for excellence in writing and in the technical preparation of your case. Prepare nice charts, tables, diagrams, and graphs. Use color and unique pictures. No messy exhibits! Use PowerPoint.
16. Do not forget that the objective is to learn; explore areas with which you are not familiar.
17. Pay attention to detail.
18. Think through alternative implications fully and realistically. The consequences of decisions are not always apparent. They often affect many different aspects of a firm's operations.
19. Provide answers to such fundamental questions as *what, when, where, why, who,* and *how*.

20. Do not merely recite ratios or present figures. Rather, develop ideas and conclusions concerning the possible trends. Show the importance of these figures to the corporation.
21. Support reasoning and judgment with factual data whenever possible.
22. Your analysis should be as detailed and specific as possible.
23. A picture speaks a thousand words, and a creative picture gets you an A in many classes.
24. Emphasize the Recommendations and Strategy Implementation sections. A common mistake is to spend too much time on the external or internal analysis parts of your paper. Always remember that the recommendations and implementation sections are the most important part of the paper or presentation.

Process Tips

1. When working as a team, encourage most of the work to be done individually. Use team meetings mostly to assimilate work. This approach is most efficient.
2. If allowed to do so, invite questions throughout your presentation.
3. During the presentation, keep good posture, eye contact, voice tone, and project confidence. Do not get defensive under any conditions or with any questions.
4. Prepare your case analysis in advance of the due date to allow time for reflection and practice. Do not procrastinate.
5. Maintain a positive attitude about the class, working *with* problems rather than against them.
6. Keep in tune with your professor, and understand his or her values and expectations.
7. Other students will have strengths in functional areas that will complement your weaknesses, so develop a cooperative spirit that moderates competitiveness in group work.
8. When preparing a case analysis as a group, divide into separate teams to work on the external analysis and internal analysis.
9. Have a good sense of humor.
10. Capitalize on the strengths of each member of the group; volunteer your services in your areas of strength.
11. Set goals for yourself and your team; budget your time to attain them.
12. Foster attitudes that encourage group participation and interaction. Do not be hasty to judge group members.
13. Be prepared to work. There will be times when you will have to do more than your share. Accept it, and do what you have to do to move the team forward.
14. Think of your case analysis as if it were really happening; do not reduce case analysis to a mechanical process.
15. To uncover flaws in your analysis and to prepare the group for questions during an oral presentation, assign one person in the group to actively play the devil's advocate.
16. Do not schedule excessively long group meetings; two-hour sessions are about right.
17. Push your ideas hard enough to get them listened to, but then let up; listen to others and try to follow their lines of thinking; follow the flow of group discussion, recognizing when you need to get back on track; do not repeat yourself or others unless clarity or progress demands repetition.
18. Develop a case-presentation style that is direct, assertive, and convincing; be concise, precise, fluent, and correct.
19. Have fun when at all possible. Preparing a case is frustrating at times, but enjoy it while you can; it may be several years before you are playing CEO again.
20. In group cases, do not allow personality differences to interfere. When they occur, they must be understood for what they are—and then put aside.
21. Get things written down (drafts) as soon as possible.
22. Read everything that other group members write, and comment on it in writing. This allows group input into all aspects of case preparation.
23. Adaptation and flexibility are keys to success; be creative and innovative.
24. Neatness is a real plus; your case analysis should look professional.

25. Let someone else read and critique your presentation several days before you present it.
26. Make special efforts to get to know your group members. This leads to more openness in the group and allows for more interchange of ideas. Put in the time and effort necessary to develop these relationships.
27. Be constructively critical of your group members' work. Do not dominate group discussions. Be a good listener and contributor.
28. Learn from past mistakes and deficiencies. Improve upon weak aspects of other case presentations.
29. Learn from the positive approaches and accomplishments of classmates.

Sample Case Analysis Outline

There are musicians who play wonderfully without notes and there are chefs who cook wonderfully without recipes, but most of us prefer a more orderly cookbook approach, at least in the first attempt at doing something new. Therefore the following eight steps may serve as a basic outline for you in presenting a strategic plan for your firm's future. This outline is not the only approach used in business and industry for communicating a strategic plan, but this approach is time-tested, it does work, and it does cover all of the basics. You may amend the content, tools, and concepts given to suit your own company, audience, assignment, and circumstances, but it helps to know and understand the rules before you start breaking them.

Depending on whether your class is 50 minutes or 75 minutes and how much time your professor allows for your case presentation, the following outlines what generally needs to be covered. A recommended time (in minutes) as part of the presentation is given for an overall 50-minute event. Of course, all cases are different, some being about for-profit and some about not-for-profit organizations, for example, so the scope and content of your analysis may vary. Even if you do not have time to cover all areas in your oral presentation, you may be asked to prepare these areas and give them to your professor as a "written case analysis." Be sure in an oral presentation to manage time knowing that your recommendations and associated costs are the most important part. You should go to www.strategyclub.com and utilize that information and software in preparing your case analysis. Good luck.

Current Readings

Kearney, Eric, Diether Gebert, and Sven Voelpel. "When Diversity Benefits Teams: The Importance of Team Members' Need for Cognition." *Academy of Management Journal* (June 2009): 581–598.

STEPS IN PRESENTING AN ORAL CASE ANALYSIS

Oral Presentation—Step 1

Introduction (2 minutes)

a. Introduce yourselves by name and major. Establish the time setting of your case and analysis. Prepare your strategic plan for the three years 2010–2012.
b. Introduce your company and its products/services; capture interest.
c. Show the outline of your presentation and tell who is doing what parts.

Oral Presentation—Step 2

Mission/Vision (4 minutes)

a. Show existing mission and vision statements if available from the firm's Web site, or annual report, or elsewhere.
b. Show your "improved" mission and vision and tell why it is improved.
c. Compare your mission and vision to a leading competitor's statements.
d. Comment on your vision and mission in terms of how they support the strategies you envision for your firm.

Oral Presentation—Step 3

Internal Assessment (8 minutes)

a. Give your financial ratio analysis. Highlight especially good and bad ratios. Do not give definitions of the ratios and do not highlight all the ratios.
b. Show the firm's organizational chart found or "created based on executive titles." Identify the type of chart as well as good and bad aspects. Unless all white males comprise the chart, peoples' names are generally not important because positions reveal structure as people come and go.
c. Present your improved/recommended organizational chart. Tell why you feel it is improved over the existing chart.
d. Show a market positioning map with firm and competitors. Discuss the map in light of strategies you envision for firm versus competitors' strategies.
e. Identify the marketing strategy of the firm in terms of good and bad points versus competitors and in light of strategies you envision for the firm.
f. Show a map locating the firm's operations. Discuss in light of strategies you envision. Also, perhaps show a Value Chain Analysis chart.
g. Discuss (and perhaps show) the firm's Web site and e-commerce efforts/abilities in terms of good and bad points.
h. Show your "value of the firm" analysis.
i. List up to 20 of the firm's strengths and weaknesses. Go over each one listed without "reading" them verbatim.
j. Show and explain your Internal Factor Evaluation (IFE) Matrix.

Oral Presentation—Step 4

External Assessment (8 minutes)

a. Identify and discuss major competitors. Use pie charts, maps, tables, and/or figures to show the intensity of competition in the industry.
b. Show your Competitive Profile Matrix. Include at least 12 factors and two competitors.
c. Summarize key industry trends citing Standard & Poor's *Industry Survey* or Chamber of Commerce statistics, etc. Highlight key external trends as they impact the firm, in areas such as the economic, social, cultural, demographic, geographic, technological, political, legal, governmental, and natural environment.
d. List up to 20 of the firm's opportunities and threats. Make sure your opportunities are not stated as strategies. Go over each one listed without "reading" them verbatim.
e. Show and explain your External Factor Evaluation (EFE) Matrix.

Oral Presentation—Step 5

Strategy Formulation (14 minutes)

a. Show and explain your SWOT Matrix, highlighting each of your strategies listed.
b. Show and explain your SPACE Matrix, using half of your "space time" on calculations and the other half on implications of those numbers. Strategy implications must be specific rather than generic. In other words, use of a term such as "market penetration" is not satisfactory alone as a strategy implication.
c. Show your Boston Consulting Group (BCG) Matrix. Again focus on both the numbers and the strategy implications. Do multiple BCG Matrices if possible, including domestic versus global, or another geographic breakdown. Develop a product BCG if at all possible. Comment on changes to this matrix as per strategies you envision. Develop this matrix even if you do not know the profits per division and even if you have to estimate the axes information. However, make no wild guesses on axes or revenue/profit information.
d. Show your Internal-External (IE) Matrix. Because this analysis is similar to the BCG, see the preceding comments.
e. Show your Grand Strategy Matrix. Again focus on implications after giving the quadrant selection. Reminder: Use of a term such as "market penetration" is not satisfactory alone as a strategy implication. Be more specific. Elaborate.
f. Show your Quantitative Strategic Planning Matrix (QSPM). Be sure to explain your strategies to start with here. Do not go back over the internal and external factors. Avoid having more than one 4, 3, 2, or 1 in a row. If you rate one strategy, you need to rate the other because, that particular factor is affecting the choice. Work row by row rather than column by column on preparing the QSPM.
g. Present your Recommendations Page. This is the most important page in your presentation. Be specific in terms of both strategies and estimated costs of those strategies. *Total your estimated costs.* You should have ten or more strategies. Divide your strategies into two groups: (1) Existing Strategies to Be Continued, and (2) New Strategies to Be Started.

Oral Presentation—Step 6

Strategy Implementation (8 minutes)

a. Show and explain your EPS/EBIT analysis to reveal whether stock, debt, or a combination is best to finance your recommendations. Graph the analysis. Decide which approach to use if there are any given limitations of the analysis.
b. Show your projected income statement. Relate changes in the items to your recommendations rather than blindly going with historical percentage changes.

c. Show your projected balance sheet. Relate changes in your items to your recommendations. Be sure to show the retained earnings calculation and the results of your EPS/EBIT decision.

d. Show your projected financial ratios and highlight several key ratios to show the benefits of your strategic plan.

Oral Presentation—Step 7

Strategy Evaluation (2 minutes)

a. Prepare a Balanced Scorecard to show your expected financial and nonfinancial objectives recommended for the firm.

Oral Presentation—Step 8

Conclusion (4 minutes)

a. Compare and contrast your strategic plan versus the company's own plans for the future.

b. Thank audience members for their attention. Seek and answer questions.

INDEX